W9-BKJ-612

Tales of Old Florida

Tales of Old Florida

Edited by
Frank Oppel
&
Tony Meisel

CASTLE

Tales of Old Florida

a division of Book Sales, Inc.
110 Enterprise Avenue
Secaucus, NJ 07094

Printed in the United States of America.

ISBN: 1-55521-225-5

Contents

1.
Subtropical Florida
(1894)

SUBTROPICAL FLORIDA.

By Charles Richards Dodge.

ILLUSTRATIONS BY CARLTON T. CHAPMAN.

THE Northern tourist who reaches Jacksonville comfortably, luxuriously, on the Limited, does the St. John's River, runs up the Oclawaha, enjoys a fortnight of gayety at St. Augustine, and then makes a flying trip through the Indian River, spending a few days on the beautiful Lake Worth, thinks he has seen Florida. Or, being a lover of piscatorial sports he may run for the Charlotte Harbor region direct, possibly resting at Tampa for a few days *en route*, bringing up on the Caloosahatchie River at Myers, where tarpon fishing for a time becomes the most serious business of life. But he has only seen a part of Florida.

Northern Florida does not differ materially in its vegetation, topography, or people from portions of South Carolina and Georgia. Central Florida is more interesting, particularly on what is known as the Orange belt; but when one crosses the boundary line of subtropical Florida, say on a line of latitude twenty-seven, he is in a new world.

After leaving Titusville, on the east coast, at the head of the Indian River, and Tampa on the west coast, the port of departure for Key West and Havana, the shriek of the locomotive becomes a memory. Perhaps the tourist—nay, call him adventurer—has heard of the beautiful Bay Biscayne, or remembers those old stories of the pirates of the keys—the wreckers of the reef—who were able to ply their nefarious occupation until Uncle Sam's splendid lighthouses and the inroads of a primitive

A Cocoa-nut Tree in Fruit.

civilization put a stop to the enterprise. Perhaps in a spirit of adventure he longs to enter this dreamland—to sail amid green isles under a genial winter sun, and imagine himself a latter-day Ponce de Leon, searching for the mythical fountain of youth. I say "sail," because the steamer, or its apology, is rarely seen in the sinuous Hawk Channel or amid the "Huckleberry shoals" of fair Bay Biscayne.

In these days of the glorification of the deeds of Columbus, it is interesting to note that the English claim priority of discovery of Florida, basing this claim upon a passage in the narrative of Sebastian Cabot, which fixes the year of discovery 1497, or just five years after the landing of Columbus. Sixteen years after Cabot's landing, March 27, 1513, Easter Sunday, Juan Ponce de Leon sighted the coast near St. Augustine, which he named in honor of the day, and landing at a more northerly point, a little later, took formal possession in the name of the King of Spain. In the fifty years which followed, such illustrious names as De Cordova, De Quexos, De Soto, Menendez, Jean Ribault and Laudonnière became associated with the history of early discovery in Florida, and with the darker history of the early struggles between the French and Spanish for occupancy. And, at brief intervals, down to the time of the War of the Rebellion, the history of Florida is a story of sanguinary conquest.

The writer has twice traversed the entire coast of subtropical Florida, once from east to west, and once from west to east, but under different circumstances, the latter experience proving the more delightful. Should the voyage of discovery begin on the west coast, Port Tampa is the objective point in planning that part of the journey to be accomplished by rail. Should there be no temptation to break the journey for a day at that huge caravansary, the Tampa Bay Hotel, in the town of Tampa, there is an "Inn" nine miles farther, at the port where, with quiet and cool breezes, the idler may await the tri-weekly steamer for Key West and Havana, and, as I was assured, fish out of the hotel windows.

At the time of my first visit to Tampa, the Plant system had in contemplation a new steamer line to Fort Myers, and the initial trip was made with three

DRAWN BY CARLTON T. CHAPMAN. ENGRAVED BY VAN NESS.

At Lake Worth.

passengers, the writer being one of the party. Passing over sundry breaks in the schedule, necessitating vexatious waits, and transference to two other steam craft before getting to Myers, the last boat reaching her wharf in almost a sinking condition, the journey proved both profitable and interesting.

At Fort Myers, which is about midway between Tampa Bay and Cape Sable, there is but one topic of conversation in the fishing season—the tarpon. The writer, fortunately, did not catch the fever, although a positive interest was soon developed in the hotel bulletin board whereon was recorded from day to day the names of those who had secured a "silver king," with the guide's assistance possibly, accompanied by the weight of the fish, and such other information as might be deemed important. The stories told on the piazza, after supper, were oftentimes larger than the fish caught, for a tarpon weighing one hundred and fifty pounds is game to the death. Men have been known to spend an entire season in the Charlotte Harbor region without once seeing their names upon any of the numerous bulletin boards at the fishermen's hotels, and I was informed upon very good authority that every fish caught in a season represents an average outlay of $500 for the whole season, for guides, boats, costly tackle, and hotel bills and travelling expenses, though there are lucky ones who find all the sport they desire during a short stay. They tell a story of a young New Yorker, who could spare but two days on the Caloosahatchie. He secured his boats, tackle, and guide in advance, and

Indian Key, where Dr. Perrine was Massacred at the Time of the Seminole War.

when, one evening, he made his appearance at the hotel in a dudish outing suit, the veterans on the piazza exchanged knowing glances. The next morning he was up bright and early and off for the fishing grounds. The next evening he saw his name inscribed on the bulletin board, against a high weight record, gave an order to have the beauty stuffed and mounted on a mahogany panel, and on the following morning started on the return journey. But such instances of luck are rare indeed.

I did not catch the enthusiasm, though it is very contagious. Fancy playing for two hours at the end of a slender bass line, over thirty fathoms long, a gamey fish weighing one hundred and fifty pounds, and some idea will be formed of the skill required to keep the fish on the line, or the line from parting, and the excitement attending the final capture.

DRAWN BY CARLTON T. CHAPMAN. ENGRAVED BY WITTE.

Source of Miami River—Entrance to The Everglades.

Sisal Thicket.

But let us imagine ourselves at Key West, and look over the dusty old town while the yacht is being made ready for the cruise up the coast. The name Key West is in one sense a misnomer, as the Dry Tortugas group are the more westerly keys, lying fifty-four nautical miles from *Cayo Hueso*, or "bone island," as Key West was known in the times of Spanish occupancy, the modern name doubtless being a corruption. There is very little of interest here to hold the tourist. Cigar manufacture is the chief commercial enterprise, the wages paid to the cigar-makers alone amounting to $3,000,000 in a single year. Key West is also the market centre of the sponge industry, which gives employment to hundreds of small boats and sailing craft, and amounting to $1,000,000 annually. The turtle trade is another local industry, though not so important now as when the sea turtles were more plentiful. It is a thoroughly Spanish city, there being less than a thousand English-speaking whites out of twenty-five thousand inhabitants, the population being made up for the most part of Cubans, Spanish-speaking negroes, and Bahamians. On

Lone Cocoa-nuts at New River.

my first evening in Key West, I made inquiry of four persons as to the locality of the post-office before receiving a reply in English.

The Government buildings and the dismantled old Fort Taylor are the only structures on the island that are at all imposing. The tobacco factories are two to four story wooden buildings, while the houses are small and cheap, a marked peculiarity being the absence of chimneys, for fires are only needed for cooking. In the markets are found the finest of fish, and tropical fruits in profusion. Prime beef is received from the North by the steamers, though the bulk of the supply is native beef, ferried across from Punta Rassa, on the mainland. Between Punta Rassa beef and semi-starvation, should such an alternative be forced upon the average Northern tourist, I fear there would be no doubt whatever about his choice.

Key West belongs to a large group of Keys lying south of the Bay of Florida and extending thirty-five miles eastward to Bahia Honda, which is the widest

Abandoned Light, Cape Florida.

open water along the entire line of keys. These islands are for the most part uninhabited, and, as they are heavily wooded, abound with game. Eastward of this large group lie the Vaccas Keys, as they are known, numbering a dozen or more islands, covered for the most part with a fine hammock growth. This brings us to an exceedingly interesting group of islands of which Indian Key is the centre, where cultivation has been attempted, and the scene of Dr. Perrine's attempted sisal hemp culture sixty years ago. From this point onward to Cape Florida there is an almost unbroken line of keys from one mile to thirty miles long, separated only by narrow channels, the more northerly of which are chiefly devoted to the culture of pineapples and tomatoes for Northern markets.

A very common, but erroneous idea prevails among uninformed people, that the waters lying between the keys and the mainland are navigable. In point of fact, it is only a shallow inland sea, the rock in many places coming to the surface, and in hundreds of years, no doubt, the coral insect and the mangrove-tree will have reclaimed the entire area, and the map of Florida will have a very different appearance.

The fact that the water is so shoal makes perfectly feasible the project to run a railroad down the east coast and over the keys to Key West, the only bridging requiring any engineering skill being the spanning of the open waters of Bahia Honda. The railroad is destined to be constructed southward to Miama on Biscayne Bay at no remote period, and from that point southward to the final terminus, it is only a matter of one hundred and fifty miles or less of construction.

For my operations along the keys and up the east coast, I was very fortunate in securing the thirteen-ton schooner-yacht Micco, at that time one of the crack boats of the Biscayne Bay Yacht Club, but now flying the Eastern Club's colors. She was expressly built for the shoal waters of the Florida coast by her designer and former owner, Commodore R. M. Munroe, of the B. B. Y. Club, and has a record of nine hundred and fifty-six miles, from Cape Florida to New York City, in six and a half days, which is creditable.

Leaving the Government dock, Key West, at about six o'clock, on the morning of February 9th, we were able to make a landing on the historic Indian Key early the next morning. This island, which is one of the smallest of the group of keys, is one of the most interesting, for here occurred the Indian massacre of August 7, 1840, in which the botanist, Dr. Henry Perrine was killed, his family escaping almost miraculously by concealing themselves for nine hours in the water under a wharf, the house being plundered and burned almost over their heads.

Early in the thirties, while Consul at Campeachy, the doctor became inter-

DRAWN BY CARLTON T. CHAPMAN.

Club House, Biscayne Bay Yacht Club

ested in the introduction of economic plants into the United States, and through his efforts, among other species, the sisal hemp plant was given a foothold on Indian Key. Descendants

Sisal Plantation at New River.

of these plants now occupying the greater portion of this key, with numbers of cocoa-palms, their feathery leaves silhouetted against the sky—for there is entire absence here of wooded vegetation —gives the island a tropic picturesqueness which does not pertain to many other keys of the group.

Landing upon these keys, the scanty soil, for the most part, is discovered to be confined to the crevices and pockets worn into the white coral rock of which all the keys are composed. A footpath is a natural pavement, though a rough one to shoe-leather, the little soil that exists anywhere being only disintegrated rock, or shells and decayed vegetation. On those keys that are more or less covered with "hammock" growth (hard-wood trees), there is quite a surface layer of decomposed vegetation, but in a comparatively short time after being cleared and "cultivated," the white, honey-combed rock comes to the surface and predominates. On some of the keys, like Long Key, twelve miles southwest from Indian Key, the surface is sand to a considerable depth, and such situations are most favorable for growing cocoa-nut trees. There is a grove of cocoa-nuts, numbering over seventeen thousand trees on Long Key, planted by Mr. Thomas Hine, of Newark, N. J., many of which have already come into bearing. The cocoa-nut flourishes throughout subtropical Florida, however, so much so that its absence would sometimes be a relief to the amateur photographer, who wishes diversity in his tropic landscapes. Apropos of the camera, this part of the world is the amateur photographer's paradise, despite the apparent monotony of a topography only a few feet above sea-level, with a vegetation often monotonous to the last degree.

During one of my trips to Long Key, an unexpected opportunity occurred to test the sea-going qualities of the Micco, which proved an experience. Yachting in Florida waters is not always accompanied by sunshine, and the dreamy existence amid balmy breezes while floating over emerald seas sometimes gives place suddenly to discomfort and anxiety, not to say positive danger. A norther, never enjoyable, is frequently to be dreaded.

One drowsy mid-February afternoon found us just inside Long Key in company with the Nethla, well known in these waters. After luncheon we parted company with the white yacht, and set sail for Indian Key, fortunately by the inside course. A sudden darkening of the sky was our only warning. Then the wind began to freshen, and we were forced to take in sail. But the wind increased in violence, and when blowing a half gale the Commodore was glad to run for a sheltered situation near Jew Fish Bush, and anchor. It blew great guns all night, and when the dawn came was still blowing. Some anxiety was felt for the Nethla, as she was nowhere to be seen even with the ship's glass. A sharpie lay near us almost down to her rail, and as the morning wore on we were much interested in the persistency with which the two men aboard of her by turns paced the deck or worked at the pumps. Despite the nasty sea that was running, the Commodore had the tender lowered and we pulled over to them. They were laden with ice, and out of coffee, and considering the chill, raw wind that was blowing, they were a pair of very uncomfortable sailors.

Best "Carriage" in Town.

"Why didn't you hail us?" demanded the Commodore.

"'fraid to," was the laconic reply.

"Afraid?"

"Ain't that a Gov'nment boat?"

"Perhaps," the Commodore answered with a smile, "But come aboard and get some coffee."

In the afternoon we landed on Jew Fish Bush which is one of the lesser keys of the group. Cutting our way through the dense growth of hammock skirting the shore we found ourselves overlooking an open stretch several hundred yards across, as level as a floor, and almost waist high in a growth of wiry grass. I paused to light a cigar. "Don't throw away the match," said the skipper.

Taking the half-burned fusee in his fingers, in an instant it was touched to a tuft of grass near, and in less time than it takes to write it, the air was hot with seething flames. The strong winds carried the fire across the area in a very few moments, the heat causing us to

Yacht Micco.

draw back toward the hammock. An hour later, when aboard the yacht, we saw little tongues of flame in the grass almost at the water's edge, and soon a half cord of driftwood that had been thrown together in a pile by some neighboring squatters, burst into a huge bonfire. Late in the afternoon we were joined by the Nethla, which had weathered the gale with the aid of two anchors, and a merry night we made of it.

The next morning dawned clear. As we ran out, the sea was tumbling over the bar in fine style, for the protecting reef is broken for some fifteen miles at this point, and we were exposed to the full force of the swell. The Micco behaved nobly, and in due time the yacht was lying comfortably in the lee of Indian Key, the landsman aboard of her heaving a deep sigh of relief as the anchor dropped. The two or three hours following were occupied in getting on a cargo of two or three tons of sisal hemp leaves, already cut and bundled by the islanders, and again we were under sail.

The sisal hemp plant is one of the most interesting growths of key vegetation. Its bayonet-like leaves will average five feet in length by four inches broad, each being armed at the tip with a stout spine of needle-like sharpness. As a ton of these leaves will contain almost one hundred pounds of strong white cordage fibre, it is a most valuable species in the vegetable economy.

A marked peculiarity is the mode of reproduction. A plant is old at seven years, when it sends up a huge blossom stalk or "mast" to a height of fifteen to twenty feet. Branches appear at the top, and in time these are covered with tulip-shaped blossoms, of a faded yellowish green color. These wither in time, and now starts forth, from the point of contact with the blossom stalk, a bud which soon develops into a tiny sisal hemp plant. One blossom stalk will support two thousand of these little plants, which detach themselves when several inches long, and fall to the ground. Those that strike soil take root and grow, but the others perish. So tenacious of life are they, however, that some plants kept by me for eight months in a pasteboard box, took root upon being placed in soil, and have grown into good plants.

An allied species of plant, known as "False Sisal," has a similar habit of growth and reproduction, though the two plants are very dissimilar. It was my wish to secure some of the fibre of the false sisal, particularly as our Bahamian neighbors had been carrying off the young plants by shiploads to stock their hemp plantations, not knowing how worthless the fibre is, commercially, and at a later period a special trip was made to Sands Key, to obtain a quantity of the leaves. This key lies almost at the mouth of Bay Biscayne and is uninhabited. Even a photograph does not do justice to the appearance of the vegetation on some of these uninhabited keys, where everything grows in rank luxuriance and the tangles of sisal, Spanish bayonet, prickly-pear, and low shrub growths, are so dense as to be almost impenetrable, save as one cuts his way in with sheath knife and *machete*.

I have a very vivid recollection of my explorations along this portion of the keys. It was in the latter part of February, and the air as balmy as a spring morning, while the pale green waters glinted and sparkled in the sunlight like a sea of emerald and tourmaline. "Dody" Curry was to be my companion for the day, and the tossing of my hip-boots into the tender was a very strong suggestion of something more interesting than lounging in the stern. The yacht lay a mile from the shore, on the inside of the key, though in the clear morning air the island seemed only a few rods away. For the first half mile the boat glided smoothly over the waters of the bay, showing an average depth of five or six feet, the gleaming white bottom clearly visible, covered with coral, sea-plumes, sponges, and many colored weeds or marine life. At this point there was a sudden shoaling, and the grinding sound made by the rough edges of the coral on the boat's bottom became audible. The rowing was often impeded, and when yet a quarter of a mile away from the shore it became necessary to don rubber boots and disembark to draw the boat after us. The walking was not as good as on Broadway, the feet often sinking into treacherous holes filled with an oozy, chalklike mud. It was impossible to find a landing on the bay side owing to the dense tangle of mangrove with its interlacing roots, and for a mile or more we floundered over the shoals, until at length the western end of the key was reached. Here the tide was running swiftly through the natural channel, forming eddies between the jagged masses of outcropping coral. The view of the island at this point was so striking that the camera was set up in two and a half feet of water, and a plate exposed. It was photography under difficulties, and was decidedly a new experience.

We now rounded the point, and turning westward, struck the shoal as soon as the channel was passed, which necessitated veering several hundred yards off-shore. It was now row and wade by turns, the open sea before us, in our progress surprising the fish that were sunning themselves in the deeper pockets, frightening the gulls or clumsy pelicans, and once coming suddenly upon a half-grown shark stranded by the outflowing tide. Dody was thoroughly tired of it, as the harder part of the work had fallen to him, and so, with the camera under my arm, I left him to reflect on the uncertainty of navigation in Florida waters, and waded ashore.

As I stepped upon the beach-sands the picture that met my gaze was one to live long in the memory, and for the moment even the camera and its use were forgotten. The silence, the solitude, the wild grandeur of this bit of sea-girt wilderness was most impressive, and the sparkling water, the glistening sands filled with shell fragments, the beach-drift, and the harmonious blending of color in the rich, rank vegetation, I recall, even now, with pleasure. I tried to imprison it all upon a $6\frac{1}{2} \times 8\frac{1}{2}$ plate. The negative made is a superb one, but the sentiment of the picture was too subtle, too evanescent, to catch and hold.

We made the entire round of the island, bringing away many trophies of our explorations, and late in the afternoon ran alongside the yacht, a pair of tired mortals. During the afternoon the Commodore and Dick had not been idle, for the spoils of a different kind of an expedition lay around over the deck. It was hard to believe that several black objects, disgusting in appearance, and as large as cabbage-heads, were sponges in the natural state, but such was the fact. Two kinds of sponges abound in these waters, that known as the "Loggerhead," a coarse form, being avoided by the spongers. A long pole with a claw or fork at the end is the implement usually employed to detach the sponge from the rock bottom. The mass of polyps covering its surface soon die, and must be removed, and the semi-fibrous mass cleaned and bleached, before the sponge takes on the appearance with which everyone is familiar. There were other interesting "spoils," including branch-coral, sea-plumes, and cup-sponges, but the object of real interest was a lot of crawfish which had been speared on the shoals. Fancy a very rough shelled lobster without claws, and a vague idea can be formed of a Florida crawfish. We had a royal supper that night, the chief dish being a kind of crawfish stew, done with tomatoes and ship biscuit, and I regret to say that nothing was left for "manners."

How some of the "Conchs," or Bahamians, who inhabit these keys make a living does not appear. On Indian Key, for example, there is a slight attempt at truck farming; the natives do a little "sponging"—I should hardly dare say in a facetious sense—gather a few sea-plumes and corals, or shells, and the story is told. Higher up, toward Bay Biscayne, however, on Elliott's and adjacent keys, pineapples, bananas, tomatoes and similar vegetable products are grown with profit. One of the largest of these pineapple planters is Mr. Edgar Higgs, who ships to Baltimore, from his own wharf, schooner-loads of pines in the season, for which he secures good prices. No doubt a quick means of transportation to the North would rapidly develop this industry, for it would enable the shippers to reach the tables of the consumers not only with fresher fruit but with that more naturally ripened. To properly appreciate a Florida pine it should be eaten fully ripe from the parent stalk.

Elliott's Key lies southeast from Sands Key, with only a narrow channel between. It is about eight miles long, by only half a mile wide, and is largely under cultivation. Landing one morning at the Higgs plantation several hours were very pleasantly spent with the manager and owner. From Mr. Higgs I learned much that was interesting regarding the rude agriculture of the keys, though it is too long a story for these pages. I have previously described the "soil" of these cultivated keys. The first operation in starting a pineapple plantation is to cut off the hammock growth and clear the area, though the stumps of the larger trees are left standing. The "slips," which are simply growths from the old plants, are usually put in with a pointed stick at the rate of twelve thousand to the acre. The first crop matures in about eighteen months, and when three crops are secured, in as many years, the fields are abandoned for this culture, the surface again cleared, and planted in tomatoes. Sweet potatoes also grow to perfection, and, as I was assured by a gentleman of experience, are frequently quarried from these fields of coral rock with a crowbar.

I was much interested in the pineapple industry, as the leaves of the pineapple contain a beautiful soft white fibre, which I have no doubt might be utilized. The leaves soon die after the fruit is gathered, to give place to the new plant, so their utilization for fibre, if practicable, would give to Florida a new industry.

A little to the eastward of Sands Key, and near the Ragged Keys, which are shoals scarcely showing above the surface, is the principal southern entrance to Bay Biscayne. Soldier Key is an isolated island lying a few miles beyond, and due south from Cape Florida; upon this key are still to be seen the Government buildings used when the Fowey Rocks Light Tower was constructed in 1878. This is the most northerly of the reef keys, and though limited in area is one of the most interesting visited. Here the "coral-insect" covers great areas of the shoals, the masses of the polyp forming a velvet like covering to the irregular rock bottom over which we waded.

When the coral structure reaches low-water sea-level the life of the coral-insect ends, and the winds and tides, and the mangrove finish the work. The mangroves live just at the edge of the shore, throwing outward into the salt water their straight, forked roots, thus forming an interlocking net-work into which the drift is carried and finds lodgement. The storms bring in solid material, and the sea is slowly but surely encroached upon, and the naked reef in time covered with vegetation. By means of the seed-vessels of the mangrove, which are in the form of smooth, round sticks, known as "cigars," the work is hastened in an interesting manner. The cigars seem to be weighted at one end, and after becoming detached and floating for a time, the heavier end catches in some hole or crevice while the tide is falling, and immediately fixing itself it begins its life as a young mangrove.

There is no more trying or exhausting ordeal, in exploring these keys, than that of attempting to force a way through a growth of mangrove, for sometimes there is no other course to be followed. An old mangrove swamp, such as I visited at Cocoaplum on the mainland, is less trying, for the growth is not so dense, and it is possible to climb or jump from root to root, with only an occasional ugly fall.

Before the Fowey Rocks Light was established, the lighthouse was on the southern extremity of Key Biscayne, or Cape Florida. The old tower is now abandoned, and the Government property about it has been leased to the Biscayne Bay Yacht Club, for a nominal consideration. We anchored and spent a night on the bay-side of Key Biscayne, where the shore goes off into deep water very abruptly. The key abounds with wild-cats, bears, and other "varmints," though we were only attacked by mosquitoes—which are formidable. Were it not for the hordes of insects which overrun southern Florida, and which flourish at all seasons, save in a few favored localities, it would be an earthly paradise, for the temperature on Bay Biscayne averages about eighty-five degrees the year round, and the nights are always cool.

The sand-flies are particularly annoying where they abound, being so infinitesimal that their presence is not known until the victim has been bitten. The Indian name "No-see-'em" is apropos. During the summer months the keys are almost uninhabitable, save to pachydermatous natives, and even they are forced at times to close the wooden shutters of their houses and live in an atmosphere of smoke. These insects will attack a yacht in clouds, though I was informed, as a singular fact, that such attack is usually made when the wind is blowing *from* the water to the shore, rather than off shore, the theory being advanced that the winds enable the pests to distinguish the whereabouts of their victims. I cannot vouch for the correctness of this theory.

Kingfishing off Cape Florida is royal sport. A stanch yacht, a few twenty-five-fathom trolling lines, and a stiff breeze are the essentials. A line is made fast to the yacht abaft the wheel, and the fisherman takes his position. A slight jerk tells when the cord has all run out, and in an instant the polished spoon sinker is seen merrily cutting the tops of the waves, away astern. The yacht is rippling through the water like a thing of life, the excitement of anticipation becomes intense, but it is only momentary—Zip! The line is suddenly taut, a beauty between three and four feet long is thrown high out of the water, the scales glistening like burnished silver in the sunlight; it is tough work starting the fish yachtward, but in a moment the hand over hand work comes easier, the line is almost in, and then begins the struggle. My first kingfish would have pulled me overboard at this stage of the game, but for the strong arm of the ever-watchful Dody. I landed the prize unaided, stunned it with a club, and as it fell into the cockpit, I felt that I owned a continent. This is kingfishing in Florida waters, and with two or three pairs of hands at the sport, a catch of two hundred and fifty fish in a day is possible. After a few hours of such exciting sport, capturing in this manner the near cousin of the kingfish, the Spanish mackerel, which also abounds in these waters, is tame indeed in comparison. We saw tarpon on this part of the coast, but they are never caught with the line as on the west coast. There are other kinds of fish, however, which it is good sport to catch, and a joy to eat, the pompano being especially esteemed as a table fish. The kingfish, also, is food for the epicure when cooked shortly after capture.

Biscayne Bay is about forty miles long by five to six miles wide, and lies along the southeastern curve of the Florida peninsula, on the very edge of the Gulf Stream. The mainland between the bay and the Everglades is hardly as wide as the bay itself, and upon this strip are located the few settlements of this portion of Florida. The bay is only navigable for boats of light draught, a yacht drawing five feet of water being sure to go aground on many of its sand-bars and shoals ; even the native yachtsmen often find navigation difficult, the sudden chalky appearance of the water in the wake of the vessel showing too close proximity to land in a vertical direction. The eastern boundaries of the bay are the narrow spur of the mainland which ends at Narres's Cut, and Virginia Key, and Key Biscayne lying just below in the same line, these keys separated by a broad inlet known as Bear Cut, the main easterly outlet to the ocean.

Were it not for its inaccessibility, the Biscayne Bay region would have long ago been one of the most popular tourist resorts in Florida, on account of its equitable climate, for which its proximity to the Gulf Stream is largely responsible, and from the easterly breezes which blow almost incessantly.

At Cocoa-nut Grove, the largest settlement on the bay, we are in a new atmosphere. Here is the headquarters of the Biscayne Bay Yacht Club, and consequently a port of entry for all Northern yachtsmen who find themselves in these waters. The Secretary of the Club, the genial Kirk Munroe, well known to these pages, met the writer, on his first appearance, as a friend of former days and gave him a warm welcome.

There is a very fair hostelry at this place, and in the winter months the society of the settlement is delightful, for with the cultivated people who are now identified with the locality, there are always a few strangers from the North, who come down here to lead a *dolce-far-niente* existence in this dreamland, all unmindful of the blizzards that are sweeping over the wintry North. One soon becomes accustomed to the absence of fresh beef and ice, though fresh venison and sea-turtle more than make up for the lack of the former, and the necessity for the latter is soon overlooked.

The roads here are mere trails through the bush, the waterways being the usual highways for travel or transportation. Madame took a trip "into the country" one afternoon, and though she had the best team in town, the experience was not altogether enjoyable.

This portion of Florida has been filling up very rapidly in the past three or four years, and now there are few, if any, homestead lands on the four-mile strip not occupied. On the bay-shore land has risen rapidly in value, and I would not dare say at how many hundred dollars an acre choice situations are held.

Three or four miles above Cocoa-nut Grove is Miami, the oldest "town" on the bay, numbering not more than half a dozen houses. As Miami is located at the mouth of the river of the same name, which flows directly from the Everglades, it is the chief Indian trading-post on the bay, the store being located on the south bank, at Brickell's landing. Just across the river is all that remains of the old Fort Dallas, which holds a conspicuous place in the history of the Seminole wars. It is now the residence of Mrs. Tuttle, a Northern lady of culture and indomitable energy, who is doing a great deal for this section of Florida. I was a guest for several days at Fort Dallas, which, under her touch has been transformed into a little tropic paradise. What with the growing of all kinds of vegetables, the planting of fruit-trees, and the advent of a herd of valuable Jersey cattle, Fort Dallas is an object-lesson to many a plodding homesteader as to the future possibilities of this region. Good transportation facilities are sorely needed, however, but the skilful manipulation of sundry wires will doubtless erelong find response in the shrill scream of the locomotive, at Miami, where now is seen only the sail-boat and the Indian canoe.

Only last season, the representative of a powerful Florida railway system penetrated and crossed the Everglades, from west to east, a bit of exploration beset with many dangers, which I think was never before undertaken by white men. The expedition was crowned with success, when the half-famished party, stepped ashore at the Fort Dallas landing.

To Mrs. Tuttle I was indebted for boat and guide for my trip into that wonderland, the Everglades. The Miami River is one of the principal outlets from the glades on the east coast, and though a sluggish stream at its mouth, it tumbles over the coral rock near its source in splendid rapids against which a boat is dragged, not rowed, with difficulty. We entered the glades by the north fork of the Miami, as beautiful a stream as ever flowed through an unbroken wilderness, the trees in places almost arching the water, its banks clothed with strange vegetation and stranger flowers, the bottom presenting a kaleidoscopic picture of many-colored grasses and aquatic vegetation.

The guide told of festoons of moccasin-snakes sunning themselves amid the branches of these trees in former times, and of prowling beasts in the bush, but we saw nothing to make us afraid. When the boat had been dragged over the point where the water makes its first plunge, at the head of the rapids, and we were rowing again in smooth water, what a surprise was in store for us! I had always associated with the term "Everglades," on the map of Florida, the picture of a low-lying, dank, dark, malarial swamp, the abode of venomous creeping things; a morass where the rank vegetation luxuriating in decay formed shadowy dells, on entering which one might well leave hope behind.

But instead I found an inland lake, of drinkable water, lying high up in the sunshine, while stretching away toward sunset as far as eye could reach was only a vision of blue waters, green isles, and vast areas of sedge-grass or reeds, moving in the balmy breeze like ocean billows. This is the picture of the Everglades in winter; in summer it might be something very different.

The water in many places is so shallow that if it could be drawn off for a depth of two feet, I fancy the Everglades would resemble a vast prairie filled with little lakes and winding streams. Some of these watercourses were too deep for the bottom to be seen; others were only a few feet in depth, the vegetation below the surface clearly visible, and with banks sharply defined, while in many places the levels varied in depth from only a few inches to a couple of feet. In one place when I wished to take a picture I stepped out of the boat, with camera under my arm, and waded to the point of view through not over eight inches of water. The bottom is old coral rock, covered with a shallow substratum of soft mud. It is not safe to enter the glades without a guide, on account of danger of bewilderment, in pushing through the winding channels and tall grass and reeds. The Indians will rarely act as guides, and intrusion upon their "preserves" is liable to be resented.

The keys or islands, which always form the distance to a picture taken in almost any part of the glades, vary in size from a mere mound a few feet across, to areas of many acres. Many of them are cultivated by the Seminoles, who are no mean farmers, though their agricultural practice extends little further than the raising of corn and pumpkins. Many of the keys are heavily wooded, and all are interesting. What gives them a particular interest is the fact that they form the abiding-places of these Seminoles, who are supposed to number somewhere between five hundred and seven hundred souls. Unquestionably the Seminole is a very decent Indian—save when he has been drinking "cider with a little Jamaica ginger in it"—(a trader told me that was the formula) and their squaws are models of womanly virtue and industry. That the race remains pure, notwithstanding the inroads of "civilization," is due to the severity of the punishment of those of either sex who are guilty of a breach of the law, for chastity is prescribed by their religion, and the penalty is death.

In late years they are pushing deeper into the glades, as the footsteps of the white man encroach upon their domain. They live upon game, fruits, and the products of their agriculture, though many wants must be supplied at the trading-posts or stores in the settlements, with money or through barter. For many years the trade in alligator skins and the plumage of birds has been a great source of revenue to them, but the alligators are almost exterminated, and the bird laws are now so strictly enforced that the trader no longer dares to buy their plumes and wings, at least in paying quantity. They still bring in game, and turtles, and a few alligator skins, or moccasins and other rude manufactures, but every year it grows harder and harder for them to get money; and as if to add insult to injury, some of their most fertile keys have recently been homesteaded by white men, after the Indians had tilled the soil for years.

The women are dressed neatly—I was told that many own sewing-machines—and they show a degree of taste in the fashioning of their garments. Although a Seminole of either sex has little love for a camera, Mrs. Dodge was able to secure nearly a dozen fine negatives, chiefly of Indian women.* The native costume of the younger men and boys is comfortable, if *not* picturesque—this is but one garment, and it resembles a shirt more than anything else. They do not wear their fine toggery at the lodges, but when approaching the settlements in their canoes, push into some sheltered nook, and in due time appear in gay turban, gaudy calico shirt, and leggins, and sometimes moccasins, although some of them wear a loose outer garment belted at the waist. They are not quarrelsome, save when under the influence of liquor, and then only in a degree, for they usually become limp in a very short time, and are unceremoniously tumbled into the bottoms of their canoes by the squaws, and taken home to sleep it off.

I had a pleasant "talk" with old Matlo, or, as he pronounced the name for me, at least half a dozen times, O-pi-o-ma-tah. He is over eighty years old, and is still a vigorous specimen of aboriginal manhood. The Seminoles do not think much of white women. They say, "White squaw pretty too much—no good." At the same time I was informed that their own women are not forced to perform *all* the work, with a hint that many New England farmers' wives are more in slavery, though doubtless the case might be stated less offensively.

Arch Creek, almost at the head of Bay Biscayne, is a romantically beautiful stream that must be seen to be fully appreciated. Like the Miami River it forks two or three miles from its mouth, the banks of the north fork in places rising to a height of twenty feet in wonderful cliffs. The vegetation is tropic to the last degree, and even more strange than that of the Miami. The creek takes its name from a natural bridge or arch not far from its mouth.

But one cannot linger forever amid such scenes. We had planned our homeward journey by way of Lake Worth, which meant a cruise of eighty miles up the Atlantic coast in a twenty-four-foot sharpie, the Egret, for only boats of lightest draught can enter the dangerous inlets in safety. As it was, we waited five days for the right kind of a sea, and at five o'clock one afternoon made a sudden departure, all things being propitious. It was dark when we sailed out through Bear Cut, with Dody at the helm, leaving behind us many delightful friends and many pleasant memories. Silently we sped on our way, the roar of the surf that was piling up on the bar a half mile ahead of us becoming each moment more audible, and seeming almost ominous. In a very few minutes we could discern vaguely the long line of white, just over our bow—a sudden plunge, a cloud of blinding spray, a sensation of settling in the water, and our little cockle-shell was on the broad Atlantic.

*See "A Forgotten Remnant," by Kirk Munroe, in SCRIBNER'S MAGAZINE, vol. vii., p. 303.

2.
Sponge and Spongers of the Florida Reef (1892)

SPONGE AND SPONGERS OF THE FLORIDA REEF.

By Kirk Munroe.

LTHOUGH sponges, in one form or another, are among the most common articles of domestic use, it is doubtful if one person in ten thousand of those who are familiar with the appearance of a sponge could tell where it comes from, or how it is procured; certainly most of them would hesitate before venturing to name the natural kingdom to which it belongs. Nor would this hesitation be at all surprising; for, while half of the sponge-fishers who have given the subject a thought, affirm that it is a member of the animal kingdom, the other half are tenacious of their belief that it is a marine plant. Even science is in doubt, and as a safe compromise calls the sponge a "connecting link." Whatever it is, whether of the lowest order of animal, or the highest form of vegetable, life, certain it is that the sponge is one of the most valuable of sea products, and is well worth more attention than it now receives.

While the sponge family is an immense one, inhabiting all tropical and temperate waters, only a few of its innumerable members have a commercial value. Such as are valuable are found in warm and shallow sea-waters on the edge of the tropics, and very nearly all the sponge used in this country comes from the Gulf of Mexico, within a few miles of the Florida coast. Here the sponge is what the oyster is to Chesapeake Bay, the salmon to Puget Sound, or the lobster to New England, and the business of sponging is so rapidly increasing in volume and importance, that it has more than quadrupled within the past five years.

The headquarters of the industry in this country is Key West, a city built on a small coral island seventy miles from the main land, and the most southerly point within the territorial limits of the United States. Here the business of sponging ranks second in importance only to that of cigar making, and provides steady employment the year through, to several thousands of the most ablebodied male inhabitants of the place. The present sponging fleet of Key West numbers three hundred and fifty vessels, of all sizes, from the well appointed 50-ton schooner, with its crew of fourteen men and towing half a dozen boats, down to the tiny sloop that affords scant room for three men and their meagre stock of provisions, but in which they will set out on a month's cruise a hundred miles or more from home with the utmost confidence in their boat and themselves.

The Key West sponger has a choice of two distinct fishing-grounds — the "Bay" and the "Reef." The former includes all the waters of the Gulf of Mexico washing the western coast of Florida, but more particularly those lying in the vicinity of St. Marks, between Cedar Keys and Apalachicola. From this locality, near a headland known to spongers as Rock Island, come the bulk of the fine sheep's-wool, or ordinary bath-sponges. Further south, near the mouth of Tampa Bay, grow the large and highly prized Anclote grass-sponges, which are destined to undergo a curious transformation of name and character before reaching their ultimate market.

Most of the larger sponge boats go into the Bay, to reach which they must traverse several hundred miles of open sea, exposed to the fury of Gulf gales. There is however little danger to be apprehended even here; for the coming storm is always heralded by unmistakable signs, and the innumerable reefs and islands of the coast, offer a wide choice of snug harbors. Besides these there are in the Gulf, miles from land, several vast springs of fresh water, that boil up from the bottom of the sea with an appearance and effect similar to that of a light oil. In these fresh water areas, seas do not break, and the great salt water combers are robbed of their terror, so that within their limits a vessel provided with good anchors and stout cables may ride out the severest gale in safety.

Such vessels of the sponging fleet as are not fitted for long sea voyages, and these number nearly three hundred, head to the eastward from Key West, and seek the somewhat inferior sponges that flourish among the countless keys of the great Florida reef. This marvellous barrier of coral forms the northern bank of that mighty ocean-river the Gulf Stream, and extends from Cape Florida on the east coast, southwesterly, for two hundred miles, to the Tortugas; while its adjacent waters offer one of the safest and most delightful cruising grounds in the world. Rising from the wellnigh fathomless depths of the Gulf Stream is the outer ledge of glistening coral, often showing above the surface and pierced by numberless deep water-channels. Inside of it flows the broad Hawk Channel, offering plenty of water for large vessels along its entire length, well buoyed and well lighted. Then come the keys fringed with the perennial green of interlacing mangroves, and ranged in a line exactly parallel to that of the outer reef. Behind them, and reached by a multiplicity of navigable channels, lies the broad expanse of shallow water known as the Bay of Florida, stretching away to the mainland, filled with low keys, sand-bars, coral-reefs, and mud-banks. These are threaded by a bewildering maze of tortuous channels, unsurveyed and unchartered, but all known to, and used by the reef-sponger. In these warm shallows lie the sponge-beds, and here the smaller boats of the fleet glean their harvests in safety. If the wind blows from any point of north they find a smooth lee outside the keys; if from the south, they run in behind them.

Although the sponger cares little for nature's beauties or novelties, he is constantly surrounded by such a bewildering profusion of both as would arouse the keenest enthusiasm of a naturalist. The waters abound in corals, exquisite algæ, myriads of vividly colored fish, and uncouth sea-monsters. The gleaming beaches are thickly strewn with rare shells; curious birds are to be noted on every sand-bar; while the waters, themselves as transparent as crystal springs, present such an infinity of tint as to be a source of constant delight. So distinct and significant are these water colors that navigation is largely dependent upon them, and the sponger guides the course of his little vessel with unerring precision by the hue of the proximate waters. To his experienced eye black water indicates rocks or grass lumps, while white marks shallows and a coral bottom. A tinge of red betokens a sand-bar that he may not cross; but where it merges into green or yellow is the narrow channel that a boat of light draught may thread with safety. Dark-green water is from two to four fathoms deep, while all shades of blue indicate a depth sufficient for large ships. Thus to the reef-sponger these colors with all their gradations are as pregnant with meaning as are the ripples on the surface of the Mississippi to a pilot of that tawny flood.

While the water is thus replete with curious interest, the land, as represented by the low-lying keys, is not less so. Here are birds and butterflies, insects and flowers, as yet unknown and unnamed. Here are palms found nowhere else in the world, besides groves of cocoanuts, broad fields of pineapples, and large areas of dagger-like fibre plants. Here grow nearly all the fruits known to tropic climes, while the ever-present mangroves, with mastics, mahogany, and a bewildering variety of other forest trees, spring from prehistoric coral that still bears the imprint of its builders as sharply outlined as when it was created.

Of all these the sponger knows little and cares less. To be sure, the cocoanuts and pineapples arouse a slight interest on account of their money value; but potatoes or cabbages would exert the same influence. He is invariably a "Conch" or native of the Bahama Islands, attracted to this country by its better prices for sponge, and has been familiar with similar surroundings from infancy. Thus while his eye is always turned upon the water, it is not to note with delight its rich coloring, nor the exquisite forms that inhabit its

DRAWN BY CARLTON T. CHAPMAN. ENGRAVED BY S. G. PUTNAM.

Key West Sponge Boats.

depths; but in search of certain black, shapeless objects that lie beneath it, and which represent his livelihood. Yet he

Searching for Sponges through a Water-glass.

passes over acres and miles of these, ranging in size from that of a cocoanut to the bigness of a hogshead, and all of a symmetrical roundness, before pausing. Apparently he is throwing away the chance of a lifetime; but if you suggest this to him he will laugh in scorn at your ignorance, and answer: "Them's honly logger'eads, vot hain't no good. Hi could load a fleet o' wessels vith them an' not go hout hof sight hof Key Vest."

A Conch is as reckless of his h's as a Cockney, and invariably supplants a w with a v, or *vice versa.*

The loggerhead is the most common of all sponges, and attains the greatest size; but it is of too coarse fibre to be valuable save as a fertilizer.

Arrived at what he fancies may prove a profitable ground the captain of a sponging schooner sends out a boat to investigate, meantime standing off and on until a discovery is reported. Then all hands, save only the cook, or, if she is a large vessel, the captain and cook, tumble into the small boats and the fishing—if fishing it can be called—is begun.

The vessel has towed astern just half as many boats as she has men in her crew, and now two men are assigned to each boat. One of them stands well aft and sculls with a long oar, while the other bends low over one of the gunwales in a most constrained position, and with his head buried in a water-glass eagerly scans the bottom as he is moved slowly over it. The water-glass is simply a wooden bucket, having a glass bottom, that is held an inch or so below the ruffled surface, and in these clear waters plainly reveals all submerged objects to a depth of forty or fifty feet. As a further aid in overcoming ripples or moderate waves each small boat is provided with a bottle of oil so hung over the bow as to slowly drip its contents into the water.

Through his magic glass the observer sees darting fish, richly tinted sea-fans and feathers, branching coral, gorgeous anemones, bristling sea-porcupines, and the myriad other curious tenants of these tropic waters. While seeing these he makes no sign until a small dark object, that, to the untrained eye, differs in no respect from the loggerheads surrounding it, comes within his range of vision. Then, without removing his gaze, he reaches for the long-handled sponge-hook or rake lying behind him, and using it with one hand, quickly tears from the bottom a black, slimy mass, that he triumphantly pronounces to be a sheep's-wool or grass sponge of the first quality.

The hook that he has just used is of iron, and has three long curved teeth attached to a slender wooden handle. This is ordinarily about thirty feet long, though the more expert spongers use handles fifty or sixty feet in length, and fish successfully in water from forty to fifty feet deep. To realize the difficulty of such a feat one has but to thrust an oar into the water and attempt to strike some object within its reach. Apparently the oar breaks at the surface, and the submerged portion darts off at a most unexpected angle. Thus the skill of the sponger lies in his ability to overcome or ignore this bewildering effect of refraction, and to detect at a glance the character of the dim object toward which he directs his hook. When the small boat is loaded, as with good luck she will be several times during the day, she returns to the schooner and transfers her slimy cargo. Heaped on deck in the heat of a tropic sun the mucilaginous animal matter with which the sponge-cells are filled quickly decomposes and emits an odor so powerful and offensive that the presence of a sponge-boat can be detected a mile or more from the leeward, and a wise sailor will always pass one to windward if possible. To the spongers themselves this vile smell might be the spicy odors of Araby the blest for aught they care. They apparently enjoy it, and at least are so indifferent to it that I have seen them eating their dinner on deck with the rotting sponges piled high about them, and unconcernedly devouring food taken from a temporary resting-place on the disgusting mass beside them. Nor do they hesitate, if the harvest is so bountiful as to overflow the deck, to stow a portion of the slimy cargo in the tiny cabin that contains their sleeping bunks. Here they will sleep soundly and peacefully with every aperture that might admit fresh air or mosquitoes tightly closed, and apparently suffer no ill effect from so doing. In fact a sponger seems perfectly willing and able to spend any length of time without air if by foregoing it he can also elude the insect pests with which the mangroves of the keys are infested. To prove this he not only closes his cabin and fills it with a dense cloud of tobacco-smoke ; but, in the insect season, he provides his bunk with a mosquito bar that is oftener made of calico than of

Using the Sponge Hook.

any other material. Carefully tucking the edges of this air-tight canopy under his blanket, he will stretch himself out with a sigh of satisfaction at having thus effectually baffled his tormentors, and will spend the night in blissful unconsciousness that he is violating a single hygienic law.

One of the first duties of the sponger on reaching his fishing-ground is to construct a "crawl" (corral?) or pen about ten feet square, of wattled stakes, in shallow water, close behind some sheltering key. To this he returns, and in it deposits his catch of fresh sponges as often as it overflows the limits of his schooner's deck. In the crawl the sponges lie and rot for several days, when they are taken out and beaten with wooden "bats" until all animal matter is thoroughly extracted; then they are washed, strung in bunches on bits of rope-yarn having an arbitrary length of five feet four inches, and laid on sand or grass in the hot sun to bleach and dry. Finally, reduced to about one-tenth of their original weight, and offering but slight resistance to almost limitless compression, they are stowed away in the hold of the schooner, which by the time its limit of capacity is reached often contains a cargo valued at several thousand dollars. Of this sum one-half goes to the vessel, which is also charged with all expenses of the trip, and the other is shared, or "sheered," according to Conch vernacular, among the crew.

As a rule the Key West sponger, white or black, and in this business the races are very evenly represented, is the most simple-minded, honest, and inoffensive of seafaring men. He seldom swears, rarely drinks, is as truthful as he is ignorant, and is above all superstitiously religious. The one form of social dissipation in which he indulges is attendance at church or other gatherings for religious exercises. His only songs are hymns, and these he renders with a heartiness that is in nowise diminished by a lack of musical knowledge or ability. He would no more think of lifting the finest sponge of the reef on a Sunday, if he should happen to discover it on that day, than he would of loading his vessel with worthless loggerheads. Nor would he fish on a Sunday, even though fish abounded and the bread locker was empty. In this connection the story is still told, with bated breath, of a hungry man who, a few years ago, caught a fish on the holy day, and was punished by a stroke of lightning on the Monday following. If there is to be preaching on any of the inhabited keys, all the spongers within a dozen miles of the place will attend it; but if nothing of this kind offers they will repair to the key beside which their crawl is located, and spend Sunday in sleeping, talking, smoking, or gathering under the shade of a clump of mangroves and singing hymns.

On one of the uninhabited keys stands a large shed-like building, erected by the builders of a lighthouse a dozen years ago for the storage of material. As there is a cistern connected with it, from which water-kegs may be filled, this key is a favorite resort for spongers on Sundays or on such days as rough water enforces idleness. As I ran in toward it one dark night last winter I was puzzled to account for a tremendous racket inside of the old building. It sounded like a riot or a free fight at least, and to satisfy my curiosity concerning it I took the skiff and rowed ashore the moment our anchor was dropped. No light was visible until I was close beside the building, when I saw that a small area of its cavernous interior was dimly illumined by a single lantern hung just within the doorway. By this uncertain light a score of spongers, full-grown men wearing palmetto hats as broad-brimmed as a Mexican sombrero, calico shirts, and jean trousers tucked into great cowhide boots, were playing tag. It was a genuine romp, such as would have been enjoyed by any boy of ten years, and the noise they made could be heard for miles out at sea. The moment they detected my presence the game came to an abrupt ending, and they gathered breathlessly about me to inquire if I were the new preacher whom they had heard was coming up the reef. They were greatly disappointed to find that I was not a preacher, and after a half hour of conversation I fell low in their estimation by asking why they could not have a dance, as I noticed that one of them had a mouth organ and another a violin. Several at once hastened to assure me that their preacher did not

Spongers' Homes.

allow them to dance; while the owners of the musical instruments disclaimed an ability to play anything except hymn tunes. So I asked them to play some of those, and of all lugubrious musical performances I ever heard I think the long-drawn wailings of those two instruments, attuned to sacred melody, was the worst. During the progress of the concert one of the tag-players took occasion to confide to me that "Hi fer one don't see no great 'arm in darncing, seeing has Hi was borned an' brung hup a Puseyite; but Hi'm the onliest one 'ere has his."

It seemed absurd to see these great clumsy six-footers playing tag; but after all it was one of the most sensible things they could do. After days of being packed like sardines on their over-crowded little schooners, with the only variant of long hours of painfully cramped positions while at work in the small boats, some vigorous exercise of this kind was an absolute necessity.

Sometimes a sponge-boat is out two or three months before "filling," though occasionally the same happy result is attained in as many weeks. Whenever the joyful day arrives that not another sponge can be squeezed into hold or cabin, and when at the same time the "grub" is so low that necessity demands a return to Cayo Hueso (Key West), then is the sponger as jubilant as a school-boy homeward bound for the long vacation, or a Grand Banker whose fish-laden schooner is headed toward Gloucester. He is all spring and activity as he hoists the small boats in on deck, hangs the now idle hooks over the side in bundles that reach from stem to stern, or sends aloft every rag of light canvas that can be packed on the bending masts, top-sails, stay-sail, flying-jib, and all. Although the cargo is a full one, it is not heavy, and before the steady northeast trade, the evil-smelling little schooner speeds merrily down the reef past the low-lying keys, leaving the empty crawls, the shining beaches, and the envious unfortunates whose holds still show vacant room, far behind. Stretched in easy attitudes wherever they can find space for their long limbs, these homeward-bound toilers of the shallow seas sing their liveliest hymns, discuss the prospect of finding a rising market, or eagerly hail outward-bound vessels with the never varying query of "Vots sponge a-fetching in Key Vest now?" For this day's dinner the cook prepares a special duff well filled with plums that have been carefully hidden away for the occasion; or perhaps the treat may be "turtle yellows"—unlaid eggs taken from the body of some turtle captured during the cruise. These, after being salted and hung for a few days in the hot sun, resemble bunches of dried grapes, big, weazened, and yellow. Raw or cooked, they are esteemed a delicacy by all Conches, although one not to the manner born would probably find snakes, snails, or train-oil equally palatable.

To the stranger the sponge market of Key West is as curious as are most of the sights in this quaint out-of-the-world town. Here, where, as in Nantucket, nearly everything, including meat, vegetables, fruits, clothing, jewelry, and sewing-machines, is sold at auction, sponges prove no exception to the rule. The sponge auction is held every day at three o'clock on the city wharf, beyond which the fleet is anchored. This wharf is really an open area of made land reclaimed from the sea, and composed largely of sponge clippings. Here the several cargoes are displayed in piles, each of which represents a grade of sponge. With a commendable ingenuity of economy these auctions are conducted without the assistance, and consequent commissions, of an auctioneer, the bids being made on folded slips of paper and pinned to the several piles by individual buyers. Among these are representatives of all the larger wholesale drug-houses of the North, and between them until recently competition was very keen; for, although handled by drug-houses, sponge is never a drug on the market. At present, however, the Key West business is very nearly controlled by one man, Mr. A. J. Arapian, a Greek, who has been in this country long enough to acquire the title of "Sponge King," and whose annual sales aggregate half a million of dollars.

While the bids are being made, each pile of sponge is surrounded by eager groups of the bronzed and brawny toilers who have torn it from the bottom of the sea. To them it represents all that is worth living for, and they will be passing rich or comparatively poor according to the price it brings. This price is regulated more by size and quality of the sponges than by the quantity offered, those of medium size commanding a better price than the very large or smaller.

Within an hour after the bids have been opened and the new ownership of the piles thus determined, they have disappeared in the various sponge-lofts of the vicinity where the commodity is in trade parlance to be "manufactured" for its final market. In the loft, each variety is first sorted into grades depending upon size, shape, quality, and the locality from which it was obtained, and to each grade is assigned a bin reaching from floor to ceiling of the spacious room. In front of these bins sit the clippers, all men and all Conches, who, with sheep-shears, trim the sponges and remove whatever coral may still cling to their roots. After being clipped, the finer grades are treated to a bleaching bath, the composition of which is a trade secret. From it they go to the drying frames, where they remain for several days, and on which they become nearly as white as the fleeces whose name they bear.

From the bleachery the sponges are borne in peculiar shaped baskets, large at the bottom and smaller at the top, made in the Bahamas from palm-leaves, to the presses, where, by means of powerful screws, they are forced into bales of the smallest possible compass. These bales, neatly enveloped in a fine bagging and tightly corded, weigh fifteen, thirty, sixty, or one hundred and twenty pounds, according to their destination, which is not always the bathroom, as many persons suppose.

Among the larger consumers of sponge are hospitals in which surgical operations are performed. This is nearly always the destination of the great Anclote grass sponges, though they do not reach it under that name. While they have the size and texture of the well-known Mediterranean ear-sponge, so called from its fancied resemblance to elephants' ears, and used, the world over, for stanching blood in large, open wounds, they have not the shape prescribed by custom. Consequently they are exported to Europe as "Anclote grass sponges;" and are there cut into the required shape before being sent back to this country as "Mediterranean ear-sponges." Quantities of sheeps'-wool and other smaller sponges are also used for surgical purposes. Many of these after having seen service, and being discarded in the hospitals, fall into the hands of unscrupulous dealers, who wash them in an acid that not only cleanses and bleaches them, but renders them worthlessly tender. They are then hawked about the streets of large cities by curbstone pedlars, who find a ready sale for their fine-looking but utterly valueless wares.

The Sponge-wharf, Key West.

Many of the larger sheeps'-wool sponges find their way to currying establishments, where they play an important part in the manufacture of leather, and to stables, where they are used for washing carriages. Coarser sponges and the small sponge clippings are worked up into "felt" roofing paper; while the larger clippings find their way into bottles of liquid shoe-polish, to the tips of mucilage bottles, and to a score of other places where they are made equally useful. Not long ago these were thrown away; but now every scrap is utilized and nothing remains in the loft but the dust of powdered lime that was once the coral to which the sponges were attached.

Thousands of bales of the finest toilet sponges, worth from ten to sixty dollars per pound, are used in potteries all over the world, for imparting that absolute smoothness of finish to delicate ware that can be attained by no other means. In most electrical machines sponge is used as an insulator, while in many other lines of manufacture its value is well established.

There are at present but four centres of sponge supply and distribution known to the commercial world, and of these the most important is Key West. In the waters tributary to this port the sheeps'-wool, which outranks all others as a general-utility sponge, attains a perfection of form and texture unknown elsewhere. Here too are to be found any number of sailors, trained to the business from boyhood, with whom to man the sponging fleet. Thus although the American sponge industry is only about sixty years old, it already leads the world in the volume of its business, the equipment of its vessels, and the intelligence with which it is conducted.

When a sponge is torn from its native bed by hooks, certain fragments or

DRAWN BY OTTO H. BACHER.

Interior of a Sponge Loft—Clipping, Baling, and Weighing.

germs are left adhering to the bottom. These so speedily reproduce new sponges that the old beds may be profitably revisited at least every two years, and in some cases oftener. As an old sponger aptly expressed it to me, "they grows just like melons." Where, as in the Mediterranean, diving machines instead of hooks are used in the fisheries, there is no chance for the beds to thus recuperate, as the machines destroy the germs and leave only barren rocks behind them. For this reason diving for sponges is prohibited by law in the waters of the State of Florida.

A similar law is now in force in the Turkish and Grecian Archipelagoes, where sponge has been taken from time immemorial, and its result has been to send the European and Asiatic sponge-divers far down on the African coasts in search of new fields. The headquarters of the Mediterranean operations is Calaimo in the Grecian Archipelago, which is second only to Key West in the volume of its business. The general distributing point for all European and Asiatic sponges is Trieste, whence come the delicate Turkish sponges so indispensable to my lady's toilet and invaluable to surgeons.

Sponging is also an important industry to the Bahamians, who extend their operations as far south as Turk's Island. Nassau is the receiving and distributing port for all sponges taken from this vast territory, and the Bahamian fisheries rank in importance with those conducted on the southern coast of Cuba, the central port of which is Batabano.

These are the present commercial sponging centres of the world, though a fine article of sponge is said to exist in Brazilian waters, and the Chinese supply their own limited demand from native beds. Sponge is also found on the Mexican and Central American coasts, so that there is no reason to doubt its existence in the South Pacific and other tropic waters in which it has not yet been sought.

From the foregoing statements it will be readily understood that the American sponge industry is still in its infancy. It is, however, an infant of most promising growth, destined in the near future to attain the proportions and command the attention it so well deserves. Then from many a Southern port besides that of Key West will the nimble schooners sail forth with flags flying, guns firing, and crews cheering as they head toward the shallow seas and coral-reefs of the distant sponge-banks.

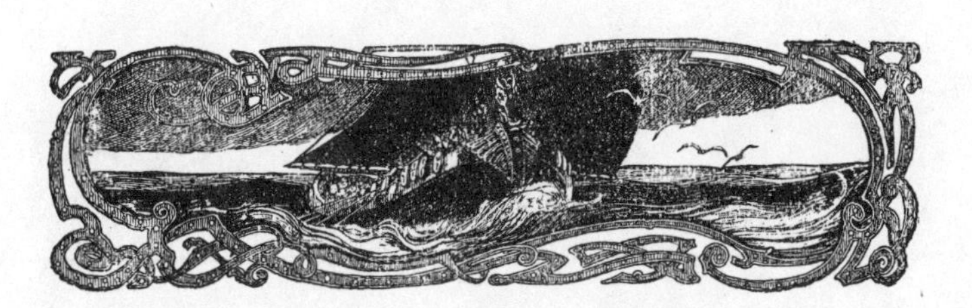

3.
The Angler's Battle Royale (1903)

THE ANGLER'S BATTLE ROYAL

THE TAKING OF THE TARPON

By CHARLES F. W. MIELATZ

ILLUSTRATED BY THE AUTHOR

THE man who has caught trout, black bass, or salmon, and has added to this the delight of shore fishing for tautog, bluefish, or striped bass, has many pleasant and exciting contests to remember; but if he should once get fast to a tarpon all his other fishing experiences—desperate as some of them may have seemed—will be eclipsed in a moment. The keen pleasure he took in recounting them will be gone. He will only remember that it was the tarpon which gave him the "battle royal."

To the trout fisherman wading down the brook, or drifting down the river with dainty tackle and beautiful flies; to the man who skirts the lily pads on quiet lake or broadening river with hellgrammite or phantom minnow; to him who haunts the rapid, and lures the royal salmon to attack some gaudy combination of color; to him who hies him to the shore to tempt the succulent tautog with crab, or chums for the voracious bluefish, or casts his bait into the swirl of dashing breakers to entice the striped bass—to each of these his first encounter with the Silver King will seem as though he had hooked one of those saucy little towboats which busy themselves towing leviathans about New York harbor.

Those true fishermen who have killed only small fish, especially those who have confined their labors to fresh water, will regard tarpon tackle as altogether too heavy for any kind of fishing. They will look at it, handle it, and then tell you that they believe in giving the fish a fair chance for his life—that they do not care for just the killing.

It would be interesting to have the opinion of that gentle angler, Izaak Walton, on the subject of tarpon fishing. But it would be more interesting to sit by and enjoy the tussle, to see the look of astonishment that would spread over his benign countenance when he beheld a piscatorial beauty two yards long break water at the end of his tackle. It would surely interrupt his train of contemplation. For he who hies him after tarpon has no use for shady nooks, wherein to sit him down with favorite author and enjoy himself till fortune smiles on him in an attack upon his lure. The tarpon fisherman must be up and doing.

Time and tide wait for no man, but the tarpon fisherman waits anxiously for the tide. The beginning of the flood is the best time, although the change to the ebb has also afforded good fishing. But the fact is that mullet, the staple article of food for the tarpon, are frequently possessed with a desire to come to inner waters in face of the ebb. This puts an end to fishing for the time being. For, when the mullet do appear, the tarpon are at once seized with a desire to kill all in sight. It is an interesting and even exciting spectacle to see a tarpon make preparations for a meal. It is not the kind of sport the fisherman is after, to be sure, but when the tarpon get started on a course of slaughter, it is not a bit of use to fish—better sit by and watch the performance. Tarpon do not make a first attack upon their food with their mouths. They have no teeth, except a roughening on the edges of the lips sharp enough to cut the best line instantly, if it comes in contact with them. They secure their food by striking with their tails, and then turning about to pick up the fish stunned by the blow. When a school of tarpon comes up with a school of mullet, the big fish are so eager to get at their prey that the second rank will often leap clear over the advance line into the thick of the company of mullet, laying about them right and left with their tails, and lashing the water into foam flecked with the blood of the small fry. The mullet, on his side, has been equipped with means of escape, for he is able to make jumps that are remarkable for fish weighing, as he does, from two to three pounds. They spit through

"The fish is out of the water, and you see your bait go sailing through the air."

the air for fully twenty feet. A curious thing about this great jump is that the mullet make a series of three leaps before stopping. The moment the mullet perceive the second line of tarpon coming over the first they jump, with an indescribable result.

The most remarkable exhibition of this that it ever was my fortune to witness took place in Biscayne Bay, near Miami. The school of mullet was fully an acre in extent. They went into the air in a mass, followed closely by the tarpon. It was a wonderful sight, and meant a frightful mortality to the mullet, for the tarpon must have killed thousands of them.

Some tarpon enthusiasts fish three tides a day. I have known them to go out as late as ten o'clock at night, if it happened to be moonlight and the tide came right. And curiously enough the fish did strike, though very few were killed. The exhibition given by the fish in the phosphorescent water made the experience well worth while.

There is one feature in tarpon fishing that the fisherman has reason to be grateful for. He does not have to sit about and wonder if there are any fish in the water. If weather and tidal conditions are right for fishing, there are always plenty of signs in evidence. The tarpon, like the porpoise, comes to the surface to blow. As the time for the change in the tide approaches, they may be seen in schools and pairs, showing their silvery sides on the crest of a wave for a moment, and then gracefully disappearing.

Some fishermen—the veterans, sometimes, but the new men always—are possessed with a wild desire to try to hook one when they see this preliminary performance. They may be seen frantically urging their boatman, first this way and then that, in the hope of cutting off a school in time to drag their bait before them, or to cast it among them. It is usually a vain effort, however, as the fish seldom begin to feed until the tide actually does turn. As a result of this unseemly haste, it is not unusual to see an impatient fisherman hooked to a jewfish (Warsaw), a follower of the tarpon, just at the time when the fish begin to feed and the propitious moment has arrived. I have seen the agony on his face while he tugged away at his jewfish, when the water all about was alive with tarpon, and a bait could not touch its surface before a fish would be there to take it. In fact, I have had experience myself, and know the feeling. Now it would seem that a jewfish, weighing from one hundred to three hundred pounds, might furnish fairly good sport in itself. But it is not tarpon, and there is nothing more to say.

Another thing you will observe about the true fisherman is that there are conditions under which his tackle counts for nothing. There are others under which he would rather do anything than give it up.

The tarpon fisherman, hooked to a jewfish at a critical time, no matter what his feelings may be in regard to the desire for tarpon, is bound to land that jewfish, and he does. It never once enters his mind that he could cut loose, re-rig, and go after the tarpon. On the other hand, a great deal of tarpon tackle, especially that for still-fishing, is so arranged that if a shark takes the bait he will cut loose the moment he closes his jaws. This will not worry the fisherman in the least. He simply puts on another snell, thanks his stars that he does not have to fight the shark, and goes on with his fishing.

But let me get back to the turn of the tide, and consider that the fisherman is not impatient; that he has made up his mind to do as his guide tells him, which is, to reserve his ammunition until the proper time. The guide will row him out to the fishing grounds, where he will see the tarpon rolling about on the undulating surface as though they had not a care in the world. They will come up and blow within arm's length. This was to me perfectly exasperating before I learned the habits of the fish.

But see! there goes one swiftly, giving the surface of the water a sharp slap as he disappears. The tide has turned. Now, if you observe, you will see the fish are moving more quickly in all directions. Here and there one comes clear out of the water. They are feeding, and now is the time to try your luck. You look at your bait, a silvery leather fish, to see that it is properly fixed to the hook, and cast it, say, forty feet or so astern of the boat, and in a moment you have an embarrassment of riches. Two or three, aye even half a dozen, tarpon rush at your bait. You are so fascinated by their action that you forget to strike until too late. None will be hooked, but your bait does not come back to you; you try again. This time a fish gets the bait. You feel his tremendous blow, and set every muscle to hook him. Probably you do. But your leather fish, hooked through the eyes, has

"You strike; * * * in another moment a mass of iridescent silver shoots into the air."

left these useful members on the hook, and shunted his body up the line. In a moment there is another strike, but as your unprotected line comes in contact with the tarpon's sharp, rough lips it parts, and away go hook and snell and fish. The programme of the tarpon fisherman is many strikes, a few hooked, and fewer killed. This is his sport, and he keeps straight on with it. No sooner does your bait strike the water again than you feel a sharp rap. On the instant, you cannot quite make up your mind whether to strike or not. But the next moment a fish breaks water and goes down immediately over your bait. He has seen it, and it looked so much alive to him that he hit it with his tail, and then simply turned around to pick it up. You are prepared for what is coming, so you brace yourself for the shock.

You feel you have hooked the fish. He goes straight to the bottom, and though you are putting all the pressure you have on your thumb-brake, you cannot stop him. He goes fully seventy-five yards before he shows himself, and when you do get sight of him you see his back as he shoots out of the water in a tremendous leap, which takes nearly ten yards more of your line. He is going straight away from you, as you sit there pressing every ounce you have in you on the brake, in the hope of stopping him. He is a hundred and fifty yards away before you see him again. You try your best to hold him. The spool on your reel is much reduced by the outgo of line. Every bone and muscle in your arms and hands is aching from the pressure. Your guide in the mean time is backing water toward the fish with all his might. It is no use, however; you cannot do it. He comes out of the water again, as the last of your line goes off the reel with a shriek. At the same time, you feel a violent pull on the rod. As the new strain comes in an entirely different way, the rod is almost out of your hands before you adjust yourself to it. But you do hold it. There is a sharp report like a rifle shot a short distance away. You look in a dazed way after the fish. You see him jump wildly into the air a couple of times, turning over and over as he falls back into the water, and all is ended.

You feel as though you had had hours of struggle; the muscles in your arms and hands fairly ache; but it has really taken little more than a minute to accomplish all this. It does not profit you to wonder how it came about. It is the kind of thing that happens to the most skilful veterans, and they can explain it no better that can the novice. They will tell you that when the fish, breaking water, is headed away from you, especially when headed toward the open sea, you might as well make up your mind that he will get your line. The fish may be counted as a dead fish, for the friction on the line will cause him to keep up the struggle until his last spark of life goes out.

You simply put on another line or take another rod, and try it again. You trail your bait for some time without any sign of fish, and you are about making up your mind to the fact that fishing is over for that tide, when you suddenly feel the now familiar shock again. In an instant the fish is out of the water, and you see your bait go sailing through the air for a distance of twenty feet. You were caught napping, and you have missed your tarpon. This encourages you to try again. You still see fish breaking water here and there, but it is invariably at the other side of the pass. You chase first one school, then another, all in vain; till, finally, in compassion for your guide who has been rowing for hours, you decide to stop. But he objects, for he is a keen sportsman and does not want to go in without a fish. So you stick to it a while longer; but, at last, after missing another fish, and having a long interval of no signs, you conclude that fishing really is over for that tide, and the guide reluctantly heads the boat for shore.

Thinking of the number of times you have been taken off your guard, you determine to be vigilant as long as your bait is overboard, and you trail it across the pass for the last time. You keep a close watch as you are nearing the shore, and just as you are about to reel in finally, you feel a gentle pull on your line. Being ready, you strike. In fact, you would strike at anything just now. In another moment a mass of iridescent silver shoots into the air and falls back with a crash. Away goes the tarpon. He is hooked, and the battle is on. He does not run the line out fast, but moves around the boat with wonderful speed, and comes out of the water only a short distance away, shaking his head fiercely, and with a defiant expression in his almost human eyes. He dashes first in one direction, then in another, so rapidly that the guide is utterly unable to

" When the fish, breaking water, is headed away from you * * * he will get your line."

At the Tarpon's Approach a Mullet Will Jump Twenty Feet, Straight Away, to Escape.

keep the stern of the boat pointed toward him. At one time he is off at right angles, and again he is right ahead of the boat, so that the line is running out over the bow. He keeps you turning and twisting in a way that is most tiring. The fish has been out of the water three or four times, giving a gymnastic performance of the first order, when down he goes to hunt for deep water. He gets there, too, in spite of all you can do to hold him. Now that he is down, he sulks. You pull and haul and lift with might and main, straining your tackle almost to the breaking point, but to no purpose. He will not budge. You have gradually worked the boat, so that it is just over the spot where the tarpon lies—a very bad place for it to be in. As you cannot move him you begin to think that the fish is off, and that your line has caught on something on the bottom. You finally conclude this is a fact. So you slack up to move the boat in another direction with a view to unhooking. This slacking of the line causes the fish to move. You put the strain on again at once, and he seems to give a little. Your tired muscles and aching fingers take on a new lease of life, and you go at him. You give him another lift. He comes up a little more. You are surely bringing him to the surface. You are putting in all the power you have. To encourage you and to be prepared for the unexpected—though he does not believe the battle to be half over—the guide makes ready with the gaff. After many pulls and much lifting, till your muscles are numb from the strain, you bring the big fish to the surface. The guide cautiously reaches out with the gaff. You are feeling highly elated, as you swing him slowly within reach, and are all ready to relax with a sigh of relief, when, in a flash, the fish, which has no intention of giving up, is away. In an unguarded moment you are the recipient of a crack on the fingers from the reel handle that makes you dizzy, and before you recover sufficiently even to think of putting pressure on the brake, the fish has not only gained a hundred yards of line, but has had a breathing spell. Well, you pull yourself together, grit your teeth, and go at him again.

Your guide is now backing toward the fish as rapidly as possible, to get in what line may be had that way before the fish moves again. Working the reel under this reduced pressure limbers you up a bit, and you begin to take notice again. But a hard fight is still before you. The tarpon recovers rapidly, and is now as fresh as ever. You reel in until you get a fairly good strain on him, doing it as gently as you possibly can, so as not to alarm him; and then you think it about time to stir him up a bit. So you give him a "yank."

He comes out of the water headed straight for the boat—and at the second jump it looks very much as though he were coming aboard. He strikes the water almost under the rod, however, and goes under the boat, out at the other end, and away. In the mean time, you have fully fifty yards of line to take in before you can get a strain on him again. This is no easy task, as your fingers tire more quickly now, and for the next half hour you will accomplish nothing beyond exasperating yourself. But then you begin to feel better. You are getting your second wind. Your fingers may be bleeding and your muscles tired, but you don't mind them. You stir up the fish as often as possible. You get in your line whenever you can, although he runs out lots of it at times. But you do not work as hard in getting it back. In fact, you are acquiring a great deal of knowledge about the sport of tarpon fishing.

At last he begins to weaken. His runs are shorter, his leaps do not lift him from the water—a final effort only brings his head above the surface. With the look of defiance still in his eye, he gives up the battle, and there is nothing more to do but to reel him within reach of the gaff. The guide puts a line through his gills, and you tow him to shore, where he is hauled out before you. What a thing of beauty he is, with his living silver sides, the deep green and gold of his back, and the wonderful iridescence of the underbody.

He measures six feet and ten inches in length, and the scales register one hundred and fifty pounds—just your own weight. As you look at the splendid fellow, a vague feeling of regret comes over you at the thought that such a thing of beauty should be dead. You would gladly give him back his life, for he has given your eye a feast of beauty in magnificent action, and he has called upon all your skill and endurance in The Battle Royal.

4.
Jupiter Inlet, Florida (1891)

JUPITER INLET, FLORIDA.

BY ST. GEORGE RATHBONE.

I WAS but one of the army of migrants when first my pilgrim steps wended Florida-ward, seeking in its to me unknown but well vouched for scenery, its balmy air and its endless varieties of sport that diversion and enjoyment which the frigid and boisterous North cannot yield after Thanksgiving Day has set the seal to the close of even the Indian summer. 'T was by degrees that its claims upon me evinced themselves. Yearly I came away with lingering steps and slow, and ever as the seasons passed my periods of absence shortened and my periods of enjoyment lengthened. From a casual and itinerant dallyer with the sorceress I became an ardent worshipper, and Florida now holds undisputed sway as my winter's queen. A hunter, a fisherman, a naturalist and a yachtsman, and yet somewhat of an epicurean, what more natural than that I should seek a camp of refuge and a permanent habitation which should yield, in the highest degree, these delights, and should find them in Eden, advantageously situate between the inlets at Jupiter and St. Lucie, the latter known as Indian River Inlet. Jupietr is about twenty-eight miles south, while Indian River Inlet lies some ten miles above, and here all that mortal can require for artistic satisfaction, sportsman's instinct or creature comforts is at our door, for fifteen miles above the St. Lucie inlet the bed of the river is covered with oysters. In sailing here two years ago, our charts having run out, we felt the way while gliding along, by sounding with an oar, and for hours heard a constant "chink" as it struck oysters. They are worked but very little, are fine in flavor, and no one has as yet thought it worth while to cultivate them.

Here also is the home of the manatee. The method of catching this fish is very curious. Two or three nets are secured across a narrow arm of the St. Lucie, the lower one firm, the second slack and the upper one loose. Then the manatee is

"EMBOWERED IN PALMETTOS." (P. 271.)

alarmed. It makes a break down the river, strikes the loose net, tears it free, gets twisted up in it, and if the second net gives the third is sure to hold. Were all the nets fastened taut, the creature would go through each like a bullet, or, if they were made very powerful, kill itself.

Here, too, we are in the best of possible positions for organizing social parties for exploration, which lend variety, the very spice of life, and thus it came to pass that on one of the typical mornings of last winter we were ready to start on a short cruise up the St. Lucie River. I had never been up the St. Lucie, although I had been some distance up the St. Sebastian two years back, when on a long cruise down the east coast.

We chartered a thirty-five-foot steam launch for the occasion, the *Eleanor*, owned by a pineapple planter, a Baltimore gentleman named Lucas, who loves Eden and has a splendid property there. He was to run the launch, assisted by a Mr. Duffy, his friend, while Harry Richards manned the engine. Frank made up the party of six.

The mouth of the river is very wide, and for several miles it is a noble stream, deep and with wooded banks. I confess I was both pleased and amazed at its appearance, but presently came a change—sudden and rather disappointing. The great river came to an end and two arms extended, one to the north for many miles and the other to the south. These branches are not one-twentieth part as wide as the main river, though generally very deep. They wind about in a serpentine way, sometimes through open reedy tracts, again past growths of pine and palmetto, and always with banks some six to eight feet high on either side.

We passed a few cranes and water turkeys, but the birds were very wild. Several herons flew up ahead of us and a couple of white ibis. Birds, with these exceptions, were very scarce, thanks to the plume hunters, who enter the rookeries and hatcheries by night and slay by hundreds egrets, ibis, herons, cranes, and even pelicans when they can. These butchers have been the curse of Florida, and it is certainly a shame that the Legislature has not prohibited such wanton slaughter.

After winding about for some time we

came to where the channel was really too tortuous to proceed further. There could be no mistake ; we were on the wrong trail and must back out. So, with setting poles, we managed to get the boat around and proceeded to the main stream, where, passing on the other side of a point, we entered what proved to be the genuine north fork of the St. Lucie. It is not here more than forty or fifty feet across and generally half of that, but very deep.

It was simply delightful. Once, however, we held our breath as a small flock of buzzards arose from a reedy bank and lazily flapped away from the carcass of a big deer, possibly the victim of some hunter who sought his venison with a blazing pine knot for a jack and a double barrel loaded with buckshot, wounding three deer to one that he slew.

We had now made twenty - five miles in all and looked for a place to camp and a good spot to tie the boat up, where a fire could be built on shore. I suggested that as the water looked suitable for bigmouth bass we have a try at them. We tumbled into the dinghy, and made an exploration of several likely arms that formed little bayous or pockets. The result was three bass, none of them very enormous in size, all caught on a Hill spoon. As we moved up a long bayou, something dropped from the bank ahead into the water with a splash.

"A ''gator!'" exclaimed Frank, although his back was turned that way.

"I see him," said I, raising my rifle.

Upon the calm water, about fifty feet away, were two peculiar objects, looking like pine knots, which I knew were the reptile's eyes. I took a quick aim and fired. There was no commotion, but Frank immediately declared I had hit him. The bullet had passed in and out of its neck, just back of the eyes.

The next day we decided to try a short tramp for deer, signs of which had been seen.

The woods were very open and we could have seen deer half a mile away.

There is only one way to get near these little Florida deer when they are browsing in the open pine barren—work to leeward and then advance slowly, watching the deer's tail, which is always jerked before he raises his head, thus giving one time to become motionless. In this way it is easy to steal up close enough to reduce the number of Mr. Deer's mess. We were given no such opportunity on this tramp, as not a deer was sighted. I raised a flock of wood ibis, and also a number of sandhill cranes, almost breaking my neck in the endeavor to get a specimen of the latter great birds. One shot I had at a crane flying, but not being a Bogardus or a Carver I failed to bag the handsome game, esteemed fine eating wherever known. I regretted not having my shot-

FLORIDA TROPHIES OF ROD AND REEL.

gun and some No. 2s just then. There were also a number of white cranes and a blue heron that kept just outside of decent rifle shot.

With the weather very hot and the wind in the west we knew what was coming full soon. Upon taking a vote it was agreed that we start down the river. We started for the forks of the river, with the current to assist our progress.

Fishing was tried at a favorite place where Henshall declared he took large bass as fast as he could get them in ; but the weather must have been against us, for we did not have a strike at the troll.

Meanwhile my premonition was verified. The wind whipped into the north and began to blow great guns. It was all very fine so long as we were on the St. Lucie, protected by the wooded shore on our port quarter, but once we struck the Indian River it would be different. There we must head directly into the teeth of the gale, and if anyone has an idea that the Indian River cannot kick up a great sea on such an occasion he makes a mistake. It has a clean stretch of some thirty miles up St. Lucie Sound to the Narrows, and is from one and a half to three miles wide. Besides, its being very shallow adds to the nasty nature of the sea.

We got it when we ran out from the St. Lucie. As far as we could see the Indian River was a mass of boiling whitecaps. No sailboat would have made progress trying to beat up against such a combination. I had been through it before, and had enough then to convince me that patience in waiting for a fair breeze was the best policy. We met one boat flying down almost under bare poles and going so fast at that as to shoot past us like a fleeting dream, the captain shouting something we could not catch, as the roaring wind carried his words beyond.

We were compelled to take the middle of the river until past Waveland, because of the grass that choked the channel.

How the billows did roar and toss! Scores of times our screw would revolve in the air as we plunged downward.

Again and again huge seas would strike the starboard bow in spite of our pilot's good generalship, and the spray would drive all over us.

It took us several hours to put behind us the eight miles between Eden and the mouth of the St. Lucie, for even the gallant little launch could make but slow headway. At about half past 3 o'clock we could plainly see the white building known as the store and post office on the edge of the water at Eden, and all of us were glad to draw near our goal, for the buffeting we received had become a trifle monotonous. Those who have gone through the checkered lines of a sportsman's career for years learn to be content with what fortune sends them, however, and take as much enjoyment as possible out of the sport itself. A few days later

DOLCE FAR NIENTE.

we decided to take a run down to Jupiter Inlet, possibly to Lake Worth, so we packed our traps, took a twelve-bore rifle, rods and tackle, a valise apiece and my inseparable *vade mecum*—the camera—and stood on the bulkhead at the end of the captain's then unfinished long pier, awaiting the coming of the *St. Lucie*. She hove in sight, and at 6:30 the tuneful voice of Captain Bravo was heard, while his well-known smile beamed on us from the upper deck.

It took us several hours to go through the Narrows, helped or hindered by the strong north wind, favorable to our passage on a straight stretch, but it sent us into many a pocket, where the darky deck hands had to throw all their strength on the setting poles in order to work her out.

The scenery was weird and fantastic—false channels or canals ran hither and thither, with the trees forming an arch overhead. We scraped the branches at times; so that it was easy to pluck the live oak or cypress leaves. On every hand lay the swamp. A few birds flew up at our approach, but otherwise the Narrows presented a dismal appearance, funereal-like in its ghostly character, and not to be forgotten.

Air plants could be seen very frequently hanging from trees and just bursting into bloom. In the top of many a palmetto I detected a young rubber tree growing. The nature of this tree is indeed singular. Starting thus thirty feet from the ground—from a seed perhaps carried by a bird—it throws tendrils down toward the moist ground. When these strike root they grow into one or more trunks—I have seen a tree with three such trunks—and eventually the palmetto that has been the foster mother of the rubber is choked to death and yields its life to the monster it brought forth.

Finally this strange region was left behind, and we passed into a channel dredged through beds of old oyster shells. Long ago this region must have been a famous place for oysters, but it has none now. At Eden there is a great shell mound erected by the ancients, and at Jupiter I saw one that staggered me; it was of great height and length.

Captain Richards advanced a plausible theory respecting these Indian mounds of oyster shells. He claims that he has always found an old burial ground near the mounds and presumes that a part of the burial ceremony was in eating great quantities of oysters and piling up the shells, as we place a monument over our dead.

After passing through Hobe Sound and stopping at one or two likely looking places on the land between the river and the ocean, where we saw luxuriant bananas growing, we came in sight of the grand lighthouse at Jupiter, whose beacon has for many years warned mariners drifting in near shore on the treacherous Gulf Stream.

It was about 2 o'clock when we landed at the dock at Jupiter. They were then building the little railway running through to Lake Worth, the ground being ready for the rails. It is now an accomplished fact, ridding the Lake Worth tourist of the abominable hacks that were wont to jolt the life half out of him during the ride across.

Jupiter is a peculiar formation; it is really the junction of the Indian and Locohatchee rivers, the one extending for 165 miles up along the coast, the other a little stream coming from the swamps of the interior not far from the head of Lake Okeechobee.

On the northern bank of what is called Jupiter River lies the great lighthouse and several comfortable white cottages, the homes of Captain Armour, who has been in charge since the war, his assistant, and the signal service man.

On the southern bank a large sternwheel steamer was moored. She looked like a Mississippi River boat, and had been brought in by the officer then in charge, Captain Fitzgerald, narrowly escaping disaster at the time. This steamer was used as an hotel, and we were served royal meals all the time we stayed.

After a while we strolled down along the sand about a quarter of a mile to a point opposite the inlet. Here, in a little bay, a party of Philadelphia gentlemen were drawing in sailor's choice, a small but rather nice pan fish, which abounds in these waters. We wandered around enjoying the warm sunshine, watching a flock of gulls and snipe on a point opposite, and finally brought up at the Chattahoochee Hotel, where several Louisville merchants had just come in from pompano fishing.

Henshall declared the gamy pompano would not take bait and could only be caught in a net, but this has been discovered to be false. During our stay at

Jupiter several score were taken. Great care must be the order of the day. Small hooks and light but strong tackle, together with a boat, sand fleas for bait, and room to allow for the fierce run of the vigorous fish, will bring success. Almost absolute silence is necessary, however, as the game is easily frightened. They are probably the finest eating fish in our country, and when taken fresh from their native waters and well cooked make a dish fit for a king.

There was a naphtha launch from New York, owned by Commodore Hughes, that won my admiration. I believe she was thirty-five feet in length over all, and with her cedar sides and brass furniture made a handsome craft. The cabin was a waterproof roof, with canvas curtains that could be raised or lowered at will. She had all the appliances to delight a cruiser's heart and I thought the boat was the neatest I had ever seen.

The Gas Engine and Power Company, of New York, its makers, have since sent out a boat that suits me better—one made to bear harder knocks, and having two short masts, being rigged with a jib in addition, so that with a fair wind the engine may remain idle. When the breeze is dead ahead such a boat, urged on by a two or four horse power engine, will climb into the teeth of the wind in a way calculated to excite envy in the heart of the yachtsman, who vainly beats against the gale and gets a tremendous ducking at little profit.

We went over to the lighthouse, and passing out upon the platform that goes around the tower we had a magnificent view, although the wind blew furiously up there, so that the more timid hugged the wall.

We could trace the Indian River a long way running north; the sinuous course of the Locohatchee until lost in the labyrinth of swamps and heavy growth; the crooked line of Lake Worth Creek a short distance, as it trended away to the south, and even get a glimpse of Lake Worth itself by careful scrutiny. To the east lay the great ocean, a magnificent panorama; to the west lay the great unknown swamps that border that wonderful and mysterious lake, Okeechobee, and terminate in the Everglades.

Monday dawned partly cloudy, with wind enough for fishing. I took views of the Chattahoochee Hotel while the people were preparing to go in quest of the finny tribes. Then we separated, one party to sail up the Locohatchee for various species of fish, a second in a couple of rowboats after pompano, while we entered the sailboat of a darky, a sort of hodge-podge, neither sharpie nor catboat, but something in the line of a skip jack with a half cabin.

The sable captain took his boy along, and we were soon making the run from the lighthouse as near down to the inlet as was safe. We soon had rods out and it was not a great while before something struck me with great force. The boat was moving swiftly, and I heard a suspicious crack that warned me to look out for that bamboo rod near the lower ferrule. I managed to save my fish, however, after quite a tug, and found him to be a large crevalle, or cavalli. This fish is not eaten as a general rule, the flesh being too oily, but he is a strong fighter in the water, and being very trimly built looks like a piratical customer. He was the first of a numerous company I took.

A few bluefish were caught that day, the party up the Locohatchee picking up nearly a dozen in some favorite locality known only to the captain of the craft.

Our pompano fishermen had better luck and brought in a fair mess of the toothsome fish. We amused ourselves between times catching mullet from the side of the steamer. This is a fish that was once said never to touch bait, and that one had never been caught on a hook. We took dozens of them. A fine leader, a trout hook, a piece of dough from the cook's galley and no sinker—the tide carries the dough along—a tiny morsel on the dainty hook, it sinks a foot or so; there is a jerk and up comes a mullet nearly a foot long, his white sides glittering like silver in the light. Small cats could be taken at the rate of one a minute. It was nothing to say "I'll fish until I have twenty-five," for they never stopped biting that I knew of, day or night. Probably the refuse thrown out from the cook's galley brought these schools of small fish around.

Crabs were caught, the largest I ever saw in all my life, but they were very scarce, and the old darky got a quarter a piece for them. They were worth it.

Boating is regarded as a *sine qua non* down in that region, and the man who does not know enough about aquatics to run his own craft had better learn before making a trip to the cruiser's paradise.

To the canoeist there can be nothing more delightful than a trip down the east coast — all sheltered work, through the great bays, known as rivers here, the Halifax, Hillsboro, Mosquito Lagoon, through the Haulover Canal and down the Indian River to Jupiter — about 250 miles in all, a winter's trip.

The only discouragements found would be the fierce northers, head winds, lack of stowage room for fresh water, and occasionally tracking over oyster bars. I have the location of all those bars well noted — I found them, as the keel and garboard streak of my cedar Rushton cruiser, *Sea Robin*, bear mute but eloquent testimony. Had I stuck to my chart all would have been well, for there is a steamboat channel, but the temptation to cut across lots often proved the cause of disaster.

From what I saw of the new steamer I was well impressed with the service. She was crowded the four times I was on her and, proving insufficient, two sister boats, the *St. Sebastian* and *St. Augustine*, have appeared on the river, so that in the future tourists down the dreamy Indian River, past the orange groves of Rockledge, the wonderful pineapple plantations of Eden, to the groves of Lake Worth may expect to be well taken care of.

We fortunately did not get aground going up Hobe Sound, and our passage through the intricate canals of Jupiter Narrows was but a repetition of the one down. Thus the halcyon days passed away and each brought its pleasures. If we did not perform great feats with gun and rod we enjoyed capturing what came our way ; we were not butchers.

If one chose to tramp a few miles back of the savannah, among the pines, deer are to be found, but it is astonishing how little one cares to exert one's self when it is so pleasant to loll in a boat and wait for the game to come to you.

Many were the phases and incidents of sport and pastime we enjoyed, now going by night with a Ferguson jack light to spear fish and securing a boat load, anon trying for alligators on the savannah.

Yet another day we netted and took two large green turtles, a number of crevalle, sergeant fish, red snapper, lady fish, mutton fish, silver catfish and a four-foot shark which I clubbed over the head and tossed away.

That night our menu for supper was flavored with game. Besides genuine green turtle soup, we had fried green turtle that beat any spring chicken I ever tasted, rabbit and coot stew, cold roast venison with guava jelly, and broiled dove and snipe.

Space would fail to describe all we saw and took part in during those glorious weeks. Their memory haunts me while I write. I am again on the lovely Indian River, sailing across for the fishing grounds, lunch and tackle and gun at my side, and T—— tightening the halliards, his sun-burned face always wreathed in a smile.

I look forward to future winters to be spent in this favored region. One may go to other parts at other seasons where game is more plentiful, often sacrificing home comforts, but at Eden it is all at your doors, among a people sociable and kindly disposed toward strangers. They are all from the North, people of education and refinement, so that in dropping off here one need not feel that he is about to encamp in a squatter wilderness.

No one has an axe to grind about Eden, simply because no one has land to sell. The available property is only about a quarter of a mile deep, running along the ridge between the river and the savannah, so that it is limited in extent. If you wonder why the captain gave his place that name, fight your way against head winds a week in a small cruiser, as I did with *Neide* in '87, and you will swear the place is a paradise as it opens on your view, with its swaying cocoanuts, houses embowered in palmettos and rubber trees, its great vistas of pineapple plants and its blooming flowers.

5.
Turkey Tracks in the Big Cypress (1909)

HERE THE ENVIRONMENT PROTECTS THE WILD TURKEYS.

TURKEY TRACKS IN THE BIG CYPRESS

BY A. W. DIMOCK

Photographs by Julian A. Dimock

WHEN the creatures of the wild were named, the wild turkey should have been christened Wise Turkey. The big bird is by nature sociable and if, at times, he seems distrustful of human beings, it is because he is quick to recognize a hostile purpose.

The Indian hunter compared his perception with that of the wary deer, to the advantage of the bird.

"Deer look up, see Injun, say: 'Maybe Injun, maybe stump'; turkey look up, see Injun, say: 'Maybe Injun,' then run away quick."

When, in the wilderness, I fired a gun which I had loaded for turkey, every chick of the family within a mile took to the tall timber. When, in that same wilderness, three years of observation had shown them that the gun was fixed for crows, the wild turkeys paid no attention to its discharge, even when it was fired within twenty feet of a brood of them, or when a dying crow fell beside them.

In many states where these birds once flourished, they may now be classed with the dodo. The one place, within my observation, where their number has decreased but little, in the last two decades, is the country of the Big Cypress Swamp in Florida. Here their environment protects them. In the dry season the turkeys scatter over the open prairies where they are not easily approached. When these are covered with water that rises to the hunter's knees, above fathomless mud in which he might disappear entirely, they gather in the thick woods of the hummocks.

On one of these almost unapproachable oases is a recently established grapefruit plantation. The owner of these three hundred acres has forbidden the killing of turkeys on his grounds. The lonesome-proof or constitutional wanderers. One day, as I rested on a log, watching a flock of turkeys which was strolling fearlessly about a lot of laborers, the boss of the gang, a weazened old man with an unfamiliar face, sat down beside me. We talked of the plantation, its history and its prospects, its work and its workmen, and then, as a bunch of turkeys came near us I remarked: "It would be wicked to kill wild birds that are as friendly as those."

AT FIRST THEY TURNED INQUIRING EYES UPON THE CAMERA WHEN THE SHUTTER CLICKED.

Indians, who often visit his place, scrupulously respect the prohibition; white hunters don't poach on the domain, because of its inaccessibility and the certainty of detection; while the negroes, who work in that isolated field, prefer not to incur the twenty-five dollar penalty, the sure enforcement of which means involuntary servitude for an indefinite period.

The plantation is a sanctuary for negroes to whom its seclusion is advantageous while its white employees are either

"Most as bad as shootin' turkeys from their roost at Skeleton Creek?" he asked.

I nearly fell off the log. A full generation had passed since I had hunted and camped with this man on the Indian-infested, buffalo-covered prairies of the Indian Territory. He had reminded me of a day when I had vainly tried to stalk some wild turkeys on the prairie and of a night when he had led me under the trees where the turkeys roosted and in sheer desperation and weariness of spirit I had shot a few out of a tree that was filled with them.

On the plantation, groups of young gobblers and hen turkeys with their broods walk freely and fearlessly among the workmen and they have often come within reach of my hand as, in the shade of a water oak, I sat idly on a stump. Yet they kept wary eyes upon the suspicious character who neither slung an ax nor grubbed with a mattock, and were more distrustful of a slight motion of my hand than of a shovelful of soil thrown beside them by a laborer. They responded promptly to the call of a tree felled by the workmen, to seek the insect life to be found in its upper branches.

Though, at first, the turkeys turned inquiring eyes upon the camera when the shutter clicked, it soon ceased to interest them, but when they observed that the unobtrusive steps of the Camera-man happened always to follow their own, they became suspicious and he had to suspend his pursuit for the day. Sometimes, when the turkeys seemed especially sociable, I sought to secure their confidence by scattering handfuls of grain among them, but they feared the gift-bearing Greek, and I only succeeded in implanting distrust, by actions which their inherited experience had taught them were of evil portent. Although the Camera-man spent much time trying to photograph turkeys on the wing, he couldn't run fast enough to make them fly. They always managed to keep ahead of him until they could plunge into the dank recesses of a cypress swamp which ended the chase.

IN THE DRY SEASON THE TURKEYS SCATTER OVER THE OPEN PRAIRIE, WHERE THEY ARE NOT EASILY APPROACHED.

Work on the plantation began but a few years ago and even now it is only partially cleared, yet generations of wild turkeys have known it as a sanctuary and within its boundaries exhibit changed natures. I hobnobbed one morning with a hen turkey and her brood and later saw them wander out on the prairie away from the plantation. On the fol-

"IT WOULD BE WICKED TO KILL BIRDS THAT ARE AS FRIENDLY AS THESE," I REMARKED.

lowing day I saw them again, several miles from their hummock homestead and was able to identify them with reasonable certainty. But their natures had reverted to type and they were typical wild turkeys, not to be approached within gunshot.

When conditions of food and dryness on the prairie invited the turkeys, they left the plantation, group by group, and brood by brood, until it was almost barren of turkey life, but the first storm that flooded the prairies drove them home again, singly and in flocks. On the prairies they were wary as the wildest of their species. In the plantation they became tame as barn-yard fowl. Sometimes a hen of the hummock hatched a brood elsewhere and brought her half-grown chicks to the old home, where it took her long days to educate them out of their wildness. Occasionally strange wild turkeys followed a home-coming flock and made their first visit to the plantation when fully grown. Day by day their distrust grew less and in a few weeks the immigants couldn't be distinguished from the well-behaved native born.

The tourist-sportsman seldom penetrates the haunts of the wild turkey in the Big Cypress country. The habitat of these birds is surrounded by moats, sentineled and guarded by fierce warders. The eye of the hunter as he walks should be keen to distinguish the ugly, coiled cottonmouth from the mud of the trail which it closely resembles. His feet must be nimble to avoid the only less dangerous little speckled-bellied moccasins that swarm in his path, and his ear quick to catch the locust-like warnings of deadly rattlesnakes that lurk in the grass. Even the few dwellers on the borders of the Big Cypress have a wholesome dread of these reptiles, which is highly protective of the game of the country.

Most of the turkeys that are killed here are shot by alligator hunters for food. The vocation of these men carries them into the very home of the reptiles and accustoms them to ignore a danger which they yet never belittle.

THEY RESPONDED PROMPTLY TO THE CALL OF A TREE FELLED BY THE WORKMEN.

Sometimes a hunter drags a torch of palmetto fans across the wind, through the grass of a prairie until it is swept by a wall of roaring flame, half a mile in width. Turkeys are unharmed; deer are even attracted by the ashes; but snakes perish by the thousand in the flames. A guide of my own was bitten by a rattlesnake while we were hunting for turkeys in the Big Cypress and although my companion, who was beside him, at once sucked the venom from the wound, the victim came near passing over the divide and it was weeks before he recovered.

The born hunter, who walks without stepping on anything, passes through thickets without touching a bush, and spots every leaf that stirs within a hundred yards, can usually pick up a turkey for supper within an hour's walk in the woods or on the prairie. It takes the sportsman longer. In former years I hunted them and have spent days vainly approaching birds that played hide and seek with me, but always kept just out of range. When I sought them by moonlight in their roosts I got them, but when I played fair they outwitted me. On the few occasions when I have successfully stalked a wild turkey there has usually been reason to suspect that the bird I bagged was not the bird I was pursuing.

One morning while in camp in the Royal Palm Hummock I heard the gobbling of a turkey which I could definitely locate in a dense thicket about three hundred yards distant. Leaving the camp, with my rifle, I told my companion that I would bring home that turkey for dinner. I then spent an hour in stealthily approaching the place from which came, every few minutes, the gobbling of the creature which I couldn't see. Before I reached the thicket the sound had ceased, but, later, was renewed from a clump of trees a quarter of a mile beyond. Again I skulked and crept until I reached the clump from which the gobbling had seemed to come, when I saw the turkey enter a mangrove swamp several hundred yards from me.

It was quite useless to go farther, but the Spirit of the Chase obsessed me and

I plunged into the tangle of mangrove, from which I emerged some hours later mud-bedraggled and worn out, body and spirit. I leaned, disheartened, against a fallen tree. For half an hour I rested for the coming interminable tramp back to camp and the humiliating arrival, empty-handed, when suddenly my turkey, or another, loomed up before my eyes. He was within twenty-five yards and looked bigger than an ostrich.

I did not dare to breathe until he turned away from me and lowered his head. Then I cautiously laid my hand on the rifle beside me and slowly turning it drew a bead on the middle of the big body of the turkey. Of course at that short range I ought to have shot off his head, but I might have missed and had to carry to camp an excuse instead of a turkey, while a shot through the body could be accounted for by the

THE HABITAT OF THESE BIRDS IS SURROUNDED BY MOATS, SENTINELED AND GUARDED BY FIERCE WARDERS.

A HUNTER DRAGS A TORCH OF PALMETTO FANS . . . UNTIL THE PRAIRIE IS SWEPT BY A WALL OF ROARING FLAMES . . . TURKEYS ARE UNHARMED . . . BUT SNAKES PERISH BY THE THOUSAND.

substitution of rods for yards in the story at the camp-fire. Thirst and fatigue were forgotten as I picked up the big bird and prepared to return to the camp. It then occurred to me that I didn't know where the camp was. I was troubled until I thought of the royal palms beside it, which lifted their splendid heads to twice the height of the surrounding forest. The towering tops of these grand old trees were never more pleasing to me than when I caught sight of them from a tree which I then climbed.

As I neared the camp I heard signal shots from my companion, to which I replied, finding him, on my arrival, much perturbed because of my long absence, coupled with his knowledge of how easy it was to get lost in a Florida swamp and how unpleasant after it had happened. That experience has come twice to me and in both instances I was led astray by wild turkeys. I think that if a balance could be struck it would be found that turkeys have had quite as much fun with me as I have had with them. But at least they have taught me that the best way for the ordinary sportsmen to get wild turkeys is to let them hunt him.

Of course the place in which he hides must be chosen with judgment. The edge of a prairie, a clump of trees, and just before sunset make a good combination. I have often had good luck while sitting quietly in a skiff as it drifted down some little stream in a turkey region. Chance counts for a lot. I once cruised with a certain well-known naturalist whose constantly recurring, unearned good luck was of sinister significance. When he went fishing, because he was too lazy to hunt deer with me, I tramped all day and got nothing while he brought back a buck which swam out to his skiff and was caught with a landing net.

On another occasion, when we were out in a swamp hunting for turkeys, he became tired and stopped to rest and write under a wide-spreading live oak for the rest of the day while I continued to hunt. When I came back with a tale of several turkeys seen, but none bagged, my friend was still writing, and a fat

THE CAMERA SOON CEASED TO INTEREST THEM.

WHEN THEY OBSERVED THAT THE STEPS OF THE CAMERA-MAN HAPPENED ALWAYS TO FOLLOW THEIR OWN THEY BECAME SUSPICIOUS.

gobbler hung to a branch of the tree beside him. It was doubtless one of the turkeys I had frightened which lit in the tree just over my friend and waited for him to lay aside his work, wipe his pen, and pick up his gun. The naturalist then resumed his writing and was in his usual philosophical frame of mind, when I returned covered with mud and full of cactus thorns.

There is a serious side to this subject, quite worthy of consideration. It would be a misfortune for this grand creature, perhaps the bird most closely associated with the progress of our race on this continent, to become extinct. Yet this has already happened in most of the States of the Union. If we are to continue to treat the turkey simply as a game bird, to be protected only that it may be killed for sport, the finish of both turkey and fun is in sight.

Year by year, more of our people hunt with cameras and fewer with guns. Turkeys shot with a camera remain to fill the forests with interest, enliven the landscape, and perpetuate subjects of study and enjoyment for generations to come. There is yet time to save this beautiful bird to the people of this country.

The one and only way to accomplish this is to back up wise laws by an active public sentiment. And this work should begin right in the big cities. It is the city sportsman who carries the automatic weapon and works it to the limit, often regardless of local law and local sentiment. The dweller on the border of the wilderness, while often indifferent to the letter of the statute is apt to live up to the law as his community construes it.

I once asked a Florida hunter if game laws were ever kept in the Big Cypress.

"We boys keep 'em," he replied, "better 'n the fellows we guide. I never shoot game for fun, and I don't kill ary deer or turkey when the law's on, unless I'm workin' in the woods and get hungry. If the sheriff wants to stop that he'll have to come and live with me."

6.
Turtling in Florida
(1890)

DRAWING THE SEINE.

TURTLING IN FLORIDA.

BY J. M. MURPHY.

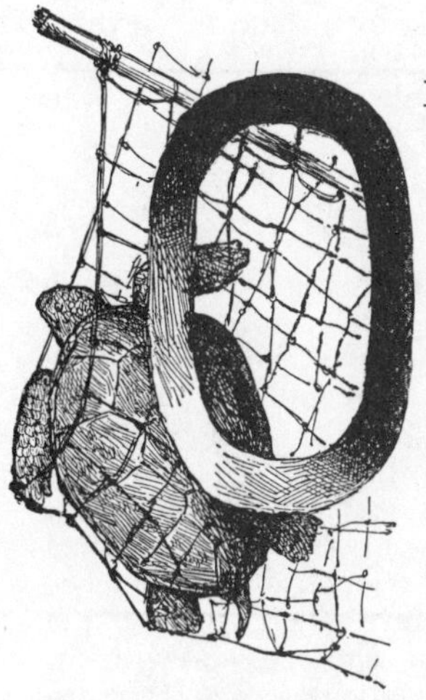

OF all the opportunities for sport in which Florida abounds, and they are many, none is so largely available and so little known as "turtling." The gunner who follows the quail, the snipe and the wild duck, and the fisherman who plays the lordly tarpum and the jewfish have each had their enthusiastic chroniclers. The St. John and the Indian rivers, the Lucie and the shallow waters of the Atlantic coast are almost as well known as the trout streams of the Laurentides, the home of the muskallonge and the sporting regions in the great Northwest; yet no champion has yet arisen to advocate the claims of the turtler or to describe the scenes and incidents of the turtler's life. Why this should be so has often been to me inexplicable, for turtling is carried on in a district beyond comparison for beauty. It has all the elements which in other spheres are reckoned sport's chief attraction, and turtles are to be caught by the adventurous when nearly every other sporting district of the United States is held fast in the grip of

"Winter lingering in the lap of Spring."

It is the arrival of that very period which the necessities of language alone make it necessary to call winter in the South that brings back to the waters of the Gulf of Mexico and to the reefs of the coast of Florida the myriads of turtle upon which the merchant and the fisherman depend, though individuals, sufficient for the sportsman, are by no means uncommon all the year round.

The season which in northern latitudes locks up the storehouses of the deep and relegates the hardy mariner to enforced idleness, in the genial South bids him prepare for his summer's harvest. The sharpies of Clearwater Harbor and of Sarasota Bay are overhauled; the miles and miles of nets are made ready for that havoc which the skillful fishermen will inevitably wreak with them, and in due time, from the inland retreat, among the palmetto and the cocoa palms of the coast, or from the Bahamas, come the amphibious "conks," whose feats of daring on and under the sea are as a thrice-told tale.

Then comes that marvelous return of life to all animated nature which, in the topsy-turvydom of terms necessary to convey full meaning to a Northern mind, must be called the spring; albeit it is with him still the depth of winter's gloom. And what a wonderful picture does Florida then present! A sky beside which that of Italy would pale into insignificance; an air beside which that of the Riviera would be debilitating; a sea beside which the Mediterranean is a capricious vixen, and a wealth of bursting foliage which has no comparison the wide world through. If ever there was a land designed to draw men's minds from the strife and struggles, the care and annoyances of life, to lull the shattered nerves and to be a refuge and restorer of those who would for a time be

> The world forgetting,
> By the world forgot,

thy name is Florida!

Follow the turtler down the coast by the mangrove, from Cedar Keys southward; live on the generous fare with which every port is bountifully supplied; spend a fortnight on such a coasting trip and I warrant me you shall have such sport as it has not entered into your mind to conceive and return to your snug hotel at Tampa, or by the Manatee River, at Charlotte Harbor, or where else among its pleasant resorts you have selected, with such a fund of health and pleasing reminiscence as it could not fall to your lot to acquire in any other resort within the United States. And all this without any preparation on your part, for that which you will have participated in is one of the standard industries of the country, followed for its intrinsic value and not for the delectation of visitors. The habitués of North American restaurants and the aldermanic stomachs of London must needs be supplied with green turtle soup whether Northern sportsmen join in the chase or not; the demand for the shell adornments, so dear and so necessary to the lady's boudoir, will be met, even if the material be gathered by the hardy Seminoles alone. The fleets of Cedar Keys and of Key West will plow the main, and the reefs of Anclote and Sarasota Bay will still be scoured for their golden harvest whether the sport be participated in by the ever-welcome stranger or not; indeed this is half the charm of it, that you are participating in a real transaction, an actual hunt, a living sport and not a put-up pageant.

Whether you follow the sport by land or sea will depend largely upon the period of the year. In the earlier portion of the season the turtling will be that of the sea, and of two sorts, in one of which the turtles are taken by nets and in the other by spearing.

Scores of boats and vessels and hundreds of men are engaged in the trade, for here are the best turtling grounds in the world, and profitable, too, in the main, though very uncertain. A hundred dollars may be realized in a day, but, like the fishermen of old, you may toil all day and take nothing. The net used is a hundred feet long and eight feet deep, with meshes a foot square. The lower part is heavily leaded and kept in position by two anchors, while the upper edge is corked and attached to two buoys, one at each end thereof. These nets are planted from a small boat whereever a shoal of turtles are seen. They are sometimes set "on chance," to drift with the tide in well-known haunts, several boats working together, pulling in opposite directions and swinging with the current until they have entangled their prey in the slowly circling nets. The great danger in this style of fishing is that, instead of gathering in the turtle, the nets are quite as likely to inclose the destructive shark or the scarcely less obnoxious sawfish. The sawfish will swing its powerful weapon through the net, much as an alligator swings his tail, and either dash through it or, in its wild fight for freedom, become so involved that it can be released only by being chopped out. The shark, owing to his immense strength, rushes more easily through the net, but plays as sad havoc with it, cutting such a diagonal sweep through it that repair becomes an impossibility. When all goes well and the green turtle only is caught the net is lifted, the fore flippers of each turtle pierced and tied together, the prizes stowed away in the hold and the nets set again.

Getting a huge turtle into a boat is lively work for a while, and one which is likely to result in an involuntary bath or a capsize if the men are not experts. The best way to do it is to lean over the gunwale, so as to bring it as close to the water as possible, catch hold of the flippers until the body of the turtle is well forward, then sit suddenly on the opposite side and in tumbles the awkward captive, sprawling amidships.

Netting, however, is not by any means so exciting as the alternative means of capture by "pegging;" this has all the incidents of whaling without its rigors. In this hunting smaller boats, broad of beam and manned by two or more experts, make their way to the "runs." One man sculls and the other stands in the bow on the lookout. Men of experience will espy a turtle almost as far as the human eye can see, even in lumpy water, although the turtle makes less commotion in the water than any other swimming creature, for only a small portion of his back shows above the surface. Its well-known snort as it comes to the surface more often indicates its locality; it is a sound easily recognized by those familiar with it, and when it breaks water, or "bolts," as it is locally termed, anybody with a good sea eye can follow it. Then the harpooner in the bow clutches his pegging pole, made of yellow pine, light and easy to handle, tipped with a sharp point and a flange to prevent its entering too far into the shell, and away goes the chase; away goes the terrified turtle out to the deep water, and away flies the pursuing boat. Quick must the marksman be, and sure. Whizz goes the pole and with it the spinning line. The peg, if rightly aimed, sinks in the shell, and if the turtle once gets a start before he is surprised and hauled in he will pull the boat with its crew several miles before yielding through fatigue, and at a pace quite surprising. It has not this chance with thoroughly efficient peggers, for every precaution is taken to prevent his scaring the other members of the shoal. He is hauled aboard with as little disturbance as possible, and a really clever crew will capture. one after another, nearly the whole shoal, without the others having a faint idea of danger.

Sometimes the harpooner is so successful that there is not time to haul the quarry aboard, in which case a keg, large enough to hold about five gallons, is tied to the peg rope and each captive is allowed to swim about until the crew are ready to take them out of the water. Great skill and judgment are required in the "striker," for a thrust that would not enter the shell of an adult would completely pierce a young one, and of course thereby materially reduce its value.

One of the means by which the struggle for liberty is counteracted is exceedingly interesting and nearly always successful, for when the turtle is struck down goes the diver, cleaving the water like a knife, and from a depth of from five to six fathoms of water he will almost unfailingly bring the turtle to the surface. This trick is in fact much easier than it looks, for all the diver has to do is to seize the shell behind the neck with his hands, lift the fore part as much as possible, press his knees against the turtle's back, and up he comes, his fore flippers violently beating the water. It is then an easy task to lasso him aboard. The best turtle divers in the Gulf of Mexico are the Seminole Indians. They have been known to bring an eight hundred pound turtle from a depth of forty feet; but the Bahamians are even more daring and successful. The easiest way in which a novice can acquire the art is to jump on a turtle while it is sleeping on the surface and then hold on like the traditional "grim death." It may be that thus rudely awakened it will attempt to get rid of its unwelcome jockey by plunging downward, but you have only to press the knees against the lower part of the back and lift the front and you will master the situation and the turtle too. This is a favorite diversion of the Seminole boys. It results in much spitting of water and shaking of long, dripping hair, but with care there

IN THE NICK OF TIME.

is no harm. The only danger is from sharks, which, in the excitement of the chase, they may fail to note the approach of. Ordinarily, so clear is the limpid waters of the bay and so white its pure, clean, white-sanded bottom, the approach of these monsters of the deep can be foreseen in ample time to avoid them.

The green turtles are the only species which move in shoals, and I have seen them so abundant in the waters of South Florida that a man could walk, if they were solid, from the back of one to the back of another for quite a distance. This may seem an exaggeration, but whoever has been at "Six Fathoms Set," off the mouth of the Shark River, when the turtle are running, will bear witness that it is almost impossible to overstate their vast number. They have certain "harbors" or "sets," which they generally frequent if undisturbed, and to which they return regularly every night. The noting and discovery of these "sets" is one of the turtler's most anxious occupations, for on it depends his good fortune.

So abundantly are the turtles caught at times that the turtlers build "kraals" of stakes on the most convenient mud banks and place the captives in them until they are required for shipping. They are fed on mangrove bushes and the parsley which grows along the shore, and although at first sulky, after a day or two they feed freely and rapidly fatten; indeed it is no uncommon thing for them to increase in weight from three to ten pounds in the short time they are there; while epicures say that the flesh becomes much more tender and delicate.

Several varieties of turtle found in great abundance in the waters of the Gulf are practically worthless: the loggerhead, for instance, and the largest of all, the gigantic trunkback, frequently attaining a length of twelve feet and weighing a ton, which looks when asleep like an upturned boot; but it is a flesh eater, and unwholesome, if not poisonous, to man, though alligators will fight desperately for it.

After the green turtle the next in commercial value is the hawksbill, not on account of its flesh, for that is worthless, but on account of its shell, which is formed of a series of scales overlapping one another at their extremities, like shingles on the roof of a house. This is the material which is used in the manufacture of combs, snuff boxes, and other ornamental articles. So valuable is this shell that at Key West it finds a ready market at from two to twelve dollars a pound; but this turtle is difficult to catch, and its haunts are dangerous. To render the shell plastic enough to work it has to be heated to a temperature of one hundred and twenty-eight degrees and allowed to soak for a considerable time. Persons who are expert in "scale work," that is, ornamental articles made out of the scales of the brilliant Southern fishes, use the shell of the hawksbill for producing some of their finest effects. The scales next in demand are those of the grunt, the grouper, the jackfish, the redfish, the yellow-scaled snapper and the tarpum, all denizens of the waters of Florida and its coasts.

All the species of turtle enumerated lay their eggs on the beaches of Florida south of the twenty-eighth degree of latitude; that is to say, they rarely lay to the north of Hog or St. Joseph Island, near the mouth of the Anclote River, and only loggerheads are found there. The other species prefer a more southern habitat. Some persons assert that green turtles do not lay on the Florida shore of the Gulf of Mexico at all, but this is a mistake, several having been "turned over" on the well-known spot called Horse and Chaise, in Sarasota Bay. As these were caught in the very act of depositing their eggs in a nest, there can be no doubt but that it was a familiar haunt of theirs. The general opinion in the northern part of the State is that this species goes to the Cuban and Mexican shores to construct its nursery, but the spongers of Key West, who know as much about it as anybody, say that its eggs may be found on all the best islets among the Florida reefs.

The eggs of the green turtle are much larger than those of the loggerhead, and are considered more palatable by epicures. This superiority of flavor is supposed to be due to their food, which is chiefly vegetable. Turtles commence laying as early as May in the far South, and continue until the latter end of August, their busiest season being during the full moon in June. This is the time usually selected by the residents of Florida for "turning turtles" on the beaches and pilfering the contents of their nests. Excursion parties are formed in different communities, and these hire crafts of various kinds to take them to the turtle grounds, which may be quite convenient or many miles away. On reaching the scene of operations they

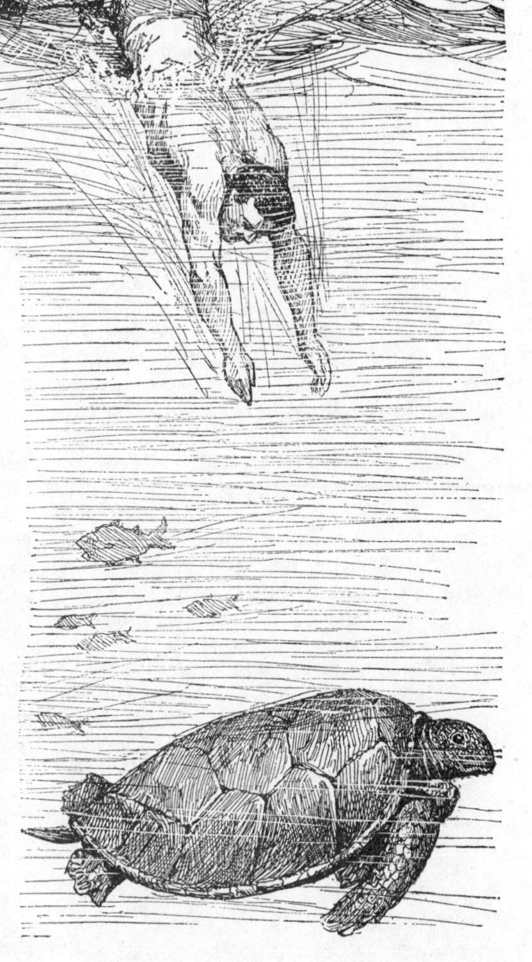

FOR "DIVERS" REASONS.

prepare a camp on shore or remain aboard the boats and go ashore in the evening. If the turtles are abundant it is nothing unusual for an expert to turn a hundred in a night, but those who capture from ten to twenty are usually well pleased with their luck, that number being more than the average small boat can carry if there are more than two or three persons in the party.

The turtle turners have to work as silently as possible in order to avoid frightening away the creatures; still they often manage to express the ecstasy of their feelings when, say, they pounce upon a three hundred pounder, by a series of eccentric gymnastic movements with arms and legs, trying to dance jigs on the sand, and making grimaces which would be a fortune to a circus clown if he could only imitate them. The irrepressible sometimes forgets everything in his delirium of joy, and whoops loudly enough to be heard by every turtle within miles, especially if the night is calm, as the Southern sea has extraordinary resonant powers under certain atmospheric conditions.

There is a spice of danger in turning turtles which makes it all the more attractive to some natures. This consists in the liability of meeting a bear any moment, for bruin, being a great lover of chelonian eggs, roams the beach all night in search of them, and devours as many in twenty-four hours as a man would in a week. If a bear is encountered suddenly, or disturbed while eating, it is likely to display a pugnacious spirit, but if it is merely ambling around in search of a meal it is more likely to run than to fight. Still, it is as well to be prepared for an unexpected meeting with one by carrying a loaded repeating rifle, as bruin will give a person little time for thinking if he has made up his mind to attack. A party of three of us killed five bears on the Indian River one night while they were searching for turtle eggs, and we might have slain more had not the sandflies bothered us so much as to affect our aim. Both bears and raccoons possess the remarkable faculty of being able to go direct to a turtle's nest, while man, with all his boasted superior intelligence, has to search for it in the most careful manner with a pointed stick, which he thrusts into the ground in every likely spot. Wherever he finds it penetrating easily he clears away the top sand and soon comes to the nicely-arranged layers of eggs, whose delicate hue gleams pleasantly in the bright moonlight.

The number of eggs in a nest varies from one hundred to two hundred, the average being about a hundred and fifty, and the maximum, so far as I have been able to learn, two hundred and eighty.

The shells are soft and elastic, and so porous that their contents evaporate rapidly. The eggs are edible for about a week, but after that they shrivel up so badly as to be little better in looks and taste than so many balls of white rags. No means of preserving them fresh for any lengthened period have yet been discovered, but those taken from captured turtles, and known as "yellow eggs" and "yelks," from the fact that their outer covering is undeveloped, are kept for months and years by drying and pickling them. To dry the eggs they are first soaked for an hour or more in strong pickle, then placed where the rays of the sun will reach them for three or four days, after which time they are ready for use. They are then almost as hard as sandstone. Turtle eggs make excellent pickles, being ready for cooking as soon as they are taken out of the pickle barrel and well washed.

Fully-developed eggs are round, white, and about two or three inches in circumference. They cannot be boiled hard like those of fowls, nor are they as delicate in flavor. The best way of cooking them when fresh is to fry them with plenty of butter, pepper and salt, or to "scramble" them well, as either of these methods modifies their strong though not disagreeable flavor. They are just as good as ducks' eggs for cakes and pastries, and are even preferred for that purpose by some cooks who take a pride in their profession. Comparatively few natives of interior Florida know what a turtle egg is good for, judging from the remarks of an old denizen of Orange County, who said that he considered it a great sin for any person to eat "sich trash and by it make himself unclean." He added that he was "no sarpint eater" and did not want to be, and had no desire "to be wusser nor an Injun." It was a difficult matter a few years ago to get even the inhabitants of the littoral to eat them, but now they are glad to pay from ten to fifteen cents a dozen for them. Captain Watkins, of Anclote, informed me that he tried to sell 5,000 loggerhead eggs in Cedar Keys at one time, but found he could not give them away, the people refusing to touch them.

An observant man will notice that the flippers of female turtles are slightly curved, and may wonder why they are so, but if he will watch the animals constructing their nests he will soon find his answer. Each turtle on reaching a favorite haunt hastens to the highest point which the sea washes, and, selecting a suitable spot beyond it, commences throwing the sand to the right and left, first with one hind flipper, then with the other, until she has dug a round hole about two feet deep and a foot in diameter. After testing it, to see that it is complete in every way, she drops her eggs, and, when she has finished laying, carefully covers the nest, makes several false demonstrations in the sand close by, in order to deceive all probable destroyers of her unborn progeny, then hastens seaward, there to remain until the maternal instinct again sends her shoreward in search of a nursery.

When the chelonia move in shoals to search for nesting places they are easily frightened by any unusual noise or the appearance of an enemy, but after they commence laying nothing can disturb them until they have finished. A person may dance on the back of one at that time and not cause it to wink an eye; but the moment the nest is covered it displays every indication of terror and scurries seaward as fast as it can travel, taking the terpsichorean with it if he does not turn it over.

The noise produced by the clashing of the shells and the scrambling of many flippers on the loose sand when a shoal of turtles crawl on a beach during a dark night is quite terrifying to a novice in "turtling," because he cannot tell what produces it, and it has a sound which is totally unlike anything he has previously heard. His heart is very likely to beat wildly at the strange and uncanny sound.

I have known a shoal to scramble through and over a large camp fire, extinguish it and rout the "campers" in the most ignominious manner. The invaders were on their way to a salt-water lagoon close by, which was a favorite haunt of theirs during stormy weather and the laying season. We found them there the next day, and were glad to seek shelter from a tropical storm in their safe retreat and secure some of them for dinner. The advance of an army of turtles is suggestive of an old-fashioned buffalo stampede so far as it seems to defy every obstacle and to push straight ahead, even if destruction awaits all in the column. This is a splendid time in which to turn turtles, but parties must work lively enough to make a living wall around them or they will be compelled to retreat or be overpowered and crushed under the weight of the obstinate reptiles.

I have heard an old settler tell of the rout of a squad of Indians who were encamped near the mouth of the Fabatchee River by an army of loggerheads, and the destruction of several of their dogs that possessed more courage than discretion.

Turtle eggs are so elastic that it is impossible for a person to put back into a nest all that he takes out of it. Few people know the cause of this, but it is easily understood by those who have seen the chelonias covering the nurseries after dropping all the ova in them. A female is so careful to conceal the nest that she scratches sand toward it from every direction, and, having made a mound over it, she rises to her full height, by straightening her legs; then letting her body drop on the mound, she packs it and the eggs as closely as if the work were done by a pile driver. She keeps packing it in this manner until it is as level as any other part of the beach. After inspecting it, to see that it is all right, she makes a few false demonstrations in the sand, in order to deceive the enemies of her unhatched young, then hastens seaward as fast as she can travel, for she knows full well the danger that threatens her ashore.

It requires six weeks to hatch the eggs, and when the young appear they issue from their retreats in such vast numbers that the beach seems covered with them, and they remind one strongly of ants pouring out of an ant hill. They are about the size of a silver dollar, but small as they are they have the instinct of self preservation strongly developed. The moment they come out of the nest they hasten toward the sea and swim away, if they are not devoured by the numerous enemies that lie in wait for them, the worst of which are the sharks, especially the species known as the "nurse" shark. These extend along the beach in water just deep enough to float them, and gobble down the juvenile chelonia as fast as they get within reach. I have heard a veteran turtler say that he found 207 young loggerheads in a nine-foot shark, and that the old fellow did not seem to have enough even then, judging from his anxiety to secure some more after being harpooned.

AFTER THE EGGS.

7.
An Easter Outing in Florida (1901)

AN EASTER OUTING IN FLORIDA

By Lynn Tew Sprague

THOUGH we of the North make much ado about spring, we know her not in all her beauty. With us she is coy, capricious and somewhat lachrymose. She is timidly here to-day; to-morrow she has fled before returning winter. But in the Gulf States she comes suddenly and to stay, with assured, sunny smiles and voluptuous arms full of flowers. By the first of March rose bushes and fruit trees are in bloom, the woods are shimmering with yellow-greens and the intense, delicious, balmy spell is felt in one's very soul. March, with us most disagreeable of months, is there a succession of golden days and odorous promises, and April is what our June is,

"The balmy month of bloom and birds,
Of song and leafy bowers."

It was an Easter day in late April when my snail-paced mule drew me up before the Major's gate. The dignified old gentleman who was to be my host, I had casually met only a few days before when a quail-hunting trespasser on his acres. He had sat with me on a fallen log in his hummock lands and talked in quaint, stately phrase of old times and old ways in the old South; and on Easter eve an antiquated negro had brought to my hotel, two miles away, a note written with the straight, strong strokes our grandfathers affected, which I knew at a glance was from the Major. It briefly asked, "Will you come and dine on the gladdest of holidays, and see how simply an old-time Southerner lives?"

So I had driven away in the soft beauty of the Florida spring morning, along a sandy track that wound and twisted seemingly any whither, like the weird Ocklawaha River, which it skirted, and was now at the Major's home. The courtly old gentleman came down the path to receive me, as though I was a hero spoil-laden from victorious battle, and there was, from that moment, a gracious old-time flavor about all his hospitality that put me altogether at ease. Like nearly everybody in Florida, the Major has known better days. The great freeze all but ruined him, but he is as erect and uncompromising as the noble old oaks in his yard. His plantation consists of some four hundred acres of sand and pine trees, with perhaps forty acres of rich hummock lands. He has a half dozen old negro servants, who raise a little poor cotton and some vegetables for market; and who cut for the Major some salable cypress timber. Before the destructive freeze, the Major used to ship about a thousand boxes of oranges.

ON THE OCKLAWAHA RIVER.

His house is large and rambling, much built on at the rear. It is sadly dilapidated and stands close to the highway, like a Northern farmhouse. But inside the weather-beaten and unpainted structure, there is the simple, delightful courtesy of long ago. Here he lives with his sister, an old maiden lady, naturally sweet and charming without effort, like all high-class southern ladies. Their days are passed without tedium or melancholy, in a climate as gentle as themselves, and as gracious as that art of living which they so perfectly retain, but which the newer generations cannot master. With simple, healthful occupations their days unroll among the old furniture and the old books; they read Walter Scott and Montaigne, and are ignorant of Emile Zola and Mr. Howells.

The Major has a little lake all to himself, on one side of which his large half-ruined orange grove stands. A little palm-bordered stream flows from it into the Ocklawaha a half mile away. Thither, after a little, we went to talk and walk, while awaiting dinner, and that leisurely promenade, under semi-tropic arcades, with the Major's kindly voice in my ears, was an experience to remember long. The balmy soul of spring seemed almost violently sweet, oppressively soft, under the palms and live oaks, by the side of the still but not sluggish stream. It stole into my blood bringing a delicious languor that made me feel kindly disposed toward everything. In the pauses of our talk, day-dreams floated through the mind, radiant and tender as the turquoise sky above us. The perfumed air was quiet, save when just a sigh of wind set the palms scraping and rasping, and made the oak leaves whisper gently. The pathside was sprinkled with beautiful southern violets. On all sides the growth was dense, and there was never any prospect along our walk, only intricate vistas through the woods where shadows lay blue across every tone of green, and where blades of yellow sunshine shifted in. How strange it seemed when a covey of robins leaped and scattered before our approach, timid as game birds. Were these shy and silent creatures really the familiar, garrulous birds of our northern summer lawns? And why were they lingering here so late?

Now and then the southern dove cooed in the bush tangled greens, and when the path bent toward the stream, two blue heron were seen dragging their long legs through bordering reeds. At a particularly beautiful spot where a spring of warm water gushed from the black earth, we came upon a flock of those divine songsters, the wood thrushes, silent and demure here in their southern retreat, where (the pity of it) they are ruthlessly shot like game birds by negroes and poor whites. Bright yellow and red wild flowers peeped from the thick tangles on either side and over our heads the arching limbs of century-old oaks were draped with festoons of gray moss. Suddenly we found ourselves at the mouth of the stream on the banks of the Ocklawaha, where the earth was soft and the path treacherous. With the decline of day miasma rises from the river banks and only negroes can live near the water. But the stream looked weirdly beautiful, as we stood beside it. Thick forests of tall cypress, live oak and palmetto fringed it; huge vines twisted among and interlaced the trees, jungles of unfamiliar growths, bright ofttimes with native flowers, were below and overhead all was draped with the eternal Spanish moss.

The celebrated river moves slowly, but is very deep, the Major told me. It seemed to have sinister shadows on its bosom and along its course are so many dark bays and coves where the deadly water snake breeds, that one scarcely knew where the channel lay.

We left the river and walked home through the pine woods. A mocking-bird sung to us ceaselessly, seeming to follow in our wake to voice his strenuous joy of the spring, and as we drew near home we met an old negro searching for us to announce dinner.

When we sat down to feast the Major read a prayer in a deeply reverent voice, and then on a table trimmed with southern holly and mistletoe, an old-fashioned southern dinner was served. We had turkey in a bed of rice, and game, and a plum pudding, and fresh vegetables, and we had coffee made as only southerners make it, and we drank some rare old scuppernong wine the Major had made. After dinner we went out to his half ruined orange grove and smoked tobacco the Major had grown, and listened to the cardinals. Then toward evening we walked back into the pines where the Major's negro hands and their friends were celebrating the day. For the Major believes the anniversary of the Saviour's rise from the dead should not be a

ONE OF THE "HALF DOZEN."

solemn day, but the very gladdest of all festivals. We sat upon a log in the resinous fragrance of the wood and listened to the snapping banjos thrumming, and heard old plantation airs sung in the rich melody of negro voices.

On the edge of a huge bonfire 'possum and sweet potatoes were roasting, and when the sun went down in a sea of yellow glory, the light of the flames on the ebon faces made the spectacle almost weird. But how happy they were—those dusky-faced children of our far South! Does the Caucasian ever attain that height of pure animal gladness? They danced for us—not dances of the feet and legs alone—but writhing, contorting dances, wherein every muscle played its part. And they accompanied all with shouts and melodious howls from the seventh heaven of negro joy.

"The old African incantatory spirit is upon them at these times," said the old Major. Nothing could exceed their respect toward him. With every new feature of the festival, a negro approached, cap in hand, to beg his sanction. He in turn was all kindness to them. But he takes an old southerner's view of their life and character.

"They are neither as well off nor as happy as in old slave days," he said. "They are naturally shiftless, idle and irresponsible. They will not work, except when driven by want and then only enough to relieve it. And I tell you, you cannot educate a pure nigger. Intelligence? Why there's Leb over there, my brightest darkey. I reckon he doesn't know who the President is."

"Oh! not so bad as that, Major, is it?" I protested.

"Leb," called the Major, and the negro drew near, cap in hand. "This gentleman wants to ask you a question." "Leb," said I, "can you tell me what is the name of the President of the United States?"

"Yas, sur."

"Well, Leb, what is it?"

"De President ob de United States?"

"Yes, Leb, who is the President?"

"Well, sur," said Leb, "Gen'al Grant wuz, but he ain't no mo!"

But the Major's sorrowful smile disdained his triumph.

It was late when, leaving the darkies feasting, we returned to the house where wine and cake were served and some more of the Major's fragrant cigars were smoked. Then, till bedtime, he regaled me with tales of old slave days, tales of the war and anecdotes of General Jeb Stuart, his old commander. But I fear the Major is one of the unreconstructed. "I have been a long time out of the world," he said. "It is much changed. It is all electricity now and no sentiment. The country has grown great, you say, and powerful. Aye! materially great and brutally powerful. Compare the men of to-day with those of my youth. It is very sad to me—this greatness of our country and its statesmen. I would rather see the nation small and weak and righteous, like Switzerland, and like Switzerland have the smallest percentage of illiteracy and crime of all nations. That is the true greatness of a people. And this freedom of the niggers down here—what is it? this boasted liberty of theirs—but a liberty to be idle, to steal, beg, and starve? What would become of them if it were not for the charity of the whites—their old masters—I should like to ask the theorists of the north?"

When at last I went upstairs, in through the wide-open windows, out of a summer-night's sky, came the pale rays of a late-rising damaged moon, and in its light I undressed and saw by my watch that it was just twelve, and a very happy Easter day was done. Back in the woods the negroes were yet singing and their soft, faraway voices came to me across the old cotton patch. A sweet lullaby to which I fell asleep.

About ten the next morning, Leb brought my sleepy mule around and the old Major came out into the road to see me off. I thanked him in my awkward best way and told him I wished there were more of his kind to sweeten and ornament life. But what a real grace these old southern gentlemen have! He did not rudely disclaim and correct me as a northerner might in an attempt to return politeness. He said, "Ah, you brought youth and sunshine into our old home, and even a blackbird may sing a little in the brightness of the spring. Promise me to come again soon. We will hunt together."

And thus I bade adieu to the straight old Major and drove away in the sand.

8.
Six Weeks in Florida
(1870)

SIX WEEKS IN FLORIDA.

WHITE SULPHUR SPRINGS, OLD ENTERPRISE.

If I were to write all that might profitably be written about Florida, more space would be required than that included within the limits of a magazine article. In its historical associations, Florida has more of romance and dramatic interest than have befallen any other locality on this continent. To these we shall refer incidentally, but the chief intent of this article will be to give entertainment and information to those who may have visited this singular region or hope to go there, or to that other larger class who are not able to journey, and would be interested to know why it should or should not have been called Florida, the Land of Flowers.

Perhaps the best way to accomplish this will be to describe the experiences of a party of us who, last winter, made the excursion. We had already accomplished some twelve hundred miles of steamboat traveling on the Mississippi River; we had passed through New Orleans and Mobile; and, a good Providence, which sometimes stands between merciless railroad corporations and a helpless public, be ever thanked, passed safely over the ragged, rickety, decayed railroad between Mobile and Montgomery, and from there to Macon. From this place to Savannah, however, thanks to Sherman and his army, who destroyed rails, ties, and rolling stock of this road, every thing is now new and of the best kind.

Savannah is the natural base of operations for the Florida campaign. You can reach this most important of the Southern Atlantic seaports by many ways. Steamboat and railroad lines concentrate here from all quarters of the country. And here you had best come if you desire to make a comfortable entry into the land of orange groves and alligators; and to this place you must return to find those comforts not to be obtained except in those localities where large communities are congregated together.

" There are two ways of getting to Jacksonville from here," was the advice of a gentleman who had spent many winters in Florida. "And whichever you choose, you will be sorry you had not taken the other. There is the night train by railroad, which brings you to Jacksonville in about sixteen hours; and there is the steamboat line, which goes inland nearly all the way, and which may land you in a day, or you may run aground, and remain on board for a week."

With this consolatory counsel we chose the steamboat and coast line for a first experiment, partially by my advice to my traveling companions; for at the termination of the great campaign of the March to the Sea it had been my experience to voyage through these wide wastes of marsh land and islands of sand, and it impressed me as a peculiar aspect of nature which ought to be seen.

It was a showery morning in February when

we got on board the little steamboat *Nick King*, and pushed rapidly out from among the crowd of shipping, down the river, past the threatening obstructions placed in the stream during the war to keep out the Yankee fleet, and finally turned into the big creek, which, by crooked and strange ways, wanders through the waste of marsh land. Sometimes there was hardly room for our little boat to make the turnings; and when, about noon, we came to a full stop, with the nose of the *Nick King* stuck fast on a mud bank, the memory of a similar occurrence came vividly to my mind. Six years before, while yet our soldiers lay in the trenches before, or rather behind, Savannah, I accompanied General Sherman on an expedition which he took, with Admiral Dahlgren, over to Hilton Head. On our way back it was so rough outside that the Admiral considered it unsafe for the *Harvest Moon* (of old a tug-boat) to combat the roaring sea; so we attempted this inside passage, and at very nearly the same hour of the day, and precisely the same spot, went aground. How long the flag-ship remained there I do not know; for the General, who had not been used to a dead halt of this kind, and who had already been absent from his brave men longer than he or they liked, became fearfully impatient, and tearing about the ship, among other places was found on the larboard or starboard—whichever was the improper side—of the forecastle deck, if, indeed, it was not an altogether heinous offense to be in that part of the ship at all. However that may be, the proper officer, with trembling limbs and pale face, at once ran to Admiral Dahlgren and reported this breach of etiquette; but the Admiral had already become aware that in his visitor he had drawn the elephant, and reassured his subordinate with the words:

"Let him run about; he will do no harm."

But the General could not wait the movements of the waters or the ship; and the polite and obliging Admiral took us into his gig and pulled up the river until we met a tug-boat, and were finally restored to the bosoms of our families.

When the tide turned we of the *Nick King* got under way, and steamed quickly along; the gray marsh, as we proceeded, stretching away farther until all around the horizon the mist and rain united land and sky, except where a clump of trees varied the strange monotony, or some other steamer came to meet us, standing out above the level of the grasses as if propelled over the land. After a while we came out into Sapelo Sound, and the sun came out from the clouds, and a fresh wind came up from the sea; and then we saw a glorious sight, such as makes the artist's heart ache with despair that then and there he can not fix the fleeting vision upon enduring canvas. Overhead the air was filled with golden mist, pierced by broad beams of sunshine, except where the sky arches to a gray and blue wall, and descends to the glimpse of the sea which we catch between the islands, and where the white breakers come rolling over the wide sand-bars; while to the left, standing out with indescribable force and distinctness, there is a low island of white sand, crowned with masses of dark cedars, and between us and it the waters spread along in wide sheets of yellow and purple. For an instant it is there, a perfect picture, and then the rain and mists swallow it all up. Soon we approached a portion of the sound which for hundreds of acres was covered with dark objects.

"What is that, captain?" asked a group of observers.

"Ducks," was the sententious answer.

"Ducks!" exclaimed an incredulous old gentleman.

"Ducks?" inquired an intelligent traveler, who came to see, and believe in all he saw.

"Ducks!" exclaimed a would-be sportsman, who rushed madly for his gun.

"Ducks! ducks! ducks!" was now shouted on all sides, with all sorts of exclamations; for as we neared this black sea the ducks rose into the air by thousands upon thousands; and, united in masses like dark clouds, they floated away toward the ocean.

When night came on we had entered Mud River. Next morning we came to Brunswick, which has a good harbor, and is the terminus of a railroad, whose business it is to bring timber to be shipped. During the same day we touched at St. Mary's, which is one of the most ancient of places on this continent, and before the war quite a village; but one day, in retaliation, it is said, our gun-boats went in and tore the houses all to pieces; and there the ruins stand as they were left eight years ago. This terrible affair is one of the unwritten chapters of the war which I would like to see recorded. Near nightfall we came to Fernandina, where, because of a storm outside, we remained all night and next day, giving us an opportunity to go over to the great beach, where we saw miles of splendid waves come tearing and roaring over the white sand with a force and majesty such as only Andreas Achenbach imitates upon canvas. From Fernandina to Jacksonville the passage is an outside journey of several hours; and as the worthy, broadly built captain of our boat, who, by-the-way, is Nick King himself, feared to take us out into the storm which was still prevailing, a party of the passengers—some thirty in all—chartered a train on the Cedar Keys Railroad, and about nine o'clock of that night we found ourselves in the town of Baldwin, where there is a crossing by the Savannah and Jacksonville Railroad. Here we took such misery as we could not avoid in one of those log shanties, which seem to have had chills and fever since their birth, which form the burg. What this place is in the summer season the demon who presides over all poisonous fevers only knows. In the morning we came forth as out from damp and mildewed tombs, and took our rapid way by rail to Jacksonville, where we arrived in time to take the steamer *Florence* up the St. Johns River.

Just at this point in the narration of our personal experiences we will halt for a space, and try to tell the inexperienced traveler what at the time and place we would have been glad to know, and could not well ascertain. And that was, where we wanted to go. To be sure, St. Augustine was our objective point, and so was the sail up the St. Johns River. But the best place to fix upon as a *point d'appui*, from which to march out and make excursions, and to which we could return for rest and comfort—that we did not know.

GREEN COVE SPRINGS.

It is barely possible that some of my readers are of those who will be content if they can only find some sheltered nook where, out of doors, they can breathe the soft, healing air, and gain such strength as the rough winter winds of the North will not permit. To any of these my advice would be to make their head-quarters at either Green Cove Springs, Magnolia, or Pilatka on the St. Johns River. For invalids, either of these places is preferable to the sea-board, for reasons which will be noted hereafter, and from them excursions can be made to any quarter. Of these three places Pilatka has more advantages than any other; for to its spacious wharves come the steamers from New York and Savannah; and the St. Johns Hotel at this place is blessed with a steward who places before you that choicest and rarest of blessings in Florida, wholesome and well-cooked food. From Pilatka also can be made those charming excursions up the Black River, and the Ocklawaha, and other small streams, which will admit the passage only of diminutive examples of steamboat architecture.

If, unlike our party, you do not desert the *Nick King*, and brave the danger of sea-sickness or of shipwreck by dancing about on the sand-bar which impedes navigation at the mouth of St. Johns River, you can be landed at either of these places; but wherever you go, we would strongly urge you to engage your rooms in advance.

From Jacksonville, which is a large and growing city, and where there are fair hotels, you can go by any of several steamboat lines to any of the places on the St. Johns River, and a steamboat makes two trips a week to St. Augustine, going by an outside passage. The other route to St. Augustine is by river steamboat and stage lines; and this we had chosen, and soon found ourselves comfortably fixed on board the new and excellent steamer *Florence*, whose business it is to take people to and from Pilatka, making stoppages by the way. We were put off at a place called Picolata, where a stage line is supposed to convey you across country to St. Augustine. A more disgraceful, disheartening abomination than Picolata and its stage line I never met with in all my travels. Ever so many years ago, when Buckingham Smith was Secretary of Legation at Madrid, he had occasion to send home to St. Augustine his wife.

"Good-by, and God bless you," he said. "You are comfortably provided for your voyage. You are all safe until you reach Picolata, and then Heaven alone can help you."

What Picolata was ten, twenty years ago, it is to-day. A shaky, rotten wooden pier, at which steamers discharge their burdens; a one-story shanty, and a ten-feet-square grog-shop on the shore—that is the forbidding exterior appearance. The outside of these buildings is all you will see; and if you arrive, as we did, at a season when a fierce, freezing cold wind is blowing from the north, and your invalid ladies are obliged to stand out shelterless in this killing cold air for hours, you will all lose your health, if you do not your patience. Personal-

PICOLATA.

"I am."

"Won't you let these ladies in?"

"No."

While we were quite ready to have committed some horrible injury upon this man, yet there was nothing for it but to bide our time. And after investing several dollars in soda biscuit, sardines, etc., the surly wretch relented, and our people were able to get into the meanly kept room, where a fire soon restored them to warmth. After waiting some five hours, about three in the afternoon we started off, leaving all our luggage at Picolata; but bringing in place of one of the trunks an English baronet, who hung on to the rack behind as best he could, preferring that discomfort to the horrible possibilities of being left. The ride over through the monotonous pine barrens was dismal enough. Half of the road was under water, and the poor tired horses could hardly proceed beyond a walk. Added to this, the wind blew cold and dreary, chilling us to the bone. About nine at night we drove into the city of St. Augustine, and at the hotel of that name found welcome and comfortable quarters.

ly, the writer was damaged in both the first and the last; and in as calm tones, and with such persuasive manners as could be mustered, he addressed a diminutive specimen of humanity, who looked as if he might have been the offspring of intermarriage for a hundred generations of Lilliputs, and who was playing "seven up" with a choice party like unto himself, in the grog-shop:

"Why are you keeping us here? Why not send us over to St. Augustine? I understand you have no special hour for starting. Our party make up a load. Please hitch up and send us over."

The man did not like the interruption to his game; but finally answered:

"Now yer wouldn't have me drive them horses right back. They come over here, eighteen miles from Augustine, this morning."

This was an appeal to our respect for suffering horse-flesh which was not to be resisted, whatever may have been our opinions of a stage line which drove a team of horses eighteen miles without change, and then proposed the same day to take them back over the same road.

"But what are our ladies to do meanwhile? They are invalids, and this exposure may be fatal to them. Why can't we get into that house?"

"Because the folks are away," growled the keeper of the grog-shop.

"All the more reason why we should get into it. Who is the owner?"

I can remember only one feeling comparable to that which impressed me all the while we were at St. Augustine, and that was when my first introduction was made into the Old World at that noble old city of Rouen in France. The same romantic interest which thrilled me then continued at St. Augustine, with an added peculiar charm. For many weeks we had been journeying through a section of our country

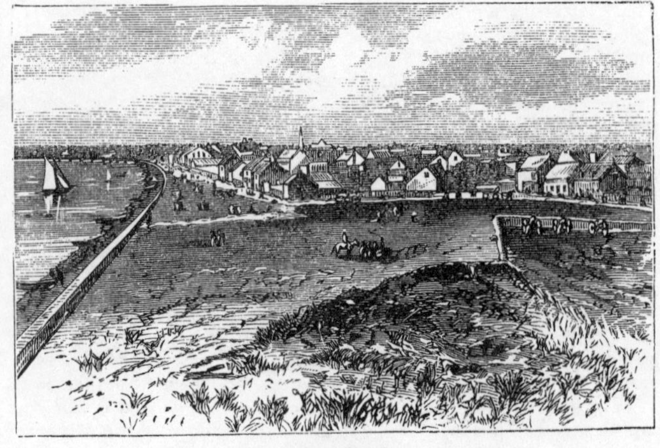

ST. AUGUSTINE.

where every thing was new and crude, and unexpectedly we were ushered into the associations, the architecture, the ruins, of three hundred years ago.

The architecture of this city is altogether unlike that of any upon this continent. The streets are very narrow, while the houses have wide balconies in the second story, which come very near to each other. The material used in their construction is very beautiful, and is called the "coquina" stone. It is formed of a concrete which has a pleasant yellow-gray tone when seen at a distance, and, when examined in detail, presents an exquisite collection of various and delicately formed shells. Although most of the habitable buildings built in the way described are of modern construction, yet, except in their pitched roofs, they probably resemble those built hundreds of years ago, and whose ruins are met with at every turn. Here you see the stained walls of a blacksmith shop, constructed by the hands of the soldiers of the Spanish governor and cut-throat, Menendez d'Avileis, in 1570. Out from graceful groves of orange-trees will rise jagged walls whose ruins came by the hand of Governor Oglethorpe, of Georgia, in 1732. Side by side with trim villas, the residences of those seeking health from the North, stand the crumbling chimneys of houses destroyed by one or another of the many conquerors who these centuries past have made this oldest of cities on this continent north of the Gulf of Mexico their battle-ground. But perhaps the most picturesque of all its ruins are the gates which stand at the northern end of the city. The pillars of the gates are Moorish in their form of construction, and are square, surmounted by a carved pomegranate. Attached to the pillars on either side are portions of the old wall which formerly surrounded the town to the east and south, while they connected with the Fort San Marco, which stands by the river a few hundred yards to the west. Proceeding from the gates outward are the remains of the causeway, crossing a deep ditch which followed the line of wall.

OLD CITY GATEWAY, ST. AUGUSTINE.

This noble example of military architecture was a delightful surprise to me; for in all my journeyings in the Old World I had never seen such a complete instance of the high state of the art of defense of two centuries ago. This fort was begun by Menendez himself, and in one and another form had resisted attacks, sometimes successfully. But in the time of Queen Elizabeth that brave old sailor, Admiral Drake, returning from one of his expeditions to South America, saw a look-out on the island of Anastasia, which is just opposite to the fort. So Drake landed, and the Spaniards deserted the place, which he occupied. He captured £2000 of money, which was in an old chest, and several brass cannon. Then he hoisted sail and steered away to report his adventures to the maiden queen. But our fort was called at that time San Juan de Pinas.

After that affair Captain Davis, one of those gentle buccaneers who made it his business to rob and murder the people of the South American settlements, came up the coast in search of a Spanish plate fleet, and, missing his prize, in a fit of spleen went into the harbor, attacked and sacked the town. The fort at this time was an octagon, with round towers, and incapable of resisting the fierce assaults of the British pirate. This was in the year 1665. During the next one hundred years, more or less, the Spaniards were hard at work reconstructing this fort upon its present plan, which I believe is called that of Vauban No. 2. I said the Spaniards were hard at work. This is a mistake—the tribes of Indians which had been conquered did the hard work, the Spaniards superintending. The Appalachians, especially, were

OLD SPANISH FORT, ST. AUGUSTINE.

employed for more than sixty years, while convicts from Mexico were sent to assist. Between one and all the fort was finally completed, and a tablet erected over the spacious portals of the main entrance, which stands for the inspection of the curious to-day, and whereon is an inscription which, being translated, declares that:

"Don Ferdinand the Sixth being King of Spain, and the Field-Marshal Don Alonzo Fernando Hereda being Governor and Captain-General of this Place, St. Augustine of Florida and its Province. This Fort was finished in the year 1756. The Works were directed by the Captain-Engineer, Don Pedro de Brazon y Garay."

As it stands, although often besieged, it has never been taken. It is what is known as a bastioned fort. Over each of the four bastions stand towers which served as outlooks. The main work is surrounded by a wide ditch; and beyond were exterior fortifications, most important of which is a demi-lune that covers the entrance to the fort. The interior of this splendid relic of Spanish domination in this country is full of interest. Out of a large "enceinte," or open space, a wide stairway, whose steps have been worn by many thousand feet, leads upon the broad rampart. It is not difficult to go back a century ago, and to imagine these iron platforms mounted with the ponderous, clumsy, bronze and brass cannon which now lie piled up in the court-yard below. We can see the royal banner floating from the walls, guarded by Spanish sentinels, in their unique costume, while all around are heard the bustle and confusion of conflict. To-day light twelve-pounders repose in the bastions; while good, trust-worthy Sergeant M'Guire is the sole representative of the power and dignity of the Republic of the United States of America.

Of course, attached to the old fort are many stories of thrilling interest; but one which has hair-raising power to every comer is that of the "Dungeon." Not in Chillon nor at Neuschloss, not upon the Rhine nor in all Europe, is there a more genuine dungeon than boasts San Marco. Only a few years ago the parapet above sunk in, revealing a cavity; and, upon inspection, beyond that another was discovered, hermetically walled in, and wherein, when opened, were found the skeletons of two persons. So much is known without question—all beyond is mystery; but the curious traveler, if he stoop low enough, may enter this coffin of stone.

SPANISH FORT AT MATANZAS INLET.

Day after day we went to old Fort San Marco, and found ample material for the exercise of the pencil and imagination; and most heartily do we commend it to the attention of the visitor at St. Augustine. Although it is of little service as a fortification to the United States government, yet it is too rich and rare an example of the art of war, and too valuable in its historical association, to be allowed to fall to utter ruin. Colonel Ludlow, of the Engineer Corps, stationed at Charleston, informed me that a small sum had been appropriated for its repair. I am sure that this officer is a gentleman of taste and judgment, who will make the restoration completely in the fact and spirit of the ancient work. Further than this, I have the personal assurance of General Sherman that the old fort shall not be neglected.

STREET SCENE, ST. AUGUSTINE.

There is another Spanish fortification, of an entirely different form of construction, situated at Matanzas Inlet, some twenty miles south of St. Augustine. It is as curious as San Marco; but little is known of its history, except that its erection was probably contemporary with that of San Marco.

We were at St. Augustine for several weeks, and had an excellent opportunity to judge of the influences of the climate. On several occasions the air was freezing cold, and then we suffered more discomfort than during the severest season in the North, for the reason that neither were the houses constructed with regard to the cold nor were we expecting it. But for the most of the time the air was mild and gentle, so that an invalid would be able to pass the hours of the day out of doors, which, I take it, is the reason Florida has become the winter home of so many thousands of persons having pulmonary complaints. Whether or not St. Augustine is the best locality for such invalids is a serious question, which must be left to the decision of the physicians who have been there; but I have known of several persons within my own limited experience who found the frequent changes which take place from the warm air of the land to the cool, salt air of the sea to have injurious results, which ceased upon going over to the St. Johns River.

Personally, I found the heat to be inconvenient for the most of the time, and arrayed myself in summer clothing. But in pursuing the occupation of sketching from nature, I was in the habit of sitting out in the open air with a white sketching umbrella over me; and at such times I have suffered more from the heat than at noonday in August in a Connecticut meadow. This feeling of exhaustion may be attributed to a lack of vitality in the atmosphere which we find in the southern latitudes. Singular as it may seem, there is not much opportunity to go out of doors in St. Augustine unless as pedestrians. For, although all last winter there must have been a thousand or more strangers, and these coming and going all the while, yet such a thing as a livery-stable does not exist. Two or three vehicles there are, which are hired by the month; but neither buggy, carriage, hack, nor even a common road wagon is to be had. It seems utterly incomprehensible that the hotel-keepers, whose interest it is to have such conveniences within reach, should not attend to these matters. This poverty in the way of conveyances is most felt when you desire to get away from the place. You can not go when you wish to, but when you can—watching the chances in advance to secure your place. When our party came away there were three ladies, with their servant, who wished to accompany us up the St. Johns River; but our people filled the stage, top and bottom, and not in all St. Augustine, for money or other consideration, could there be found a conveyance. A few riding horses there are—safe, comfortable little ponies—who will take you about on the road by the river, or across the plain of palmettoes to the "Magnolia Grove"—a picturesque place called by that name because in this tangled bit of woodland there is only one magnolia-tree. While upon this subject of the discomforts of this place that portion of my conscience lying in the region of the stomach will not permit me to be silent. The food furnished you at the public hotels is simply dreadful. Fresh, nutritious meats there were not. Even chickens would not come at our call; or if they did, it was evident they had made a long journey. We were in the land of wild game, but it rarely ever came to the refreshment of our fainting bodies. This was the soil and the atmosphere from whence proceed early vegetables; but no friendly hand ever strove to induce their appearance aboveground, so far as we knew. In place of wholesome, well-cooked food, we were served with canned meats, canned vegetables; and, as if in compensation, all sorts of fancy tarts, and "méringues à la humbug," and other indigestible jimcrackeries under foreign names, were served up *ad nauseam.*

If excuses could justify this ill-treatment, surely we had enough of them; but under no circumstance is there justification for this disobedience of the Divine command to "feed the hungry," more particularly when the consideration of four dollars a day is exacted.

St. Augustine is not singular in this matter of poor food and bad cooking. It is common to almost all the hotels in the country, especially where they are kept upon the American plan, which abominable system is being fast driven out by the more sensible European method of paying only for what you get, and having that especially cooked for you.

Among the objects of interest in St. Augustine is the sea wall which protects the town from the encroachments of the water, which extends from the water battery at the fort, some three-quarters of a mile, to the arsenal—a handsome building, which is only occasionally used by the government. Every body visits the orange groves of Mr. Buckingham Smith and Dr. Anderson. Orange-trees are not very plentiful in the city or neighborhood, although the perfume of the blossom often enough greets you as you walk through the streets. Indeed, this odor is sometimes so intense as to become unpleasant. The fruit of the orange is quite as costly as in the North. "Uncle Jack," a very small, very ancient, and very peculiar negro at Mr. Smith's, will pull them from the tree at fifty cents per dozen. The most palatable orange we saw came from Indian River, some seventy miles south of St. Augustine, and these found ready purchasers at one dollar per dozen. I was told by the owners of the large orangeries on the St. Johns River that they had sold their crops at about two dollars per hundred. The orange crop of Florida is not so profitable as has been supposed. In 1842 there came an insect known as the "orange locust," nearly destroying all the trees in the country; but that difficulty is fast disappearing. Now and then, however, there comes from the north a yet more terrible invader, in the person of the Ice Fiend, who freezes the life out of the trees, destroying millions of property in a single night.

THE CATHEDRAL.

Although the ruins of former greatness are to be seen at every hand, yet by one and another means the most venerable are passing out of sight. The palace of the British attorney-general, which, it is said, was grand in its proportions, has been torn down so that its material could be used in the construction of other houses. And I was told that one Logan, who was an army quarter-master stationed here, tore down an old powder-house, one of the rarest of the ancient remains of the Menendez régime. Mr. Logan used the stones of this unique ruin for his personal benefit. What shall be said of a person who had so little regard for these priceless relics of the past? There still remains the "Residence of the Spanish Governors," fronting the public square, and now used by the United States authorities. These buildings are highly picturesque, as is the striking façade of an old Spanish treasury building on St. George Street. But the cathedral, of simple Moorish architecture, and which also fronts the square, will attract marked attention. One of the priests who minister there is Father Rousse. A gentle, kind-hearted, humane Frenchman he is, who does his best to take care of the bodies and souls of several hundred negroes and white people, the most of whom are of the poorer class. During our frequent peregrinations we had reason to know of this, and also formed a friendly acquaintance with the good father.

When we came one day to bid him good-by, he said: "Ah, you will become a good Catholic sometime, will you not, *mon ami?*"

"I hope it is not necessary," we replied. "Be sure we shall meet each other in the better world."

"Je l'espère," he answered, sadly, making the sign of the cross.

Certainly the lower, and especially the negro

class here, and, in truth, in all other places we visited in the South, needs the care of some spiritual and religious instructor. Before the war it was for the interest of the master that the slave should be under the control of a religious sentiment. It was one means of subjection, of obtaining obedience; but emancipation loosened that cord, so that the negro in his ignorance is falling from grace, and the elective franchise, with all the carpet-baggers in creation, won't save him. At one of the Protestant churches here, and subsequently at Jacksonville, we saw shocking mummeries, which belonged to the fetich worship of savage Central Africa, and not of Christian America. The necessity of taking care of themselves will be a great assistance to these poor people, but it will require many years to bring about that condition when they can provide for their own needs. Meanwhile the present generation will disappear, and a better intelligence will come with those that follow. But it is my conviction that the present political system will not achieve the desired end. The larger number of the negroes are in darkest ignorance, and in the matter of voting are used by designing men to accomplish their bad selfish ends. It is sad, indeed, to see how these people have in one way and another been made the tools of the white man; but in all their misery they continue to exhibit in a marked way their keen sense of the ridiculous. In illustration of this fact a comical incident occurred to me in one of my sketching expeditions.

One sees a deal of humanity when out of doors making sketches from nature. The people of all ages, colors, and both sexes gather around you, and sometimes in most unpleasant nearness of proximity; you are obliged to listen to lively criticisms of people and things in general; and not unfrequently you, and what you are doing, are made the subject of sharp if not wholesome remark.

One morning I planted myself, with white umbrella, camp-stool, and paint-box, in one of the principal thoroughfares of the city. It would have been called a narrow lane any where else. In front of me was a most romantic picturesque view, such as could be found nowhere but in this charming old Spanish city. There was a bit of ruined broken wall of what had once been the palace of somebody two hundred years ago. It was built of coquina stone, gray and brown, a patch of old brick, with stained plaster in places, making up a rich mass of shadow, with brilliant dashes of light on the top giving emphasis to the whole. Beyond this precious old wall there was an ancient stone house of one story, with a pitched roof. A window opening in the gable showed dark in the midst of the iron-gray of the wall. Further on—this was at my right—there were the high palings of a fence, then another gray gable end of a house, and against the sky beyond that, the roof of a building glittering in the sunlight. On the left and opposite side of the street there was a wee bit of an open place called a square, alongside of which ran a wreck of what may have been a respectable dwelling-house a century or two ago. It had yellow, black, and blue walls, and a shattered shingle roof, violet and brown in color. The end to the street was patched with stone and plaster, and had doors and windows, which were hardly visible in the short perspective, but what little there was shone bright in the direct rays of the sun. On the other side of this was a fence, and then a wooden cabin, and then the branches of a tree dancing green in the light; finally another house, with a high pitched roof and a balcony, which almost touched another balcony on the opposite side of the way, both of which ended the line of the street; far beyond that there was a strip of green grass and gray sand; then, following the sea wall, the blue waters of the river in the dim distance, the purple and yellow of Anastasia Island, and above that a sunny sky, such as is found only in these Southern latitudes and by the sea.

This was the picture I was trying to sketch—with indifferent success, I was informed by one of my bare-legged critics.

"He can't draw, Jake," he said to his companion. "This feller can't draw as dat odder man who's takin' the church down. Dat ar's Aunt Phœbe's; isn't down right. He can't draw."

I made no reply to this and similar remarks shouted in my ear, but I had a pretty positive opinion that my spectators were a "poor set;" and this opinion was confirmed when at noon I came to gather up my apparatus, and did not find the leather strap with which I bound in one parcel camp-stool, staff, and umbrella. All about I searched for the missing article, in the fence corner, and on the road; but it had disappeared with my juvenile critics. While yet I was looking I became all at once aware of the presence of one of the most extraordinary of all these astonishing black people. She—for I still believe it was a female—was costumed in a blue infantry jacket, which was buttoned tight over her bosom; below this a pair of bare feet and legs straddled from underneath a dress of many materials, but of a nondescript and indescribable color. I speak as an artist. I should say it had so many shades that the *ensemble* was neutral. On the kinkiest sort of a head, whose perpendicular front side showed all eyes and teeth, was perched the funniest scrap of a dirty frayed straw hat. It had been stuck there for the purpose of covering, whatever other office it served. This person, with both arms akimbo, yelled at me:

"Wha' yer lookin' fer?"

"A strap—a leather strap."

In a second she exploded: "Yah, yah, yah, yah, yah, yah, yah, yah, yah, yah, yah, yah, yah, yah!"

I gazed at the creature in silent astonishment. What cause of merriment was there in the search for a lost strap? But she was not at all depressed by my look, but burst forth

"LOS' HIS STRAP."

with another scream, at the same time bending forward and clapping her hands upon her knees.

"Yu-yu-u-u! Yee-ee-ee! Yah, yah, yah! He's los' his strap! Yah, yah, yah!"

At this point I could resist no longer, and began to laugh most heartily. Up to this time the surrounding crowd had kept a quivering sort of silence in their polite hospitality, not knowing but that I might be offended. The moment, however, I began to laugh, there was a succession of reports such as one hears on a Fourth of July morning from a bunch of double-headed fire-crackers. At first one, and then another, went off, until it got to be an insane mania. Young and old, male and female, gave free vent to their exuberance of feeling. They screamed, roared, and yelled in every key of the chromatic scale. In their extravagance they clutched at each other, shouldered the old wall, hung upon the fence, and rolled in the sand.

Such an extraordinary sight and sound I never saw nor heard; and very soon I beat a safe retreat toward my hotel, followed at a respectful distance by the woman with the infantry jacket, who would erupt at intervals with her thundering laugh. And after that day, whenever I met her on the street, she would scream forth, "Los' his strap!" with a prolonged chorus of "Yah, yahs!"

I have already said that one of the objective points of our expedition was the St. Johns River. If this trip had not formed a part of our original intention we most surely would have adopted it subsequently, for every pilgrim who came within our acquaintance would at once shoot off the question:

"Have you been up the St. Johns? No? Then you must not miss it. Splendid scenery. Alligators. Lots of fun."

So one day, when one of our folk who had been laid up with a bad cold was sufficiently recovered, we got into the stage, where our places for a week had been engaged, and started back toward Picolata. The prudent reader will wonder that we should go a second time to that wretched place; but there was no alternative short of a voyage by sea to Jacksonville. From this place started the steamer *Starlight*, upon which we supposed we had engaged state-rooms for the round trip up and to Enterprise, the head of the St. Johns River, and back. We expected to take the *Starlight* at Picolata, and if she had failed us, there were other steamers passing, which would have conveyed us somewhere, any where away from Picolata. I ought to have mentioned that our luggage followed us over to St. Augustine some two days after our arrival; so upon our return trip we took good care to start it off several hours in advance in a separate go-cart. We passed that affair half-way on the road over, and some of the passengers avowed that the driver was asleep, and the mule chewing palmetto leaves by the road-side. We ourselves proceeded safely on to Picolata, and, after waiting four hours in the hot sun, found ourselves on board the steamer *Starlight*, and, to our chagrin, learned that our message had not been received, and there were no rooms awaiting us.

This apparent misfortune proved our greatest happiness, for, lying over at Pilatka at the St. Johns Hotel, we obtained delicious food wherewith to assuage the pangs of hunger. Think not, good reader, this is an unnecessary exhibition of feeling over a small matter, for great had been our suffering, and great was our delight. Delicious waffles, noble wild turkey nobly served, tender lamb, adolescent chicken, light, sweet bread, potatoes, green pease, and other delicacies that ravished the heart and made glad the digestive apparatus.

The trip of the *Starlight* to Enterprise, back to Jacksonville, and the return to Pilatka, occupied about three days, and this interval was pleasantly passed, for we saw, for the first time, the distinctive characteristics of physical nature in Florida. Heretofore we had passed through pine barrens and over plains covered with palmetto, but these may be seen in Georgia and the Carolinas; now, however, we were presented to a new, a strange aspect, which filled us with wonder and surprise.

Unlike the mountains and the sea-shore of the North, the scenery of the tropics is greatest in its little things. And so in a row-boat we wandered along the shore, past forests whose sombre depths were veiled to us by vast screens of drooping moss, or, pushing our little craft over and through the wide-spread beds of water-lilies, we entered within the precincts of this solemn Hades.

What weird, wondrous visions then greeted our thrilled senses, as, gliding silently on, the bright heavens were almost shut out from view, and there rose up beside and around us trunks of trees which looked as if they might have been human once, and, like the lost souls of Dante's vision, condemned to this imprisonment!

"We had put ourselves within a wood
That was not marked by any path whatever:
Not foliage green, but of a dusky color;
Not branches smooth, but gnarled and intertangled;
Not apple-trees were there, but thorns with poison;
Such tangled thickets have not, nor so dense,
Those savage wild beasts that in hatred hold
'Twixt Cecina and Corneto the tilled places."

Now stooping as we passed underneath some fallen monarch of the place, we brushed aside the thickly trailing vines, or passed into the embraces of that parasite of death, the pendent moss; and then our keel would disturb the perfect surface of the most marvelous of mirrors, reflecting countless forms of leaf and twig and moss and tree, with here and there bits of blue which told us that there was a heaven above. How intense is the silence of this place, broken only by the splash of a single blue heron, who, wondering at this intrusion, gazes, and then, spreading his great wings, rises slowly and disappears, leaving a deeper silence than before! This is not the forest of Ohio, with its cheerful life and health, its varied growth of beech and birch and oak and buckeye and elm, and a hundred other varieties of tree and bush, with all their beauty, grace, and strength, and glowing youth. All this seems to be in fullness and reality what the spectacle at the theatre suggests. It is not life: it is the funereal pageant of nature.

It was at Pilatka also we first saw that rare and most beautiful of birds, the swallow-tailed hawk, with his gray back and wings, his snow-white breast and exquisitely graceful flight. The natives will tell you he is the "snake-hawk," because he makes war upon those creatures. They will also tell you that this bird, who rises from the shallow water with wedge-shaped bill and red neck thrust far out from his body, and whose flight is swift and straight, is the water-turkey; but the vulgar are apt to give names without reason. In a day or two, as we ascend the river, you will see this same bird, increased to enormous size, one of that vast flock of black objects which, far in the blue ether above, is circling round and round; and then the ornithologist will tell you he is the "cormorant."

The sky was filled with masses of gray clouds, which roofed in the wall of green through whose narrow avenues we were swiftly gliding. It was the morning after the night we had gone on board of the *Starlight*, and I stepped out of my state-room to gaze upon this most entrancing of all the moods of nature, when the gray clouds seem to sweep the tree-tops, and there is that subdued harmony not to be found in the garish sunlight. As the little steamboat plowed along its narrow channels, the water, rushing in to fill the vacuum she made, would sway the countless lily-pads and bending ferns to and fro, sometimes baptizing them with its generous flood. The forest trees were the same all along the way. Cypress, maple, pine, and live-oak, while the palmetto would sometimes choke out the other growths and send forth for acres around its umbrella-shaped tops. The vines grew every where, and along the bank would trail in masses, sweeping the dark waters with their leafy fringe. Very often the dead, gaunt form of some towering pine would rise above its fellows; and here that noblest of birds, the ospray, would leave his nest, secure from harm, and then, sitting upon some outstretched limb, would dash from his height into the waters and bear his prey aloft to his waiting offspring.

Now and then the steamboat would shoot out into a more open space, and where there did not appear to be any outlet, where the bow of the boat seemed about to be crushed against the land; but it parted before us, and what appeared to have been the solid earth was but a floating island, which went dancing and torn in the wake behind us, its long roots thrown up to the troubled surface of the water. At every turn in the river—and it had an endless twist and turn—the tall forms of the blue and white heron would rise from the shallow waters and fly before us. Thousands of ducks were feeding among the water-plants; and not seldom it was a comical sight when, coming suddenly upon them, they would attempt to rise, but, too fat to achieve speedy flight, would tremble and flutter and finally scamper away into the tall weeds. Later in the day the sun came out, and then the torpid bodies of huge alligators would be seen lying on the banks.

"That ar's a 'gator slide," said a tall, sunburnt native to me, at the same time pointing to a smooth spot on the river's bank. So I watched for such places, and soon saw all I desired in the way of "'gators."

On the bow of the boat, and in fact all over the boat, wicked people had stationed themselves with all sorts of fire-arms, firing at every helpless creature they could see. One of these more especially bore the marks of imbecility in face and form. He sat in the extreme bow of the boat, and blazed away at every thing at one time, very nearly shooting some ladies who were stationed near the pilot-house. On another occasion a magnificent female ospray rose from the water near us, and with strong pinions bore a struggling fish to its nest, upon which it settled. Our noble Nimrod at once leveled his gun at her.

"Stop!" cried an alarmed and indignant gentleman. "Surely, you're not going to shoot the mother feeding its young?"

"Well, I guess I'll scare her, any way," was the brute's answer, as he sent a bullet, fortunately not wounding the bird. Shortly after, this same wretch was about to fire at a heron which had evidently been winged by some other coward; for it could only run away, and in the direction of some cattle feeding in the marsh near by. Again this fellow drew bead.

"Take care!" cried one of his companions; "you will kill the cattle."

"They are not mine," was the answer; and this time his bullet hit the mark, and the poor bird was left fluttering and struggling in death. And so, all the way up and down the river, these men sat there and fired at the beautiful birds, which by thousands inhabit the river-bank and the swamps; now and then getting a shot at an alligator; but in no single instance did they hope to fulfill that first requirement of a sportsman—never to shoot at game which you can not bring away. The cowardly fellows shot all day long, without the least prospect of getting a feather. If the officers of the boat can not stop this mean business, the game laws of the State ought to be put in force to the condign punishment of the offenders.

To me the most charming feature of this trip to Enterprise is the presence of these large birds, which I saw for the first time. Nothing could be more beautiful than these flocks of white swan, curlew, cygnets, and heron, constantly rising before us. Powder and ball will soon drive them away, however.

The boat makes several stoppages by the way, usually where some venturesome settler has a place where the sand rises a few feet, has built a hut, and grafted some of the wild orange-trees, which grow in profusion. If the settler be an enterprising man from the North, he will plant a patch of pea-nuts or vegetables; or he may go further, and put in a few acres of the long-staple cotton; but, except in the products of oranges and pea-nuts, he will obtain very little for his pains. So far as my observation goes, there is very little soil in this region fit for agriculture. Unlike other States of the South, which have received from the great rivers of the North rich alluvial deposits, this is made up chiefly of sand not prolific of vegetable life.

At one time, where there was no evidence that man had ever placed his foot, the boat ran alongside a bank and left a plow-share and a keg of nails—two very significant signs of civilization. At another place we found the oddest sort of an apology for a steamboat, which lay at the bank awaiting our coming, so that it might continue its voyage up some of the smaller tributary streams. The owner of this craft, it appears, had put up in some portion of this benighted region a steam saw-mill; but finding none who wished for lumber, he changed his business and set up his engine in a small flat-boat. A belt, pieced of leather and canvas, ran from the engine to a drum attached to the paddle-wheel, which was about eighteen inches wide, and at the stern. The efforts of this engine, which was laboring under a severe attack of influenza, to turn the wheel were laborious in the extreme. There was not much room to speak of in this little box; and so, to make a place for two ladies and a gentleman who were transferred from our boat, the dog-kennel and chicken-coop were placed over the wheel, much to the horror of the animals, who howled and cackled in unison with the wheeze of the ancient saw-mill engine.

As you approach Enterprise the river widens out into a large lake, which is bordered by swamps filled with the ugly palmetto. Enterprise receives its name from the fact of an utter lack of that quality, which, in places of public resort, brings comfort to the traveler. There is one large hotel, which is open to the same objections noted of hotels at St. Augustine. Enterprise is otherwise celebrated for a very large sulphur spring, out of which the milky-looking water pours in a six-inch stream, and as being one of the means by which whoever wishes can cross the country to Smyrna, on Indian River. At Enterprise I met an interesting character in the person of an old negro, who was the owner of sixty acres of sand and palmetto near the sea-coast. Asking this man a leading question as to his health, he volunteered a good deal of valuable information. He said:

"De fac' is, I wus in de Souf durin' de contineration of de wa'. But I thort dat I would seek my fortins in a new country, and so cum down here wid some odder cul'd people, an' bot sixty acres lan' fur two dollars an' a half, which I paid at de office. Dat Freedman's Buyo played de debil wid a lot of our people dat a rascal of an agent brot down dar ter Indjun Ribber an' lef ter starve. It wus a heap better ter lef um be whar dey wus. I could git along, cos I'se eddicated by Colonel Orr, an' could git along any whar; but de plantation niggers don't know nuffin."

"Have you ever voted?"

"Oh yaas, I've voted twice; once for de Presi*dent*, and todder time fur Colonel Hamilton, member fur dis deestrict."

"Hamilton! Why, he lives at Pilatka, and was a rebel. How is that?"

"Yaas, he wus a rebel, but dare cum down hyar a free nigger, a carpet-bagger, from Ohio, or sum odder place Norf, an' put himself up. But wha' did he know 'bout de interests of de people of dis deestrict? Nuffin. Ef he'd bin a freedman belongin' ter der Souf I might a voted fur him; but"—and here the old man spoke with great energy—"we've had nuff of dem carpet-baggers. Dey are lookin' out fur demself. Dey don't care fur de cul'd people. Colonel Hamilton has bin in Congress afore, an' knows what we wants. Dat's why I voted fur him."

It seemed to me that the old man had the true philosophy of the matter.

Our journey down the river was not marked with any new subject of interest. We reached Jacksonville in due time, took the more than excellent sleeping-car to Savannah, and so on north to Washington in safety, notwithstanding the danger from the shocking condition of the railroads.

I can not depart from Florida, however, without a word with regard to that for which she is most famous, her wealth of flowers and foliage. Perhaps if we had remained until April we should have been treated to a more brilliant spectacle in the way of flowers; but, in all the redundance of the growths peculiar to her soil or swamps, we saw nothing comparable for one moment to the magnificent, glorious transformation of the spring in our Middle and Northern States. There is but one season in Florida. We have four, with their infinite moods and changes of majesty and beauty. And of all these, most wonderful is the spring, with its tender green, its leaves, its buds and blossoms, its songs of many birds, its skies of clouds and sunshine; and, more than all, that sense, which never came to us in the land of the Everglades, of elasticity, gladness, hope, that aspiration of the soul for THE NEW BIRTH.

9.
A Visit to Death Lake, Florida (1888)

A VISIT TO DEATH LAKE, FLORIDA.

BY LIEUT. W. R. HAMILTON.

SOME years ago, I was stationed at Fort Barrancas, on the west coast of Florida, and at the mouth of Pensacola Bay. It was the custom of the military authorities every summer, as the sickly season approached, to order all the troops stationed in garrisons along the southern coast into camps among the pine-trees to escape the fatal yellow fever. The camps were selected with a view to health and isolation combined.

In the year of which I write, we were ordered up into the pine woods about thirty-six miles north-west of Pensacola. The camp was several miles from the only line of railroad then existing in that country, and fifteen miles from the nearest settlement, which happened to be a railroad and telegraph station also. The yellow fever had already broken out with terrible violence in New Orleans, and all the southern coast was alarmed. Of course, we were obliged to maintain the strictest quarantine to prevent any communication between our camp and the outside world. This was necessary, as the country soon became filled with refugees from the plague-stricken districts, yet it made our existence particularly doleful. We received fresh meat only once a week, and, as it was brought in an open cart thirty-six miles in the hot sun, the term *fresh* was about all there was of that significance about it. We lived on potted meats and canned vegetables and fruits almost entirely. Nothing was allowed inside the lines except the mails, and even they had to be disinfected outside before admission. News of the outside world was from a week to ten days old, and as the weather was extremely hot, it can be easily imagined that our existence was not particularly rose-colored.

Judge, then, of the delight and pleasure we all experienced when, one sultry evening, when the very air was quivering and dancing with heat, an old man came into camp with a large basket full of beautiful little fresh-water fish. How he passed the line of sentinels no one cared to inquire, the probability being that the guards, knowing what a boon he had in his basket, winked at his passing. He came direct to the line of officers' tents, and in five minutes had sold all his fish at a good price. We asked him where the fish came from, and he answered "Death Lake." I had heard of "Death Lake" a number of times, and the negroes in the neighborhood always spoke of it with bated breath and a mysterious air, so that my curiosity concerning it was much aroused. I therefore asked the old man to my tent, where I could talk to him about it. After he had seated himself and taken a drink of cool water, fresh from the spring, I asked him the name of the fish and when and where he caught them.

"They be brim, mister, and they wuz caught by me early this mawnin' in the lake."

"But where is the lake?" I inquired, "and why is it called Death Lake?"

"Wal," he answered, "it lies about six miles from here, in the middle of a big swamp, and it is called Death Lake, I reckon, because no one can't git there without losing his life."

"Yet you have been there, and you are alive," I replied.

"Yes, but I've most lost my life as much as a dozen times, and I'm only forty years old."

He looked fully seventy, and he was much bowed and broken. His eyes were deep sunk, and had a watery opaqueness; his cheeks were sallow, and there were only a few straggling white hairs on his head. His answer surprised me, and I pressed him to tell me his story, which, after a while, he did, although he was much averse to it. After a time I prevailed upon the old man to take me to the lake next day. "But it is at your own risk, young man," he said; "remember, if you dies, I told you all about it, and you can't blame me."

"Not if I die," I replied; "but I am strong and healthy, and willing to take the risk."

I easily obtained the necessary permission to leave the camp, as I was not going near the settlements, or where the fever existed, and I moreover promised to bring back a good string of fish for the commanding officer. The next morning I met the old man at daybreak, just outside the lines, and off we started together. He carried his large basket and a couple of fish-poles made of reeds he had cut in the swamps. I carried our lunch and a coffee-pot.

We tramped for about two hours through the woods, till we came to a small river called "Perdido," from the Spanish word for "lost." "Lost River" was a very good name for it, as it had its origin in Death Lake, and lost itself completely in the swamps after many turnings. Close to the bank, the old man had a flat-bottomed skiff moored, in which we paddled up the stream for a half-mile, when we reached the confines of the large swamp in which Death Lake is situated. The scenery here is of the typical Florida nature. On either side the stream was bounded by the swamp. Huge cypress trees lifted their weird limbs upward, and long streamers of trailing moss floated from them, and even at times formed a swinging arch across the entire width of the stream. The water was dark and sullen, and on the banks, wherever a little sunshine happened to strike, half a dozen alligators might be seen basking, which, on our approach, would flop into the water with a tremendous splash. After paddling up the sides of the swamp for a couple of miles we came to an archway, which appeared to have been cut by man through the foliage of trees and vines. It was not over four feet high and about eight wide, and from it the water flowed with a scarcely perceptible current.

"Now, Loot'nent," said the old man, "we've got to go up this creek, and you'll have to kneel down like this, for we have to stoop pretty low in places."

Once inside the arch, it became very dark, for though the sun was shining brightly outside, it could not penetrate through the dense foliage of the vines. The little stream turned and twisted in the most tortuous channel I ever saw, and often it was with difficulty that we managed to turn the boat round the sharp and narrow corners. At length, after paddling in this fashion for over half a mile, we emerged into the famous Death Lake.

Right well had it been named, for the very feeling one had in breathing its atmosphere was of death. It seemed more like a river than a lake, for though by its various windings and twistings it was several miles long, it was never, in its broadest part, over sixty yards wide, and throughout most of its length not over twenty yards. The banks were lined by immense cypress trees that towered upward to a height of eighty feet or more. From their branches hung long festoons and trails of Florida moss, while the roots of the trees, half out of water, assumed such weird and fantastic shapes that they seemed like immense serpents that had become suddenly petrified in their writhings. So dense was the foliage that it formed an impenetrable wall to both sun and wind, and the sunlight never touched the water except between the hours of 12 and 2 P. M. Not a breath had stirred the waters for years, and they were covered to a depth of several inches with a green vegetable slime, so that the first appearance was that of a beautiful level floor, on which one might walk.

We reached the lake about ten minutes before the sun, and there was consequently a very strange light over the water. It had much the effect of a twilight above, through which the sun was breaking, while close to the water hung a mist, heavy, silent and motionless. But the tops of the trees the sun had touched with his master-strokes, and created tints more beautiful than could any painter's brush. So still was the place that the silence was actually oppressive, and, though we were startled at the sound of our own voices, we would have been glad to have heard the noise of some animal life.

But all round us was death; no sign of life anywhere. No birds in the trees; no insects in the air. Even the reptiles and snakes avoided the fearful place. To breathe such air for an hour, except when the sun was directly over the water, would be death to any living creature. Even the water was lifeless, and the trees and all vegetation were dead, except the moss, which lived at the expense of all else. The old man had told me in his queer parlance that the lake had no bottom, for although he had dropped 900 feet of line, he had never touched. I had taken the precaution to bring with me two of my sea trolling-lines, and fastening them together, I had a line 250 feet long. With this I sounded in several places, but only proved the old man's words, for I never touched bottom. I afterwards learned, as the explanation of this, that all Western Florida is of a limestone formation, and so I presume this lake is one of those wonders that have their sources far away down in the bowels of the earth.

As soon as the sun touched the water we let our fish-lines down to a depth of about thirty feet, and soon began to pull out very quickly the "brim"—a corruption of the name of bream. Although, when the hand was thrust through the slime, the water had a horribly slimy, warm feeling, the fish came up cold and firm, showing that below the water was clear and cold. The fish had the same dull, opaque eyes as fish of subterranean caves, proving that the vegetable mould on the water's surface had for many years formed a bar to any light in the water.

In the two hours we managed to nearly fill our boat, for the fish bit as fast as we could throw the line overboard; so about two o'clock we stopped, and paddled out as quickly as possible to avoid those poisonous vapors that killed all animal life. Notwithstanding the sport, so weird and unearthly strange was the place that I was glad to leave it. I could well understand its name now, and as we passed through the tortuous archway, I thought of the many negroes in the old slavery days, that escaping to this swamp to find liberty found death instead.

After reaching the river, the old man suggested our stopping at a place on the banks, where the ground rose in a little knoll, and cooking some of our freshly caught fish. I agreed to the proposition, and as we reached the bank I jumped out and took three or four steps inland, when the old man sharply cried, "Look out, Loot'nent! See there!" at the same time pointing, as he stood up in the boat, to something directly in front of me. I looked and beheld, about a yard from me, a huge moccasin snake, the most deadly poisonous reptile of the South upreared to strike me. I involuntarily took a step backward, and as I did so I heard another hiss behind me, and then others on all sides. One quick, horrified glance showed me that I was surrounded by at least a dozen of these fearful reptiles, all coiled and ready to strike. For an instant I was paralyzed and unable to move, and it was, perhaps, well that it was so, as I should probably have stepped on one and been bitten.

"Move carefully and come away," the old man cried. "If you don't git close to them they can't hurt you; they're casting their skins."

So it proved. It seems that this spot of ground, being drier than its surroundings and more exposed to the sun, had, by the natural instinct of the creatures, been selected as the place for the annual changing of their skins. While this process is going on they are almost incapable of motion. As a rule they will move off when disturbed, provided they are not attacked, but in this case they could not; but had I got within striking distance they would have bitten me. I picked my way out very daintily, and stepped into the boat, with no further desire to eat fish till I got back to camp. Indeed, I felt quite faint as I realized my narrow escape. We paddled down the river, soon reached our landing-place, and then made a bee-line for camp, which we reached just at dark. With such a string of fish, my return was heartily welcomed; but after hearing my adventures, no one else seemed anxious to make the visit to the lake.

I wanted to revisit the lake, till one morning, about two weeks after my visit, I was taken suddenly ill, and before the day was over I was unconscious with the terrible "swamp fever." I had a long and hard fight for my life, and though I conquered in the end, I lost all desire to ever see the horrible place again.

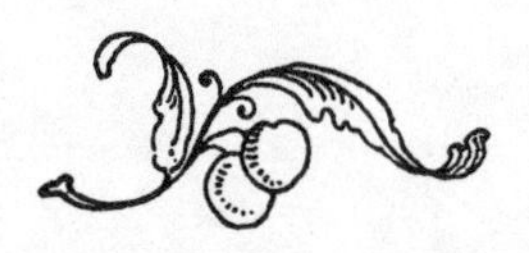

10.
Winter Shooting in Florida (1889)

WINTER SHOOTING IN FLORIDA.

BY F. CAMPBELL MOLLER.

WITH the middle of December the upland shooting in the Eastern States comes virtually to an end. To be sure, a couple of weeks remain before the curtain of legal protection descends over the game still to be found in the dead fields and snow-whitened coppices on the first day of the new year, but the remnants of the quail bevies are wild, and, in much shot-over districts, begin to approach in their watchful behavior and antics the typical wariness of the hawk. As for the ruffed-grouse, one needs to be a thorough workman, both in shooting and stalking, to render even a tolerable account of these birds. The last woodcock was seen nearly a month ago, this mid December day, as one fired and missed him among the black alders, and he is up and away on the next stage of his journey to the swamp-lands of the Carolinas or the Mississippi.

The sportsman resident of the country may at this season of the year have an occasional sun-gilded winter's day with the setters, when the breeze comes warm from the south. But more often will he be listening to the tinkling, musical notes of his beagles as the brown hare leads them a circling chase through the brier-fields, or the deeper notes of the fox-hounds will strike upon his ear as they echo among the gray cliffs of the brown-treed mountain-side.

Yes, it may not seem to be quite the correct thing to my English readers, but we shoot foxes from a "runaway" in the rough, wooded, hilly country of the Eastern States, where it would be impossible to ride to hounds, and gladly do we accept this chance to rid our farmers of this destroyer of game and poultry.

After the 1st of January, comes the exodus of fashion, sport and ill-health from the rigors and blizzards of a Northern winter, and many are the queries from brethren of the gun, visiting for the first time the land of Spanish-moss and palm-trees, to those who have shot quail among the wild violets and sweet jessamine in the Carolinas during early springtime, or "plugged" alligators in some muddy "backout" of the Upper St. John.

No matter whether he knows how to use a gun or not, nearly every man off for an outing in the South thinks it necessary to take with him some such weapon for the destruction of animal life. This fact, in brief, is sufficient reason for the scarcity of game along the shore and in the waters of the traveled portion of the St. John's River. Continual bombarding has driven the denizens of flood and field to remoter districts, and if one wishes really good sport, he must literally hunt for it.

The majority of men going South solely for sport take the Charleston, Savannah or Fernandina steamers, continuing by rail, if necessary, to their destination, which is certainly the most economical procedure, especially if one's dogs be taken. This should always be done, if possible, as a dog fit for a sportsman to shoot over can rarely be hired or even bought in Florida until the end of the season.

If quail-shooting be the expressed desideratum, one had better confine one's self to the Carolinas or to Georgia, both for quantity and proper ground to shoot over. But if he desires a variety, such as snipe, deer, 'gator and quail shooting, all on diverse grounds, lying, however, in the sweep of a short radius from the spot he makes his headquarters, Florida must needs be his objective.

If one is not going below the Carolinas, a rifle will be an unnecessary encumbrance. Bird-shooting alone will be obtainable unless you visit the wild mountainous country far from the paths of the Northern tourist. Here the shotgun and buckshot are the chief agents used in killing deer, and, in this sport as practiced in that section of the wildwoods, one must nearly always be able to ride well; and unless one is shooting on some friend's invitation, he must also pay well for the auxiliaries necessary to secure a shot at the denizens of the woods.

The same directions will apply to "jumping" deer with dogs from among the stunted scrub covers of the Florida brakes. One generally shoots from horseback at the small deer of this region, because the saddle affords a much better opportunity of seeing over the clumps of dwarf oaks or palmettos than would be obtained on foot.

For alligator shooting a heavy bored rifle—especially an express—will be indispensable. A forty-four calibre repeater will, however, be found to answer very well for all-round work on the river. And here, let me at once dissipate any tyro's fallacious belief regarding the invulnerability of the American saurian, save in the eye. I have known them—aye, big ones at that—to be killed with buckshot from a close-carrying shotgun, at a distance of thirty-five yards by planting a few pellets behind the fore-shoulder, and in the thinner skin of the lateral abdominal walls. Frequently a second or even a third shot at close range will be necessary to finish them as they lie floundering in the shoal and blood-stained shore-waters by the side of a half-submerged old tree-trunk. But more of 'gator shooting anon.

Tweed clothes of light color and loosely woven texture should be worn for Florida sporting, as it is warm shooting there even in midwinter. When shooting or outing generally, it is much better to increase the thickness and warmth of the underclothing as the coolness of weather renders such advisable, than to encumber one's movements by heavy coats and trousers. A pair of thick, oil-tanned grained-leather knee-boots with legs made as narrow as permissible, to be worn with thick-ribbed, long hose, will be found the best shoeing to be used in the Florida bottoms. The long boots, coming over the buttonings of the snug-fitting knee-breeches of whipcord—not knickerbockers, mind you—where they fasten just above the swell of the calf, will be found the most comfortable and consistent rig, whether splashing through the sloppy prairies, along the river after snipe, or tramping the waste fields in the clearings between the pine woods. Should you wear ankle-boots and the baggy knickerbockers, always don a pair of thick leathern leggings as an indispensable precaution against the musical and larksome rattler.

Along the St. John's, from Magnolia to Enterprise, increasing proportionately as one nears the latter place, fair sport may be had with all the before-mentioned varieties of game by driving or boating far enough into the recesses of the back country, away from the spots easily reached by the average hotel lounger. But for really good shooting one must get over into the Indian River region, or, better still, the Hummocks on the Gulf coast, and especially about Homassassa, if he wants good accommodation and an abundance of deer, quail, and snipe as well as bass fishing. Below Lake Georges and extending toward the Everglades is an immense breadth of country, comparatively unknown, rich in sport and adventure to the exploring tourist who is willing to endure much rough travel by canoe and portage, and to pitch his tent o' nights in the great dense swamp-lands.

In Florida, quail are mostly shot in the open of the stubble fields or clearings, or in the slight cover underlying the tall, shadowy pine-lands, for the simple reason that the "thickets" in the far South are almost impassable. I remember once following a bevy of quail, flushed from an old maize field, into a bordering covert of prickly plum, cactus and palmetto, with the same indifference with which I generally plunge into the many-stemmed alder-brake or waist-high cat-briers at home. I shall never do it again. Let the bevy go! Start up a fresh one, and trust to your skill in "driving" them into lyings more favorable for your purposes, if not for theirs.

For shooting in the country back from one's hotel a wagon and pair will be needed, and, unless you are well acquainted with the region, a driver and guide combined, be he "Cracker," "Nigger" or Indian. As most of these gentry do a little pot-shooting themselves, in season and out, they will generally insure you good sport, particularly if the man is made to understand that an extra "tip" may be forthcoming, when you return in the evening, proportionate with the amount of game found.

A deal of shooting is done driving through the rough country, among the pine woods, leaving at times the sandy road for miles together, provided the undergrowth be not too dense. And with the dogs quartering on each side of the wagon, one has but to get out and shoot when a point is obtained.

I find No. 10 shot, backed by a heavy charge of powder, the best size for shooting Southern quail, which, by the way, are a trifle smaller than the Northern bird, although identical in all other respects. No. 10 shot is also the proper size for snipe. Some capital bags of these migratory birds may be obtained even on the meadows—or prairies as they are called in Florida—suburban to Jacksonville.

But quail and snipe shooting in the South, with trifling differences as to covert, haunt and lyings, inseparable from the richness of the tropical setting and coloring, will be found so analagous to the same sport in the North that further comment is unnecessary. However, it will prove a new and delightful experience to the Northern sportsman to flush birds, as is frequently done, in the scent-laden atmosphere amid the glorious coppery splashes of color of an orange grove, and see through the tree-stems the blue St. John's flashing its sapphire width in the warmth of golden sunlight, and the solitary giant palm rising here and there along the far, sandy shore.

A day with the alligators is not bad sport when properly undertaken and provided for; and the hide, teeth and feet will put you in possession of much valuable material to be made into bags, leggings, slippers, shoes, whistles, and gun-racks. But since the utility of the 'gator's hide has been discovered, they, too, are fast disappearing from the places wherein they formerly abounded.

This sort of sport does not demand an early morning start. The best time to approach within easy range of the alligators is while they are taking their siesta at midday or early afternoon, sunning themselves on the bog burrocks, which, in lieu of a beach, mark the line of demarcation between the waters of the bayou and the swampy forest bottoms.

Your skiff and man—who, by the way, should be a good paddler and familiar with the haunts of the quarry you intend pursuing—having been engaged over-night, you may breakfast as late and as leisurely as you will, provided you have not too far to row to your proposed ground before high noon. So, enjoy your repast of fresh fish and game of the region, after having previously coolingly and deliciously prepared your palate with a goblet full of pure orange juice from fruit plucked that morning. Your sable attendant is waiting outside in the warm, genial sunshine, in which all of his color love to work for periods almost indefinite, and relieves your waiter first of all, because to him the most important, of the luncheon hamper, grinning the while, and giving a soft "chaw! chaw!" as he hefts its portentous weight and eyes the claret and beer bottles protruding from one of the partly raised lids. This all being to his entire satisfaction, he will pick up your macintosh coat and shotgun and precede the way to his boat. You take a gun as well as a rifle, as doubtless you will get some shots at ducks and shore-birds as you row to the creek and back, especially the latter, because the evening flight will then be on.

Your man may have pulled you for nearly an hour, and as you near a bay which marks the outlet of a creek leading to the lagoon where you intend paddling for 'gators, an object well out from shore attracts attention. It looks like a water-logged dead branch floating under water, save for three knotty protuberances rising above the placid surface. It is the snout, orbital bone and topmost spinal joint of a 'gator, at least eight feet in length, judging the distances between the slightly exposed portions of his scaly frame. No use firing at him; even if one did hit the small mark he gives at 200 yards, he would only be lost, for a dead or wounded alligator will always sink to the bottom, and there, where that old chap is floating in silent content, the water is much too deep to use the long boat-hook or the grapnel to fetch his body to the surface.

Entering the bayou, the darky exchanges the oars for a thing he calls a paddle. Not as delicately shaped is it as are those you have used about Bar Harbor or on the Adirondack lakes, but it will answer the purpose admirably. You seat yourself in the bow of the boat with your repeater across your knees. There is a fascination in this coasting along the weird, shadowy banks of the tropical creek, with its wealth of beautifully and vividly colored birds. Rounding into the entrance of the lagoon one sees a flock of white heron with wings glistening and flashing in the sunlight as they fly over yonder moss-hung headland; and the brilliant flamingo dyes with a gliding streak of salmon-pink his reflected flight in the shaded, still waters underlying the wild tangle of the wooded shore along which your boat is silently creeping. The skiff rounds the headland.

"Look yaar, sah! Dere he be—ole 'gator on a lorg."

"Where? where?" is hastily whispered, as you anxiously scan the shore-line for a hundred yards ahead. Nothing, however, meets the inexperienced eye but a wild reach of water-grass, rushes, bog-burrocks and partly submerged fallen tree-trunks.

"Dar, sah! under dat big cypress, 'bout ten rod ahead, and lying on de lorg on de show. Shoot, or he'll 'be orf next minit," hurriedly whispers your "gillie."

"Ah! there he is." One holds just back of the fore-shoulder. Bang! "He's hit!" Then his tail wildly beats the air, and he rolls into the water, which just covers but does not conceal his frantic contortions, only to expose himself to a second shot as he flounders up on some sunken logs. The man has grasped the oars after the first shot, and is rowing rapidly to the spot where the mud and spray are being whirled vigorously about.

"Give him a shot in the neck." Missed! but no matter.

Now we're within twenty yards of him. "Stop, Joe; don't row up any farther. Keep well out of the reach of his tail." Now, pump another ball at his head or neck to break his cervical vertebræ. "Good!" He rolls off the log, but "rolled off dead, shoo," says woolly-head, showing his ivories, and getting the long-pointed hook ready for use when the blood-stained waters shall have cleared away.

While the darky busies himself with removing the alligator's skin, you start off for a shot at a flock of teal which has come dangerously near, and perhaps you also secure some plover. There is every reason to be satisfied as you turn your boat down stream for home. The waters are aglow in the evening sun; not a breath of air is stirring; everywhere calm and quiet. You puff away at your pipe, and as you gaze at the 'gator skin in the bottom of your skiff, you find a use for every tooth and every inch of hide, and you picture to yourself the pleasure you are going to give to numerous friends. It is well to dispose of your cargo in this way before you make your landing, for there at the wharf you will find assembled the usual contingent of pretty girls waiting for the evening steamer and the return of the different boating and shooting parties. Hard-hearted will you have to be to withstand the pleadings for mementos, etc., and there is every probability that when you reach your hotel all that you have left will be the memory of a pleasant afternoon with a 'gator.

11.
The St. Augustine Lawn Tennis Tournament (1890)

THE ST. AUGUSTINE LAWN-TENNIS TOURNAMENT.

BY THE TENNIS EDITOR OF OUTING.

SO varied are the climates of the United States, so widespread the votaries of lawn tennis and so fashionable its gatherings, that one is not struck with the sense of incongruity at the announcement of a lawn-tennis championship progressing at St. Augustine in weather that is pleasant to the eye and grateful to the senses, while in the Northern States one is battling against the bitter spring winds. Everything conspires to mark St. Augustine for lawn tennis' own. Its climate is perfection alike for players and spectators; there is little or no wind, and the temperature, while not too hot for exercise, is sufficiently high to be enjoyable to outdoor spectators. Its company is the most appreciative, being largely gathered from those sections of society which in the ordinary summer season of the North are themselves contestants in many a local battle. And just so much as St. Augustine and the sunny courts of Ponce de Leon are specially adapted for winter lawn tennis, so lawn tennis exactly meets the requirements of Ponce de Leon. Its environments are all that luxury, good taste and refinement can require. The opportunities it offers of enjoyment are not restricted to the contestants or to age or sex. The proverb that the spectator sees the most of the game is more than verified in lawn tennis, for the spectators not only see more but enjoy more of the game than the combatants. It is especially the ladies' game, too, and its tournaments afford just those occasions for social intercourse and pleasant gatherings which tend so much to bring out the happiest and pleasantest sides of human nature.

Furthermore, the St. Augustine tournament comes at a time of the year when it holds the field with undisputed sway. At other times — from the opening of the season late in May or early in June at Flushing, until it culminates in the glories of Newport—there is always a choice; one can pick and choose. The Middle States championship, or the Western States, or the United States or some college tour-

PLAYERS OF 1888.

nament in which one is interested is always then either approaching or is in progress, or has just passed; for, with all the care which authority and mutual arrangement exercise to prevent the national events in lawn tennis from actually competing with each other in dates, it is impossible to prevent them from conflicting in interest.

On the other hand, the Tropical Championship at St. Augustine has a season to itself, and it is the premier season, too. It comes like the flowers in the spring, a welcome harbinger of the greater glories approaching, but doubly welcome on that account. The contestants are not left with the pleasant satisfaction only of being for the week the lions of society. The prizes which mark their practical skill are more tangible and perhaps more alluring; for to the title of Tropical Champion was added, by the generosity of Mr. H. M. Flagler, of New York, in 1888, a beautiful and massive sterling silver trophy, representing in design the ancient city gate of St. Augustine, and he who first wins the championship the fourth time, not necessarily in succession, will become its owner; and for the next in succession of merit—the defeater of all comers except the champion—there is annually provided a magnificent silver pitcher.

Although, up to the present, the giants of the courts, Messrs. H. W. Slocum, Jr., and R. D. Sears, have not entered the lists at St. Augustine, it has had attractions for men in the highest ranks of lawn tennis, and, seeing that Mr. O. S. Campbell, a foeman worthy of the steel of the mightiest, has already scored two victories toward the four which will make him the owner of the St. Augustine trophy, it may rather be expected that new contestants will next year

THE FINAL SINGLES OF 1890.

enter the field. One drawback only exists, if such it can be called—the soil of Florida does not admit the cultivation of good grass courts and asphalt has been adopted. But this slight drawback weighs but little in the balance against the many countervailing attractions, and year by year, since 1887, when the Tropical Tournament was first held in the private grounds of the Moorish Villa Zorayda of Mr. Franklin W. Smith, it has grown in public favor until it has gathered round it more and more a galaxy of social enjoyments. Riding, driving, boating and fishing supplement the tournament, while this year a tennis german was in the programme.

It is no wonder, then, that under such circumstances, with such surroundings and for such honors, the entries in the courts by the picturesque Alcazar Casino have rapidly increased and have attracted players from both sides of the Atlantic. Lord Hope, brother of the Duke of Newcastle; the Hon. Maxwell Scott, of historic Abbotsford, and Mr. Garrett, have all at one time or another been tempted into its arenas, but the honors have always stayed at home.

In 1888 Mr. H. G. Trevor, of New York, after a five-set match, in the final round defeated Mr. Beckwith, of Cleveland, and thereby became the first of the tropical champions, and Lispenard Stewart, C. E. Garrett, L. H. Dallas and George Worthington were then among the entries.

The spring of 1889 witnessed a large accession of Northern experts, including the youthful, slight-built O. S. Campbell, of Columbia College, who took there for the first time his racquet and his mascot straw hat; Mr. Deane Miller, Mr. I. Stuart Smith, Mr. A. E. Thomson, of New York city; Mr. R. V. Beach, of Yale College, and Mr. A. E. Wright, of Trinity College.

The courts, which had up to that time been of wood, were then asphalted, and good tennis resulted. Wright won over Miller after a brilliant match of five sets, but was defeated by Campbell, who won the silver pitcher in the final all-comers' match by three sets to one, and followed that by taking three sets and the championship from Trevor, while Wright and Campbell won the doubles and Beach the second prize in singles.

This year the numerous attractions of climate, society, pastime and competition brought to St. Augustine on March 17 fourteen players, the most prominent among whom was again O. S. Campbell, his old opponent and erstwhile champion, H. G. Trevor, Mr. T. S. Beckwith, who stood at the head of lawn tennis in St. Augustine in 1887, the year preceding the establishment of the formal championship tournament, and R. V. Beach.

The weather was favorable throughout the whole week, with the exception of an occasional shower—of trifling consequence, for the asphalt courts soon dried and the porches of the Alcazar Casino, made more picturesque by their fair occupants, afforded ample shelter.

This year's tournament was of exceptional interest. Trevor, the champion of 1888, played a brilliant match with Beach and lost it. Beach in turn suffered defeat at the hands of Beckwith, who had been the champion of 1887, and in that way Beckwith, by the laws of the survival of the fittest governing the tournament, became the runner up or challenger to single-handed combat of the holder of the championship, O. S. Campbell. Beckwith is a brilliant but inexperienced player in tournaments, and the result gave Campbell again the championship honors.*

The red-letter day of the tournament was not, however, the final in the singles, but the final in the doubles, which was played on Thursday morning between Campbell and Smith and Beach and Trevor — a day which may well mark the high-tide point of the social pastimes and pleasures of St. Augustine's lawn-tennis season.

* The scores of the whole tournament will be found in the Records in the May number of OUTING.

1—T. C. HARRISON. 2—L. H. DULLES. 3—F. WHITTRIDGE. 4—H. G. TREVOR. 5—O. S. CAMPBELL. 6—R. B. WHITTRIDGE. 7—G. S. SMITH. 8—O. GOLDY. 9—R. V. BEACH. 10—H. A. PEACOCK. 11—T. S. BECKWITH.

12.
The Log of a Filibuster Correspondent (1903)

THE LOG OF A FILIBUSTER-CORRESPONDENT

By RALPH D. PAINE

DRAWING BY FLETCHER C. RANSOM

ON New Year's Day of 1897, the ocean-going tug *Dauntless* was laying a course for Cape San Antonio at the western end of Cuba. Behind her were the Florida coast and several disappointed cruisers ordered to patrol those waters and capture any vessels suspected of engaging in the lawless traffic of carrying aid and comfort to the insurgents across the Straits of Florida. This was the second voyage of the expedition which crowded the hold and decks of the *Dauntless*, and the munitions of war and the Cuban volunteers on board were battered and sea-stained, after one hazardous flight on the filibuster *Three Friends*. But one unsuccessful attempt to land in Cuba had not discouraged the notorious "Dynamite Johnny" O'Brien, who guaranteed to deliver such cargoes regardless of obstacles.

It was due to my misguided endeavor to stay with this expedition that the voyage of the *Dauntless* began amid scenes of excitement that were positively painful. While the cargo of arms and munitions and the Cuban party had been hidden on a key off the southern coast of Florida, awaiting rescue by a filibustering steamer, I had made my way to Key West in search of information, and returned to the refuge in the fast steam yacht *Vamoose*, placed at my disposal by the newspaper for which I was acting as an amateur bucaneer.

The *Dauntless* lay four miles off shore, while a fleet of sponging schooners and sloops was bringing on board the cargo of rifles, machetes, dynamite, and other necessities of the strenuous life.

The *Vamoose* was long, low, white and rakish, and her torpedo-boat outline was not familiar to the hard-working company off No Name key, so when she slid round the nearest key, and headed for the *Dauntless*, the fleet of sloops and schooners scattered like a flock of pigeons at sight of a menacing hawk.

A torrent of black smoke from the stack of the *Dauntless* showed that furious stoking had begun below decks. The *Vamoose* approached the *Dauntless*, before the filibuster could slip her cable, and the crew recognized the harmless character of the yacht. But on the hurricane deck there was one figure in violent agitation. Even before I could order a boat lowered to board the *Dauntless* I knew that the man in a rage was General Emilio Nunez, in charge of filibustering operations in Florida, who had come to command this expedition in person after the first failure of the *Three Friends*. I was pulled alongside, and when within point-blank range, the language of General Nunez was nothing less than a broadside. Spanish and English expressions of his state of mind volleyed like the sputter of an automatic gun. An occasional Spanish oath of unusual complexity choked him, as if the mechanism had been jammed.

At least one-half of the cargo had been between ship and shore when the *Vamoose* hove in sight.

The imbecile spongers and fishermen had waited not for orders, but had fled at first glimpse of what they thought was a revenue cutter or torpedo boat.

With a cunning that made matters worse they were heading for the shallow passages among the keys through which a steamer could not follow them.

General Nunez comprehended the significance of these rapidly diminishing white patches, fleeing every way but toward the *Dauntless*. The whistle of the filibuster was bellowing reassurances, trying to tell the frightened lunatics that the strange vessel was friendly, but no recall could reassemble the small craft. Greatly condensed and sweepingly expurgated, the opinions of General Nunez conveyed the following convictions:

"You have ruined the expedition. How can we catch these crazy swine? What do you mean by coming here in that imitation of a man-of-war, and smashing all our plans to pieces? This cargo has been carried half way round the island of Cuba,

The Cubans on the Shore of Corrientes Bay. . . . . "'Patriots, homesick and seasick, with the stuff piled around them like the wreck of a hardware store.'"

it has lain on this key for weeks, and now when I come to see that it is landed, you have scattered the expedition all over the coast of Florida, and a revenue cutter or a cruiser will be down here by to-night from Key West. It is too much for words. Alas, poor Cuba!"

There was a deal of common sense in the remarks of the Cuban general, although, as delivered, they blistered the paint on the deck-house of the *Dauntless*. Dazed, and profoundly unhappy, I ordered my two sailors to pull for the nearest sponging sloop, a hopeless chase. I helped at the oars, and we crawled half a mile, in the vague hope that one of the fugitives might sense our peaceful intentions. But this symptom of pursuit in small boats seemed only to make the panic-smitten flotilla struggle more desperately than ever to escape beyond the horizon line. The expedition had simply exploded in as many fragments as there were boats running away with installments of the cargo.

I boarded the luckless *Vamoose* and ordered the boat's captain to put after the runaway craft, in the hope of getting one of them in a corner, and sending a small boat within hailing distance. The yacht tore through the deep-water channel for a mile, and then had to slacken speed, and feel her way. The disgusting ability of the spongers to smell their passage through the shoals baffled the deeper-draught yacht, and her keel ripped over more than one fragment of reef before the captain gave up the chase and confessed himself beaten.

I had no wish to return to the *Dauntless*, and my ardor as a filibuster was sufficiently dampened to call it an inundation.

An incident which added to the gaiety of the scene was the sight of a surf boat filled with Cubans, rowing madly back to the key from which they had started. They did not wait to beach their craft, but fell into the surf, as the *Vamoose* came near, and scampered into the mangrove jungle, a rapidly moving picture of ludicrous terror, if one's sense of humor has not been submerged in woe. The idea of returning to Key West on board the *Vamoose* became immensely attractive to me, the more I dwelt upon the impossible situation.

Help came in this darkest hour. A small steam launch, bringing a party of Cuban sympathizers from Key West to wish the expedition *bon voyage*, had hailed the *Dauntless*, and now bore down on the *Vamoose*, seeking to assist, if possible. The nearest of the distant fugitives was pointed out, and the launch put away in chase. The little craft drew no more water than her quarry and in half an hour succeeded in getting within hail of a hysterical sloop, despite the efforts of the latter to escape by any method short of taking an overland route. The sloop turned back, and with a quartering wind was able to head up for the *Dauntless*. This change of mind was observed by the skippers of two other runaways, and they also turned, taking it that all was well. The remainder of the fleet began to hesitate, then to put about, and within an hour two of the boats had reached the *Dauntless* and the others were on the way. The work of transferring the cargo was resumed, and continued without further interruption until late in the afternoon. I had disrupted a large and important filibustering expedition, and accomplished the feat single-handed. But there was no pride in the achievement as I sneaked on board the *Dauntless* after sending the *Vamoose* back to Key West.

The voyage around the western end of Cuba was made distressful by a heavy gale and head sea, that washed over the *Dauntless* as if she had been a floating bottle. Forty odd men were trying to sleep and live on her decks without shelter of any kind, and they were drenched and chilled two nights and days on end.

Nobody except the captain of the tug and General Nunez knew the destination, and there was no joy on board when early in the morning of the third day at sea, it was learned that "Dynamite Johnny" O'Brien, commanding the *Dauntless*, had been instructed to put his cargo ashore in Corrientes Bay, where the province was overrun with Spanish troops, and the prospect of being thrown ashore was not a consoling one to the patriots.

General Nunez and Johnny O'Brien, however, were not selling return tickets for their personally conducted excursions, so, over a smooth sea on a cloudless morning, the *Dauntless* slipped close into the mountainous coast. Her cargo was piled on the lower deck, ready to be thrown into surf boats as the landing party made ready to make the last move in the filibustering game.

Not a smoke blur was visible. The Cuban shore was a curtain of palms and close-woven jungle, and there were no signs of human presence or habitation.

If ever a ship wished to conduct herself as unobtrusively as possible it was this same *Dauntless* slipping shyly along within rifle range of a hostile coast. But something went wrong with the whistle valve, as the steamer was beginning to sheer in toward the mouth of Corrientes Bay. The *Dauntless* had a whistle whose volume of sound would not have discredited a transatlantic liner, and suddenly the roar of it burst upon the vigilant silence. For several minutes the crew's frantic efforts to quiet the whistle were ineffective, and when it was silenced, men jumped if a match was scratched alongside of them.

But there were no responses to the unhallowed invitation of the *Dauntless* to hasten and shoot her full of holes, and with uneasy lookouts, she kept on up the wide and beautiful bay. Strategetically, the place was not praiseworthy. Should a hostile vessel pass along the coast while a filibuster was within, there was no concealment possible, neither was there any way of escape with the entrance of the bay blockaded. For this reason, the crew was prepared, in the matter of arms and rations, to take to the beach and desert the ship, if a Spanish blockader was sighted off the bay. His cargo once landed, Captain O'Brien was not deeply concerned about the fate of it.

The *Dauntless* was made ready for flight by bending a rope hawser in place of the chain cable, and a deck-hand stationed at the bitts in the bow, with orders to cut, if there was no time to get up anchor. The safety valve was clamped down, and fires were freshened. A lookout was swung to the fore-masthead in a boatswain's chair, and his orders were to yell at the first show of smoke outside the bay.

When the first boatload was safely started for the heavily wooded beach, a mile away, there was considerable anxiety over the possibility of a surprise somewhere in the screen of undergrowth that came almost to the water's edge. But the patriots were not molested, and they dumped their packages of rifles and machetes at the edge of the surf and scrambled back for another load, not at all anxious to remain without reinforcements. Then the little band of undisciplined Cubans from the cigar factories of Tampa and Key West were taken ashore and set in the midst of the heap of boxes and flags, like the survivors of a shipwreck. And they had pictured a landing with a brave array of Cuban cavalry drawn up on the beach to welcome and protect them, flags flying and bugles blowing.

The doleful landing violently affected the most flamboyant of the adventurers, a former cavalry bugler of the regular army, Jack Gorman. He had expected to kill a large number of Spanish officers, and receive a heavy reward for his marksmanship. He went ashore with a boatload of ammunition, and returned to assist in filling another. There was an air of gloom about him that clung closer than his faded canvas leggings.

"It's the hell of a place," said he. "It would take a mowing machine to get a man started on a march through that jungle. There ain't a Cuban soldier in sight, and from all I can hear there ain't none within a hundred miles, and the dozen or so that's left in this province is hidin' in the tops of the tallest trees in them mountains back yonder. And this gang of patriots is sittin', homesick and seasick, on the beach, half of 'em in plug hats and cutaway coats, with the stuff piled up around them like the wreck of a hardware store. I was promised a commission in the Cuban army, but where in blazes is the army? How am I goin' to pick off Spanish officers at a thousand dollars apiece, if we are supposed to go after the Spanish army with that God-forsaken outfit? An' here I am burnin' up with fever and no hospital in the nearest seventeen counties."

The devastating Gorman grew rapidly worse in the next hour. Before the last boat had gone ashore, he had declared himself unfit to walk a step, and was in a genuine fever. Nothing more pitiful could be imagined than the contrast between the former jaunty figure of a fire-eater and the huddled and discouraged heap of Gorman, his trusty rifle neglected in a corner of the deck. I went ashore with a crew of patriots who were transferring a dozen cases of nitroglycerine and dynamite shells. The boat grounded a hundred yards from the beach, and the Cubans tumbled into the surf, each hugging to his breast a package of explosive sufficient to jar the island off the map.

If one of them had stubbed his toe on the coral reef, there would be an excavation in place of an expedition. The possibility was realized a little later, but fortunately the Cuban involved had lingered in the surf boat to beach it some distance from the cargo and party, and was alone, by a distance of several hundred yards, when he tripped and dropped a case of nitroglycerine. It is needless to say that the patriot was obliterated, and the explosion caused new astonishment that no Spanish vessels appeared.

One American continued to play his part undisturbed by conditions, favorable or otherwise. He was an Irishman, Mike Walsh. The landing of the expedition was not up to his expectations, but he showed no uneasiness at the absence of a Cuban force of welcome and protection. He hustled cargo ashore, and grinned at the forlorn aspect of the party with whom he had cast his fortunes.

"I turned filibuster and pirate on the high seas to look for a scrap," explained Mike, as he threw a reluctant Cuban in a surf boat, and pitched a bundle of machetes after him. "I got a jewel of a scrap on the *Three Friends*, and why should I be kickin' when I fired on a Spanish gunboat and made myself the hero of the only naval engagement of the Cuban war? This outfit of lone patriots has got to scrap as men seldom fought before to get them arrms anywhere, and I'm with 'em to the finish. Av coorse I'm goin' to land and stay landed, and if you get unaisy about me, have patience and prisintly you'll read in the papers that Major Mike Walsh of the glorious and iver-victorious army of liberation is capturin' Havana with that same bold company of warriors that is sittin' there on the edge of the jungle, lookin' as disconsolate as the survivors of a Mississippi flood. Grab that oar, you pig-headed son of Castillio, or I'll put you in irons."

No sooner was the surf boat clear of the filibuster than Captain O'Brien gave the order to get under way. The landing had been handled with admirable skill. In two hours the cargo was put ashore, and the steamer under all the steam she could carry, dashing toward the mouth of Corrientes Bay. In the shadow of the clustered palms that hung over the white thread of beach the company of Cubans were gathered in a black mass, and a straggling cheer came over the summer sea. There was pathos in their seeming abandonment. They had not seemed like soldiers before this moment, but the serio-comic side of my adventures with them was now eclipsed by admiration. Among them was one Irishman, for whose safety I had small fear, and this faith was justified more than two months later when the first news of Mike Walsh, the gunner's mate, reached the United States. The information was brief but cheering. Somewhere in the hills of Pinar del Rio, Mike Walsh, in command of a small squad of Cuban soldiers, had dynamited a train filled with Spanish troops, and had considerably reduced the fighting strength of the regiment involved.

The misfortunes of the expeditions by sea seemed to have passed over the *Dauntless*, and the lucky vessel fled around the end of Cuba and toward the coast of Florida without sighting a Spanish steamer of any sort. The crew toiled to obliterate all traces of cargo and passengers, and the outlaw craft became a respectable sea-going tug returning from a cruise in deep water. She passed in the St. John's River, almost under the guns of the *Dolphin* and the revenue cutter *Boutwell*, but having no reason for flight, the tug was not stopped and overhauled. It seemed as if there would be rest for the weary in this home-coming, after several weeks of adventurous living, but dreams of seemly raiment, a hotel *menu*, and a real bed under a real roof were blown away in an hour after the *Dauntless* had crossed the St. John's bar. Captain O'Brien addressed me in this discouraging style: "We are going to set you and Gorman ashore about ten miles below Jacksonville, as we must go to the dock with the vessel's crew and no extra hands. You had better sneak into town, or keep out in the woods for a day or two, until you can get word to the Cubans. If you want to go back with the next expedition, it isn't going to help your programme to be tangled up with warrants for filibustering, and from what I hear from Nunez, you are wanted. So am I, for that matter, but perhaps I know the ropes better than you amateurs."

In the early evening a yawl left the *Dauntless* and once more marooned the writer, with his despondent comrade in arms, Jack Gorman. The landing place was within a mile of a winter resort hotel at Roseland, several miles below Jacksonville, and I had visited the place in happier days. It promised a welcome refuge for keeping under cover. We entered the hotel grounds and five minutes later were in full retreat, but I could not blame the proprietor. The hotel had been turned into a sanitarium and "rest cure," and when the two bucaneers walked into the office, a dozen or so of nice old ladies and pallid elderly men were playing cards or chatting drowsily. Highwaymen could not have caused a more violent flutter in this peaceful company. I became conscious that our appearance might not be conventional, and a pier glass in an alcove explained the general agitation. The two ragged, dirty, unshaven and warlike ruffians were enough to cause a general relapse among all the patients afflicted with nervous disorder. Our hand-baggage consisted of blanket-rolls, saddle-bags, rifles, and similar *bric-a-brac*, and when we dumped the pile inside the door, there were signs of hysterics over by the fireplace. There were no vacant rooms for us; there would not have been if half the house stood empty, and the clerk was rude enough to say as much. He was making a suspicious move toward the telephone when we bade him good evening and slid into outer darkness. Homeless and hungry, we walked miles, fearing to board a trolley car, and came at length to a saloon at the lower end of Jacksonville. It was one of the times when there seemed urgent reasons for the existence of the saloon. Timidly advancing to the bar, a brief order was given. It was filled, but not consumed, for, from a table at one side, arose the voices of three men in argument. It was the following announcement that caused upraised glasses to stop in mid-air:

"I tell you, the *Three Friends* did land that expedition, and some of the gang were captured. The Spaniards got Ralph Paine, the correspondent, all right. I used to go to school with him here in Jacksonville. Just listen to this from the *Times-Union:*

> "Havana, via Key West.—It is known here that the steamer *Three Friends* had landed at Juaraco the expedition carried from Fernandina, and it is reported that Ralph D. Paine, the correspondent who was on the filibuster, has been captured and, with three Cubans, has been placed in the Cabanas fortress."

We did not stop to deny the report but fled without explanation. The sign-board of a sailor's lodging-house faced us at the next corner, and we went no farther. Twenty-five cents a day was the charge for an alleged room, and I bore a week of this extravagance. Later I found a more comfortable hiding place at Green Cove Springs, and awaited sailing orders—but both the *Three Friends* and the *Dauntless* were in disgrace, carefully chaperoned by deputy marshals who never left them day or night. And so I passed one month. The chief embarrassment in this shy and retiring life in Florida was that I changed my name so often it was necessary to consult a memorandum book before asking for mail.

When it seemed probable that no more expeditions could be got away from Florida for weeks or months, newspaper orders called me to other fields of work, and a career of filibustering on the Spanish Main was cut off in its prime.

13.
In the Cape Sable Wilderness (1903)

White Ibises in "Flight-Line" for Rookery.

IN THE CAPE SABLE WILDERNESS *

By HERBERT K. JOB

PHOTOGRAPHS BY THE AUTHOR

IT was a cool, sparkling morning with a bracing northerly wind, the 26th of April, when we shoved the tender over the slippery "soap-flat," and stood upon the shore of the southernmost mainland in the United States. An almost unbroken wilderness lay before us, with all its interesting possibilities. A handful of settlers had taken up government claims along the shore, and built their rude cottages or curious palmetto shacks. Back from the strip of timber along the water's edge is a moderate area of marshy prairie which is flooded in the summer rainy season. Aside from this, all the Cape Sable peninsula is a wild, tangled, pathless mangrove swamp, extending back a number of miles to the open saw-grass marshes of the Everglades. In the embraces of this swamp lie a series of shallow lakes with muddy bottoms, connected by various channels through the thickets, and more or less overflowed by the sea, especially when strong on-shore winds heap up the waters into the shallow bays. The whole region is as flat as a floor, and hardly above the level of the sea.

The first lake we visited after an arduous tramp over mangrove roots and through the jungle was a mile long, with densely wooded shores, a mere layer of water over a bed of mud of the consistency of molasses. Up near the further end we could see an islet with a lot of snow-white birds roosting on the trees, and, as we neared, I saw that they were the great wood ibis—technically, a stork

* This is the second of a series of articles by Mr. Job, illustrated by photographs he made during a recent trip taken especially for OUTING into this great untraveled swamp land.

—the American representative of that much reputed bird of the Orient, and, like it, our bird is also an imposing creature, standing nearly as high as a man, and clad in spotless white, save for the black extremities of the wings. The stork is apt to nest high; in the interior of Florida I have found them nesting more than a hundred feet from the ground, in inaccessible security. Here it was delightful to see them on the tops of low mangroves, evidently breeding. And so it proved. The great birds left when we were at quite a distance, and circled far off over the swamp, together with a vagrant crew of buzzards.

As we landed on the muddy islet densely overgrown with red mangroves, we heard the hoarse voices of young birds beyond, that in almost human tones seemed to reiterate, "Get out, get out." It was not easy to transport the cameras over the treacherous tract full of deceitful mud-holes, but after a struggle I arrived under the nests, whitewashed and stinking. Very soon I was overlooking them. There were eighteen, all told, within an area of a few rods, and each contained two or three young birds, pure white in color, about the size of large pullets, with heavy-looking bills. It was the first time in my life that I had looked into a stork's nest, and happy was I in the blazing Florida sun, upon the mangrove-tops.

To photograph these stork houses, which were merely large platforms of sticks, proved to be a problem indeed. Built some fifteen feet from the ground, upon the topmost twigs of very slender trees, almost bushes, it was hard enough to get one's head above them, to say nothing of the camera; and, of course, there was nothing on which to fasten the instrument. Finally I selected the most convenient trees, tied several of them together with cord, and had the guide hold them up as I mounted and stood gingerly on the top, overlooking the nests, but with nothing to hold on to. With no less care I hoisted up my ten-pound 5 x 7 camera, and, thanks to the good light, was able to make several snap-shot pictures. This

White Ibises.

A Fledgling Wood Ibis.

being done, I descended safely, taking with me one of the young ibises, which I posed for a portrait upon the ground.

Along the "Capes" there are no mud-fiats, but deep water close in to the fine beach of shell-sand. Here a chain of lakes approaches near the coast, and we took the opportunity to explore them.

The first was several miles long. We poled past several little mangrove islands, starting some brown pelicans and cormorants from some of them where they were roosting on dead stubs. Then we followed a narrow channel through the mangrove forest into the next lake, white ibises and yellow-crowned night herons flying up before us to enliven the scene. The next lake was also very shallow, with mud-flats here and there, on which were scattered quite a host of birds. Conspicuous and noisy were a flock of laughing gulls. Less conspicuous, but more interesting to me were the shore-bird ranks both in this spot and as seen during the day. Right before us on the flat a splendid band of the large black-breast plover, and around them a humbler host of sandpipers, ring-necks, dowitchers, and the like, were feeding, sedately or nimbly, as the case might be. But dwarfing them into insignificance by physical contrast stood sleepily a pair of splendid white

Young Wood Ibises in Their Nest.

A Young White Ibis.—These are dark in color, while young wood ibises are white.

showed myself, they were up and away.

We visited in all four or five connected lakes, examining a number of islands, but without finding any rookeries or breeding birds, or seeing any more white pelicans. These last were plenty here a month ago, but they had now evidently departed for their northern breeding-grounds, and there is no likelihood that the species ever breeds in Florida. Yet we

pelicans, with bodies as large and plump as the roundest pillows of the daintiest couch. I skulked along shore under shelter of the forest till I was delightfully near the unconscious birds, and ready for an exposure—when away they went, alarmed, evidently, by the boat. They alit about a mile off on a flat, where I stalked them under cover of an island and secured some telephoto pictures, though at longer range than I could wish. As soon as I

were glad that we visited this chain of lakes. Hawks and eagles circled about, herons and ibises flapped along, shore-birds of many interesting varieties prodded the mud and whistled their piping notes. In fact, nature was so lavish that, in one narrow place in the lake between an island and the shore, two young tarpon of fair size for eating leaped into the boat.

After the rest of the party had returned home I camped for a week with a guide

Young Wood Ibises in Nest.

at the old spot east of Cape Sable. Poor forlorn country! Though the soil is suitable for the raising of tropical fruits, the lack of fresh water and the terrible insect scourge makes it simply torture to stay there. Clouds of mosquitoes give their victim not a moment's peace. One must wear thick clothes, and either don gloves and a screen hat or fight all the time. In camp must be maintained a constant blinding smudge of dead wood of the black mangrove, which "skeets" and men alike detest. Photography under these circumstances is comparable to the Spanish Inquisition. Settlers who pretend to any comfort at all screen their houses and keep outside the door a brush of palmetto leaves with which every visitor must beat off the stinging swarm before dodging within. Other settlers keep the smudge-pot going and live in smoke. There are also swarms of a terrible great fly, an inch and a quarter in length, whose bite is like a knife-thrust, with corresponding flow of blood. No domestic animal except the mule can support life in such a country, and that hardy beast only by being kept in a screened stable and bundled up in burlap when taken out to work.

The Last Lingering White Pelicans.

One of my most interesting and roughest excursions was to a lake six miles away, or rather to its vicinity. When we neared the edge of the lake, which was more properly a sort of everglade morass, and tried to get into the swampy woods where the birds were flying into the rookery, troubles began, compared with which the clouds of "skeets" were as nothing. Rivers of soft treacle-like mud proved absolutely impassable. Finally we got across a wide ditch, and encountered a tract of impenetrable dead saw-grass. A match was applied, and, after the roaring cauldron of flame had passed, we went on. Then we encountered a tropical jungle—a solid mass of roots, vines, scrub palmetto and the like. The guide went forward with his caseknife, and cut openings, through which we crawled. After half an hour of this came a saw-grass bog quarter of a mile wide. How we ever managed to flounder across, dragging one another out of holes, I hardly know. But we reached, at length, the swampy tract of woods into which returning ibises, herons and egrets were dropping, and from which we could hear a confused murmur of distant squawking.

I shall never forget the sight which greeted me as I emerged from the slough and came through the woods to the edge of one of the impassable muddy bayous, about thirty feet wide, bordered by thickets of mangroves. The trees were fairly alive with splendid great birds and their half-grown young. The most abundant was the white ibis, a fine creature, snow-white, with black wing-tips and brilliant red legs and bills, both long, the latter down-curved. They are locally called "white curlews," and are esteemed one of the best food-birds of the region. Their young are of a blackish-gray color, with white on the rump, and were now in the stage when, though unable to fly, they had left the nests. The woods were fairly alive with them, and droves raced over the ground under the mangroves, or climbed among the branches in all directions.

In the Mangrove Swamp.

Next in abundance was the little Louisiana heron, the common blue-gray species with white under-parts, whose young were in about the same condition as the young ibises, and mingled with them. Across the bayou we could hear, but not see, the large, graceful snow-white American egrets and their young. As with the peacock, beauty of form and plumage is not matched with sweetness of song, and this lovely dream of a bird speaks in harshest rattling grunts. Much the same is true of the elegant little snowy heron, a few of which we could see dropping into the swamp beyond our muddy Jordan. These last two species are the wearers of the so-called "aigrette" plumes, the fatal ornament which has led almost to their extermination.

But what made me thrill with special excitement was the sight of half a dozen

Young White Ibises and Louisiana Herons.

or so of large rosy-pink birds quietly perched upon the trees just opposite us across the barrier, the roseate spoonbills on their nesting-ground. What a spectacle—the dark green mangrove foliage dotted with ibises of dazzling whiteness, "pink curlews" (the local name), and blue-tinted herons! I felt that I had here reached the high-water mark of spectacular sights in the bird-world. Wherever I may penetrate in future wanderings, I never hope to see anything to surpass, or perhaps to equal, that upon which I then gazed. This is the last remnant and the last place of refuge of hosts of innocent, exquisite creatures slaughtered for a brutal millinery folly.

Climbing a tree, to get above the undergrowth, I screwed my 4 x 5 camera to a limb and proceeded to take pictures of the surrounding birds, with telephoto attachment and with long-focus single lens. Then, with this camera and the 5 x 7, I followed along the bayou, hoping to find some way to cross. Every time I tumbled into a mud-hole or snapped a twig, there was wild confusion. The air was white with ibises.

The day was now nearly gone, and yet we had not crossed the bayou into the main part of the rookery. But at length we reached a place where a small tree had fallen across, and managed to reach the other shore. The very first nest which I examined, about five feet from the ground, in a crotch, contained four young snowy herons. While I was standing there, the queenly mother, exquisite with her back-load of elegant drooping "aigrette" plumes, flew down and fed her white-robed princely children. About twenty-five feet up the next tree was another nest of twigs in a fork of the main trunk. A sort of rosy flush around its edge led me to climb to it, and I gazed upon three young roseate spoonbills. They were, perhaps, one-third grown, and were clad in a rosy-pink down, through which feathers of the same hue, especially on the wings, were sprouting.

My plates were nearly all used up, and I tried to expend the few remaining ones judiciously amongst this mass of wonderful material. Then the guide fairly dragged me back, for it was very necessary to be out of the morass before sun-down.

14.
Following Audubon Among the Florida Keys (1903)

A Man-o'-War Bird in Flight.

FOLLOWING AUDUBON AMONG THE FLORIDA KEYS*

By HERBERT K. JOB

PHOTOGRAPHS BY THE AUTHOR

FROM off Miami, out beyond Key West, nearly two hundred miles, extend a series of submerged coral reefs which form a breakwater for a parallel chain of long narrow islands of rough coral rock formation, densely overgrown with trees and jungle. Inside these islands are great shallow bays with immense flats of white clay mud, containing hundreds of low islands. These last are not of coral, but are groves of red mangrove trees growing out of the mud in shallow water, around whose roots the soil has gradually lodged by the action of the tides. The seedling mangrove drops off from the parent tree, and is borne by the current until it grounds on a mud flat and takes root. Here it spreads out by sending down new roots from the branches—like the banyan tree of the Orient—then drops off seedlings, which take root around it, and thus, in a few years, another key is formed.

In Audubon's time this great inaccessible wilderness was the resort of pirates and wreckers. Even now, so shallow and difficult of navigation is it, a sail is a rare sight upon its waters. Few naturalists have penetrated its inner shallows, and many of the keys are still nameless. Even indefatigable Audubon only entered the portals of Florida Bay, never reaching Barnes' Sound. Naturally, then, our little party of three on the 7-ton schooner, *Maggie Valdez*, was that night an enthu-

* This is the first of a series of rather remarkable photographs made by Mr. Job on a special exploration trip to Florida for OUTING; others will follow on birds of prey—shore birds, for which Mr. Job is gathering material for this magazine.

siastic one on the borders of this land of promise, harassed though they were by mosquitoes and by troops of horrible-looking cockroaches, each two inches long—with which boats in this region are infested, as well as with scorpions.

Early the next morning we sailed out through the coral reef into the open sea to cruise outside the keys further westward, since the *Maggie*, drawing four feet of water, was too deep for the flats of Card's and Barnes' Sounds. The ever-wonderful migration of the birds was now at its height, and thousands of little land-birds were making their long, weary flight from the West Indies, or even farther, across the sea to our shores. Even with Florida in sight, those last two miles often proved heart-breaking. The tired little creatures often would alight on our spars, or even on deck, sometimes allowing us to take them in our hands. One such was a male bobolink, in a curious mottled transition stage of plumage. Another male bobolink tried to alight on the end of the boom, but was too much exhausted to gain a footing, and fell into the water, where he lay struggling pitifully, unable to rise. Thus, undoubtedly, do multitudes of the little migrants perish. Besides this kind we also identified water-thrushes, redstarts, and black-poll warblers.

Toward evening we ran in to anchor under the lee of Indian Key, where Audubon, in 1832, began his famous entrance into Florida Bay, coming there on the U. S. revenue cutter *Marion*. Here he was entertained by a resident customs collector, and with him made boating-trips among the keys. It was with absorbing interest that I gazed upon and explored this beautiful tropical islet. Though I could not trace the great naturalist's literal footsteps upon the littoral stretch of hard coral rock, I could recall his words of admiration at the beautiful little birds he saw flitting among the bushes—this very same time of year, it was—migrants that had happily escaped the dangers of the sea. And here, now, many warblers, thrushes, finches, doves, and the like, were happy among the luxuriant growth of cocoanut palms, century-plants, and the thorny thickets—in which last the mother ground-doves were brooding young in their frail nests—as the evening shadows fell. When the sun rose, they were all jubilant with song. We drank milk from the green cocoanuts, rambled about and took photographs, and talked with the old man, who, with his wife, represented the human population. The old fellow had never heard of Audubon, and cared more for the boat he was building than for antiquities. This island was the scene of an Indian massacre in the Seminole War, and later was occupied by an enterprising rascal who ran a drinking and gambling dive, which was resorted to by smugglers and outlaws. Shades of Audubon!

Audubon narrates that, immediately landing on Indian Key, he was conducted by his host across to a neighboring key, where he and his party inspected a rookery of Florida cormorants. From his account I should judge that this was Lower Metacombe Key, which we could see about a mile to the westward, a long, dark strip of mangroves some four miles long. We did not visit it, as the guide said that the cormorants did not resort there, but frequented some smaller islands further in the bay. So, hoping to happen upon the route of Audubon's second-day excursion, which he made between 3 A.M. and dusk, to a key evidently some miles away, where he found the man-o'-war birds resorting and beginning to nest, we got under way about 8 A.M. Our course lay between Lower Metacombe and Lignum Vitæ Keys, and on into the mazes of "soapy mud-flats," or "soap-flats," as Audubon called them. The simile is an apt one, for the sticky, whitish clay mud has a very soapy appearance, and the tide running over the flats stirs up a whitish lather suggestive of soapy dish-water.

Approaching some small flats marked on the chart as the "Boot-leg Keys," six or eight miles north of Indian Key, the schooner stuck hard and remained fast for the day. But it proved an interesting day, for noticing near-by keys we set forth with camera and note book, and rowed the tender as far as we could, dragging it the rest of the way over the slippery white "soap," in which we sank half way to the knees. On the first island there were some twenty pairs of Louisiana herons nesting, and one pair of the red-bellied woodpecker. As we neared the second island I waded on ahead, camera in hand, ready for a snapshot when the birds rose, and when I appeared around the end of the island great

" Spent their time making vicious lunges at me."

Young Great White Herons—" These were of the sulky sort."

Man-o'-War Birds—"A plate full of graceful soaring birds."

was the commotion among its inhabitants. A confused mass of wings were seen and heard beating the tree-tops and the air as two or three hundred birds rose—the brown pelicans, cormorants, and man-o'-war birds. The first two flew directly away, the latter separated from the others, and, in a flock, soared higher and higher overhead, giving me time for two more pictures.

Eager to see the nests, we forced our way through the tangle of mangrove roots and branches. Everything was as filthy as should be in a great nesting-place, but great was our surprise and disappointment to find that there were no nests. It was merely a roost, but one constantly resorted to. The birds, though now dispersed, returned that evening in much larger numbers, and when we sailed by here later on the trip, one night at dusk, there were hundreds of them, both in the trees and hovering, mostly man-o'-war birds. Ever since he had known the region, the guide said, this had been their principal place of resort in that vicinity. Inasmuch as water-birds are very tenacious of their resorts when not too much persecuted, it is very probable that this was the rookery which Audubon visited on his second day's excursion.

It was not before sundown that we succeeded in warping the schooner out of her sticky resting place. We sailed on, dodging shoals, or scraping over them, until about nine o'clock, when, in the dark, we ran aground once more, but got free, and anchored for the night. At daybreak we started on, and that day managed to keep afloat. The wind was light, and we worked leisurely along, seeing a big turtle, now and then, floating on the surface, and an occasional sea-bird—pelicans, laughing gulls, a very few terns, and once a parasitic jaeger. In the afternoon we passed Sandy Key, the farthest point that Audubon reached. A few splendid great white heron—the largest heron of North America, snow-white, which Audubon discovered on these keys, and named—were perched appropriately on the trees. As the guide was in a hurry to get home, we postponed our landing here and kept on toward a spot on the now visible mainland, about ten miles east of Cape Sable.

Here we remained for a week, making trips into the interior and to neighboring keys. Some of these keys, owing to the shallowness of the water, we could best reach in small boats. One day, approaching a small key, I saw several great white herons—splendid birds, nearly as tall as a man—flying uneasily about, well over the tops of the trees. On landing and clambering about for some time amid mangrove roots and slippery, sticky mud, never ceasing, withal, to fight mosquitoes, I was finally rewarded by finding several of their nests, built in crotches, twenty to thirty-five feet above the ground, bulky, saucer-shaped platforms of good-sized sticks. Each of them, of course, was profusely whitewashed, as were the surroundings, and contained two or three snowy white young, in various stages, from callow nestlings to those nearly matured and almost able to fly.

One nest especially interested me. It was conveniently situated, about thirty feet from the ground, and was occupied by an imposing young heron of almost full size, which stood on the nest and received me in dignified manner, not scrambling or fluttering out, as young herons are all too apt to do. While I admired him and screwed my camera to a branch, he never moved, nor did he at the critical moments of exposure. Then, as I would stir him up a bit, he retreated out beyond the nest, where he stood like an obelisk, showing his good breeding in every inch of his stature, as I again took his picture.

Not so well bred were a trio of half-grown scapegraces in a neighboring nest. These were of the sulky sort, that threw themselves prostrate in miserable attitudes, refusing to stand up and behave, despite of all that I—even assisted by my guide—could do. Another nest with two tiny fledglings also gave me trouble, from the difficult combination of wind, movement, and shadows. However, I conquered them, and then climbed to a rather lofty nest near by of the great blue heron, whose two youthful inmates spent their time in making vicious lunges at me, accompanied by the harshest expletives of the heron tongue. I did not catch sight of their parents, but now and then a vision of white, ghost-like, passed silently overhead, safely distant.

Having secured another (and nameless) vessel of lighter draught than the *Maggie*, we started off on a general exploration of

Young Great White Heron—The species Audubon discovered on the Florida keys.

mangroves. Purple herons rose at almost every step we took, and each cactus supported the nest of a white ibis. The air was darkened by whistling wings, while on the waters floated gallinules and other interesting birds." Next morning, at low tide, he was amazed to see the flats covered with feeding birds in all directions. But now, as we reviewed these same scenes, traversed the long beach, searched the groves of red and black mangrove, examined the little interior pool and swamp, and the patches of cactus, we found a different state of things. Too convenient a landing place for the "conch" fishermen, there were no longer "acres" of ibis nests. We found these later, back from Cape Sable, on the main, in the inaccessible swamps to which they have been driven. A few pairs of great white herons, probably nesting, flew out from the mangroves and alit on the flats, where there were also great blue and Louisiana herons feeding, as well as some laughing gulls, black-breast plovers, and other shore birds. A lot of black-crowned night herons flew up from around the pond, and kept returning, as though they had nests somewhere about. Some brown pelicans, fish crows, and buzzards were flying around, and a pair of bald eagles, soaring conspicuously over the island, had their nest, a great pile of large sticks, six feet in height, about fifty feet up a giant black mangrove. On a number of other keys we afterward found similar eagles' nests. The young had long since flown.

As we walked along the beach, we noticed, a few yards out from shore, a

the inaccessible shallows and keys of the inner bays. First, however, we sailed westward to Sandy Key, to examine this remote spot, six miles off Cape Sable, where Audubon passed the night under his mosquito net, and which he so vividly describes in one of his "episodes." With a good easterly wind, we were there by noon, and hastened to go ashore. The key is about a mile long, in two lobes, connected by a narrow grassy isthmus. The rest of it is mostly wooded. It is one of the few Florida keys that boast a genuine beach—of the regulation Cape Sable shell-sand.

When Audubon landed there seventy-two years ago he records that "our first fire among a crowd of the great godwits laid prostrate sixty-five of these birds. [This was before the days of "Audubon" societies!] Rose-colored curlews [roseate spoonbills] stalked gracefully beneath the

beautiful specimen of the Physalia, or "Portuguese man-o'-war," floating on the water, its transparent jelly-like form flashing in the sunlight, resplendent with blue, purple, and rosy hues. It had the curious habit of rolling completely over and righting itself again. It swam by means of tentacles that streamed down below, and was constantly accompanied by a pretty little fish, that we afterward saw dead, killed by the dangerous tentacles. One of our party laid hold of the creature, and began to drag it ashore, but he soon let go with an exclamation of pain. The captive had well used its means of defence, and for the next hour my friend was in torment, his arm being nearly paralyzed up to the shoulder, and aching severely. He will be chary of these warriors hereafter.

Sailing on again, this time south and east, late in the evening we approached Man-o'-war Keys, two islands, one of them a mere "bush," or clump of mangroves, another reputed resort of the frigate or man-o'-war birds. Early in the morning we rowed the remaining mile over the soap-flat, to find that there were very few "men-o'-war," but plenty of Florida cormorants, which resorted to both the islands, though not to breed. They afforded me some flight-pictures, and some amusement, too, when, wading around a corner of the "man-o'-war bush," I came suddenly close upon a number of them on the trees of the submerged inlet. In their terror many of them dropped like stones into the water, as though they had fainted, and were lost to sight; others, partially recovered, went fluttering along the surface. The only evidence of nesting was on the larger key, where there were a number of great blue herons and their empty nests, and another nest belonging to a pair of eagles.

From here we started on for a long hard beat to windward, still south-east, to reach a little settlement called Planter, on Key Largo, where there was a store—the only one in all the region—for provisions were running short. It took two days of hard work, even to getting overboard to push. The rough clearings on the key amid the outcropping coral rock certainly looked

"Stood like an obelisk."

"Now they begin to rise."

very unpromising for agriculture; but the profusion of all sorts of tropical fruits was convincing and delightful. Potatoes are dug, they say, with crow-bars instead of shovels.

Having now plenty of provisions, fruit galore, and a fine mess of craw-fish, we proceded to explore many of the inner keys. On most of them there were no resident water birds, save a few herons. On one large key, along the shores of two salt lakes in its interior, we found least terns, Wilson's plovers, and black-necked stilts, breeding, and a colony of laughing gulls about to do so. The migration of the shore-birds was interesting, and I found the best opportunities for photographing them that I had ever met.

Despite all our efforts thus far, we had not found the man-o'-war birds actually breeding. So one day we were more than glad to anchor near a small key to which the guide said thousands of these great birds constantly resorted. It was back under Key Largo, farther up the sound than we had yet been. We reached there just before sunset, and at once I started out in the tender, the other ornithologists deciding to wait till morning. As the guide rowed me through a narrow passage in the mangroves, a break in a long peninsula, there lay before us the little round green islet. First of all some cormorants flew from a mangrove clump out in the water. Then, as we approached within long gunshot of the island, began a wonderful scene. A few man-o'-war birds had been visible, alighting on the trees, or flying about; now they began to rise in scores, in hundreds, and then in thousands. When one realizes that these birds measure nearly seven feet in extent of wing, it will give a better idea of the imposing spectacle before us. The area of the island was hardly an acre, and it seemed incredible that so many of the great birds could have found footing in the trees, or that anything short of the toughness of the red mangrove wood could sustain them all. I secured a picture of them as they began to rise from the island, and then a number more as they soared overhead, fairly covering the sky. One only had to point a camera upward almost anywhere and snap to get a plate full of gracefully soaring birds. After a few moments the cloud gradually drifted away, to hover for hours over a distant key.

Then we hastened to the island. Several reddish egrets—the only ones met with on the trip—started out from the trees close beside us, as did some Louisiana herons. The island itself was entirely under water, and the trees were white with filth. But even here the elusive men-o'-war were not yet nesting. The Louisiana herons had eggs, and there were about a dozen rude, empty nests of sticks, lined with some frigate feathers, just like what these birds are said to build; yet they may have belonged to cormorants. The man-o'-war bird is not now known to nest in Florida, and we had hoped to be able to re-discover this fact, to which Audubon was witness. Since these birds are said by the guide—a careful and accurate observer—to remain here in immense numbers throughout the entire year, and as they are known to breed very late, I am confident that a visit to some of these roosts in June or July would find the host settled down to family cares—and what a sight it would be!

On the way back to the vessel, a pair of the exquisite pink roseate spoonbills flew close over our heads, giving me a splendid and memorable view of their glories. Alas for the delaying naturalists! The birds did not return that night to the roost, and next morning a single straggler mocked the camera of the delinquents.

All along on the cruise we had watched longingly and carefully for a sight of the great rosy flamingoes feeding on the mudflats. That pleasure was not for us. Small bands of the wary creatures are yet seen in this region, mostly in fall and winter. Our guide saw the last bunch in early April, before we arrived.

Audubon, describing his cruise among the keys at this same season of the year, speaks of the intense heat and of the necessity of a fish and cracker diet. Our experience was that the temperature was very equable, with fine cool nights, ideal weather for living and sleeping outdoors—very different from the heat of the interior of Florida. We enjoyed a hearty and varied fare without any ill effect. Indeed, it would be hard to recall a more enjoyable outing in all my experience than following the great pioneer of American ornithology among the keys of Florida.

The Schooner *Maggie Valdez.*

15.
A Good Day's Tarpon Fishing (1890)

FOUR SILVER KINGS

OUTING.

FEBRUARY, 1890.

A GOOD DAY'S TARPON FISHING.

BY O. A. MYGATT.

SIX weeks passed after our arrival. Tom and I had had but indifferent luck. He had caught two and I one, when his day of days came. It was 9 o'clock in the morning and a glorious day, such as Florida in Spring alone can show, when Tom, directly after his breakfast, strolled down to the pier. At the foot of the stairs Raphael, his Spanish boy, was getting things ready for the day's sport. It was about four miles across the bay to the ground, and half an hour later saw Tom anchored on what he considered a favorable place. This is on a sand-and-mud bottom, covered with thin patches of seaweed. The boat was anchored about 300 yards from shore in six feet of water. A stake was driven in the mud at the stern and the sailboat fastened to it to prevent swinging. The rowboat was removed from the stern and fastened on to the anchor rope forward, giving a free field behind and preventing any possible bumping between the boats. Tom was ready to begin his day's attentions to the tarpon. Cutting off the tail of a mullet just above the dorsal fin, he passed the hook through the bait so that the point came out through the skin at the dorsal fin which he had cut off. Standing on the stern, he cast his bait in shore some twenty-five yards. Having successfully cast, he took hold of the line at the tip of the rod and drew off the reel some twenty feet of line, which he coiled on a smooth surface. Sitting down, he lit his cigar, holding the line lightly between his fingers above the coil, and waited patiently for a friendly tarpon to take pity on him. Some men have waited three months for this, and then the tarpon did not take pity. The day was warm. A brisk south wind made the water quite choppy and turbid. Everything pointed to a good day's fishing, so Tom eagerly gazed around for signs of tarpon.

Half an hour went by. Suddenly he saw the dorsal fin of a tarpon, not eighty yards off, appear an instant out of the water. He straightened up and saw that his line was all right. "By jove!" he involuntarily exclaimed. The large and beautiful tail appeared for one moment out of the water not ten yards from where his bait lay. He knew that the fish was feeding, for when grubbing his snout down in the seaweed a tarpon generally shows his tail above the water when it is not deeper than six feet. Again everything was quiet, then there was a swirl immediately above his bait; again the tail appeared and the line was pulled from between his fingers at a steady, even rate. Slowly the line disappeared overboard as the coil unwound. Tom, in the meanwhile, had grasped his rod, holding one hand placed well up; the other firmly grasped the butt, the thumb lightly grasping the leather brake of his reel. The rod he pointed directly in the direction of the fish, keeping one eye, however, on the coil, lest it might tangle or catch in a splinter, when the tarpon would be as good as lost. At last the coil disappeared overboard. Tom waited with the rod still pointed toward the fish until the strain on the line was sufficient to cause his reel to click, when he knew that a strike might be of some use. Click went the reel, down went his thumb on the leather brake, and with a long, steady movement he swung his rod to the vertical position, when he took most of the pressure off the brake. Whiz! went the reel with lightning speed in the fraction of a second.

Then, with a glorious leap, out sprang the king of game fish. His tail was three feet above the water, his head perhaps eight, while his six feet of polished silver side flashed in the sun. As he appeared Tom, ready for him, tipped his rod, allowing his line to grow slack, so that as the monster, gleaming and dripping in the sunlight, shook his head fiercely in vain, the hook remained firmly fixed. With an immense splash he was in the water again and off like lightning; but the instant he was again in his element Tom had full strain on his line, and wherever he now rushed he must drag this eight-pound strain with him. Give a tarpon a few moments of slack while in the water and such are his retching powers that, firm as the hook may be caught, he will at times loosen it and at his next jump cast out bait and hook. While the first few rushes and jumps had been taking place Raphael had brought around the rowboat to the stern, and both springing in they followed the fish in his wild career, allowing him, however, a fair percentage of towing. Again and again the tarpon sprang clear of the water, fiercely shaking his head; each time the rod was tipped at the right moment and the jerking strain avoided. The tarpon's course, fortunately for the angler, is an erratic one. Each jump will change his direction. Were it not for this you might as well play a torpedo on a rod and line as a tarpon. Time and again he dashed straight for the boat, and, safe in the boat as Tom felt himself to be, it was nevertheless uncomfortable to see the monster cleave the water, dashing straight at him.

But Tom was ready for him each time, and, thanks to his large multiplying reel, took in his slack in time and dipped his rod in the water as he passed underneath the boat. Now the tarpon stopped his rushes, and lying on the surface flapped his tail, feebly an inexperienced angler might think. Tom, however, did not flatter himself that he had already tired the

CASTING THE MULLET OUT.

brute, but telling Raphael to row up alongside the fish as near as possible, he began a sort of up-and-down sawing motion with his rod. He was trying to get the snell of the hook caught in the strange cut or slit beneath the upper jaw of the tarpon. Once in it, Tom knew that it would not slip out and

A TARPON JUMPING.

that the tarpon could not possibly chew through the snell. I have found that, with a little care and after some practice, the snell can always be placed or worked behind this slit, thus removing all danger of its being bitten through. Instructing Raphael to get still nearer the tarpon as he sulked on the surface of the water, he ordered him to touch the fish with the gaff. An electric shock could not have produced a greater effect. Once more the tarpon was all motion. Now, out of the water, shaking his head, now dashing this way and that, taking the sharpest curves, sometimes even grinding his nose in the sand! Gradually the jumps became weaker and weaker until soon nothing but the tarpon's head appeared above water when he tried to jump, and he feebly shook it, as if protesting at his magnificent life being cut short.

A few more splendid rallies, when he dashed off endowed with new life, and then suddenly, as if his heart had broken, he rolled over, belly up. Tom prepared to gaff him now, but, miserably weak and played out as he knew the tarpon to be, he was very careful that Raphael should not gaff him until he was sure of holding him, while he himself stood, rod in hand,

ROD AND FISH.

prepared for that final mighty convulsion of the fish which often at the last moment will wrench away the gaff and snap the line. Only when Tom had passed the rope through his gills and fastened it securely to a cleat did he feel perfectly sure of his game. Then, indeed, with a sigh of relief he stretched his aching arms, rubbed his cramped thumb, almost paralyzed with pressing on the brake, lit a cigar and, smoking, leaned over the stern, gazing at the tarpon as it swayed to and fro flashing in the light as he was towed back to the sailboat some two miles off. Here the tarpon was lifted out with some difficulty and thrown on deck. Again Tom cast out his bait. For half an hour he had no strike, but about two hours after midday he struck and hooked his second tarpon and once more went through the same excitement, finishing by capturing his fish.

Nor was this the end of that day's sport. By 5 o'clock he had laid four tarpon on the deck of his boat. Their weights were 84, 85, 110, 115 pounds; their lengths respectively 5 feet 9 inches, 5 feet 11 inches, 6 feet 1 inch, 6 feet 2 inches. There were still many signs of tarpon being there, and it was much against his will that he set sail for the hotel, but he was completely tired out with the four struggles he had gone through, and had to give in through sheer physical weakness. So, happy as a king, yet wishing he had been strong enough to try and catch more, he returned to the hotel in that very customary mood of man, a strange mixture of satisfaction and dissatisfaction.

Meanwhile, although Tom had been covering himself with glory, poor I, fishing some fifty yards from him, had only managed to land a little fifty pounder. To describe the state of envious jealousy and the hatred I felt toward Tom would be impossible. Imagine sitting within casting distance of another man, seeing him hook five tarpon inside of four hours and land four, while you yourself get but a little fellow and three sharks! I registered a vow that I should equal or beat his catch, but vows are not much use when fishing. For several days following this great catch of Tom's but few tarpon were caught—not more than two by all the fishermen. The fourth day—a beautiful, warm one—six boats anchored off Blanco all day, but one tarpon being caught. Toward evening, however, as the boats began leaving, I noticed several tarpon swirls near our boat. I begged Tom to stop, pointing out to him the signs of fish. His only answer was "Bosh! Those are nothing but shark. I have had enough fishing to-day." As we only had one sailboat I had to sail back to the hotel with him. As soon as I had landed him, however, I said to the man, "And now off to Blanco." Tom sat on the wharf with several other men, and in chorus they jeered at my energy, while they assured me that all my efforts would prove in vain.

Just before sunset we arrived at Blanco and anchored in shore in about four feet of water. I have always found that the tarpon bite best in shallow water. Putting on baits I cast them from the sailboat, using both my rods, intending to fish from the large boat only. Hardly ten minutes had passed; the men were preparing supper when, above the glassy surface not ten yards from the boat, a magnificent tarpon tail appeared immediately over one of my baits. This was followed by a sudden swirl which almost caused my two men to fall overboard with excitement. Seizing my rod I pulled off and gave the rapidly-moving fish some thirty feet more of slack line, then waiting till my line was taut, I gave a good strike. There was a mighty leap, a fierce shake of the head and whiz went my reel. "Thank heaven, he is hooked!" I gasped.

Getting into the rowboat I followed the leader. Now and then from the sailboat came encouraging remarks from my excited cook. Supper, I need hardly say, suffered sadly from lack of attention. Meanwhile I was going through the ordinary evolutions of catching a tarpon, enjoying its exciting rushes and beautiful leaps as they took place under the reddish glow of the fading sunset. Already I had him well tired out and was pulling him in gradually to gaff when I noticed a huge fin some eighty yards off. The fin cut the glassy water like the bow of a steam yacht. The tarpon, becoming aware of this immense shark's presence and endued with new life, shot off in his intense fear. But he was fagged out, and I soon stopped him. The shark meanwhile had slowed up and was slowly circling about tarpon and boat, perhaps hesitating between two appetizing dishes. I felt a chill run down my back and my hair seemed to creep, when slowly coming straight up to the boat he passed not three feet underneath, revealing not more than twelve feet of a spotted back. He doubled and prepared to play the same trick. Feeling that a strike of his tail under the boat might throw one or more of us in the water, I yelled to Joe, "Strike him in the jaw with an oar!" Joe gave him a powerful blow that caused him to swerve aside for a moment, but in an instant, turning on his side, he made a vicious snap at the oar. Joe, nothing daunted, was about to hit him again. "Leave him alone!" I cried. "You are only making matters worse. Let us gaff the tarpon and get him in the boat and we will get a revolver." Meanwhile, standing in the bow, my mind was divided between my fear of falling in the water where the shark might interview me and losing my tarpon. The tarpon, by the way, all this time had been acting in a most eccentric way, evidently frightened crazy by the presence of this large shark. The latter, however, ceased his attentions to us and began to circle around the tarpon, who made frantic efforts to get away, while I, realizing that it was nip and tuck between the shark and I as to who would get that tarpon, risked all the strength I dared on my line and tried to get the fish within gaffing distance. I had succeeded in getting him within twenty feet of the boat, and seeing him come in belly up, bleeding greatly from the gills, was beginning to flatter myself I had added one more to my record. Suddenly, cleaving the water like lightning, with a fierce rush, the shark made for him. There was a horrible splashing—I saw the tarpon lifted clear of the water, while the spot became blackened with blood. For a moment I was dazed, not to say scared, by the sudden turn matters had taken.

Joe, too, was kneeling in the bottom of the boat, his eyes starting out of his head. He finally said, his voice gradually rising into a shriek, "Well, if I ever saw anything like that may I be d——d!" Recovering myself I wound in my line, feeling nothing but a dead weight attached to it. As I pulled this came to the surface, the water gurgling round and round through it. With a shout of laughter Joe screamed

UNDER THE PALMS.

A FLORIDA SCENE.

out, "Well, you have got his head, anyhow!" Sure enough, there was the tarpon's head, with shreds of skin hanging from it. But Joe spoke rather too early, for the twisting mass was suddenly seized and dragged beneath, while my line snapped. Throwing the rod down in the boat and uttering a strong cuss word, I seized the oars and rowed silently back to the boat. Here we were accosted by the cook, who had taken in the whole thing from the boat and was in a frenzied condition of excitement which almost equaled ours. Supper I found going to chips, but I was too mad even to swear at the cook. The tarpon, so far as I could judge, would have weighed between 120 and 130 pounds, and measured from 6 feet 2 inches to 6 feet 4 inches in length. The shark was of the species known as "leopard shark" on the coast. After two cups of black coffee I began to feel better, and told Joe to get the boat ready once more. Meanwhile I got out my Winchester rifle and a Smith & Wesson .38 calibre revolver, determined that that shark should not fool me out of tarpon again. Meanwhile the shark had disappeared, evidently satisfied with his supper. It was pitch dark when I got into the rowboat; with an ordinary miner's lamp darkened with a paper cover on one side, and rowing to a spot in about fifteen feet of water, I cast out my lines.

Having pulled off the proper amount of slack I coiled the line on the stern seat, where it could not tangle if suddenly taken out, and sitting down I lit my pipe and sat listening to the fish as they jumped in the darkness all around me. The light, meanwhile, had been placed in the locker forward and all was dark. All around me small fish kept continually jumping, while now and then I would hear the deep swirl of some larger fish. There was no wind at all and the water was perfectly smooth. There was no light around except such as was given by the stars and the phosphorescent zigzags of fish as they would rush now and then under and around the boat, leaving a trail of light behind them.

Thoroughly enjoying the lovely evening I was puffing away at my pipe when I heard a deep swirl near the boat, while simultaneously one of the lines was pulled from my hand and in the quiet darkness I could hear the rustling of the line as it was pulled over the edge of the boat. Handing the other rod to Joe to wind up I quietly seized my rod, holding it firmly in my hand until the warning click of the reel told me that all the slack had been taken out. I then gave a steady strike, which was immediately followed by the sound of a heavy splash — then all the strain left my line. "Hang the luck!" I cried, almost ready to weep at the hard luck I was having that day. Bang! went something against the boat, splash came half a barrel of water in, while the boat rocked. Falling on my knees to keep my balance I quickly pressed my thumb on the brake, ready for the rush that was sure to follow. Whiz! whiz! whiz! went my reel.

Joe hurriedly untied the boat from the stake we were fastened to and we drifted slowly off into the darkness in tow of an unseen fish, whose leaps we could only hear and imagine; and then began the same struggle as in the daytime, but with the novelty and mystery of complete darkness, which gave an additional excitement to it, for all had to be done by the feeling of the line, while the whereabouts of the fish were generally judged by the noise he made in jumping. Seventeen times I counted that fish jump, and time after time he would double on his tracks after jumping and come back straight for the boat, the sensation each time being that the line had broken, all strain on it suddenly being removed. But, warned by my first mistake, I always took for granted that he was on and simply took in the line as quickly as possible, holding the point of my rod well underneath the water in case he should pass underneath the boat, when the line might otherwise catch in a splinter or some other unevenness and snap.

Joe now produced the lamp and turned its light on the fish: he had so far been too busy reeling up the other line and getting the boat in order for the struggle. Once the lamp was in use matters became simplified, provided the glare was kept carefully out of my eyes. By the aid of the light I could follow my line and approximately judge where my fish was at any time. When he jumped, if not too far off, I could see him clearly—a magnificent mass of flashing silver, surrounded with sparkling drops of water against an ink-black background. A tarpon dropping on a dark night by the light of a strong lamp is a far more beautiful sight than one seen in the daytime, or even by moonlight. At last, tired out, I got him close to the boat. He was a most beautiful sight in a different way. There he lay, within six or eight feet of the boat, working his tail, as slowly and clearly visible to me as if behind a glass aquarium. There was no reflection on the water, as in the daytime, to dazzle the eye of the onlooker. Every scale was clearly outlined while, with his bulldog-like jaw and large fierce eye, he seemed to be meditating some devilish trick. Now and then, as he turned on his side, the opalescent green and purples on his back would flash in the light.

Gaffing at night I have always found a most difficult thing to do successfully. One of the two in the boat must always hold the lamp so that its rays shine directly on the fish, while the fisherman should have both his hands free to manage his rod in case the fish should not be gaffed. For it is just at this moment that many tarpon are lost, the line becoming entangled in a rowlock, splinter or cut on the bottom of the boat by the fish suddenly darting under it. A remedy for this last accident I have always found to be successful is to hold the point of the rod well underneath the water while the fish is being gaffed. While holding the rod in this position makes no difference which way the fish goes, your line is sure not to catch in anything. On the other hand, the gaffer should have both his hands, for a tarpon is no easy brute to manage when he is gaffed, tired out as he may be.

I once had one of these so-called tired-out tarpon spring into the boat when being gaffed, barking off my shins with his jaw, while with his tail he broke the end of an oar. We wisely retired to the end of the boat, leaving the fish all the room he wanted for his playful kicks ; but if a tired-out tarpon can break the blade of an oar with his tail, what would a fresh one do if he should happen to get into a boat?

I finally ended the matter as to who should hold the lamp by holding the lamp myself in one hand, while with the other I held my rod, one thumb pressed against the leather brake of the reel, the tip of the rod being quickly put underneath the water just as the fish is being gaffed. But this method is not a great success till after some practice has been had at it, as I lost three tarpon one night when gaffing, the line being cut by barnacles which were on the bottom of the boat. This fellow, however, we safely gaffed, towed back to the sailboat and threw on deck, returning at once for more, wishing to take advantage of the rising tide.

I had three more strikes that night. landing two out of the three tarpon, Thoroughly tired out by the many strange mishaps of the day I returned to the sailboat and got into my bunk and fell fast asleep. The next morning at sunrise we started for the hotel. The fish, on being weighed, scaled as follows : 88 pounds, 114 pounds, 142 pounds ; lengths respectively 5 feet 9 inches, 6 feet 1 inch, 6 feet 5½ inches.

It was now nearly the 1st of May, and the fishing became excellent. All the fishermen had left, excepting Tom and myself. Hardly a day passed but we caught a tarpon. The day I had been longing for, namely, one in which I could equal Tom's catch of four, came at last. It was a more or less glorious repetition of this day's sport, with one exception. Both of our men were off catching bait with a large drag net. Tom and myself were left alone on the sailboat. I had two rods out, one on each side of the boat, while Tom was reading. Suddenly I heard a swirl close to the boat, and jumping for the rods was just in time to strike the fish as the line grew taut. With a leap he was out of the water, and with a leap Tom and I were in the rowboat. Neither noticed that we had forgotten to take in the other rod and line. After fifteen minutes or so the tarpon sawed through the snell, which was an old one, and was lost. Rowing leisurely back to the sailboat I heard a splash and looking over my shoulder I saw the water disturbed as if a fish had jumped. Almost at once the tarpon sprang out again, shaking his head. "Thunder and lightning !" I yelled, "we forgot to take in the other line." As we rowed for the boat as fast as we could I could hear the reel buzzing away at an awful rate, and every now and then giving a jerking hum like a buzz saw at full speed, when the fish jumping would jerk out the line more rapidly. Fortunately the click was a strong one and the reel did not overrun. Exerting ourselves to the utmost we endeavored to arrive before all of the 200 yards of line were out ; but when within thirty yards of the boat, looking over my shoulder, I saw the tip of the rod bend, and then the rod was jerked in the water and sunk.

"There goes my new split bamboo rod

and my best reel!" I was too mad to swear. We climbed out on the sailboat and stood for a moment motionless, without an inkling of what should be done. Meanwhile the tarpon was still merrily jumping and working gradually in shore.

"Let us take the gun and try and shoot him!" suddenly burst from Tom. It was an inspiration. To seize the gun and spring into the boat seemed the work of a second. For once the New York Fire Department was nowhere in comparison. Pulling with all our might we rowed toward the spot where the tarpon was jumping. Everything was in our favor. There was hardly two feet of water where he had got. "If we can only shoot him before he breaks the line we may trace the rod," muttered Tom. The tarpon, tired of jumping, was now lying on the surface of the water, flapping his tail and blowing out bubbles from his open mouth. He had jumped nearly thirty times, more than any fish I had ever seen. Standing in the stern, I pulled the boat quietly toward him, while Tom stood ready to shoot, well up in the bow, his gun being loaded with buckshot. He got within twenty feet of him, when, his back being flush with the water, or a little out, perhaps, Tom stood high up in the bow and blazed away at him. The tarpon made the water boil, and then jump, jump—he was at his old games again.

"I'll be hanged," said Tom, when the shot went all around the fish without having any effect on him. Suddenly I saw Tom look intently into the water close to our boat, then seizing the gaff, reached over and made a gaff at something. Pulling the gaff back he triumphantly seized in his hand a moving No. 15 linen line.

"I saw it dragging down on the seaweed!" he said. "Now we've got him."

"Is he still on?" I eagerly asked.

"Rather," said Tom; "and so is your rod, probably—at the other end. Grab the line and pull in on it! I will try and work the hand-line racket on this tarpon in the meanwhile."

Doing as he suggested I was delighted to feel a resistance as I pulled in on the line, careless as to how it got tangled in the boat. Very soon I had my beloved rod and reel safe again in the boat, long pieces of seaweed hanging on the reel.

It was indeed a miracle that the tarpon in rushing and tumbling had not broken the line, especially when dragging the rod about through the seaweed, but then I have always been the luckiest of mortals. Meanwhile Tom was trying to catch the tarpon, using the thin linen line as a hand line and getting his fingers well cut for his trouble. He succeeded in getting the tarpon, which was tired out, with its lips almost up to the boat, when the strain on the line ceased, and Tom pulled in the second snell for that morning.

Two days afterward I hooked and landed a tarpon weighing 148 pounds, and 6 feet 8½ inches in length, after a tough fight of about fifty minutes. We had hauled him out of the water and laid him upon the roof of the cabin. Tom was admiring his size and his shape and cursing my luck, as he generally did, whenhe suddenly called me up with a yell.

"It is our friend of the day before yesterday," he said. "There are the marks of the buckshot."

"Nonsense, you are dreaming. You allow your imagination to run away with you."

"I will bet you anything you like," insisted Tom, now thoroughly aroused, "but this will settle it." As he said this he took out a large clasp knife and, cutting a large slit in the fish's throat, he forced the cut open. Feeling around in the throat he pulled out a piece of snell. Feeling around once more he pulled out a second piece. Twisting the two pieces around his hand and pulling vigorously on the snell, the shanks of two hooks became revealed. There could be no doubt now any more. It was our friend of the day before who had taken my rod off for a trip.

Upon May 15 the bow of our sailboat headed toward New York. Thirty-four tarpon had been caught by us and placed on the *Marian's* deck that trip.

16.
An Intimate Study of the Pelican (1905)

AN INTIMATE STUDY OF THE PELICAN[1]

BY FRANK M. CHAPMAN

Associate Curator in the American Museum of Natural History

WITH ILLUSTRATIONS FROM PHOTOGRAPHS BY THE AUTHOR

NO one can look a pelican squarely in the eye without being impressed by the bird's reserved, grave dignity. The same patriarchal bearing in a man suggests years of fruitful experience and the learning of sages and prophets.

Is the bird a feathered caricature of a human prototype, or does its white head contain even a fraction of the wisdom its owner's outward appearance so strongly proclaims? In short, where in the psychological scale shall we place this bird of imposing presence?

To answer this question, I decided to go to the land of pelicans; establish, if possible, personal relations with the inhabitants; and from an intimate, minute study of their daily life attempt to determine their mental status. At the same time it was proposed to secure photographs and information upon which to base an accurate representation of pelican life in the American Museum of Natural History.

[1] Readers of THE CENTURY will recall Mr. Chapman's remarkable article, "A Flamingo City," in the number for December, 1904.—THE EDITOR.

"THE BROAD-PINIONED BIRDS SWEPT BY ME WITHIN ARM'S LENGTH"

THE PELICAN AT HOME. No. 1.

We have in America two kinds of pelicans, the white and the brown. Of the former, I can only say that it does not encourage the advances of the avian psychologist. Invasions of its strongholds on remote lake islets in Manitoba and in Nevada have resulted in their complete desertion by every white pelican old enough to spread a wing; and success here is doubtless not to be looked for so long as this snowy-plumaged bird remains a shining mark for every roving rifleman.

THE PELICAN AT REST

With the brown pelican I have been more fortunate, having obtained an opportunity to study its home life, domestic and social relations, such as has been accorded to few students of birds in nature.

HISTORY OF PELICAN ISLAND

IN that long, narrow lagoon on the east coast of Florida known as Indian River, there is a muddy islet three or four acres in extent. Originally it doubtless did not differ from hundreds of similar neighboring islets; but, for some reason past finding out, this islet, and this alone, forms the nesting - resort, the home, of all the pelicans of the Indian River, if not, indeed, of the east coast of Florida.

The brown pelican, unlike its white cou-

THE INITIAL UPWARD STROKE OF THE WING IN FLIGHT, REVEALING A SURPRISING DIVERGENCE OF THE FIVE OUTER FLIGHT-FEATHERS

sin, nests normally in low trees and bushes; and there is evidence that when the original pelican colonists landed on the islet which now bears their name, it was well grown with black and red mangroves in which the birds placed their scaffolding of sticks. Exceptionally low temperature and high water—perhaps also excessive use by the birds, which sometimes build as many as seven nests in a single mangrove—have killed tree after tree, until at present only three serviceable trees remain. Still the birds come back, the impelling motive which prompts them to return to this particular spot being evidently stronger than that which induced them to nest in trees.

ILLUSTRATING THE ELLIPTICAL OPENING TO THE POUCH, FORMED BY A DRAWING IN OF THE TIP AND SPREADING OUT OF THE SIDES OF THE LOWER MANDIBLE

No one can remember when pelicans did not nest upon their chosen land, and on only two occasions have its feathered occupants failed to establish on it their yearly pelican nursery. Once they were driven away by a number of singular creatures who seemed either to fear or to hate the great birds which, to most people, form so picturesque and pleasing an element of Florida coast life. Landing on the pelicans' islet, they shot the inhabitants in large numbers and left them to rot in the mud. The survivors retreated, but established quarters on the nearest islet.

The second time the pelicans deserted their ancestral home they were driven away, not by enemies, but by friends. Prior to the passage of the present admirable bird-protective law in Florida, the pelicans were at the mercy of every man with a gun. A demand from milliners arose for their wing-quills, and it was feared that at any time Pelican Island might be attacked. An effort was made to buy it from the government, but the red-tape knots of the Land Office defied untying until, on presentation of the case to President Roosevelt, he promptly disentangled them and created Pelican Island a Federal reserve. The Audubon Society immediately appointed a warden, who was empowered to prevent trespass, and erected on the island a large sign proclaiming its population the wards of the government.

The future safety of the pelicans now seemed assured, when, to the surprise and disgust of their would-be friends, the birds expressed their disapproval of the whole arrangement by deserting the island in a body. Not a nest was made or an egg laid upon it, but two smaller neighboring islands were covered with the dissenting birds.

At the beginning of the next nesting-season (1904–1905), when the pelican clans began to gather, it was evident that the great sign announcing Federal possession of the home of their forefathers appeared to cause them much uneasiness, whereupon the warden, who had long suspected the root of the trouble, removed the offending boards, and the birds at once returned to their heritage, built their homes, and reared their families, as the accompanying pictures, made during the season in question, abundantly prove.

"THE BIRDS BEGAN TO RETURN TO THEIR NESTS"

Consequently, we may infer from this incident either that the pelican can read and has strong political prejudices, or that

THE PELICAN AT HOME. No. 2.

it lacks sufficient discrimination to realize that a board painted white with black marks and held upright by two posts is perfectly harmless. However this may be, the fact remains that, to the great satisfaction of their well-wishers, the birds have accepted the guardianship of the government. One of the most remarkable and easily accessible bird-resorts in America should, therefore, long continue to delight visiting nature-lovers, as well as to supply our South Atlantic coast with a singularly interesting form of life.

A BATHING SCENE

THE PELICANS' YEAR; A SKETCH OF THE ISLAND'S LIFE

YEAR after year, in the first week in November, with singular exactness the pelicans come to their unattractive little mud flat. Some come from up, some from down the river, all evidently moved by a common impulse. What is it? It is not a question of food, for the pelicans rarely feed near their nesting-place; it is not a question of climate, for they do not go far enough from their breeding-ground to experience climatic change when returning to it.

The journey is doubtless prompted from within. With birds the season of reproduction is periodic, and with migratory species, whether the journey be to a near-by island or to another zone, the return to the breeding-ground is only one phenomenon in a physiological cycle of development which includes, in regular order, migration, courtship, egg-laying, incubation, the care of the young, the molt, and the retreat to winter quarters.

Even in the tropics, birds, as a rule, do not nest until spring and early summer; but the pelican woos his mate in November and begins housekeeping in the first month of winter. Among such dumb and undemonstrative birds courtship must be a very solemn affair, but no one seems to know much about it. Apparently, however, it is conducted to the satisfaction of both contracting parties, and with the happiest results; for never have I seen indications of domestic troubles among the indigenes of pelicanland. The warden, to whom I am indebted for these dates of arrival and nesting, tells me that the first mated birds resort to the trees, where a bulky nest of sticks lined with coarse grasses is built upon a platform made by laying heavier sticks from crotch to crotch. When the arboreal sites are taken, the remaining birds, numbering about one thousand pairs, build upon the ground a nest containing, as a rule, more grass and fewer sticks than are employed by their relatives in the trees.

Unfortunately, the island is so low that a "norther" raises the water sufficiently to flood all but a sand-bar at its eastern end. Only those ground-nesting birds which build upon the sands, therefore, are secure from the waves. Consequently, if one should visit Pelican Island in April, after the season of northers had passed, and see the close-set nests on the sand-bar, with the rest of the island unoccupied, one might credit the survivors with ability intelligently to select a nesting-site above the reach of the waters. Whereas, in truth, the earlier homes of many of these same birds, built on low ground, had been inundated, and their eggs, washed from the nests, were still scattered about the island. Apparently, then, there is here no conscious selection evolved by experience. Year after year, birds nest on the low ground and suffer the consequences, while, by elimination, the high-ground colony is established through the disaster which befalls all those that do not resort to it.

The first of the three eggs to which the pelicans limit themselves is laid by December 1. One might imagine that even in Florida winter was a singularly inappropriate season for hatching eggs; but pelicans are large-bodied birds, and husband as well as wife is faithful to the duties of incubation, one going on the nest as the other leaves it. Normally, therefore, the eggs are never exposed, and after about four weeks' sitting the little pelican announces itself by a characteristic choking grunt, uttered even before it leaves the shell.

A PELICAN YAWN

It is not an attractive creature at birth, but in about eighteen days its black, naked ugliness is concealed beneath a down so thick, soft, and white that it might grace a swan. The young of tree-nesting pelicans do not leave their nest-tree until they make their first attempt at flight; but if the young pelican chances to be born on the ground, it will go swimming for the first time when about six weeks old, and at the age of ten weeks it will have learned to use its wings.

In March, if all goes well, the pelicans may close their house for the season, take their family, and go traveling; but June 1 sometimes finds birds still occupied with domestic affairs. This extension of the nesting-season is doubtless due in part to some individual irregularity in the time of laying, but more largely to disaster of one kind or another which befalls early efforts at housekeeping.

High water, cold weather, or exposure to the sun before they are clothed, are all factors in creating a high mortality among young pelicans; and few, indeed, are the parents which succeed in raising a family of three.

A VISIT TO THE ISLAND; PELICAN LIFE STUDIED FROM A BLIND

THIS marked variation in the dates of the phenomena of nesting-time makes a visit to Pelican Island far more interesting than one to an equally large colony of birds whose eggs are laid and hatched and whose young take flight at approximately the same date. A day with the pelicans gives one an epitome of their home life, from the building of the nest to the flight of the first-born.

Furthermore, we have to encounter here no dangers of sea or cliff such as threaten one when visiting the birds of isolated rocky islets; no flood and desolation of Bahaman "swash"; no mosquitos and moccasins of noisome marsh. On the contrary, a trip to Pelican Island is as delightful an outing as one may take in Florida. One has only to secure the needed permit of Warden Kroegel at Sebastian, when all the rest is plain sailing or "motoring," as the case may be.

While the birds have become comparatively tame since the appointment of a warden has assured them safety from marauders, they are still far from regarding man as above suspicion. If, therefore, one would enter the inner circles of pelican society, he must adopt some disguise or method of concealment which will not attract attention. An umbrella-blind, successfully employed on former occasions, was found to answer admirably the needs of the case. Erected among the thickly set nests, the nearest of which was only four feet away, it was shortly accepted as

"THE NEW-COMER ALIGHTS NEAR THE NEST, AND, WITH BILL POINTED TO THE ZENITH, ADVANCES SLOWLY"

a part of the landscape, and, so far as the pelicans were concerned, I might have been a spirit of the air.

There is a wholesome sense of satisfaction and a quite indescribable fascination in being closely surrounded by wild, shy creatures, that, unaware of your existence, live their lives in an absolutely natural manner.

On several former occasions I had attempted to study the life of Pelican Island; but, whether from a boat moored for days near by or from the shelter of the island's scanty vegetation, probably at no time were the birds wholly at ease.

Within three minutes after I entered my blind, however, the birds began to return to the nests which they had reluctantly deserted at my approach, and in a few minutes more the routine of Pelican Island life was resumed. With a wing-spread of between seven and eight feet, a pelican is an impressive bird even at a distance; but when dozens of the broad-pinioned birds swept by me within arm's length, or alighted almost at my feet, I realized that, given the excitable, courageous nature of terns or gulls, which dart and dive so threateningly at invaders of their nesting precincts, the pelicans might dispense with the services of a warden.

It is true, a bird which had placed its nest on a stump six feet from my shelter snapped its bill loudly at me when I peered through the slit in my blind nearest to her. The young defend themselves in a similar manner until their wings will bear them, when, like their seniors, they show their faith in the valorous discretion of flight.

YOUNG BIRD FEEDING

The croaking, wabbly little creature helped itself to the predigested fish

Birds of all ages and voices, from the grunting, naked, squirming new-born chick, or the screaming, downy youngster, to the silent, dignified, white-headed parent, were now within a radius of a few yards. At a glance, I could see most of the activities of pelican home life: nest building, laying, incubating, feeding and brooding young, bathing, preening, sleeping, fighting,—all could be observed at arm's length. Surely here was a rare opportunity to add a footnote to our knowledge of animal life.

When several thousand birds of one species not only select the same bit of ground for a residence, but build their homes side by side, one infers that they possess marked sociability of character and looks for manifestations of it. But I waited in vain for any positive evidence of friendly or communal relations between the thickly grouped pelican households.

Under only one condition have I ever heard an adult wild pelican utter a note, and this virtual voicelessness implies in itself a limited means of communication. The birds steal one another's nesting-material with an air which plainly bespeaks a knowledge of their guilt and that they expect to be attacked by the bird they have robbed. Such an attack may lead to a bloodless fight, when the contestants grasp each other by the bill, snapping their mandibles together with a pistol-like report. Theft and battle, however, are not usually considered expressions of loving friendship, and my studies leave the colonial life of pelicans unexplained.

In the pelican family, as one might suppose, there are evidences of communication between the parents and of recognition of their young. The first was best shown by a very pleasing little performance which I have called the ceremony of nest-relief. It appears that both sexes incubate as well as brood; and as it is quite essential that neither eggs nor young be exposed, it follows that, unless disturbed, the bird on the nest does not leave its charge until its mate arrives to take its place. The new-comer alights near the nest, and, with bill pointed to the zenith, advances slowly, waving its head from side to side. At the same time the sitting bird sticks its bill vertically into the nest and twitches its half-spread wings while uttering a low, husky, gasping *chuck*, the only note I have ever heard issue from the throat of an adult wild pelican. After five or six wand-like passes of its upraised head, the advancing bird pauses, when both birds at once, with apparent unconcern, begin to preen their feathers, and a moment later the bird that has been

"THEY EXTEND THEIR FEEDING EXCURSIONS INTO THE THROAT OF THE PATIENT PARENT"

THE BILL OF A FISH MAY BE SEEN EXTENDING FROM THE POUCH OF THE LOWER RIGHT-HAND BIRD

on duty steps off the nest, and the other bird at once takes its place.

Doubtless this act possesses some sexual significance, but since male and female pelicans are externally alike, it is not possible to tell which part either plays on these occasions. Observation, however, leads to the conclusion that the relieving bird is the male, and that the ceremony is omitted when he gives place to his mate.

There was apparently no such regularity in this event as one finds, for example, among incubating pigeons, in which each sex has its appointed time to come or go.

The relieved bird usually flew directly to the water, there to bathe with much loud flapping of the wings and dashing of spray; after dressing its feathers on a neighboring sand-spit, it would make a leisurely start for some fishing-ground up or down the coast: for it is not a little remarkable that the pelicans rarely, if ever, fish in the waters about their home. If the birds are not hungry, the morning bath is followed by an aërial promenade, when they rise a thousand feet or more above their home, and, on set wings, sail in wide circles for long periods of time, apparently for pure enjoyment of the exercise.

With the addition of triplets to the pelican family, domestic problems become more complicated and correspondingly more interesting. For at least ten weeks the young are wholly dependent on their parents for every morsel of food which passes down their capacious throats. The fishing excursions now receive added importance. The old bird has not merely to satisfy its own hunger, but the insatiable and growing appetite of its offspring. Nor is it merely a matter of quantity which has to be considered: quality as well must be taken into account, and the size of the fish

NEARLY GROWN YOUNG ONES STRUGGLING TO BE FED BY AN ADULT JUST ARRIVED FROM THE FISHING-GROUNDS

captured be regulated by the size of the throat it is intended to go down.

Ten miles up the coast I have seen pelicans headed for still more distant fishing-grounds; and it is said that some go to the Canaveral Shoals, forty miles from their home.

Early birds leave the island at the first hint of dawn, and the last arrivals return to it when it is too dark to distinguish the minor details of the landscape, sweeping by with a rush of wing so near that it is evident they do not see one in the gloom. Generally leaving alone, they fall in with fellow-fishers by the way, and gather thus in parties of from six to a dozen or more, flying diagonally, one behind the other, all flapping and sailing in unison; traveling high in the air, before the wind, or low over the curling breakers when going to windward.

They are daring, dashing fishermen, these sedate birds, and from a height of thirty to forty feet plunge headlong and with a resounding splash on their prey. At the moment of striking, the tip of the lower bill is drawn in and its sides bowed widely out, forming an elliptical opening to the

pouch, and enabling them to capture fish fully fourteen inches in length.

Menhaden form a large proportion of the fish captured, and, large or small, they are carried in the crop, not in the pouch. When returning, the single-file formation is maintained until the birds reach the occupied part of the island, when they proceed directly to their nests, situated, perhaps, in widely different parts of the colony. No time is lost in administering food to the expectant and clamorous young, and this operation of feeding is the most remarkable performance which the watcher on Pelican Island will observe.

Long had I wondered how the naked, apparently helpless pelican, a day or two old, was fed by its great-billed parent. But with the utmost ease the croaking, wabbly little creature helped itself to the predigested fish which, regurgitated by the parent into the front end of its pouch, was brought within reach of its offspring.

This method is followed until the young are covered with down, when, evidently requiring a larger supply of food than their parents can prepare for them, and no longer needing partly digested nourishment, they extend their feeding excursions into the throat of the patient parent, finding there entire fish, which they swallow before withdrawing their head. Two and even three well-grown chicks will thus actively pursue their search for food at the same time, and only their extended and fluttering wings seem to keep them from disappearing in the depths of the cavernous pouch.

Not for a moment do they stop a high-voiced squealing, and the rise and fall of their partly muffled screams indicate the nature of their success in getting food.

Occasionally the poor judgment of the parent, allied to the greed of the young, leads the latter to attempt to

THE YOUNG AFTER FEEDING

"THRUST HER BILL DEEP INTO THE NEST, APPARENTLY SEARCHING FOR HER CHICKS"

swallow too large a fish, when the old bird saves its offspring from choking to death by forcibly pulling the fish from the throat it refuses to go down.

More frequently the young pelican secures a fish not too large, but too long for it, when it swallows it as far as it will go, and, with the tail sticking from its pouch, quietly waits for the head to digest before it can encompass the whole prize. In one such instance, the victim chanced to be a needle-fish, which, refusing to go down head first, was finally taken in the reverse direction.

It is, however, when the brown wing feathers begin to grow and the young leave the nest that feeding occasions the greatest excitement. Although each bird has its own particular abiding-place, from which, unless disturbed, it does not wander far, it never hesitates to demand food of any grown bird which comes near it. When, therefore, an old bird arrives from a fishing expedition, all the nest-graduates in the immediate vicinity rush toward it, with a resulting riotous uproar and clashing of wings; but the old bird is not to be "held up" so peremptorily: with threatening motions of the bill it resists the entreaties of the struggling mob until its own offspring approaches, when the pouch is opened and feeding follows. At once all the other loud-voiced claimants subside, and in not one instance are they seen to disturb their more fortunate comrade.

As the young increase in size, feeding becomes a more serious proceeding for all concerned. At the age of flight, the young birds average slightly larger and heavier than old ones, and the physical shock of feeding is so great that the parents supply only one bird at a time, and that at long intervals; while the young seem so overcome by the prolonged stay in the parental pouch, as well, doubtless, as by the size of the meal they have secured there, that on emerging they are in a dazed and helpless condition. Laying the head on the ground with wings relaxed, they act as though they had received a violent blow at the base of the brain. This apparent semi-consciousness is followed by the most violent reaction, as the reviving bird sud-

"DEVOURED BY A SCAVENGING VULTURE, WITH WHOSE MEAL THE SURROUNDING PELICANS SHOWED NO CONCERN"

THE PELICAN IN FULL FLIGHT, THE HEAD DRAWN IN, THE POUCH HIDDEN

denly grasps itself by the wing and whirls about like a demented creature, pausing only long enough to bite at the other wing before turning in the opposite direction.

If this surprising exercise be intended as an aid to digestion, it is evidently effective, since, at its conclusion, the bird settles down to sleep.

Beyond supplying them with the food and shelter essential to their existence, the parent pelicans seem to take very little interest in their offspring. In one instance, however, a parent whose family of two had died through exposure to the sun showed evident concern at her loss. For two hours she (I assume it was the mother) stood near the nest containing the bodies of the unfortunate little pelicans, returning to it at intervals to thrust her bill deep into the nest, and toss the material about, apparently searching for her chicks, which, disguised in death, she seemed not to recognize. Happening to touch one of them with her bill, it was flung from the nest as an object of no interest, and later was devoured by a scavenging vulture, with whose meal the surrounding pelicans showed no concern.

This incident was virtually the only variation observed in the routine of pelican existence. While it expresses a certain individuality, it emphasizes also the limited range of the bird's intelligence. But as one considers the conditions under which pelicans live, there appear to be no factors to stimulate mental development. Their food-supply never fails, and is secured without competition; after the first few weeks of their lives their climatic surroundings are favorable in the extreme; in disposition they are non-combative; while the nature of their nesting-resorts protects them from predatory animals.

Man alone appears to threaten their continued existence, and from him, fortunately, those of their kin who live on Pelican Island are now happily protected. While they cannot repay their defenders with the music of thrushes or a display of those traits which so endear the higher animals to us, they may at least claim success in filling their place in nature, while the charm of every water-scene is increased by the quaint dignity of their presence.

17.
Caught on a Lee Shore (1893)

THE CENTURY MAGAZINE.

JUNE, 1893.

CAUGHT ON A LEE SHORE.

PLEASURES AND PERILS OF A CRUISE ON THE FLORIDA COAST.[1]

TOWARD the end of 1890 we matured our plans for a cruise (our second) in Florida waters. Accordingly, about the end of December, my wife, I, and the steward of our yacht *Galatea* left England in the *Umbria*, and arrived at New York December 29. There we remained for a week, completing our camp outfit and fishing-gear, not forgetting charts and sailing directions.

Arriving at Jacksonville January 11, 1891, we made our final preparations, and departed for Titusville, at the head of Indian River, where we were met by our old acquaintance Captain Vann, the owner of the sloop *Minnehaha*, which we had chartered. Deep-draft vessels are useless for Florida waters: a maximum of three feet is all that is admissible. The *Minnehaha* was of a type common on Indian River, locally known as a "skipjack." She was flat-sided, with a rise of floor of about fifteen inches, and drew, with all her stores on board, about twenty-six inches of water. Over all she was 28 feet 7 inches; extreme beam, 12 feet 9 inches. She was decked as far aft as the cockpit, and had a deck-house, or booby-hatch, over the cabin, which gave about 4 feet 10 inches head-room. The cabin itself was 13 feet long by 10 feet wide, divided fore and aft by the center-board trunk, which rose about 2 feet 6 inches from the floor. The cabin extended underneath the fore deck, and in that part of it all our light gear was stowed. There were two rudely constructed trestles, which did duty for bedsteads. My wife appropriated the starboard one, while I occupied the port. All the fittings were of the very roughest description; there was nothing yacht-like about them, but it was the best boat available that we knew of. Abaft the cabin was an open cockpit 7 feet by 5 feet. In this space the crew—consisting of the skipper and the steward—lived, cooked, and slept, except at such times as we were able to pitch the tent and make a camp on shore. An awning spread over the main boom gave them shelter at night.

The rig was a simple one, consisting of two sails, jib and mainsail, both laced to booms. She spread a large area of canvas for her size. Although she had less than five hundredweight of ballast, she carried her canvas well, and in smooth water was very fast to windward (her draft was seven feet with the center-board down); but in anything of a lop or seaway she spanked and pounded, and proved very wet. Off the wind she was hard to steer, like all her type. She was good enough for smooth-

[1] This paper is a condensation of portions of a manuscript diary by Lieutenant William Henn, the well-known naval officer and yachtsman, who, in 1886, sailed the *Galatea* against the *Mayflower* for the *America's* cup. The pictures are after drawings by the author and photographs by Mrs. Henn.—EDITOR.

water work, but was very uncomfortable in the least bit of sea, and soon after we started she began to leak badly.

At 9:30 of a lovely morning, January 15, we cast off from the wharf. Properly speaking, Indian River is not a river, but a long, shallow salt-water lagoon running parallel with the Atlantic Ocean. This lagoon is about 150 miles in length, and, except in the narrows, is from one to five miles in width. It has two communications with the ocean, one opposite St. Lucie or Fort Capron, about ninety miles south of Titusville, and the other at its southern extremity at Jupiter. The depth varies from ten feet to as many inches, but channels have been dredged through the principal shoals and oyster-bars for craft drawing four feet of water. An hour or two after starting, the wind shifted and came dead ahead, and we had an opportunity of seeing what the *Minnehaha* could do to windward. Slowly but surely we caught up and passed boat after boat, and I could see Skipper was getting "the last inch" out of her, and doing it well. At 4 P. M. we were off Rockledge, twenty-two miles from Titusville, and there we decided on anchoring for the night. After midnight on January 17 the rain came down in torrents, and lasted until morning. The downpour soon searched out all weak places on deck, and, to our great disgust, we found the water had penetrated in quantities, which showed that the leaks were serious. Skipper "guessed he 'd find them out and fix them," but this he never was able to do, and throughout the cruise we suffered much inconvenience and discomfort from this trouble. January 18, in Indian River narrows, we ran hard and fast on an oyster-bar. All hands, except my wife, who worked away with a "setting-pole," had to jump overboard to shove the sloop off — a style of navigation called by the Indian River boatmen "shirt-tailing."

DRAWN BY CARLTON T. CHAPMAN. ENGRAVED BY F. A. PETTIT.

AGROUND.

At 6:30 on January 19 we were under way with a fresh breeze from the north, bound to Jupiter, forty miles to the southward, and the *Minnehaha* made short miles of it. About noon the lighthouse was abeam of us, and we were steering for the point near the inlet where we had made our camp four years before. We soon cleared the ground and pitched the tent. While engaged in this work, our old friend Captain Carlin, who is in command of the life-saving station at Jupiter, made his appearance, and welcomed us warmly. The fishing proved as good as ever, large numbers of bluefish and pompano being caught daily.

One day Captain Carlin brought a young racoon on board as a present for my wife. The little creature, which we named "Cherokee Kate," was nine or ten months old, and was still very wild and vicious.

At sunrise on January 23 the weather was fine, so I gave the order to strike the tent and prepare for sea. Skipper showed signs of being unwilling to start, and was very dilatory, but by seven we had everything stowed on board, and, hoisting our sails, finally got off. We had to help her along with the setting-

DRAWN BY CARLTON T. CHAPMAN. ENGRAVED BY J. HELWELL.

JUPITER INLET.

poles, as a strong flood was running, but at the inlet we had wind enough to burst through it, and we crossed the bar without shipping a drop of water, disturbing in our passage over it several large sharks and saw-fish, some of which were close enough to be touched with the boat-hook. Shaping our course south, we ran parallel to the beach, keeping about a quarter of a mile outside the surf to avoid as much as possible the current of the Gulf Stream, which here sets close along the shore. We were at last fairly started on our cruise, and the *Minnehaha*, for the first time in her existence, was breasting the waters of the broad Atlantic. The sea was smooth, the wind being light, and Skipper's spirits revived; but in spite of it all he was not very cheerful, and opined "that a 'norther' was brewing," and "hoped we 'd be lucky enough to reach a harbor before it struck us." We soon passed the life-saving station, and the crew turned out and gave us a cheer, at the same time running up the American ensign at the flagstaff. We dipped our burgee, as an acknowledgment, little imagining that the next time we saw them we should be in dire distress and in want of their assistance.

At 9:25 P. M. we were off New River Inlet, about fifty-three miles distant from Jupiter, and Skipper's forebodings as to being caught by "a norther" were not going to be fulfilled. We had intended to stop at New River for a few days, as the fishing there is excellent, and game abounds in the vicinity; but as it was dark before we reached the inlet, and there being only three feet of water on the bar, we decided on proceeding to Biscayne Bay, about twenty miles further south. At 1:30 we sighted the light on the northern extremity of the Florida Reef, and at 2 A. M. arrived off the passage between Virginia Key and Key Biscayne. Here we anchored to await daylight, having sailed seventy-three miles from Jupiter.

On approaching Cocoanut Grove, we observed several yachts at anchor, their white sails glistening in the bright morning sun. A signal was flying from a wharf, which proved to be the burgee of the Biscayne Bay Yacht Club. We hauled down our private signal, substituting for it the burgee of the Royal Northern Yacht Club. A yacht now got under way and came out to meet us, and we were warmly welcomed by her owner, the secretary of the club, who piloted us to the anchorage. Our "mud-hook" had hardly reached the bottom before the genial commodore, whose flag was flying on board his sharpie, the *Presto*, came on board, and tendered to us all the privileges of the club.

The sharpie is, without doubt, both for build, rig, and accommodation, the best type of craft for navigating Florida waters that I am acquainted with, especially the type which finds favor with the yachtsmen of Biscayne Bay. These sharpies are round-bottomed, and carry several tons of ballast, but the draft, without the center-board, does not exceed three feet. They are far superior to the flat-bottomed type, which pound heavily in the least lop of the sea, and are wet and uncomfortable except in smooth water. They sail fast both on and off the wind, are easily handled with a small crew, and are good and safe sea-boats. They are ketch-rigged, with one head-sail, and have a peculiarly cut topsail, which is very effective off the wind.

We left Miami on January 29, bound to Key West, distant to the southward about 150 miles, and after several stops reached there February 4. About noon we anchored among a fleet of small yachts whose crews appeared to regard us with a certain amount of curiosity, for our craft was of a build unfamiliar to the Key-Westers, and their interest was further aroused by seeing the signal of the Royal Northern Yacht Club fluttering at our topmast-head, and observing a lady on board.

February 6 we set sail for Cape Sable; but our bobstay snapped before we reached the bell-buoy, so we had to return for repairs, making an early start on the 7th. About four o'clock we ran on a bank of coral mud and grass, and stayed there till 9:30, when, getting afloat, we anchored for the night. The next evening we were moored alongside a shelving bank of sand in Little Cape Sable Creek, about ten miles west of Cape Sable. Skipper and I started to explore the creek, which was hedged in with an almost impenetrable growth of tall mangrove-trees. Presently the air became dark with mosquitos, and, pursued by the pests, we pulled back to the sloop, which, to our dismay, we found had been left aground by the ebbing tide. Night was rapidly approaching, and the mosquitos were more numerous and fiercer than ever. We were literally devoured by them; our clothes were little protection; they penetrated everywhere. So, leaving the sloop, we made two large fires on the sand-bank, cutting down and piling on the green mangrove-branches — anything to make a smoke, or smudge. To a certain extent our efforts were crowned with success, and, wrapped in wreaths of smoke, we made a hasty dinner, and anxiously watched the rising tide. The light of the fires threw a ruddy glare on the surface of the creek, lighting up the dark, impenetrable walls of mangroves, and now and again we could see the dorsal fins of the sharks that were coming in on the flood-tide. In spite of our sufferings we determined to fish for them, and in a few minutes the shark-line was rigged. Baiting the hook with a four-pound Spanish mackerel, we pitched it out a few yards from the shore, and, making the end fast to a tree, waited developments. We were not kept long in suspense; in less than five minutes the slack line, which was coiled on the sand, began to run out. After twenty feet or so had disappeared, we seized it, and held on, jerking it hard to drive the hook well home; in an instant we felt we were fast in something, for in spite of the combined efforts of Skipper, steward, and myself, all

DRAWN BY CARLTON T. CHAPMAN. ENGRAVED BY A. HAYMAN.

FROM JUPITER INLET INTO THE OPEN.

DRAWN BY CARLTON T. CHAPMAN. ENGRAVED BY C. W. CHADWICK.

A WHARF AT KEY WEST.

of us were swiftly dragged toward the water's edge, and the next moment the quiet waters of the creek were lashed into foam, as a huge shark plunged and rolled on the surface, vainly endeavoring to get rid of the good steel hook with its three feet of chain. The struggle was of short duration, for after a momentary "tug of war"—twelve feet of shark versus seventeen feet of man—we dragged the great brute's head on the shelving sand, and sent a four-pound ax crashing into its brain. The hook being then cut from its jaws and rebaited, was again cast out. In less than an hour we had hooked five, and landed three ranging from nine to twelve feet in length, and, feeling we had done our duty by the sharks, we were satisfied. At 9:30 the next morning we were sailing up the coast. We were all feeling very sorry for ourselves, suffering terribly from mosquito-bites, and many were the imprecations we uttered against "Little Cape Sable Creek." I have had considerable experience with mosquitos and their ways, in many parts of the globe; but except on one occasion, when elephant-hunting in Ceylon, I was never so badly bitten, nor have ever suffered as much. We afterward heard that this creek was notorious as being the worst place on the coast for these pests.

At 4 P. M. we were abreast of Pavillion Key, which seemed to be alive with pelicans sitting on the mangrove-trees, while many frigate-birds were soaring high overhead. On landing, we found the sand covered with the tracks of racoons and possums, and we saw traces of a deer. Returning on board, we rigged up and baited the shark-line, putting it overboard after dark, and securing the end to the mast. Soon after midnight we were awakened by the violent motion of the sloop. At first I was at a loss to account for it; then suddenly remembering the shark-line, I roused my wife and crew, and hurried on deck. Sure enough, something was hooked, for the line was as taut as a bar, and the sloop, tugging and straining at her cable, was sluing and sheering about in a very lively fashion. We soon got hold of the line, and then it was a case of "pull devil, pull baker," the huge fish plunging and lashing on the surface and nearly dragging us overboard, and with blows from his powerful tail making the phosphorescent water fly in all directions. At last we mastered him, and, dragging him alongside, bent the fore-halyards on to the line for a purchase, and succeeded in lifting the brute's head clear of the water. Then the question arose, How to get the hook out of his jaws? My wife was equal to the occasion, and appeared on the scene with her 45-caliber Smith & Wesson pistol, loaded and ready for action, four rounds from which fired into his brain had the effect of quieting the monster, when, after wetting us all over with a final convulsive lash of his tail, he turned "belly up." We quickly cut out the hook with an ax, after first measuring the fish's length with a boat-hook (it proved to be a little under twelve feet), and then turned in again.

Seven o'clock A. M., February 10, saw us under way with a light southeast wind, bound to Great Marco, distant about twenty-five miles.

At noon the temperature of the air was 82° in the shade, and the sea-water was 74°. Off Cape Romano the wind fell very light, and on the numerous sand-banks in its vicinity we saw great numbers of pelicans, both white and brown, the white variety being the more numerous. At 4 P. M. we were off Caximbas Pass, and the wind had almost died out. The sea was alive with porpoises, which were leaping clear out of water, and presently we sailed through a shoal of great devil-fish, some of them being close enough to strike with a harpoon; but although we had on board the weapons and lines, I had no desire to use them—devil-fish, as I well know from former experiences, being awkward customers to tackle, even in a properly equipped craft with skilled hands to throw the irons, and afterward to manage the lines and boat. Some of the fish we passed seemed fully eighteen or twenty feet across, from wing to wing, and would probably be the same length from the tips of their horns to the ends of their tails. Many years ago I assisted at the capture of one near Port Royal, Jamaica, which towed us for more than two hours. We were in a 5-oared 27-foot whale-boat, and had no less than three whale-irons fast in the fish; but before we killed it the boat had shipped a great deal of water, and we were all soaked to the skin by the shower of spray which the monster threw over us. This specimen, which was considered by no means a large one, measured sixteen feet in length, about seventeen in breadth, and was estimated to weigh more than a ton. Wonderful stories are told about these fish, of their lifting ships' anchors, and enveloping swimmers with their enormous wings, and drowning them; but I cannot vouch for their accuracy. Skipper, who had never before seen nor heard of these creatures, seemed relieved when we saw the last of them. Just as the sun was setting we arrived off Great Marco Pass, the wind being so light that we were barely able to hold our own against the tide, which was setting out by the channel with a velocity of nearly three knots an hour; but at last we succeeded in passing the inner fairway buoy, and "brought up for the night."

The settlement on Marco Island consists of two or three families, and here there is a post-office. We anchored off the dock, and soon settled with Mr. C—— about hauling out the *Minnehaha*. She had been leaking badly ever since leaving Indian River.

At Marco I met "Joe," the skipper of a 30-foot sloop, which was undergoing repairs, who offered to pilot me on a tarpon expedition. After rowing for half an hour we headed for a bight which Joe called Tarpon Bay. We anchored in five feet of water on the edge of the channel, and began operations by several exciting encounters with sharks, which bit off the hooks. Then we lighted our pipes, and patiently watched. Half an hour passed, and still no sign. The tarpon had disappeared, and so had the sharks; not a fin was visible, but the sun was blazing hot, and I was beginning to think tarpon-fishing a delusion. Even Joe was not very sanguine, and said it was rather early in the season for them to bite well. We were discussing the advisability of shifting our ground, when once more the line began to move, very gently and slowly, but evenly and with increasing velocity. The slack had almost run overboard when, a hundred feet away from the skiff, a dazzling mass of silver some six feet in length shot high into the air, and fell back with a crash which whitened the water with foam, and could be heard half a mile off. "Tar—pon! Tar—pon!" shouted Joe. To pick up the rod was the work of an instant, and then the reel began to whiz as the noble fish dashed away at a tremendous speed, throwing a succession of magnificent leaps, shaking his head (as a dog does with a rat), and making extraordinary contortions in the air in vain endeavor to eject the hook. In a jiffy Joe had the skiff under way, and we followed the fish, which was tearing down the channel, as fast as we could, while I put on all the strain I dared, trying to check or turn him; but I might as well have tried to stop a torpedo-boat. He had now got about one hundred and fifty yards away, and the line in the reel was getting low, when out he jumped again, and, on regaining the water, turned and made straight for the skiff, passing within a few yards of it long before I had time to get a taut line on him.

"Keep a level head, boss, and I guess you 'll get him; he 's got the hook well down. Start in now and work him for all you 're worth," said Joe, who was handling the skiff admirably. I soon got in all the slack, and was bearing hard on him, yet could make no impression. The fish was swiftly and steadily heading down the bay, keeping in the deep water, and we followed, sticking as close as we were able. Then, for the first time, I realized that I had a pretty big contract on hand.

Another wild rush was followed by a couple of grand jumps. "Now 's your time to make him tired. Worry him; don't give him a rest." I worried him all I knew how, until the tension of the line made it fairly sing again. The fish slowly yielded, and I succeeded in turning his head toward the shallow water. The last jumps appeared to exhaust him somewhat, and, by putting on all the strain the gear would bear, I at last got him out of the channel on the flats, where the water was barely four feet deep. He was now moving lazily

DRAWN BY GILBERT GAUL. ENGRAVED BY C. SCHWARZBURGER.

SHARK-FISHING, LITTLE CAPE SABLE CREEK.

along; we were literally towing him toward the shore. But it was hard work; my hands and arms were getting tired, and my garments were soaked with perspiration. Suddenly the tarpon stopped, and, turning rapidly, made another desperate rush for the deep water. The reel whizzed like a buzz-saw, and, in spite of all my efforts to check him, full eighty yards ran off before "the king" again flung himself high in the air; another spurt, followed by more leaps, showed that he had taken a new lease of life, and I began to despair of ever being able to tire him. It was a stand-up fight between man and fish, and so far the fish seemed to be the less tired of the two. More than an hour had elapsed since the first jump, and to all appearances "his majesty" was as fresh and lively as ever. I was feeling sore and strained about the hands and arms, and my fingers had scarcely strength to turn the crank of the reel. Joe now volunteered to "give me a spell," but I declined the offer, and, getting a fresh grip of the rod, sitting well back, and bracing my feet against the bottom boards of the skiff, put on all the strain the rod would bear, and again brought my huge antagonist to a standstill. Then I started in to pull at him and to worry him, and presently he gave way, and again I led him into the shallow water. He was now much easier to manage, and soon I succeeded in getting him two or three hundred yards away from the channel, within twenty yards of the skiff, butting him hard, and doing all I could to bring him within reach of the gaff; but my efforts were in vain. Suddenly he came to the surface, and blew like a porpoise. "Now, look out," said Joe; "he 'll be off again." That breath of air had undoubtedly put new life into him, for like a flash he ran out fifty or sixty yards of line, and again broke water. "That makes twelve jumps; he 's a bully one. Hold on, and turn him again," roared Joe, and almost immediately the fish came straight for the skiff, actually passing under the bottom, though fortunately the line went clear. Again he rose to the surface to breathe, then another frantic rush, and two more leaps. But these were his last. We were now close to a small mangrove island, in shallow water, and the great fish was unmistakably beginning to tire, for now and then, as he turned, we could see his magnificent broadside; but still he was far from being "played dead," although I was very nearly played out. "Try to lift him," said Joe, who had unshipped the oar. The fish was now within six feet of the skiff, almost motionless, and we could see that the snell outside his jaw was badly frayed. Joe then stealthily seized the gaff, and as quick as lightning struck the tarpon through the shoulder. A desperate struggle ensued, but Joe held on, and so did the good barbed gaff and its long hickory pole. After an exciting ten or fifteen seconds, which

"CHARMING BILLY" AND HIS PAPOOSE.

DRAWN BY CARLTON T. CHAPMAN. ENGRAVED BY C. SCHWARZBURGER.

EVERGLADES AND INDIAN CAMP.

DRAWN BY CARLTON T. CHAPMAN. ENGRAVED BY J. W. EVANS.

"HANGING ON BY THE EYELIDS."

to me seemed a lifetime, we had his head above the gunwale of the skiff, which was nearly half full of water (shipped during the final act), and reeving a stout line through his gills, secured it to the after thwart, cutting the snell, which was almost frayed through, adrift from the line; five minutes more would have done for it, but Joe's clever strike secured the fish. I felt thoroughly tired, my hands and arms were cramped and stiff, as were also the muscles of my back and shoulders. The fight had lasted for an hour and twenty-seven minutes.

Then, taking our prize in tow, we proceeded homeward; but on the way we nearly lost part of him, as a huge shark made a dash at the body of the defunct monarch, and just missed getting a mouthful. As it would not do to run any more risks, with considerable difficulty we lifted the tarpon into the skiff, and reached home without further adventures. The figures were: Length, 6 feet 6 inches; girth, 3 feet 2 inches; weight, 145¾ pounds. Joe said the fish "was lean," and not in the very best condition, or it would have weighed 160 pounds. After it was photographed, Joe took off the scales, my wife securing the best of them for preservation.

On February 14, the *Minnehaha's* repairs being complete, we sailed in company with the *Gipsy*, owned by a friend, for Charlotte Harbor, the limit of our cruise up the west coast, and Skipper's spirits rose when he saw the light on Sanibel Island. In the afternoon an old friend, ex-Commodore C—— of the New York Yacht Club, arrived in his 38-foot water-line sloop *Atala*. We had been antagonists in more than one hard-fought race since we first met on the Riviera. We decided to fish and sail in company, and had many days of pleasant sport. On February 25 I hooked a tarpon, which after a hard fight of over two hours was cleverly struck by the commodore's "goffer."

On March 1, the *Minnehaha*, in company with the *Gipsy* and the *Atala*, cruised up the Caloosa River twenty miles to Fort Myers, a thriving settlement with a population of about 700. Here we had varied experiences with tarpon. On March 5, at 5 A. M., when the first streak of yellow light brightened the eastern sky, and while the good people of Fort Myers were wrapped in sleep, we weighed anchor, and with the last of the ebb-tide, and a faint draft of southerly wind, we dropped slowly down the river, followed by the *Atala*. We had reached the farthest point of our voyage, and henceforth every mile we sailed would be bringing us nearer to Indian River again. It was a quiet and lovely scene: the broad river was like a mirror framed on each side by the dark pine forests, and there was not wind enough to ruffle its surface, which reflected the exquisite hues and colors of a glorious sunrise. Our progress was very slow, and as we soon would have the tide against us, we began to think we were in for a long passage, when we saw smoke ascending astern, and presently the little steamer which plied between Punta Corda and Fort Myers hove in sight, and, on coming up to the *Atala*, took her in tow; she then steered for us, and, hailing Skipper to throw our line, pulled us down to Punta Rassa at an eight-knot speed. We landed, and after collecting our mails proceeded to St. James's City, arriving there about 10 A. M. Taking leave of our friends, we prepared to set out on the return voyage, which was begun on March 6. A week later we arrived at Indian Key.

DRAWN BY CARLTON T. CHAPMAN. ENGRAVED BY H. E. SYLVESTER.

LAUNCH OF THE SURF-BOAT, JUPITER LIFE-SAVING STATION.

The first streak of light of March 17 saw us under way, with a fresh southerly wind, and under a double-reefed mainsail we went flying up Hawk's Channel. Off Key Largo we were struck by a sharp squall from the southwest; we dropped the peak of the mainsail to it, and afterward close-reefed the sail; then skirting the shore of Old Rhodes Key, and keeping close to the northeast point, we sailed into Cæsar's Creek, having done the forty knots from Indian Key in a little over six hours. After passing Rubicon Keys we were once more in Biscayne Bay, and, the wind having moderated, we shook out all reefs and steered for Cocoanut Grove, off which place we anchored at 4:30 P. M., receiving a hearty welcome from the members of the Biscayne Bay Yacht Club. My great ambition was to catch a tarpon in Biscayne Bay, as several noted New York anglers had fished for them without success, and I had been told "it was useless to try, as the tarpon there lived principally on shrimps, and would n't look at a mullet." I made up my mind to give them a fair trial, and on March 21 took one which in length was 6 feet 3 inches, girth 3 feet 2 inches, probable weight about 130 pounds.

On Sunday, March 22, we made an early start, and under a double-reefed mainsail, with a slashing northwest wind, soon reached the sheltered waters of the Miami River. A friend had very kindly arranged for us an expedition by land to the Indian village on the edge of the Everglades; and as there was no church service to be held at Miami, a mission to the Seminoles was decided on. Crossing the river to old Fort Dallas, we set forth. The track was rough; the coralline rocks everywhere cropped up, and the tough roots of the saw-palmettos protruded across the trail. Our wagon plunged into the midst of the great pine forest and a jungle of palmetto undergrowth, pitching and rolling in a manner that threatened destruction to the vehicle, but which served only to increase the mirth of the passengers. Soon all semblance of a track ceased; then the colored coachman's navigation was marvelous, and the way in which he avoided disaster against the trunks of the huge pine-trees proved him to be an old helmsman. At length the prairies which mark the beginning of the Everglades hove in sight, and we soon emerged from the forest. A collection of palm-thatched huts on the edge of the great pine-woods which extended away to the north and eastward, and skirted the vast level expanse that stretched away to the south and west as far as the eye could reach, came in view, and the home of the Seminole was before us.

We soon drew near the camp, and found at home only "Charming Billy," his squaw, and papoose. All the others were at work in their fields in the Namak, some distance off. These Indians are very quiet and friendly. They cultivate sugar-cane, pumpkins, sweet-potatoes, etc., and they also make a good deal of starch from the root of the cassava, quantities of which grow in the pine-woods. They hunt in the fall and winter, and find their way frequently by water to Miami, bringing with them venison, skins, alligator-hides, birds, plumes, and starch, which they exchange for tobacco, calico, ammunition, etc. Billy expressed no curiosity as to the object of our visit, the real purpose of which was to enable my wife to photograph the Indians and their homes. Upon broaching the subject there was some slight demur, but after a little persuasion, and a friendly chat in which it was explained to Billy that we were "strangers from beyond the sea," he was won over, and consented. Mrs. Billy, however, utterly declined being pictured, but I managed to get a rough pencil sketch of her without being perceived.

On our way back we had gone scarcely a mile from the edge of the prairie when we became aware of a strong smell of burning wood, and on reaching an open spot observed great columns of dense smoke rising in the southwest. We were well to windward, and out of danger, but a strong west wind was blowing, and between the lulls we could plainly hear the hoarse roar of the flames, and the crashing of trees and branches, as they were overwhelmed and fell in the fierce conflagration, while clouds of light ashes were floating in the air, and falling all around us. We reached Fort Dallas without mishap, when, bidding adieu to Andrew and our kind host, we crossed the river to Miami, and regained our little vessel.

On March 24 we had a splendid morning, with a light northeast wind, and all of us felt sorry it was to be our last at lovely Miami. Our friends came down to the wharf to see us start, and fairly loaded the *Minnehaha* with green cocoanuts, tomatoes, and flowers. After exchanging salutes with the commodore and the Yacht Club at Cocoanut Grove, we turned our head toward "Bear's Cut," and steered for the open sea.

On nearing Bear's Cut, the wind, which had been gradually dropping, died out to a light air, and as it was impossible to stem the strong flood-tide which was setting through it, we anchored for the night near the Key Biscayne in about six feet of water. The next day broke fine, with a flickering wind from the northward, and after sunrise a light fog rolled in, but soon lifted, and we got under way, and afterward anchored off the south beach of Virginia Key. At 10:30 the wind had shifted to the northeast, and the weather was looking fine and settled. As we could lay our course up the coast, the water being smooth, we weighed and proceeded to New River, distant about twenty miles.

We put out the trolling-lines, and were soon busy with the kingfish. We made good progress, and at 3:30 P. M. arrived off New River bar, which seemed to be smooth; but we decided on anchoring outside until we saw what the weather was going to do, for if the night promised well we made up our minds to give up the expedition to New River, and make a dash for Jupiter Inlet, the state of New River Bar auguring well for finding Jupiter Bar passable.

We were now about to undertake the longest and most dangerous run on the southeast coast of Florida; for we had between fifty and sixty miles to go, with no available harbor, if the sea should rise, for more than two hundred miles, unless we could regain Biscayne Bay. Jupiter Inlet had no more than four feet of water on the bar, and except in fine weather and with smooth water was a dangerous one to attempt. Hillsboro' and Lake Worth inlets, both of which we would have to pass before reaching Jupiter, were no better. If Jupiter Bar was impassable, we would be in an awkward predicament. But everything appeared to be in our favor — settled weather, a fair wind, and smooth water; so, congratulating ourselves on our good fortune, we made the requisite preparations for a night at sea, and at 6:30 P. M. let her go north.

Until midnight all went well. We had passed Hillsboro' Inlet, and were some twenty miles to the northward of it, when suddenly the wind increased, and hauled farther ahead, with passing showers of light rain; but the water was still smooth, so we reefed the mainsail and held on. At 3 A. M., having then passed Lake Worth Inlet, and being within ten miles of Jupiter, we ran into a heavy swell setting from the northeast, and at once knew that Jupiter Bar was impassable. We could already hear the thunder of the surf on the beach, and see the line of white breakers on our lee beam. The wind all the time was increasing, so we now close-reefed the mainsail and stowed the jib. For a craft of her size the *Minnehaha* was doing right well, but it was trying work. She was shipping water, and I could see Skipper was anxious. I must confess I felt the same. It was no use disguising the fact, we were "regularly caught on a lee shore," and cut off from gaining any harbor. However, we remembered the life-saving station at Jupiter; if we could manage to gain it, I knew I could depend on the captain and crew to do all in their power to save us. We spoke but little, for all were aware of the danger we were in; but we drove the sloop to the best of her powers, and longed for daylight.

About four o'clock we caught sight of Jupiter Light, the bright flash of which sent a ray of hope into our hearts, for it seemed like an old friend, and told us we should soon be within reach of assistance. Would the night ever pass away? The *Minnehaha* was pounding and smashing into the short lop on the long, heavy swell, sending the spray flying all over us; but we were making headway, and gradually "clawing off" the shore. The little craft, however, was straining and leaking badly, and the pumps had to be kept going without intermission. At last a dim light appeared on the eastern horizon, and the white crests of the waves to windward seemed more distinct; then, as the stars began to pale, a gray light came stealing over the water, and soon it was bright enough for us to distinguish the white beach with its darker background; and to our great relief a dark blurred mass appeared about two points away on our lee bow. This quickly took a definite shape, and proved to be the buildings of the United States life-saving station at Jupiter. But to leeward, as far as the eye could distinguish to the north and south, ran several lines of furious breakers, the spray from which rose in sheets of vapor enveloping the sand-hills in clouds of mist. It was anything but a pleasant sight, and then I think we all realized the peril we were in, and the small chance we had of gaining the shore, if, as a last resource, we should try to beach the boat.

DRAWN BY CARLTON T. CHAPMAN. ENGRAVED BY GEO. P. BARTLE.

CROSSING JUPITER BAR.

We were now within a mile of the station, and about half a mile from the beach. There was no time to lose, so I ordered Skipper to hoist the ensign "union down," and to half-mast our private signal, which was flying at the topmast-head. The moment had arrived to "lay the boat to." Would she do it? Skipper said, "No"; but try it we must. We watched for "a smooth," and eased down the helm. She came up nearly head to the wind; then, gathering sternway, fell off in the trough of the sea. The next moment a crest struck her amidships, and sent the water flying half-way up the mainsail. Then she came up to the wind, only to fall off again. It was no use; she would not "lay to." But we had still one resource left before trying to run her through the breakers. "Get the anchor ready!" was the order. "She 'll never hold on; she will go clean under," declared Skipper, a bit scared. "Do as I tell you; see everything clear, and let go." It was no easy matter to get forward, but at last he managed to reach the bow, and, cutting the lashings, hove the "mud-hook" overboard, paying out the cable to the last inch. "Will it hold?" we involuntarily asked ourselves, and some moments of intense anxiety elapsed, as heaving and tossing on the heavy swell she drifted astern, the mainsail flapping and banging from side to side.

Suddenly she stopped, and drove her bowsprit clean under, trembling from stem to stern with the heavy jerk, and then swung head to the sea. She was holding on, but would she be able to ride in such a sea? "She 'll go bows under," said Skipper; "better chance it, and try to beach her; the cable will never stand." "Lower and stow the mainsail," was the next order, and this was quickly executed.

She did make some wild plunges, at times going bows under, right into the mast, sending the water flying into the cockpit; but she held on, and if the cable should not part or the sea become heavier, there seemed still a chance of saving her. We went forward, and, watching for an opportunity, secured the end of the cable to the mast, and served it round with a bit of small rope to prevent it from chafing on the bows, at the same time seeing everything clear, in case it should part, for setting the jib, as in that case the sole chance of saving our lives would be to run her ashore.

We now turned our attention to what they were doing at the station, and saw the United States ensign flying in answer to our signals, and the life-boat on the beach with the crew about her. They made a gallant effort to launch her, but the breakers proved too heavy, and to our great disappointment they desisted from making any further attempts. We afterward learned that the boat had swamped. The crew remained on the beach, standing by the boat, watching for a chance to come to us.

We still held on, but were in a very critical position. At any moment the cable might part, as a portion of the rope of which it was composed was, according to Skipper, "old and untrustworthy." This information was not likely to raise our spirits much, so we prepared for the worst.

We had no life-buoys, or anything on board that would float, except the oars of the skiff and the setting-poles, which would n't have been of much account; and, to add to my anxiety, two of our ship's company, my wife and the steward, were unable to swim. The danger in beaching the sloop was very great, as there was an outer line of breakers, with deep water between them and the shore. If we were swamped in crossing it, we should sink before we could reach the beach, and there was the additional risk of encountering sharks, several of which were actually visible. We emptied the water-casks and improvised a couple of life-buoys by slinging and attaching to them beckets for life-lines. Then we could do no more but await developments.

The swell was now very heavy, but the wind was not increasing, evidencing a strong blow somewhere up the coast, which was sending this big sea down to us. We were anchored in four fathoms of water, about half a mile from the shore, and within two hundred yards to leeward, in a depth of eighteen feet, the swell was topping and breaking.

The *Minnehaha* was making much better weather of it than we had expected, but now and again she would almost stand on end when an unusually steep sea rolled in, and then, sliding down the opposite slope, would bury herself to the mast, sending green water over the fore end of the deck-house. Still, if the sea became no worse and the cable held, we stood a good chance; on the other hand, we were literally "hanging by a thread," and at any moment might be fighting for our lives.

Skipper had lost all heart, and was seasick into the bargain, poor fellow. The sloop was pretty nearly all he owned in the world, and I think he had made up his mind that he was going to lose her. Our feelings were not enviable, for even if we escaped with our lives, we were nearly certain to lose everything else. It was, however, reassuring to see the crew of the life-saving station standing about their boat, watching us, and we knew that every man of them would risk his life to save us. They had hoisted a signal at the flagstaff, but, having no signal-book on board, we were unable to ascertain its meaning.

Toward noon there was a decided lull, and we saw the crew gather round the boat, and run her down the beach. They were going to make another attempt to launch her. Would they succeed? It was about as anxious a five minutes as ever I spent, for when they got near the water's edge they were hidden from our sight by the heavy rollers. We could not speak, but we watched with mingled feelings of hope and almost breathless anxiety. Even poor Skipper, who was utterly prostrated, raised his head. Five minutes elapsed,—less perhaps,—but to us

DRAWN BY CARLTON T. CHAPMAN. ENGRAVED BY R. C. COLLINS.

CAMP AT JUPITER INLET.

it seemed an hour; then, tossed high on the crest of a great sea, appeared the boat with her gallant crew. They were clear of the beach, and the boat was coming over the breakers like a sea-gull.

The feeling of relief was intense; our dangerous position was forgotten, and soon Captain Carlin and his boys were within hail. They approached cautiously, and the bowmen, laying in their oars, flung a grapnel to us, which was quickly made fast; then, hauling up alongside, Carlin and two of the crew sprang on board. A warm grasp of the hand, and then to business. We had no need to explain the situation; a few hurried words settled everything. "Carlin, you must take my wife and the steward ashore, for they can't swim. Lend us an anchor and cable, and a couple of cork life-jackets, and I think we can hold on. We want, if possible, to save the boat and gear. What do you say?" "All right; we'll manage it for you. We had a hard job to get out; the surf on the beach is the heaviest we have had for a year. Look alive there, boys, with an anchor and line. Pull well out to windward, and let go." This was quickly accomplished; then Carlin and a couple of his hands went forward and re-secured the cables.

By this time my wife, who was very unwilling to leave, was persuaded to go, as her presence on board only added to my anxiety; and, taking with her a few valuables, including "Cherokee Kate" and another coon which had been given to us a few days before, she and the steward were quickly put on board the life-boat, and cork life-jackets fastened round them. Then Carlin tossed two to us, and, saying they would keep a watch on us, and show a light during the night to mark the best place to run ashore, gave the order to let go. In a few minutes the boat was among the breakers. We watched her shooting on the crests of the rollers, losing sight of her in the hollows, and at last, to my great joy, I saw her run up on the beach, and all hands land in safety.

The sea had now moderated, and the sloop was riding easier. Having a second anchor down made us more hopeful, for we now had "two strings to our bow," and I began to feel more cheerful, and as if I could eat and drink something, having had nothing for nearly twenty-four hours. I rummaged about, and finding the "ribs and trucks" of a ham, a box of sardines, and a box of crackers, made a good meal; but Skipper, who was lying prostrate in the cockpit, could n't touch anything. It was the roughest sea he had ever been in.

Standing on the deck-house, I took a survey of our surroundings. Away to the north and west, distant about a mile, was Jupiter Inlet, across which a furious sea was breaking. The rollers on the bar wildly tossed their great white crests, as they curled and broke in a smother of foam, and a smoke-like mist hung over the coast, rendering its outline almost invisible. Inside the line of breakers I could see the placid waters of Indian River, "the haven where we would be," and the tall, symmetrical tower of Jupiter Light on its wooded bluff. Wistfully I gazed at it, and longed to be safely moored in the smooth waters that it overshadowed. Abreast of us was the life-saving station, and I could see the life-boat on its carriage, all ready for launching, and some of the crew on watch. To seaward the weather looked fine; the swell had unmistakably decreased, and the wind was dropping and veering to the southeast.

Telling Skipper to rouse up and keep a lookout, I lay down and took a nap; but in an hour or so was awakened by an unusually heavy plunge, and found that both wind and sea had increased, and things were not looking very rosy. The flood-tide was making, and the *Minnehaha* would not lie head to the sea; she was shipping water, taking it green over the deck-house. I felt anxious again, and Skipper was in decidedly low spirits, and called my attention to a twelve-foot shark which was slowly cruising to and fro. I admitted that he would n't be a desirable companion if we had to swim for it, and remarked: "We are not going to get to it this time. Cheer, oh!" But Skipper would not be comforted, and "wished to goodness we had gone into New River."

We took another look at the cables to see that they were not being chafed, got our anchor-light ready, and before dark saw everything clear for making sail. About eight o'clock the weather became finer, and the wind fell, and hauled more to the south. We could see the light on the beach, and knew that our friends were keeping an eye on us; then, being thoroughly tired and wet, we lay down, both of us falling so soundly asleep that it was daylight before we awoke.

During the night the wind moderated, and shifted to the westward of south, with heavy rain-showers, which put down the sea considerably; but at daylight of March 27 there was still a big ground-swell, and the surf on the beach and the breakers on the bar looked very formidable, and Skipper agreed with me in thinking the bar was impassable. However, all immediate danger was past; for, barring the long ground-swell, the water was smooth and the wind inclined to come off the land. So, lighting the stove, we put on the coffee-pot, and started breakfast. Skipper seemed to be quite himself again, and had forgotten all the perils and dangers he had been through since leaving New River. At 8:30 A. M., Carlin and his crew mustered on the beach in front of the station, and hoisted a flag; then, waving to us and pointing in the direction of the inlet, they all walked toward it, evidently meaning that we should attempt to "take the bar." I must confess that I did n't like the look of it, but having implicit confidence in Captain Carlin's judgment, we got under way and prepared to run in. Then, stripping off everything with the exception of our trousers, we clad ourselves in the cork jackets, and steered for the bar. On nearing it, the skiff, which was towing astern, swamped, and as she was much strained, and would have been a hindrance to us, we cut her adrift, and never saw her again.

We sailed along the outer edge of the rollers, looking out for the channel, but the breakers extended right across the inlet,—four formidable lines of them,—roaring and flinging their snowy crests in the air as they curled and broke. A surf never looks so dangerous from seaward as it is in reality, and I hesitated. Sharks were visible, plenty of them—an additional risk. But Carlin and his crew had arrived at the inlet, and were ranging themselves on the beach, with their "life-sticks and -lines" all ready to heave. I also caught sight of my wife; she too was there, standing near Carlin, and I felt more than thankful that she, at all events, was on "the right side of the hedge." Being about high water, it was the most favorable time for attempting the passage, and we had a nice steady breeze. The chief danger lay in broaching to; and as we would have to raise the centerboard on account of the shoal water, the chance of doing so was thereby increased. We hove to, and reduced the after sail; then, steeling our hearts, we pointed her head for the breakers, and let her go.

The men on shore were still in line, as if on parade; suddenly it struck me that this was not merely accidental: they had been placed in range to show us the best course through the breakers. By keeping them "end on" we should strike the deepest water on the bar. We instantly altered course, and, jumping forward on the deck-house, I held on to the mast, directing Skipper how to steer. We rapidly approached the broken water, and seemed to fly. As the first roller lifted and literally hurled us forward, the water seethed and boiled in over our decks, but comparatively little of it found its way into the cockpit, as it broke ahead, expending itself in an acre of foam. We were still moving fast, but a great transparent wall of green water was rapidly coming up astern, ominously curling and hissing. I held my breath; the critical moment was at hand, for if the roller did not break before it overtook us, to a certainty we should be swamped. Skipper's teeth were hard set, and his whole weight was thrown against the tiller to keep the sloop straight. Suddenly I felt her dragging; she was touching the ground, and the roller was almost overshadowing us, when in an instant the green wall changed to a flood of milk-white foam, which, surging down on us, lifted the sloop, tossing and bearing her onward at a tremendous pace. A flood of water swept in over the stern and weather-quarter, and half filled the cockpit, nearly washing Skipper overboard, as we almost broached to; but we were safe. We had crossed the shallowest spot, and when the next breaker thundered astern of us, we shot into smooth water, and all our troubles were over.

A loud cheer went up from our friends as we ran the *Minnehaha* alongside the beach at our old camping-ground, and there securely moored her.

Indian River once more! Farewell to bars and breakers; good-by to the Gulf Stream and its clear blue sea, to coral reefs and sandy keys; henceforth smooth water and sheltered anchorages! Skipper hailed with delight the change to landlocked waters; but for myself, knowing our delightful cruise was nearing its end, I could not help feeling sorry that it was so. We had just finished mooring the *Minnehaha* and clothing ourselves when my wife, with Carlin and his men, appeared on the scene; and after exchanging congratulations we heard all that had taken place since parting from us. They had landed without mishap, and Carlin had taken my wife to his house at Jupiter, where Mrs. Carlin showed her much hospitality and kindness. From first to last Carlin and his crew behaved admirably. The zeal and intrepidity they displayed were worthy of the service to which they belonged, and we must ever feel grateful for the assistance they rendered to us.

The coasts of Florida, from the head of Indian River on the east to Tampa Bay or Cedar Keys on the west, are about the best cruising-grounds for a small or medium-sized yacht that I am acquainted with. As for the fishing, for variety, gameness, size, and quantity of the fish, I believe it to be the best in the world. And game, both fin and feather, is more or less abundant, according as the country is more or less settled.

William Henn

18.
A Winter's Sport in Florida (1889)

A FISHERMAN'S LUCK.

FROM PHOTOGRAPH, ENGRAVED BY J. HOSKINS.

OUTING.

NOVEMBER, 1889.

A WINTER'S SPORT IN FLORIDA.

BY O. A. MYGATT.

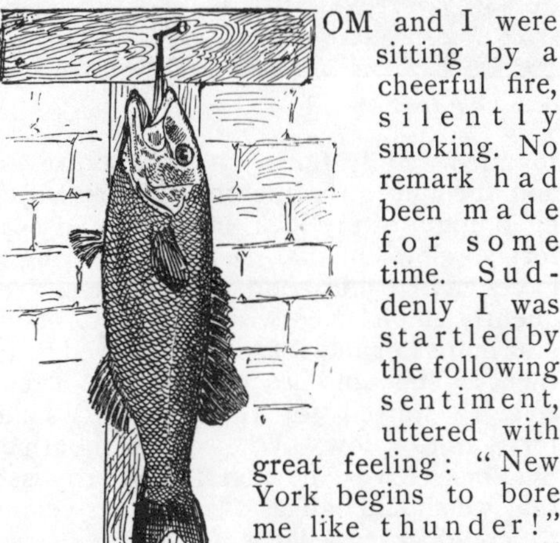

TOM and I were sitting by a cheerful fire, silently smoking. No remark had been made for some time. Suddenly I was startled by the following sentiment, uttered with great feeling: "New York begins to bore me like thunder!" "Well," said I, "if New York bores you there are two courses open for you—either go shoot yourself or go to Florida and shoot something else." Tom was a bit brightened at the suggestion. "Right you are, old boy! Florida is the place, but no shooting trip; let it be fishing, pure and simple. Besides, you know, it doesn't pay very well to take a gun to Florida nowadays. What do you say to skipping from this civilized metropolis on Saturday?" "Saturday suits me," I answered. Saturday at midnight we boarded the Jacksonville express, rods in hand, and with a goodly supply of tackle in our trunks. Tuesday saw us at Rockledge, on the Indian River, bargaining for a sailboat and two rowboats. The same afternoon, having laid in a large stock of provisions, flour, eggs and canned goods, we started down the lagoon. For a skipper we had the genial, well-posted McGruger, while dusky, good-natured Peter acted as cook and aide-de-camp.

It was a beautiful Florida winter's day, warm, but pleasant. As Tom and I lay on the cabin roof smoking our pipes and the boat glided along, we mutually congratulated ourselves on the change from New York, with its snow and slush, its unhallowed but civilized delights, to our present enjoyment of floating along, caring not whither we went. Next day we arrived at the Indian River Inlet. Here I had often found good fishing on former trips, so we decided to put in several days at channel bass. During the first of these, owing to a cold north wind, the fishing was poor, but the fourth day the wind went south and the weather became warm. Tom, disgusted with our poor luck, refused to move from the sailboat, so, taking a boat, I left him to row up one of the channels that run from the inlet to the Indian River. I stopped at a large deep pond caused by a sudden curve in the creek. Putting on a spoon bait I cast it astern, then letting the rod down so that my feet controlled the handle of the reel I proceeded to lay around, letting out line when I thought necessary. I have always had a mania for fishing entirely alone whenever I could, and have found that with practice, calling to my aid traits of forgotten ancestors, and using my feet as

GOOD DIGESTION WAITS ON APPETITE.

well as my hands, I could do very good trolling by myself. I had rowed barely half a minute and not thirty feet of line had run out, when there was a sudden jerk and the reel buzzed. Dropping the oars I seized the rod and then followed fifteen minutes of such pleasure as only a fisherman can feel.

At the end of this time I had brought the bass alongside the boat and gaffed him. On weighing him on my scales he pulled beyond the twelve-pound notch. Casting him in the bow I began again to fish. Within two minutes I had another one, and once more I was in the seventh heaven of a fisherman's delight, playing my catch. The day turned out to be a red-letter one. For four hours, until full tide, my good luck continued. At 5 o'clock I started to row back to the sailboat to get my well-earned, but, unfortunately, canned dinner. Nineteen channel bass lay in the boat, glittering proofs of a great day's sport. The lightest weighed six pounds, the heaviest sixteen; the total weight being something over three hundred pounds. As I went back I passed two sailboats whose occupants had been fishing at the inlet. Their surprised, not to say disgusted, faces when they saw my catch gave me most excessive joy. Tom, whom I found reading where I left him, was dumfounded. Only for a moment, however, and then he gave me the full benefit of his opinion of my luck in a style of oratory so eloquent that Demosthenes might have envied him had it not been frequently emphasized with profanity. Several more fair days' fishing followed, and then as the sandflies became too attentive we started for Jupiter Inlet, some forty miles below. When off the mouth of St. Lucie River, however, Tom proposed that we should sail as far up the river as we could to see what was there, as he put it. Having heard that the river was most beautiful, and that fresh-water bass were plentiful, I offered no objection, so our course was altered and set for St. Lucie River.

After the first few miles the river, which was broad, with pine woods on each side, narrowed down to a couple of feet in width. The banks grew lower and were covered with palm trees, live oaks intermingled with other trees forming a background. The water grew deep and of a transparent dark-brown tint, becoming almost black in places. Lily pads covered the whole surface at times; then the water was hidden by a mass of bright yellow flowers. Kingfishers darted about, with their harsh, exasperating cry. Now a white crane slowly crossed the glassy surface, its reflection as clear as the bird itself. Then a large silver-gray heron, suddenly startled, would rise slowly and majestically and disappear around the curve of the stream. Small bright-blue and cardinal-red birds darted in and out among the trees, while now and then pairs of wood ducks, rising suddenly from many a little pass, would for a moment show their brilliant metallic colors, as, like pieces of jewelry, they flashed in the sunlight. The whole scene was really enchanting. No thought of shooting or fishing entered the mind. Either seemed out of place in such a paradise. For three days we roamed up and down the river, paddling up side creeks, reading, dreaming, smoking and thoroughly enjoying the beautiful scenery. But soon the spirit of the fisherman awoke in us once more, and, tearing ourselves away from our fascinating surroundings, we sailed for Jupiter Inlet. The trip was uneventful. While passing through Jupiter Narrows we caught a dozen or so of sea trout, trolling with a phantom minnow. The sea trout cooked in brandy and washed down with true old English Bass makes a delicious meal. On arriving at Jupiter we inquired as to the fishing there that year. The lighthouse keeper informed us that but few parties had been there so far and that the fishing was poor. This we found to be true enough, as only a few stray bluefish and channel bass rewarded our efforts.

An old cracker from the upper part of Jupiter Creek luckily turned up a few days after our arrival, and, as we had found out from experience that something was always to be learned from the oldest inhabitant, we entered into conversation with him on the subject of fishing. To our delight he assured us that he had seen hundreds of tarpon up the creek, that they followed his boat like sheep and that they would snap at a piece of rope trolling in the water. We made up our minds that he embroidered well, even if the whole fabric was not a gigantic lie, but determined to investigate the matter nevertheless. We questioned him as to how many miles up the creek he had seen the most tarpon. Next day found our sailboat tied to a pine tree about a mile

A ROYAL FISH.

LOOKING OUR BEST.

below the spot described. It was about 4 o'clock in the afternoon when we reached our anchorage or treeage, but Tom and I determined to take a row up the creek and see whether the cracker had been greening us or not. So, taking one rod along for any stray chances that might turn up, we started. I rowed around several curves, Tom reclining in the stern, when I saw his face suddenly illuminated with the most angelic expression, while his lips parted in a rapturous smile.

"Great Cæsar's ghost, just look at that!" he cried, pointing behind him. Dropping my oars, I looked around. A stretch of about a hundred yards lay before me, the water smooth as glass, the slanting rays of the setting sun touching only one side of the creek. In this stretch of water some fifty to sixty fish were rolling about like porpoises, but the silver glitter and the large scales visible on the nearer ones made me cry out at once, "Tarpon, by Jove!" They were the first we had ever seen, so our excitement may be well imagined. Suddenly one rose within twenty yards of the boat, and, making a beautiful curve, showed almost his whole side and disappeared. I took the rod, and putting on a large bone squib, cast it far out, drawing the squib rapidly back over the surface of the water, winding swiftly on my reel.

Two or three times I cast, and suddenly there was a swirl and a splash. A large tarpon had dashed at the squib and missed it. Time after time this was repeated, sometimes two or three following it right up to the boat, but evidently without trying to seize the bait. It was most exasperating. Here we were surrounded by these large and beautiful fish, who seemed entirely bent on tantalizing us. After half an hour they ceased to do even that, and we saw the whole band go splashing and cavorting up the stream, where they disappeared around a curve. It was now nearly dark, so, disgusted with our treatment, we returned to the sailboat. During dinner and all that evening tarpon was the only subject of conversation, and many were the plans proposed to decoy one of these lordly fish to his doom next day. Early in the morning Tom and I started off up the stream once more. We had a good supply of squibs and spoon baits of all sorts, but no bait, as the men had been unable to get any mullet owing to the depth of the water in the creek. For four hours we wandered up and down that stream, but never a tarpon showed itself. Half a dozen alligators were scared, and we saw them jump from the banks into the water; but we were not after alligators, and had no gun any way. At last, disheartened, we started back for lunch. Suddenly on turning the curve we met our friends of the day before at the same old game. Putting on a spoon bait and a lead for bait I cast it over the spots they were breaking in. After one or two playful rises by tarpon that didn't mean business, the spoon was seized by a big fellow, who, coming up with a rush, showed himself half out of the water. Whiz went the reel, snap went the line, and my first tarpon had been hooked and lost. Three more spoons went the same road.

This being our first experience with tarpon, we were not aware of the necessity of a thick cotton snell above the spoon for a couple of feet, to counteract the file-like action of their jaws. I was growing desperate at my frequent losses and almost sick with the constant excitement and disappointment, when a smaller fellow seized the spoon and disappeared with it. The line didn't break this time, and the fish seemed well hooked. This tarpon behaved like a lunatic. Probably it seemed so to me, as he was the first one I had ever trifled with. He would dart with lightning speed for fifty yards, spring several feet out of the water, wriggle and shake his head fiercely in the air ; then dash back on the same track he had come and disappear under the boat. Now and then he would vary this performance by taking double somersaults in the air backward and forward, being evidently an adept at either. Of course, this sort of thing could not last long, and in fifteen minutes I had him alongside the boat and Tom gaffed him. When gaffed he made a final rally, struggled for freedom and almost succeeded in dragging Tom into the water, but instead Tom jerked him into the boat. "What a beautiful fish !" we both exclaimed at once, and sat gazing admiringly at it. Without a doubt the tarpon is the most beautiful fish in the world, if we take into account shape, color and size. Fresh from the water its sides are a brilliant silver ; its back a dark opalescent green, giving purple and red metallic flashes when looked at from various angles. Its belly is white mother of pearl, its tail and back fin gleam with purple and green iridescence. When we consider that to this flashing mass of silver and brilliant coloring a good, gamey shape is added and a fierce head, we easily understand why the tarpon is called "The Silver King," and is the king of game fish.

An exclamation of Tom's drew me from my pleasant contemplation. "Stolen as usual," he sarcastically said, and so it was. The fish was hooked in the cartilage just behind one eye. Soon after all the tarpon disappeared. It was, probably, their dinner hour. We took the hint and returned to ours. On weighing the fish he scaled forty-two pounds, measuring four feet two inches in length. For a week we tried that creek again with spoon squib and fresh bait, but, although we saw many tarpon playing around, not a rise nor a strike rewarded us. At last, weary with futile attempts, we sailed down the creek and back to Jupiter, entering off the light-

LANDED AT LAST.

house. Here we heard that up in the bay, just before getting to Jupiter Creek, plenty of big crevalle had been seen sunning themselves, so we decided the next day to try our luck with them. Starting about 9 o'clock, Tom and I rowed up to the lagoon, some four miles away. This lagoon was really part of the creek, but was three-quarters of a mile wide by two miles long. Paddling about here we arrived at a spot two hundred yards from the southern side, where the frequent brakes, screws and small mullet informed us that some large fish were feeding. Allowing our boat to drift, we placed ourselves in each end of the boat with a rod. Having cut pieces of mullet about six inches long and about an inch wide, we tied these to the hook and line, allowing about half to hang loose below the hook. Casting the bait as far as possible, we would wind in, jerking them to the surface of the water.

At every cast the water would actually boil behind our baits, but somehow the crevalle would not bite just then. Half an hour later, however, when the tide began to run in, Tom hooked the first fish. The crevalle made a splendid fight, and although on a heavy rod it was fifteen minutes before we could gaff it. He weighed fifteen pounds. Two more I landed soon afterward. They made splendid sport. Tom had just played the fourth some ten minutes and was gradually rolling him in for me to gaff, when, within ten feet of the boat, a shark, about seven feet long I should judge, sprang at the crevalle, and, presto! the deed was done.

Twice again during the afternoon the same thing took place. Each time the shark was successful and obtained the free lunch he coveted.

UP THE LAGOON.

At one time there were five sharks struggling around our boat, no doubt attracted by the blood of the crevalle that had been bitten. Only quick work with the gaff saved our fish several times. We had altogether landed twenty-three crevalle, averaging from three to seventeen pounds, when, the sky in the north becoming threatening, we headed back to Jupiter. It was too late, however to escape the storm, for before we could reach our sailboat it struck us, and in five minutes we were soaked and the boat half filled. For several days we repeated our crevalle excursion, each day catching from a dozen to two dozen of this gamey fish, than which, in my opinion, none pulls harder for its size. Finally, having spent a fortnight very satisfactorily in the neighborhood of Jupiter, we set sail and started north once more. We decided to go to Titusville and from there to Puntagorda, on the Gulf side, by Enterprise, Sandford and Bartow. From Puntagorda we planned to go to Puntarassa, which we had heard was the headquarters for tarpon enthusiasts. This programme we carried out. At Puntagorda we engaged a thirty-foot sloop with two men and two rowboats, in which we sailed to the Tarpon House, Puntarassa.

The reader must not be led by this ornamental name of Tarpon House into figuring for himself one of the typical hotels of the southern United States. It only became a hotel after passing through a certain evolution of its own. Originally a provision depot during the last Seminole war, it became for years a terminus of the Havana cable, which it still is. A few years ago, however, the genial operator, Mr. George Schultz, adapted it to fill, in a measure, a want long felt by anglers in these regions, and now it affords a shelter during the night to the few but energetic tarpon fishermen who visit Puntarassa. Notwithstanding the fact that Mr. Schultz has accommodation for some twenty guests, he has every spring to send as many more away. Imagine to yourself a large, irregular, painted wooden house, surrounded by a veranda, with a pier fifty yards long jutting out from it. Place the whole of this on a sand spit stretching out into the bay and you have a very good idea of the place. Not attractive, no doubt you think. Wait until you have returned once from a good day's tarpon fishing to its comfortable shelter, to its good—though invariable—fish supper; wait till after supper, when sitting on the veranda you are smoking and glorying about yourself, always supposing you have caught a tarpon, and then, not till then, give me your opinion.

Here Tom and I put up, glad to escape from the narrow confinement of a sailboat which we had endured for six weeks on the Indian River and had had quite enough of. Our sailboat we simply used for cruising about to the various fishing grounds. At the hotel were some ten or twelve energetic fishermen, generally New Yorkers, most of them good at all sorts of fishing. During the daytime nobody was visible, all being off to court the lordly tarpon. In the evenings all would meet on the veranda or in the smoking room, when the events of that day were thoroughly discussed. The number of swirls seen or imagined; the number of tarpon fins or tails that had been spied; who had had a strike, with generally a wildly excited discussion as to whether that identical strike had been a shark or a tarpon. These were the topics we discussed. If a tarpon had been caught the lucky man was the hero of that evening. He was surrounded and questioned; every detail was eagerly demanded; the number of times his fish jumped, how high, how far; whether he had made more than one somersault in the air; how he took the bait off, slow or fast; did he show his tail out of the water or simply swirl, or had he given any indication of his intentions at all? Then the noble catcher was interviewed as to how he had played his capture and how he had gaffed it. And then a man would presently leave the group and go to the end of the pier, and with a lamp would examine the fish carefully and put his finger in every suspicious hole, lest by chance that fish might have been shot or speared; and perhaps the fish would seem shorter than the length announced, and at once a tape would be procured and the fish remeasured, perhaps even be weighed. The difference of a quarter of an inch in length or of half a pound in weight would be welcomed with shouts of laughter and the lucky man guyed on his deceitful proclivities.

Verily, the lover's jealousy may be a green-eyed monster, but compared with the jealousy of the tarpon fisherman toward his brother sportsman it counteth as nothing. Dark hints, suggestive winks, sarcastic smiles and harassing whispers can be seen all over the hotel the day one or more tarpon are caught. If you saw two old sports of an evening whispering in a corner, their faces indicative of subdued delight and exchanging every now and then a soft chuckle, you might be sure that the reputation of so-and-so as a fisherman was suffering badly at their hands, or rather tongues. Aside from the weakness of thinking that every fish was not caught exactly as it should be, or in quite a sportsmanlike way, a more genial or perfectly satisfied set of men it would be hard to find anywhere.

19.
Our Florida Garden
(1910)

Illustrated with Photographs

I BOUGHT a few acres in Florida at a venture, without having seen any part of the State and not having very accurate knowledge of what I bought. I had only a general idea that some day I might like to get away from the grippe and zero climate, and Florida offered the only chance in sight. Three years after the purchase it became decidedly wise for me to take advantage of it.

Going southward as if into a foreign land, or on a voyage of discovery, I found things very different from what I had expected. My ten acres were covered at each end with huge pines, standing from sixty to one hundred feet in height. In the middle there was a ruined orange grove, with a wide belt of plums that had died below the graft, making a thicket full of birds' nests. It was a curious place to Northern eyes.

The ground was full of rabbit holes and gopher-turtle holes, and there were a lot of other queer fellows in possession, while all the ground that was not covered with pines was given over to a tall, rank, coarse grass, seven or eight feet high. The turtles would come out at midday, lugging their houses on their backs, to dine on almost any vegetable matter, but always retiring into their holes before sundown. Up from the lake also came water turtles and snapping turtles, wabbling about clumsily, but giving visions of future soups.

I grubbed out most of the orange stumps and grafted the rest. There was little to do with the plums but to grub them also, and to do it very thoroughly, for the ground was full of roots. Under the pines, at the ends of the lot, were innumerable young oaks and persimmons; oaks of half a dozen sorts, the willow, and the scrub and the black jack being most common. A few water oaks could be selected for making future trees, and the black jacks are very beautiful when carefully trimmed and kept free of moss.

The persimmons were of the native sort, most of them probably barren, but they were good stock for grafts, and we filled them full at once of the Japanese sorts. We grubbed out the oaks, excepting a few of the better sorts, and we pulled the moss from the smaller trees. This moss was one of the curious features of the landscape to us, but it is something of real importance when it hangs down in long tresses from the tall pines. It does away with the necessity for weather vanes, as it will tell you precisely and volubly which way the wind blows.

The front two acres, with their fifty huge pines, after the underbrush had been cleared out, was a superb building lot. It overlooked Lake Lucy, a lake about half a mile across and as pretty a piece of water as you could ask for. Facing it from the east, it gave us such sunsets as I had never seen before.

These two acres or thereabouts I intended to clean up, and make into a lawn, something like what we have in the North. When I began to inquire about grasses, I found that very few of our Northern varieties would thrive here at all, not liking either the soil or the heat of summer. Before I had begun to experiment with St. Lucie grass

WHERE MR. POWELL HAS FOUND A WINTER HOME ON LAKE LUCY.

and Bermuda grass the winter had so far gone that the wild flowers were coming into bloom in rapid succession.

In November I had found violets and some other exquisite flowers here and there about the lake, but about the first of March the procession opened amazingly, and by mid April I had made up my mind that I would rather have this wild-flower garden than any lawn that was ever created with blue grass or any other grass. Wonderful and beautiful, they made a substitute far beyond my conception of wild flowers.

I had lived in Missouri and Illinois and Michigan, but had never seen anything to equal this display—legumes of all sorts, several varieties of sensitive plant, flowers as exquisite and large as sweet peas, two or three kinds of dandelion and coreopsis, and I know not what else. You see this ten acres of mine had not been burned over for fourteen years, and there had been accumulating, all the time, bird-sown seeds of everything collectable in central Florida.

Now, after I have built my house, although I have large beds for roses, cannas, gladioli, etc., still these wild flowers are not ashamed of themselves, resting their arms or their heads on tufts of grass or huckleberry bushes and looking up to me with a pleasant greeting every morning. Grandest of all was the Cherokee bean, an exquisite bush, out of which springs, all through March, April, and May, long stalks of the most brilliant carmine flowers. Most of our wild flowers have bulbous or large roots of some sort, on which they can feed during dry spells.

Turtles rapidly disappeared after we began cultivation, and so did all the rest of the wild animals. Rabbits still linger where they can find a neglected corner, yet they are doing very little mischief. One of the turtles which the natives call the gopher turtle has a hole on a slope of about forty-five degrees into the sandy soil, out of which he comes at about eleven o'clock in the morning, for a lunch on almost any vegetation he can find.

These holes vary from four inches in

OF COURSE THE ORANGE IS THE TYPICAL CROP IN FLORIDA.

diameter to twenty, and the inhabitants vary as much in size. A well-grown turtle will weigh about ten or twelve pounds, and of course is an unwelcome visitor in a patch of green peas. It is an easy matter to catch these fellows by planting boxes just under the mouths of the holes. As they make their exit for dinner, the clumsy fellows tumble into the boxes and cannot get out. They make excellent feed for hens, and the gopher turtle is a welcome addition to a vegetable diet, in soup or stew.

Foxes we occasionally hear in the distance, and they have been known in our hen yards. The real gopher is not a turtle at all, but a ground squirrel, with pocket jaws; and a mighty busy fellow he is, plowing through your garden or yard. Every few feet he throws up a heap of dirt, and then tunnels forward—going several rods in a single night. It is very interesting to watch him bring up the dirt from below in his pocket jaws and dump it in an orderly way.

The ground mole, here, as in the North, is not at all an enemy, although he has the credit of doing all sorts of mischief, the fact being that he lives on grubs and is of decided economic value. The real gopher or squirrel is the only pest that we have difficulty in controlling. He is fond of sweet potatoes, and his raids are sometimes very destructive. On the whole, the enemies to our vegetation are not seriously troublesome.

We mowed the weeds and made huge piles for compost, just as we would in the North. The folks advised us to burn it, but this we refused to do. Florida has, for time out of mind, been burned over once a year, until there is hardly a shovelful of humus to a square rod. Nitrogen can be so easily obtained by plowing under legumes that the loss of this element is not so badly felt, but there is need of more phosphorus and potash.

You would suppose that the ash left by the fires would supply the potash, but the ash of pine needles and scrub bushes leaves very little except a bit of carbon. As a substitute the gardeners and farmers buy commercial fertilizers, for which they are compelled to spend at least one third of all their earnings. This stuff is little more than a gad for a worn-out soil, and, like a whip to a worn-out horse, can only serve for a little while.

Instead of following our neighbors, we began at once making soil and humus, that is incipient soil. No State in the Union furnishes more annual material to make soil and to fatten it than Florida. There are legumes of all sorts, from three inches high up to the velvet bean, which grows seventy feet in a season. These can be mowed for hay or silage, then foddered, and finally plowed under. This adds an enormous amount of raw material for soil making, and the nodules of the roots furnish a splendid deposit of nitrogen.

Results That Count

In a compost pile of half-fermented stuff we grew a sweet potato weighing eighteen pounds. Placing this on exhibition, we left it for an argument, better than words, against the plan of burning up the material we had used for the compost pile. Into such a pile one may throw any sort of wasting stuff, even pine needles. Comminute all this with sand, at the end of each year, and work it into your garden for soil. We found pile after pile to be accumulating, and in the course of three or four years had better success with vegetables than could have been secured by the use of fertilizers.

This annual burning over of the State is very startling to newcomers. Early in January we saw to the west of us a huge fire, sweeping under the pine trees and flaming up to and among the limbs. It was a terrifying sight, to which, however, we soon became accustomed. We found that there were fire lines about houses and orchards, made by plowing a dozen furrows, and, with the people always alert, nobody was in serious danger.

You may expect to see these flames in any direction any time before the end of February. By that time nearly everything outside fire lines has been burned over. The pine trees you might expect would easily catch fire, but they do not—unless tapped or wounded; and tapped trees are always hoed about. So back into the universal ether goes all that vast mass of stuff that Nature has woven of the air to add to the riches of the soil.

It costs millions to the State annually, and the only object is to let a fresh growth of grass come up quickly, to feed the range cattle that roam the woods. But even this is false logic, for these wild pastures are yearly growing slimmer, and they last through a shorter season. So it happens that range cattle are half starved in the winter, and not unfrequently die for lack of food. The two things that Florida needs are a stock law and to stop the burning over of her wild lands.

You do not know the turpentine tappers, but if you come to Florida you will soon find them out. It is a curious business that will deliberately destroy all the forests of a half dozen States, for a little immediate gain; and still more curious is the lassitude that allows the destruction to go on. The French have a method of tapping trees which gives a profitable return and leaves the trees practically uninjured. In this way an industry is perpetuated, but our American tapping is another thing.

The trees are cut with a broad ax, hewing out great slices and leaving scars from which the resin flows into boxes at the bottom of the cut and is scraped once a month into casks. The cut is repeated each year, and in six or seven years the tree is exhausted. So go great forests of pine that stand eighty to one hundred feet high, leaving us thousands of acres of standing lumber which will be cut down by portable sawmills. The end of it all is a haggard waste.

The government of Georgia has instituted an investigation as to the more conservative methods, and I believe is enforcing something of the kind in that State. The principle of the whole business is "After us the deluge." Georgia and the Carolinas are pretty nearly stripped of pine, and Florida is following close after.

SMALL LAKES ARE SCATTERED EVERYWHERE ABOUT THIS SECTION OF FLORIDA.

A forty-acre untapped pine wood I found lying along the lake to my left. I immediately bought it and am dividing it into homesteads, with convenient cottages. We call it Ozone Park, and have named our first homestead Rest Cottage and the second one Peace Cottage. This gave me something like fifty acres of beautiful pine, to which I was able to add lake frontage of twenty acres more.

Word came that the tappers were about to buy the pine bluffs across the lake. This would ruin the whole landscape; be not only a financial damage, but rob us of the glorious sunsets. Bidding quickly, we got it ourselves, and little by little we have been able to get possession of nearly the whole lake and its surrounding acres.

Still the range cattle were everywhere, and forty cows would be at our garden fence every day. There was nothing to do but to fence in our property, clean it up, and put up notices that forbade shooting inside our lines. The quail soon found it out, and came to us, calling out Bob White, which does not happen to be our name, although we respond by feeding them at our doors. The range cattle trailed up and down the road for a while, but now we rarely hear a cow bell or see a pair of horns. The cattle ticks in the grass are disappearing with the cattle.

But the pig is another question. This "razor back" is the most irrepressible and irresponsible inhabitant of Florida. He has the law, even if you have the recorded deed. You must not shoot him nor maim him if you find him in the middle of your potato patch. If you do, it will cost you probably fifty dollars, if not a lawsuit and a deal of trouble. He can run like a hound, and he can get back in five minutes. It needs two pickaninnies to each hog.

Hog-tight fence costs heavily, and they can root under it. To put such a fence around two hundred acres would cost more for wire than you had paid for the land. So it was nip and tuck for two years, and we used up those two years in fencing and consideration. Never, never were we more tempted by Providence.

We were glad to hear guns, which might mean that somebody had shot a hog. The owner of twenty-five groaned over the fact that he got only one of them home in the fall; what became of the rest nobody knows. We are promised a stock law before long that will give ordinary human rights to hogs and hog rights to human beings. Legislators are afraid to tackle this question for fear of losing votes, yet nine out of ten of the people hereabouts know of nothing more diabolical than to call you a "razor back."

We shall get by the plague within the next two or three years. It is slow work changing old customs. Half the people of Florida still believe that burning of the State is good economy. Just at this moment, with a stiff breeze, a huge fire has started to the southwest—a mile away—and the farmers are off on horseback and on foot to help those who are in danger with back fires.

An Easy Answer and a Soft One

One simple-hearted neighbor tells me that "it is Nature's way; for, if the grass is not burned away annually lightning may strike somewhere, and the accumulated vegetation will make a furious blaze." I tell him that lightning sometimes strikes a Northern church or school house, a thing which could not occur if we had the forethought to burn them ourselves annually.

But it is really wonderful how Nature provides soil-making material all about us. The lakes are low at present, and the vegetable deposit which has been made under the water is many feet deep, in the form of black muck. While the lakes are low we can haul this to our fields and gardens. Treated with lime, or aërated for a year, it makes superb plant food.

The whole of Florida should to-day be covered with vegetable deposit, and it would be but for the annual burning. We make great use of beggar weed, which we call the alfalfa of the South —a plant that grows five or six feet high, and can be mowed repeatedly for hay and then plowed under. The leaves are very sweet to the taste, and horses prefer it to any other hay that we can secure.

There are a dozen wild grasses, nearly all of which can be utilized by cutting early, but they are badly neg-

WHEN THE RIPE FRUIT DEMANDS ATTENTION.

lected by the farmers. When fully grown they are dry and woody. The velvet bean was an importation for ornament. It grows from fifty to seventy feet in a season and was used to cover the cottages. The bean is eatable, but it is coarse, and the vine is so rank a grower that it is unsuitable for orchards.

The cow pea, of course, thrives here, and makes a very excellent summer cover crop. In the North you need a winter cover crop against cold; here we need something of the kind against the heat. Nature undertakes this business of covering the ground well against the scalding noondays, but man persistently antagonizes her beneficent work. The larger part of our wild flowers are also legumes, and as useful as they are beautiful.

Our ten acres with which we started we found to be an ideal homestead. Starting at Lake Lucy, in front, the land sloped upward to the east and then rolled on down into Lake Emerson. The beauty of Lake Lucy was startling from the first; an almond-shaped sheet of water, about half a mile across, the banks, after a rim of flat rich garden muck—splendid for celery and lettuce

CELERY IS A GOOD CROP IN SOME PARTS OF FLORIDA.

—rise to a bluffy height, which makes superb building sites, all of them holding the lake in front. It was a curious and complete retreat, two miles from the village; a few select neighbors within reach and lofty pines crowning the whole lake rim, occasionally running down to the shore.

Those that stand near the lake look at their own beauty in the still water, where they are more conspicuous than on the land. It was not greed, but sympathy with Nature, that led me to buy all that I could secure. Lake fronts and knolls soon became inseparable. These small lakes are scattered everywhere about this section of Florida. They vary from a few rods in diameter to half a dozen miles. Some of them are mere ponds, but most of them will some day be utilized by those who desire winter homes, out of reach of frost.

Of course the orange is our typical crop, and an orange grove or orchard is a thing of beauty and a joy forever. Either in fruit or in blossom the tree is a model for lawn or grove. After the freeze of 1895, which killed the trees to the ground, suckers came up and were grafted or budded. Five or six of these starting at the ground made round-headed bushlike trees, about twelve to fifteen feet in diameter. These are covered with golden balls, that ripen from November first to June.

Blossoming takes place in March, and then the whole orchard will be an orchestra of bees. The waves of perfume roll off for half a mile. The grape-fruit tree is very similar, but more inclined to droop. Peaches do quite as well as oranges, and with half the care would give better financial returns. The orchards, however, are neglected so badly that they do not give perfect crops for more than two or three years.

I have fifty fig trees, or bushes, and the magnolia fig is pretty sure to be very profitable. The Japanese plum and the native plums thrive very well indeed, but the European varieties not so well. I have in excellent condition the Bing and Lambert, and a few other cherries, as well as the sour sorts, like Morello and Suda Hardy. With pears experiments have been confined to Kieffer and the other sand pears. They grow well, but are irregular bearers.

The loquat is a semi-tropical evergreen tree, the fruit shaped like a pear but flavored like a cherry. It is delicious, one of the best of the semi-tropical fruits; but slightly in danger of frost—which we get in mild degree once or twice a year. I have over one hundred quince trees, and every variety that I have tried thrives admirably.

In March and April we have huge mulberries, and in such quantity that we can use them as freely as we please and let the birds take all they want. I was told that apple trees would not grow here, but this positive assurance was untrue. Some of the very finest varieties, notably King David, Red Astrachan, Maiden's Blush, Stayman's Winesap, and Winterstein stand the test as well as they would in Michigan. The key to success with all such trees is heavy mulching; then over the mulch a good layer of sand.

The sandy soil conducts heat quickly, and at midday, with the thermometer at eighty or ninety, the sun scalds the fine young roots. Mulching prevents this; only slope your mulch inward instead of outward, so as to catch all showers. Remember all the time that observation down here is keen, but not trained. It reports on inadequate data and will mislead you if you are not accustomed to experimentation yourself.

Your first winter in the South will be a puzzle. Everything is just as you did not expect it to be. In the first place, it really is winter, although it does not feel like it. The deciduous trees know December from June quite as certainly as in Massachusetts, dropping their leaves in November and not putting them on again till March or April. The birds stop singing for the most part, although you will get an occasional outburst from the mocking bird. The cardinal bird sings all winter, and you will hear other Southern songsters often enough to know that they are about.

Alligators sink down into the mud, and stay there until March, although they occasionally come up to investigate. The water turtles at the same time crawl out from the water and march up almost anywhere to deposit their eggs. It takes our Northern trees some time to find out what to do down here. So it happens that to-day, in my young orchard, we have peaches one quarter grown, while on other trees there is not yet a sign of life. On the shrubbery some bushes calmly wait for spring as it used to be in the North, while other sorts are running chances.

Nature understands this friskiness and has a way of sending out a succession of blooms; that is, she holds back a part of the limbs, while others are allowed to go ahead with their sportiveness. I never saw a second bloom on a judas tree in the North, but a large one on my lawn, here in Sorrento, gave me two complete blossomings, one in January and the other one just as the leaf buds started.

A Haven for the Gardener

In the vegetable garden there are just as many surprises as there are in the fruit and flower garden. The Irish potato grows quite as well as the sweet and gives as good crops as in Maine or New York. They are ready for shipment, so as to reach the Northern market about the time that we are planting potatoes in the New England States. Cabbages are ready by the first of January, and the October-planted garden is giving carrots, beets, and green peas about the same time.

I find that my pole beans and my bush limas particularly like Florida. Melons cover all the high lands and ripen in May and June. Of course they get into New York City ahead of any rival and command their own prices. Among the nut trees the pecan is coming into decided prominence, and many more groves would be planted if the nut harvest could be realized a little sooner. For the present, while potatoes can demand three dollars a bushel and sweet potatoes one dollar, they will stand among the favorites. I suppose that no larger and finer melons grow in the United States than right here. We can ship them by the car load, averaging over forty pounds to the melon.

Celery might be a favorite crop, only that along the St. Johns River irrigation is so much more easily secured that the energy of our people can best be applied to something else. The pine tree has a happy faculty of renewing itself by seedlings. A Northern forest of beech or maple is always followed by other sort of trees, but here the succeeds itself.

he annual fires destroy millions of the yearlings, still you will find everywhere little groves of pines that have not been scorched. I think that we shall see Florida pines restored to their control after the turpentine fellows are also under control of law.

Our neighbors are of four sorts; the genuine "Cracker," the negro, the relics of a race that came to exploit Florida and was conquered by the freeze of 1895, and a more recent influx of home makers. The last class is a well-sifted lot, and pretty sure to be able to take a stout grip on the land. The trouble with the exploiters of 1880 to 1890 was that they were not farmers at all and came with money borrowed at twenty per cent to plant orange groves. They spent every dime they had clearing a place in the forest and planting an orange orchard.

The Neighbors

The freeze took from them all their investments, and drove them pellmell from the State. They were teachers, ex-ministers, worn-out lawyers, while very few of them knew how to hold a plow or plant a garden. The negro of central Florida is a pretty good fellow; moderately industrious and civil. I have never seen one who was either rude or drunken. Even if we had no prohibitory law in Florida, this town has not one saloon, as it has only one church.

There is no loafing place of an evening except about the post office, and on Sundays the people all gather together for hand shaking and possibly to listen to the parson. I do not think the church has any special influence, except of a social sort. Theology is softening here at the South almost to the degree that it has in New England. The negroes, of course, have their own church and they have their own theological squabbles. The negro woman is much more industrious than the negro man and generally speaks of her husband as something that she has picked up somewhere to take care of. He is her man.

The Cracker is often a first-class farmer and peculiar only for his twang and his curiosity. He is a Southern Yankee and looks upon every bit of news or information as something that he may ask all the questions about that he likes. He will listen, if he can, to a private conversation, and his manners are his own. But in the Florida Cracker there is a lot of making. Only a very small minority of them desire to live in the old, half-savage style of fifty years ago.

The people who are coming at this date are also to be divided into two classes, those who only hire a cottage for a winter and those who buy in order to create a home for themselves. Migratory farming, as we call it, is a growing fashion. Northern farmers find it possible to work seven months in the North and to close up their apple picking and corn husking and get down here early in November, in time to harvest their oranges and plant a winter garden. In the trucking region the farmer gets here in time to take care of his celery and lettuce gardens.

The negro question exists only at the North. Here there is no more distinction between whites and blacks than there is between employers and employees in New York, with the exception of two or three conspicuous features that can be talked about. Separate churches and separate schools are sure to pass out, only so far as the negro himself prefers them. The negro car is a nuisance every way, and yet when well filled with the lower class of field negroes it is not a desirable place for a decent white person. Industrial education is slowly but surely making a change with both whites and blacks and injecting a good deal more of common sense into social relations.

Some features of the old slave life had an element of the beautiful, but the old "mammy" has gone forever. Where one of them is to be found she is merely a curiosity. The new type of negro woman is a laundress. She takes your washing at ten cents an hour, carries it to the side of a pond or lake, often half a mile from her house, where she has her big iron kettle hung over a wood fire. Her garden has lettuce, tomatoes, and sweet potatoes, which she cultivates herself. She is probably living with her third or fourth man. They are all alive, but she prides herself on having only one at a time.

So it is that the civilizing process zigzags somewhat, and only in the long run can you discover that there is any progress. The negro makes a good teamster and some of the preachers are really shrewd if not pious. My plowman tells me that he picks up his "textes mosly round de fields, case de good Lawd has sown 'em mose everywhere, and mighty good ones. Yes, suh, I picks 'em up right down here, in your lot, suh! and den I rolls 'em over, and talks about 'em with old Billy here, suh! till my heart gets mighty warm and happy, suh."

What have we done and what are we going to do? We have at least built a home where we can be out of doors nearly every day of winter and most of the time in our shirt-sleeves. In January the thermometer averages somewhere about seventy, going up sometimes to eighty and at night dropping to sixty-five. We have four fireplaces, and about sunset a few blazing pine knots make a delightful place to think and rest. We pull off our shoes, push our feet to the fire, and are soon ready for a dreamless sleep.

We can sleep out of doors, if we prefer, in hammock beds which are swung in our broad veranda at night, but drawn up to the ceiling during the daytime. We see very little meat and have never seen a butcher or a butcher shop. However, fresh meat comes into the village once a week. We live mostly on eggs, sweet potatoes, and oranges. Our bees work all winter and furnish us plenty of sweetening. Our hens lay as well in January as in June, and we have plenty of pasturage for cows. A bowl of bread and milk, filled to overflowing with mulberries or blackberries in April or May, tastes as good as it does sitting under our Northern apple trees in August.

An overcoat is rarely touched, although there are a few chilly days dropped in, at no regular date. The atmosphere is simply delightful, and roses understand it as well as we do, for they are in blossom all winter. Grippe is sometimes brought down by tourists, but it cannot live here. At this moment I can step into my garden and pull for dinner fresh peas, fresh cabbages, fresh carrots, or I can pick a mess of collards, or a huge eggplant, and at any time can dig a mess of sweet potatoes, while there is a supply of cassava for puddings and pies.

This is the kind of garden we have in Florida. Make it at any time that you please, but if made for winter in September or October, you must look out for a possible frost. Have plenty of loose compost to throw over the plants, if the thermometer should happen to drop as low as thirty-three. I have seen it once as low as twenty-eight, but zero, or anything like zero, knows not Florida.

20.
The Tarpon of Turner's River (1911)

THE LARGEST ONE WAS OVER FOUR FEET LONG.

THE TARPON OF TURNER'S RIVER

BY A. W. DIMOCK

Illustrated with Photographs by Julian A. Dimock

MARCO is the name of a post office, but the place is called Collier's. Ask any child on the West Coast of Florida about Marco and he will shake his head, but mention Collier and the infant will brighten up and say: " Dat's Tap'n Bill! "

Island, bay, hotel, houses, boat-building plant, and even the atmosphere are, and always have been, Collier's. When Ponce de Leon was cavorting about the peninsula pestering the inhabitants with his inquiries about a spring, he stopped at Collier's. Everybody who goes down the coast stops there. The only way to avoid a long detour around the Cape Romano Shoals is to go through Collier's Bay to Coon Key, and one cannot pass through Collier's Bay without calling at the store.

Summer is the time to visit Collier. When the little mail boat lands me with my family at the dock Captain Bill meets me with:

"Well, how are you? The hotel isn't open, you know."

"Glad of it. That's why I am here. Where's that baggage truck?"

Then I wheel our baggage to the hotel, we select the choice rooms, and spread our belongings all over the place as if we owned the whole business. When the dinner bell rings we sit down with the family and occasional tramps like ourselves who stop in on their way down the coast. Instead of the colorless crowd of tourists who occupy the tables when the hotel is open, we meet itinerant preachers and teachers, lighthouse keepers and land seekers, scientists and Seminoles. Best behaved of the lot are the Indians, for they sit quietly, saying nothing, while their eyes take in everything, and they touch neither knife, fork, nor spoon till they have seen how others handle them.

We take possession of the island, and wandering forth with big baskets return laden with a score of varieties of fruits from avocado pears, bananas, and cocoanuts down through the alphabet to sapadilloes and tamarinds.

As evening approaches we sit on the sheltered piazza that overlooks the bay, and, if the tide favors, watch the porpoises at play, and, more rarely, witness the dizzy leaps of a dozen or a score of tarpon each minute.

From Collier's Bay to Coon Key the channel twists and turns among sand flats and oyster reefs, between wooded banks and around tiny keys without blaze or buoy, stake, or sign to point out the path. After years of observation and practice I can take a boat over the course, if the day is clear, without running on a bank more than once in three trips.

Yet a boy to the manner born has piloted me through the maze on a night so dark that I could scarcely see his face as I sat beside him. He chatted with me throughout the trip with his hand resting carelessly on the wheel which he idly swung to and fro without apparent thought or purpose. His every act was so casual that I had just figured out that we were hopelessly lost somewhere in the Ten Thousand Islands when he leaned past me to shut off the gasoline from the motor. A minute later the boat rubbed gently against some object that I couldn't see.

"Where are we?" I asked.

"At your own dock," was the amazing reply.

My captain carried us over the same course in the same mysterious manner and I was only sure we had passed Coon Key through the broader sweep of the wind and the gentle rise and fall of the boat on the slight swell from the Gulf. Going down the coast I got my bearings and felt rather than saw its familiar features. I was conscious of the nearness of Horse and Panther Keys, and off Gomez Point I had a mental picture of the old man for whom it was named as I last saw him at his home. He was then well along in his second century, and year by year his recollection of the first Napoleon, under whom he served, became clearer and the details of their intimacy more distinct.

Sand-fly Pass, leading to Chokoloskee Bay, was our goal for the night, and nothing but a nose was needed to find it even in cimmerian darkness. Its mouth was guarded by a pelican key, from which a rookery of the birds sent forth lines of stench as a Fresnal lens radiates light.

In the morning we entered Chokoloskee Bay, and crossing it anchored within the mouth of Allen's River, near the Storter store.

For nearly two miles Allen's River is a considerable stream. Beyond that distance it divides and spreads over flats until it is only navigable to a light draft skiff. Near the mouth of the river we caught and released a few tarpon of good size, but when a mile up the stream I struck a ten-pound fish I returned to the *Irene* and rigged up an eight-ounce fly rod. The fish rose best to a tiny strip of mullet, cast and skittered along the surface, or trolled. They preferred light flies to those of more brilliant coloring. Yet their tastes changed as often as the colors of a chameleon, and they turned up their noses to-day at the lure that best pleased them yesterday.

The light fly rod is too flexible to fasten the hook in the hard mouth of the tarpon with any approach to certainty. In the beginning the fly fisherman will fail, nine times out of ten, to fasten the hook in the mouth of the striking tarpon. Then he will learn to thrust the butt of his rod away from the fish when it seizes the bait, and clutching the line or reel bring a strong, straight pull to bear on the hook in the mouth of the fish.

My first fish on the fly rod in Allen's River weighed about four pounds, but it took longer to land than its predecessor of twenty times that weight. It led me into a narrow creek where an out-thrusting branch from the bank forced me to step out of the canoe into water waist deep. I followed the fish up the shallowing stream, walking on

WE TAKE POSSESSION OF THE ISLAND AND, WANDERING FORTH WITH BIG BASKETS, RETURN LADEN.

the bank when the bushes permitted and wading in the channel when trees came to the water's edge.

When the tarpon had had fun enough with me in shallow water it led me back to the deeper river. I nearly capsized the canoe as I got aboard while playing the fish, which cavorted up and down and across the stream, leaping several feet in the air every minute or two for a quarter of an hour before yielding.

In two days I had a score of strikes and landed half that number of tarpon after an average contest of an hour with each. The largest one was four feet long and weighed therefore about thirty-two pounds, but it was an exceptionally active fish and wore itself out in half an hour by a series of frantic leaps, one of which took it over the bow of the canoe within reach of my hand.

During the two days' fishing there was seldom an interval of ten minutes between the landing of one tarpon and the strike of its successor. On the third day the tarpon were as abundant as ever and jumped all around the canoe, but not a strike could I get. If Solomon had ever fished for tarpon he would have added the way of a tarpon in the water to that of an eagle in the air, a serpent on a rock, and the other things that were beyond his comprehension.

We sailed to the south end of Chokoloskee Bay, where Turner's River connects it with the network of waterways through which tidal water flows in all directions around the big and little keys of the Ten Thousand Islands which extend from Cape Romano to Sable. Channels navigable to tarpon of the greatest draft connect Turner's River with the Gulf of Mexico, while from scores of tiny streams and shallow water-courses it collects the output of many tarpon nurseries.

I began business on Turner's River with an eight-ounce fly rod, and soon was fast to a ten-pound tarpon which thirty minutes later was captured and freed half a mile up the stream. Scarcely had a fresh lure been thrown out when there was a tug on my line and, as I believe, the largest tarpon that was ever caught on a fly rod shot a dozen feet in the air. Three times in quick succession it leaped violently, shaking its head to dislodge the hook.

Down the river the tarpon dashed till only a few feet of line was left on my little reel. The slight strain I could put on the line wouldn't have feazed a fish one tenth the size of the one to which I was fast. I needed more yards than I had feet of line to offer a chance of tiring this creature whose length exceeded mine by a foot. One more stroke of that propeller tail and my goose would be cooked.

I yelled to the captain to paddle for his life, regardless of the fact that he was already putting in licks that endangered it. Soon he was gaining faster than I could take in line and I shouted to him to slow up, changing the next instant to a cry to go ahead. When the trouble was over I asked the captain if I had screamed at him very often.

"Most all the time, but I didn't mind. I knew you was excited and didn't rightly know what you said," was his reply.

The line never again ran so low as in that first dash of the tarpon. Yet a hundred times the end of our hopes seemed near, but always the fish swam slower, or the captain paddled faster. The wild leaps of the creature were startling but welcome, for they tired the tarpon without carrying away line. We had followed the fish up, down, and across the river, and after an hour's struggle were well out in the bay, yet at all times we had kept within two hundred feet of our quarry.

Always we feared the tarpon's getting too far away. Sometimes the danger was of its coming too near, and more than once it sprang at us with wide-open jaws, falling short of the canoe by inches only, and once it sprang fairly against the captain, nearly capsizing the craft.

The sport of fishing is in inverse ratio to the size of the tackle compared with the activity, strength, and weight of the fish. Linus Yale, as skillful with trout as he was ingenious with locks, used to hitch his horse to a tree by a mountain brook near his New England home and forget for the day the anxieties of the inventor and the burdens of the manufacturer.

AS I BELIEVE, THE LARGEST TARPON THAT WAS EVER CAUGHT ON AN EIGHT-OUNCE FLY ROD SHOT A DOZEN FEET IN THE AIR.

NO SOONER HAD WE TURNED LOOSE AN EXHAUSTED TARPON THAN A FRESH ONE PRESENTED ITSELF.

All trouble was left behind as he constructed a line from hairs in his horse's tail, attached a hook of his own forging, tinier than was ever made before, with an almost microscopic fly, and with a reedlike rod, made on the ground, captured the wariest trout in the brook. When with this flimsy tackle he landed a trout of large size he rejoiced more than when picking the Hobbs lock gave him world-wide fame.

As I followed my big fish the game increased in interest. It was more like chess than fishing. Strength availed little, for the utmost strain I could put on the line through the light rod was no restraint on the powerful tarpon. The creature must be made to tire itself out and do the chief work in its own capture and at the same time be kept within the narrow limits that the shortness of my line established.

When the reel was nearly empty the line was held lightly, while the captain paddled strongly. As we neared the quarry a quick twitch of the line usually sent the tarpon high in the air and off on another dash. As the reel buzzed the captain invited apoplexy by his efforts, while I encouraged him to increase them.

At times the fish seemed to be on to our game and refused to jump when called on. It even became immune to the splash of the paddle and made an ingenious move that threatened checkmate. The tarpon was beside us and the line short when it dived beneath the canoe and swam swiftly away on the other side. There is only one move to meet that attack, and it usually ends in a broken rod and a lost fish. I dropped the rod flat on the water, thrusting it beneath the surface elbow deep, while my finger kept a light pressure on the line. Happily the tip swung to the tarpon without breaking and the fish was played from a rod under water until the captain had turned the canoe around.

The strain of a single pound on a fly rod is more exhausting to the fisherman than ten or even twenty times that pull on a tarpon rod, and I was glad when the camera man said he had used his last plate and offered to change places with me. Usually when plates were out we got rid of the fish as soon as we could, but this was an unusual fish, destined to hold long the record for an eight-ounce rod capture, if once we could slide it over the side of the little canoe. The craft might be swamped the next minute, but the record would be safe.

The tarpon noticed the new hand at the bellows and went over his repertoire brilliantly. He traveled a mile up the river in search of a place to hide from the human gadfly that worried him and sulked under a bank for some minutes before allowing himself to be coaxed out. He pranced down the stream to the bay, with occasional leaps by the way, and the captain struggled mightily every foot of the course to keep within the limits of the line. In the bay a new terror possessed him and he dashed about as if crazy.

He saw his fate in the thing that he couldn't shake off, as the creature of the forest knows when the wolf is on his track, and he exhausted himself in his panic. Then he rolled over and lay quietly on his back with gasping gills in apparent surrender while the canoe was paddled beside him.

"I'm afraid we'll capsize if I take it aboard," said the captain.

"Get it in the canoe first and capsize afterwards all you want, only don't move till I measure it," replied the camera man.

After the tarpon had been found to measure six feet six inches, the captain got a grip on the corner of its mouth, and lifting its head over the side of the canoe was about to slide it inside when a powerful stroke of the fish's tail sent the head outboard and the captain was given his choice between swamping the canoe or releasing the fish. He let the tarpon go, for which I abused him at the time, but forgave him later when I saw that the hook was still fast in the creature's mouth. It was many minutes before the captain got another chance at the fish, but when he had renewed his hold and was ready to haul it aboard he sang out to me:

"I'll hang on to him this time if he lands me in—Halifax, so look out for the pieces of your canoe!"

But the tarpon slid into the canoe without a flutter, and slipping under the thwarts lay flat in the bottom. The trouble came later when, the rod having been laid aside, camera man and captain worked together to get the slippery thing out from under the thwarts and overboard. They would probably have swamped the canoe anyhow, but the tarpon made the thing sure and secured his revenge by a flap of his tail that landed him in the bay with his tormentors. It was a fitting end to the adventure, for, after the final scrimmage, canoe and canoe men sadly needed the scrubbing they got in the nearby shallow water to which they swam.

We hit the top of the tarpon season at Turner's River, on the West Coast of Florida, and for three days the fish stood in line, waiting their turn like metropolitans seeking good seats at the opera or holding their places in the bread line. No sooner had we turned loose an exhausted tarpon than a fresh one presented itself for the vacant chair. Twenty tarpon a day was our score, of fish that ran from ten to thirty pounds each. Most of them were taken on the fly rod, for which they were too large, as their weight was light for a heavy rod in such blasé hands as ours were becoming by that time.

Much of the action of a fly rod is wasted with a fish of the tarpon type weighing over five pounds, and much time lost from the camera standpoint, since it is hard to hold the fish near the canoe. A stiff, single-action, tournament style of fly rod fits the agile baby tarpon down to the ground, while a withy, double-action article couldn't follow for a minute the fish's changes of mind.

"These fish are too little for the big rod, too big for the little rod, and we have nothing between," I observed to the camera man just after landing on a tarpon rod a ten-pound fish in as many minutes.

"Let's go down the coast," was the reply. "There are big fish in the big rivers and babies in the creeks at the head of Harney."

I agreed to this as I threw out a freshly baited hook and trolled for another ten pounder. But it was a tarpon of ten stone or more that struck before twenty feet of line had run out, and as the creature shot up toward the sky I shouted:

"There's a seven footer for you, the biggest tarp. of the trip!"

It may have been the biggest, but I shall never know for sure. I threw myself back on the rod with a force that would have slung a little fish to the horizon and my guaranteed rod snapped like glass. I hung on to the broken rod and the tarpon played me for a few minutes, after which he sailed away with half of my line as a trophy.

Before running down the coast we went back to the Storter store in search of a substitute for the broken rod. The captain said he could make a better rod than the old one out of anything, from a wagon tongue to a flag pole. We bought a heavy hickory hoe handle which looked unbreakable, and furnished it with extra fittings which I had on hand. As we sailed down the coast I mended the broken rod and we entered on the new campaign with three heavy tarpon rods in commission.

We were cruising in the land of the crustacean. There were reefs of oysters along the coast. Oyster bars guarded the mouths of the rivers and great bunches of the bivalves clung like fruit to the branches of the trees. Beneath us was one vast clam bed, and dropping our anchor we drove poles in the mud down which we climbed and to which we clung with one hand while digging clams out of the mud with the other. We gathered a hundred or more, as many as the most sanguine of us believed we could eat. They ranged in size from that of the little neck of New York to giant quahaugs, of which single specimens weighed over five pounds.

Our anchorage that night was beside the little pelican key that separates the mouths of Broad and Rodger's rivers, and we roasted clams on the beach beside the latter. It was the toss of a copper which stream we should fish in the morning. Their sources and mouths were the same in each case and a creek united their middles like the band of the Siamese twins. We chose Rodger's River because of its beauty, the great

THE BAIT WAS SEIZED BY A SPLENDID SPECIMEN OF THE SILVER KING.

I HAULED ON THE LINE TILL THE FISH WAS TWICE HIS LENGTH FROM ME, AND WAS TRYING TO HOLD HIM THERE.

royal palms that adorned it, and the tragic legends connected with its abandoned plantation, rotting house, and overgrown graves.

Big herons rose sluggishly from flooded banks before us and with hoarse cries flew up the river, dangling their preposterous legs. Fly-up-the-creeks flitted silently away, while lunatic snake birds, made crazy by worms in their brains, watched us from branches that overhung the stream, and when we were almost beneath them dropped into the water as awkwardly as if they had been shot.

We admired beautiful trees, great vines, fragrant flowers, and blossoming orchids as the tarpon bait was trolled from the trailing canoe, and from the mouth of the river to the cut-off no tarpon disturbed our meditations. Hurrying sharks showed huge fins above the surface, slowly rolling porpoises turned keen eyes upon us as they passed, otters lifted their little round heads, and a great manatee, frightened by a sudden glimpse of our outfit, left a long wake of swirls like those of an outgoing liner.

Crossing to Broad River by the crooked cut-off, we traveled a mile and a half to gain a third of that distance. Projecting roots held us back, overhanging branches brushed us harshly, while with bare faces we swept away scores of great spider habitations, suspended from bridges which their occupants had engineered across the stream. Yet I had little cause of complaint, since the only spiders that ran down my neck were the few that escaped the camera man, whose position in the bow of the leading craft gave him the first chance at the arachnids, or vice versa.

As there wasn't a tarpon in Rodger's River, we looked upon trolling down its companion stream as a mere formality, yet no sooner had I put out my line after turning down Broad River than the bait was seized by a splendid specimen of the silver king. The camera man missed the early leaps, for he had been slow in getting out his artillery, but after it had been brought into action he was kept busy. We were carried up into Broad River Bay, where the channels were so overhung with manatee grass that at every turn my line was loaded almost to the breaking point.

When the motor boat, maneuvering for position, got out of the middle of the channel, the propeller twisted a wad of the grass about the shaft and the motor stopped. Then Joe leaned over the stern of the boat, with head and arms under water as he tore at the clinging mass, while the camera man relieved his mind by energetic exhortation.

The tarpon led us through Broad River Bay to a series of deep channels which we had long known as the home of the manatee, several specimens of which we had captured there. The surrender of our quarry came after we had entered the broad, shallow, island-dotted bay that stretches from the heads of Broad, Rodger's, and Lossman's rivers across to the narrow strip of swamp prairie and forest that separates it from the Everglades.

After releasing the tarpon I fished no more till we were back in Broad River, when, again, on putting out my line, the bait was seized by a tarpon whose length we estimated at five feet since we never had a chance to measure it. The fish attended strictly to business, and after a few brilliant preliminary jumps, made straight for the cut-off, where, after turning a few corners and tying the line around some snags, it leaped joyously high in air, free of all bonds and in full possession of a valuable tarpon hook and a goodly section of costly line.

We traveled a mile down the river before throwing out another lure, and found ourselves in a tarpon town meeting. There were scores of them, leaping and cavorting, dashing hither and yon, and behaving as if at a big banquet, but it was a Barmecide feast, for not a food fish could be seen.

"Hang to 'em, if you can," called out the camera man as I baited my hook, "for I've had bad luck with the fish so far to-day."

"The next tarpon stays with me, or I go with him," was my reply, and the next minute one of the family was over my head, fiercely shaking his wide-open jaws to get rid of the hook. But the hook was fast and I hung to the line through the tarpon's first run, though the canoe was nearly capsized before the captain could head it for the flying fish. The thwarted creature, after three wild leaps, headed straight for the canoe, and diving under it brought the strain of his weight on the tip of the rod, which broke in two parts. I clung to the butt, and as the fish was of medium size soon brought it to the captain's hand, despite the broken tip.

We had now no rod nearer than the *Irene,* which was five miles distant, but the fish were in biting humor and the opportunity was not to be lost. There was a hand line in the motor boat, and I handed it to the captain, for my muscles were aching, and I thought to rest them with the paddle. The broken rod was left with the camera man, for both the hand line and the captain were strong, mixups with big tarpon certain, and a swim in the river the probable outcome.

One tarpon turned back so quickly, after towing us steadily for a quarter of a mile or so, that I couldn't change the course of the canoe till the fish had torn a dozen yards of line from the captain's hands and was that far behind us. The captain pulled fiercely, and the creature turned again and seemed to leap at me with wide-open jaws. Its weight fell on my arm and the side of the canoe, which would have capsized but for some quick balancing by my companion. Thereafter that afternoon the captain played the fish a bit less savagely, for which I was not sorry.

I had no dread of being swamped by a tarpon. It had happened before and would happen again, probably that very day, but I wanted it over, and expecting it every minute for hours got on my nerves.

It was late when the crisis came and we were near the mouth of the river, for each fish we struck had carried us down the stream with the ebbing tide. It was a tarpon of the largest size that turned away from an approaching hammerhead shark, and swimming beside the canoe shot high in the air directly above it.

I held my paddle without moving, waiting, waiting for the canoe to sink under me as it had done before. The captain rose to his feet as the tarpon turned in the air, and by a seeming act of volition threw himself clear of the craft.

"Glad I didn't wait for the spill," said the camera man as he turned the plate holder in his camera, "but I don't see how he missed you. What's become of the fish? Can't you get him to do it again?"

The tarpon had escaped. He had given the line a turn about the canoe, and of course it had broken.

The *Irene* was in sight off the mouth of the river as I tied a new hook on the broken line and told the captain I would troll till we reached the boat. But a tarpon lay in wait for me among the oyster reefs, and, after he was fast, started back up the river. He was a hard fighter and so erratic in his dashes as he tacked up the stream that every few minutes I had to give him line to keep from capsizing.

"Can't you get that fish nearer the canoe?" shouted the camera man. "How can I photograph you when you're a mile apart?"

"I'll take him inside the canoe, if you want," I replied, though I had no notion of doing it.

I hauled on the line till the fish was twice his length from me and was trying to hold him there when the creature dived till the line ran straight down. Then it loosened, and like an arrow from a bow something shot up from the depths, dashing gallons of water in my face as it passed. I couldn't look up, but I wondered what would happen. Just as I concluded that this tarpon, like the last, had cleared the canoe in his fall, the craft gave a twist, a roll, and plunged me, shoulder first, beneath the surface!

It was a few yards' swim to an oyster reef, where the captain and I reëmbarked and were soon paddling for the *Irene.* It isn't worth while to change the few garments one wears when fishing for tarpon just because one has been overboard, so we sat on the deck as we were and ate clams on the half shell while Joe made clam stew for a second course and gave us our choice of stewed smoked turtle or clams for the next one.

Photograph by Grace E. Mounts.

WHERE MINNOWS ABOUND.

21.
Crossing the Everglades in a Power Boat (1907)

The Motor-Boat towed us through Channels of clear Water

Crossing the Everglades in a Power-Boat

BY A. W. DIMOCK

Illustrations by Julian A. Dimock

"THREE days, me think so," said Tommy Osceola, when asked how quickly he could cross the Glades to Miami in his canoe; but he only shook his head negatively when I inquired how long it would take a white man. The camera-man and I had decided on the trip, and I asked Tommy if he would go with us, when the trader chipped in:

"What do you want of a guide? Don't you know where the sun rises?"

We fell in at once with the enchanting suggestion of our Florida friend, and invited him to join us in crossing the Everglades with no other guide than a compass, to which he nodded instant acceptance. We arranged to take the two boys from our cruising-boat, and with launch, skiff, and little Canadian canoe go down to Osceola's camp in the Ten Thousand Islands. There we would borrow an Indian canoe for the trip, leaving the launch and skiff with the Indians until our return. As we were about to start, the sand of our sailor-boy ran out, and, in the language of the hunter-boy, he "skipped his job"; but his place was quickly taken by an older sailor, who had cruised and hunted with us in former years. As our purpose was really to cross the Everglades, we dispensed with such conventional obstacles as tent equipments, prepared foods, medical and surgical outfits, and big armaments, and told our hunter-boy, who bossed the galley, to put up a spoon, cup, fork, and plate for each of us; to take a coffee-pot and frying-pan, and pack enough bacon, corn-meal, and coffee to feed us for a week. An old single-barrelled shotgun, which we took along on the chance that we might get bird-hungry, was found convenient to blow off the heads of venomous snakes, but was not used otherwise. Each of us had a blanket, mosquito-bar, and rubber sheet, and, generally speaking, a change of underclothing.

As getting some real pictures was part of the project, we were liberal with the camera-man, and he filled what space was left in the canoe with two big cameras, plate-holders, and heavy boxes of $6\frac{1}{2} \times 8\frac{1}{2}$ glass plates. The population of Everglade, consisting of our friend's family, turned out to witness the departure of the flotilla in tow of the power-boat, in which the captain held the tiller-ropes, while the camera-man acted as engineer. The skiff, which was next in line, contained the Florida man, the writer, poles, provisions, and our personal bundles; while stretched out at full length on top of the loaded canoe our hunter-boy enjoyed his *otium cum dignitate.* Our course lay among the Ten Thousand Islands, through Chokoloskee Bay, Turners River, and bays Sunday, Huston, and Chevalier. We camped on a plantation which bore the name of the last, but had been recently abandoned by its late owner, who had gone to a country where the titles to property are clearer than in the unsurveyed Ten Thousand Islands. We respected the padlock on the door of the house, and lay on the ground in front of it, where my slumbers were undisturbed until dawn, when a possum sought to share my bar. We here added to our stores by gathering a few avocado pears, a bunch of bananas, some stalks of sugar-cane, a few sweet potatoes, and a lot of guavas. Some plantations in the Ten Thousand Islands have their private graveyards, but all have histories, and as we continued our placid voyage my companion told me of the one we had left, which was known by the name of its founder. He was a harmless individual who once weakly consented to join two of his associates, whose names have been too numerous to mention, in arresting his nearest neighbor, one Wilson, upon a bogus warrant. Arresting Wilson upon a genuine warrant had long been recognized as a form of suicide, and it is believed that nervousness arising from his acquaintance with the man induced the leader of the trio to begin the service of the warrant at long range. The return shot neatly shaved off one side of his mustache, and he fled, followed by his fellow conspirators. Mr. Wilson chased them as far as Cape Sable in his boat, and is believed to be still on the lookout for their return. He is said to wax indignant at the suggestion that his course was justified by the bogus character of the warrant. and insists that his action was quite uninfluenced by that feature of the case. The ringleader must have experienced a change of heart, since Lieutenant Willoughby, who employed him as a guide despite his reputation as a bad man, writes of him in his *Across the Everglades* that he often sat up an hour beyond his usual time that he might tuck the lieutenant in bed before retiring.

Early in the day we entered a narrow creek completely covered by branches of trees that interlaced overhead, and so crooked that the power-boat at the head and the canoe at the foot of our procession were usually travelling in opposite directions. During two miles of snake-like progress to Alligator Bay, dragging over roots, pulling under branches, smashing an occasional wasps' nest and striking at impertinent moccasins, we saw more varieties of orchids than I have found in a single locality elsewhere, including specimens colorless and full of color, scentless and filled with odor that made the surrounding air heavy with their fragrance; some garbed sombrely as a Quakeress, and others costumed to rival a Queen of Sheba.

On one of the keys of Alligator Bay is the principal plume-bird rookery left in Florida. It had been shot a few days before our visit and twelve hundred dollars' worth of plumes taken. The mother birds had been shot, the young birds had starved.

Of important rookeries, this is one of the least accessible, and birds nest here when driven from others. If a trustworthy warden could be found and kept alive here for six months in each year, a long step would be taken toward perpetuating two or three species of the most beautiful of birds, now far along on the road to extinction. Probably two wardens would be better than one, for the sake of preserving their species also from extinction in this land, where the Court of Appeals is a shotgun. In continuing our cruise eastward we cut our way through two miles of an even crookeder creek, across which many trees had been felled by plume-hunters from north of the rookery, who sought thus to block the road of their rivals from south of the bay, or of a possible wandering game-warden. A few more miles of navigation through creeks, lakes, rivers, and among keys brought us to Possum Key, with the area of a good-sized room, where for many months an escaped convict lived with his family, while officers of the law sought far and wide for him with varying degrees of diligence. At Onion Key—a Lossmans River landmark — we ate grapes and figs while coffee was being made for our luncheon. The afternoon was spent exploring in the Glades the many trails leading from what we thought was Rocky Creek, vainly looking for signs of the Indian camp of which we were in search. When night came we were miles from the nearest camping-ground we knew, and our choice seemed to lie between sleeping in our boats or searching through the blackness of the night for a bit of dry land that might not exist. At this crisis the captain remembered having seen near the river some banana plants, indicating the presence of land above the water. We waded to the place, and by beating down high grass and weeds made room to spread our blankets and stretch our bars. In carrying the baggage to camp we groped our way fifty yards through a thicket and waded in the mud half leg-deep.

I was glad that the moccasin I stepped on turned out to be a bullfrog, and that the crawling things that got under my bar didn't prove venomous. A family of rats running around and under us disturbed our slumbers during the night, and when one woke me up by prolonged squeaking near my ear I hoped a snake had got him and that I would get the snake in the morning. We held a council of war beneath our bars, definitely abandoned search for the Indian camp, and decided to tote the power-boat all the way to Miami. In the morning, by

POLING THE LAUNCH THROUGH SHALLOW WATER

channels which our manatee-hunt had made familiar, we found the head of Rodgers River, and descending to its mouth, sailed three miles down the coast to the mouth of Harney River. Miami now lay sixty-five miles east-northeast of us. Twelve miles of this were made easy by the river and an intermediate bay, for of them we knew every fork, bight, bunch of grass, and island; and as the sun set and a few acres of bonnet stopped the motor, we were within a quarter of a mile of the Glades and half that distance of a beautiful Indian camping-ground surrounded by lime and lemon trees. The approach to this site was overgrown, and when my Florida friend and I reached it, after wading through knee-deep water among weeds that grew far above our heads, we found it occupied by a big rattlesnake which was much alive and most musical. While keeping the reptile at bay with oars, waiting for the shot-gun which the camera-man was bringing us, we estimated his length, in the hope that he would prove worthy of being captured alive for the Zoo in New York. Big as he was, he failed to qualify for that honor, and we blew his head to pieces. His mate could be heard rattling in the near-by thicket, but this was so dense and so filled with the thorny branches of the untrimmed lime-trees that we didn't trouble her. I was sorry afterward, when the darkness of the night brought to my memory gruesome tales of venomous serpents following the trail of the bodies of their mates, dragged with murderous purpose across the beds of innocent victims, and reflected that one of my hips was resting in the hole in the earth which the shot from my gun had made as it slew one of the pair. In the morning we gathered from the ground a bushel of limes, to correct, if necessary, the lime-water of the Glades, and as we added them to our stores I thought with disrespect of the widow's cruse, which only maintained its original supply, while under our system each day doubled it.

Here our real journey began. We looked out upon the Everglades, and innocent enough they appeared. Miami was fifty-three miles east-northeast of us as the crow flies. But we were not crows. The only record of crossing the Glades at this point which I had seen was by Lieutenant Willoughby, and he had treated the subject with much seriousness. But the lieutenant was burdened with official responsibility, a cargo of scientific machinery, a heavy armament, and a weight of ammunition that suggested provision for another Seminole war.

Climbing a Tree for Observations

In 1883 the *Times-Democrat* sent an expedition through to Okeechobee from Harney River, but I had not seen its report.

In 1892 one of the chief officials of the East Coast Railway, with an engineer and twenty men, conducted a *de luxe* surveying expedition from Fort Myers to Miami. Unfortunately the surveying portion of

HEADS OF THE RIVERS CHOKED BY "BONNETS," A KIND OF WATER-LILY

the work had to be suspended because of unexpected obstacles and privations, even the leaders of the expedition having been compelled, it was stated, to sleep in wet clothing.

We endeavored to feel impressed as we plunged into this mysterious region. But the motor-boat towed us gayly along in bright sunlight through channels of clear-flowing water, among beautiful keys, over meadows covered with the big white-petalled, pink-tinged pond-lily of my New England memory. Sometimes strands of heavy saw-grass drove us north, or shoaling water forced us to the east, but we kept a running account of our digressions, and compensated for them as we found opportunity. We lunched on a key of cocoa-plums, myrtle, and sweet-bay, where we found about a square foot of earth for a camp-fire. I sat on a log, with my feet in the water, exchanging glances with a water-moccasin coiled on a root within six feet of me as I ate my lunch. It became more and more difficult to keep the propeller free from grass, and we finally gave up its use almost entirely and worked steadily pushing with oars and poles. The best of these poles, which had been obtained from an Indian, had a wooden foot formed like a lady's shoe with a French or cowboy heel. The heel held on the coral rock, which is never far from the surface in the Glades, and the foot sank but little in the soft ground and heavy grass. That night we found no key with land enough for a camp-fire, but the boy managed to heat some coffee on a pile of brush, and we slept in our boats. It was not convenient to rig our mosquito-bars, and we dispensed with them, as we found the pests so scarce in the Glades as to be hardly worth considering. The captain curled up in the motor-boat; the camera-man slept on oars laid across its gunwales; our Florida friend and I were comfortable in the bottom of our skiff, where the croaking of frogs had just soothed me to sleep, when a tropical thunder-storm burst upon us and half drowned us before we could get up. The hunter-boy had shown woodcraft by stretching his bar among the trees and piling up branches enough to keep him out of the water beneath him, while the canvas top of his mosquito-bar measurably protected him from the torrent from above, and if the disturbance awakened him, he gave no evidence of it. When the storm had gone by, my companion said he wanted to be dry once more, and put on his extra undergarments. Before he was fairly in them the black clouds came back and it rained worse than before. The next day we were in the water a good deal. The motor-boat had to be pushed and hauled. The open water, which we followed when possible, often led so far from our course that we had to drag our boats over water that was shoal and through grass that tugged against us. During this day our work was hard as that of pleasure-seekers in the North Woods or campers among the Canadian lakes and rivers. A bit of dry land was secured for a midday camp by blowing the head off of a cottonmouth moccasin which had preempted it. We discovered in the afternoon a beautiful camping-ground of Indian antecedents, half an acre in extent, dry, level as a floor, covered with pawpaws and fringed with wild grapes and cocoa-plums. Piles of shells of turtle and snail, bones of deer, and remnants of fish told how life might be maintained in the Glades. That afternoon our course was guided by the dead top of a tall mastic-tree, at the foot of which was an Indian camp with the fire still burning.

We camped beside it among pumpkin-vines, and ate roasted taniers and pumpkins which we gathered from the little field where grew oranges, bananas, corn, and sugar-cane. The song of birds awakened me in the morning, and I recognized cardinal, king, and mocking birds, and saw one horned owl, several black hawks, and many crows. There was a greater variety of trees and higher land than we had seen since leaving the west coast. From the top of the mastic-tree a fringe of pines could be seen to the east, and I

Slow Progress

fancied once that I heard the whistle of a locomotive. Soon after starting we saw the smoke of Miami factories and an occasional Indian in the distance. The water grew shoal as we worked toward the coast, and the iron shoe of our launch continually pounded the upthrusting pillars of coral. We turned back often for little distances, and pushed and pulled the power-boat for hours, stumbling along the uneven, rock-based, grass-covered formation. We tried to lunch on a promising bit of ground on a small key, but finally yielded possession to a few million big ants who seemed to possess some squatter interest in the property. In the afternoon we met an Indian, who was spearing turtle and fish with much skill. He told us that his village was "three miles," and although it was off our course we invited ourselves to visit it; and as the water and grass permitted, towed the whole outfit, including the Indian and his canoe, with the motor-boat. The village was attractive of its kind, consisting of three or four large buildings, neatly thatched, with large tables three feet above the ground, which served as floors. There were clocks (not running) on the walls and sewing-machines on the tables or floors, while accounts hanging on a hook showed frequent dealings with a Miami tradesman. The little colony consists of four or five families and less than thirty members. The men wear shirt-waists and bare legs, the women beads above, skirts below, and a middle zone which seems to have been forgotten.

At night we camped near the village, and I made my bed in the lower end of an Indian canoe that was twenty-five feet long and lay upon the sloping bank of a little canal. My companion slept just above me, and must have dammed the rain, when the usual deluge came suddenly in the night, with his bar, blanket, and himself; for when he got up, the rush of water nearly swept me away; but I was getting used to this, and only feared that I might get dry some day and take cold from the exposure.

We cooked breakfast by the Indians' fire, and then, after a short run with the motor-boat, poled leisurely for the last few miles, during which the current of the water on which we floated changed from the southwest course it had maintained since we left the west coast to about the opposite direction. This would suggest that the maximum elevation of the southern Everglades may be measured by the fall in its course of the Miami River, and that the current stories of eighteen feet of elevation above sea-level may be looked upon as fairy-tales.

It was late when we found the south fork of the Miami River, and dark when we sat down to a square meal at a hotel. The return trip around Cape Sable, although under power, was more trying than the one through the Glades. Shoal water and the sticky blue mud bothered us at times, and the closing of a creek by the railway added many miles to our course, mosquitoes and sand-flies afflicted us, and our supply of fresh water ran out, producing in all of us, when we discovered it, a sudden and intense thirst.

Around East, Middle, and Northwest capes we encountered waves so high that their tops gently lapped over the coamings of the power-boat, while we in the skiff bailed continually, and only the little canoe kept its contents dry. During an all-night run up the coast a rain-squall flooded us and stopped the motor, while the whole flotilla tossed about in the darkness and rain and drifted seaward for an anxious quarter of an hour, even the imperturbable hunter-boy remarking, "Looks like we've got to swim."

But we had crossed the Everglades in four days with no other guide than a compass, travelling seventy miles to make fifty-three, which seems to us like an air-line under the circumstances.

I estimated that from Everglade to Miami across the Glades we travelled 146 miles in six and a half days, and from Miami to Everglade around the cape 148 miles in three days and one night.

We saw no game during the trip and the track of but one deer. Two alligators and a good many turtle appeared. Birds were scarce, but there were enough to keep one from being hungry if other food gave out. Fish abounded from coast to coast. In most of the deeper channels tarpon could be seen. Big-mouthed bass, called trout in Florida, were plentiful, as were gar, bream, and several other varieties, and a few mullet were seen.

THE RETURN TRIP PROVIDED ALL THE EXCITEMENT OF THE JOURNEY

Our experience was that one meets delay in the Everglades, but not danger. The water is pure and sweet and food plentiful enough. Limpkins taste like young turkeys; all members of the heron family are likely to be found in the Glades and most other birds are fair food. Snails, which abound, are delicacies when called periwinkles; you would pay a dollar a portion in New York for the frogs that are yours for the catching in the Glades. There are plenty of turtle, which possess all the good qualities, except cost, of the green turtle or the terrapin. A few fruits can be had for dessert—cocoa-plums, custard-apples, and pawpaws,—while the leaves of the sweet-bay make a fragrant beverage. Crossing the Everglades of Florida in a canoe is not an adventure, it is a picnic.

22.
Cruising on the Gulf Coast of Florida (1907)

Cruising on the Gulf Coast of Florida

BY A. W. DIMOCK

IT is now a score of years since the hospitable *Karena,* known to the natives as "The Ark," threaded most of the waterways and ran aground on all the bars of the west coast of Florida, from Cedar Keys to Key West. It was the prototype of the cruising house-boat of that coast of to-day, and, as its owner with prophetic instinct once remarked, lacked only a little steam-tender to run its errands. In place of the *Karena* we now see floating houses, with every attribute of a home, from a *chef* to a canary, from a library to a pet cat, with sixty-horse-power engines in the basement, in which the owner changes his residence while he sleeps, and only knows where he is living when his captain tells him. Glittering launches, polished dinghies, and a uniformed crew go with this outfit, which suggests yachting rather than the cruising I care for. Stately yachts at stated times rattle their anchor-chains just within Boca Grande, while near by their chartered craft lodge the guides who know the tricks of the tides and the tarpon and reduce the labor of the fisherman to a minimum. I have seen a well-known yachtsman quietly enjoy his magazine and cigar on the deck of his boat while his guide trolled for tarpon within a few hundred feet. When a tarpon was hooked, the sportsman laid aside his magazine and was rowed out to the skiff of his guide, from which he captured what was left of the fish. There are house-boats of simple construction which are moved about by tugs, and often anchored for the season in one place. They make inexpensive homes with attractive features, but they are not cruisers. Occasionally, a should-be cruiser becomes conventionalized, and goes back and forth from Fort Myers, to Punta Rasa, and Boca Grande, fishing in orthodox fashion on the predetermined dates.

The interest of a cruise is often in inverse ratio to its cost. Two young men, with some knowledge of sailing and a genuine love for the camp-fire, arrived on the west coast of Florida with two months in time and two hundred dollars to spend. They bought a sloop with a small skiff for one hundred dollars, enlarged and fitted up the cabin at a cost of seventy-five dollars, invested twenty-five dollars in supplies, and buried themselves among the Ten Thousand Islands. Two months later they emerged with clothing in tatters, faces and arms red as the Indians with whom they had consorted, bodies rugged, and stores of experience sufficient to illuminate their lives. They sold their outfit at cost, reducing their net expenses for two months to the twenty-five dollars paid for supplies, to which the wilderness had contributed, without cost, fish, game, and fruit.

My latest cruise began as a family affair, with the girl, the camera-man, and a captain. Another girl was needed, so we borrowed the tree-lady, who, having just evolved from her inner consciousness a tree-book, which was counted authoritative, was now anxious to see some real trees.

Our equipment was the result of compromises between the requirements of deep-water cruising and shallow-bay exploration, and between cabin capacity and seaworthiness. It consisted of a yawl-rigged, flat-bottomed boat 37×14, with a draught of three feet, a cabin 20×12×6 feet, two skiffs, and a small launch. Fittings and furnishings were severely practical, and included dark room, tools for all ordinary repair-work, and fishing, hunting, and photographic outfits.

Starting from Marco, we gave the tree-lady her choice between tarpon and crocodiles, and as she selected the former, sailed for Charlotte Harbor and the tarpon resorts of Captiva Pass and Boca

THE HOUSEBOAT AT ANCHOR

Grande, where the season was at its height. On the first day at Captiva Pass the tarpon scored. The tree-lady was in a skiff with the camera-man, making tarpon jump while he photographed them; the girl was on Captiva beach gathering shells, leaving me to fish by myself, which I did by placing my tarpon-rod on the seat beside me, with the bait trolling behind the skiff as I rowed in the swift current of the pass. There came a highly pitched buzz of the reel, a wild leap six feet in air of a frightened tarpon, and my rod flew over the stern of the skiff, leaving a straight wake to the Gulf. I fancy that the whole outfit—rod, massive reel, and six hundred feet of costly line—was an exhibit that night at some club of tarpon devoted to the baiting of fishermen. I should like to see the legend attached to it, to know the estimate of my weight, and to hear the account of the contest, that I might compare the stories told by fish with those told about them.

We were fishing for the camera, and when the hooked tarpon ceased to pose they were turned loose, with a single exception. The tree-lady wanted some tarpon scales big enough to weigh the fish-stories she was preparing for her family. At Boca Grande we anchored north of the pass, safe from everything but a gale from the northeast, which is what came to us with the going down of the sun. A strong tide held the boat in the trough of the sea, and a wicked roll caused havoc in the cabin, where a bottle of oil breaking on the floor made walking thereon distressing. As the tide rushed past, it created a wake of phosphorescent fire, and an occasional wave breaking over us bathed the boat in liquid moonshine, while filling the cockpit with water that had to be bailed out. We hoisted the jigger to hold the boat across the seas, and gave the hurricane-anchor a few more fathoms of chain. Our captain was on shore unable to join us. Four times he dragged his skiff through the surf and tried to row to us, but four times he was capsized and swept back. As the night wore on, the launch filled and sank, and the remaining skiff was swamped, broke her painter, and was washed ashore. In the morning the captain succeeded in reaching us, although his skiff sank under him just as he caught the line we threw him. We made tackle fast to the launch, lifted it until it could be bailed out, and then hoisting a sail with many reefs, spent an exciting quarter of an hour in clawing away from the beckoning beach. Following the storm, the fishing at Boca Grande was marvellous. The mile-wide pass was filled with minnows by the thousand million, making dark patches upon the water, often many acres in extent. Among them porpoises rolled, thousands of tarpon leaped, the fins of hundreds of great sharks cut lanes through them, uncountable cavalli, Spanish mackerel, bluefish, ladyfish, and other predatory small fry, devouring and being devoured, beat the water into surflike waves; while, moved by a single impulse, here, there, and everywhere, minnows by the yard or acre were leaping three feet in the air, filling it with rainbow-tinted masses of spray. Everywhere the water was covered with dying minnows and spangled throughout with their scales. As our skiff was rowed among them, tarpon leaped about it, drenching us with water and throwing hundreds of minnows and other little fish into the boat. A small fish, which had fallen aboard, was put upon a tarpon-hook, and as it dropped overboard was swallowed by a jack-fish, which in turn was seized by a tarpon. A great shark took up the trail of the tarpon, and a moment later had bitten him in two, at the same time striking the skiff so vicious a blow that I was glad to remember that, contrary to current superstition.

Cocoa and Date Palms near Shell Mounds
Relic of the Aborigines

SHARK PURSUING TARPON

A fraction of a second lost a record picture. The wake of the pursuing shark may be seen, but the camera was too late to catch the fish himself

the shark in this country never attacks a human being.

Tarpon-fishing with the camera is the apotheosis of sport. There is yet to be discovered anything more picturesque and thrilling than the leap of the near-by tarpon, filling the air with prismatic drops, and the gleaming silver of its gracefully contorted body brilliantly reflecting the rays of the sun.

Only less spectacular, because of its Lilliputian scale, is the leap of the lady-fish, which rises to a fly and gives an acrobatic performance that makes the best work of any known game-fish look very tame. Sea-trout, Spanish mackerel, channel-bass, and other game-fish kept the larder full and gave continuous sport at every pass in Charlotte Harbor and Pine Island Sound from Gasparilla to Punta Rasa. Half an hour with a landing-net on the shore would fill a bucket with crabs, while on any moonlight night from May to July great turtles could be found crawling on the beach, and turned over for stews and steaks, or followed to their crawls for the one hundred and thirty to one hundred and eighty eggs which would be there in the morning. We beach-combed for shells from Gasparilla to Big Marco Pass—all but the tree-lady, who explained that she was under contract to produce a standard work of reference on conchology and must approach the subject with a mind that was blank. Later when she sailed for the north from Marco, we turned south for the crocodile country. From Coon Key to Sandfly Pass our course lay outside the keys, and we ran before a gale under jib and jigger, landing disgracefully among the bushes when we tried to stem the tide that flowed from Chokloskee Bay. Here we found a party of Seminole Indians, paved the way for a visit to their camp, and obtained a full-grown wild-cat, or lynx. We made a cage for "Tom," who day by day grew more ferocious and had to be fed at the end of a stick. He nearly ate up his cage in his efforts to get free, but when his door was opened, hesitated long before he came out. He then walked slowly, growling at everybody, but so surprised by the indifference with which he was regarded that he soon began to make advances, and finally laid a tentative paw upon the hand of the captain as he stood at the wheel. Thereafter he became friendly, sometimes too friendly, occasionally playfully jumping upon any one who happened to be sleeping on deck, which, until we got used to it, was exciting.

From Pavilion Key south the coast is one vast bank of clams, perennially inviting the cruiser to go overboard and tread for them. One night when anchored with light tackle a few miles below Pavilion, a gale from the southwest dragged the anchor, a big wave lifted us, and at the very top of a spring-tide dropped us on a high coral reef. The next morning we were many yards from water, with the chances that we were settled for a month; but happily a favoring wind that day raised the water enough to enable us to haul the boat back into her element. As our cruise led us through crooked channels in the shallow water of the Bay of Florida, we often ran aground, but by promptly going overboard could usually push off into deeper water. Once we had to dig the boat out, loosening the mud under it with a hoe and washing it away by a current from the propeller of the launch.

At Madeira Hammock we anchored for a crocodile-hunt, in the interest of the camera, and for ten days in skiffs explored creeks and bays in the pursuit. Once we turned aside to follow with a harpoon three big fins travelling tandem that belonged to a thirteen-foot sawfish, whose thousand pounds propelled a broad four-foot saw, armed with fifty-two teeth, through schools of smaller fish. He belonged to the detested shark family, and we wasted no sympathy on him as he towed us at racing speed through a mile of creek and bayou. We caught a number of crocodiles, but their story belongs to the camera-man. We took with us for shipment to the Bronx Zoological Gardens, at Bronx Park in New York, one ten-foot specimen which we had captured in his cave, and sailed for Marco, where the camera-man left us for New York. On the way up the coast the cat and the crocodile quarrelled, and to save the eyes of the saurian we put him overboard one evening with a rope around his body. During the night he died—mysteriously. The lynx swam ashore in response to the crowing of a cock, and perished in a hen-roost, but not mysteriously. Both had been prematurely promised to the Zoo in New York, and I was mortified; so I visited a rookery, captured and shipped a dozen pelicans for the Zoo, and again sailed for the crocodile country. We started on Friday, wherefore the girl predicted disaster, and reminded us thereof on the following day when a heavy rain-squall struck us, shut us up in semi-darkness and proceeded to box the compass with the boat. When the squall got through with us we were under bare poles, with the jib our only hoistable sail. Two days later at Madeira Hammock I stood again, harpoon-pole in hand, in the bow of the skiff, which my perspiring boatman patiently sculled among the keys, over the flats, and through the labyrinthic rivers that lie between the Bay of Florida and the saw-grass of the Everglades. The harpoon was simply a pointed bit of barbed steel, only capable of penetrating one inch beyond the barb, and intended merely to maintain communication with the quarry until it could be secured by other means.

One morning, just after we had started on our daily cruise, a series of swirls in the water near us, the language of which was then unfamiliar, seemed to tell of a frightened crocodile and that the hunt was on. We followed the zigzagging trail of muddy water as fast as we could scull and pole, getting occasional glimpses of a fleeing something, until the full view of it under the bow of the skiff gave me the chance I was seeking. As the harpoon struck a broad back, which was not that of a crocodile, the creature rose above the surface, and a big beaverlike tail deluged me with half a barrel of water as it struck and nearly swamped the skiff, and told me that I had at last found the manatee which I had vainly hunted during many years. For hours we chased the creature, keeping a light strain on the harpoon-line, frightening him as he came up to breathe, until, exhausted, he rose more and more frequently, and I made a score of unsuccessful casts of a lasso at this specimen of the wild cattle of the sea. Finally the manatee came to the surface to breathe so near the skiff that I put my left arm around his neck as far as it would go and tried to slip the noose over his head with my right. The sudden lifting of his head threw me upon his back, while a twist of his big tail sent me sprawling. We were swamped four times while working the manatee into shallow water, where we got overboard, fastened a line around him, and soon had him under control, although when the captain got astride of the creature he was promptly made to

Looking for Shells along the Beach

turn a back somersault. Docile as our captive had become, he was yet eleven feet long, of massive proportions, and a weight which was difficult to handle. We tore the seats out of the skiff, sank it, and succeeded in getting the creature over it. Then, having bailed out the water, we were paddling the overladen craft out in the bay, when a cataclysm left us swimming side by side, while a submerged skiff was being towed Gulfward by a rejoicing manatee. We soon recaptured and persuaded him into shallow water, where I herded him while the captain went to the big boat for an anchor and cable, with which we made our captive fast, giving him two hundred feet of rope in an excellent sea-cow pasture.

We were now candidates for a dungeon and liable to a big fine because of our unlawful detention of a highly protected mammal, so we sailed for Miami in pursuit of an *ex post facto* permit. The authorities were good to me when convinced of the educational destiny of the manatee, and in a week I returned with permits in my pocket, promises of free transportation by rail and steamer to the New York Aquarium, telegrams of congratulation from the Zoo people, and lumber for a tank for the manatee, only to find no trace of anchor, cable, or captive. Our boat had been struck by lightning in Miami, but the shock to our nerves, although serious, was light in comparison with this.

For a day we followed the zigzag trail of the anchor flukes, through a water glass over half a mile of the bottom of the bay, until we came upon the anchor, cable, and worn-through harness from which the manatee had escaped. I returned to Marco; here I left the girl, took aboard gasoline for a thousand miles' trip, four weeks' provisions for two, and sailed south with my boatman to capture a manatee. We explored the waterways between the

Everglades and the Gulf from Capes Romane to Sable. We sailed up broad rivers which narrowed until the bowsprit plunged into the bushes at every tack and the towed skiff gathered oysters from overhanging mangrove branches as it swung against the bank. We followed the contracting channels with the launch, until we were flying at full speed through crooked creeks, with bushes from the banks sweeping our craft on either side. When the branches closed over the stream, we dragged the skiff under them to the everglades or the end of the creek. We struck waterspout weather off Shark River, when conical clouds sent swirling tails dancing over the surface of the water, which they sometimes touched and drew upward in huge swaying columns. The next day our boat lay becalmed at the mouth of the Rogers River, which we explored in the launch.

As we started, graceful frigate-pelicans floated high above us with motionless wings, while on the water about us their awkward namesakes filled pouches with food for their families, and flew homeward with the curious intermittent strokes peculiar to these birds. The round head and bright eyes of the grass-eating green turtle bubbled up for a moment above the water, in pleasing contrast with the grosser head of his loggerhead cousin. Water-turkeys dropped heavily in the river as we passed, then quickly thrust snakelike heads above its surface to gaze at us. Herons, big and little, blue, white, and green, flapped lazily out of our way with discordant cries; brown curlews, roseate spoonbills, and white ibises sat undisturbed upon near-by trees; egrets and long whites forgot the bitter lessons that man's cupidity and woman's vanity had taught them, and even a monkey-faced owl, big and white, unknowing how rare a specimen he was, turned goggle-eyes upon the gun beside me. At the head of the river a tropical storm burst upon us, followed by a calm, and filled the western sky with massive clouds wonderfully colored, which were duplicated in the mirror of the water, until the illusion of a sky beneath us of infinite depth made me cling to the boat for dizziness. At the end of a long vista the middle ground of slim palmetto

THE PET WILDCAT

CRANES FEEDING ON MUD-FLATS

and towering royal palms completed an unforgettable picture.

We had explored Lossmans River to the Everglades, and were cruising the bays near its head, when, about dusk, we saw a big rattlesnake swimming towards a mangrove key. To cut him off compelled us to run the launch full speed into the key. The skiff in tow came surging up beside us, and the snake was between the two boats. We got the snake in the skiff, where the captain held him down with an oar until I had him safely by the neck. After extracting the fangs of the reptile, which was six and a half feet long and had ten rattles, I tied him in the boat to be skinned for mounting the next morning. Sometimes, as we cruised, the big eyes of a wondering deer gazed upon us from a bit of meadow; once I snapped the camera-shutter on a black face with white eyeballs, framed in an opening in the mangrove bushes, and on the same day in the depth of the wilderness we exchanged nods of half recognition with an alligator-hunter upon whose head was a price.

The days left us were few. Sweet bay-leaves had supplanted coffee, palmetto-cabbage was our vegetable, cocoa-plums, custard-apples, wild limes and lemons our fruit, and hour by hour we measured the gasoline left in the tank. One morning, with scant two inches in the launch, I estimated that we could go through Shark to Harney River, up that to the Everglades, and return. Far up the river we went, among beautiful keys, between richly wooded banks, past Golgotha camps of alligator-hunters and trappers of otter; in channels choked with moss and grass, which had to be cleared from the propeller every few minutes; along shores covered with wading birds; over waters alive with alligators and thickly dotted with the heads of fresh-water terrapin, until the launch was stopped by a solid mass of lily-pads, covering the stream and held in place by stems eight feet long, through which startled alli-

SUNSET OVER THE GULF

gators made their way along the river-bed, setting the pads above to dancing mysteriously. Forcing our way in the skiff through half a mile of pads, we reached the Everglades, and following an Indian trail, pushed far out on its surface for a final interview with a region which, although desolate, was yet strangely fascinating. When but a mile of our return trip was left, a frightened manatee, just ahead of our launch, rolled his body half out of water, like a porpoise, and throwing his tail in the air, started down the river. This was our last chance, and we followed his every turn. When he headed up-stream to escape us, we were so near that again he leaped half out of water, and soon was so exhausted that he rose for breath every few seconds. My hopes, which had died, were resurrected, and already I was drawing up the skiff for the final act, when the engine stopped, with its last drop of gasoline, and the manatee-chase was ended.

As we silently poled the launch homeward, my mind ran over the results of the hunt. We had seen a dozen manatee and had a calling acquaintance with half that number. We were familiar with their slightest appearance above the water and with the signs they left beneath it. We had seen them as Romeos and Juliets, and often when within a few feet of one had only been thwarted by the darkness of the water which in the rainy season pours from the cypress and mangrove swamps. A tiller-rope broken during the excitement of a quick turn had saved one from probable capture, and as I remembered that an impulse of emotional insanity had held my hand when a mother manatee with an unweaned calf pressed close to her side rose beside me, I thought with bitterness of the poet who wrote, "The quality of mercy is not strained." But I knew where the creatures lived, and when we reached our boat, just as the stars came out, I had determined that in the hunt for a manatee it was only the first chapter that had closed.

23.

Along the Florida Reef (1871)

ALONG THE FLORIDA REEF.

[First Paper.]

A MANGROVE SWAMP.

PURPOSING to aid the Cuban Telegraph Company, our government considered it advisable to make a reconnoissance of the great range of keys upon the Florida Reef.

A cable from the main land at Cape Sable to Key West has since been laid; but at this time it was thought that wires could be laid upon the trees and carried across the inlets upon poles set in the mud of the extensive flats between the islands. Several obstacles appeared after the examination, the principal one being the interference with the passage of the numerous sponge-boats that find occupation here. The wild and rugged nature of the forest rendered it more difficult and expensive than the cable plan.

Major M'Farland, of the Engineers, was ordered to take charge of the survey, with the schooner *Oriental*, then in his employ. An examination of the Pine Keys had been made previously. Our destination was to Knight's Key, where we arrived after one night's sail, some sixty miles from Key West. The Reef and islands or keys that have been formed upon it extend in a line nearly parallel to and within two degrees of the Tropic of Cancer, Dry Tortugas forming the western, and Virginia Key the eastern extremity. The keys here, as well as most of the others, are raised to a uniform height of about two feet from high-water. Either the water has subsided, or the islands have been raised, as they represent the accumulated tenements of once living bodies—bodies that can not live and build above water. The old dead corals massed into a solid, continuous ledge. Brain corals embedded in the broad, extended blocks of astræans present a rough, unyielding base, whereon is a meagre layer of earth, the débris of the sea, with the accumulated vegetable matter from the shrubs and trees.

Two prominent features seem superimposed on the Atlantic face of our coast: the peninsulas of Cape Cod and Florida. The latter is still growing, and it is well ascertained that nearly all of the peninsula has been built up from the sea bottom by species of corals and other marine animals now living and operating there. Centuries must have passed while this vast tract has been built up. But erroneous notions have been formed regarding their rate of growth.

A brick, having a specimen of meandrina upon it one inch in diameter, was placed under water in the year 1860 by the writer, at Tortugas, with the view of determining the rate of growth of corals. When taken up in 1861, just one year after, it had increased to *two* inches in diameter, and was over half an inch in thickness. The large aquarium, which was built at the water-side for observation of marine objects, contained many other specimens, and it was observed that the branch corals grew even more rapidly, some attaining five to six inches in one year.

The various forms of branch corals, brain and star coral, and the sea feathers and fans are familiar to most. Our museums are well stocked with fine specimens. The Free Academy at New York has a fine collection of every species known to the waters of our shores. A large fragment of the Reef, as it appears with many of its various inhabitants, and two fine

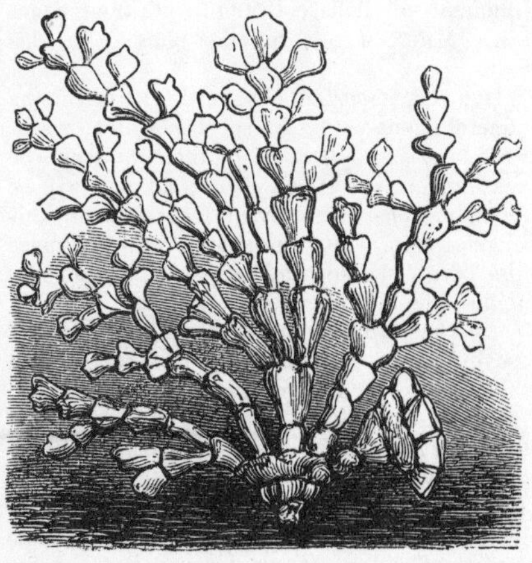

CORALLINE.

CIGAR-SHAPED MANGROVE.

heads of brain coral, each two feet in diameter, are among them.

One species of astræa, unlike most of the corals that have a circumscribed growth, spreads out ledge-like, and knows no boundary, no definite form. This particular species seems to be the principal element in reef-building; its individual polyp is small, but the congregation is vast, and tier after tier rises until the surface is reached, when acres, miles of this one variety lie dead and decaying, and furnishing a strong foothold for another element of land-making, not less sure and irresistible.

The mangrove now performs its part. A long, cigar-shaped fruit is formed, the seed of which germinates within the small inconspicuous flower before it drops, and presents the strange spectacle of a young tree, already rooted and ready to put forth its leaves as soon as it drops and finds foothold. These young trees are much like the young magnolia; designed to live and thrive in the salt soil, they float over the shallow water, and take root wherever they touch the bottom. The rootlets then make fast to the reef mud, throw out side shoots like so many flying buttresses, and put forth from the top or smaller end a tuft of rich glossy green leaves. The trunk does not reach below the spreading roots, but is supported by them above the water. Here is a network of rootlets wherein the débris of the ocean is entangled, and within which dead leaves and fragments of shells collect to form the meagre soil. Miles of reef become planted in this way.

One very important element in the soil is the mineral frame-work of a species of alga or sea-weed. A handful of soil taken up from the beaches, or upon the keys more inland, will be found to consist largely of fragments of this singular alga. Its vegetable portion is a mere film of green, covering a series of bead-like joints—the latter composed of lime.

Another and very effective method the mangrove has of extending its boundaries, and thereby also contributing more help toward land-making. Some of the fruit, instead of dropping and taking root as independent trees, grow downward until they reach the water, still remaining attached to the parent, root in the mud, throw out leaves, and assume the part of offshoots. Even these offshoots throw off others, which bend over and form knees, and in this way multiply to an indefinite extent.

These knees and the long, pendent suckers are curiously uniform in size, being only about two-thirds of an inch in diameter, smooth, brown, and pliable as a gutta-percha tube, holding the same uniform cylindrical shape throughout the entire length, and quite resemble the branches of the banyan.

Key Vaccas and Knight's Key lie parallel to each other. Here the water was so shallow that we were forced to leave our boats and push through the mud to deeper water.

These keys near the water-line, and for some rods inland, were nearly bare. The ledge of astræan coral was black and jagged, looking like rotten ice. Here and there were heads of brain coral embedded, some of them three feet in diameter. Upon this ledge stood several varieties of trees of large size, holding to the bare rock and sending rootlets into the numerous cracks and inequalities where the scanty soil was collected.

Along the entire border, and for some distance inland, were fragments of wrecks, carried there by some unusual high tide.

After a short sail we reached Boot Key. Here were groups of mangroves of great beauty. Osprays were disturbed in their fishing; and on the rocks, just below high-water mark, were great numbers of that peculiar armor-like multivalve shell, the chiton—the largest species. Here, too, were great numbers of the beautiful bleeding-tooth nerita. On no other of the numerous keys were these shells found.

One of the most gorgeously colored actinias, or sea anemones, as large as a coffee-cup, here spread its beauties in a little pool left by the receding tide, and a variety of the more common kinds was frequently seen.

Next day we visited Plantation Key. This is a large island, several miles in length, and has a good beach. The mangroves are here replaced by larger trees, and a variety of shrubs and small trees is supported by the deeper soil which has accumulated. A strong growth of coarse grass and many flowering plants thrive well.

In the soft, wet sand of the beach, among the numerous tracks of beach birds and gulls, were some which we conjectured were made by a large feline; and as no other of that family could be expected here, we anticipated the jaguar, or American panther. After tracing his steps for a mile or more, we came to a hut temporarily occupied by wreckers. The occupants were thoroughly frightened. They had not seen the animal, but had heard him prowling around their premises; and two young dogs were missing. Later in the day we had crossed a channel to Metacomba Key, where the same kind of tracks was visible. On reaching a hut where two men lived we heard doleful stories of fright and damage. Their dog had been taken and left maimed and half dead in the bushes; and a hog that reposed in quiet slumber against

THE ATTACK.

the side of his pen had lost an ear, the panther having bitten the appendage completely off, and taken it with him.

It was just before dark when we came up, tired with the day's tramping. Our party sat upon the beach, and listened to the tale. The surroundings and features of the scene were exceedingly sombre and striking. As is common near tropical homes, however humble, the cocoa palm was here conspicuous, rearing its grand plumes above the dark back-ground, and relieved against the starlit sky in all the beauty of its flowing leaflets. The dense undergrowth, cavern-like now where the clearing held the rude habitation, reflected fitfully the lurid blaze of the camp fire. The broad, glossy foliage of the banana sparkled with the play of light, the fire-flies here and there broke the broad patches of darkness, and the figures of the two wreckers, whose scared faces were lighted by the glare, all made a picture impressive and grand in artistic elements. Our party were now thoroughly aroused to the fact of a first-class hunt awaiting them, and the most feasible method was promptly pronounced to be that of stalking; an inglorious but safe one, as even the mosquitoes would prove formidable in the jungle. The panther would unquestionably return at night, as he had only moistened his teeth in the flesh of the poor dog that was curled up before the fire, trembling with fright and pain from his lacerated limbs, and had only a taste from the ear of the hog.

Fowling-pieces and rifles were thoroughly inspected, and the party arranged to watch in the hut, placing a board across the door, behind which Pableau, our cook, was stationed as a look-out. A fearful attack from the mosquitoes rendered this style of hunting far from agreeable, notwithstanding the fire was kept burning briskly before the door, ostensibly to draw them away from the house. True to his instincts, "Painter" put in an appearance about midnight.

"Golly! folks; look at them eyes!" says Pableau; and bang went his rifle, out of all proper time, and against orders.

The creature leaped over the bushes, and crossed in full view of the blazing fire, just in time to receive a broadside from the reserve; who presented a comical appearance, crowding the doorway, and aiming over the prostrate form of Pableau, who had been kicked backward by the combined effect of a big charge and fright. The monster proved to be a full-grown puma, or American lion, nearly five feet in length, and standing over two feet high. The paws were very heavy and powerful, measuring four inches and a half in length, and four inches broad.

Several instances of attacks upon children have occurred in Florida, and one very recently in Upper Florida. A child was seized, and the animal was making off rapidly when the father gave chase; the panther dropped the child and fought desperately with the man, but was soon overcome by a shot from a neighbor who had fortunately witnessed the fearful attack.

TURTLE-TURNING.

On the following day we sailed into Angel-fish Creek, a channel within the vast field of young mangroves. The space between the main land of Florida and the outer line of keys is a vast mud flat, nearly dry in some places, and having numerous channels. Upon the Reef border the young mangroves find a foot-hold, and a steady increase is made toward the final filling up of the bay, even to the main land.

Tavernier Creek is another of these open water-ways, quite like a river—open runs produced by the tides. Here is the favorite haunt of the young sea-turtles, a good feeding-ground, secure from the numerous enemies of the outer water. The green turtle here finds in abundance the peculiar sea-weed which it prefers, and on which it thrives and fattens. During the breeding season they are easily taken while crawling upon the beaches to lay their eggs; but many are taken by pegging, as the turtler terms it. A prism-shaped pointed steel peg is fitted to a socket in the end of a stout pole. A line holds the peg, and serves to draw the creature toward the boat after it has been driven into the shell and loosened from the pole.

Fine specimens of the hawk's-bill turtle are caught here, having the elegant shell plates, or scales, so valued in jewelry and comb manufacture. The green turtle is most valued as an article of food, and the Key West market is usually supplied from these back bays and creeks. The loggerhead turtle, a coarser and larger reptile, attaining the weight of several hundred pounds, feeds mostly on flesh, and is caught upon the beaches during the breeding season. In the summer months, and on moonlight nights, turtle-turning is practiced, and the visitor in these regions finds in it exciting recreation. Lying on the clean sand of the beach, with an eye athwart the sparkling ripples of the shoal water, an eager listener; presently a slight break is seen, hoarse breathing heard, and all is still for a moment, when a huge form rises from the edge of the sea, turns its big head to either side, and toddles hurriedly and awkwardly up toward the highest point, where it loses no time in excavating a deep hole for its eggs. So persistent are they when once at work that one can take the eggs one after the other as they are deposited, leaving only the empty hole in the sand, to be as carefully covered by the simple creature as if it contained its proper complement. They are exceedingly shy in landing, and will not come on shore if an intruder is discovered; but once out of water they seem to realize their helplessness. The favorite method is to turn them on to their backs, and this requires the whole strength of at least one man. Hundreds of eggs are laid at one time, and are covered about eighteen inches in the sand. The heat of the sun hatches them, and the young work their way out and toward the sea with unerring precision.

As we floated on the smooth surface a fine view was had of these haunts of strange, unfamiliar creatures. The water, clear as crystal, and the white coral mud, revealing every object distinctly. Nature reigns here undisturbed, save by the sponge-hunter, who pushes his boat through the labyrinthine channels, year after year, in continuous search. Young green turtles are very numerous; darting away as the boat passes over them.

One is reminded of a gay pantomime: gorgeously colored angel-fish flit by, crossing and recrossing like so many richly dressed columbines, their gay bands and wing-like fins resplendent with color. Harlequin morays, darting in and out of the shadows of the sea fans and feathers; groups of gorgonias brilliant with iridescence; clowns, pantaloons, and supernumerary shapes innumerable among the conchs, hermit-crabs, and devil-fish. A small species of saw-fish was frequently seen, a sluggish creature of the shark family, rather neatly formed, but furnished with an unaccountably long and broad snout, armed with a row of stout teeth on either edge—a prolongation of the upper jaw as long as the body of the fish, seemingly formed altogether as a defensive weapon, which can only be worked sidewise as a scythe.

Sponges were very numerous, though we were told that a large portion were not worth gathering. The sponger could readily distinguish the best as he pushed his boat over them. Some of the coarser kinds, not marketable, are four feet in diameter. They are all more or less concave at the apex. A black membraneous tunic covers them, and soft jelly-like portions project into the pores and cavities, constituting the slight claim they have to a place in the animal kingdom. Animal mucus and fat oil have been found in their analysis; so the vexed question is settled by chemistry, and they are unquestionably admitted to the ranks of animated nature, though far from active members. A slight current is observable over the openings, and nourishment is probably absorbed as it circulates through them. The frame-work is made up of silica, a wonderful proportion, in the form of spiculæ or splinters. Unlike most other marine objects, sponge is less attractive in its living state; only after the soft parts are removed is it pleasing to the eye. The pretty urn and other shaped sponges found on the beaches are merely the skeletons.

A large trade is now carried on at Key West in this article. Small schooners, from ten to twenty tons burden, are employed. They are much the shape of half an egg, and as flat as is consistent with due regard to sailing qualities; approaching, probably, as near as is possible the mythic craft that is said to "float in a heavy dew." These vessels lie at anchor in the channels, while the spongers push their small boats over the flats to gather the sponge. In some places they dive for it, and in shoal water grapple them. The specimens are very heavy, being loaded with water and the jelly-like animal matter. They are buried in the sand of the beaches until the matter is decomposed, when they are washed and carried to Key West, collected upon strings of convenient length, and bleached in the sun. That portion of Key West called Conchtown is the principal depository, where the yards and fences are loaded with them. For many years nearly all the sponge collected on the Florida Reef was sold at Key West to an Israelite of New York, one Isaacs; latterly others have entered the trade, and a very respectable income is derived from it.

A "CONCH."

To the naturalist, of whatever "persuasion," these mangrove thickets afford a wonderful field for observation. If he is an ornithologist, the homes of the herons and the eyries of the ospray are here at hand; is he a conchologist, how rapturously he views in the still water the winged aplysea, the rich tints of the triton, or, as it climbs the buttress of the mangrove, the mottled mickramock; a lover of crustaceans, the great hermit-crab, with his imbricated armor and formidable side-arms, most potent for defense, at the mouth of his confiscated castle; mayhap a gorgeously colored strombus of the larger growth. Radiata? the enthusiastic star-hunter finds his type cloaked in many strange devices, from the great cucumber-shaped biche la mer through many forms to the undisguised conventional star of the order, the pretty five-finger. To the botanist, not a varied field; but to him with artist eye, a never-ending succession of grand scenes and choice aspects. Nature seems to have varied the grouping of the mangroves in such manner that new charms are presented at every remove. At sunset the play of light and shadow, the chiar-oscuro of nature, was particularly charming, and new beauties were added by the strong reflections in the still water.

The great white herons, bright as snow, here make their homes; congregating at certain points they settle down upon the topmost branches to roost, contrasting their ermine vesture with the rich green of the foliage. Frequently we came up suddenly and surprised them, standing in the shallow water where they watched patiently for shell-fish. Particularly in the twilight the scene was of great interest. Like a panorama, as our boat moved along through the narrow channels, appeared each side of the thicket. A constant rising on either side so long as we continued to float on. Here a big sand-hill crane rises, flapping off to settle down farther inland. On the other hand the richly plumed night-heron; anon a lazy bittern; all around us the snowy egrets; at our bows the grebes and cormorants, and the curious snake-birds, diving, pushing forward, and looking furtively behind them; and where the channel spreads out into bay-like openings, the pelicans and gulls and terns were disporting in great numbers. Frequently long lines of white, looking in the distance like neat picket fences, proved to be white cranes standing listlessly in the shoals. With the rich green back-ground of the thicket a beautiful picture was presented.

THE WHITE EGRET.

The bald eagle and the ospray were often overhead, and now and then their nests could be discerned away in the midst of the thicket, an immense concourse of twigs spread across the top branches of dead button-wood. Some of the divers, the snake-birds, would seem to dive at the flash of the gun, and in several instances when our party had shot at one we failed to find it, although it occurred in open water, far from the banks. The wreckers hold strenuously to the opinion that they make fast to the weeds on the bottom with their bills, and there remain until danger is past. We were certainly puzzled to account for those fired at; for if killed they would float. It is well known that they swim well and for a long distance under water, and at such times, when frightened, expose only the tip of the bill or nostril, as the porpoise or whale brings its blow-hole to the surface to breathe. In this way they could go on indefinitely. The water was perfectly smooth, and we watched closely, but could never detect the bill or see the bird rise again.

The herons and egrets are generously provided with lanterns to aid them in fishing, and are said to practice the same method as certain fire-fishermen. Upon the breast of these birds, concealed by the long plumes, is a patch of soft yellow down just covering a bare spot. As the heron stands in the water at night, or twilight, this patch is exposed, exhibiting a phosphorescent glare which attracts the luckless fishes within striking distance of the lance-like bill. The beautiful night-heron has this curious appendage more bountifully endowed, as it feeds mostly by night.

The scarlet ibis and the roseate spoonbill are occasionally seen here. The glossy ibis, a rich maroon-colored bird, and the elegant purple gallinule are more common. These birds are exceedingly beautiful, and come into the landscape as rich bits of color where grand masses of green foliage and the sombre breadth of the shadowed still water are harmonized by them. The long, graceful necks and bodies of the great white egrets, and the light blues of various shades in the plumage of the herons, the velvet black of the coots and ducks, were constant elements in pictures ever before us so long as we drifted within this sanctuary of Nature. Eleven different species of herons and several of the bittern family frequent this region, and the multitude of individual members of these families, or genera, to speak in the language of the naturalist, makes up a heronry of such respectable dimensions that none shall here remain ignorant of the difference between a "hawk and a hernshaw."

In the full moonlight we drifted down with the tide on our return to the vessel. New beauties were discerned at every turn as the moon shed her peculiar light over the scene, now nearly quiet and noiseless, save where we passed the eyrie of a querulous old bald eagle who seemed to be scolding some one at home, and fluttering uneasily on her nest. A tardy war-hawk here and there came into view, skimming over the channel roostward, and the hoarse croak of a cynical bittern broke upon the still air as he half unfolded his wings and relapsed into listlessness. We were fatigued, and Nature was nearly at rest; a smart pull brought us to the outlet of Tavernier Creek, where we joined the vessel.

Pableau had served green turtle, young and tender, in all its seductive forms, plover pie, barracuda, and king-fish, and wild-ducks of rare flavor. During a cruise in these waters the table can be constantly supplied with the choicest wild game and fish.

In the morning the yawl was refitted for another day on shore. We were anchored off Old Rhodes Key, and now stood off toward Plantation Key, and took to our boats as soon

A PINE-APPLE CLEARING ON KEY LARGO.

as the water became too shoal to admit the schooner farther in. Every where along the beach were fragments of wrecks. Old hulks are seen on the shoals, and at high-water mark winrows of wood lined the shore. Here was a Turkish maiden, the figure-head of some unlucky ship, lying half buried with splinters and fragments of gilded panels, the remains of a wrecked steamship. Farther on a handsome sign-board bearing the Yankee name of Joseph A. Davis in gilt letters. Figure-heads in scroll-work, handsomely carved. On another key, great numbers of new hogsheads and bundles of staves for barrels; part of a cargo, no doubt, destined for the "ever-faithful isle."

Plantation Key has considerable good soil; many of the trees here are seventy or eighty feet in height. Here was a large plantation of cocoa-nut palms, several hundred in number, and a patch of young pine-apples. A late paper gives an account of the products of this patch, which have been materially increased since the writer was there. Mr. Baker, the owner, who resides at Key West, is reported to have realized seven thousand dollars this season from his crop of pine-apples. The great draw-back is the prevalence of mosquitoes, throughout the whole year, in such swarms that few persons are willing to suffer the annoyance; otherwise these keys would richly reward the cultivator.

We now ran across to Key Largo, the largest one of the group, being near forty miles in length, though not much wider than others. There is no beach here, but the mangroves grow to the very shore, where the coral ledge is irregular and broken, presenting many indentations and inlets. It was impossible to walk any distance, consequently the party remained in boats, beating up as near the shore as possible. Here the muddy bottom was loaded with gorgonias and sponges. The old coral is here replaced by a crystalline lime deposit within the openings. Fragments freshly broken present the appearance of stalactitic formation. Near Angel-fish Creek a large crack extended in shore from the water. This is the only instance observed where the original deposit has been disturbed. This crack was open, and about two inches in width.

The fine summer-like weather which makes up the greater part of the winter in this latitude is now to be interrupted by the almost regular fortnightly visit of a "norther"—a strong cool wind which subsides usually in two or three days to give place to the grateful trade-wind. Meantime we get under way for Indian Key, the grand rendezvous of the wreckers, fortunately for us, near at hand. Indian Key is one of the few islands of the Reef that can be called inhabited. Here for many years the wreckers have resorted, as it is convenient as a midway station and the safest harbor in heavy weather. Like the island of Key West it is increased in height by a lime formation called oolite. The foundation is probably the same as the other keys, but nearly twelve feet of extraneous matter has accumulated upon it. The soil is excellent, and various tropical trees and shrubs thrive well there. The whole island seems to have been under cultivation. Fine cocoa palms and many flowering shrubs are there, and what with the several houses the place looks quite village-like and picturesque. Wrecking was a lively business when the highway of commerce bore great numbers of ships richly laden with cotton; and here those hardy mariners found convenient resort. The anchorage is safe and valuable for that class of vessels. Other places, more or less protected, were frequented; and certain stations were recognized, mostly within sight along the Reef.

The wrecking vessels are usually small schooners, much like our pilot-boats, owned frequently by companies who fit them out, and divide the profits with those concerned. Vessels consort with others, and a system of signals is used. They anchor within sight of each other along the Reef, and readily exchange signals when a wreck is seen. A vessel unluckily strikes upon the Reef, the fore and aft canvas of a wrecker is seen bearing down upon

A WRECK AMONG THE BREAKERS.

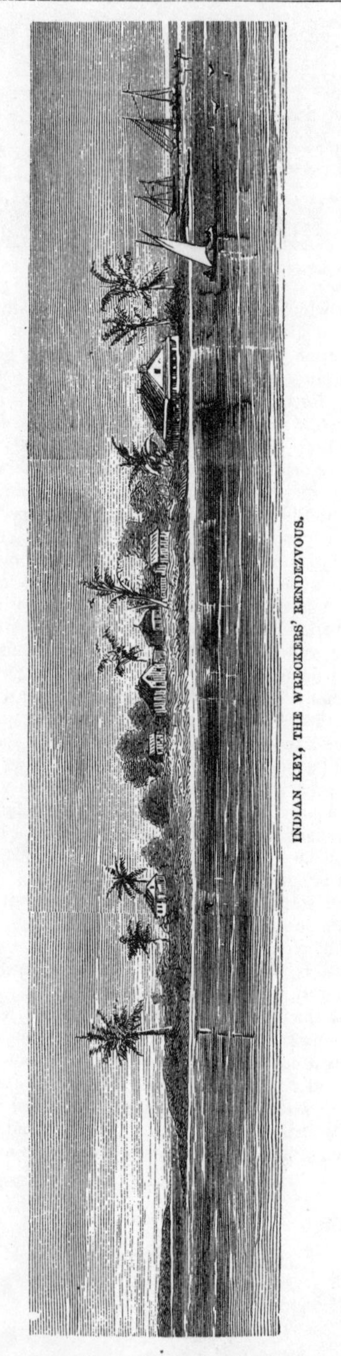

INDIAN KEY, THE WRECKERS' RENDEZVOUS.

her, and ere the hull is quite visible above the horizon white specks in the distance grow spectre-like into life, and soon spread a protecting cordon around the hapless craft. So promptly do these vessels come to the rescue they are likened to the condor that swoops down upon his prey; but the valuable aid to life and property rendered by the wreckers of the Florida Reef should be a subject of more just appreciation. Rather let these "toilers of the sea" be seen as they are: watchers by day and night; sea-faring sentinels in their snug craft, pacing the deck under the tropic sun heat, or peering forth from mast-head as they are tossed upon the gale. Good men and true most of them. They are average men, not pirates.

Let humanity make requisition on the schooner *Oriental*, and Dave Ellis will guide her helm as long as he can hold her tiller. A good fat salvage is a thing to be talked about, and with pleasure; but when life is in danger his big heart is in the right place, and prompts him on as far as man can go. Bob Rand and Long John may be gushing with terebinthinate Hollands; the spirit and flesh are both strong.

How quickly would these craft come to grief in the hands of others! No sea-faring people approach them, save the pilots. Theirs is a rough, perilous lot. Inured from youth to all the sailor's craft, the wrecker pursues an advanced course of duty.

At a time when every sail is reefed or furled, when angry clouds curtain the fair sky, and ocean boils with fury—when others seek shelter—then the wrecker is on the alert. A trusty hand is at mast-head, a sure one at the helm. The schooner frets heavily at her moorings; the spare hands quit their uneasy stride upon deck, and slip down the companion-way for support; the reefing points are made taut, bonnet is off the jib, foresail snug at home, fore-hatch tight as a bottle, and deck clear forward and aft. The spars shiver and the shrouds whistle with the wind. All is snug alow and aloft, and ready for the hoarse cry that comes, mayhap, from the look-out: "On deck there! Brigantine ashore to leeward, hard on Tavernier."

A fair taste of this wrecker life we had, for our schooner, the *Oriental*, was an old wrecker, and its crew experienced hands. A gale was now upon us, and Indian Key and a harbor our goal. Plash comes a heavy sea aboard as she swings to the wind; her jib flaps for an instant, and quickly "tautens" to its full. Merrily, cheerily, up goes the main—what there is of it, for she is necessarily close-reefed. The main sheet is "eased off a trifle," and her course is made; before the wind, a little on, a point or so, free. On the billow, down, down, beam under, rising upon the next with a cataract rush athwart the bulwarks; the crested mountain combing over behind, and the strong, skillful arm at the helm easing her just in time to keep her in trim, *on*, not *under*, that fearful billow! How like driving a spirited horse this holding the tiller in a heavy sea! Presently other sails were seen, all bending to the breeze, and in one gay fleet we "fell off and stood in" to the anchorage.

This picturesque island has a few of the old houses remaining that were built during the Indian war. At one time the whole place was burned, and was the scene of a fearful massacre. The present proprietor of the island, now living there, was one of the few who escaped with their lives. It was the old story, whisky and close bargains. The Indians were incensed, and came in a body, burning and destroying. There was, however, one notable exception, the family of Mr. Howe, who had always treated the Indians with kindness and fairness. They were not harmed, though the savages who had made the attack were insane with liquor stolen from the stores, and ready for any act of cruelty.

Dr. Perrine, a gentleman who had located here for the purpose of pursuing studies in natural history, was burned to death in his house, his family escaping by boats. We were led to the end of the island, and shown where the savage Seminole warriors crept softly from their canoes in the darkness to ply the fire-brand and tomahawk, and to "frighten the isle from its propriety" with their terrible war-whoop. Near by was an ambitious-looking slab, covering a brick tomb. Considering the result of the incumbent's dealings with the Indians, one is apt to reflect upon the old adage, viz.: "Such is life." The inscription which we found written on the slab is the following:

Sic transit gloria mundi.
Here lyeth the body of Capt. JACOB HOUSEMAN, who died by accident.
To his friends he was sincere; to his enemies kind; to all men faithful.

Houseman and some others were fortunate in reaching the revenue cutter, which was lying at anchor in the harbor, but died some years after.

In olden times, when cotton ships were frequently ashore on the Reef, and wreckers were numerous, this island resounded to the high reveling of its frequenters. The large storehouse was made redolent with fumes of Jamaica rum, and resonant with tones of the violin. Jig dances and clog dances and walk-arounds, checkers and old sledge, were their amusements. Pableau is a good violinist, and now, responsive to a loud call from the interested islanders, who had collected at the old store, he furnished music to a rehearsal of the old time scenes.

Among the residents was an old hulk, who had been driven ashore here years ago, and now lived on Lignum-vitæ Key, near by, where he raised a few water-melons, and so kept hunger from his door, selling his produce to dealers in Key West. Old in the service of the sea, Captain Cole is yet hale and hearty, a temperate man, and one well worth the acquaintance of any one who should happen to drift that way. He is a Norwegian by birth, and a very intelligent man; having no friends, he prefers to live here alone, almost a hermit's life. Boats for the sponge trade are built here; one upon the stocks was quite egg-shaped; made to carry largely, and to run in shallow water.

CAPTAIN COLE.

We were quite amused at a scene which we encountered on our first landing; but were told that it was of almost daily occurrence. A brace of Indian pullets—*Aramus giganteus*—alighted on a tree, when forthwith several women sallied out and "drew bead" upon them. The lucky ones bagged the game and withdrew, wringing the necks, and resuming work with an air of practiced hands.

From Indian Key to Virginia Key and Cape Florida, the extreme eastern point, the islands are separated by wider and deeper channels, and here it became quite evident that so much cable would be required between the keys nothing would be gained by adopting this route. The survey was rapidly made here. At Cape Florida light we anchored, after a two weeks' sojourn on the waters of the Reef. In our boats we proceeded across the sound, seven miles, to the mouth of the Miami River, at the southernmost extremity of Florida, where we met the overland party in camp at Old Fort Dallas.

ALONG THE FLORIDA REEF.

[Second Paper.]

BAY BUISQUINE.

CAPE FLORIDA, a point of great interest and solicitude to the mariner of these waters, is Key Buisquine, forming with Virginia Key the eastern extremity of the Florida Reef, and situated seven miles from the nearest main land of the peninsula, at the head of Buisquine Bay.

A light of the highest power is here mounted, which, with the great Loggerhead light at the extreme western end, and the intermediate cordon of skeleton towers and beacons that rise from the waters of the dreaded reef, forms a mighty arm of protection. The labors of our party being over, we left the *Oriental* at anchor for the night, and sailed across the bay to the mouth of the Miami, where we were to meet the overland party of telegraphic surveyors.

Though dignified by the name of river, the Miami is a mere outlet of the fresh water of the Everglades, yet picturesque and full of quiet beauty, derived from the luxuriant foliage of its banks.

The old garrison of Fort Dallas is in full view as we approach. The neat cottage-barracks, with broad verandas, arranged pleasingly around a fine sloping parade—tall cocoas, lime-trees, and rich groupings of poncianas and elders loaded with their brilliant blossoms—altogether form a cheerful scene of much beauty. The entrance to the little stream is particularly pleasant; the banks are green to the water's edge with tall flowing grasses and water-plants. On the clear amber surface are deep shadows, and the reflections of beautiful forms contrast picture-like with the opposite bank, where a broad patch of sunlight tinted quite to brilliancy the shelving white sands of the beach. Climbing vines and flowering plants and shrubs hang over the cliff. There is a charm unspeakable in the view of these broad leaves and nodding plumes of wild, tangled way-sides.

At the close of the last Indian war this fort, like many others in the State, was abandoned. Indications remain, however, to show that the plan was an excellent one. The oolitic rock of the region was used freely in the construction of the buildings. Ledges of this rock crop out abundantly, and it is easily worked to the required shape by axes. Resting upon the old coral formation, it seems to be composed of agglutinated masses of calcareous sand and mud. In some instances large portions have a crystalline structure, like calc spar.

The old barracks are now occupied by two

MOUTH OF THE MIAMI RIVER.

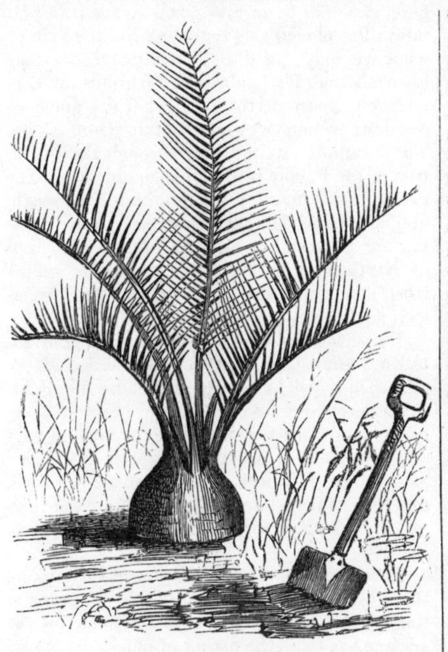

ARROW-ROOT.

gentlemen, who have a grant of land from the State, and are authorized to encourage the colonization of the region. The families of the party were with them, and a number of Swedish immigrants were expected. Those already in possession were enterprising and assiduous in their endeavors to bring out the resources of the country. At the house of Captain Hunt, the chief sojourner, we were entertained very kindly and pleasantly. We here found the overland party of the Telegraph Company, who had traveled the whole length of the State through the forests bordering the east shore.

We were attracted by an unusual display of fine books in the office of our host, and found that the selection was valuable and appropriate to this undertaking, as well as very large; comprising scientific standard works, and works of reference in most departments of knowledge. Many scientific instruments and the most approved agricultural implements indicated a plan for intelligent beginnings that deserves success. Single-handed the settler can not expect to succeed here, but intelligent co-operative undertaking must, to a reasonable extent, be successful, if not highly remunerative. Many attempts have been made to colonize this section of the country, and many avenues to industry and profit have been opened, through the value of the indigenous productions; and it must be through its productions that this part of the State prospers, as the whole Atlantic coast is barred in from the sea.

The arrow-root has proved very profitable, and the farina produced is said to be equal to the best product of Bermuda. It is called *coontie* here, probably from the Indian designation of the root. The plant is the *Zamia integrifolia*. The root from which the fecula or starch is obtained grows in the rich soil of the forests, and resembles in size and shape the ruta baga turnip. One-half of the root grows above-ground, and the top is a tuft of fern-like or, more properly, palm-like leaves, the genus to which they belong being just removed from the palms. In its crude state the root is poisonous. Our troops, during the war, eager to avail themselves of so valuable an article of food, without first obtaining the necessary information concerning its nature, were frequently poisoned by it. The starch, of course, prepared properly, is a valuable article, and is used in this region as flour for bread. The wife of our host presented us at breakfast with exceedingly nice white bread made of it. To extract the starch the tubers are first beaten in large wooden mortars or troughs to a pulp, which is thrown into tubs of water. The fibrous parts are then thrown out, the milky liquor, being passed through a hair sieve or coarse cloth, is suffered to settle, and the water drained off. A white mass is left, which is again washed, and the pure starch is dried upon sheets in the sun.

A species of agave or aloe is very abundant on the keys and in this region. Many attempts have been made to render it profitable. It yields the Sisal hemp of commerce, from which our best cordage is made. Large plantations are seen at Key West, and some machinery was erected there and in this vicinity, for the purpose of crushing the fibre into proper form for the market. Like many other channels of industry here, it remains for more persevering efforts or less expensive methods of preparation.

This agave, unlike the *A. Americana*, which blooms so seldom as to be designated century plant, bears blossoms after the third year. A more impenetrable chevaux-de-frise can hardly be conceived, and it is used extensively as hedges around

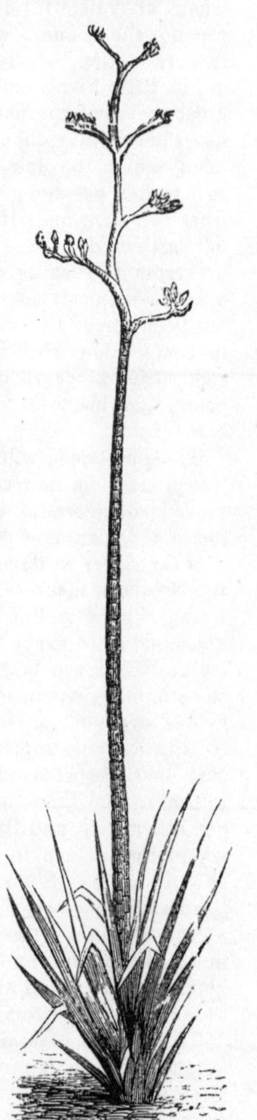

SISAL HEMP.

plantations; its long pointed leaves interlocking each other form a formidable barrier. The growth of the flower stalk is very rapid, amounting sometimes to seven inches daily. When fully grown they attain the height of fifteen feet, and are eight inches in diameter, resembling somewhat the bamboo. This curious candelabra-shaped flower stalk, shooting out from the centre of the plant, is a striking and effective object in the picturesque of tropical scenery. The whole plant is interesting; the flowers are not so attractive as the white ones of other smaller species, but each flower is at maturity a young plant, a perfect facsimile of the parent plant, with rootlets already started and ready to take hold of the earth as soon as it shall drop. The root being the heaviest, they are sure to drop right side up. Thus the plant is propagated, when under other circumstances it would fail. It occurs to us that possibly this is a provision of nature to insure the increase of this plant in sterile regions, where, if fruit with its seed fell on the dry ground, the chances would be greatly against its germination. Here the plant is ready formed, its little leaves exact counterparts of those great spears of the parent plant, and provided like them with a channel adown their centre, along which the dew, be it never so little, is sure to find passage; eventually the dew nourishes the plant and stimulates the roots to put out earthward.

Across the leaves of the agave were webs of that gorgeously colored spider, epiera, which has been forced to contribute its silken threads in competition with the silk-worm. Like a rich setting of pearls and rubies this spider appears, and his web is a marvel of geometric beauty.

The pine-apple will probably become a staple production, now that the experiment has proved so successful at Key Largo, where immense crops are now raised. Like the orange, it is far richer in flavor than those brought to the Northern markets. It is surprising to the stranger here to find the Florida oranges so much better in every respect than the foreign fruit. They are larger, perfectly round and smooth, often red inside and out, and of a delicious sweet flavor, far surpassing the latter. So with the pine-apples. And this fact will insure for those who cultivate them a profitable return. The limes are more abundant than any other fruit, and literally cover the ground, where they return to the baser uses for want of consumers. Limes are much preferred to lemons, having very thin skins and rich juice.

The shattuck—*Citrus decumana*—is another much-prized fruit, and, like the lime, requires quick transportation and early consumption, as they do not long remain intact after ripening.

The banana, plantain, and cocoa-nut furnish as good fruit as is produced farther south; as also do the guavas, sapodilla, pomegranate, mammee, and tamarind.

In view of the fact that the frost never comes here, it would seem that when steam transportation has placed this region within the pale of what we may call diurnal commerce, we may have all that Bermuda now furnishes, and, in addition, many of the tropical fruits and productions which we now obtain from Cuba. The example lately shown through the operation of the Pacific Railroad is significant. The great Pacific market is brought within reach, and certain productions are already daily reaching our Eastern homes. At present the crops of North Florida are liable to be cut off by frost, and much loss is occasioned thereby, as well as discouragement.

When the fashioning hand of intelligent enterprise shall bring out the capabilities of the soil, then it will be possible to realize a delightful and prosperous condition here. Among other new trials the olive-tree has proved very successful, and it is said that the oil is as good as the best of Lucca. Figs are easily raised, and several fruit-like products that are delicious salads. The castor-oil plant is also very productive.

Though the solid substructure of this region, the main land proper of Florida, is the same as that of the more recent keys and reef, yet the surface has more the aspect of older portions of the country. The soil is deeper, and extensive deposits of oolitic and crystalline calcareous formations in some instances materially increase the elevation. As at Key West and Indian Key, the calcareous rock crops out abundantly, and the detritus which readily accumulates, associated with vegetable matter, forms a rich soil, which only requires the addition of animal manure to be equal to the support of a heavy growth of crops or timber.

That trend of coast which forms the terminal portion is an old range of keys, precisely like those now forming the outer barrier bordering the Gulf Stream. As extensive mud flats now form between these two ranges, so extensive mud flats did similarly form on the northern side of that old range, which is now called the Hunting Grounds; while the flats, now called Everglades, have become overgrown with rank grass and shrubbery.

Another range of old keys occurs again, alternating with what was once mud flats; and so on this series is continued, quite the length of the State.

Large bodies of fresh water accumulate and find outlet through the Miami. It is believed that a considerable flow is maintained also through the old reef, as fresh water is observed to bubble up through the salt water of the channel which borders the south shore.

One remarkable point has long been the resort of wreckers and sea-faring men, where they could obtain an unlimited supply of fresh water. A hogshead is sunk in the soft mud over the bubbling outlet, and as the salt water is shallow, the fresh flows in perfect purity and abundance.

This locality has long been known as the

AN EVERGLADE.

Punch-Bowl, and is so notably valuable and accessible that passing vessels not unfrequently haul up there to refill their exhausted beakers. Coast-wise shipping hug the shore here to avoid the Gulf Stream, as the four-knot current is a serious obstacle, especially to sailing craft. Northward-bound vessels take the centre of the stream, and consequently receive the benefit of the current.

This terminal strip of land, which we have noticed as one of the old lines of keys, is designated the Hunting Grounds, and has long been the favorite resort of the Seminoles. The small remnant, less than a hundred, still remains here. Not until lately have they made any effort to support themselves, otherwise than by hunting and fishing. The chief, a son of Billy Bowlegs, and two other braves, visited Key West lately to make arrangements for commercial intercourse, attracting great attention there not only for their extremely elaborate toilets, but for their unusual business-like demeanor. Since the death of Cocheco, a notoriously ugly chief, who was hung by General Harney, the tribe has remained peacefully within its reservation.

Of the Everglades a late writer says: "There is a great deal of truthfulness and poetry in the name that has been given to the beautiful openings which occur in the swampy scenery of the peninsula of Florida. Formed in a low, yet not absolutely level country, these magnificent examples of semi-tropical richness strike the beholder with surprise; and it seems a waste of nature's grandest exhibition to have these carnivals of splendid vegetation occurring in isolated places, where it is but seldom they are seen by the appreciative eye of cultivated and intellectual observers."

During the war with the Indians our troops under Taylor and Scott and Jessup, and a host of lieutenants who are now, many of them, prominent in the different arms of our service, were familiar with the Florida Everglades; but suffering and death came to be the lot of many brave ones. Nature here is profuse to an extent marvelous indeed. Grand towering trunks, loaded with strange parasitic plants, and vines of enormous dimensions, like huge serpents, coiling around them. The singular forms of air-plants, vying in color with the birds and insects that alight upon their blossoms—an enchanting, wondrous scene.

With the same prodigal variety and numbers that characterize the outer keys, many others are here added. The deer and black bear roam within the forest. The panther makes his lair in the long grass, and climbs the extended limbs of the live-oak to spring upon his prey. The cypress is draped and festooned with the gray moss. On its topmost branch sits the bald eagle, with watchful eye, mayhap, upon the industrious ospray; while he, unconscious of his foe, bears the finny prey toward his rude eyrie. The sweet tones of mocking-birds and the numerous warblers charm the ear; and the gorgeous colors of the wood-duck, the ibis, and the gallinule, with hosts of other varied tints upon plumage and foliage, fill the eye with wondrous delight.

We leave this region of beauties with reluctance; but, *entre nous*, dropping gently from the sublime to a sober truth, it must be recorded here that mosquitoes do seem to thrive in direct ratio as these beauties increase.

Leaving the Miami, we ran down along the southern shore. The water covering the flats is barely sufficient in some places to float the boat. A part of this water is distinguished by the name of Card's Sound. Myriads of gulls and wading birds are seen on all sides, the latter standing in the shoals feeding, or quietly waiting the return of hunger. We were reminded of the amusing observations of Audubon respecting the pelicans as we came up to a long line of them sitting upon a shoal belt of sand. He says: "Ranged along the margins of a sand-bar, in broken array, stand a hundred heavy-bodied pelicans pluming themselves. The gorged pelicans patiently wait the return of hunger. Should one chance to gape, all, as if by sympathy, in succession open their long and broad mandibles, yawning lazily and ludicrously." The white pelican, according to Audubon, has a habit in fishing quite different from that of the brown pelican that is so common here. The latter dives upon a shoal of fishes, but does not go under water; he scoops them with his open bill, and remains on the water until he has adjusted the fish within his pouch. He is not very expert, and usually depends upon hunting the smaller kinds, that so congregate upon the surface of the water that they can not easily escape. He often misses his aim, and, considering his voracious appetite, nearly all his waking hours must be occupied in feeding himself and family. The white pelican has been noticed to swim against the wind and current with open bill, wings partly extended, scooping the small fishes and stowing them away in the ample pouch. They would then rise and fly back, to commence again and repeatedly the same process. Several hundred small sardines are found sometimes in the great pouch which hangs beneath the bill.

The water being perfectly smooth, the white muddy bottom, when undisturbed, as we passed over presented many beautiful objects to our view. A large species of sea-anemone was very abundant, and varied greatly in color. The beautiful flesh tints, and occasional touches of purple and lake, heighten the pleasing effect.

The gorgonias, including the sea-fans and several shrubby kinds, are abundantly spread over these flats, and it is easy to see their agency in holding whatever extraneous matter comes near them, and thereby helping on the work of building up the soil to the level of the sea—up to and even above that point that the mangrove requires to gain foothold and continue the work with its entangled buttressed roots.

One solitary plantation is seen upon the borders of the Hunting Grounds. The proprietor was raising sugar-cane in addition to his usual crops. It is here cut into short pieces and planted out in rows. They continue to grow and give out shoots yearly, only requiring to be occasionally renewed. Like many plants in this region, they become perennial. The tomato gets to be a stout bush, with hard, woody stalk, bearing continually.

At Cape Sable more thorough and successful experiments have been made in agriculture. Parties in Key West own large tracts, and considerable income is derived from the products of the plantations.

To the Northerner the scene here is charming beyond description. At the close of the day, when the clear western sky is toned delicately from the azure zenith through the rich blush of amethyst and berylline to the golden-rayed horizon, a sumptuous back-ground is presented for the noble plumes of the royal palms, and the elegant flowing tops of the papaw and the date.

The royal palms of Cape Sable have an extended reputation, but few ever get to see them,

WHITE PELICAN.

ROYAL PALMS.

as this region is wholly out of the world of travel, though the entering wedge may be said to have been driven with the electric wire. This is already one of the great highways of thought; and one day the great palms may shade the weary traveler, and give, in his own country, that measure of delight which so long has met the visitor in the neighboring isle of Cuba.

The cabbage palm or palmetto—*Sabel palmetto*—is here very abundant. It is a notable and striking example of Providential care for man's well-being that on this wide-spread sea-board of the tropical shores, where the construction of marine works requires material to oppose the relentless, irresistible encroachments of the teredo, the palmetto alone is invulnerable. Straight, smooth, and tough, it possesses all the requisites for its use, and grows in profusion near those regions where the ship-worm is most destructive. Other wood, either hard or soft, after one year's immersion, becomes so occupied by the brittle shells of the destroyer as to be dangerous; and in two years nearly the whole interior structure is replaced by them. Minute punctures on the surface of the pier indicate the presence of the young shell-fish that have just been hatched from the spawn deposited there. Gradually the creatures progress, growing larger as they go toward the centre of the log or along the grain, wearing a smooth, devious channel, which they line with a white, brittle shell. The whole interior of the log may be occupied by these shells, and yet the exterior remain intact, unless the structure is broken through, which requires very little force. It has long been a puzzle to account for the work done by some species of these mollusks. Some bore into limestone, and others into flint. The theory of acid secretion from the mouths may hold good with the limestone, but it seems unaccountable how the harder stones are perforated.

A commission of Dutch naturalists has lately reported on the subject, and M. Kater affirms that he has seen the teredo in the act of boring in wood by a rasping motion of the minutely denticulated portion of the valves. He also asserts that the teredo has an enemy in the worm called *Sycoris fucata*. The teredo has a well-marked rasp upon the anterior end of the valves, which is characteristic of the family; and it would seem possible that in most cases the result is through voluntary action of these teeth. Systematically this is a bivalve mollusk, of the class Conchifera, and family of Pholads; generic title, Teredo; specific name, Navalis—*Teredo navalis*—a sea-borer. It is therefore not a worm, but a shell-fish of the clam kind.

So valuable an article for building purposes as the palmetto proves to be is of course in great demand, and those who own the land which produces it set a high value thereon. The terminal bud, resembling somewhat a cabbage, is edible, and many trees are killed by removing it, as they will not survive the loss.

On the gray mossy branches of the large trees bright scarlet sprays of the air-plant seemed almost ablaze with the splendor of color. Full-blown flowers of a species of tillandsia they were, of the same genus as the long moss, though so curiously different in general appearance. In popular descriptions of natural objects, intended merely as conveying a general notion of what the object is, its relations to nature generally, and its aspect as a thing of beauty or worth, to the end that we may have a comprehensive knowledge free from mere technicality, it seems more direct to the purpose to omit the term *genus*, and use the expression *family*. The systems in use, as methods of properly studying and placing objects of nature, are of course indispensable; but there is a large class of readers who, it seems, would read with more zest and profit if the aspects, nature, relations, and intrinsic value of natural productions were exhibited with a light untangled woof holding the thread of narration. We are constantly meeting in our rambles upon the sea-side and the wood-side with singular objects, which we are told by our systematic mentor, much to our surprise, are only another form of some one very familiar to us. We do not at first recognize the resemblance. Do we not often meet with a person who looks so much like an acquaintance that it *seems* impossible that he is not closely related, while the *true* relative would not perhaps be recognized? Yet a closer inquiry reveals certain characteristics which are unmistakable.

THE LIVE-OAK.

In the case of this tillandsia, what a wide difference in the appearance of the two species or *members!* We will now call them, of the same *family*, using the terms *members*, *families*, classes, and grand divisions of nature, through which we get a ready comprehensive view of nature. The pine-apple and the scarlet air-plant, both members of the bromelia family, quite resemble each other in most parts; but another member of this family, the long moss—*Tillandsia usneoides*—would hardly be regarded as such by the stranger; yet there are certain characters common to all. The bromelia is represented also by a tree which produces the delicious fruit called sour-sop, resembling the pine-apple fruit in external appearance, but quite different in taste. Another bromelia is a large-leaved plant, which bears the pinquin fruit, from which a wine is made of great strength and pleasant flavor. One of the most familiar examples of a large family, with members wearing nearly similar vesture, is found in the tomato and potato kind—*solanias.* Here we find strange forms—some of doubtful repute, really claiming relationship of very close nature with our steady, domestic tomatoes, potatoes, egg-plants, peppers, and others—no less disreputable forms than the night-shade, tobacco, henbane, belladonna, thorn-apple, bitter-sweet, etc.

In most of the above-enumerated the flower is strikingly similar, both in shape and color; and the leaves, in odor, form, and color, group the whole family together; and the unanimous opinion would be that they all strongly possess family likeness, though each has its peculiar or characteristic habits and properties. Some are climbing vines, others are shrubby plants, that seem to revel in the most uncomely places of the earth.

The scarlet tillandsia* looks like a small yucca, or pine-apple, and has a flower stalk composed of branches like heads of rye, of the brightest scarlet; the stamens a rich azure-blue, tipped with golden anthers. The dew accumulates within the trough-like leaves, and thus the plant is cared for during the dry season. This plant sometimes germinates upon a rail-fence; and fastening its twine-like roots around the wood, seems to thrive as well there as upon the trunks and branches of trees.

The *T. usneoides*—the long moss which hangs in such profusion from the cypress and live-oaks of the South—is another true epiphyte; growing *upon* trees, but deriving no nourishment from them. Having no roots, it hangs in festoons and clusters as if thrown over the branches by accident. Its flowers are inconspicuous. Its seeds are so light they are blown easily through the foliage, vegetating wherever they fall. Different is the parasite, which not only grows *upon* the tree, but derives nourishment therefrom. The mistletoe—*Phoradendron flavescens*—that of old Druidical fame, which grows upon the oaks of England, is a fair specimen of a parasite. It also grows in this region. Its berries furnish the well-known glutinous component of bird-lime. The dodder—*Cuscuta*—of the North, is another example, though belonging to a different family. Five other species grow in the swamps of this region; some

* Presented on the dead branch of the live-oak as an *air-plant*.

of them very delicate and wax-like, climbing the trunks of trees.

The long moss is quite an important article of domestic commerce. The outer gray tissue, when dry, is easily separated from the black, wire-like heart, which bears strong resemblance to the horse-hair of the upholsterer. It is much used for mattresses, and gives a good return to those engaged in its preparation.

As we wander along the coast, now northward, leaving Cape Sable, the early labors of Audubon are continually in mind. Labors of love to him no doubt; yet one can not help reflecting how constant and enduring must have been the enthusiasm for his favorite pursuit, to support and cheer him alone in these wild and then more dangerous regions. Through these swamps and along this coast the great naturalist roamed for months, to cultivate an acquaintance with the rarer birds, and to see them in their homes.

Punta Rassa, at the mouth of the Caloosahatchie, was an important place during the Indian wars. A fortified block-house and other government buildings yet remain. The banks of the river in many places are enormously increased in height by the dead shells left by Indians. A little above the mouth is the more pretentious garrison of Fort Myers, a delightful situation. On the bank of the river are the graves of our officers who were killed in the terrible Dade massacre. A decent monument marks the spot. Oysters of the largest kind and of the best quality abound here, their southernmost habitat.

Flowering plants abound in greatest profusion, and frequently we met with old friends of the garden, that seemed out of place here, yet were in their own homes. The lovers of good fish will find rich mullet, and so large are they that the spear is used in their capture; in a novel manner too. A two-tined spear with long slender handle is tossed in the air, to fall vertically among or upon the fishes. A line attached serves to haul them in.

The barracouda, a most excellent fish, is also taken by the spear, but by another expedient, also somewhat novel. The fisherman selects a time when the tide so runs that he can float quietly with his back toward the sun; the light is then directly in the eyes of the fish. Like the pickerel, the barracouda floats warily and darts like an arrow; but with the sunlight in his eye his enemy has the best of it, and strikes unerringly.

In the shoals about here many beautiful seaweeds were seen with exquisite colors, ranging from delicate tints of green to browns, tipped with crimson and scarlet.

Tampa Bay is the next most important place in our route. It is distinguished as the home of a most remarkable animal; no less than one that forms a connecting link between the present and a past geological age—the *manatee*, or *sea-cow*, one of three species known to inhabit the globe. As among terrestrial carnivora the lions, wolves, and dogs are represented in the water by the seals, so the great terrestrial pachyderms, the elephant, the mastodon, and the dinotherium, have an aquatic representative in the manatee. Curiously enough, the only locality where this animal is found in this country is a fresh-water creek leading into Tampa Bay. One distinct species inhabits the Amazon; another the Red Sea. The three species comprise the whole race known to science. A township and a river derive their names from this creature; and manatee sirup has more than a local reputation. It is believed that the cane or sorghum produced in the manatee country is of surpassingly fine flavor. It is consequently in great request.

The manatee prefers the fresh water, but is not exclusively aquatic in its habits. Like the whale, the body tapers to a fish-like form, and terminates in a flat, horizontal tail, which consists of the rudimentary legs united within fin-shaped integuments. The arms are like the seal's, short, flattened, and inclosed within a fin-like palm. Rudimentary nails upon the

THE MANATEE.

BROWN PELICAN AND SEA GULL.

palm serve to hold the young while swimming. The head is round, and the upper lip is covered with a stiff mustache. The recently discovered dinotherium, the largest of terrestrial animals, is closely related. The characteristic features of the elephant, the tapir, and the whale family are united in this huge form. Like the manatee and elephant, it has an enormous pair of tusks directed downward, and, like the whale, is deficient in posterior extremities.

One calm day, as we were lying at anchor off the shore, a long, devious band of ripples was observed, contrasting sensibly with the still water of the Gulf. Eventually it approached, and proved to consist of myriads of small fishes —young "sardines." Here was a wonderful illustration of the maxim, "Eat and be eaten." First, the spawn of these small fishes is hatched upon the surface of the sea, and forthwith acres of fishy forms live, move, and have their being —gregariously, and almost as one mass of animation. So uniform and simultaneous are their movements, they seem like the result of one impulse. Large fishes, the Jacks, so called, make vigorous onslaughts among them, and carry many captive. The dash and uniform simultaneous movement of a squad of Jacks as they make a raid upon these solid columns of sardinian infantry are interesting to witness. The sardines are continually leaping out of the water to escape their enemies, presenting in the sunlight their sparkling silver sides, and attracting the attention of the watchful sea-fowl. This vast animated patch soon became a scene of the greatest interest. As the "streaky fingers of the morn" began to fade, and the sun-rays to glisten on the silvery wings of the flying fish, and glow in iridescence on the rippling masses, the brown pelicans drop from their roost and come flapping heavily toward the scene. Fluttering for an instant over the prey, down he plunges, with open, dip-net bill, resting on the water to adjust the game in his capacious pouch. The laughing-gull—inglorious bird!—with eager and accustomed eye, hovering near, essays to help himself, and, *nolens volens*, settles on poor Pelec's head—a head, albeit, none of the smallest, but one amply rotund and roomy. Now is the moment of his discontent. As the fish is tossed to bring it right end down the gull adroitly snaps it away, laughing his derisive *ha, ha!* as he goes. The pelican seems to submit to it as an inevitable operation, and makes no resistance, but flaps heavily up again to renew his search. Meantime the lazy gull is brought to grief, even in the midst of his hilarity. The war-hawk is on his track. Listening and ogling from the neighboring shore, he spies when he can leave his roost to profitable purpose. The exultant laughter of the gull soon gives place to shrill cries of alarm. The war bird, conscious of his power, bears a wary eye; cautious, and sure of his mark. The weaker darts fitfully in zigzag lines, striving with all his power to escape. Fatigue and fear prevail, and losing faith, he lets the choice morsel drop. Down darts the hawk; clutching the prey ere it reaches the sea, he soars straightway to the nearest roost. So the struggle for existence goes on.

The sun was now fairly up, and new intruders came to the feast. The air was alive with winged watchers and hunters. On the outskirts of this river of fishes the little terns were busily engaged; and they deserve all they get. Brisk, expert little fellows, their faith is "total immersion." Quick as thought they dart into the sea, and seize their prey wholly under the surface. With a nervous flutter and pleasant chirp they rise upon wing again—pretty busy-bodies indeed.

The great gray gulls and the gannets and cormorants hang around like so many vagabonds, ready to pick up a dead fish or floating fragment—too clumsy and inexpert to fish legitimately.

Stranger creatures now came to the festival: a dozen or more of those great *sea-devils*—not those of "The Toilers" memory, but sting-rays, or stingarees, or ocean-vampires, or sea-bats—

THE SEA-DEVIL.

Cephaloptera vampyrus—nomenclature enough to scare the whole army of sardines, aside from their hideous shapes. The huge forms were swaying up and down through the line, creating sad havoc. By this time a strange scene was before us—a contest wherein the strongest or most expert came off best. We could not assert that the vampires ate the fishes, but they seemed to be so active, and confined their operations so undeviatingly to the shoal, it was natural to suppose they did. It was rather an unusual occurrence for such a variety of creatures to get together in one struggle of the kind. Shoals of fishes are frequently beset by gulls and pelicans, but here were congregated many forms not often seen. Could we have looked under the surface, other expectant marines, with open countenances, might have been seen. The voracious bonito and the hyena-faced barracouda linger near the outposts to snap the stragglers, casting an eye, meanwhile, to their own foe, the tiger-like shark, which sculls in gyratory survey of the manœuvres. Jelly-fishes—animated rafts—float over and through the columns, throwing down their deadly missiles: threads of electric potency, which wound and lasso at the same instant. To name all the enemies of these unfortunate fishes, those we know as probable enemies in addition to those actually in sight, would require much enumeration from all the various branches of zoology. The great variety of animal life in these waters is made strikingly manifest at such times as these, and when the sea is perfectly smooth.

The sea-devil is not uncommon off the Atlantic shores, but the larger ones seldom go near the land. The dimensions are enormous, and may seem exaggerated; but in this instance, like every other where the measurement or approximate size is given in these papers, it is from *actual* personal experience, or from reliable scientific sources. The breadth of one measured by Dr. Storer, of Boston, was eighteen feet;* its length was seventeen feet, exclusive of the tail, which was nearly as much more. Those observed by us were about ten feet across. This is the only time we have ever seen them in numbers. Their movements were much like the larger butterflies, as their wing-like expansion of body is used in swimming. A smaller species of the family, the whip-ray, or whip-eree—*Rhinoptera quadriloba*—is seen frequently on the reef, and is distinguished for its long, slender, whip-like tail, four to five feet in length, round and supple as gutta-percha, tapering to a point.

The rays are furnished with most singular eggs: dark green leather-like cases, rectangular in form, and with four slender threads, which serve to hold, entwined around the floating algæ or other drifting objects. Within the case is a reddish yolk. Floating on the surface, the sun-heat brings to maturity the imprisoned young, which are liberated from the case through a

* Represented in our cut with leather-tortoise. Its attitude is just as when they turn, bringing a large part of the fin out of water.

split in the edge, which was until now impervious. The sides contract, and the young ray comes forth, still attached to a considerable portion of the yolk, which serves to nourish him until proper functions develop. Eggs of the common skate having these characteristics are often found on the beaches of the North, from which the young fish can be taken alive.

The spines of the large rays prove terrible weapons, and wounds from them are exceedingly dangerous. Experienced seamen seldom care to attack them, as their huge forms move with such impetus as to crush all before them. It is a fact perhaps not generally known that a species of ray was formerly known in the waters of Cape Cod that possessed considerable electric power, like the torpedo. It was called the cramp-fish. Latterly it is seldom seen.

Along the whole shore from Charlotte's Inlet to Cedar Keys, where we now come to anchor, a fine white silicious sand is the prevailing component of the soil. Sea-Horse Key, a high mound-like island, fifty feet from water-mark, the highest land south of Hatteras, is of the same character. As the substructure is of coral formation, this sand must have been carried from the great outlets of the upper trend of the Gulf coast. It is said to be found as far south on the Atlantic coast as Jupiter Inlet. It is fair to suppose, allowing that the peninsula was at one time much shorter than it now is, that the Gulf Stream has had an agency in the distribution of this sand, carrying it on along the Gulf shore, sweeping round the southern end, and leaving it heaped upon all sides.

With the round tower of the light-house, Sea-Horse Key, at the entrance of Cedar Keys Harbor, forms quite a pleasing object. The harbor is very shoal, but narrow winding channels lead to the town on Way Key or Dépôt Key, where the railroad from Fernandina terminates.

THE CRACKER.

Steamers plying between New Orleans and Havana touch here to take and deliver freight and passengers. The village is prettily situated on a mound, which is shaded completely by grand old live-oaks. Long moss hangs in wonderful profusion from the limbs. Palmettos and yuccas abound, and what with the lumber trade, good oysters and fish, they contrive to make it a tolerable abiding-place. As we have hinted with regard to co-operative husbandry or intelligent application of agriculture in South Florida, so here it is possible that a paradise almost can be realized. The accessories of nature are so profuse and grand, so full of use and beauty; but how stupid are the people, the indigenous race, called *crackers!* Pale, sharp-visaged, sandy-haired people, ignorant beyond all reason; little can be expected from them—or *nothing*, but to vegetate.

Upon a long wide beach at low-water we met one of those curious armies of soldier-crabs, or *fiddlers*. A space of many rods was wholly occupied by them, and so closely did they march that their various movements seemed simulta-

SEA-HORSE KEY.

neous, like the sardines. One arm, like an immense club, is raised in front, while the other is too small to be conspicuous. The females have no large arm, and march under protection of the males.

The stone-crab is here used as food, and reaches a large size. The shell requires the heaviest blows to fracture it.

On our way down the coast, returning to Key West, the vessel ran very near a medium-sized leather-tortoise — *Sphargis coriacea* — a species thoroughly oceanic, and of such rarity that we give some statistics of its history. The first one found on this coast was taken in Boston Bay, in 1824, and sold to the proprietor of the old Museum for two hundred dollars. It is now in Mr. Kimball's museum in Boston. This creature measured seven feet and one inch in length. Rondelet speaks of one nearly eight feet in length, taken at Frontignan. The body is covered by a black leather-like shield, divided into seven prominent longitudinal ridges. In general appearance the reptile resembles the snapping-turtle, but the flippers are purely fin-like. A small specimen, three feet in length, came into the possession of the writer at Nahant, where it was cast upon the beach. A bullet-hole in the neck indicated its probable fate.

In connection with these observations by the way, along the shores of Florida, it may be appropriate, and possibly of service to some, to record here certain facts concerning the climate, and its suitableness in cases of disease. So many different opinions have been expressed, the invalid is puzzled to know what to rely upon. As a physician, and one having no possible interest in the success of the commonwealth of Florida, beyond the ordinary desire to see all parts of our country yield the best and become duly appreciated, living now far away, and with no prospect of ever returning to the country, I wish to be exact, and "nothing extenuate." After a residence of nearly eight years on one of the fortified keys of the reef, I venture to tabulate a few *facts*, offering no arguments. The localities under notice are the Dry Tortugas, Key West, Indian Key, and that portion of South Florida below Charlotte's Harbor or the mouth of Caloosahatchie.

The keys upon the Florida Reef are wholly exempt from frost.

Very rarely frost appears as far south as the Caloosahatchie.

The keys of the reef are never visited with a temperature, in summer, above 92°. Twice only in eight years was the mercury above 90°. It averages 87°.

In winter the average temperature is about 70°.

In winter about every thirteenth day and the two succeeding ones are cooler, from the prevalence of a north wind; then the mercury is down to about 60°. A pleasant easterly trade-wind prevails at other times. The atmosphere is dry and bracing during the northers; no rain falls. Rain seldom falls during the winter.

The intermittent fever is never known here. Pneumonia and affections of like nature are exceedingly rare. Diseases of the alimentary canal, as dysentery and diarrhea, are remarkably infrequent. Bilious remittent is an occasional visitor, less frequent than it is in other portions of the South. Dengue, or break-bone fever, is also an occasional. Yellow-fever is a stranger; it never originates here, and is easily kept away by good quarantine regulations.

The extreme equability of the temperature, and the benign influence of the tempered sea-air, suit the delicate breathing organs of the consumptive in winter. The debility caused by the long-continued, though not excessive, heat of summer is counterbalanced by the great gain derived from the absence of rude, irritating winds. A marked difference is seen in this respect between this latitude and that of North Florida. In the latter section the mercury reaches a much higher and a much lower point. This delightful equability of temperature is the great and valuable point to be considered by the invalid who determines to "go South" for health. Many have had occasion to be thankful for the manifest comfort and extension of life gained by leaving the rude winds of the North for the genial air of the extreme South.

The great drawbacks are the want of good public houses and a proper diet for the sick. It is reasonable to suppose, however, that as the wants increase, methods will be found to supply this present lack. To compare Key West with Havana, we would say that every season finds disappointed invalids returning from Havana for want of the ordinary comforts of home. The city is too close and noisy, and too Spanish. Key West would be a *paradise* for the sick or invalid were there decent accommodations. The house of Mr. Russell is well adapted, and it is fair to presume that as company increases the proprietor will find means to procure all the necessaries for the comfort of his guests. It is a truth long patent, that a good public house on the higher part of the island of Key West would be a godsend to the many who seek health or pleasure along the Florida Reef.

ALONG THE FLORIDA REEF.

[Third Paper.]

SPONGE FISHING.

THE Northwest Light twinkles an instant on the southern horizon, and disappears as the flush of the coming morn reveals its iron cage suspended in the broad space of waters. This is the entrance beacon of Key West Harbor, from the north. Our course is now clear for the low lines of waving tree-tops that mark our goal.

In due time the vessel is made fast at the pier; and the *Rosetta*, our much-prized boat, which was left behind in charge of "the Bos'n," is brought alongside and made ready for further service in the morning. A finer day, and one less portentous of evil, could hardly be recalled.

It is like the many in this latitude—fraught with cheering influences. Nature, on every side, seems in her best aspect. The summer-like air is pleasantly tempered by the east wind. The rich azure of the sky is heightened to wondrous beauty by the moving volumes of day clouds; and the still sea mirrors the scene, adding deeper touches of olive and brown where the reef lies near the surface.

As the day wanes the wreckers and the spongers make sail and stand in for an anchorage. The barometer indicates no immediate change; and the wharf-loungers agree with Captain Gieger that "we'll have a fair day to-morrow." Yet a change comes; a low line of leaden clouds lifts gradually at sunset and shuts in the richly colored scene.

Presently heavy curtains of sable shoot upward. The Squire confirms the Judge's remark—that a norther is brewing—and steps home to change his linen for kersey. Meantime a heavy rain has broken upon us, and speculation is at once rife. In the cooler months such rains are rare. The torrent continues through the whole evening, and is unabated at bedtime. The wind strengthens, and the darkness, with the rain, shuts us in from the scene. To sleep is impossible. The rain blows so furiously against the windows; and the puffs that come intermittently—now here, now there—it seems a thorough gale. The blinds that have rattled, and the signs that have creaked, and the tin roofs that have crashed, all give way, and go rattling and crashing together into the streets, adding to the piles of débris from wharves and yards; floating up and down with the driven tide; choking the highways and by-ways, and holding general carnival of chaotic noises. The wind, after going all around the compass, is plying steadily from the south, driving in the sea through the streets, with timber and fuel from the docks. To look out or go out is unsafe, as slates and tin are flying from the roofs; and lumber even is driven through the air by the wind. To wait and watch is our only lot through the long hours of the night. The house remains whole, but not tight; torrents of water pour through the soaked walls and the tinless roofs. The furies ply their utmost. Whirling continuously, seemingly with all power, an occasional lunge sways every thing with enormous force.

At daybreak is a lull. Slate tiles yet fly from the roofs; but with considerable effort we gain the scene of our great solicitude. Piles of tin roofing, lumber, trees, and broken chandlery are left high and dry where the tide swept them. The sea was even now fearful to behold. Heavy surf was breaking against the buildings upon the wharves, crushing and destroying many of them. Half buried under the timbers of a wharf a steam-tug was pounding and beating her way, and now had cut clear through to the opposite side, where she jammed and chafed what was left above water of our good schooner, of which little else was visible but her tapering top-masts.

The wind is yet a gale in strength, and its wild howlings, with the flying scuds of spray, render a view of the whole scene impossible.

"But where is the *Rosetta?*"

"She went to pieces, Sir, early in the night."

"And the Bos'n?"

"He has not been seen since, Sir."

The Bos'n had held on by the schooner until obliged to retreat. She was sinking, and as he leaped to the shore the skipper tossed his valise after him, which he unluckily caught by one of the two handles. The off side went overboard by stress of weight. But what was the Bos'n's astonishment and indignation when he discovered that the half which was now subject of immediate salvage was worthless compared to that now open to the law of flotsam and jetsam! The truth is, Bos'n had occupied his spare hours in selecting, and expended his spare change in purchasing, some fine neckties and fine linen, with a proper selection of under-clothing, and had placed them carefully in the one half of the valise which was now so cruelly snatched from him, while the part which was saved held only the less valuable shift of old clothing.

A WRECKER OF THE REEF.

We looked around to find even a fragment of the lamented boat: the little cove between two piers was literally choked with broken lumber. Presently a form was discerned standing so motionless among the stranded fragments that it seemed like a half-buried spar, with its rag of canvas fluttering in the wind. There the Bos'n stood, and at his feet lay all that remained of the once gay *Rosetta.* He did not move nor speak. The old man had deemed it incumbent on him early in the night, as it looked, as he afterward remarked, a good deal like foul weather, to fortify himself; and nothing is more sure than that he became firmly intrenched. An expression of face indicative of great calamity was now all that was possible.

As the wind and rain subsided the people went forth to view the wreck: The tall old cocoa palms, which had not felt such a shock for many years, were stripped; and many of those that escaped the late destructive fire were wrenched and sadly denuded. The streets were blocked by great limbs and brush-wood. At the barracks a very long frame building that was perched upon stones four feet in height,

THE HURRICANE.

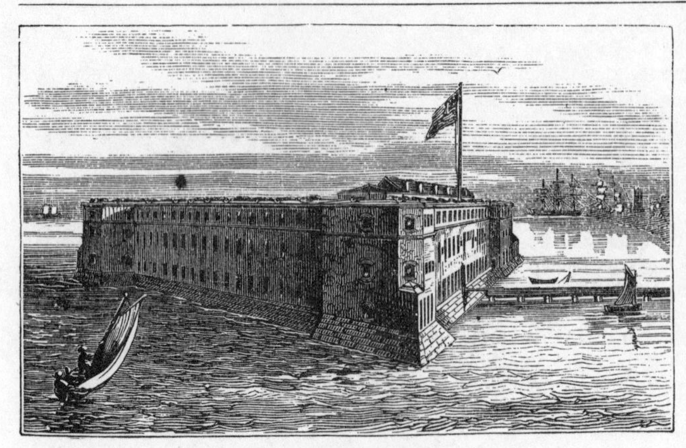

FORT TAYLOR, KEY WEST.

and under which several cows had found shelter, was lifted and dropped, unbroken, its whole width away from the spot, crushing the cows, that in some instances broke through the floor and remained unharmed. The front of one house opposite a lumber-yard was riddled with holes, and one plank went entirely through the end of the house. Vessels of all classes were ashore; and several gun-boats, kept under steam, were constantly plying their screws to prevent dragging the anchors. A large bark, that was quietly standing into the entrance of the Moro at Havana, was suddenly driven seaward, and, with incredible speed, across the Gulf, over the shoal reef, high upon the beach near Fort Taylor.

This is a fair specimen of the hurricane of the West Indies. The hurricane of 1850 has long been quoted, and used as a convenient point to date from. This gale of 1865 will now take its place. Some say it is greater, some say less; but it is probably much like the average—severe enough, and one that comes once in about fifteen or twenty years.

Key West, now shorn of its beauties, presents a dreary aspect. We must therefore speak of it as seen before this scathing blast.

The island of Key West is about five miles in length, and one mile in greatest width. The town is situated at the western extremity, where the reef protects a large and safe harbor, one of great depth, and of incalculable importance to our navy.

A ridge of calcareous rock crops out in the central part to the height above water of ten or twelve feet, and in other places about water level. Within the hollows and inequalities of the rock a rich soil has accumulated, consisting of decayed vegetation and animal remains. On this soil trees can not attain a large size. Yet the island is well wooded with a strong growth of shrubs and small timber. Approached from the sea, Key West has quite the appearance of an important maritime town. The intricate and dangerous nature of the reef navigation is brought to view by an early appearance of the pilot, while yet out in the Gulf, and by the occurrence of buoys for miles along the devious channel.

You are naturally puzzled concerning the harbor. Where is it? For is it not all out at sea here—an island in the ocean, with no protecting points or arms of inclosure? All such protection is here, but under water. The solid reef is an all-powerful barrier, and breaks the heavy sea as it rolls inward on either hand. Deep channels lead between in several directions, and open into a wide basin off the western end of the island, where the town is; and that is Key West Harbor.

From the top of Sand Key Light, on the great iron-framed tower, near the edge of the Gulf Stream, may be seen in a calm day, mapped by the various brown tints of coral and algæ, these protecting arms of reef, divided by the blue of the channels. Or, when the north wind in all its potency has wrought tumult in the ocean bed, and the troubled sea moves shoreward in majestic columns, the falling crest, complete dispersion and retreat, denote the presence of a resisting power—mighty bulwarks of the myriad polyps, whose galaxies of bright stars spread their open mouths, and take with every wave fresh aliment.

Projecting from the seaward face of the town, Fort Taylor commands the entrance. A fine front of granite and brick work, with castellated walls, bastions, and towers. Along the beach, at intervals of a mile, are several martello towers, works of great strength, each with a casemated wall surrounding it. These towers, with Fort Taylor, give to the island prominent features.

The town is laid out in squares; and, before the rebellion, was pretty and prosperous. Many of the merchants owned pleasant estates, and much pains was taken to add new beauties from tropical regions to their already semi-tropical surroundings. Nothing can exceed the pleasurable feeling experienced on the sudden arrival from the cold north to the perpetual summer climate of this island. Landing here in December, in a moonlight night, before rebellion had laid its heavy hand upon the people, we sought the abode of one of the merchants of the place. The tall cocoa palms were then at their best, and presented a spectacle strange yet lovely in the extreme. The bright moon was soon lost to view, except where its beams in places penetrated the thick, overhanging foliage. A long stretch of handsome stone fence, loaded with vines, and nearly concealed by flowering shrubs, inclosed the estate of our friend. On the gateway the pendent branches of bergamot gave forth rich perfume. Buried within a complete canopy of foliage was the quaint cottage home. Broad verandas were furnished with wicker seats, lounges, and with the ever-acceptable hammock of grass netting. Choice birds—the red-bird, the canary, and the mocking-bird—were pleasant, cheering occupants. The good people, in white linen and in lawns, welcome with the heartiness characteristic of the Southern home. With the then accessionals, African slaves, passing the tempting bits of fruit and the refreshing draughts of cocoa-nut nectar and jelly, and the constant perfumes of jasmine, of lemon, and the endless odoriferous fruits and plants, the scene was one altogether novel to the unaccustomed Northerner.

The unusual wealth of rare vegetable forms on this estate makes it a fit subject of notice.

On all sides, overshading every thing, is the cocoa-nut palm; and beyond every thing for grace of form in vegetation is the young of this tree. The leaves rise directly from the earth, or nearly so; in the centre a stout mid-rib, bending with exact curve, upward and over, bears its leaflets in exquisite outline and comb-like regularity.

Uninitiated, we wonder at the peculiar aspect of these trees. Large trees, fifty or eighty feet in height, yet with no branches; growing with leaves from the top like plants—leaves sometimes fifteen or twenty feet in length. Of the three great classes of vegetation—Exogens, Endogens, and Acrogens—outside growers, inside growers, and top growers respectively—the Endogenous class, to which the palms belong, is profusely represented in the tropics, and as meagerly represented in the North. The most prominent of the class in our Northern States are the cereals, maize or Indian corn, and the orchids, cattails, and grasses. If we compare the cornstalk with the banana we shall be led a step further, and see how much the palm is like it. The banana, which is one of the most common plants here, and stands in splendid groups around this estate, throws up a leaf much like that of corn; another comes up within, and then others, alternately facing to right and left, until a great fleshy stalk is grown. The first leaves wither and die, and the stem supports a few of the latest leaves at the top. It is a green, succulent trunk—soft, almost, as the cornstalk. So the palm grows up, soft and stringy in its fibre—its long leaves dropping as it attains certain height, leaving behind the triangular scars which give this family a characteristic feature. And thus, as the cornstalk has no branches, so has the palm none. When the cocoa palm brings forth its first flowers and fruit, in its seventh year, a striking resemblance is seen to the flowers and fruit of the cornstalk. A large yellow spathe puts out, and falls over to reveal a bunch of elegant florets of the choicest "corn-color," which soon begin to branch like the tassel of corn, presenting a beautiful feature of this much-admired tree. The tassel is unlike the corn tassel in one respect—the young fruit appears upon that of the cocoa, and eventually there is a bunch of nuts formed from

COCOA PALMS.

DATE PALM.

material for the construction of the huts of the poor. The midrib is formed into oars and various articles of use along shore. The terminal bud, like that of the palmetto, is a delicious article of food. The leaves are useful for thatching and for hats. The ashes yield an abundance of potash. The juice of the flowers and stems, replete with sugar, is used in the manufacture of arrack. From the spathe, or flower-covering, flows, when cut, a grateful beverage. An excellent oil is expressed from the kernel; and every body knows the uses of its well-known fruit.

The banana is not tree-like, but is annual in its growth; the root being perennial, and permanent. In one year the banana grows from the root to about twelve feet in height, bears its one bunch of fruit, and dies. Other shoots meantime are coming up from the same root; they in turn bear fruit; each after a year's growth. Such a method of growth brings the plant into extensive groups. Every yard in Key West has its banana patch; and the grand glossy leaves lend great beauty to the surroundings of the humble cottage as well as to the more pretentious domicile. The flower-bud of the banana is purple, and contrasts finely with the rich green of the leaves.

One of the handsomest trees of this garden is the date palm, which bears the dates of commerce. The leaflets of this palm are so beset with sharp spines at their base it is a matter of wonder that the fruit is ever gathered.

Closely resembling each other as do the palms, a wide difference is seen in their products. Sago, coquillo-nuts, wax, dates, cocoa-nuts, and a great many more less familiar. The date palm requires about the same length of time to arrive at maturity as the cocoa-nut. We remember visiting several date palms here in 1859, when they were then small plants, just brought from Cuba. These and a group of cocoa palms, of the same age, at Tortugas, were watched with great interest. In 1866 both groups were in bloom, and young fruit soon formed on them.

The great leaves of the palm and their leaflets have on the surface of the midrib or stem hollow troughs, and in extremely dry weather

it weighing many pounds. The corn tassel is the male blossom; the silk being the top of the female flower, from which comes the fruit.

Endogenous plants are those that do not grow by successive layers, added year after year, so that the rings of growth can be counted, as on our trees and shrubs, when they are cut cross-wise. They have no bark, but uniform bundles of fibrous woody matter added from the centre as sap rises, and there deposits it. A most interesting provision of nature is seen in the fibrous development of the base of the leaves. From that portion which clasps the one above it strong fibres issue, and extend around and form a close and regular net-work. The fibres are crossed and interwoven so as to resemble an artificial matting. Being dry and gray, they are at first sight supposed to be extraneous wrappings. It becomes at once apparent that they are intended to hold the immense weight of the long leaves; which would otherwise be split from the trunk during the prevalence of high winds. The cocoa palm varies much in its aspect. Beginning to bear when it has arrived at the age of seven years, its leaves at this time are of immense size compared with the trunk; but as the tree grows older it towers to the height of sixty or more feet, bearing only its top-most leaves; while the fruit still continues to form at their base. Fruit in all sizes is seen on the same tree, as they continue to put out blossoms in every month of the year. The uses of the cocoa palm and its productions, both in this climate and elsewhere, are wonderfully extended. The hard trunks form an easy

the leaves are more erect; thus allowing every drop of dew which collects upon the surface to run toward the centre of the tree, moistening the bundles of fibres which make up the solid structure of the trunk.

The plantain is quite as common as the banana here, and is so much like the latter that it deserves no special notice. The fruit is not pleasant except it be cooked.

In the front corner of this estate we observe a most singular tree; and in our rambles around town we meet it frequently near the street. One remarkable specimen is within the parade at the barracks. This is the *Ficus pedunculata*, or wild fig. Its habits are very similar to the banyan of the East, or *Ficus indica*. As is frequently the case, the one we are observing is supported by another tree. The seed of the fig has been left by some bird upon the branches of an iron-wood-tree, and now the latter seems to be wholly within the grasp of the fig. Rootlets or aerial branches are thrown down, while the young tree derives nourishment from the iron-wood, and a rapid growth soon covers it entirely. Branches shoot out and hang in the air until they reach the ground, where they take root, and present the novel aspect characteristic of the banyan. The leaf of this fig is large and oblong, unlike the indented leaf of our edible fig—*Ficus carica*. Like the India-rubber-tree, it has the thick white milky juice common to this family. One of the members yields a rich and wholesome milk, much prized by the natives, and is consequently called cow-tree. Bread-fruit is another product of the class. Many, however, yield poisonous juices; the famed upas is one. The gum-resin of commerce called shellac is from another of the family.

One of the taller and more conspicuous trees here is the almond. It is a striking feature in the scenery—not the less that it is the only tree that shows the autumnal colors in the cooler season. The branches are thrown out horizontally around the tree at a certain height; then a straight, limbless trunk rises a few feet, and another whorl of branches spreads out. Frequently three of these whorls or umbrella-shaped groups are seen. The leaves are very large and thick, and in many respects the tree is remarkably attractive. The fruit is imperfect here; though probably this is not the species that bears the finer kinds of commerce.

The tamarind is prized much for its fruit. Fine groups of them are common, and they are now loaded with ripe pods. The inner part of the pods is a most grateful, acidulous morsel, and when preserved is much esteemed. The delicate tracery of the tamarind leaves is quite rivaled by that of the chaparral. The latter resembles the weeping-willow, has smooth, rich green trunk and branches, and a flowing, airy spray of foliage of the finest feathery character, with slender stems of golden-yellow blossoms. This tree is more like the mimosa than chaparral, and is probably misnamed.

The guavas, several varieties, are thrifty in all parts of the island. In this garden are some fine trees. The fruit is rich and luscious, and furnishes the well-known jelly of the West Indies. The trees are low and straggling, like the peach, but have a rich, glowing foliage and smooth, mottled bark, like that of ash. It is worthy of remark here that nearly all trees and shrubs of these warm regions are destitute of the rough bark so common to trees of the North. It occurs to us that this is parallel with the fact concerning animals. The Northern animals are provided with thick coats, and shaggy ones in the extreme North, while those of the tropics are smooth and thinly clad. The pitch-pine is loaded with thick, shaggy bark. The palm is naked, its smooth skin quite exposed.

The sapodilla is a straight, elegant tree of the middle size. Several fine ones here, near the front walk, are completely shaded by the cocoa palms, yet they are fresh and thrifty, and full of the russet-apple-like fruit. The tree resembles closely the *Magnolia glauca*. Maumee-apple and maumee sapoté are beautiful trees, and bear large egg-shaped fruit, most excellent in quality. The peculiar form and grouping of the leaves, and their curiously arranged veins, make this tree conspicuous and interesting in this delightful exhibition of foliage.

The sour-sop and custard-apple are small shrubby trees, bearing fruit that is much valued.

The shaddock, with its great pumpkin-like oranges, grows in abundance.

Limes are in great profusion, and the woods are full of them. The juice is considered much more agreeable than that of the lemon. The latter is not of much account here, as, like the orange, having tap-roots, they do not find sufficient depth of soil.

Of all the flowering shrubs the oleander is the most prominent. Trees they are here fifteen or twenty feet high. Our friend, the Judge, can show us his neat cottage quite o'ertopped with them; and if we visit him at evening, and sit under his cheerful veranda (always allowing him to retain the wicker *rocking*-chair), he will show us a display of the gorgeous cups of the night-blooming cereus, which "excite our special wonder; while the air nimbly and sweetly recommends itself unto our gentle senses," fraught with the perfume of the festooned jasmines and roses.

What a wealth of gay blossoms these oleanders display! Marvelous, indeed, and one would think sufficiently so in this garden of gay beauties. Yet our benign friend, noting the fulsome exposition of the beauty and rarity of certain plants duly catalogued from the North, essayed to procure and plant a few seeds of the *marvel of Peru*, judging correctly, as he thought, that—a marvel from Peru, a land renowned for all that is gorgeous—the plant would certainly prove a desirable acquisi-

BANANA AND NIGHT-BLOOMING CEREUS.

tion. The Judge could have borne the disappointment, he said, "with some degree of equanimity had he not from time immemorial been bothered by the plaguy *four-o'clocks* coming up all over his garden. Why don't they *say four-o'clocks*, and done with it?"

These same four-o'clocks prove quite acceptable at Tortugas. We maintained a hedge of them several years. They become, like many plants, perennial, and grow quite shrubby. They were cut neatly in square shape, and continued blooming the year round. The agave, or Sisal hemp, grouped with the various shrubs, is an effective object in the garden. The vines and flowering plants that climb and hang gracefully over the walls are delightful objects, and each deserves a nearer view. The effect at night, while the moon is shining through the thick foliage, is exceedingly pleasant; and when a gentle breeze is stirring, the great leaves of the cocoanut palm, rasping each other, give forth a sound like a gentle fall of rain. The birds make free with this little forest, and give sweet music in return. Rambling out from the main street we gradually emerge into a low wooded expanse. Here the curious candle cactus rears itself above the surrounding shrubs, with here and there a stalk of agave relieving the uniformity of the outline. How strange and various are the forms of this family! This is a member of the cereus family, and is as prim and straight and angular as Mr. Burton tried to be in his inimitable personation of the head of a similar one. The grand columns of this plant in Mexico are wonderful objects compared with others, or considered as mere plants. The flower is exceedingly beautiful, like others of the cacti, but pure white.

The night-blooming cereus is native, growing luxuriantly upon trees; fastening itself, each joint as it puts forth, by rootlets. The houses are sometimes loaded with this plant, as it fastens readily upon brick or wood. In many of the yards in Key West the large trees are seen every evening during the warmer months decked with the great cups of this elegant plant. It is easily propagated by the joints. A curious example of that tendency in nature to adapt itself to circumstances is afforded here. This cereus, when not climbing and fastening itself by rootlets which are thrown out of the angular borders, contracts regularly at about every foot of growth, where a woody fibre is formed to strengthen it. It then enlarges to its proper size and shape, growing one of these joints every month. But if the plant is allowed to fasten itself by the rootlets it continues on for many feet in one unbroken angular column, somewhat like that of the columnar cereus, or candle cactus, but triangular in form. In the former case no rootlets are thrown out, as they are not called for; at the same time the fibrous contracted parts *are* called for to render the plant service as *acting backbones*. This would be a pretty example for the "development" theorists were it not true that, like every other object subject to such changes, the plant is ever true to its sphere of creation, be it never so "plastic" notwithstanding. Here comes closely to us the question, Has the creation been put forth by some unknown cause, endowed with innate power, with laws that work blindly, indefinitely; or, is there an Omnipotent, an Omnipresent Author who has devised the all-wondrous plan of nature, and yet guides and directs its workings? It seems impossible for one to take the former view without blindly setting adrift, and either denying the existence of the Creator, or attributing to him "resources so meagre that in order to create a human being endowed with reason, he must first change a monkey into a man. Without question this diversity of thought arises from two opposite qualities of mind. It is most likely that those who embrace the "development theory" are all of the same class of minds, the mathematical, say, or metaphysical. On the other side are found practical minds; those that see Nature as she is, and accept her plan as laid bare before us. A gentleman of great culture, yet given to useless speculations, remarked that he "could wish that the theory was correct, as it offered a grand field for thought." *There lies the secret.* Not satisfied with a devout contemplation of Nature as presented in her manifold forms, lacking the sense of appreciation of her beauties, forgetting for the time how little is our power of comprehension comparatively, impatient of the slow yet sure steps of exact science, they can only be amused by risking the accepted faith of the Christian for a wild reverie after a "simple and easy solution of the fact that we live."

From the angles of the cereus the buds put forth, and bloom with very little stem, the large cups appearing to open directly from the surface. Fully spread, the flower is of pearly whiteness. The stamens are very numerous, and have the effect of the plumage of the bird of paradise. Mingled with the perfume of the jasmines, the air is often nearly oppressive with the odor.

Other species of cacti are numerous in the forest—among them the opuntia, from which the cochineal bug of commerce is obtained. This plant in Mexico yields many thousand pounds yearly. The prickly-pear, a low variety, covers extensive tracts, and several delicately formed species are found in single groups. In the gardens are cultivated many of foreign growth.

In the midst of the bush lives an old negro called Sandy. Every one who has visited Key West has heard of or made acquaintance with this odd genius. The old man, now white-headed with age, has lived here with his wife, as he says, a heap many year. Sandy is shrewd, intelligent, and provident. He has read much and pondered, he says, and for many years has held forth to his colored brethren. His voice is voluminous, enduring, and cumulative—interesting his hearers, and plunging them into the most profound agitation, physically, if not mentally, agonizing to behold. The old man is very fond of plants, and has a very extensive variety of tropical productions.

"Well, now, I know I'm gwine to hab rain, Cap'n—suah, stranger," says Sandy, as we approached, in company with our friend. "Yes, dat tree is Susannah's tree—dat is, I keeps dem trees for her sake, and I comes out dere and reads in de Bible and ponders." The tree that we were examining is the mastic, which yields the gum-mastic of the shops. We failed to see the connection, however, concerning Susannah.

Fine grapes are growing here trained upon frames. In his garden near the house are fine guavas—an orchard of them—and sapodillas. On an old stump near the house is a bald eagle, which Sandy has kept for many years. Date palms, oranges, lemons, pomegranates, limes, grow here in perfection. Pine-apples, tobacco, coffee, and sugar-cane also thrive, with more or less luxuriance.

Near Sandy's house are the remains of an old mill, which was once used to crush the leaves of the agave or Sisal hemp, from which the Manilla or Mexican hemp is made for cordage. The manufacture was abandoned on account of undue cost in working the mill. Labor being cheaper in other countries, the hemp is imported for less price than they can afford to manufacture it at Key West.

The pawpaw is a striking and singular object — rising with bare trunk, showing scars where the long-petioled leaves have dropped. From the top a cluster of leaves shoots out, and altogether the tree resembles a fan palm at a distance. The fruit hangs from the base of the leaves. An unusual number of terrestrial shell-fish are seen lying on the ground and crawling over the stones. In the North, land-shells are so small and inconspicuous they are seldom seen. Few are probably aware how large a number of shell-fish live upon the land, permanently adapted to terrestrial life. Several species of helix, or snail, and a large achatina are plentiful here. Myriads of dead shells lie upon the ground. Some of the islands in the Indian Ocean are wonderfully stocked with land-shells. Ceylon has one hundred and twelve known species; and in the Philippine Islands there are over three hundred.

A rambling style of gardening is that of old Sandy's; but he succeeds in raising a good deal of nice fruit.

The garden of Captain Pffister is probably one of the finest on the island. More care is taken there to produce good fruit, and plenty of it. He has all the usual varieties, and in great profusion.

In these gardens we meet with nothing familiar; all is strange, yet full of interest. An epitome of the tropics is here, in our own land, and proves a pleasure to those who are unable to go from home to enjoy the views in foreign climes. At New Orleans and throughout the Southern States we meet with many strange forms of vegetation, but mingled with those more familiar. Here all is strange. It is so far south that a new zone is presented with peculiar productions, animal as well as vegetable. The pelican and the frigate-bird at once attract our notice. The palm and banana are equally strange to our sight.

UNCLE GEORGE'S CABIN.

In the outskirts of the town are many quaint cottages and cabins, where as quaint old people live. Old Uncle George puts his snow-white head out from the door and says, "Come in!" We are enthusiastically fond of these choice bits of living pictures. A friend who is quite as enthusiastic, and an artist of great culture withal, once, in the suburbs of Havana, in the midst of a pouring rain, from which his companion was hastily urging him, insisted on having the umbrella held over him while he sketched a rude cabin, "full of the picturesque." We are almost afraid that it will be thought absurd to stop by the way and enter and admire this "picturesque" cabin of Uncle George's. But let us take a glance, and not tarry. Plumes of cocoa-nut palm, long lance leaves of banana and plantain, rich russet foliage of almond, glossy green globes of guavas, towering over and nearly concealing what little space is left on the thatched walls not decked with flowering vines of ipomœas and jasmines. Gorgeous oleanders break the green masses, in varied tints, from the rich crimson to the lightest blush of pink. Slender sprays of coral-bush tipped with lake, peach blossom roses, and gay cups of the many-colored elders and cordianas, come into the picture; and the quaint old colored folk, quite in keeping, complete the scene.

The profusion of flowering plants and trees impresses the stranger with pleasure. A stroll up and down the streets is quite enjoyable, particularly in the early spring, when there is rather more than the usual floral display. All through the winter plants bloom, birds sing, and insects flit and hum.

One of the most singular and striking flowering trees is called the Gieger tree here, from the fact that Captain Gieger first brought it from the West Indies. The exquisite tint of scarlet, and large size of the flowers, render it very showy and ornamental. The pomegranate is a graceful shrub, throwing up long, slender branches, which bend with the weight of the rich, red-cheeked fruit. The flower is an elegant sculptured cup of scarlet, quite unique and wonderful as compared with others.

Though there are few houses here of any pretension to style, there are many tasteful cottages and domiciles. The house of Mr. Ferguson is a pretty Grecian structure, standing on about half an acre of land, and almost hidden from view by the numerous palms of all sizes. This place is exceedingly attractive to the stranger. The Marine Hospital is creditable, and is a pleasant feature, surrounded by noble trees. The Episcopal church and the parsonage are appropriate structures, and are embellished finely by the grand row of pine-trees—a tall species of Southern growth.

Were the streets shaded by palms, which grow so rapidly here, the town would present additional graces, greatly to the credit of its inhabitants and charming to the stranger. Across the island, to the northward, lie extensive salt ponds. Years ago these ponds were remunerative. Slaves were then employed, and other labor was low-priced. Lately the works have been re-established on a more scientific footing, and there can be no doubt but the intelligent enterprise of the proprietor will prove eventually successful. Key West salt has always maintained the highest standard, the highest reputation, in the whole list of localities, being placed at the head of the list by competent authority. This fact will stand always to its credit, and must be the means of bringing a considerable income to the town.

This, with the sponge trade, and the usual wrecking business, gives to Key West at present a good earnest for the future.

The bay on the northern side bears a lively little fleet of vessels, small craft, nearly all of which are engaged in the sponge business. Opposite this bay is the government reserve, where is situated the United States barracks—an artillery post, and one of the neatest in the army. Six handsome cottages are arranged on two opposite sides of a square. Barracks for the privates are on the third side, facing the fourth, or front, which borders the bay. A handsome parade ground is within; and a hospital, with other appropriate quarters, is situated near.

Fort Taylor is a strong work, with two tiers of casemates. Besides the two towers, with their surrounding casemated works, two others are to be constructed—one upon the extreme eastern portion, and another upon an island in the inner harbor. These square towers are arranged to mount four guns of the largest kind on the top or parapet. Loopholes for musketry are in the walls. Covered ways and casemates are in the works surrounding the towers.

Along the south beach, facing the broad waters of the Gulf, grow most delicate and brilliantly colored algæ, mossy sea-weeds, and corallines. At low tide, when the little pools are left on the rough ledge, exquisite forms are seen, simulating in the clear mirror of still water the daisies and the ferns of the forest. Here is a form quite unique, even among the algæ. Long, slender stems bearing shallow circular cups, prettily radiated in the manner of the mushrooms. We so often meet with bright faces like these turned to the sunlight from the sea-side, learning to regard them as animal nature, that here in the same pool with such forms as tubularias, anemones, and others, it seems odd that the delicate fringes of this little cup do not instantly recoil on being touched. This is certainly one of the most interesting of all the algæ.

That species called *Acetabularia crenulata* grows in pretty bunches, and looks like so many mushrooms, barring the color—a delicate green.

Algæ vary much in their composition, from the purely vegetable structure to those that absorb or assimilate muriate of lime of the sea-water to form within their tissues a carbonate of lime, which in some species is hard as stone. Some of the nullipores are quite like stalactites or coral forms.

The laminarias, those long-leafed kelps with hollow stems, are not found here. Around the rocky shores of the North immense beds of them are seen in a calm day, swaying in the sea like tall grain.

Marine vegetation here forms a distinct province, differing greatly from that of the eastern coast, and strongly resembling that of the Mediterranean. Nearly one-third of the species are identical. Near one hundred and fifty species are found upon this island.

The caulerpas, comprising those elegant trailing plants with feathery fronds, most remarkable in their close resemblance to pinion plumage, constitute the entire forage of the green-turtle, so prized as an edible reptile.

After a heavy gale from the southward the beaches are loaded with algæ from the reef, and great numbers of the various species of sponge and gorgonias, sea-fans, sea-feathers, and other forms, attached to dead coral or shells. At such times the wonderful display of curious zoophyte forms cast upon the shore is worth a visit.

Our lost boat seemed likely to place an obstacle in the way of rambling along the reef; but we were fortunate in coming into possession of an almost duplicate of the one so much prized—one no less celebrated than the cutter of the yacht *Wanderer*, that was sold here, the noted slaver. We christened her *The Curlew;* and as our schooner is no more also, and the Bos'n having brought himself to a peace footing, we embark in the new boat, intending to run ashore along the reef as we head for the western end, or "leward"—"Down to the Tugasses," as the wreckers say; "Tight and snug," says the Bos'n—and we head her for the Marquesas.

As we shove ashore innumerable light-colored crabs run up the beach and suddenly disappear. Spirit-crabs! Appropriate name. Singular, square-bodied creatures, of the same color as the surrounding sand. Here they burrow for retreat, and sally forth by hundreds to feed on carcasses.

Low trees or shrubs, called bay-cedar, completely cover these islands. Crawling upon the branches were great numbers of hermit-crabs, each with his stolen coat upon his back. This is truly a *freak* of nature. Many of the species are aquatic, but this one is terrestrial, and does not go into the water. With chest and arms of formidable strength, this creature ignobly tapers to a soft, worm-like posterior. Like Richard, not shaped for sportive tricks, curtailed of fair proportion, cheated of feature, deformed, unfinished, sent before its time into this breathing world scarce half made up, it seeks to usurp and intrench itself within the castle of another knight of the shore.

As soon as the young crab has attained sufficient size and strength to assume its wonted responsibility, and struggle for existence, it forthwith looks about for "its size" among the cast-off univalve shells; first thrusting a long claw into the chambers to make sure that all is well and the castle vacant. Should a smaller or weaker knight of his order chance to be the occupant, battle is given at once. The sally-port is closed by the stout mailed arms, and the castle held strictly on the defensive as its only safety. The ambitious knight is on the alert, however, and eventually succeeds by strategy. The weaker party relaxes a little, and peeps forth to survey the field. A well-aimed blow and quick passage of arms place the incumbent *hors de combat;* he is dragged from the gates, and quick as thought the conqueror throws his rear within the castle, winds up the spiral turret, and presents a bold front of mailed armor at the gate. This strong-hold is held unless some party yet stronger gives battle anew.

These hermit-crabs are exceedingly pugnacious, and seemed to be continually disposed to rout and plunder. Several large ones were sent North, packed in a small box. One individual remained; he, the strongest, had devoured all that was edible of the others, leaving only the shells and claws. The survivor was kept under a glass bell for a year. He moulted once successfully, casting a perfect shell, an exact fac-simile of himself; but he died in the act of casting the second time. This crab became quite tame; eating from the hand, and remaining partially out of the shell when touched, though usually they remain "closely mewed up" when approached.

It is a ludicrous sight at times, when great numbers of these creatures congregate about a carcass, or climb the bushes after a rain to sip the moisture from the hollow leaves. An officer of the post at Tortugas, lately arrived, filled his pockets with the pretty shells so profusely scattered upon the keys. On landing at the wharf, homeward bound, he was much surprised at the manifestly improper expression that met him in every face of the guard, from sergeant to private. A friendly voice called his attention to the crawling multitude which now well-nigh likened him to the tawdry shell-work of frames and fancy boxes. The crabs, in many instances, can retire within the shell so far that they are not readily observed. One, enthusiastic in his first blush of delight at finding so large a number of pretty shells so near each other, is quite likely to fill his pockets greedily, without stopping to examine them, then and there. The shy creatures withdraw, and hug closely the inner chamber of the shell the instant a footstep is felt, and so remain until all danger is past—hence the possible mistake of which our friend really became the victim. An amusing sight was afforded in the office of the engineer in charge at Fort Jefferson. The officer—now our distinguished Quartermaster-general—had a large number of these crabs, from the largest to the smallest, placed upon the floor. Then commenced a novel scene—battles and combats, sparring, and rough-and-tumble fights; while numbers of them crawled upon the walls, and manifested every phase of curiosity by examining closely all parts of the room. A large species, which usually selects the turbo, a shell about the size of a large tea-cup, had the habit of living under houses or logs, and seemed to sally forth more at night. Occasionally they would crawl into the house. One particular individual became notorious as a constant visitor, and regularly crawled up the corner of a book-case to drink water from a dish—never, of course, leaving his shell behind. They present an exceedingly grotesque appearance shambling along with

CONTEST OF CRABS.

THE HERMIT AT HOME.

their heavy stolen shells. Diogenes must have learned his habit from these creatures. Some naturalist has given the philosopher's name to one species.

These hermits seldom adopt an imperfect shell; but the height of the ludicrous was reached when we discovered an individual ensconced within the bowl of an old black clay pipe nearly stemless. It required all the taction the poor weak abdomen could muster to keep a sure tenure of possession. Commiserating his forlorn condition we gave him a chance to change quarters; an opportunity which he seized with alacrity; not unlike in that respect some in the army who delight in "turning each other out according to rank." The hermit is opposed to "commutation of quarters," and takes his "in kind"—*casemates* though they be, of *one story*, and *no back window*.

Few freaks of nature exceed this of the hermit-crab. It seems so unaccountable that an animal, in every other respect like its kind, should be so half finished, and given the instinct which induces it to adopt the rejected covering of another—the dead shell of a totally different class. The "developmentists" can take comfort, for here is an excellent opportunity for the exercise of the imaginative faculties. Here is a species trying very hard to establish itself by "natural selection." Can we not imagine the hermit eventually *stuck* to his stolen shell? or, seriously, in accordance with the theory of Darwin, we may imagine a single hermit-crab centuries back suddenly afflicted with paralysis of the abdominal muscles, which renders the part impotent, and in consequence the members attached become shriveled and useless. As this class of philosophers assume certain conditions when necessary, we will have to assume that the hermit was originally built as perfect, and on the same plan, as others of its family. The hermit now presents an aspect exactly of a paralytic. It is most reasonable to *imagine* this weak creature crawling into, as he naturally would—following the "law of natural selection"—the first available hole or by-place for protection in his "struggle for existence." What more likely than that a shell, a cast-off, dead shell was the first object in his way? Hence results an "unconscious selection." Once within, *imagine* him forever there. Clad in armor, which he moves with reasonable celerity, he never will give up his strong-hold; not he. Darwin says: "Under nature, the slightest difference of structure may well turn the nicely balanced scale in the struggle for life, and so be preserved." Now, our hermit, possessing unusual means of defense in his adopted shell, gives battle to his tribe, and kills off, assisted by his offspring, the weaker portion (the imagination indulges fondly here), while the soft, inactive, palsied posterior of the crab relies upon the kindly offices of the spiral conch, and perpetuates its degenerate form; preserving a favored race in the struggle for life, and offering a splendid example of the "origin of species by means of natural selection."

So reason the "developmentists." Let us rather have faith in the wisdom of the Creator, and believe that this *apparent* anomaly is designed for some good purpose, remembering that our wisdom is finite.

On the beach of the Marquesas are found the finest varieties of gorgonias seen upon the reef. Some of the most elegant yellow and purple sea-feathers are cast ashore here.

Gopher-turtles and terrapins abound here, and both are much prized as food.

Before the steady east wind we run along over the reef and Rebecca Shoals to East Key, the largest and outermost of the Tortugas group. Miles of reef, of uniform depth of water, here spread out before us. On the western border of this group of islands is a deep channel, much used by shipping bound to the Gulf ports. A dangerous quicksand and projecting points of reef are localities of many serious disasters. The map of this reef, kept at Fort Jefferson, indicates many names of vessels wrecked there. The channel is safe to those accustomed to its bearings; but strangers too often attempt its passage.

Were we approaching this key in the month of May, before the low white sand-bar was distinctly visible, we should see a cloud of moving specks directly over it. Nearing it, the cloud is seen to be made up of mottled sea-birds—sooty and noddy terns—members of the gull family, the prettiest of their class. Nearer, we are met by one and another, and presently by many, flying straight at us, as if determined to see who comes, and stop him at once. But suddenly they wheel, utter a shrill cry of alarm, and fly directly back to join their companions. As we reach the shore, myriads of these garrulous birds fly over and around us, disputing every inch, darting with all vigor at our heads, and filling the air with their shrill cries. The island is nearly covered by the bay-cedar, which forms a close brush, about ten feet in height. Under this brush, in all directions, are eggs of the terns. A slight depression is scooped in the sand, and one brown, spotted egg is deposited. Barrelfuls of these eggs are collected by the soldiers in the course of a few days, and they prove, unlike the eggs of most sea-fowl, most excellent eatables. Besides the immense numbers on the ground, pure white eggs are found on the top branches of the bushes, laid by the sooty tern or noddy—a lovely bird, with eye dove-like, and expressive of all gentleness, its plumage quite in keeping with its character. Darwin was impressed by the beauty of the little white tern which we have seen hovering over the *river of fishes*. He says: "There is one charming bird, a small, snow-white tern, which hovers smoothly at the distance of a few feet above one's head, its large black eye scanning with quiet curiosity your expression. Little imagination is required to fancy that so light and delicate a body must be tenanted by some wandering fairy spirit."

The noddies build a rude nest on the very top of the slender bushes, and in no instance did they appear to be hollow, but almost always quite the reverse, so that the single egg is only held in place by the twigs. Often the nest is of considerable dimensions, and requires much time in its construction, notwithstanding it is so crude. It is believed that the sun has much to do with hatching the eggs; for the parent bird is seldom seen sitting upon the nest, but usually near it. The egg of the noddy is nearly pure white, and the yolk is as yellow as that of a hen's egg, closely resembling it as an article of food. They are regarded as a great luxury, and prove of inestimable value to the command during the hot weather of the first weeks of summer. The birds continue to lay about six weeks. Though their numbers are enormous, and a cloud of them hangs over the island during this time, it seems difficult to account for the great numbers of eggs unless it is true that they deposit more than one. Only one being found in or near a nest, it is supposed that they lay in different places. A custom is to clear a space which can be recognized, and take the eggs from that place daily, or on alternate days; in this way for several weeks a fresh lot of eggs is taken with no risk of gathering those partly incubated.

A novel effect is produced by shouting loudly while in the midst of this chaos of voices; instant silence—fearful, almost, in its intensity; every voice is hushed, but only for a moment; the vast chorus, *una voce*, bursts forth again as if it had not been interrupted, but as if we had suddenly lost and immediately recovered our sense of hearing.

Spirit-crabs and hermits, Bohemians of their class, gather around and filch away the small fishes that chance to drop from the greedy chops of the young birds. The hermits drag their heavy shells to the top of the bushes, and lay in wait for a grab at the young noddy's victuals.

This is the season for turtle-turning. It is now that the green-turtle and the loggerhead crawl upon the beaches to lay their eggs. All the rest of the year they swim in the great deep. We have seen how shy they are, and knowing that, we wonder why they should select moonlight nights as suitable time to perform this important work. Perhaps they have poor sight, and are beholden to the sweet silver light of that luminary. Ten to one, Bob Rand and Long John are to be found just round the bend of the key, killing two birds with one stone; not literally, but in the way of watching for a chance to pilot in a vessel, and keeping a sharp eye to any reptile that may "break" near the island.

The Bos'n is beckoning, and tugs on with unwonted energy, which betokens some extraordinary good luck. The boat at anchor and the shelter-tent — leg-o'-mutton sail stretched over an oar — confirm our suspicion; and all doubt is removed concerning the presence of the renowned turtlers as we discover the Bos'n placing his affections between a pot of hard-boiled noddies' eggs and a black bottle labeled "Kitchen and Henderson's Hair Restorative." To sit upon the clean white sand, and eat hard-boiled noddies' eggs dipped in pepper and salt, "with a sup of Bob's cawfee," was, as the Bos'n says, having "dead loads of comfort."

The Bos'n says he "remembers the day, 'twas of a Chewsday—four year come Michaelmas—sin' he'd exparunced ony thing like ut." Certainly nothing but a Daniel Webster, Boston cracker chowder, with crispy rashers tried out of sweet pork, and eaten on the rocks at Nahant in the hot term, equals this bivouac and its accompaniments of hard-boiled noddies' eggs and Bob Rand's hot coffee.

The turtlers camp here for the season. They make fast those that they catch, and send them into market as occasion offers. Some of these huge reptiles weigh over six hundred pounds, and require all the strength of the two men to turn them. When once on their backs, they are entirely helpless. As they are all females that come out of water, they are allowed to lay their eggs before they are turned. The eggs are much esteemed by the native population of this vicinity. Most of those taken here are loggerheads; the green-turtles are more abundant within the creeks and channels of the older part of the reef, where, as we have seen, they feed and fatten in the extensive fields of algæ. The loggerhead is carnivorous, and is not esteemed a delicacy.

Middle Key and Sand Key are two smaller islands, with no vegetation, forming with East Key a line of barrier, with the intervening reef, which is continued by the larger Loggerhead Key, Bird Key, and their reefs; completed by Long Key and Bush Key, between which and East Key, where we now are, the main ship-channel passes.

Winding in almost zigzag course, the channel opens within this barrier an expanse of deep water that proves of great service as a safe harbor. In the centre of this harbor is the island formerly called Garden Key, now wholly covered by Fort Jefferson.

ALONG THE FLORIDA REEF.

[Fourth Paper.]

WITHIN the barrier reef which incloses the group of islands called the Dry Tortugas is one broad lagoon, hemmed in on all sides by sand-spits and shoals, and opening to the sea only by a narrow cut called the Five-Foot Channel. The water in most parts is just sufficient to float our small craft.

The Five-Foot Channel affords a convenient passage for the small boats of the pilots, that would otherwise be compelled to navigate the long, winding, main openings of the harbor.

The lagoon is a notable field for the naturalist. A wonderful variety of animal life is here, and often it has been the scene of considerable fun and merriment. A species of shark, some eight or nine feet in length, was often seen here in great numbers, reminding one of a drove of hogs, their habits being so peculiar. Though frequently in close contact with them, we never succeeded in killing one of the larger kind. It is, without doubt, a species of scyllium, called here the *nurse*, and in Havana *gata*. The "nurse" of the Northern waters is a scymnus, another genus. This shark, gata, has a very small mouth, which is placed far underneath its exceedingly blunt and club-shaped head. We judge so from the appearance of a small one which we speared under a coral rock, where they are frequently seen. They appear to be very sluggish, and often wedge themselves between the rocks, and resist all efforts to dislodge them. They appear by their huge forms very formidable, but are quite harmless. Dr. Storer, in his "Synopsis of the North American Fishes," gives the dimensions of the gata as fifteen feet in length in some instances. Those frequenting the lagoon were not over nine feet, and all seemed about the same size. They evidently came in there to feed on the shoal bottom, and on several occasions we had come upon them when they were in water so shallow that the mud would be turned up in furrows as the creatures scampered off with their big fins projecting above the surface.

Charley was wild with excitement at this sight on one occasion. Putting the helm down, he gave chase. The Bos'n was along, and Fat Charley—all members of the *Curlew's* crew, introduced in a former article. Running with a free wind, the boat—then the old *Rosetta*—was very fast; but they never would have caught up with the sharks had the creatures made a straight line out of the lagoon, but they crossed and recrossed, and ran around the boat in every direction. This was too good to be lost. Giving the helm to Bos'n, Charley sprang forward, and made fast a line to the grains (a kind of fish spear, with slender wooden handle). The boat was brought up in the wind, and Charley jumped over, making a lunge at one as he passed. The line ran out rapidly, and just in time he gave a turn around the thole-pin. Now came a jerk, and the boat swayed around, and was off in a moment, cutting water in fine style. Bos'n dropped the helm, and hugged the stern-sheets with terror.

Fatty was elated. It was fun for him; and Charley shouted in the full enjoyment of his fast team. There was no way to make fast and hold on. The creature was so large and strong that the boat and its crew were no adequate resistance; so they could do nothing but let him run, or cut the line. On another occasion, when a "man-eater" started off with the same crew in a heavy flat-boat, and in the deep channel, more danger was apprehended; here, it was all sport, and little danger. The fun was soon up, for the keel struck a coral head plump and square, sharky kept on, snapped the grains, and Fat Charley pitched head foremost into the mud. The Bos'n was too well fortified to sustain much damage, but remarked, with much force, as well as truth, that he was "—— if he could see ony profit in such a wenter. The cussid critters," he said, "hadn't ony ile in 'em, ony how."

They could not give the chase up so. Consequently the blacksmith was applied to at once for a regular harpoon. After a little tinkering they produced a stout steel-pointed spear, well rigged with chain and stout line. The Bos'n begged off for this trip; so, again fitted out, the boat is headed in a bee-line for the fishing-ground, or, more likely, a butterfly-line—a zigzag—for the lagoon lies to windward from the fortress, and nine times out of ten we have to beat up there, when the wind is a trade from the east, which is most of the time; if it blows a norther, there is little comfort; or if there is a dead calm, it is just as bad for sailing.

THE BOS'N AT HOME.

The shoals were black with these huge creatures, but they were getting shy. The only chance was to float gently near them; in doing so they approached pretty closely, and Charley, regardless of boat or any thing, leaped over and made a plunge at one of the beasts, driving his harpoon "clean home," as Fatty said, "sure enough." The water was just deep enough to make it difficult walking, so Fatty tumbles in and essays to help. Charley, in his eagerness to do the whole thing, lost his hold, while Fatty suddenly appeared to be running off in a most extraordinary manner.

The shark had gotten so much line out that he had full play, and was now running at full speed, towing Fat Charley, like a big log, endwise on the surface.

This was amusement for Fatty; and nothing can exceed the novelty of the scene, when all around the lagoon, back and forth, from one side to the other, the huge boy was seen driving his single team, and kicking out behind in the greatest glee. Imagine the astonishment of the rest of the herd, now huddling in some remote part of the lagoon, and then suddenly dispersed by the furious onset of their excited companion, snorting and turning up the mud as he skimmed the shallow bay! All this time Charley was half crazy with disappointment at losing the fun; but the good laugh enjoyed all round was some compensation. By the time Fatty had gotten pretty well tired of the sport the lagoon was well cleared of the creatures; and as there was no chance to get a bight on the line, he had to cut it and let the animal go, though he made every effort to bring him "in to the death."

As long as we remained at the fortress we never could get a sight of them again; though previously they had been often seen feeding in great numbers within this inclosed shoal.

The boat was then gotten under way, and Fatty bestowed himself amid-ships to look after the fore-sheet and take a quiet smoke, while Charley bethought him, at the helm, what report he should make to the Bos'n, who was discerned, as they approached the shore, taking observations over the top of his famous telescope.

At the head-quarters of our crew, the old hospital, a description of which has been given in an early Number, the evenings were sometimes enlivened by unusual fun and jollity.

The summer of 1863 was remarkably hot, and the rebellion at its height. Prisoners of all complexions were thronging the fortress, and still they came. Too many were here already, yet loads of them continued to arrive. Nearly all were badly tainted with scurvy; and no more unfavorable place could be selected for such as were thus afflicted, particularly on account of the scarcity of vegetables. Crowded as they were in the jails at New Orleans, many were broken down before they reached here; others were taken sick on the long voyage of the half-rotten tubs sent from the Northern ports.

Altogether a serious aspect was gathering upon our pleasant garrison. Nearly nine hundred prisoners and a regiment of infantry were quartered within the walls of the fortress. Though the medical department was usually well provided with the necessary supplies, antiscorbutics were wanting, and no fund was available for the purchase of such. The surgeon suggested and carried out a plan which proved a godsend to the wretched creatures. It must be remembered that the great bulk of these prisoners were men with families, who had been hastily picked up and court-martialed for various infractions of discipline, and not for crime. Men they were who had found it difficult to succumb to the exactions of petty officers, who in many instances were their inferiors. Many decent men were thus punished unjustly; and many instances occurred wherein it was found that officers of their regiments had preferred charges from mere personal revenge. We are glad to record that such instances, when brought to the notice of the officers in charge, were considered, and the individual in nearly every case released from confinement.

Still there was much to do to provide for those who were to remain. Men were dying of scurvy, and those that were apparently well had no employment. The different departments worked all they could use, but many were cooped within the close casemate quarters, and subject to the very conditions that favor the increase if not the origin of the dread disease. The leaden complexion, that unmistakable index of the complaint, met one at every turn.

The surgeon's first thought was, what indigenous productions are possible? The boat is manned, and a thorough search is made of the islands in the group. It was found that purslain, a succulent vegetable that is well known in the gardens of the North as a troublesome weed—called there *pusley*—grew in profusion on most of the islands, and particularly where the earth had been newly cleared and turned up. This was the only available, the only eatable, plant to be found. Boats were sent out, and loads were brought in and distributed among the various messes. The purslain was boiled, and used as *greens*, with vinegar and pepper. This, of itself, was not only useful in a wonderful degree as an antiscorbutic, but it proved a luxury as an article of diet.

Those who have never made use of this article will find it an excellent *greens*, and also a pleasant substitute for asparagus, boiled, and eaten with butter, or dressed with toast, like asparagus. A most grateful article it proved to be to the sick and wretched of this garrison.

The juice of limes is far beyond any other remedy for scurvy. Limes were to be obtained at Key West, but the quantity required constantly was so great that we were unable to meet the expenses. The Sanitary Commission sent useful articles, but the prisoners, who needed the most, were left out, and would have died in great numbers had not some extra measures been taken to provide for them. Money must be had at some rate to purchase the necessary articles. The surgeon hit upon a plan whereby he accomplished two important ends by very simple means. He would turn out from the vast throng all who could sing, dance, play a tune, or tell a story. Here was a chance to stir up this mouldering mass of humanity, give

SHARK-FISHING.

them exercise—as we have seen they had none, one-half being unoccupied—interest them, cheer them, and make some money out of the performance to purchase the much-desired articles of diet and regimen.

FORT JEFFERSON.

There are always to be found, even in a company only of soldiers, some who are musical or have a notion for fun, some who are dramatically inclined. What, then, is there not possible in two regiments—a regiment of soldiers and a regiment of prisoners?

All those who desire to take parts in music, dancing, minstrelsy, or the *very* light drama, etc., are requested to report, etc., etc. An order of this import was promulgated in the quarters both of the prisoners and soldiers.

Such a motley assemblage! "Then came each actor" (from his cell)—"the best actors in the world" (upon their own showing), "either for tragedy, comedy, history, pastoral, pastoral-comical, historical-pastoral, tragical-pastoral, scene individable, or poem unlimited." Unquestionably there were some who could, upon occasion, invest a scene with all the interest belonging to a real tragedy. *Low* comedy was well represented, as well as the comic drama.

From the eager throng seventeen performers were selected; others were held in reserve.

The old building was fitted up with comfortable seats for the audience. A decent stage was erected; suitable scenery was painted, and a gorgeous drop-curtain procured, upon which was a painting of Fort Jefferson. On the painting, which was very large, and the fort well in the fore-ground, were the two light-houses. A pleasant trick was perpetrated by Charley just before the opening, when the audience were admiring the unexpected scene. He punctured the lantern of the light-houses, and placed a candle behind each, which gave a very pretty effect, and, in the parlance of the theatre, brought down the house. What with the drop-curtain, a few pieces of appropriate side scenery, and a pretty display of flags and bunting of all colors, the interior of the little theatre was quite cheerful and inviting.

The Bos'n was made usher and door-keeper, and was busy as a bee in all the various duties appertaining to his office.

Fat Charley was to be drop-tender, to have charge of the curtain, and act as "supe" as occasion required.

The green-room was above stairs, in a large room—as was requisite, it may be imagined, for seventeen performers.

To start with, it was deemed prudent to adopt the minstrel style of performance.

The rehearsal revealed a personage who was at once elected as manager—Dan Sullivan.

Who of that assemblage will ever forget Dan Sullivan and his inimitable performances? Dan was a snug-built, devil-may-care Irish boy; sharp as steel; with a peculiar mark in one eye, that, with his pock-marked face, gave him a look wherein mischief was read clearly. Dan could do any thing in the line of the "profession." He didn't brag—not at all; he only said "Yes, Sir," and opened that sinister eye in a peculiar way in answer to inquiries. The first rehearsal proved all; he was sufficient, and was pronounced a fit man to be a manager; though he was to be strictly subordinate to the *directorship*—a position that the surgeon held for himself as the supreme guide of the affair.

An amusing crowd they were for minstrels, for nearly half were black—negroes. Bones was black as the ace of spades—a perfect African. Of course there was little need of burned cork in their case. Bones realized all that was possible in his part; he played every thing that could be put into the "instruments," and put himself into every conceivable position in doing so; but he had not a particle of humor in his composition, and only varied the stolid look which settled upon his countenance by an occasional exhibition of white ivory—a big mouthful—when the audience applauded with more than usual vigor. His bone-playing, in a word, was really a piece of perfection. Bones danced a jig also, with the same precise, mechanical method. Dan Sullivan danced in like manner, but always embellished his jig with humorous remarks and "taking" situations; expressions of face conveying humor, effective in the same manner as that of Grimaldi, or other successful clowns. There seems to be a *fund* of such humor in men of his class—an inexhaustible mine from which well up sparkling ideas that set the muscles of the face afloat, and the voluble tongue into electric-like fluency, on the slightest occasion. On some trifling theme the audience—

though, as we have remarked, not unused to sportive tricks and first-class merriment—burst with simultaneous roar at a sudden turn in the fun then going on. We are often reminded in Dan's performances of Grimaldi's unsuccessful shave by the barber's daughter—showing how a "face" will sometimes create great merriment. "Grim" had walked up and down to look up a barber's shop. Seeing a pole near by, he stepped in, and observing that there was only a pretty little girl within, who was sitting at her needle-work, he retired, saying as he did so that he would step in again. Strolling about the market-place a while, he called again, but the barber had not come home. Grimaldi was walking down the street when he met Mr. Howard, the manager, who walked back with him, and stepped in. Her father had not come in yet.

"That's very provoking," said Grimaldi; "considering that I have called here three times already."

The girl agreed that it was, and stepped to the door to see if he was in sight.

"Do you want to see him on any particular business?" inquired Howard.

"Bless my heart! no; I only want to be shaved," said Grimaldi.

"Shaved, Sir!" cried the girl. "Oh dear me, what a pity it is you didn't say so before, for I do most of the shaving when he is at home, and all when he is out."

"To be sure she does," says Howard. "I have been shaved here fifty times."

"You have?" said Grimaldi. "Oh, I am sure I have no objection. I am quite ready, my dear."

Grimaldi sat himself down in a chair, and the girl commenced the task in a very business-like manner—Grimaldi feeling an irresistible tendency to laugh at the oddity of the operation, but smothering it by dint of great efforts, while the girl was shaving his chin. At length, when she got to his upper lip, and took his nose between her fingers with a piece of brown paper, he could stand it no longer, but burst into a tremendous roar of laughter, *and made a face* at Howard, which the girl no sooner saw than she dropped the razor, and laughed immoderately also; whereat Howard began to laugh too, which only set Grimaldi laughing more; when, just at this moment, in came the barber, who, seeing three people in convulsions of mirth, one of them with a soapy face and a gigantic mouth, making the most extravagant faces over a white towel, threw himself into a chair without ceremony, and dashing his hat on the ground, laughed louder than any of them, declaring in broken words, as he could find breath to utter them, that "that gentleman as was being shaved was out of sight the funniest gentleman he had ever seen," and entreating him to "stop them faces, or he knew he should die." When they were all perfectly exhausted, the barber finished what the daughter had begun; and, rewarding the girl with a shilling, Grimaldi and the manager took their leaves. After this amusing description, which is from the pen of Charles Dickens, it is worth while, for those who love the humorous, to see George Cruikshank's drawing of the scene in Dickens's "Life of Joseph Grimaldi."

The tambourine-player, or Tambo, familiarly, was a wiry little mulatto, who called himself St. Clare—a mere boy. He was a perfect monkey in mimicry, and proved a great "card," as the managers say. St. Clare, as well as Sullivan and others, had been connected with strolling companies—bands of "minstrels," circus followers, etc. St. Clare had a funny way of singing the popular songs of the day, and particularly those of the *break-down* kind. He was good in "Ham Fat" and "walk-arounds," and particularly strong in "H'ist up the Flag" and the "Baby Show."

Tambo led off usually with song in the minstrels, and the company joined in the chorus. Conundrums were introduced, and many local hits. On one occasion St. Clare—Tambo—was given a part to perform which "brought down the house"—"highly gratified the aujence," as the Bos'n remarked. A light-brown dog had long been the pet of the garrison, belonging to no one person, but making his home at the guard-house. He came to be called "Sugar," and always answered to that name. Sugar had a habit of always meeting the ladies and officers of the garrison at the sally-port, and accompanying them in the usual walk around the walls, first saluting, which was accomplished in the usual manner of dogs—by coming to attention, arching gracefully the spinal column, extending the jaws to a right angle, and gaping.

Sugar was the garrison dog. Just as engine companies have their dogs, so do battalions or companies of soldiers have theirs. Sugar was just the color of the brown sweet that you see in long boxes marked ——, Cuba. He was much attached to the guard-house, and, for the time being, the officer of the guard was his commanding officer. Tambo was bright enough, and played the tambourine acceptably. He had a good deal of original humor; but he could not remember new things with certainty. On this occasion he was drilled for the local joke, and after a few rehearsals he was charged, and ready to fire off on the coming evening. Evening came, but not without some misgivings on the part of the director. Full of humor as St. Clare was, he was unaccountably stupid in learning any new joke. Sam Douglass, another mulatto, one of the sentimental kind, who *would* always sing "Rock me to Sleep, Mother," or one or more of the numerous paterno-pathetic ditties, had just been informing the audience that "poor dog Tray's never ugly," when St. Clare commenced: "I's gwine ter perpound fur yer eddification a conundlecumdrum. Kin enny you ign'ant darkies 'splain ter me why —dat is, can yer—can yer"—("Grocery store," says the prompter in his ear; for Tambo sat purposely at the extreme end under the folds

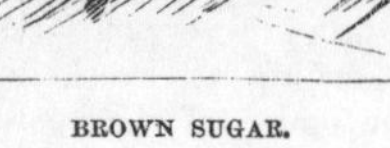

BROWN SUGAR.

of the flag-curtain)—"why dis yer box dat I's settin' on am like a *grocery store?*"

"Why, I don't see dat," says Violin, "'less your breff smell ob old Jamaiky."

"Go 'way, dar! be sensible."

Bones scratched *his* head, and looked about as much like getting the true answer as the side of a stove-pipe.

"I kin tell yer why dat box am like a grocery store. Dat box am like a grocery store 'case dar's a pocketful ob terbacker on it what was stole from de sutler!"

"Who-o-o ya fesultin' dar? Jes' you hole yer lip! I'll *tell* yer why dis box dat I's settin' on am like a grocery store—becase it is chock-full of *Brown Sugar.*"

"Bress us, honey! Well, now, de gen'l'man *hab* lef' his mind, shuah," says sentimental Sam, with an expression of mingled indignation and ridicule.

"*Git back*, now! Wha-wha-what der yer mean, foolin' the gen'l'men ob dis yer stage? *Whar's* de sugar?" says Violin.

Tambo stood up, lifted the box by the edge, when *Sugar*, the dog, who had been curled up in the small space of a candle-box, leaped to the front, shook himself, came to a "right-shoulder shift," and left the stage by the "right oblique" in "quick time." It is needless to add that the house was then and there "brought down."

Here was a minstrel troupe of real Southern plantation darkies, the "violins" only being white. Some could sing from personal experience of the "Louisiana Lowlands Low." Others were familiar with the "Yellow Rose of Texas" and the "Suwannee River;" while Sam, the sentimental, sighed, in truth, for his "Old Kentucky Home far Away."

Among the negroes was one most mysterious individual. He never wore a hat, and had a scraggy mat of yellow hair, and decided Arab features. He hailed from Texas, and put in his claims for a member of the *troupe* on the strength of his proficiency on the *conch!* He had selected one of the largest shells of that class that he could find—one about the size of his head—had cut the point away; and the music that he got out of that contrivance would have arrested the attention of Ned Kendall's ghost. In the chorus, loud above the din and rattle of the various instruments, the hoarse croaking of Pedro's conch was heard. Sam, the affectionate, beat the triangle; and it was as good as a play to see him fondly gazing at the wonderful performance of Pedro in his occasional "conch solos."

Pedro came out stronger afterward in a new rôle. He was a magician. The Bos'n remarked that "that yellow fellar had an oncommon look o' the devil aboot him." Pedro was allowed to spread his throne of mysteries, and come out between the second and third parts with an astonishing array of articles appertaining to the mystic craft. He gave quite a creditable performance, and several tricks were new to the audience. Among the best performances, or we ought to say the *very* best, was the "song and dance," by Dan Sullivan, which always came in *secondly*, after the minstrels; we might say, also, that the "song and dance" *always* meant "Off to Brighton," for never was performance better received by any audience. Dan was repeatedly "brought out," "encored," in this part, and as long as he remained at the post on each night of performance he was called on to sing that part. It is a pretty good test, even though it be "away down at the Dry Tortugas." Here was the same audience, night after night, calling and recalling out our "Minstrel Star"—a star, maybe, with less of the glory and radiance that attaches to the saint, and one whose light beameth upon the unjust probably oftener than upon the just. Yet with all thy faults, Daniel, thou inimitable mime, may thy rays continue to shine, and, for thy good, get wisdom, Daniel, and get understanding, and die a Christian—if so be thou art not already with the worms.

Dan made an occasional venture with other songs, and the "Ghost of the Pea-nut Stand" was very successful. Dan was pardoned after a while; and on the occasion of his last appearance it was proposed to give him a benefit. The usual programme was announced, and with it, as a closing piece, the "Pea-nut Stand." Dan had worked hard, appearing in his usual jig-dance, the dance in "Off to Brighton," and in the first part with the minstrels. In the last part, the curtain rising revealed Dan with an extra accompaniment of a basket of pea-nuts. During the song he passed the basket in among the audience, after throwing a portion among the "pit." At the close he was cheered by loud shouts, as well as by a pile of currency within the basket on its return amounting to twenty or more dollars. This was quite a lift for the scape-grace on his departure, if he made good use of it—a matter, we are afraid, that admits of serious doubts; particularly as we afterward learned that he was temporarily incarcerated within the dread structure known as the Sweat-box of Key West for assault and battery and contempt of court. Vale, Dan!

Among the scape-graces of the prison were two who professed to be vaulters and tumblers. One, a fair-complexioned boy of eighteen, affirmed that he was brought up to the business in a circus—that his father was a vaulter by occupation. The other, about the same age, was much like the first in appearance. Fat Charley suggested they be called the "Kerosene Brothers." These fellows were so constantly in the guard-house, and not only that, but decorated with bracelets of eight-inch shot and chain, that it seemed hardly feasible to make use of their limbs, under the circumstances, for the general entertainment. Circumstances, however, rendered it necessary to remove them, as well as others, for a time, on account of the fearful effects of the prevailing disease. The officer in charge saw no reason why the chains should not be removed occasionally to allow the cramped limbs to regain their wonted suppleness, and the stage was thought as safe a place as could be found for that purpose. The guard could remove the bracelets, and allow the poor fellows a little stretch of limb

THE "KEROSENE BROTHERS."—MORNING.

then and there, just as they were allowed to wash in the pleasant waters of the seashore.

So the Kerosene Brothers were on the boards; and never was somersault like that of Dill exceeded in its wonderful perfection. To take two or three quick steps upon a bare stage only eight feet in height from floor to ceiling, and throw the body over in somersault, without extending the arms, forward and backward, is about as far as human power extends. This was done by one of them often, and always with complete success. The two together performed many very pleasing and difficult parts; in fact, they exhausted the circus rôle, as far as they knew; and, with St. Clare as clown, were a "strong card" in the programme of the little theatre.

THE "KEROSENE BROTHERS."—EVENING.

St. Clare was compelled to use a goodly quantity of flour to whiten his face to the requisite aspect, an African clown being rather foreign to the conventional notions of the stage.

Among the various parts taken by one of the "Brothers" was lifting of heavy weights. The balls, it must be confessed, were more gracefully handled in this exhibition than during the day, when the same eight-inch shot and shell were dragged by the Kerosene Brothers around the garrison on police duty. An amusing burlesque was brought on at the close of the performance with heavy weights. Tambo, as clown, had prepared a pasteboard box resembling in size and shape a fifty-six pound weight; being painted carefully to resemble the weight, and as carefully marked with the figures. Attached to this was a rope. Seizing the rope, and winding it with all caution around his hand, the weight was swung, very slowly at first, in precise imitation of one performing the same motions with a *solid* weight. After a number of swingings, back and forth, apparently with great exertion, the weight is allowed to leave the hand, and goes out over the audience, fearfully near the heads of those in the pit, causing a general and instantaneous stampede. The light pasteboard box, as it is, returns by a jerk of the hand, and a sigh of relief is heard "all along the line."

A small fee for admittance was charged, and thereby was obtained a sum quite adequate to the full accomplishment of the design. Limes were constantly procured, as well as vegetables and fruit; and in a short time the surgeon had the satisfaction of seeing a rapid and steady improvement. At the commencement five hundred men were on the sick-list; and that number were prescribed for every day for several weeks. Many were too ill to leave their quarters. Tents were put up for them in the fresh air, and every attention paid to give them sufficient and generous diet, with the lime juice, which was served three times a day; when rapid convalescence followed. The garrison had been highly entertained, and great good had come out of the proceeds.

A movement of this nature would hardly be considered proper in ordinary times; but when we consider how many there were, among the hundreds of wretched creatures, who were probably suffering for a trifling breach of discipline, and dying for the want of the actual proper food, it will be seen that the means used were justifiable. The walls of the fortress were too small to accommodate more than half the number, and maintain the ordinary conditions of health. Disease was upon them, the season was midsummer, the climate tropical. The theatre plan was manifestly a sanitary measure, and proved so most thoroughly not only to the sick, but to the well. To the latter it was a rational prophylactic.

Many of the troops were sick at the time, but all seemed to be enlivened and to receive new energy after the hearty laugh at the evening entertainment.

The excellent band of the 110th New York Infantry, the regiment then on guard there, furnished the orchestra with superior string music, and helped materially toward the success of the enterprise; particularly as Helmer, the leader, gave really very fine sólos on the violin. Few of those who attended, night after night, will forget the pleasure derived therefrom. The little *Théâtre de Hôpital* has, we are gratified to learn, since been refitted, and has not ceased to be one of the *institutions* of the Dry Tortugas, though the motley throng that once crowded its corridors and "green-room" has long since dispersed. Pardons came "thick and fast," and hundreds of the poor fellows, many of them with anxious families awaiting their coming, were released. Hundreds that had gone unwittingly astray were now at liberty, but had felt the full measure of penalty, in some instances to a most serious extent.

Another day dawns upon the reef, and we muster our crew. There were great numbers of curious cucumber-like creatures, or things, lying upon the bottom of the lagoon. Every visitor here is sure to spy them, and, of course, desires to know what they are. A peculiar habit which we have noticed connected with them we will also look into. Driving the boat into a shoal place, Fatty gets over, and stooping with head under water, eyes wide open—a trick we can hardly conceive as agreeable—seizes a cucumber, which makes hardly more resistance than its namesake of the garden; spirting a stream of water, though, with considerable power, and slowly contracting itself, as if to show that its position in society is not so low as you thought. This is the *bêche de mer* of the French, the trepang of the Chinese, and the holothuria of science.

For a long time the Chinese have been in the habit of eating these creatures; and American ships, particularly those fitted out and owned in Salem, Massachusetts, have long been in the trade. The animals are gathered in the waters of Madagascar and in various parts of the Indian and Pacific oceans, are then cut and dried, or smoked, and carried to the Chinese ports by the shipload. After our view of them here, we should hardly be prepossessed in their favor as an article of luxurious diet, though probably they would prove quite as grateful to the taste as the birds'-nests of the Chinese.

This trepang is one of the wonderful modifications of the radiated animals. Belonging to one of the four great divisions—the Radiata—it seems at first strikingly different from the more familiar forms of star-fish and sea-anemones. To understand more clearly why this long-bodied member of the family is like the flat ones, or built on the same plan, we may take an orange, which is something like, in shape, the more round sea-urchins. Now if we roll out the orange-formed urchin, or jam down the long cucumber-like trepang, we have a nearer approach to the type, and see the plan expressed equally clear in both forms. If we peel the orange in quarters, or fives, and not only throw back the peel to form the star that it will, but the whole, in its divided parts, we have a star shape which indicates the star-fish, one of the most familiar forms of the plan. The mouth, it will be observed, is always at one end. Then, again, we take a star-fish, fold in backward his arms so that the points touch each other, then a sea-urchin is represented. To express the form of the holothuria, which seems so different, if we could roll this sea-urchin into a cylinder the relation is seen at once. No more interesting example or proof of the presence of Mind in nature is found in the whole range of creation. The greatest diversity exists in this division of nature, and yet the most mathematical exactness is proved in the adherence to the plan laid out for that particular class. But we came out here to have a little recreation, and not to meet dry matters in science. We want you to see what a curious parasite there is in this strange animal. We have spoken of its value to the Chinese because the circumstance seems to be not generally known to readers; and it is probable that few have ever heard of so strange an instance as this of the trepang's "hanger-on." Now the old gentleman Webster, of the "Dictionary," says that a "parasite is, literally, a trencher friend—one that frequents the table of the rich, and earns his welcome by flattery—a hanger-on." We see none here, but drop the trepang into the tall glass jar which we have brought along for the purpose. The creature soon begins to exhibit numerous small white tubes arranged in a line along the body, just as they are (the same kind of organs) in the arms of a star-fish, or on the five quarters of the sea-urchin. The tubes have sucking-disks, and fasten themselves upon the glass. Now the creature crawls with considerable skill. It is a great tube itself, with a nearly straight intestine running through it. At the mouth it is provided with a row of soft tentacles, not unlike the sea-anemones, instead of teeth like the animals very much higher in the scale of life. Instead of the brittle shell of the urchin, or the rough spiny armor of the stars, the trepang has a leathery tunic covering its fleshy body. One species, however, of its class has a beautiful armor of scarlet-colored scales, and spreads a wonderful array of tentacles from its mouth—a soft tree-like branch with innumerable branchlets. This is often brought up on the lines of the fishermen off the New England coast, and is only the size of your hand. Our captive here is over a foot long, and as large as your wrist. It looks always so much like a cucumber, with its rough knobby sides and oblong shape, that the term sea-cucumber seems quite appropriate.

FAT CHARLEY AND THE TREPANG.

Well, we have been talking just long enough to give the trepang a chance to exhaust the air—the oxygen, as the chemists say—and you must know that so large an animal will require a large quantity. The small jar would not long afford him the all-important life-giving element unless it were very frequently renewed. The first indication of this want of air is seen by the creature's anxiety to reach the surface, the same as in the case of the golden carp that are kept in glass globes. But another and more important member of the animal world puts forth a remonstrance. He is not only more delicate, physically, but he belongs to a very much higher class of society, and has lungs to be refreshed with the grateful element—or gills, rather. As the trepang begins to stretch up his mouth toward the air, a fish's head is seen bobbing up and down, peering out into the external world from the interior. Now "a joke is a joke;" and we at first thought some one had perpetrated a joke upon us; but no. On various and numerous examinations this particular species of fish is found living *within* the intestine or stomach of the trepang! Is it not unaccountable that a fish, well formed and perfect in all its parts, should be placed in such a position for life? A "hanger-on" he certainly is. Though a "trencher friend," and "one who dines with others," he looks like one born for better things. Out he comes and swims feebly, then drops heavily to the bottom. He seems to be unable to support himself, or is too lazy. This fish is about the size and shape of a small smelt. It has a long slender fin along the entire length of its back, and altogether is as well provided with means for self-protection as any other fish. The only difference is seen in its extreme transparency; and this is a very interesting sight. Holding the glass before the light, you can see the pulsation of the great vessels, and nearly the whole anatomy, at one view.

The trepang has no apparent objection to his presence, and in most instances they are found to have this for their companion, their "hanger-on," though never more than one.

On examining the anatomy of the trepang we find that the intestine doubles upon itself, in a measure; and it is probable that no secretion is formed within that portion of the intestine occupied by the fish, except, perhaps, mucus. Then, possibly, the fish is provided with an extra secretion of mucus, which prevents any undue action of the fluids of the internal structure of the trepang. Wonderful as it is, the *fact* remains; this fish is wholly dependent on the kindly offices of this low, simply organized creature of another division of the animal kingdom. The fish would not survive out of his accustomed protection, though we have carefully tried the experiment, with frequent changes and renewal of water. For some wise purpose this apparently absurd situation is created, and it affords another illustration of the presence of a Guiding Hand in this wondrous world. This was a new fact even to naturalists; but since we made these observations Dr. Collingwood has discovered on the shores of the China Sea an enormous blue sea-anemone, two feet in diameter, in which little fishes take shelter. Some of the jelly-fishes also have been found to protect fishes and carry them within their ample folds. A very remarkable instance of this habit we will endeavor to illustrate in another part of the lagoon at some future time.

As we come about, and sail toward the fortress, a dark cloud, hanging like a curtain over the eastern horizon, is all that interrupts the otherwise brilliant sky. This is a scene of frequent occurrence during the summer months, and furnishes that form of cloud which drops from its borders to form the water-spout. As we look, the slender line of smoky hue has reached the water, and seems like a spiral prolongation of the cloud above. Presently the water is seen to boil and curl upward; while onward it goes, whirling and bending, a tall black column, until it strikes the shore of Sand Key, when a sudden and complete collapse ends the seaward portion of it. A slender thread remains, hanging from the margin of the cloud, but is soon absorbed; and the sooty curtain vanishes slowly and completely, leaving a fair sky, illumined by the gorgeous radiance of the setting sun.

24.
Mr. Wegg's Party on the Kissimmee (1886)

MR. WEGG'S PARTY ON THE KISSIMMEE.

BY HENRI DAUGÉ.

THERE were eight of us, four being ladies and four gentlemen—all of us wearing old clothes, and most of us big straw hats—who came down on the tri-weekly "construction train" of the South Florida Railroad, then running from Sanford to Kissimmee City. We were all perched on a pile of lumber on a flat car, the only place for passengers or luggage. Our party was a youthful and adventurous one, bound on a "camping-out" excursion; still it hesitated on the brink of the unknown, and having reached Kissimmee City, we pitched our tents at first on an island near it, at the head of the big blue lake Tohopekaliga. The new town, with its sixteen houses, none painted or white-washed, but all looking as new and yellow as only fresh pine lumber can look, had at least the beginnings of civilization—a bakery, a restaurant, and hotel in process of erection.

Our third night in our first resting-place was passed by a glorious camp fire in solemn conclave, the great live-oaks and hickories and cabbage-palms of that beautiful "hammock land" around us. Four of us were ready for the projected journey down the river, encouraged thereunto by the optimistic owner of a sail-boat, who had haunted us during our stay. He did not hint that no ladies had ever attempted such a trip before: far be it from him to daunt our courage! On the contrary, he discoursed fluently of the parties he had been in the habit of taking to visit this remoter Southern country, of their successes in hunting and fishing, of the excellent camping grounds, and of the wild beauty of the Kissimmee River. The owls hooted, the fire danced, the discussion was lively, and farewell glees and choruses were sung with good-will.

On Friday morning, then, after cheerful good-byes, the four restless spirits set forth in a sail-boat owned and manned by the person who acquired with them the name of Wegg. "Maginnis," our bachelor, and the erect and rosy young lady whom we called "the Major," the tall young fellow who was dubbed "Leggins," and his wife, our "Matron," formed the party. The luggage consisted of bedding rolled within two small light tents, guns and fishing-tackle, a few cooking utensils, sacks of meal and potatoes, and some cooked provisions in a tin can. Our handbags, a couple of folding canvas cots, and two closely tied up hammocks completed our outfit; while beneath the stern seat, which Mr. Wegg occupied, rudder in hand, was stowed an old sack containing his belongings.

The little boat, nineteen feet long and five and a half wide, went gayly before the breeze, past the islands that crowd the upper lake, and at a moderate pace across the blue waters of Tohopekaliga until we had passed Steer Beach. But the lake is twenty miles long, and as the breeze died away, becoming fainter and fainter toward noon, Mr. Wegg first manifested his surprising facility for "dropping into poetry," doubtless to cheer us. He burst forth into a recitation beginning,

CABBAGE-PALMS.

"Sweet lake of Oneida, thy aqueous flow,"

and after rendering several stanzas paused, and modestly but firmly observed, "It was I who composed these verses."

Here was "a literary man" with a vengeance! We complimented him upon his talents, and he then, with another burst of good feeling, demanded a song. As no one was in haste to render it, he himself, untroubled by false shame, cheerfully broke forth with an old war song on the theme of the *Monitor* and the *Merrimac*. (He had told us that he had been a Union soldier.) The three rebels of the party listened to this as calmly as the placid, pretty young lady from New Hampshire.

"'Raise your voices, every one,
Give three cheers for Ericsson,
Who gave us such a vessel, neat and handy O!
For the Union thirty cheers,
For the Yankee volunteers,
And three for Yankee Doodle Dandy O!'

"The breeze seems to be failing us," Mr. Wegg blandly concluded.

"We shall have to take to the oars, I suppose," Maginnis said.

"Oh, why be in such haste?" Mr. Wegg playfully remonstrated. (Mr. Wegg and his boat were hired by the week, and not by the trip.) "When you get into a boat you prepare to loiter or to speed at the wind's will. You experience diversity, and sometimes adversity. Do any of you remember the anecdote of Mrs. Partington," Mr. Wegg continued, still more joyously and playfully, "how she called on Isaac, when in later life he was settled in his pallyshul mansion, and how, dropping her carpet-bag upon the velvet roses of his parlor floor, she rushed forward, and seizing his hand, exclaimed, 'Ike, I've been with you in diversity, and I'll never forsake you in posterity'? Besides," added Mr. Wegg, reflectively, "as to *rowing*, it would not be my wish to work you gentlemen too hard, but as I told you, I was a soldier in the Union army, and I had a waound in that service, since when my back has been weak. A healthier man, till that occurrence, was probably never seen."

This was news indeed! Mr. Wegg's weak back had previously been, as it were, kept in the dark. He had been, in his own language, as he afterward proved to be, "about as tough as you make 'em." However, merely to help the sail along, and to take a little healthful exercise, Maginnis and the Matron each took an oar by-and-by, and entered the Kissimmee River rowing.

The stream here at its beginning is a narrow one, and winds and turns sharply upon itself. Its course between Tohopekaliga and the next lake is twelve miles, though the distance in a direct line is said to be only four. The eight-foot oars struck the lily leaves on each side as we went down the current. We saw paths and narrow beds, trampled and bewallowed, in the mud of the marshes now and then, which were made by the alligators; then, after long stretches of cane-brake and of marsh and willows, we came upon the beauty of Gum Swamp. The tall trees drooped over the stream at right and left; wild calla-lilies flourished on the margin of the river, the bud greener without than on the cultivated lily, but white within, and with its golden rod; here were grasses and vines as graceful as Nature's hand could fling abroad—and all so near that one was almost within arm's-length of this loveliness all the way. After leaving this we came again to level savannas, and saw rice-birds flying over them, and ducks, but too far away for a shot. Maginnis brought down a strange white bird with his gun, which we secured. And toying with thoughts of supper, we got out a fishing-rod, and Mr. Wegg offered to fish, and did fish, and speedily caught a fine "trout," or black bass, which must have weighed at least seven pounds. After this, Mr. Wegg, elate with success and boastful withal, condescended to take the oars, and at about 5.30 P.M. we emerged from the river into a lake apparently five or six miles long, which Mr. Wegg stated to be Lake Cypress. Across this lake we flew before the breeze, which had happily sprung up, crossing it in about half an hour.

The sun had sunk, and we searched in the twilight for the river. As yet Mr. Wegg was confident in tone; he said that "he didn't presume that there was a guide on the river that could strike the Kissimmee *first off* within a quarter of a mile or so, the shore was so deceivin'," and so we could not blame him for the weary half-hour in which we skirted along the southern lake shore looking for the outlet. But we were a little annoyed by his repeated suggestions as to "tying up in the saw-grass for the night"; we were determined to find dry land and a camping place. The ladies were especially decided in their rejection of all such suggestions, for which cause Mr. Wegg launched forth into pensive reflections as to the ease with which a party could be made comfortable "when composed of gentlemen only"; and added sadly that he didn't know as he ever heard of ladies comin' down here in a sail-boat before this; they were generally too afraid of roughing it. However, Leggins, who had mounted the prow, discerned at last among the cypresses an opening that seemed broader and more promising. The fish were darting about us with startled leaps and splashes; a good two-pound trout actually leaped into the boat, slapping the Matron's cheek with his cold body as he came. We wound through the mazes of the river hour by hour without finding any landing; finally we came upon a broad opening, apparently the mouth of a lake. Here Mr. Wegg gave up completely, confessed himself entirely lost, and unable to find his way in the darkness. "*No* guide could go farther with certainty," he maintained; "in daylight he could do as well as any man."

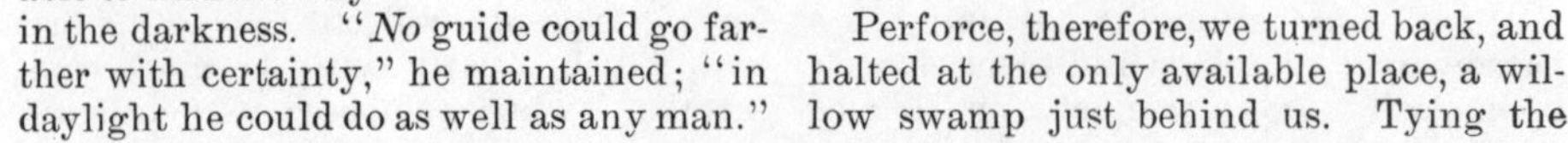

GUM SWAMP.

Perforce, therefore, we turned back, and halted at the only available place, a willow swamp just behind us. Tying the boat to an old stump, Mr. Wegg laid a plank from the bow to the roots of a tree, and all the men got out and explored the country. They could only find a footing by stepping from root to root across the black mud, vines and bushes entangling each step. There was nothing to do but to wait for daylight. The hatchet was produced, and some small boards which had lain in the boat split up, and laid on the willow roots to make a fire; but they refused to burn until the Matron (who thought with a pang of her lectures to impatient Dinahs) produced a brown bottle of kerosene and drenched the sticks with the oil. The fire blazed up royally now, and by its illumination the stern of the boat was curtained off for the ladies' apartment by means of a rubber cloth and two sticks; bedding was unrolled, and the ladies stretched themselves between blankets, shielding their heads with their large hats from the drenching dews.

Maginnis curled up on two seats in the middle of the boat, wrapped in his long overcoat, a blanket thrown over his feet, and slept the sleep of the just. Mr. Wegg folded himself in his patchwork quilt and reclined upon the bow, snoring gently; but Leggins, rendered wakeful rather than sleepy by the unwonted surroundings, sat up in his place by Maginnis, his rifle at hand, and counted the alligators swimming silently down stream. None offered to molest the boat; only one old monster, after swimming close and apparently investigating the craft, retired across the stream to a thick bed of lily leaves (or "bonnets," as they are called in Florida), and there made night hideous by noises which were variously described by members of the party as "barking," "bellowing," "croaking," and "grunting." Leggins counted eleven alligators between ten o'clock and one, which swam by; but the procession continued after he had fallen asleep, for the ladies awakened from their first slumber about two o'clock, and watched them go by until dawn. The sight and sound of these dark, stealthy objects, the continual splash and leap of fish here and there, the slow revolution of the constellations about the north star, the far sound of owl hootings in the swamp, made the night seem strange and weird. The Matron, sitting up in her place, kept singing in a small, low voice little hymns and songs, beneath whose influence the Major now and then dozed off. Then Mr. Wegg awoke, and began the recital of some remarkable dreams from his perch on the bow; and then—oh, so slowly!—the faint dawn revealed tree and stream and boat and shore; and everything was stowed away as securely as possible, and we made haste to reach some landing where fire and breakfast could be had. Passing grassy stretches with bright birds darting over them, wild and shy, at last a lake widened before us, which Mr. Wegg hailed as Lake Kissimmee; and tacking across to escape a grassy point of land, we shortly came to a high white sandy beach with huge live-oaks upon it, and cypresses and cypress knees stretching out into the water, and this he announced as Gardiner's Island, the point at which we hoped to find deer.

After some difficulty we made a landing in the shallow water, and again stood on dry land. Among our first discoveries were deer tracks in the sand, and following them over the sandy ridge, behind the groups of saw-palmettoes, we saw them wind away to the marsh beyond. But alas for hopes of hunting! the bog cut off human feet from the mainland and piny woods far away, and there was no place to cross to the covert of the deer.

However, at present our thoughts turned more to repose than to adventure. We had soon a big fire roaring on the bare white sand crest, fed with dry oily stalks of palmetto leaves and abundant dead wood. The cooking utensils and provisions were brought from the boat; seats and benches were easily found on the roots of the great oaks which stood out above the white sand to almost as great a circumference as that of the branches; plates and cups were laid out; in a wooden tray corn meal was hastily mixed with water and salt, fashioned into five "pones," and fitted into the skillet; setting this upon a bed of glowing embers and covering its iron lid with more live coals, the kettle was next set on to boil, the bacon sliced, the frying-pan made hot. The Major rolled in meal a fish freshly caught and cleaned by Mr. Wegg, and the fish was fried immediately upon the removal of the meat from its own lard. To make the coffee completed the task, and that gypsy breakfast, with the help of sugar and condensed milk, and some crackers from the square tin can, was to our taste a delicious one.

After an hour of repose we all returned

ON THE KISSIMMEE.

to the boat, for on finding no way to get at game from this point, Mr. Wegg declared that this was only the north beach of Gardiner's Island, while the *south* beach was the real hunting ground. So we skirted the beach, but found no southward opening—only grasses and lily leaves as on the margin of a lake. Still we sailed on, westward from the beach, and sailed for hours, a great lake opening before us, and finally Mr. Wegg remarked that he didn't believe we were in Kissimmee Lake after all; we must be in the lake the Indians called Hatchinineha. But the game was a great deal more plentiful on Hatchinineha than on Gardiner's Island.

"Make a landing, then, anywhere, and let us get up the tents and have a night's rest," was the general cry. But, alas! this was impossible. All around this lake we circled the hot day through, with little breeze and steady rowing; whenever we saw what appeared to be a high bold shore we put in for it, and, arrived there, the pines had always receded a mile or two, and impassable marsh and bog divided us from land.

It was only at sunset that we at last wearily made the beach we had left in the morning, and there we encamped for the night. It was Saturday; this was to be our resting-place for two nights and a day.

Mr. Wegg's assurance was but slightly subdued. He cheerfully performed a share of the labor in erecting the tents beneath a big live-oak on the beach, and informed us as he moved about:

"Well, now you can say that you have seen Hatchinineha, and when folks tell *you* about the good hunting there, you can tell them there ain't a landing on the lake—*can't* you? It's *worth* something to know that lake."

The gentlemen bore with Mr. Wegg with admirable good-nature; but the Major and the Matron eyed him "with sick and scornful looks averse," and would none of his good cheer. They did not in the least believe that they had traversed Hatchinineha; had he not first called it Kissimmee?

Our Sunday fishing was brief, and resulted in a fine trout for breakfast, and a huge one weighing about eleven pounds, which was successfully baked for dinner, after this fashion: having been cleaned, washed, and rubbed with salt inside and out, the great fish was wrapped in brown paper and laid on palmetto leaves, on a hot place left bare by raking away the ashes from the former centre of the fire; it was covered then with palmetto leaves, then with cooler ashes, and then with hot glowing embers; and there it was left for hours. Potatoes were baked at their leisure for dinner, too, and while Maginnis and Mr. Wegg took the boat and went off to cruise about and hunt for the river, the ladies vanished down the beach, and found the firm white sand to be a delightful bathing floor. The water was clear and soft, warm enough in the shallows to be called a hot bath, while by wading out to the knee—always with smooth, snowy sand under foot—it was cool and exhilarating. Leggins later found refreshment in a similar

"I THINK I SHALL REST FOR THE BALANCE OF THIS SACRED DAY."

experience; and there was some reading aloud and some drowsing before the other two returned with good tidings; they had found the river—we were camped within a half-mile of it; better than that, they had seen a sail-boat coming up the river, and Mr. Wegg eagerly assured us that it was handled by the best guide in the country, and doubtless he would give us full directions as to the route to pursue.

This boat soon came in sight, and paid us a brief visit; it held two handsome and courteous young sportsmen from the North, the bluff and welcome figure of an Orlando (Florida) hotel man, and Mr. Jack Rooney, of Kissimmee City, the vaunted guide, a man whom Mr. Wegg could have embraced in his joy, for now he would have reliable information. We all hung upon Mr. Rooney's words as he described to us the various landings on Lake Kissimmee, and advised us of their merits.

"Ever been there before?" Mr. Rooney asked Mr. Wegg, with a suspicious look. "You can get lost on Lake Kissimmee mighty easy if you don't know it."

We were looking at the half-smoked venison displayed by the hunters in response to our inquiries, but we did not miss the answer.

"Well," said Mr. Wegg, reluctantly, "I've been there once—with another man as guide, though—and not so very lately; so I may ha' forgot some."

Oh, Mr. Wegg! Mr. Wegg! You who had regaled us with stories of your trips hither, and of how you "us'ally" advised as to this and that! But no one lifted a voice against him; only all questioned and admired the other guide, who looked picturesque and capable; and when the other boat had gone on—hastening northward day and night because tidings of a relative's illness had been brought by a cow-boy—the ladies made some complimentary remarks about Mr. Rooney. This was wormwood and gall to Mr. Wegg; the praises which had sprung to his lips in the joy of deliverance died away. He tried to subdue the enthusiasm by hints that the ladies wouldn't have liked a guide fond of whiskey; and finally, perceiving them to have no faith in this insinuation, mournfully declared,

"Well, now, you wouldn't 'a liked Jack Rooney; he 'ain't got any principles to speak of—*nor* religion."

"He probably has more principle than to take a party of ladies to explore a country he doesn't know," retorted our young Matron, tartly.

Mr. Wegg looked a little sheepish.

"Well, now, you have got that on me, haven't you?" he said, slowly, seating himself close at hand. "Well, I am very tired"—stretching himself in an easy attitude. "I think I shall rest for the balance of this sacred day."

On Monday morning the whole party was off betimes, sailing down the river, which was broader and more tranquil than above, after an entrance had once been effected through the concealing "bonnets." The shores here are high and grassy and beautifully wooded—splendid camping ground, every foot of it. On the bank of the river was an Indian canoe, dug out of a huge cypress log; there was also a large flat barge, without seats or rowlocks, tied up to the shore. Further on, the lake gave its usual tokens of being near—wide stretches of marshy land and willows—and we entered the great beautiful blue Lake Kissimmee, with Brimmer Island twenty-five miles below us, where the others had found deer; West Hammock and the Indians to our right; and to the east, beyond the Rookery, Camp Hammock, with a new and empty house and a reputation for abundant game. The westerly wind decided our course to the last-named point, fifteen miles away. We pushed through some yellow grassy stretches, and slowly crept up on the Rookery, the round heads of its cabbage-palms for our landmark. As we approached the island we saw flocks of beautiful white birds rise in the air and float away like clouds beyond gunshot range. We had seen these flocks before on our way, floating high and far, now with the sunlight on their white wings, shining like snow, and then melting from sight like a dream, to re-appear faintly, but brightening as the sun smote their plumage, and so, like visions of angels, fading and shining forth by turns. Turning due east to pass to the right of the Rookery, we came, for the first time in Florida, upon the true water-lily (*Nymphæ odorata* of the botanist), faintly fragrant, with its exquisite chalice of white and gold.

The lake looked enormously big and blue in its eastern expanse after we passed this island and the wastes of grass and lilies; but beneath the trees of the farther shore we saw a tiny yellow speck.

"Do my eyes deceive me, or *is* that the new house we are looking for?" Mr. Wegg inquired.

It was unmistakably a new house—the house Mr. Jack Rooney had told us of.

It was just as the sun sank that we reached the landing. And having carefully refrained from describing the beauty of the sunsets so far, I claim indulgence for a tribute to this of Monday, March 20, 1882. The sun lay like a golden ball set on the dark blue rim of the horizon, into which the trees of the Rookery had melted. The lake, looking west, lay wide and placid, a band of deep soft rose-color around the far western rim, all silver between that and us; a more perfect sky and scene never smiled in lonely loveliness before the eyes of man.

All day Tuesday we rested at Camp Hammock, the woods where deer or turkey *might* be seemed to recede before the advancing steps when one tramped toward them over the prairie-like stretches, and Leggins and Maginnis returned from a fruitless exploration of one strip of woods observing that this was merely a voyage of discovery anyhow, and unless a man had plenty of time it was of no use to attempt a hunt without a guide.

That night the wind blew almost a hurricane; we fastened up what we could on the windy side of the house to break the great draughts of air that swept in through the logs and threatened to elevate the dividing tent into a horizontal position. All night long, when any one awoke, the wind was heard booming through the air, and the fear of an equinoctial storm was upon us.

There came no rain with Wednesday morning, however, and the wind had somewhat abated. It was now from the north, and would permit our departure; so we made what haste we could and got aboard. As far as we could see, the broad lake was covered with white-caps, but the little boat headed gallantly into them; the waves looked enormous, and were less the work of the present wind, though that was a stiff one, than of last night's gale. The boat rose and fell with a slap into the trough of each succeeding wave; the ladies, enjoying the excitement, sat covered with rubber cloths that streamed with the water dashing in, laughing as wave or spray washed their faces; and Mr. Wegg appeared somewhat grieved at their good cheer.

"Would the ladies like to put back?" he asked.

"Put back?—what for?" they indignantly demanded.

"Oh, I can stand it if you can. Thumping across the waves this way *might* start a plank. Yes, sir, it *is* a stout boat, as I told you. Only—well, ladies us'ally are liable to get scared at such times as this."

SHOOTING ALLIGATORS.

We had crossed the roughest water, though still in a strong wind, and were making a tack by the Rookery, when, with a sudden crash, the sail fell rushing down.

"The oars! the oars! Don't let the wind get us out to sea!" Mr. Wegg yelled, springing forward; but Leggins and Maginnis had the oars in an instant, and headed the boat into the grasses. It was only the sailing tackle broken by the strain; a new rope, and we would be ready for the lake again; and fortunately we descried a landing just ahead. We pushed in, and as we did so a large blue heron rose and flew from her nest in a low spreading tree. No other birds were seen, for this further shore of the Rookery was almost bare of trees; but Maginnis added the rare eggs of the blue heron to his collection, previously enriched by an eagle's egg, cream-colored and with flecks of chocolate brown: the heron's eggs were as large as a goose egg, three in number, and of "robin's-egg blue." A moment later we found better sport at hand. Leggins seized his rifle, fired, and there was a great commotion in the shallow water close at hand; then a dead alligator turned on his back, and held up all four feet, as is their way in death. When drawn ashore and measured he lacked about three inches of the length of one of our eight-foot oars—a respectable size, but not half that of some we saw. The Matron, who had been promised some alligator-skins, now declared that she should like to carry away this.

"He won't be dead any more'n a snake till sunset," Mr. Wegg declared.

"With a rifle-ball through his eyes?" Leggins demanded.

"Oh, he's done for; but he won't die till dark."

"Then kill him," the Matron commanded, with the prompt inconsequence of that sex which can even be cruel, it is said, when one offers to cross its will. "Cut off his head and sever the spine, and I know he's compelled to be dead."

Mr. Wegg did not refuse her. The head was cut off and thrown a yard away, and taking out his knife, he began to skin the white breast of the beast, this being the only desirable part of the skin. The monster, headless, moved a foot or thrust with its formidable tail now and then, but the horrified exclamations of the ladies were met with assurances that this was only muscular contraction; still, it looked awfully like life, especially as the contortions grew more agonized when the stomach was being skinned. But the task was swiftly finished, the skin heavily salted and rolled in a piece of bagging; and we took our leave of the Rookery with only one more trophy—a duck which Maginnis shot, and whose breast afforded a skin thick as fur and soft as down in beautiful shades of brown; the wings, of the same hues, had a space of vivid peacock blue toward the tips. The Major and the Matron prepared these carefully to make a feather turban for Maginnis's young sister at home.

That evening we went no further up the river than the spot which we called "the Indian camp," where we found the barge and the dug-out. Thursday night we camped on the "north beach of Gardiner's Island" once more. Leggins, by request, cheered the camp fire that night with old Georgia corn-field songs; and the chronicler fell asleep to the cheerful music of a lay full of iteration and monotone, but with the peculiar melody of long rounding notes, and the negro gasping of the breath and soft sweetness of occasional "dying falls." By Friday night, after a long day of hard work against the eddying sweep of the current around the sharp river bends, we reached Lake Tohopekaliga. The next morning we beat up the lake against a heavy wind and chopping seas; and when we danced into view of Kissimmee across the blue waves of Tohopekaliga, we heard the engine of the tri-weekly train whistle as it came in.

We caught it in time for the return trip, however, and also had time for an excursion to the bakery. Brown, unshaven, with worn and torn raiment, and a cheerful appreciation of baker's bread, we took our places in the fresh and new passenger coach which awaited us. Kissimmee City and the South Florida Railroad seemed to us the heart of civilization.

We met friends that told us that the others of our party had returned home after a delightful sojourn; they had lived on such luxuries as poached eggs, fish chowders, cake, and baker's bread from Kissimmee City. We, the more adventurous four, were content; we had subsisted on corn bread and coffee for the most part —and *venison*, of course. We did not disclose the fact that the deers' horns we had brought home were purchased from the Seminoles.

25.
Sport in Florida
(1886)

SPORT IN FLORIDA.[1]

BY JAMES A. HENSHALL, M.D.,

Author of "Book of the Black Bass."

Indian River is an extensive but shallow sheet of water, 150 miles in length, and above the Narrows varies from a mile to five miles in width. It is not a river, properly speaking, but a shallow salt water lagoon, or sound, with two inlets from the sea — one opposite Fort Capron, and the other at its extreme southern end, at Jupiter River. From Jupiter Narrows to the head of the river there is no current, and the mean rise and fall of the tides is but three inches. From Jupiter Inlet to the Narrows there is a strong derivative tide-wave of greater mean. The general course of the river is N.N.W. and S.S.E. The variation of the compass at Titusville is 2° 54″ E. It is a magnificent body of water, separated from the Atlantic by a narrow strip of land, generally from a fourth to a half mile in width, though in places the intervening strip is not more than from 75 to 200 yards wide.

Being so near the sea, there is a good sailing breeze almost every day, and with an easterly or westerly wind one can lay his course either up or down the river. While the breezes are almost always fresh, gales are very infrequent during the winter season. "Northers" are dreaded most, chiefly on account of their coolness, but a "sou'wester" is the most treacherous, baffling, and squally wind that blows on Indian River.

[1] The publishers of this entertaining work have kindly consented to our making these extracts. They have also placed the cuts at our disposal.

OUR CRUISING BOAT.

The entire carrying or freighting business is done by small yachts and sail-boats; consequently there are plenty of boats and experienced boatmen that can be chartered to convey parties or individuals to any portion of East Florida. These boatmen are, as a rule, intelligent and accommodating. An Indian River boatman is *sui generis* a peculiar and unique combination of sailor, fisherman, hunter, guide, cook, woodman, and philosopher — an animated salmagundi, full of all kinds of expedients for all kinds of emergencies.

The boats are necessarily of light draught, and center-boarders. There are the "skimming-dish," the "pumpkin-seed," and the "flat-iron" models, all half-round yacht-built boats, broad and beamy, cat-rigged or sloop-rigged; they all pound and spank in a sea-way, and are very wet. Then there is the "skip-jack," a much superior model for sailing, will go to windward much better, but, as they are built very flat, with little or no sheer, and with chubby bows, they are also wet. There are a few ships' boats, picked up on the beach, mostly, built over and usually schooner-rigged; they do very well sailing free, but on the wind are loggy. Last and best is the "batteau," of good length, little beam, and flat bottom, with "pirogue," or "periauger," rig — that is, two leg-o'mutton sails like the "sharpie."

I will say here that, if the "sharpie" is ever introduced into East Florida, it will rapidly take the place of all other boats, for it is undoubtedly *the* boat for Florida waters, being fast, safe, weatherly, easily handled, of extremely light draught, great carrying capacity, and cheap.

The day after we arrived at Titusville was Christmas day; but it was hard to realize it with the thermometer at 75°, with the birds singing merrily, and tuberoses and hyacinths blooming in the open ground; while all around were trees and shrubs luxuriant in their green and graceful foliage. Eager to begin our cruising and camping, I hastened to the river in search of a suitable boat for our party, and, by a stroke of extreme good fortune, I hit upon a "skip-jack" yacht, cat-rigged, eighteen feet long, seven feet beam, and drawing fifteen inches when loaded. She was decked over, forward and aft, with a very roomy cock-pit. I examined her thoroughly, and found her tight, in good order, and sound condition. She was called *Blue Wing*, and proved to be one of the fastest and safest boats on the river. I purchased her for quite a moderate sum — about one-half her real worth.

Of course, my purchase was soon "noised abroad" among the boatmen, and at night there were "all hands and the cook" mustered in the office of the hotel. With an eye to the main chance, many were quite anxious to go with me in the capacity of skipper and guide. They were quite solicitous in regard to our welfare, and I was entertained graphically with the difficulties of navigating Indian River, with its intricate channels, rocky reefs, treacherous shoals, oyster bars, variable winds, and sudden squalls. I was regaled, mysteriously, with highly-colored descriptions of the best fishing-grounds and hunting localities, known only to a "chosen few."

But as I deemed my past experience in sailing — ten years of my youthful life on Chesapeake Bay, and later on Long Island Sound, and still later on the Great Lakes — sufficient for Indian River, I declined their kind offices with the best grace possible, and put a bold face on the matter, as the following colloquy may witness. After I had been interviewed by a number, one who appeared to be a kind of "oracle" amongst them approached me, and cast off his "jaw-tackle" in this wise: —

Oracle (patronizingly) — "Doc, I'd like to sail the *Blue Wing* for you fellows, and learn you the ropes. How long will you be on the river?"

"About four months."

O. (surprised) — "Why, most parties only go down for two or three weeks; but I 'spose you'll run down to Jupiter, and make long camps all the way down?"

"I shall stop but a day or two at Horse Creek and Elbow Creek; a few days on Banana River; then Crane Creek and Turkey Creek; a week on Sebastian River; through the Narrows and Capron for another week; then St. Lucie River and through Jupiter Narrows, and Hobe Sound to Jupiter River. After a few days at Jupiter, I will go to Lake Worth."

O. (emphatically) — "But you can't get the *Blue Wing* through the saw-grass to Lake Worth!"

"No; I shall go over Jupiter bar, and sail outside to Lake Worth Inlet."

O. (amazed) — "But she has never been outside; and, if you'll take my advice, you won't try it."

"And from Lake Worth I will sail to Biscayne Bay."

O. (astonished) — "Jerusalem! why, that's a hundred and fifty miles *outside* sailing!"

"No, only about seventy-five miles, with two good harbors between: New River and Hillsboro' River."

O. (vanquished) — "Well, Doc, you'll excuse *me* — I don't want any of that outside bizness in mine — not in an eighteen-foot boat, no how!"

"Then I may cruise along the keys to Key West, and if the boys stand the racket pretty well, I will sail up the west coast to Charlotte Harbor and Pease Creek, where I will sell the boat, hire an ox-cart and team, and go across the country to Lake Okechobee and come out at Fort Capron, where I will charter your boat to bring us up to Titusville, provided you are on hand."

O. (admiringly) — "Why, Doc, you must be a regular old salt!"

"Yes, I can discount Lot's wife for saltness; I am the saltiest of the salt — saltpeter and Epsom salts — a double dose."

O. (reflectively) — "Are the rest of your party good sailors?"

"I don't think any of them ever saw a sail-boat before they reached Jacksonville, and I am certain that none of them were ever in one."

O. (decidedly) — "Well, they'll have a rough time of it if they follow you."

"That's what I brought them to Florida for, to *rough* it."

THE NATIVES.

The alligator is one of the institutions of Florida. To most persons he is a repulsive and dangerous-looking reptile; but I rather like him. He is a familiar feature of the sub-tropical landscape, and is withal perfectly harmless if let alone, and will get out of one's way fast enough if given the chance; but when wounded or cornered, look out for him, and keep out of reach of his lively and powerful tail, for he is then an ugly customer, and "means business."

In the lonely fastnesses of a cypress swamp, with only the alligator for company, I have felt on terms of confidential fellowship with him, as he lay upon a bank, or floated noiselessly with only the top of his small skull and wicked eyes above the water, silently watching me; and his eye is the only ugly feature about him — snaky, treacherous, and malevolent.

OPEN FOR BUSINESS.

I have hid myself in the saw-grass or saw-palmetto, bordering a placid pool in Southern Florida, where alligators do most abound, and by making a peculiar, grunting noise, have seen a score of heads silently appear above the surface of the water and swim noiselessly toward me; but upon the least movement on my part they would instantly disappear, without leaving a ripple to mark their course.

Paddling along a quiet stream — and all streams in Florida are quiet, however swift — they can be seen lying motionless on the banks and sand spits, sunning themselves, and slipping and sliding into the water as one gets nearer, without the least noise or confusion, and as silently sink out of sight. But it is rather startling to have a big fellow, who has just discovered you as you get abreast of him, come crashing and floundering through the brush and saw-grass, and plunge into the water, not twenty feet from your boat, with a noise and commotion like the fall of a large tree from the bank. These are the big ones that are always fifteen or twenty feet long — but if measured with the tape-line they would not exceed twelve feet.

An alligator is easily killed by a well-directed shot, if put in the right place, but he will stand a good deal of indiscriminate shooting. Just back of the eye, and close behind the fore-leg are the vulnerable points. Immediately back of the eye is a a slight depression, or flat space, at right angles with the top of his flat skull, and a bullet fairly planted there is instantly fatal.

SEEDY CITIZEN.

If one is above and behind him, the only vulnerable spot is where the skull joins the neck.

The alligator lives upon fish, turtles, snakes, and wild-fowl, to which diet he adds, for reasons best known to himself, pine-knots and cypress-knees. He is especially fond of dogs, pigs, and calves; and young alligators who are strangers to him he takes in like a Christian. In his throat, or gular region, under the lower jaw, are two small slits, the mouths of the musk glands. The odor of the secretion is similar to that of the muskrat, but stronger.

The nest of the alligator resembles somewhat a large muskrat house, and is formed in a similar manner, of grass, leaves, brush, and muck. In the center of this the female lays from twenty to forty, sometimes more, whitish, oblong eggs, an inch or more in diameter and three or four inches long. The female is frequently seen lying on top of the nest, but the heat generated by the decomposition of the heap is sufficient to hatch the eggs.

The bull alligators have regular pitched battles in the spring of the year, in which they engage "tooth and toe-nail," and with a liberal use of their powerful tails. The bellow of the alligator is a harsh, hoarse, jarring, and discordant sound, which can be heard for a long distance. They are very active in water, but clumsy and awkward upon land. When wounded they will put to blush the best efforts of the most finished acrobat. The flesh of the alligator is red and clean-looking, and when well boiled is said to be somewhat palatable, though fishy in taste. The natives often feed their dogs and hogs boiled 'gator meat.

In addition to the alligator (*Alligator Mississippiensis*), a true crocodile (*Crocodilus Americanus*) is found in Southern Florida. A number have been killed on the tributaries of Biscayne Bay, and at the lower end of Lake Worth.

To the casual observer there is no apparent difference between the Florida alligator and crocodile; but upon closer observation it will be seen that the head of the crocodile is somewhat narrower and longer, and that the long canine teeth of the lower jaw project through holes in the upper jaw, while in the alligator these holes are only blind pits, into which the lower teeth fit.

The crocodile likewise has a ridge of projecting scales along the outer surface of the hind legs, which scales are absent in the alligator. The hind feet of the crocodile are also webbed nearly to the toes, which is not the case with the alligator, the web being much shallower. The crocodile grows to a larger size, usually, than his congener, though they are similar in habits.

A CLOSE CALL.

The wind being favorable, we sailed up the south fork, called South Halpatiokee River, some four miles, being altogether about twelve miles from the mouth. Here we moored the schooner for a camp of several days, and had fine sport, there being an abundance of deer, turkey and quail.

One morning I entered a clump of bushes near a spruce-pine thicket, where I had seen some turkeys the day before, and began calling or "keouking," with the intention of enticing some old gobbler within range. Just outside of the clump of shrubbery was a large bare space of white sand, which I had examined carefully for deer or turkey tracks before concealing myself. After a half-hour's fruitless endeavor, I came out of my ambush, and was surprised to find the fresh track of a large panther, who had approached within six feet of where I was concealed. He evidently mistook my efforts at "keouking" for the complainings or agonizing cries of some turkey in sore distress, and thought to make a meal of it, but seeing me, he beat a hasty retreat, for his tracks led to and fro between the thicket and my hiding place.

A SURPRISE PARTY.

26.
Florida:
A Winter Playground
In the Blackjack
(1909)

FLORIDA

A WINTER PLAYGROUND

BY KIRK MUNROE

IN its winter playgrounds the United States is the most fortunate country of the world; for, while Europe has within its borders only shivery Italy, every portion of which suffers from cold weather through January and well into February, we have California, Arizona, Texas, and Florida, all of them warmer than Italy, and offering a greater variety of natural attractions.

Foremost among these by virtue of its accessibility, and its possession of the only tropical area of United States mainland, stands Florida, the largest state east of the Mississippi, and having an area equal to that of combined New England. At its most southerly point it is six hundred miles nearer the equator than Los Angeles, and three hundred miles farther south than New Orleans; while it extends toward the tropics a whole degree beyond the latitude of Brownsville, Texas, which is the next most southern bit of the United States. Moreover, its entire coast line is bathed by the warm waters of the Gulf of Mexico, and those of the Gulf Stream, which give it the winter climate of Upper Egypt at Assouan, or of northern India. Thus, through its geographical position, Florida gains its chiefest asset, the most equable climate of the world.

Although the topography of Florida is

There's no end of opportunity for canoeing on swift or still waters.

by no means as varied as that of California, and while it is entirely lacking in mountains or in fact any elevation greater than three hundred feet above the sea, it is far from presenting the monotonous level of swamp, pine barrens, and sand, imagined by those who ignorantly speculate as to its natural features. The northern portion of the state is a high, rolling country of red clay hills and fertile valleys, heavily forested, dotted with blue lakes, and intersected by many swift-flowing rivers fed by crystal springs. Most notable among these rivers are the St. John, (Sp. San Juan) which, like the Nile, flows due north, and the Suwanee, (Sp. San Juanita or Little St. John) known to the whole world through Stephen Foster's song.

The central portion of the state also boasts of hills, only they are of sand instead of clay, and of an incredible number of spring-fed lakes.

In the three most southerly counties, Dade, Lee, and Monroe, are located the Everglades, the Big Cypress Swamp, Lake Okechobee, and that long-extended line of coral sea islands, known as the Florida Keys. The first of these is a limitless prairie, occupying thousands of square miles, covered with giant grasses that grow in clear, clean, drinkable water, and dotted with an infinity of small, wooded islands. On these islands dwell that remnant of Seminoles who successfully resisted expatriation to the Far West, and who remain to-day the most picturesque Indians of the United States.

West of the Everglades lie those dark, watery woodlands known as the Big Cypress; a trackless labyrinth of swamp, fresh-water lagoon, creek, and low but wonderfully fertile islands on which the Seminole makes his most prolific gardens. All these are deep buried in the shadows of a vast cypress forest that, in turn, is bordered by a dense, interlaced, and impenetrable fringe, miles in width, of mangroves, that grow equally well in salt or brackish waters, and extend to the Gulf an unbroken mantle of perennial green.

At the northern end of the Everglades lies Okechobee, the largest fresh-water lake, next to Michigan, within the limits of the United States. On the south, all these are girdled by the Florida Keys, a wonderful chain of coral islands that, beginning at Miami, extends for two hundred miles south and west through the warm waters of the Gulf Stream, which gives them the climate of Cuba.

Now all this, with every portion easily accessible, is thrown open every winter as a playground for the people of the North. Here, beyond the reach of snow or ice and amid tropical surroundings, they may hunt, fish or loaf, cruise on summer seas, or speed automobiles over ocean beaches hard and smooth as a floor. They may play golf, tennis, or bridge, at the most fashionable of winter resorts, or with canoe and camera they may explore the depths of an uncharted wilderness, widespread, primeval, and occupied only by gentle savages who dwell in huts of palmleaf thatch, as strangely picturesque as those of the South Pacific. They may share the curious lives of sponge fishers and turtle catchers on the coast, or of Florida cowboys and cypress loggers in the interior. They may take a launch trip into the Everglades and witness the operations of draining one of the world's greatest swamps; or in the same launch they may adventure among the coral Keys and study one of the mighty engineering problems of the age, the building of a sea-going railroad. Thus in this particular winter playground is provided plenty of occupation and amusement for all ages and tastes, and for the slender purse as well as for "predatory" wealth.

Twenty-five years ago Florida as a winter playground meant only Jacksonville, St. Augustine, the St. John, and the Ocklawaha as far as Crystal Springs. To the tourists of those days all else was a vast space, vaguely alluring but unknown and unattainable. Then there were but two railroads; one running west from Jacksonville to the Chattahoochee, and another from Fernandina to Cedar Keys, with a branch to the St. John. About this time, however, a Pennsylvania steel man built a little thirty-five mile railroad from Jacksonville to St. Augustine, to which he gave the big name of Jacksonville, St. Augustine and Halifax River Railway, and with this enterprise the vast system of tourist routes that now cover the whole state, was inaugurated. After a while Mr. Henry Flagler, since known as the "Magician of Florida," bought this little railway as a plaything. Then, to make business for his

The seashore was made for the children, with it's gentle sea and beach strewn with shells.

plaything, he began the restoration and upbuilding of America's oldest town, to which, within a year, he had not only given one of the most beautiful hotels in the world, but he had in other ways so added to its existing attractions that its fame as a winter resort has since become as widespread as the English tongue.

But this was only a beginning. The Magician who had accomplished these things soon began to plan other and greater enterprises. He cruised down the Indian River, touching at such beauty spots as Daytona, New Smyrna, and Rockledge, and still pushing southward beyond its ultimate waters he finally discovered Lake Worth with its charming but isolated little winter colony at Palm Beach. This was the most beautiful place the Magician ever had seen, and at once he made a large tract of its choicest lands his own. Then, that Palm Beach might be opened to the whole world, he ordered that his railroad be brought to that point with all speed. At the same time he began the erection there of the largest hotel in the world. So impatient was he to witness results that these great undertakings were begun and finished between two seasons, and Palm Beach sprang full-fledged into the foremost rank of famous winter playgrounds.

For a time the Magician paused here, devoting himself to the beautifying and perfecting of what he already had acquired. To meet the demands for still more ample accommodations, he built other hotels at both St. Augustine and Palm Beach, and established a third playground at Ormond, midway between the two. Then came the great freeze of 1895 that extended its icy fingers even to the Palm Beach paradise, and despoiled it of much beauty. While the Magician sadly gazed upon withered foliage, dead flowers, and citrus trees shorn in a night of their glorious bloom, he was presented with a great bunch of orange blossoms, as perfect and fragrant as had been those so recently destroyed. Until that moment he had not known that there was an orange bloom left in all Florida.

"Where did they come from?" he asked eagerly.

"From the Biscayne Country, nearly one hundred miles to the southward," was the answer.

"What is there?"

"One of the most beautiful salt-water bays of the country."

"How large is it?"

"About forty miles long, and from two to ten broad"

"Is there any reason why our road cannot be extended to that country?"

"None at all."

"How can one reach it now?"

"By two days' ride over a trail almost hub-deep in sand, and through an unbroken wilderness, or by a night's run down the coast in a yacht."

A little later Mr. Flagler had seen for himself the orange trees, untouched by frost, from which his blooms were gathered, and the living green of scores of other tropical trees that form an encircling forest about the amber-crystal waters of Biscayne Bay. At that time there were a dozen houses at Lemon City, near its upper end, two at the mouth of the Miami River, midway down the length of the bay, and a score or so more, six miles south of the Miami, at Cocoanut Grove, then the largest settlement between Palm Beach and Key West. All else was wilderness, exquisite in its primeval beauty and already famous as being the only rock-bound portion of Florida. In those early days the rocks of the Biscayne country were regarded with lively curiosity by those who knew Florida only as an area of sand and swamp, and in these later days of development the rock houses, rock walls, and rock roads of Dade County are its most notable characteristics.

A year after the Magician's first visit, or in May, 1896, the railroad, now known as the Florida East Coast, had reached this land of perpetual summer, of perennial bloom, rugged contour, and swift-running streams, and had established what was thought to be its final terminus on the banks of the Miami. Tracts one mile square, on each side of the river, had been laid out in town lots, the sixth of the great East Coast hotels was in process of construction on a point of land between river and bay, and the embryo city of Miami had sprung into existence. To-day this most southern of mainland cities boasts eight thousand inhabitants, many miles of paved streets, electric lights, a score of hotels, two banks, two daily papers, a deep-water

With ox-teams and prairie schooner, trips mediæval in speed, nerve-restoring in effect, can be taken.

channel dredged across its shallow bay to the sea, terminal docks at which ocean-going steamers may lie and discharge cargoes, an ever-increasing foreign and coastwise commerce, and a widespread surrounding of prosperous farms, and thrifty groves, threaded by hundreds of miles of the finest rock roads of the state.

Here, for six years, the Magician rested, only extending his transportation facilities by the establishment of steamship lines to Key West, Havana, and Nassau, and building at the Bahama capital another of his splendid winter hotels. Then his attention was attracted by two other great undertakings in line with his own. One was the construction, by Sir William Van Horne, of a railway, throughout the entire length of Cuba, from Havana to Santiago, and the other was the resumption of work, with a certainty of its completion, on the Panama Canal.

Key West is a long way nearer to both Havana and Colon than any other port of the United States, and a railroad to Key West necessarily must receive much of the freight from both places. Such a road could be built along the line of Florida Keys, and besides promising to do well as a freight proposition, it would open a most unique and fascinating playground to the ever-increasing number of tourists searching for just such places.

Then why not build it?

No reason at all, since our Magician is amply possessed of the magic wands of to-day, and finds his greatest pleasure in testing their powers.

Then let it be built.

With the edict thus issued, work was begun on the sea-going extension of the F. E. C. Ry., and last winter (February, 1908) passenger trains were run to Knight's Key, more than one hundred miles beyond Miami, and four hundred and seventy-five south of Jacksonville, over a roadbed unique among all the railroads of the world. Key West is only forty miles beyond Knight's Key, but, in covering this distance an immense concrete viaduct, spanning a deep channel three miles wide, still remains to be built. Thus at least another year must elapse before F. E. C. locomotives, and steamships from the Orient, via Panama, can rub noses at Key West. In the meantime, however, the best of the Florida Keys are being traversed by through Pullmans from all principal Northern points, and this new playground is ready for the entertainment of the many thousands who will seek its charms.

While Florida's eastern coast has thus been transformed into nearly five hundred miles of winter playground, the many delightful localities on the West or Gulf Coast have not been overlooked by railroad builders. These have extended their lines to Homosassa, known and loved by two generations of fishermen; to Tarpon Springs, headquarters of the Gulf sponge industry, and of a happy winter colony of yachtsmen; to St. Petersburg at the southern end of the Pinellas peninsula; to Tampa with its interesting cigar factories and its great Moorish hotel; to Manatee amid its orange groves; to Sarasota with its shell beaches and fine salt-water bathing; to Punta Gorda at the head of Charlotte Harbor; and finally to Ft. Meyers nestling in the shade of its cocoa palms, on the south bank of the Caloosahatchie, and having the same latitude as Palm Beach. Here are the largest grape-fruit groves of the world, also the finest tarpon fishing. Ft. Meyers is furthermore an interesting place as being the winter home of Thomas Alva Edison, and the outfitting point for cruises down the lower West Coast, among the bird-haunted labyrinths of the Ten Thousand Islands; into the mysterious waterways of Whitewater Bay; or on past Cape Sable, to the Keys; and, if one chooses, around the southern end of the state to Biscayne Bay and Miami. Of course this trip may be reversed, with Miami as the outfitting point, and Meyers, Punta Gorda, or Tampa, the objective.

To those who do not care for salt-water fishing or cruising, or who find the sea breezes of the coast too bracing, the interior of Florida offers hundreds of delightful playgrounds, beside spring-fed lakes, shaded by rustling palms, moss-hung live-oaks or orange trees laden with fruit, dead-ripe and luscious, that may be had for the picking. In these groves the yellow fruit and the scented blooms hang side by side; for oranges ripen in the winter, and at the same time the trees cover themselves with fragrant bridal wreaths of the next year's fruitage.

Most of these pleasant places can be

Palm trees and clouds make a trip along the west coast a trail into fairyland.

reached by train; for the vast territory that twenty-five years ago held only two railroads, now is so threaded with these arteries of travel that only two of its forty-six counties are without them. Then, too, the waterways of the state, its rivers, creeks, and canals, its myriad lakes and lagoons, are so intimately connected one with another, that a canoe or light-draught launch may traverse them in any direction throughout the length and breadth of the peninsula. Thus, for instance, the inland cruiser may start from Jacksonville and go up the St. John to Welaka, where he may enter the Ocklawaha, follow the windings of that crooked stream past Crystal Springs, and so on for a hundred miles farther, into the "Lake Region." Here, in close proximity, lie Lakes Griffin, Eustis, Harris, Yale, and Dora; and the last-named is connected by canal with Lake Apopka, the largest of all. Bordering these lakes are great orange groves, and fine winter estates, besides towns and villages at which supplies may be renewed. From Lake Apopka a short railway carry may be made to Kissimmee on Lake Tahopkelaga whose waters flow south by way of the Kissimmee River to the great lake Okechobee, which, through the Caloosahatchie, finds outlet to the Gulf near Ft. Meyers.

Or the cruise from Jacksonville may be continued up the St. John, past the mouth of the Ocklawaha, through Lakes George and Monroe, to Sanford, where another all-rail carry of about thirty miles, forms a second connecting link with the south-flowing waters of the Kissimmee.

If he chooses, the cruiser may keep on past Sanford, still farther up the St. John, making his way through widespread marshes, and innumerable ponds, all connected by navigable streams, to distant Lake Poinsett. From its eastern shore a wagon carry of five miles will land him at Rockledge on the salt waters of the Indian River, with a clear inland passage all the way to Palm Beach and Biscayne Bay.

Still another cruise may start from Jacksonville, with a thirty-five-mile rail carry to St. Augustine, or a short, outside run from the mouth of the St. John to the same point. From there it may be continued to the extreme southern part of the state by salt-water lagoons, connecting canals, the Indian River, Lake Worth, Biscayne Bay, and the sheltered waters of the Bay of Florida, lying behind the long-extended line of Keys.

The route of any of these cruises may, of course, be reversed, by starting from Key West, the most southerly city of Florida, which has direct sea communication with New York and Mobile. By thus working northward, for some eighty miles along the Keys to Cape Sable, and so on up the West Coast to the mouth of the Caloosahatchie, or along the entire stretch of Keys, one hundred and fifty miles to Miami and the waterways of the East Coast, the cruiser stands a good chance of having warm and pleasant weather during his entire trip. This most desirable feature of a cruise cannot be assured to him who makes his start from Jacksonville or St. Augustine, for, from the middle of December to the middle of February, the northern half of Florida is more or less subject to the discomforts of frosty nights, cold winds, and chilling rains.

On any of these expeditions, whether undertaken from the northern or the southern end of the state, the cruiser need never be more than three or four days, or a week at most, away from a base of supplies, including gasoline for his motor. Thus, on Florida cruises, it is never necessary to over-burden the cruising craft with cargo.

While every county in Florida demands from the non-resident sportsman the payment of ten dollars for a hunting license before he may so much as take aim at bird or beast, the angler is subjected to no such restriction. He may take fish by fair means, in any Florida waters, without price or question; and as all these waters, fresh as well as salt, swarm with fish of all degrees of excellence and pugnacity, the cruiser, who also is a fisherman, will find every opportunity for the pursuit of his favorite sport. Nor need he fear going hungry while traversing these prolific waters, if he is provided with tackle and bait. If he would fish only for sport and the excitement of battle, the mighty tarpon, "Silver King" of finny tribes, often tipping the beam at two hundred pounds; and the agile bonefish, weighing less than ten, but darting with the swiftness of a hawk, and fighting with a hawk's persistent energy, will give him every opportunity for testing his skill and power of endurance against theirs.

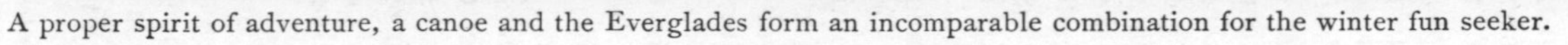

A proper spirit of adventure, a canoe and the Everglades form an incomparable combination for the winter fun seeker.

If he must fish at the command of appetite, he will find pompano and Spanish mackerel, kingfish, and grouper, big-mouthed bass and perch, mangrove snapper, and yellowtail, besides scores of others, all admirably adapted to the frying pan or the chowder pot, awaiting him at every mile of his Florida cruising. Besides these, he will find crawfish, as large as lobsters and more delicate, oysters and clams by the bushel, shrimp to be scooped in by the netful, turtle and terrapin to delight the heart of an epicure, and turtle eggs freshly buried in warm beach sands. Ch, no! the Florida cruiser need never fear hunger, even though his entire supply of "boughten grub" should become exhausted without chance of renewal, if only he has the knowledge and skill to help himself from nature's abundance.

He must learn, probably from experience, for he is not likely to profit by written advice, especially if he be young and self-confident, that many biting and stinging insects abound in certain parts of Florida at all seasons. To meet these he should provide himself with netting for mosquitoes, and with dope for sand flies; or, better still with a fine cheesecloth bar for both; with ammonia for all insect stings, though salt water is nearly as efficacious; and with a hypodermic syringe and a solution of potash permanganate for venomous snake bites; though the chances are ten to one that he will not see a snake of any kind during his entire cruise. He must learn that the ubiquitous, but microscopic redbug has colonized every bunch of grass and moss and dry seaweed in Florida, as well as every log and bit of dead wood, and that, given the opportunity, they will promptly incorporate themselves with him, until he has good cause to imagine that he has been set on fire. To war with the redbug, the cruiser's most convenient weapons will be kerosene, a salve of lard and sulphur, spirits of ammonia, or a saturated solution of salt.

He will furthermore learn that scorpions are no more to be dreaded than spiders, that if a centipede crawls over his bare skin it will leave a painfully inflamed trail; that, when bathing in salt water, if he touches the long, streaming tentacles of a purple physalia, or Portuguese man-of-war, he will fancy that he has run afoul of a bunch of particularly vicious stinging nettles, and that if he comes into contact with a whip-ray he probably will receive a wound that will be acutely painful and a long time in healing. But, as an old Floridian says:

"What's the use in naming all them biting an' stinging critters, when I've lived here all my life an' haint run up agin nary one of 'em, 'ceptin', of cose, redbugs an' moskitters, an' scorponiums, an sich trash that don't count, only to make a feller scratch *and* cuss?"

Florida is very easy of access nowadays, Jacksonville being but thirty hours from New York and forty from Chicago by the fast trains, or three days from New York by steamers that also touch at Charleston; while the Keys, only just across the Straits from Cuba, and now reached by through Pullmans from all principal Northern points, are but twelve hours farther away. Thus, within forty-eight hours, one may change his environment from arctic to tropic, winter for summer, a zero mercury for one between 60° and 80° above, ice and snow for blue skies and bluer waters, ever-blooming flowers, and singing birds. And all this without leaving the mainland of the United States!

On the Keys, this winter, the traveler in search of a new playground will find half a dozen new hotels; small to be sure, but clean and well appointed; and here will be unfolded a wonderland to delight and interest him.

IN THE BLACKJACK

A DAY WITH THE QUAIL IN FLORIDA'S TANGLED SCRUB OAK

BY MAXIMILIAN FOSTER

NOON—high noon, you'd say, since a sun like Joshua's stood midway in the round of staring cloudless sky. But every man to his choice. We'd chosen this day of many Florida days for our sport; so here we were. Across the open, the blurred landscape swayed drunkenly—sand and a waste of scrub pine, oak and palmetto wavering in the glassy heat flung back from the baked and arid earth. But who hunts in a half-tropic land like this suffers a penalty in days of just this kind. We hunted; and I think Bert and I each had a clear opinion of the other's idiocy. And each of his own, as well.

Yet hope tempted onward. Beyond, and through a fringe of live oaks standing on the southward bluff, we caught a glimpse of blue, a strip of color gleaming like naked metal beneath the foliage that of itself was as stiff and fixed as bronze. There was the Gulf, and by and by, a landward breeze would rise upon its width, and for a while, wake to life again the dead world around us. So we drifted on, hunting shade, the silence broken only by the tires grinding along the road's deep, sandy furrows; the steam-like panting of Mac and Doris under the wagon body, and our own patient, thoughtful sighing. But when the breeze came——

"Birds?" observed Bert, and grinned. "Oh, shucks!"

And I believe he was right, at the time. *Birds?* If there were any, we'd quite failed to locate their whereabouts. "Say, if you did find any birds today," said Bert oracularly, "I'll bet a dollar they'd be squatting on a slice of toast."

Which was hopeless of Bert, who was nominally hopeful.

"Cheer up," said I hopefully, and utterly without hope, "we'll cross over to the bayou heads for a while. We'll find them coming down to the swamp to drink."

Bert looked at me over his shoulder, grinning feebly, though it were benignly. "*Unh hunh*—oh, yeah," he remarked distinctly. "Regular formula to find birds, isn't it? You hunt 'em early in the straw—oh, yeah! Fine! They're all there just where they roosted. And afterwards, when they've moved, we find them all out in the pines, feeding on the mast. Sure! That's it. And then a little later, they retire to shady nooks to scratch and dust. By 'n' by they go down to the swamp for a drink. Right you are. *Hmph!*" Bert sniffed lightly, and the sniff was voluminous with its scorn. "Only they don't," said Bert tartly. "Not on days like this anyway. They just dissolve. Hey!—get ap, you Dolly!"

Dolly, the mare, belonged to our friend the dominie. And a more thoroughly quiet and seemly Dolly no parson ever drove on godly ways. Times when the dominie carried the gospel afoot we exercised Dolly at his behest, and he was glad. But to exercise Dolly required as much exertion on our part as on Dolly's; for Dolly owned to a kirkly repose equal to that of the dominie's richest parishioner dozing in a pew corner. To keep Dolly awake was an art as well as a manual effort, a kind of progressive carpet-beating, only a little more dusty. "Git ap!" said Bert, turning off the road into a piece of pineland strewn with down-timber. "Git ap, you!" Accordingly, Dolly awoke long enough to rattle us over a fallen log, a jolt that was as if meant to remind us a buggy is not a steeplechaser. "*Unh*—whoa!" snapped Bert, and weariedly stood up.

"I'm looking for a way," explained Bert, "and there isn't any. I want to find a short-cut, because it'll be the longest way to get there."

"To get where?"

"Oh, down by the swamp heads where all the quail are drinking," said Bert coolly. "Wasn't it there you said we'd find them?"

I stuck my gun between my knees and reached for the reins. "You give me those lines, Bert."

"Willingly," said he, and thrust them on me. "Hie away, bullies!" said Bert listlessly, leaning over to look under the wagon body at the dogs. "Hie away, there!"

Doris, after a glance to make sure he meant it, linked away across the open, stretching herself in a hopeful burst of speed. But Mac—big, lumbering, clumsy Mac sidled off uncertainly, scuffling dispiritedly, and with a look almost of reproach in his wistful eyes, as if he had settled with himself that to hunt to-day meant only a waste of precious effort. "Mac," said Bert, addressing him pointedly, "you hie away there, or I'll get down and say something real personal to you. Git!" said he, and Mac got, picking up speed as he reached out across the open. But one could hardly blame the big, blue-ticked setter. Beyond, the pineland thinned out again, and between the tree boles we could see what lay beyond—another waste of scrub, but scrub of a different kind than the desert of palmetto, oak and pine straggling behind us on the sandy plain. "Blackjack!" snorted Bert, and lurched to his feet. "Hey, you, Doris—come out of that!" he cried sharply, and instinctively reached for the dog whistle strung from a button of his coat.

For we'd been there before; we were fully informed concerning that particular stretch of thicket—a desert of stunted oak sun-dried to a dingy rust color, square miles of it lying like a jungle and thicker than a summer woodcock cover. Back three weeks or so, on a December afternoon, the dogs had popped into that tangle before we could head them off, and there the two had hunted quail on private account while, for a sad two hours, we had hunted them. Sad, I say, because the dry, rasping foliage gave off heat like an oven; sad, because we wandered blindly through the blind maze of it, hot, weary and futile—and still sadder, hotter and more wearied because we knew that Doris and Mac must have found birds, or, long before they would have come in to Bert's incessant shrilling, piped Pan-like on the dog whistle. And then, when he had chanced on Doris frozen to a covey in the depths, we added a new vexation to our emburdening woe; for the birds, trod up from underfoot, whirred headlong against the wall of brown, rattling foliage and were gone at the first jump off the ground. So we had collared Doris, and Mac coming in at the crack of my ineffectual dose of No. 9's, had been collared, too, and forthwith we fought our way out of the trap, growling our vows to the future. "Don't No. 1," I said at the time: "Don't go into the blackjacks before the leaves are off."

So now—"Hey, you come out of that!" muttered Bert again, reaching for his whistle, and, at the call, strident and commanding, Doris headed up again, quartering out into the more open ground of the pineland.

"And here's 'Don't No. 2,'" remarked Bert reflectively: "Don't go into the blackjacks at all. Not scrub like that, anyway. We'll just stick to the open, I guess."

But one might just as well have hunted birds in a picked cotton field as to look for them in the midst of these open pine fields at noon. Particularly in the midst of bland, glaring sunlight like this. I knew it and Bert knew it, too. "It's about a mile to the heads," he mumbled, settling back and half-asleep; "we'll hunt along."

But man proposes and—well, in this case it was Doris that shaped the way, disposing of our plans in a measure that left no other alternative. For, as the buggy turned, Doris swung with it, streaming up to our right, going at the pace of a quarter-horse and heading straight for the jungle of blackjack. "Hey, you come out of that!" yapped Bert again, and snatched swiftly for his whistle. "You Doris!"

She was gone though, a flash of white gleaming an instant against the rusty edge of the scrub oak, flitting like a wraith. But as she plunged headlong into the thick of it, we'd seen her sharp head flung upward—seen her swerve and then ply onward with an added sign of making game in the way she flattened in her stride.

Bert's whistle dropped from his lips. "Say, look at old Mac!"

Away along the blackjack's edge, the scuffling, clumsy bigger dog—a dog keen and true in despite his seeming awkwardness—there big Mac had swung across the other's line, and now, with his head outthrust and shoulders hunched together, he was stalking on in the train of vanished Doris, his eyes fixed on something unseen to us in the scrub. *Pop!* there he froze; and prodding Dolly into a trot, we rattled up toward him, tumbled out of the buggy; and, for form's sake, if not for other reasons, we hitched the dominie's dozing mare to a jack pine, and walked in to see what was doing.

It was Doris that old Mac had his eye upon, and there in the scrub oak's edge we found her, fast on a beautiful point—beautiful, I say, though not one of the head-high, upstanding points that fashion dictates. But Doris, cracking headlong into the thicket, had been left no chance to pose, for, stooping to trail, the full blast of the covey scent had caught her straight in the face as she swung. There she was now, crouched sideways, her head screwed back to her shoulder, all four legs propped together, and almost toppling over in the tense, guarded stress of that exquisite, anxious moment. One saw that the birds were almost under her, and the bitch's eyes rolled slowly as we pushed our way into the thicket.

"Wait," said Bert, eyeing the ground ahead. "Let's try to drive them out into the open."

"All right—but we can't do it, Bert."

Still Bert said we'd try, and try we did. Also I fail to recall a more complete and hapless fiasco—as it should have been—this imbecile effort to herd the covey to our liking. Out in the clear we might have headed them one way or another after a fashion, but to drive them willy-nilly away from close cover like the scrub and out into the open pine-lands. Have you ever tried it? But Bert, I suspect, knew fitly what would be, for, as we circled in ahead of quivering Doris, I saw him out of the corner of an eye, squinting backwards into the blackjack, and edging in sideways, a sure sign that he had no faith in the maneuver and meant to swing when they flushed.

And—well, as might be expected. *Hurrh-rrrh!* I still have a clear, unfailing recollection of the way that covey burst out from underfoot and climbed scrambling, beating a way through the latticed twigs. For the moment the air was full of birds, their wings whirred in my face as they rose, streaming overhead, and in that brief, disordering moment, I swung sharply about, a bird at my right shoulder battling clumsily against the boughs, and another plowing by straight overhead, so close that I could have reached up and clubbed it down with the barrels.

Yet, as I swung, the thicket seemed to open narrowly, a half-blurred lane seen beyond the length of gun rib, walled in on either side, but still open enough to show me that overhead bird hustling on his way. There was no time, though, to dwell on the scuttling fellow; in some respects it was like squibbing at longbills, a shot such as you get when you kick up a cock from among the birch poles; for the gun, pitched to the shoulder, cracked instantly the butt-plate found its rest. *Bang!* said Bert's gun, and then again—*Bang!* Somehow you always see the other man's downed birds when you're drawing on your own—Bert had managed a right and left—and *bang!* I had him—and then *bang!* again, this time at a hen bird streaming off at the right. A nice clean snap at her, and—well, a nice clean miss.

We broke our guns and dropped in fresh shells. "Dead!—fetch, Doris—Mac. Three are pretty good," said Bert, and then added: "*Hmph!* three when we didn't deserve any. Why, you'd think we were punching cows, the way we tried to round them up. Hey! where are you going?"

"After the singles," I told him. "And into that scrub!" protested Bert, peering into the thicket. "Hey," began Bert, peevishly, and then halted with an exclamation. "Why, I declare!" he cried, "it's almost open enough to shoot. Why, the leaves are nearly gone."

"Come on, Bert."

He took another look. "Hie away there, you Doris—Mac!"

Bert, with a look on his face of a Cortez exploring unknown worlds, plunged ahead into the jungle, Doris and Mac racing on before.

For, as Bert had said and, by chance, I had already seen, the leaves were almost gone. Looking at the scrub from a distance it had seemed to be as walled-in and as thick and blinding as before, as traplike and impenetrable as on that day when we had sadly hunted our missing dogs. But three weeks of year-end wind and weather had stripped the maze of its foliage; there was room to shoot now, even in the thickest parts—if one shot quickly—so Bert and I braved it again. But I'll admit, we stuck pretty close to the dogs.

That venture proved to be a pretty lucky try for us, a full repayment of the morning hours' blank and fruitless effort. And for many hours, too, when we had wandered far and near, wondering where the birds had gone. For here was their natural refuge, a place in which to hide and keep, and in that waste of scrub, that day, we found shooting to last us many weeks—covey after covey strung together in a way we'd never dream to find them in wasted, shot-over grounds we'd known before. And here it seemed to make no odds to our success whatever time of day we hunted—morning, noon and evening—it was one and the same; the birds were nearly always there—always I had almost said—always there when we hunted them.

"Steady, Mac!"

But the blackjack had its disadvantages, too—more than one, I can tell you. Out in the open, a bungle is your only chance to make a miss. Very nice and pretty, of course; you can drive straight up to your birds, if the down timber isn't too thick; and the birds stand no chance at all, until sad experience has taught them to light out at the first jump for the cat-brier swamps along the head of the draws. And, if you don't care to get your hands scratched, you can shy off from the cat-briers and hunt another covey in the open. Only you don't always find the coveys in the open, though in the blackjack——

"Steady, Doris!"

A hundred yards within the scrub Doris dropped, and Bert nodded for me to take the bird.

Now, that particular cock quail was like a great many other birds we found in there—big, well-fed and strong, not at all like the weazened, half-hearted starvelings one finds so often on Florida's sandy plains. For food in there was a-plenty, and these birds were like their Northern fellows because of it—stout and hearty birds, prone to lie close at any hazard, and then to rush from cover, bustling fiercely like a grouse. This bird I have in mind now, had squatted in a little bunch of tuft grass, verdure strewn with withered oak leaves exactly matching his own mottled tans and grays. And though I trampled the tuft to and fro, kicking gingerly in the fear of stamping him underfoot, he would not budge until I very nearly trod on him. Then, like his fellows, he burst from cover straight away—*burr-rrh-rrh!*—bent on departing forthwith and regardless of the way he went. *Burr-rrh-rrh-rh!* That first jump took him straight forward—not upward—and about on a height with my knee. Most disconcerting—*bang!* Prettily missed. *Bang!*—again. I'm not at all certain where he went after that, though I could swear to it that the charge of No. 9's went elsewhere.

"*Hmph!*" said Bert consolingly, "he lit out along the ground just like a rabbit. But your shot hit the brush just where he was before he bounced upwards. If he hadn't you'd have got him."

"Thanks!" said I.

"You're welcome," said Bert. "Where's Mac?"

And a moment later there was added to this question, its companion query—a question we were pouring always into each other's wearied ears: "Oh, say, where's Doris, too?" There was but one variation to the plaint: "Say, can you see either of the dogs?"

For, above all other places I have ever hunted in, this particular stretch of blackjack owned the ability of swallowing our dogs at odd moments, as if the ground had opened and sucked them in, or, as if they had run down an unseen hole. "Where's Doris?" "Where's Mac?" Conversation in the blackjacks was reduced inevitably to this form, querulously persistent—Doris and Mac hunted quail; we hunted them—and in nearly every instance when we'd lost the two and then found them again, one or the other was fast upon a covey.

So now, the beginning of that plaint: "Where's Doris? Say, can you see Mac?"

Ten minutes later—and more by good luck than by good management—we found the two, each fastened to a bird. Mine skied, and clearly outlined against the sky, seemed too easy. But as I pulled, the bird ducked, stooping back to cover, so that it took a hasty snap from the left to pull him down. Bert's bird was like that first single of mine, flushing close and skimming the earth like a rabbit, his bustling wings almost fanning the ground as he tore away. Furthermore, his flight took him under the lower branches of the scrub oak, a safe screen for him had Bert tried to crack away standing upright. But my friend knew a thing or two; I saw him squat on his heels, the gun cracked, and by the nonchalant, airy way Bert arose and broke his gun, I knew the bird was downed.

"Shucks!" he remarked, "it was just like shooting through a water main. I couldn't possibly have missed him."

But others could, I among them. I could have missed that bird with ease.

We picked up four other singles after that, and then again the setters disappeared. "See here, Bert," said I, after a hot and wearying scramble to and fro, "we'll never in the world be able to follow the dogs afoot. I'm going to get the wagon."

"Hey?" Bert turned to stare at me with a fishy eye. "You going to try driving in this blackjack. Say, I guess Dolly will need a set of climbing irons if you do."

But we tried, and the effort, I'm bound to say, was very nearly a success. Dolly aimed straight at the tangle—"Get ap, Dolly!"—Dolly, headed into the thick of it, ambled peacefully along. But not for long. "Git ap, there!" chirped Bert, and to the staccato accompaniment of the oak staves rattling on the spokes, an ear-racking clatter like unto a small boy dragging a lath along a picket fence, we plowed our way into the scrub. But not for long, as I've said—"*Unh!* whoa there, you!"—and then again, "*Unh!*" as we brought up with a bang, wedged in firmly between two blackjack boles that disputed our right to ride them down.

"Don't No. 28—say, I forget the rest," drawled Bert peevishly, "but Don't No. 28—don't go into the blackjacks with a parson's mare and buggy."

I turned about, looking behind me for a way to back clear of the mess, and I caught another fishy gleam from Bert.

"Because," said he, still petulant, "you've knocked about a dollar's worth of paint already off the parson's buggy, and you'll knock all the hair off Dolly, too, and besides, I can see language coming not fit for a perfectly respectable parson's mare like this."

Nor was Bert wrong. I backed and then went ahead again, and it was Bert that supplied the language as a blackjack limb sprang back from the forward hub and rapped him on the knuckles. Somehow we plowed through the worst of it, learning a lesson by the way—the lesson that follows one's dogs properly in any field—particularly in scrub like this—one must take to the saddle. We had the lesson driven home that day.

"Whoa, there! Look!" cried Bert.

We'd burst out into a little swale, an opening where the down timber lay hidden in the thick, upstanding straw, and there in the center lay a little puddle, a hollow into which the drainage of past rains had flowed. On its edge stood big Mac, stiff and rigid like a statue, and off to the left, Doris, with one paw curved beneath her and her back to the other dog, hung quivering.

"Pretty, pretty!" chuckled Bert, as we tumbled out. "See old Mac backing Doris—why, it's all of seventy yards." But Bert had no sooner clucked his satisfaction than he cried aloud again. "Back nothing!" he exclaimed. "Each one has a covey!"

Which was true.

We walked in on Mac's birds first, and as the guns cracked the other covey flushed at the sound. But we were looking for that; we marked their flight, and as they scaled along, hustling over the blackjacks, we saw them wheel and swing in ahead of the others.

"Gee! Come on—let's hurry!" urged Bert joyously. "Two coveys down together. We'll get some shooting now."

But again man proposed and—well, there was the providence that disposes things to the advantage of the little birds. I've said we'd marked their flight, but in that tangle of sun-dried scrub, all of a hue of the birds themselves, there was no marking them down. Furthermore, we had not marked them far enough—pure carelessness on our parts, for though the birds may be said to have gone away in a bunch, there were outlying strays—at least three or four I'd seen out of the corner of an eye to screw away from the main flight—and these I had not marked at all. But live and learn. We walked out with the dogs ahead of us, and then Bert and I began to grumble peevishly.

For we found no birds; the two coveys were gone as if stricken from the world about. About where we thought they'd dropped, we circled, and, running the circle home, drew a blank for our pains.

"Farther out," said Bert reflectively, and ranging on, we tried it farther out. Another blank, and—"Oh, shucks!" said Bert. Afterward, we went still farther, drew another blank, and, the Gulf wind having raised itself, puffing gently, we hunted up that gentle whisper of a breeze, found nothing—turned—came back—and once more lost our dogs.

"I was looking straight at Mac," protested Bert; "I had my eye right on him not a quarter of a minute ago. Where's Doris?"

How could I know? I gave thanks only in that Doris was lemon and white—not a brick-red Irish setter or a black and tan Gordon, for if she had been we'd never found her at all in the cover of the blackjacks.

"What we need in here," said Bert dispiritedly, "is a red, white and blue dog—in stripes, too—something we can see. Oh, here we are!"

It was old Mac. He came slouching in out of the depths, took a look at us, and promptly plunged back into the blackjack again. "And there you go," said Bert, sotto voce, as Mac dissolved from view. "Say," demanded Bert, "did you mark where the birds went, anyhow?"

"No—did you, Bert?"

Bert protested he had been too busy marking down a dead bird dropped to his right barrel, and a cripple tumbled over at his left. The long and short of it was, that a half-hour later we found three scattering birds lying far out to right of where we thought the coveys had gone; the others we never found. But to find the dogs seemed enough to be glad for. Mac we stumbled over behind a fallen tree, and when we had cleaned up that single, Bert neatly wiping my eye after I'd missed with a right and left, Mac went on and picked up the two other singles.

But Doris, a swift and widely ranging dog, we saw nothing of for an hour.

"Catch me in here again afoot or in a buggy," vowed Bert wrothfully, "and I'll——"

But I never learned Bert's provision for what he would do, for there in another little rift among the blackjacks, an opening carpeted with straw and the strayed leaves drifted from the scrub oak, we found the missing bitch, poised head high and outstretched, and holding fast to a smashing covey of quail.

Now, two shots may match each other, bird for bird, in the open, but in the close thickets like this sweep of blackjack, the man who keeps an eye to his p's and q's is the one that gets the quail. By that, I mean the one that walks in for the rise where there will be room to shoot—one that picks the likeliest opening in the brush. Every time, he will be the one to get the birds, and Bert and I—well, I think we bungled that covey handsomely.

For Bert and I, stumbling unexpectedly over the bitch, hilariously burst our way toward her, forgetting utterly how long she must have held the steadfast point before we came along. Indeed, the birds had long run out from under her, and as we crashed through the blackjack they got up almost behind us at the right, whirred frantically, and again, at the first jump, dissolved forthwith into the walled background of the thicket.

Bang! Bang!—then *bang! Burr-rrh-rr!* A stray bird, rising late—*bang!*

"Oh, shucks! never touched him at all."

"Same here, Bert."

Four shells like votive offerings burned on the shrine of carelessness. "Oh, shucks!" mumbled Bert, more loudly than before.

Yet armed by past experience we made that covey pay for it.

"Mark!" snapped Bert under his breath. The blackjack was thinned out enough to give a view, and with our eyes, we followed, till with a sudden lift, the birds turned sharply to the right and were gone.

Bert grinned grimly. "Got 'em now?" he asked.

I nodded, and sending on the dogs, we walked straight up to that scattered covey as if there had been a sign post to show us the way.

There were many things we learned about—and all about—that day. One, in chief, was that it wouldn't do to lift one's eyes off the birds until the last bird was lost to view; then one must gauge the distance through the blackjacks to where they'd likely drop; and after that, to swing off both to the right and left in widening circles. For in that listless air there was no way to tell how they'd turn, whether on one hand or the other, and the only way, after all, to find them, was to hunt far and wide—if we missed them then, we came back to the starting point and hunted far and wide anew. For, in that close thicket, as I've said, there was no close marking of the spot; we must take their line—and take it closely, too—and then follow the formula of far and wide. In that way only we found our game—not always, I'm bound to say, but times enough to make it pay.

Evening dropped and found us still at it, a day big in doings, though not, perhaps, in the number of the slain. But we had birds enough and in plenty. At dusk we came out on the blackjack's edge, and there in the straw of the rising pineland, we had a half-hour's clear shooting in the open that was child's play to what we had left behind.

"Oh, shucks!" said Bert, "it's too easy. Let's go home."

So home we went through the dusk, leaving behind us a scattered brood piping its covey call, but taking with us more than had dropped to our guns—much more, in the memory of that day's events in the blackjack.

"Well, well!" exclaimed the parson, peeping into the wagon box, "you've certainly had a day."

"A day and a half," promptly answered Bert, "and we owe you, too, for about nine dollars' worth of buggy paint."

But the dominie, busy pocketing the plumpest of our birds for the sick and needy of his flock, was too absorbed to hear.

27.
Alligator Shooting in Florida
(1899)

ALLIGATOR SHOOTING IN FLORIDA.

BY JOHN MORTIMER MURPHY.

Author of "Sporting Adventures in the Far West."

DARING sportsmen who visit Florida during the winter months never desire to return home without having shot an alligator, and the larger it is the better pleased is the successful man. Many fail to accomplish their purpose, nevertheless, and for the simple reason that the saurians are hibernating at that season of the year and seldom emerge from their cosy retreats except when pressed by hunger or deluded by unusually warm weather.

To kill them at such times a person must be familiar with their haunts or have the good fortune to meet them while he is in quest of better game. They seem exceedingly stupid and lethargic on such occasions, as if they were not fully aroused from their slumbers and were weak from long fasting. If they are encountered suddenly on dry land, they make their usual display of bad temper by swelling the body to its fullest dimensions from throat to tail, hissing forth their anger in musky tones, and lashing the ground with their elastic caudal appendages. Their little piggish eyes also gleam with a mingled expression of fear and ferocity, and frequently their elongated jaws snap viciously together, as if they would like to devour their human foe.

If not stopped, they try to escape, as they do not relish fighting on land; but if any determined attempt is made to bar their way they become aggressive immediately. Their first movement is to try and hit the enemy with the muscular tail, and if that fails they sometimes advance open mouthed. The latter action is more of a demonstration than a real attack in most instances, yet it looks formidable enough to startle a novice, or even a veteran hunter unacquainted with the characteristics of the saurians. The person who understands them pays little attention to these feints, unless the animals are within biting range, for he knows that he can easily elude his fleetest assailant, owing to its rigid, scaly armor, which prevents rapidity of movement, and its comparatively awkward legs, which nature seems to have destined more for weight carrying than speed. If the reptile charges, the hunter merely steps aside and lets it pass on, or tumbles it over with a load of shot in the eyes or a bullet through the brain.

Most of the 'gators killed in winter by Northern sportsmen are shot while they are sunning themselves on a bank or beach, after a long sleep in the muddy bottoms of lakes or rivers, or while migrating from one body of water to another. The novices who kill large alligators at such times generally like to have themselves and their victims photographed by a knight of the camera, that they may be able to furnish ocular proof to their Northern friends that they actually destroyed a "Florida dragon." These gentlemen also seem anxious to get a lady or two into the group, and no picture is thought complete without the usual black butcher engaged in flaying the carcass. Colored men are quite anxious to become dissectors at such scenes, for, besides the liberal pay usually received, their vanity is highly flattered by having their features portrayed in the foreground, and surrounded by distinguished company. Many of these photographs may now be seen throughout the Northern States, and the friends of the gentlemen who killed the saurians no doubt look upon them as the most daring of heroes, yet if the facts concerning some of these victorious scenes were told they would bring the Nimrods less praise than ridicule. One of the photographs which made the deepest impression on my mind depicted a man, in full sporting toggery, sitting on a camp stool, with a rifle across his knees, in front of a huge alligator, which a negro was carefully dissecting. A large tent occupied the background, and groups of palmettoes were visible on the right and left. The picture looked innocent and real enough, yet the accessories were grouped for the occasion, and all the principal figure in the scene had to do with the alligator was to help tow it to where it was photographed after the negro had killed it with an axe while it was enjoying its noon siesta.

These remarks are not intended to imply that the majority of sportsmen do not kill the reptiles in a thoroughly sportsman-like manner, but rather to explain how so many photographs of Florida scenes make the skinning of alligators seem so common.

Before describing any of my experiences with the saurians it may be well to note some of their traits, for these are not well known even to persons who have spent years amid the haunts of the reptiles. Alligators are, primarily, the most marked feature of animal life in the Southern States, and the most interesting to the sportsman and naturalist, though each looks upon them from different standpoints. To the former they are too often nothing more than skulking, cowardly and destructive thieves which gobble down his wild ducks as fast as they touch the water, or his loved companion, the dog, while attempting to retrieve the dead birds. Their open countenances carry no indications of generosity to him, but, on the contrary, are typical of all that is truculent, sardonic and hideously repulsive. Man and the alligator seem to be natural enemies, for the former rarely misses an opportunity of destroying the latter. It is a common belief in Florida that the reptile will boldly attack a sleeping man, but hurriedly flee should he arise; for man erect is to the alligator what he is to the tiger, "the lord of creation," and it pays him voluntary homage by scampering off at its best pace. It is also said that an alligator will not attack a white man while he is bathing, but it has no such respect for a black or a red man. In fact, to use the vernacular, "an alligator likes a nigger better than a hog, and a boy than a man."

It seems more probable that the negro's dusky hue in the dark and often muddy waters prevents the saurian from detecting his dangerous character until after the assault has been made, and then it has things too much in its own jaws to care for the result. I am also inclined to think that fear of the white man has become an hereditary instinct with modern alligators, for they appear to avoid his haunts as much as possible—though they may be quite numerous near negro quarters—and will flee from him where they pay little attention to the presence of his black brother. That this should be so seems quite natural when we consider the perpetual war waged on the saurians by the Caucasian race for centuries.

According to the book of Genesis the waters brought forth the fish and the birds, and according to paleontologists that book is correct, the reptiles being the source from which emanated our feathered creation. Birds are, therefore, simply modified saurians, the scales of the latter having become transformed into feathers on the former, and the fore feet into wings. How many eons it took to make this wonderful transformation of mud-crawling, hideous reptiles into winged and beautiful songsters no scientist can determine. Yet that one is the product of the other is apparent to every student of primitive animal life. Look, for instance, at the picture of the ichthyosaurus, compare it with that of the bat-like reptile, the pterodactyl, and note how similar in form they are, though differing vastly in size: the former was a finned reptile, twenty feet or more in length, the latter a winged reptile, about the size of a pigeon, which had teeth, and a long, pointed tail like that of a lizard. It was at this period of the earth's history that both forms of life began to form into distinct groups, and the divergence has been getting greater ever since, until, at present, few persons besides students of zoology would think that one bore any relationship to the other. The penguin is probably the nearest living type of the pterodactyl, and the crocodile and alligator of the ichthyosaurus.

It may not be generally known that both the crocodile and alligator are denizens of Floridian waters, but such is the fact. The former is more southern in its habitat than the latter, and also shows a more marked preference for running streams and sandy beaches near the seashore. Its favorite ground for a siesta is a sloping beach which commands a good view of the environments. When alarmed it dashes into the rolling billows, should any be near—for it is far more marine in its habits than its congener—and swims boldly into the open sea. It is evidently capable of making long voyages, for it has been found among the keys of the Florida Reef, having, apparently, reached them from Cuba. Many persons in this State, well acquainted with the saurians, cannot tell an alligator from a crocodile ; yet each has distinctive traits so well marked that a single glance is enough to enable an expert to distinguish them apart.

The alligator has, in the first place, a shorter snout, a broader head, and more teeth than its congener. It does not possess the two holes in the upper jaw into which the two great tusks of the lower jaw fit, which are so prominent a characteristic of the latter, nor do the teeth protrude through the upper jaw, as they do in the crocodile. A glance at the snout will therefore enable a novice to tell whether the saurian he espies is an alligator or a crocodile.

Two species, or varieties, of the former are supposed to be residents of Florida, one being known as the black and the other as the brown alligator. The first, which is quite plethoric, if not aldermanic, in proportions, ranges from eight to thirteen or more feet in length, and makes its home in the bank of some sluggish stream, cosy lagoon, tranquil lake, and saw-grass savanna, while the second is attached to rapid rivers, its favorite haunts being deep pools, sheltering crags or bushes, and sandy banks. It also frequents brackish streams—which the first generally avoids—and is, on the whole, longer, more slender, quicker, and more active than its congener, and seems to have no objection to the sea, to which it often makes trips during the fishing season in August, September and October. I have found both varieties—for I do not consider them distinct enough to be classed as species—at the mouths of rivers emptying into the Gulf of Mexico as far south as the Caloosahatchee, their place on the lower keys being occupied by crocodiles.

I do not recall any scene more expressive of hideous horror than a mangrove morass swarming with ferocious mosquitoes, filthy-looking saurians, and slimy snakes of various hues, whose lightest sting is as fatal as a dose of prussic acid, while the deadly miasma which fills the air is quite palpable. It is fortunate that such spots are infrequent, and more so that they are difficult of approach, for they are usually located amid a dense mass of green shrubbery, which shows light and life above and gloom and death below.

The nests of the crocodiles and alligators look much alike, the main difference being in size. The former commence building their nurseries as early as June, and the latter from July to August, the dates varying according to the character of the weather and their northern or southern habitat. It is only the female of each species which engages in architecture, and, primitive as that may be, she works at it with a persistence and determination most worthy of praise until her domicile is completed. Her first movement is to fill her mouth with dead leaves, grass, shrubs or wet soil, and carry them to where she intends to build her nest. After laying the foundation, which has a diameter of six or seven feet, she piles her material carefully by using her head as a trowel, and sometimes her forepaws. When the walls are from four to seven feet high she opens a hole in the top and drops her eggs, separating them into layers by means of earth, dry grass and leaves, and when all are laid she covers them with another layer of the same material, arranging it carefully, in order to make it as protective as possible. This done, she retires to a convenient shelter close by, leaving her eggs to be hatched by the heat of the sun and the steam arising from decaying vegetation. The eggs are about as large as those of an ordinary goose, have a decidedly musky odor, and, like those of all reptilia, have a tough, membraneous covering instead of a shell. They are eagerly devoured by bears, pumas, wild cats, cranes, herons, and other furred and feathered enemies, but if they secure them it is only when the female is absent or sleeping, for she will fight any living thing in defense of her nest. Each nursery contains between forty and eighty eggs, and, as nearly all prove fertile, it is quite evident that the country would swarm with the saurians unless Nature placed a check on their numbers. These checks are numerous enough, and embrace fur, fin and feather. Moccasin snakes, darters or water turkeys, members of the *Grallidæ*, and many species of fish prey on them constantly, but their worst enemy is, in all probability, the male alligator, for he will devour all the young in a nest in a few minutes. The mother knows this only too well, hence she seldom strays far from her nursery, and when the youngsters announce their birth, by vehement croaking, she is generally the first to answer their summons and escort them from their prison. On emerging from this retreat she leads them to water immediately, and carefully watches over their welfare until the following November or December, when all separate to hibernate during the cold weather.

As soon as a male alligator hears the cries of the juveniles he becomes exceedingly alert, and steals toward the nursery with all the cautiousness of his nature, for he knows full well what is in store for him should the female discover him while on his cannibalistic expedition. If he finds the coast clear he hastily tears open the nest with jaw and paws, and devours as he digs; yet, no matter how thoroughly he may be enjoying his feast, he retreats in the most ludicrously precipitate manner on seeing the female approach. The latter often pursues him until he seeks refuge in the water or his home in the bank of a contiguous pond or stream; but should she overtake him she attacks him with the utmost fury, using teeth and tail with extraordinary effect, and generally routing him or leaving him badly crippled. An assault on her progeny drives all timidity from her nature, and she is then as ready to face a man as a mouse. I have never known an alligator to pursue a white hunter over land and through water except when defending her young; in all other instances that I recall, the saurian, when brought to bay, was only too glad to escape, if it had the opportunity.

An acquaintance of mine once fired at an alligator which he saw lying under a bush close to the river, and planted his bullet solidly in its side, but the reptile did not make the slightest move. He fired a second time with the same result. Thinking the animal was dead, he advanced rapidly and incautiously toward it with an empty rifle. On approaching to within fifteen or twenty feet of the saurian, he was horror stricken to see it charge open mouthed, and at a pace of which he thought it incapable. He had just time enough to glance at the spot the animal had quitted and note that it was covered with crawling, croaking little 'gators, before the musky hissing of the mother got so strong as to induce him to face about and dash for his boat, which was anchored about a hundred yards out in the stream on account of the shallowness of the water. He dashed through the bushes, sprawled through the muddy beach, and half ran and half swam through the river, after throwing away his rifle, but the enraged reptile still pursued him, its eyes being of a greenish-red hue and gleaming with the most demoniacal hatred. Running and terror combined had so exhausted the fugitive that he was unable to clamber into the boat after reaching it, and there is every probability that he would have fallen a prey to the infuriated brute had not his comrade promptly "yanked" him in on finding him hanging listlessly to the side. A couple of bullets sent the motherly saurian hurriedly shoreward, where she rejoined her squalling offspring and led them to a place of greater security. The fugitive picked up his rifle when the

A FLORIDA LANDSCAPE.

mother disappeared, and vowed to never again go gunning for alligators without a full magazine. This incident strongly impressed him with the fact that an alligator is not as stupid as it looks, nor so slow as its ungainly legs would indicate.

Another female alligator attacked a horse and rider while crossing a stream because they frightened the youngsters in her company. The horse was so badly injured about the hind legs that he was hardly able to reach dry land. The rider on seeing this was rendered so furious that he went to a farm house close by, borrowed an axe, and wading to his arm pits into the river, boldly assaulted the reptile. He swung his weapon much as a Crusader his battle axe among the Saracens, and, although the saurian used all her skill and power in defending herself and progeny, she was killed in less than ten minutes, her skull being broken in several places. She was then towed ashore, and left there as a feast for the buzzards. The horse subsequently recovered, but it was many a day before he was fit for service.

A SOUTHERN BEAUTY.

Tales of this sort could be extended into a volume, but I think those related are sufficient to prove that a female alligator is no mean foe when she is trying to protect her offspring.

In passing through low, swampy lands, in summer persons should reconnoitre the ground carefully, as several nests are frequently found close together in such places, and some are so carefully concealed that one cannot tell their character until he is in their midst. If his presence is then detected by the lurking mothers, he is liable to be charged from various directions simultaneously, and if he does not prove nimble of foot and quick of eye, he is in danger of bearing the impression of some brute's tail on his leg for many a day.

The chief weapon of offense and defense with an alligator is the caudal appendage, and as it has to bend itself into almost a half circle to deliver an effective blow, the person who keeps his wits about him may readily avoid it, unless he is taken by surprise. A fair blow from the tail of an adult will easily break a man's leg or arm, and I have known it to knock a large hog a distance of several feet. An alligator will always first try to strike its prey with the tail, on land, but in the water it will seize it round the body and sink immediately to the bottom. The saurians have killed some dogs of mine by just one squeeze of their huge jaws, and I have seen them pull young cows under water by the nose and hold them there until suffocated. The strength of their muzzles is almost inconceivable to a person who has never noticed the weight of the animals they seize and the ease with which they drag them along the bottom of a stream or pond to where they bury them. It should be remembered that, although the saurians have an abundance of teeth, yet they are so scattered and irregular that they cannot tear flesh until it has become soft. This is why they bury their prey until it becomes putrid. This does not apply to fish or other tender-bodied creatures, they being gulped down without much effort.

The female alligator is more destructive than the male, particularly when she has her young by her side. She will then watch for a dog, a hog, a duck or a goose for hours, and even days, with a patience unparalleled by any living creature I know of, except an Apache on the war-path. I have even known one to lie in ambush for weeks to capture some special dainty, such as a dog or a hog. I remember one that waited at least three months in and around a certain place where she saw a terrier of mine cross the river occasionally, until she finally succeeded in capturing it. The children, knowing the danger that threatened the dog in its frequent passages across the river, used every means at their command to make it stay at home, but their efforts were unavailing, as it would follow their boat as soon as it reached the opposite shore. One day, after driving it back, it stood watching them from a sand bank which was covered with about six inches of water. It might have been there ten minutes when the lurking alligator seized it, and before the poor creature could give more than one scream of terror it had disappeared. I knew that saurian was watching for that dog, but as I was very ill at the time I felt myself unable to do anything more than prevent my pet from going to the river when I saw it rushing for a swim across. I have not killed that alligator yet, but I hope to do so ere long.

Although the alligator has its own ideas as to what constitutes a dainty morsel, and will often risk its life to secure it, yet it is generally ready to swallow anything from an oyster to a king crab, terrapin, mussel, mullet, or piece of rotten wood. It is exceedingly fond of flies, and, in summer when insects are numerous, it is estimated that an adult swallows from half a bushel to a bushel a day. The reptile is, therefore, as excellent a fly trap as it is an aquatic scavenger, so that it fulfills some good in the economy of nature. Its mode of capturing flies is to take possession of a log in the water, open its cavernous mouth, and let the insects settle in it. One fly attracts another, and all buzz about the mucilaginous cavity until it is full, then the trap closes suddenly and the cunning 'gator gulps down about a quart of the choicest provender in a moment. The trap is reset, and the trapping continued until the saurian has had enough. It remains as immovable as the log all the time it is engaged in catching its dinner, and one observer, who must have used a telescope in his observations, says it does not even wink its eyes. An alligator has been known to eat two pecks of flies in five hours, as that quantity was found in the stomach of one shot on the Myaka River, after being watched for that length of time. All alligators are popularly supposed to swallow pieces of wood to aid digestion, yet I have seen some dissected which had none in their digestive organs.

The young, which are exceedingly pugnacious even the moment they leave the nest, certainly show a strong dislike to wooden fodder, for I have seen them shake a piece, much as a terrier would a rat, when it was pitched at them. I have known a mother to do the same thing when she thought her family was endangered by it, then drop it suddenly, and bellow loudly, as a command to them to hasten to the water. They appeared to understand her, for they scampered with a waddling gait toward the lake, and sought safety in its muddy bottom. Alligators, as a rule, have a regular place of retreat in the bank of a stream or tarn. This is excavated with the forepaws, and, according to some crackers, the dirt is carried away in the mouth of the engineer, who backs into deep water and disgorges its load, then returns to renew the operation, until it has made itself a capacious home under water. This will readily account for the size of the mouth, for it must not only procure food, but also act as a mud scow. The female adopts the same method for building her nest, and not only fills her mouth but also takes a load between her forelegs when she is in a hurry. She can, by this means, accomplish much work in a day, for she never seems to tire. It is quite amusing to watch a young mother build her first nursery, she being not only fussy and vigilant, but so suspicious that a few fluttering leaves startle her out of her wits. I came upon a juvenile matron engaged in architecture one day before I was aware of her presence. She seemed at first undecided what course to adopt toward me, but recovering from her surprise she chose her plan of action by advancing toward me and hissing out her anger. I picked up a piece of a pine bough and waited her approach. Seeing that I did not retreat, she stopped suddenly, and began hissing more energetically.

"Did you ebah see sich a sassy thing in all you bawnd days?" asked the intelligent colored man who was with me, as he gazed at her in astonishment. "Why, she's sassier 'n a preacher's daughteh 'n a camp meetin'."

I tried to poke her out of the way with the club, but she would not yield an inch of ground, and snapped viciously at the stick whenever it touched her. I was quite amused at her determination, so I was content with tapping her sharply across the tip of the nose, and then leaving her in her glory.

I have said that the teeth of an alligator are irregular and scattering, yet that peculiarity does not prevent one from being able to cling to an object with as much tenacity as a bulldog.

(To be continued.)

ALLIGATOR SHOOTING IN FLORIDA.

BY JOHN MORTIMER MURPHY.

Author of "Sporting Adventures in the Far West."

Continued.

ESIROUS at one time to secure a young saurian, in order to have it mounted, I shot at the neck of one which was about forty yards from my pier. All that I could see of the animal was the end of the nose, so that I had to guess at the position of the neck, yet I was fortunate enough to send a bullet through it from side to side. It did not move after being hit, so I sent one of my negroes in the boat to bring it in. He grasped it by the head, paddled ashore, and placed it near my feet on the veranda of the house. I examined it carefully, then measured it, and found it to be a few inches over four feet. I was quite pleased with my capture when I found that the hole in the neck would not be prominent when the skin was stuffed, and that the size was about what I wanted. I left it on the veranda for dead and started to attend to some other business which kept me engaged for two hours. At the end of that time I returned to the house and was surprised to find my captive gone. I sought for it eagerly and finally saw it crawling under the house. I poked a long stick at it to hasten its movements, and was astonished to see the creature seize the prodder and shake it viciously, but still keeping its hold. Thinking I could pull it to me without much trouble, I tugged at the stick and the alligator tugged against me, bracing its feet, as if it had learned the art in a regular saurian tug-of-war team. I proved the victor in a short time, yet the determined creature would not let go its hold, even when I held the stick and itself off the ground to a height of four feet. The outer curtains of the eyes frequently blinked while I held it out, proving that the sunlight was too much for them; still it clung, and shook its head and swept the air with its tail, and displayed its meanness generally. As it would not quit its hold, I put a rope around its neck, but not tight enough to choke it, and handing the cord to the negro, he dragged it after him, as he would a struggling cur, until he put it in the boat. On reaching the village in which the taxidermist lived, the colored man hauled his captive ignominiously through the streets, much to the enjoyment of some of the inhabitants, who asked him what kind of a pup that was, and if he was training him for the 'coon-hunting season. The fate of that pugnacious saurian was as ignominious as its march, for an inquisitive pig and itself became engaged in a quarrel the same day and the porker not only killed but devoured it. This being an unusual turning of the tables, it brought piggy some compliments for its bravery.

The flesh of the alligator is white and edible, but quite fibrous. Were it not for the choking musky odor which renders it so repulsive to white people, alligator steak would be preferable in many instances to that taken from a Florida cow. Hogs and dogs devour the fresh meat with keen relish, and negroes and Indians are glad to get it when other pabulum is scarce. The tail is a favorite dish with some of the natives of South America, and, as a luxury, ranks next to the flesh of another reptile, the iguana; and how good the latter is may be inferred from the fact that epicures consider it to combine the flavor of the chicken with the tenderness of the frog and the green turtle. It is, in fact, as highly prized by all classes as the *murœna* was by the ancient Romans.

When the Seminoles of Florida wanted alligator steaks in the early part of this century, they went to a lake where the animals were numerous, and by thrashing the water with sticks and paddles, and shouting lustily, drove the game shoreward, where it was killed by old and young with all sorts of weapons and missiles. No wonder these tribes fought long and bravely for their hunting grounds, for it is doubtful if any equal area on the continent could furnish savages good food in such wanton abundance as Florida, particularly along the coast.

It is quite an easy matter to "corral" alligators, by building fires in a circle over certain areas. They seem to have the greatest fear of a fire on land, and not only will they not come near it, but they will go as far from it as they think advisable. The hunter who has lain in his blankets near a blazing fire and close to a Florida stream or lake, must have been deeply impressed by the loneliness of his surroundings when he heard the complaining cries of the saurians on beholding the strange and fearful glare. These cries are frequently sounded in many keys, from the impatient grunt of disturbed repose to the plaintive, measured groaning of lazy contentment and the deep bellow of suddenly-aroused anger. The volume of noise which an adult bull alligator can produce when trying to drown the voice of a rival is most remarkable, and hardly to be believed by a person not acquainted with his lung capacity. When several are exercising their vocal organs at a time, the air seems to vibrate and to send the sound through the forest like the rolls of muffled bass drums. One can, therefore, imagine the nasal power of a canoeist of national fame, whose snoring at Homosassa was generally supposed by the guests of the hotel to be produced by a grand chorus of all the adult saurians in Florida, until an investigation revealed the truth.

Alligators were formerly shot only for sport, but since their hides have become valuable for the manufacture of purses, hand satchels, slippers, and hunting boots, a certain class of persons, generally known as "'gator scalpers," have made a special business of killing them. These men carefully reconnoitre a region before commencing work, and when they find one where the saurians are abundant they pitch their camp in a sheltered spot and lay in provisions for a certain length of time. A scow or skiff is then built, if none has been brought with them, and the guns and jack lamps are put in order. If the men work during the day they frequently use a hound or a hog for bait to lure the saurians within gun range. To make the one howl and the other squeal is sufficient to bring every alligator within hearing to the top of the water, where it lies like a log until it has located the animal, then sinks noiselessly and swims shoreward. It rises frequently for bearings, and on approaching its intended victim scarcely makes a ripple. When it is near enough to attack, it bends its tail into a half circle, and letting fly backward gives the live bait a tremendous whack which either kills, cripples, or throws it into the water, where it is instantaneously seized by the powerful jaws. The captive animals are so terror stricken on seeing the alligators approach that they appear to become paralyzed, and unable to utter a sound, or so crazed with fear as to scream in the loudest and most heartrending manner. It is not often that professional hunters allow the reptiles to capture their live bait, for the moment the saurians lift their heads above water a ten gauge, loaded with buckshot, sends its contents into their eyes, causing instant death, or a magazine rifle empties its bullets into their brains. Most hunters pursue their calling at night, this giving them not only a better opportunity of luring the animals within gun range, but also preventing the latter from seeing the character of their foes. These men scarcely utter a whisper while at work, and move about on the inky water as noiselessly as phantoms.

Three men generally form a "gang," but two are sufficient if the saurians are not very abundant, and a jack lamp is used instead of the ordinary fire pan. When the former number get into a boat, one man is stationed as a lookout behind the lamp, a second sits amidships with a loaded breechloader in his hands, and the third uses a long pole for pushing the craft. When the lookout espies the glittering eyes of an alligator he waves his hand to the steerer, who poles the boat in the direction indicated. Not even a "'coon's whisper" is uttered by any person, and this renders it necessary that the poler and lookout should readily understand each other's sign language. On approaching the alligator, the craft is pushed so slowly and silently that the most cautious saurian only looks at it in bewildered astonishment or blinks sleepily at the unusual glare. On drawing quite close the armed hunter pours the contents of his gun into the eyes of the animal, and kills it almost instantly, as the leaden pellets reach the brain without meeting any obstruction. Were a rifle used instead of a shotgun, the number of misses would be much greater, and the probability is that many alligators fatally wounded would escape and be lost. The person who has not tried rifle shooting at night would be surprised at the number of apparently easy shots missed, especially in fire hunting, when objects seem so near and are yet so far. Very few men can feel much assurance of killing a saurian at night with a rifle, for unless it is hit in the eye or the brain it will carry off a good load of lead without seeming any the worse for it. The great difficulty in killing alligators is to get at the brain, that organ being unusually small and pointed; hence, a rifle ball is more liable to miss than hit it. An experienced "gang" of hunters will capture from ten to fifty alligators in a night, and more if they have unusually good luck. This is paying work, as a salted green alligator hide is worth from fifty cents to a dollar and a half, the average price being about a dollar. The most successful hunters I ever met were two crackers who slew three thousand saurians in six months and pocketed as many dollars for their hides.

I asked one of these men if he had ever been attacked by an alligator. "No," was the reply, "because I never gave one a chance. I always kill my 'gator before he gets his mad up bad enough to pitch into me, though I have often seen one grab at the boat or lash it with his tail. Green hands at the business get hurt, however, by taking hold of the 'gator's tail before the critter is dead."

"Are alligators inclined to fight when wounded?" I asked.

"That depends," he said. "They will jump at anything when they're crazy with wounds, but if you don't put yourself in their way they're more likely to try to get off than to fight."

"Did you ever know an alligator to make an unprovoked attack on a white man?"

"Not a bull 'gator," he an-

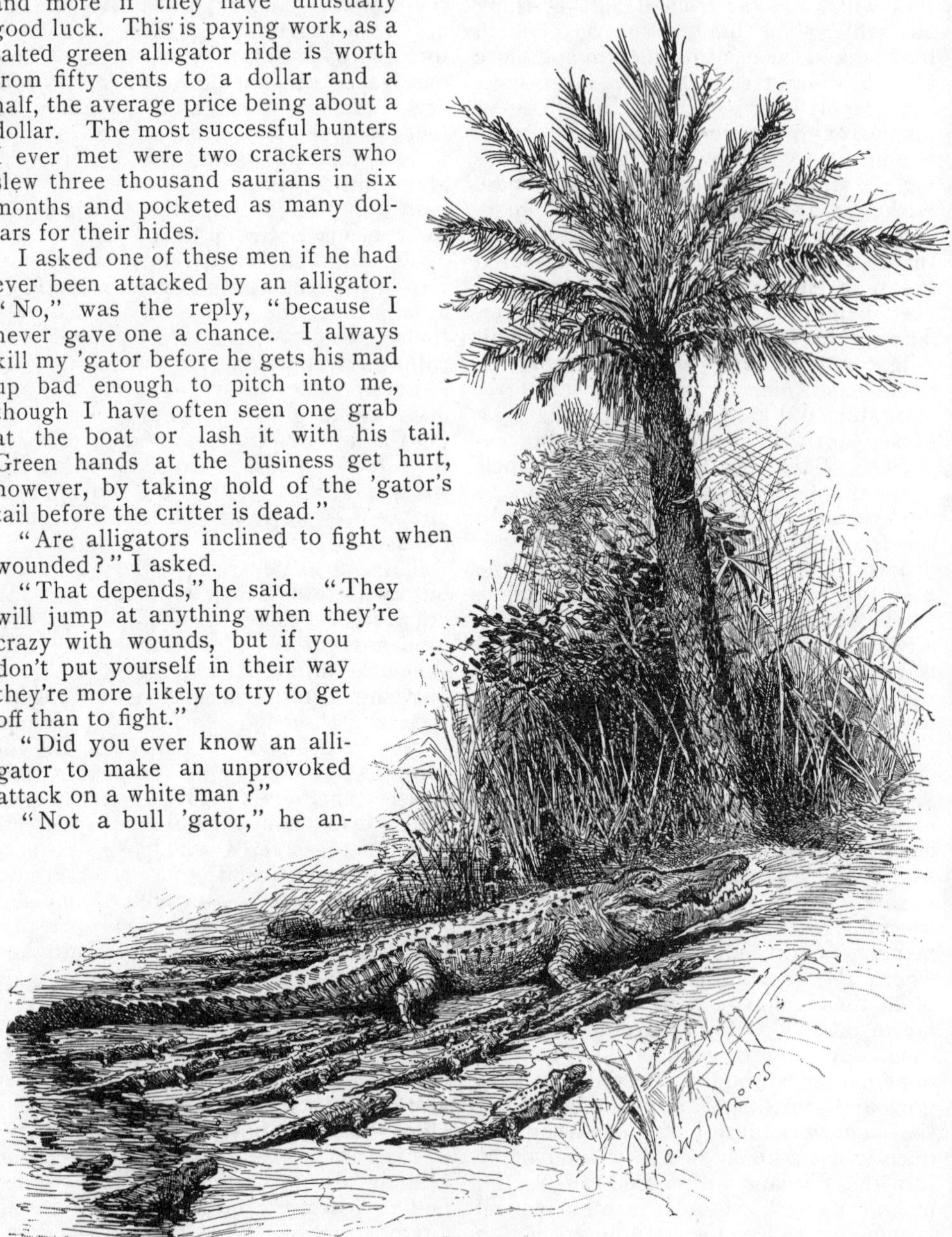

THE 'GATOR'S NURSERY.

swered, "except in one instance, and perhaps that might be called a provoked case. The man was cleaning fish at the mouth of the Cootee River, and throwing the entrails into the water. There were some 'gators round the head of a bend that were devouring the offal, and as it became scarcer they drew closer to the pile of fish on shore. The fisherman wasn't out that day to feed 'gators, so he began thrashing the water and throwing sticks and stones at them. A huge old bull 'gator, who must have been the father of all the others, didn't like this, and made an open-mouthed rush at the man. That fellow was scared, I tell you, for he went ashore so fast that he made as great a noise and raised as high a sea as if he was a porpoise charging into a school of mullets. The 'gator put off after scaring him, and Bill Smith told me that the old bull had a grin six feet long on his face, and was shaking his fat sides with laughing."

"What made him grin so?"

"Why, the bull was so old and toothless that he couldn't hurt anything, and of course it made him laugh to see how easy it was to frighten some people."

"Is that the only case you know of?" I queried.

"It's the only one I know of myself, but I could tell you lots of yarns 'bout fellows who were supposed to have been killed by 'gators in Dade and Monroe counties."

I told him that I had a large stock of such tales on hand, and his prompt reply was: "Very likely; but ain't you found most of them to be jest only lies—regular nigger lies?"

I replied that I had traced some of them, and knew they were partially true.

He looked at me in a very scrutinizing manner for a few seconds, then blurted out:

"Blame me if they ain't keerful in talkin' before you, or else they'd stuff you as full of blood-curdling 'gator stories as a dime novel is full of Injun blood. There is many an 'Alligator Pratt' in this part of the State."

His candor was most amusing, so I asked him if he had any idea as to the number of alligators shot for their hides every year.

"No, and I don't b'leeve you can find out," he said. "Those Tampa and Jacksonville hide buyers wouldn't tell you, even if they could, for thousands of 'gator hides go out of the State without passing through their hands."

That the number of saurians in Florida is diminishing rapidly may be inferred from the fact that the cattle men in the southern part of the State complain of the destruction of the animals. This complaint seems strange coming from persons who are so often compelled to deplore the voracity of the saurians, but it seems they have cause for it. The alligators excavate holes; these holes fill with water, and the cattle resort to them in times of drought when the streams and lakes are dry. The slaughter of the saurians causes these holes to fill up with weeds and rubbish, consequently there is no water for the cattle, and they sometimes suffer severely or die from thirst.

This is another plea for the life of the alligator from an economic standpoint, but I fear it will carry no more weight in this case than it did in that of the buffalo, whose water-filled wallows saved the lives of many pilgrims of the plains. There is little fear, however, that the alligator will become extinct in this century, for it is not only very prolific, but it has food in abundance and many means of escaping its great enemy, man, which more valuable animals have not. Were the real value of the alligator known, it would be destroyed more wantonly than it is. The hide is, primarily, the most valuable part, then come the teeth, which are made into watch guards, breast pins, earrings and other articles, which meet a ready sale at good prices. Teeth in the best condition are worth from one to five dollars per pound, and at retail sell for ten times that amount. The flesh is eagerly devoured by dogs, pigs and fowls, and the oil extracted from it is worth from twelve to twenty-five cents a gallon. When the meat is deprived of its oily matter and smoked or dried, it makes an excellent food for some domestic animals. Here is an opportunity for an energetic person to start a factory and prepare the flesh for this purpose. The article is good, the market is open, the field of operations large, and no opposition.

I have been trying to obtain some accurate information as to the number of alligators destroyed every year, but have not succeeded thus far. I notice that two firms in Jacksonville advertise steadily for 100,000 green salted hides; by allowing that each receives this quantity annually we have a basis of 200,000 to start on. Admit that tourists kill 2,000; that twice as many are slaughtered for sport by natives, and that 20,000 or 30,000 hides are sent direct to Northern and Western markets, and we have 246,000, or say, in round figures, 250,000 alligators destroyed each year in Florida. Add to this number those slain in Alabama, Mississippi, Louisiana and Texas, and I think it would be safe to estimate the annual destruction at half a million.

The highest number that fell to my rifle in one day was twenty-eight, though I shot several more, and my best score in a night, using a shotgun, was seventeen. The toughest alligator I ever met was one which carried thirteen of my 40-60 rifle cartridges and a short .22 pistol bullet in its head before I was able to tow it ashore. I was engaged for four hours in killing this one, and when I finally got a rope round its tail, it took two men pulling in a boat and myself walking in the water, and heaving with all my might, to get it to my pier. Its head was one mass of holes, which presented a hideous appearance owing to the protrusion of the bones, yet the reptile had so much vitality that it was able to drench me from head to foot, and shove my boat off its back after receiving my last bullet. This animal was exactly nine feet seven and a half inches in length, and we estimated it to weigh nearly 200 pounds.

The largest alligator to fall to my rifle was twelve and a half feet long—as measured with an eight-foot paddle; this was so heavy that I let the tide take the carcass away after I had secured the head. I killed it by a shot in the mouth while it was yawning, the bullet coming out at the spinal column. I fired at it from an estimated distance of 500 feet, and in the presence of a large "gang" of negroes who were clearing an orange grove for me, and eagerly watching the success of the shot. Their exclamations of approbation were quite flattering when they saw the alligator close its mouth suddenly and disappear in the muddy water; one individual expressing his opinion by shouting emphatically:

"I don't nebeh want you to fire at me, boss. I'd be a gone 'coon, shoo, if you did."

"Nor me nudder," exclaimed others, in a diplomatic way, which was quite amusing.

I never before saw such a tremendous cavity acting as a mouth for an animal, and the fact that I was able to plant a bullet in it at the distance mentioned proves that it was large enough to be no disgrace to a stump orator.

I have enjoyed some ludicrous situations while engaged in saurian hunting with our colored (green) brethren, for if there is any living thing of which they have a wholesome fear it is an alligator, and next to that, a "bad dog." Bayonets have no terrors compared with the jaws of these two creatures. I asked one athletic individual why he was so much afraid of alligators, and he replied:

"I heard a man in Jefferson County say dat de reason 'gatahs was so black was, kase in old times, 'bout de flood time, 'gatahs used to live on cullud people, and dat made 'em so bad they was kicked out o' d' Ark by Noah or his mudder. Now, I don't want 'em to get any blacker by eatin' me; not if I kin help it. No, sir, you can't get me to tech de tail of a possuming 'ole gatah. I ain't ready to die yet."

28.
The City of the Pelicans
(1903)

"The young pelicans * * * reminded me of boys as they gathered here and there in groups, chattering in gutteral tones."

THE CITY OF THE PELICANS

By HERBERT K. JOB

Author of "Among the Water Fowl"

PHOTOGRAPHS BY THE AUTHOR

TWO of us left New York just before midnight on the 8th of last April, bound for Florida. Hardly a sign of real spring had yet appeared, and one of a long series of cold, easterly rain-storms was raging. The next afternoon, in Virginia and North Carolina, we gazed upon blossoming peach trees and bursting buds. One night more, and, in early morning, at Savannah, nature was in the full glory of summer's leaf and flower. By middle afternoon, half way down the east coast of Florida, on the bank of breezy Indian River, the journey ended. Easterly storms were forgotten, as for three weeks—one day excepted—the sun shone brightly, with a daily warmth of 80 to 85 degrees, tempered by the fresh breeze that arose regularly about nine o'clock in the morning.

On the morning of the 16th we were starting in a small sail-boat for Pelican Island, twelve miles farther down the Indian River—scudding along, rejoicing in the balmy air and the beautiful tropical surroundings. Shiny, silvery mullets were leaping high out of the water in all directions, falling back with resounding splash, at times almost into the boat; flocks of bluebills rose from before us every few minutes; eagles and fish hawks were wheeling about, ready to descend upon unwary fish. By ten o'clock we began to see lines of great pelicans, with slow, measured wing beats, flying down stream past us, and before eleven the guide pointed out Pelican Island.

No tremendous cliffs were there, as at Bird Rock. Indeed, it was hard to distinguish this small, low island from the adjacent shore, half a mile away, with its jungle of palms and mangroves, until we had come quite close. Then we could see many beating wings, and, with our field-glasses, a great crowd of birds, the brown pelicans upon their nests. With eager anticipation, we made ready our battery of cameras for the bloodless fray, casting anxious glances at the heavy, cumulus clouds, that threatened to spoil the light at the critical moment. And now we were close enough to take in clearly the whole situation. Here was the low, flat islet of only about three acres, somewhat triangular in form. A few small palmettos, low mangrove bushes, and stumps were standing, but most of the area was an open expanse, overgrown with tall weeds and grass, except for two considerable sandy tracts at the east and southwest corners. Each of these barren places was fairly covered with an army of great birds, about the size of geese, of a grayish color above and dark brown beneath, with long brown and white neck, and enormous bill with pendant pouch, that was held pointed downward in most ridiculously solemn, pompous fashion. A few birds were located at the northwest end, and there were also small, overflow colonies on at least two other islands a short distance eastward. These brown pelicans are a southern species, entirely different from the white pelican, the only other kind found in North America, that occurs mostly in the interior and on the Gulf, and breeds on islands in lakes from Minnesota northward.

From time immemorial this little island has been the principal, if not the only, breeding-ground of all the brown pelicans of the east coast of Florida. Though there are hundreds of other islands, apparently just as good, this one alone attracts the pelicans. Dastardly plume-hunters have, at times, all but annihilated them; egg-collectors have robbed them of every egg in sight; yet they remain faithful to the home-land of their ancestors. Creatures of habit, they are, like chickens that persist in roosting in the orchard, despite the advent of winter, cold and storms.

Our boat was now closely approaching the eastern end of the island, and we camerists held ready our instruments, expecting at every moment to see the birds rise in a cloud and leave the vicinity, as do the white pelicans in the North. To make sure of present opportunity, we took snapshots of the birds as they yet sat upon their nests. Then we

"Nests on the bushes or trees were built of sticks, lined with grass."

"Even when we sprang on shore the birds on the farther side remained on their nests in utter unconcern."

prepared in earnest for the grand flight. The boat was run ashore abreast of the colony, but without alarming them. Then we stood up and shouted, but only the nearer birds flew. There they sat upon their nests, hundreds and hundreds of them, many within about fifty feet, solemnly gazing at us. It was not until we sprang upon the shore that there was any general flight, and even then the birds upon the farther side of the group remained upon their nests in utter unconcern. We also noticed with delight, as we went back to the boat for more plates, that the flying birds, after a short circuit over the water, returned at once to their nests. The fear that it would be impossible to secure pictures at close range was groundless.

Equipped with all needed photographic implements, we now started out for a tour of inspection. Hundreds of nests were before us, a few of them built on the spreading limbs or tops of the mangroves; but the great majority were on the sand, usually about a yard apart. Those on the bushes or trees were built of sticks, lined with grass, and were quite bulky, while those on the ground were small and rude, composed only of grass and soft materials. The contents of the nests were greatly varied. Though the nesting season of the pelicans begins in January, many of the nests still had their complements of great, dirty-white eggs. These may have been second or third layings, owing to previous depredations, though to what extent individual pelicans may be irregular in their time for laying, I cannot say. In other nests there were young, in various stages, from the naked, newly hatched, and rather repulsive looking things, to the more sightly, yet not altogether handsome, downy stage. Still other nests were empty, but that their mission had not been fruitless was evident from the numbers of well-grown young that were running about in all directions. Many of them were all but able to fly, though their bodies were more or less downy and ragged. In color they were very different from their parents, being of a lighter gray, and mainly white on the under parts.

These young pelicans afforded us no little amusement. Though they evidently inherited somewhat of the true pelican gravity, their childishness could not be concealed. For one thing they were, like most children, eminently social. They reminded me of gangs of boys upon the street corners, as they gathered here and there in groups, chattering away in peculiar guttural tones, that often rose to loud, harsh screams when individuals got into a fight, which was all too often. They could not have learned these disagreeable manners from their parents, who are peaceable and

"The flying birds, after a short circuit, returned to their nests."

silent. For want of better reason, we shall have to lay it to innate natural depravity, that only the grace of further education and experience overcomes. Then the gang would scamper away, perhaps bent upon some gay prank. Those on the mangroves could not run from us, but gave, as we approached, a rousing reception, making terrific lunges at us with loud snaps of the bill, with screams that would repel any enemy.

The pelicans secure food for their young by plunging headlong into the sea and catching fish in their seine-like pouch. Though all youngsters are supposed to be in a chronic state of hunger, these children require to be fed only twice a day—morning and afternoon, we are told. Strangely enough, though the river seems to he full of fish, the pelican parents do not fish anywhere near the island, though the young may do so later. In flocks they fly across the narrow strip of "hummock," or jungle, that separates the river—which is properly a salt-water lagoon—from the ocean, where they may be seen off the beach sailing about and plunging after their prey. It was not the regular feeding time while we were on the island, and we saw the curious feeding process but a few times. The youngster thrust head and neck away down into the parent's gullet, with greedy violence, and gobbled away at the partly digested fish. In the case of the older children, roaming about in bands, it may be a question whether the parents can identify their own, or whether communism is not, for the time, the order of pelican society.

Presently we made a visit to the other large group of pelicans at the southwest corner of the island, about a hundred and fifty yards from the first. Here we found a similar state of affairs. Each of the many occupied nests was brooded over by a devoted parent—whether the male or female, I could not tell. The citizens all dress well, and look remarkably neat and clean. But let not the visitor hope to vie with the pelicans in neatness of apparel or cleanliness, upon *that* island. The passing birds are continually dropping a watery excrement as they fly, which, though it does not seem to stick upon the oily plumage of the pelicans, certainly does not allow the garments of human visitors to remain unspotted. The ground, too, is very dirty, infested by swarms of insects, and in a short time our clothing and cameras were well besmeared.

Naturally, we were interested to make an estimate of the population of Pelican Island. As nearly as we could count, there were 450 nests at the east end, 512 at the southwest, and 14 at the northwest, making 976 in all. This means 1,952 adult birds on the island.

"Many nests still held their complement of great, dirty-white eggs."

"Naked, newly-hatched, repulsive-looking things."

"The not altogether handsome, downy stage."

The most common number of eggs in a nest was three, but quite frequently there were only two. In only one nest did we find four, and in one other five. If we assume that each pair raises two young, the colony would double its numbers every season, if not disturbed. Though we did not land on the adjacent islands, where the other pelicans were nesting, we sailed close by, and estimated, from appearances, that there were over 200 nests. Supposing, then, that there were 1,200 nests in all, the total adult population of the colony can be placed at 2,400.

Mr. F. M. Chapman has recorded that on a visit to this island, in 1898, he counted 845 nests, and noticed a very few on another nearby island. Assuming that there were then 900 nests in all, the colony has apparently increased about one-third in four years. This desirable result may be due to the better enforcement of strict laws in Florida against the destruction of plume-bearing birds, the efforts of the American Ornithologists' Union in appointing a warden to guard the colony, and a bettering of

"She would settle down, * * * seeming to say:
'I'm all ready now; pull your string.'"

"There they sat upon their nests, hundreds and hundreds of them, many within fifty feet."

public sentiment in Florida, owing to a realization of the great value of wild life in attracting tourists. Our own party is a case in point. To see this pelican colony, heron rookeries, and other bird resorts, three of us—one more having followed—had come from New England, distributing several hundred dollars among railroads, boarding-house keepers, outfitters, traders, stablemen, and guides. And thousands of others do likewise. The people of bought another four-by-five camera, and adapted it so that I can use the lens (an astigmat) of the five by seven interchangeably on both. This gives a somewhat larger image of a bird at a given distance than with the smaller lens. As it is seldom possible to secure a larger image of a wild bird or animal that can readily find room on a four by five plate, I prefer to use the small camera and large lens for most of my work, since the weight of a large camera, with a sufficient

"Well grown young * * * were different from their parents, being of a lighter gray."

Florida, or other states, are short-sighted indeed, if they allow vandals and plume-hunters to massacre these interesting and valuable wild creatures.

A little account of our photographic work on Pelican Island may be of interest. I brought with me two long-focus cameras, five by seven and four by five, the former mostly for view work, the smaller one for birds and nests at close range, and for long, hard tramps. Since returning from Florida I have

number of holders and plates for a day's work—especially in wading marshes and penetrating swamps in a hot sun—is almost prohibitive.

To this equipment I have added a high power telephoto lens, which I find very useful, especially in bird colonies, or places where large and shy birds congregate. It gives sharp definition, even at full aperature, especially on a small plate, and thus allows of quite short exposure—half a second, or less—

in bright sunlight. The one essential is that it be kept absolutely without jar or movement during exposure; and I usually find it best to prop up the front with a stick, or with a light rod carried for the purpose. With a focal plane shutter on a long-focus camera of the reflex type for flight pictures, the same lens interchangeable, the battery is complete for every emergency in practical bird photography. Yet one good instrument alone is very satisfactory, and if I were to select one instrument for general work in nature photography, I would have a long-focus four-by-five camera, of any reliable, well-known make; preferably with a larger lens than the ordinary, and a high-power telephoto attachment.

Now about the actual photographic work on the island. First I took a number of general views, snapshots with the camera in hand, of the pelicans on their nests and in flight. Then, with the camera on the tripod, I photographed nests at close range, with eggs and young, using a ball and socket clamp, which makes it possible to point the camera in any direction. When these routine matters had been disposed of, I had the rest of the precious time for that fascinating, but often nerve-wearing, branch of the subject, —bird portraiture. In general the method is to place the camera, preferably not on the tripod, concealed as well as circumstances will permit, near a nest or place to which the bird is likely to return; attach a spool of black linen thread or rubber tube to the shutter of the camera—I much prefer the former—retire to a more or less distant hiding-place, as the case may require, and, awaiting the return of the subject, pull or squeeze at the opportune moment. I always use the lens at full aperature, one-fiftieth of a second in bright sunshine with the quickest of plates, or the briefest timed interval, if the light is dull. If the day be dark, the case is almost hopeless, for birds are very active, and are nearly certain to move when they hear the click of the shutter—for there is no shutter which I have been able to find that is really silent.

Over at the farther end of the southwest settlement the area of nests extended almost to a tract of tall weeds. Here I found it convenient to plant the camera on the shortened tripod, allowing the weeds to arch over it, where it commanded a view of a number of nests at moderate distance. When I withdrew a few yards, the birds at once returned, and I pulled the thread. Then, after two or three such exposures, I placed the camera on its case upon the ground, and focused upon a near-by nest, covering the camera with the rubber cloth and then with dry grass. The birds did not seem afraid of it—though in similar cases they usually are—and returned very soon, giving me all the exposures I wished.

Over in the eastern colony a pelican that had her nest at the foot of a stub returned readily to her eggs, though I had placed the larger camera on the sand, without concealment, but little over a yard away. She would waddle past the camera and onto her nest, settle down, and draw in her chin in the usual dignified attitude, seeming to say, "I'm all ready now; pull your string!" I also set the camera on the tripod in the open, near some nests on a mangrove, and pulled the thread when some of the old birds alighted on the empty nests, near the large youngsters. Another successful method was to drive a company of these well-grown young down to the shore, where they would stop and allow me to creep up within ten feet before taking to the water.

We stayed on the island until half after four, but were careful not to remain in any one spot near nests, thus keeping the birds away. Newly-hatched young will soon die in the sun, if not brooded; and visitors to bird colonies will do well to remember this, or they may do great damage.

During the day the wind, which had started up from the north, had steadily increased, and all the afternoon had been blowing a gale down the river. We waited in vain for it to veer to the southeast, as such a wind on the Indian River usually does by night, and at length we had to start on our long hard beat to windward. Our craft was a wretched sea-boat. Every wave broke fairly over her, and after the first few moments we were all soaked to the skin. By dark we had hardly made four miles, and were almost perishing with cold—yes, even in Florida! We debated leaving the boat, to walk across the strip of jungle and up the ocean beach, the character of the river shore making walking there impossible. But the fear of stepping on rattlesnakes in the dark deterred us, and we pounded wearily along. The night was dark, indeed, when the wind canted a few points to the eastward, and at a late hour, weary, shivering, hungry, we reached Oak Lodge again, not sorry, however, that we had visited wonderful Pelican Island.

29.
Trailing the Sea Bat
(1900)

TRAILING THE SEA-BAT.

By Charles Frederick Holder, LL.D.

FLASHING AND SOMERSAULTING IN A CIRCLE.

THE outer Florida reef, where the army of coral polyps has made its last stand against the Gulf Stream, was lying on the surface of what seemed a sea of molten steel. The wind was dead, and the blue expanse of the gulf had that strange oily appearance so often a characteristic of a dead calm in the tropics. In the west vermilion-tipped clouds—mountains of the air—rose high in the heavens, casting deep shadows over the green-topped creations of the wind, hurricane, or the prevailing tides. The keys appeared to be formed without rhyme or reason, but in reality nature could not have ordered better, as with their outlying banks and reefs they constitute a perfect harbor, a deep blue channel winding clear and distinct against the coral-covered lagoon, completely encircling Garden Key, the headquarters of hunters, sportsmen and anglers who find their way to the outer reef in search of adventure.

Some wit has described fishing in Florida in the summer as sitting in a Turkish bath holding a string, and I think the author of this mot found his inspiration on the reef on a warm day while trailing the sea-bat.

The heat was appalling, pouring down with such intensity that the shallows were too hot for comfort, and thick vaporous clouds waved upward from the bleaching coral sand, distorting every object along shore. For days the dead calm had continued; the long sleepy summer was at its height, and one had to pick his time for sport and diversion. There was an hour or two at sunrise for barracuda spearing, or for the beating jacks; a long siesta at midday, then a while toward evening perhaps when one could lure the dainty gray snapper or test conclusions with the big sharks which swam the blue channel at all times. Then came the night, often cool, to be spent on the water listening to the melody of negro rowers, the weird tales of Chief, a Seminole, who preferred the heat of the outer reef to the mosquitoes of the coast.

On such a night, when the only sound to break the stillness was the distant roar of the surf, there came out of the darkness, near at hand, a rushing, swishing noise; then a clap as of thunder, which seemed to go roaring and reverberating away over the reef, like the discharge of cannon. So startling was the sound, so peculiar, that the negroes stopped rowing, and one or two dropped their oars in consternation.

"Vampa fish, sah," said Paublo, the

stroke oar, in a hushed tone, "an he mighty uncomfortable near, sah—jes over yander."

I thought so myself as the eight-oared barge now rocked in the sea made by the fish. In a few moments another jumped some distance away, and we could hear a splashing sound, which Paublo said was caused by the fins as the fish rushed through the water. The darkness was of that quality that could be felt, yet it was that described by Milton as

"Dark with expressive bright"

as the lagoon scintillated with phosphorescent light; every oar set the sea ablaze with silvery radiance, and ahead of the boat waves of fire seemed to go rippling away. Now another seething, hissing sound was heard, and a blaze of triangular light above some huge, dim fire body below, glided swiftly along; then a volcano seemed to rend the very sea, and out of a blaze of phosphorescent light that sent its radiations in every direction, rose a dim shape, cleaving the air to drop into another volcano, which opened to receive it with loud intonation.

IT APPEARED TO FLY INTO THE AIR.

"Sea Vampa, sure," Paublo whispered, as though he feared that the unknown would hear him. "Dey jes wheelin' an' wheelin', leapin', an' I reckon we'se in a bad place."

"Sea bat," grunted Chief, as the ladies expressed alarm. "They jump five, yes, eight feet high."

"How heavy are they?" I asked, thinking of possibilities.

"Three or four tons," replied Chief, sententiously.

This answer was unsatisfactory to some of the party, so we hauled close in shore near Long Key, where we listened to the explosions, as they seemed to be nothing else, caused by the crash of the return of the leaping fish. A school of sea vampires, sea bats, or devil fish, as men call them, had wandered into the lagoon I knew them by reputation and hearsay, but never had seen one alive; and when I announced that I was going to take one on the following day, if they were still there, the boys, as the negroes were called, all protested.

"Why, marster, one of dem vampas yander is twenty feet wide, 'deed he is. Five years ago a schooner seventy-ton burden, was layin' jes offen de pint yander; de capten had dun done gone ashore an' all de crew ceptin' de cook was a pickin' micramocs on de reef, jes ober yander wha yo' see de ole wrack a-layin', yes sah, jes yander under de cross. All at once dey hear de cook a-hailin' an' screamin' jes lak he crazy, an' lookin' up dere was de schooner, sails furled, anchor down, a-sailin'outen de channel. De cook he ran 'bout lak he crazy; he don' want to jump overboard cause he fraid of de sharks, so he jes yelled; an' de schooner sail on for half a mile, den stop, an' de men what had been follerin', clim board. What done it? Why, de vampa fish. Yes, sah, he jes pick up de anchor an' tote it off."

Each boy had some particular story

to relate as to the dangerous character of the fish and its gigantic size and strength, intended to convince the listener that its capture was impossible. I found that some of these stories were true. A sea bat had towed a schooner up the channel, and while several attempts had been made to take one of these fish, it had never been accomplished in this locality. When I asked for a volunteer, after announcing my intention of trying this sport, the men were strangely silent. There was a superstition among them, that the fish had some demoniac power; that it could seize a man in its claspers and hold him beneath its cloak-like body and smother him. I finally secured the services of Chief and Paublo, and by daylight the following morning we were on the water, the men pulling across the channel to the long lagoon which formed the breakwater of the group to the east.

My boat was a light cedar affair, built in Boston, thoroughly seaworthy and prepared for the rough weather that is often experienced among the keys, by having under her forward and side decks rows of airtight cans, which more than once had proved to be of good service.

For weapons of offense I had the ordinary grains of the reef with which I had often taken large fishes. This harpoon consisted of a two-pronged spear attached to a steel cap which fitted closely upon a long, pliable yellow pine handle. The barbs of the points were movable; when they entered a fish they closed, but when the slightest strain came they opened and prevented the harpoon from tearing out. A stout line or rope was made fast to the grains and led up the pole, and three hundred feet of it coiled forward in a large half barrel. Besides this I had a sharp coral chisel to use as a lance in case of necessity. Thus equipped, we were ready for almost any game, at least of the sea.

The early mornings were usually ushered in by transformation scenes of splendid possibilities--staged in the heavens—and this was no exception. Long before the sun appeared, the east was a mass of crimson clouds; first deep, dark and ominous, gradually increasing in brilliancy, color and tint, until the sun burst forth in all his splendor.

We soon reached the spot where we had heard the thundering of the sea bat the preceding night, but the lagoon was apparently deserted. At Chief suggesting that the fish did not come so far up until full flood tide, we turned and rowed to the south, parallel to the great fringing reef against whose sunken coral rocks the surf broke sullenly. Long Key—a sandy spit since destroyed by a hurricane—Bush Key and the long fringing reef two or three miles in length, formed three sides of the lagoon, which at high water was from ten to twenty feet in depth and through a part of which ran a deep blue channel. Acres were covered with branch coral, while the rest of the bottom was either white sand, or had a scant growth of algæ—the home of craw fish, crabs and various shell fish upon which I believed the big rays fed.

The men rowed slowly down the reef by an old ship blown in by a hurricane years before, now lying ghostly and still, with a corporal's guard of pelicans, frigate birds and gulls; down by Bird Key whose population of terns rose high in air with bewildering cries. I had begun to think that the morning was a poor time for vampire fishing when Chief stopped rowing and pointed to the east. I turned in time to see a black triangular object waved above the surface; it might have been the dorsal fin of a shark, yet no shark had so black a topgallant sail, or, indeed, so large a one. Paublo was gazing at it with protruding eyes and parted lips; it was a rude awakening for him as I believe he had considered it a forlorn hope, and secretly prayed that we might not see the dreaded fish. I turned the boat in the direction of the fin and bade the men give way. The trim cutter shot through the still water like a gull. Where I had sighted the fish the lagoon began to dip into the deep channel of the Gulf Stream as it flows between Cuba and the Keys, and until nearly one hundred feet is reached every object on the bottom can be seen, so clear is the water.

We had almost reached the spot when not one, but five or six fins appeared, my exclamation causing the men to look around. I gave the tiller to Paublo, Chief taking the oars, and crept forward. As I picked up the grains I noted that I could see the bottom distinctly thirty-five feet below. We had happened upon a school of the monsters which were indulging in some game of the sea. There were, perhaps, ten or twelve in all, moving in a circle one hundred and fifty feet in diameter, and churning the water into a veritable maelstrom. Chief was slowly and noiselessly propelling the boat ahead, and we drifted about thirty feet from the circumference of the circle.

Surely these fleeting, glistening figures were the witches of the world of fishes, as no more diabolical creature could be imagined. They resembled enormous bats, and in following one another around the circle, raised the inner tip of the long wing-like fin high out of the water in a graceful curve, the other being deeply submerged. Imagine a fish shaped like a bat, the wings ending in graceful points, a vivid black on the upper surface and white beneath, a long whip-like tail, while from near the large and prominent eyes extended forward a pair of writhing, clasping finger-like tentacles three feet in length. Endow such a creature with marvellous activity

"WE WERE UNDER WAY DRIVING THE FISH WITH A SINGLE REIN."

and a constant desire to change its position and assume some extraordinary attitude, and possibly a faint conception of the actual appearance and personality of these strange creatures circling before me may be obtained.

As we slowly drifted nearer I could see them deep in the water, apparently going through a series of fantastic figures; now gliding down with flying motion of the wings; sweeping, gyrating upward with a twisting vertical motion marvellous in its perfect grace; now they flashed white, again black, so that one would have said they were rolling over and over, turning somersaults, were it possible for so large a fish to accomplish the feat. Since then I have been informed by one who had opportunity to watch them on many occasions, that this is what they were doing, and is really a common practice of the big rays. As I recall this strange performance, the huge creatures would suddenly turn over and shoot along upon their backs, thus displaying the pure white of the ventral surface, then again turning at the surface, move along with the remarkable, undulatory, bird-like motion. All this passed in rapid review, and fearing that they would become alarmed I gave the word, and Chief moved ahead.

I wished to select my game and make the throw as the fish turned, and to accomplish this I waited until several had passed. Finally we drifted directly in the path of the remarkable procession, the fishes paying no attention to the boat. One dived beneath her, another came careening up from below, standing directly on edge, as nearly as I could determine, and fairly exposed its broad back, not ten feet away; and as it glistened in the sun I hurled the grains into it with all my strength. The pine handle seemed shot into the air as it rebounded, then we became witnesses to the extraordinary agility of this monster ray. It appeared to fly into the air, rising, an appalling mass of flesh, out of the seething waters, its side wings beating the heated air as it rose, then falling with a crash and the reverberating sound we had listened to the night before; fell as a square eighteen by ten feet and weighing tons might fall.

As the heavy waves from the impact struck the boat, I stumbled into the bottom, rolling out of the way of the jumping line that was now hissing from the barrel. The fish, after its first leap, had headed directly to the South, or out to sea, and the line was rising upward in coils. The Indian oarsmen rowed the boat ahead to lessen the strain when it should come, but so furious was the rush that I decided to check the fish before the rope was exhausted, and taking a piece of sail-cloth I grasped a coil and held on.

The boat was well under way, but the shock was terrific. Arms and muscles snapped, and for a moment the rope smoked through the cloth; then Chief dropped his oars and took it, and we were under way driving the fish by a single rein. I had used the boat to capture man-eater sharks, and as a precautionary measure to prevent the line from getting over the side, had a deep notch cut in the bow, in which it rested. With no little difficulty we succeeded in lifting it in place, the bow of the boat at the water's edge riding a heavy sea, which rushed ahead of us as an advance guard. In a short time the fish towed us into deep water, and then surged downward, keeping near the bottom, and we were forced as far astern as possible to keep the bow from going under. I noticed that Chief had taken out a big sheath knife, which he habitually carried in a leather scabbard, and held it in his teeth—a significant movement that was not lost on Paublo, whose terrified glance shot from the fast-disappearing keys to the hissing line ahead and back again.

We were headed far out into the gulf, and for two miles the ray towed us at rapid pace. It was evident that if something was not done the line would have to be cut away or we would follow our wild steed indefinitely. I therefore directed the men to ship the oars and pull against it while I took a turn with the rope around the forward seat; but this powerful brake had no effect upon the fish. Then I determined to haul in and try to lance it. We were now a mile and a half, perhaps more, to the south of Bird Key in the open gulf and began to feel the long swell that ever rolled in from the west, while an ominous squall cloud as black as night, to the south dead ahead, did not add to the pleasures of the situation. The line was passed astern and we all "boused on," as Paublo expressed it; now gaining a foot, again slipping back, hauling, straining every muscle, slowly but surely forcing the light boat upon the fish to the accompanying shouts of Paublo and Chief—"ah ho ah," "ah he ho," "all together now," "ah ho!" Then would come a rush; the line would smoke through our fingers for ten or twenty feet, and lying back until the flurry seemed to die away to haul again.

For some time we worked in this way, and I estimated that the fish was not more than twenty feet away, and had crawled out onto the little deck to peer down into the water, when the line rapidly rose, then turned so sharply to the left that I was nearly thrown overboard. The Seminole, who was in the stern, grasped an oar and aided in hauling the boat around; but she yawed and careened so that the water poured in; then the fish appeared at the surface forty feet away, its wing waving in the air like the black piratical flag it was, perhaps in derision, perhaps in defiance, then disappeared. The fish had turned the keeled boat in little more than its length and was now towing us directly back to the reef—a proceeding more than satisfactory as a storm was rapidly coming, and if caught we should have to cut away; so we sat with a turn of the line about the thwart on the alert for any move. Steam could hardly have towed us faster; we flew through the water throwing clouds of spray over the deck, racing with flocks of gulls that eyed us curiously, plunging among schools of Portuguese men of war and velellas, and in a short time without incident entered the lagoon, where I decided to bring matters to a finish and cut away rather than go to sea a second time.

Whether the great fish was accustomed to go to a certain feeding ground and now returned in its terror from mere force of habit, I do not know, but the fact remains that it was rushing up the lagoon between the Long Key and the outer fringing reef, into an almost perfect *cul de sac*, the water shallowing at every flap of its wonderful wings. I stood on the little deck and could see every movement of the strange fish, that in swimming over the white sandy bottom in water not over four feet in depth displayed its outline perfectly

Chief had the oar, steering the boat after the fish, which, it was expected, would turn at any moment, while Paublo stood amidships holding the rope, which had a turn about the seat. The lagoon narrowed rapidly, and at high tide a small boat-channel was formed; at other times being too shallow and easily waded. Perchance the fish having passed this at flood tide, was again making for it, hoping to reach deep water, which was but a stone's throw away. The graceful,

"AGAIN AND AGAIN I LANCED THE FISH."

bird-like movements of its fins was a fascinating spectacle ; a waving, undulatory motion which sent the ray along at a remarkable speed, and the slightest increase of which forced it over the white sand like the shadow of a dark cloud.

We were running parallel to the beach, and some negroes stopped and waved their hats as we shot by. Suddenly, without the slightest warning, the fish turned. I saw the pointed fin leap into the air until it stood upright, as the fish seemed to breast the water in the turn. I stepped back and shouted a warning to Chief. But it was too late. The bow of the boat was jerked, shivering and trembling, almost completely around, throwing Paublo over the rail into the lagoon, and was away almost before he recovered his feet and stood in water nearly up to his armpits looking at the retreating boat doubtless with amazement seasoned with relief, as he could easily wade to Long Key.

The fish headed for the outer reef, on which a heavy sea was breaking ; drawing little or no water it could doubtless plunge over while the boat would either ground, or if it succeeded in making the reef, would doubtless be swamped in the surf. We took the line as Paublo dropped it, and surged upon it with all our strength, and were encouraged by finding that the fish was weakening. But we were rapidly approaching the reef ; another haul and we were nearly on top of our quarry, whose long tail was under the boat, the mighty wings pulsating just ahead. A patch of coral now loomed up, and this fortunate obstacle turned the fish and in the whirl the fin seemed to rise almost over the boat, hurling the spray over us, and once more we were off up the lagoon headed for the *cul de sac*.

I gave Chief the rope, and taking the big square-edged lance sent it into the black mass. A cloud of blood followed, while the speed of the fish was increased so that the bow was well under water, flush with the deck. Again and again I lanced the fish, but the blade was a chisel-like affair, and did not penetrate more than five or six inches. There was a duplicate pair of grains in the boat, and this weapon was also hurled into the ray's back, but still it rushed on, seemingly as vigorous as ever. I fully expected to see it turn again, but it held its course, heading directly for the narrow tide channel between Long and Bush keys toward which Paublo was running along the beach of the former key. It was an exciting moment. The fish was alongside, yet we were going, as near as I could judge, at full speed.

Nearer we came, flying over the roots of mangroves, over patches of coral and sea-grass, into a narrow channel hardly four feet deep and not thirty feet wide, with a flat on each side partly bare. Not a tenth of a mile away the sea was beating on the reef, which meant liberty, if not life, to the fish. But fishermen's luck was ours. The tide was so low that it left but two feet in the upper head of the channel into which we ran. The fish discovered its error too late, but made a gamey attempt to rectify it, turning and lifting itself partly out of water, rolling the boat over, throwing oars, grains, and fishermen into the lagoon.

The turn cost the fish its life, as it ran high on to the narrow mud flat, where it beat the shallow water with its powerful wings, opened its cavernous mouth with great sucking gasps, every movement urging itself further out of its native element. Paublo, who had waded across the little channel in his exuberance, bounded on to the flat back of the monster and waved his hands aloft, while Chief ran in shore with the rope and presently had the fish securely fastened to a mangrove tree not fifty feet away.

We had earned our game and were well exhausted. Had it been high water, and could the ray have gone through the channel, which doubtless it often passed, it would have escaped.

Stretched upon the hot sands beneath the straggling mangroves, Paublo humming a low baccarole of his own invention, Chief silent, but with a long smile fixed upon his countenance, we could not believe but that the writhing black mass was a monstrous bird, one of the uncanny pterodactyls which geologists dream about; yet it was a noble quarry, "the struck eagle stretched upon the plain, no more through rolling clouds to soar again." The weight of the ray we could only conjecture, but it was doubtless several tons; and had this light and airy jumper sprang upon the boat it would have crushed it like paper.

When the tide was at the ebb the black vampire, as the men called it, was high and dry, and was paced off. It was eighteen feet from tip to tip, ten feet long from its mouth to the base of its tail, which was about seven feet in length. It is impossible to convey any adequate idea of the appearance of this devil-fish, sea vampire, this *Manta brevirostra* of science, which is so difficult to take that it more often runs away with boats than is captured, and of whose habits very little is known. Indeed, vampire fishing will never be a popular sport except among those who delight in an element of danger.

THE SEA-BAT DRAWING PILES IN PORT ROYAL SOUND.

Mr. G. E. Northrop, of Chicago, captured a very large sea bat in the Gulf of Mexico in the Summer of 1898, and in a letter to the writer described it as remarkable sport. The fish gave a hard fight, towing the heavy boat a long distance. Unfortunately the photographs of this fish turned turned out unsatisfactorily. In this connection, it is a singular fact that none of the popular works of the day appear to have a thoroughly correct figure of the fish, nor are photographs of it available so far as I know.

The big ray was almost jet black upon its upper surface, the back being rough; the under surface was white, with gray cloud effects here and there, giving it a marbled appearance. Popular fancy has given the fish a sting above the base of the tail, but this is a misnomer; it is without the serrated lance which marks many of the tribe which I took in these waters, one of which wounded a companion by striking its lances across his foot.

The mouth of the ray as we pried it open was of ominous dimensions, and afforded ample room for a man to lie very snugly coiled up within. The teeth were very small, but the extraordinary feature of this fish—the one which has given rise to many tales, true and legendary—is its two tentacles or claspers, fleshy objects about four or five inches wide and three feet long, which extend outward from each side of the mouth. Their office is undoubtedly to aid in securing food. When the fish is moving they are in constant motion, being whirled about like the tentacles of a squid, and that they are muscular and powerful has been demonstrated on many occasions. The natural movement of the claspers is inward, and when any object strikes between them it is instinctively held—a proceeding which explains the undoubted fact that these fishes can run away with large vessels.

At least five instances of this were heard of on the reef occurring from Tampa Bay to Garden Key, and the Hon. Wm. Elliott, formerly of Beaufort, S. C., a famous hunter of this game, reports two instances from that State. In every case the vessels, always at anchor, suddenly moved off in a mysterious manner and were towed greater or less distances. The ray had collided with the chain, and, true to its instincts, threw its two tentacular feelers or claspers around it and rushed ahead, thus lifting the anchor. That the claspers are very powerful is well shown by the experience of Mr. Elliott, who, in endeavoring to kill a large fish, which he had harpooned and run down, with a knife, felt his arm seized and held so securely that it became numb. He called to the men to hold the fish at all hazards; but it is obvious that if the animal which they had just hauled to the boat had made a rush and broken the harpoon or rope the sportsman would have been carried off in its embrace.

I never heard of an attack being made by the bat on the Florida reef; there it was supposed to catch cray-fish, and employ the feelers to whip the food into its mouth.

That so enormous an animal can leap so easily and so high is remarkable, and I believe that this is a common pastime, as in later attempts to follow the fishes at night, I frequently heard the resounding crash that told of the return. The ray which I struck seemed to clear the water three feet, but Chief said that he had seen them jump five feet, while Mr. Elliott, already quoted, states that he has seen them bound ten feet into the air.

On the reef this fish was considered a dangerous animal, and never followed. Some years previous an attempt had been made to catch one which fouled a vessel's cable. The fish became impaled on the anchor, and when brought up broke away. It was then harpooned, but escaped after leaping partly on the boat, breaking the oars on one side, and seriously injuring the crew, who were crushed into the sinking craft. So the sea vampire, which was supposed to suffocate its victims with its cloak-like wings, was dreaded, and that anyone should consider it sport to follow such a creature and hunt it down was more than the ordinary reef negro could understand.

The negroes of upper Florida, Georgia, and the Carolinas, where the fish is also found, are equally afraid of it; yet, in 1845, to take one of these monsters was considered in these States the highest phase of sport, and the visitor to any of the hospitable plantations near Hilton Head would be sure to be invited to a sea vampire or devil-fish hunt. The sport was followed with great abandon, and one gentleman had a record of sixteen sea vampires taken with the harpoon in one season, the fish towing him from ten to twenty miles, and fighting from one to five hours.

The waters of Port Royal Sound were the breeding grounds of the fish, and it is a singular fact that the wild excitement embodied in the sport was discovered in an attempt at retaliation on the part of the planters whose property had been destroyed by the rays. Those whose property abutted the Sound had water fences which marked the limits of their plantations seaward, and some had piers extending out into the water. The heavy posts, which would be in deep water at flood tide, were mysteriously hauled up, and I am informed by a gentleman from this section that the piles of wharves were occasionally similarly treated. For a long time the cause was unexplained, but finally a school of large rays was seen to sweep along and collide with the piles. The fish evidently threw their claspers about them and in the violent struggles which ensued wrenched them loose.

The sportsmen made the attack in eight oared barges propelled by negroes, and when the strike was made the barge rushed away toward the ocean, several other boats being caught as they passed until the fish was towing a procession of craft. This was the initial fish, which measured twenty feet across, and from that time on the exciting pastime became the sport above all others of the Sound region. The catches were marked by many sensational features. On one occasion Mr. T. R. S. Elliott was the harpooner, and when the fish was struck it cleared the water, striking the boat in the bow, sweeping away all the oars on one side, and sending her astern so violently that every man in the barge was thrown from his seat and one or two severely crushed. The man at the helm, James Cuthbert, was pitched headlong on to the deck, while Mr. Elliott took a flying leap into the air, landing upon the back of the struggling fish. He was fortunately hauled aboard before the ray got under way, and stood on the little deck, drenched, and raised a cheer as the boat moved off behind the wild steed.

The legend heard in the Pacific that this fish envelops its prey with its cloak-like wings may be traced to the ancient authors, among whom Oppian writes, "It is the broadest among fishes" (*Eurotatos pantessin metichthusin*); and he further describes its habit of seizing mariners, sinking with them and smothering the victim beneath its wings. This belief is still held by the pearl divers off the Southern Gulf Coast. The truth is that while the fish makes a remarkable fight for its liberty, it is timid and never attacks; the fouling of anchors, the leaping upon boats being mere accidents attendant upon the movements of a large fish in agony and fear.

In following this sport in Port Royal Sound the sharks were often a factor to be dealt with, attacking the wounded sea vampire in such numbers that while being towed by a fish Mr. Elliott took with a line as many as six hammerheads which were following the trail of blood; vicious monsters ranging up to nine feet in length.

In its peculiar somersaults the bat is not unique, as I have repeatedly observed the California banded sheepshead roll over and over; yet in so large a fish it is a remarkable act. Merely venturing an opinion I am inclined to think that this may be a feature of courtship, and nowhere have the strange gambols been so often observed as in Port Royal Sound. Here the fishes were repeatedly seen by Mr. Elliott, as I saw them once in the Gulf of Mexico, swimming in a circle, black and white flashing at intervals as they somersaulted; now swimming upon their backs; now vaulting into the air and while in this position falling upon the back. Sometimes the act would be performed in deep water, the flash of the white ventral side alone telling the story of the turn; again the water would boil at the surface, the horns appear and the huge fish would roll completely over until its tail lashed the air in its descent. So commonly was this trick performed that more than one of the fishes taken by Mr. Elliott was harpooned in the belly.

It is believed that specimens measuring nearly thirty feet across have been seen. Mitchell refers to one caught in the West Indies which required six oxen to drag it up the beach; but the average ray taken on American shores, which the sportsmen may expect to find in the summer months from Port Royal Sound to Garden Key and up the west coast of Florida, and in Lower California, will rarely exceed eighteen or twenty feet in width—large enough to afford some of the most exciting experiences in the annals of sport with the spear at sea.

30.
Snapper Fishermen of the Gulf (1904)]

SNAPPER FISHERMEN OF THE GULF

By HENRY C. ROWLAND

PHOTOGRAPHS BY ARTHUR HEWITT

ONE February day about ten years ago I found myself aboard a snug little fishing schooner which had sailed from Pensacola, Florida, for any place in the Gulf of Mexico where might be found the lordly red snapper, even though the quest led as far as the Florida Straits, Campeche Bay, or the Tampa Banks.

Feeling that a passenger would be regarded as a useless piece of dunnage aboard a vessel of this character, I had simply shipped as a "hand."

The crew of the schooner I liked from the first. All were Americans and men of good heart. The most entertaining character aboard was the grizzled old cook, who was known as "Neddy," and who, aside from his profession, was what might be called a "graduate hobo." Summers he roamed the face of the North American Continent and winters he signed on as cook aboard some vessel bound for balmy climes. He was a genial old fellow, surprisingly well read in classical literature and history, and professionally I have never met his equal in any part of the world. It takes an accomplished chef to convert a sea-gull or "hell-diver" into an appetizing dish; yet Neddy could accomplish it, and even find time to fish or to read Shakespeare during the process.

The system of a red-snapper fisherman is interesting. Each man of us, including the skipper, but not the cook, had his trick at the wheel and lead. As there were six, this divided the twenty-four hours into even periods, each man having two hours at the wheel, day and night. The trick at the lead is irregular, as over a bottom where there is but slight chance of striking fish it is hove but a few times, at intervals of varying length, perhaps every half hour, while at night it is seldom used at all.

To each man there is allotted a certain space of deck, where, opposite a well-worn groove in the gunnel, he keeps his bait-tub, bait-board, knife, lines and "gulletin'-stick," this latter being usually a piece of an old swab-handle, two feet in length, having one end whittled down to a flat point, from which is cut a V-shaped piece. When a fish swallows the hook, he is first stunned with the butt of this club, after which the flat end is rammed down his gullet, the nick in the end keeping it on the line until the hook is reached and loosened by the downward thrust, the point coming in contact with the flat point of the stick, when a tug on the line brings out hook and stick. Over the knife which transfixes a little pile of prepared baits hang a pair of "nippers." Nippers are loops of cloth into which the hands are slipped to protect them from the friction of the line. These are frequently disdained by veteran fishermen whose palms have acquired the texture of sole-leather.

The leadsman, standing on the weather bulwarks, over the chains of the main-shrouds, grasps his line by a toggle lashed about a fathom from the seven-pound lead, which with one or two powerful full-arm swings he sends flying ahead. A strong and skillful man can throw off about fifteen fathoms of line, thus giving the lead scope enough to reach bottom before its drop is checked by the schooner's speed. This lead is concave at the bottom, the hollow space being filled with a composition of soap and wax to which particles at the bottom adhere. When the lead brings up "live bottom," as shown by little pieces of live coral, crustaceans and the like, one may expect to find fish, for this is their feeding ground. Mud, sand, rock, and dead bottom is less promising.

Two baited hooks are fast to the line near the lead, and in case of a bite the leadsman is not slow to announce the fact. The third day out we had an alarm of this character.

It was after dinner, and at the time I was enjoying a siesta on the stay-sail, which when not in use was thrown into one of the dories. The wind was fair and had lightened a bit, although we were still slipping along at a speed which gave the leadsman all that he wanted to do to fetch bottom in about thirty fathoms of water. All at once my peace was riven by a piercing cry:

Typical Gulf Residence.

"*Bite-O!*"

I flopped out of the dory more from fright than zeal; for Sam, who was throwing the lead, had in sheer deviltry leaned over and yelped directly in my ear. The man at the wheel was crowding the helm hard down as fast as he could claw the spokes. Two of the others, Jim and Oscar, were below, and, in their mad rush to be first up the companionway, had jammed in the hatch, where they were admonishing each other heartily until a powerful boost from the skipper, who had been dozing in his bunk, sent them sprawling against Billy, who was steering. Of the lot, my line was first over the side. Sam was frenziedly hauling in the lead-line, and a moment later slammed on the deck a big copper-colored fish, with the disappointed comment:

"Red grouper, begawd!"

As I hauled in the slack of my line there came a gamy tug which told that the bait had landed in the right place. Old Neddy had come on deck at the first wild cry, and stood watching me with interest, a potato-knife in one hand and a grimy volume of "Scott's Poetical Works" in the other. I slung my fish on the deck and looked upon it with surprise, for it proved to be a porgy twice the size of any that I had ever seen.

"Po'gy," quoth Neddy. "Good bait." He laid his literature carefully upon the house and picking up my fish-knife sliced the porgy behind the gills, ripped off the skin, split him lengthwise and cut off a good-sized bait. As he did so, I saw that the fish had a leprous looking spine which seemed in spots entirely necrosed.

"What's that?" I asked inquisitively.

"Pox," says Neddy, apparently surprised at my ignorance. "These here Gulf po'gies mos' allus hev it. They ain't fitten for nothin' but bait."

Interested in this bit of fish pathology, I was about to inspect the matter to greater length, when the skipper, who was next me, observed:

"Don't git discouraged, matey. There's lots more o' sound ones down where he come from just cryin' to be took aboard."

I got my line over again, but aside from a few more porgies, groupers, a "spotted-hind," and a jew-fish, nothing was accomplished, and soon we gave it up and stood off on our course again.

For several days following we cruised over good fishing grounds, but with poor success, never seeing as much as a scale of the fish that we sought. The men began to grow restless, casting about for some "hoodoo" on which to fasten the blame, and I was beginning to feel a certain sympathy for Jonah when at last we struck a small school. It was my trick at the wheel, and Oscar, who was at the lead, had just hauled up a big black grouper, giving the customary hail, when Captain Dave, whose line was first over, suddenly threw upon the deck a great

The Local Fisherman and His Boat.

gleaming fish whose sides shone and sparkled like burnished gold.

"*Snapper-O!*" he yelled exultantly.

"*Snapper-O!*" chorused the others. "Cap'n Dave's high-line! Whoop!"

This landing of the first snapper gives to the performer the honorable title of "high-line" for the rest of the trip. At the welcome shout old Neddy came flying from his galley, where he was skillfully preparing a dish which he called "lobscouse a lar new-brig." Leaving this dainty relish to burn in the pot he hurried aft to take the wheel, for this is one of the duties of the cook when catching snappers under sail.

One of the Types.

I had luffed the schooner at the first hail, and if the school had been a large one we would have bouyed the spot and got the dories over; but since the fish seemed few and the breeze was light, we drifted back and forth over the spot until they stopped biting altogether.

For several days following we frequently "struck fish," but only in small scattered schools. This did not annoy me to the same extent that it did the others, for as the fish are caught just off bottom, and we were fishing in anywhere from twenty to fifty fathoms water, one does not need to haul up many twenty-pound fish with a five or seven pound lead to get a satiety of the sport. It is not the tax to the back and arms which trouble the beginner if he be fairly strong and lusty, but the damage to the hands is terrific. The "green hand" will find that the line is forever slipping off the nippers and cutting into his fingers, where, with the "fish-gurry" and slime, and an occasional jab in baiting the hook in a hurry, one's whole being soon seems concentrated into one great pair of smarting, aching "flukes." In addition to this, I was unfortunate in getting a bad start, from which, while it did not impair my usefulness, I suffered for the length of the whole trip.

I had hauled my first big "count snapper" over the side, and as he hung from the line in a beautiful arc I eyed him in some perplexity, not knowing just how to get rid of him with safety and despatch. Well forward of the gill there is a knife-edge plate of cartilage known as the "razor." Just behind the razor there is a pocket which is not apparent, but into which with a little dexterity one may slip a thumb by which to hold the fish suspended while the hook is twisted out. Behind this pocket is another dangerous weapon known as the "spear." Either the spear or the razor will cut a man's finger to the bone if he goes about it properly.

Putting the Catch into Fish Boxes at the Wharf, for Preservation.

I had seen the others whip the fish from the line in the twinkling of an eye, although I did not see just how it was done. Sam, noting my perplexity, came to the rescue with a true sense of deep-sea humor.

"Nab 'im be the eyes, matey," says he.

Although suspicious, I took the suggestion seriously and tried to grip Mr. fish by his two rolling orbs. The result was like trying to pinch an icicle by the tip, and a roar of laughter from the others showed me that this advice was but a pleasantry. The next hint savored of the brutal.

"Shove yer flipper up under his gills!" called Oscar. "What ye want to josh him fer, Sam?"

The reproach of his voice misleading me, I promptly followed the direction. It seemed reasonable enough, especially as I had taken other fish that way without mishap. If I had shoved my already smarting hand into a saw-toothed steel trap it would have been pleasanter, because I might have got my foot on the spring and drawn it out again. As it was, the fish's gills, which seemed like opposing metal saws, shut down on my fingers, cutting into the flesh and holding me a prisoner, while a roar of laughter from all hands gave evidence of the real humor of the situation, which for the moment I had overlooked. In silent agony I laid the fish upon the deck, when he began to flop without letting go, which made things worse. I looked around for my knife, but it was at a distance, and I felt disinclined to walk over to it.

I said that all hands were amused, but this is a mistake. My good friend Neddy had watched the whole performance from his perch on the coaming of his booby-hatch, where he was wont to sit at times like a grizzled old prairie dog, bobbing down now and again to look to his professional duties. He dipped down now, to emerge in a second with a snarl like a bear and a huge carver in his hand.

"Ye blankety-blank, lop-eared, shad-bellied, swivel-eyed brush-cutter!" he growled at Oscar, and kneeling on the fish slashed off his head with one scientific stroke of the knife. "Ye grinnin' band o' sea-goin' galoots, d'ye want to ruin the lad?" says he. With another swift stroke he split down the detached head so that I could draw out my bleeding fingers, whereupon he turned again to Oscar.

"Don't you never come sniffin' around my galley fer a hand-out agen, ye son of a scuttle-butt, or I'll lam the fool head offen ye. Tryin' ter cripple the pore feller!"

Later, Oscar tried to make his peace with me.

"I wouldn't ha' told ye that, only I didn't think that ye'd be sich a dam' fool as ter do it."

"It's all right, Oscar," said I. "I don't bear malice, but I like a good laugh myself once in a way. This trip isn't over yet, so just look out, my son, that's all."

The very next day I got even with Oscar by locking him in the ice bunker while we two were stowing fish. If the others heard his muffled howls they gave no sign. He was lightly clad, and when I let him out an hour or so later he was blue and could hardly move hand or foot. When he got thawed out again he seemed inclined to go more deeply into the affair, to which I made no objection, being still a little in his debt as it seemed to me. Captain Dave, who was on deck at the time, put a stop to it, however.

"Stow all that, boys," says he. "Shake hands and call it quits. If you want to fight wait until you get ashore and then lam some Dago or Dutchman." Captain Dave, be it understood, detested all foreigners as much as he loved his fellow-countrymen.

Another time I got the laugh on the joker. I had gone to relieve Billy at the lead, and Sam was at work hard by, giving the deckhouse a coat of ornate green. When I had made half a dozen casts he lounged idly over to where I was stationed.

"Leave us look at the bottom, matey," says he, casually.

I handed him the lead, a little nettled at his not being satisfied at my report of "black sand."

"That's right," says he. "How much water ye gettin'?"

I told him.

"The reason I ast," he went on, "is becus' the skipper says there was a Spanish treasure ship went down here onced, and a feller that I knowed on a fishin' schooner told me that when they was fishin' here one o' the hands fetched up a skull on his hook. He says they buoyed the spot, and about a year ago another feller told me that when they was cruisin'

Cleaning the Catch at the Market.

somer's around here, some o' their lines got fouled on bottom, and they found some grains of gold dust on the bottom o' the lead."

I swallowed this yarn without a gulp, especially as I had heard the skipper discussing the matter at breakfast. We were almost becalmed at the time, and although there was no necessity for very frequent casting, I kept the lead going steadily until relieved by Sam.

After he had made a few casts he called to me:

"Take her a minute, will ye, matey. I want to fill me pipe."

I took the line and let the lead drop. Then as I hauled it in again and glanced closely at the bottom my heart gave a sudden throb, for there, imbedded in the composition on the bottom, was a small silver coin, rough and corroded, but none the less actual.

I was about to announce the wonderful discovery, when something impelled me to look closer. Extracting the coin, I turned it in my hand, and lo, on the impression which it left in the white soap was the slightest smear of fresh green paint.

My eyes took in the coin, the newly painted roof of the deckhouse, and the labored look of innocence on Billy's face as he pumped some of the melted ice-water out of the bilge. Slipping the coin into my pocket, I took another heave of the lead, and at the splash Sam reappeared in the companionway. His face wore an expression of artful indifference as he took the line from my hand, but after a throw or two this gave way to an expression of pained inquiry. At last he could stand it no longer.

"Hain't found nothin', hev ye?" he asked kindly.

"No," said I with a grin; "but I think we must have passed over that wreck you were talking about."

"Why?" he demanded eagerly.

"Why, because I thought I saw a paint smear on the soap," said I, "and I don't see how it could have got there unless it landed on her side."

Billy subsided to the deck in a paroxysm of mirth. Sam grew very red in the face and cursed softly. I don't believe he has heard the last of that yet. At any rate, he never got up the nerve to ask me for the coin.

Supply and Demand.

Billy told me afterwards that it was Sam's intention to claim it since I had brought it up in his watch, and then sell it to me as a souvenir for a dollar or two.

The element which contributes most to the life of ease aboard a snapper-fisher is the fact that there is no cleaning nor salting down. Schooners of this type, which because they make long cruises are known to the craft as "high flyers," carry bunkers filled with ice, where, as soon as there comes a lull in the fishing, the catch is quickly stowed. The decks are then sluiced with water from draw-buckets, after which the vessel is as clean and sweet as a yacht. As the space in the ice bunkers is limited, a captain who has confidence in his ability to find fish is not anxious to fill up with those of a low grade; at any rate, not until the end of an unsuccesful or "broken" trip, when his chances for getting over a large school of snappers is slight and the ice is dwindling fast. Consequently, we did not spend much time in "shackin'."

I do not believe that there is any sort of nautical life in which there is found the same "dolce far niente" existence which one enjoys aboard a snapper-fisher. The climate is delightful, the sea interesting and full of marine life, and the food excellent; for these fishermen believe in living well, not knowing but that some one of the occasional hurricanes that occur in those waters may cause this trip to be their last.

Many of the vessels, with their crews, that fish out of Pensacola, hail from "Down East," and are the identical schooners and men who sail out of Boston, Gloucester, and other New England ports. I had noticed that beneath the name upon our schooner's stern, the new port of hail, "Pensacola, Fla.," failed to entirely conceal other dingy letterings, among them a tell-tale "Mass." Captain Dave told me her story.

"She was a Boston vessel, come down here five years ago, meanin' to fish the winter an' go no'th in the spring. She's ben here ever since. Skipper owned her; a likely young feller and engeged to be married to a little schoolma'rm out Marblehead way. He got in debt for his store bill an' all, then this Gol-darn country tuk him by the throat an' he ran wild. Mortgaged his schooner, then got sold out and finally went square-riggin' on a wind-

Where the Boats Tie Up.

jammin' lime-juicer. We most of us stay. Make one or two good trips o' fish an' blow the money, then a broken trip or two an' get in debt, then git lazy an' keer-less an' never go back. It's poor pay, but easy livin'."

It is not always "easy livin'" however.

A few days later we struck fish in good earnest and for three days we worked as it is my fervent prayer never to work again. My hands were in a frightful condition and for some time afterwards when I awoke I would have to take each finger in the other hand and work it into suppleness again. We took, as I remember it, fifteen hundred snappers besides the many other fish which we threw back. At any rate, I know that the haul was an unusually fine one and all hands were consequently jubilant, except perhaps Captain Dave, who did not lose sight of the fact that there is a big difference between fish in the bunkers when the ice is getting low and fish unloaded in good condition at the wharves of the Company; and I noticed that as soon as we were in a fair way of being loaded up, his interest in conditions overhead was far keener than it had been heretofore.

Up to the time when we were ready to start upon our homeward course the weather had been little short of perfect. Towards the evening of the last day of our fishing, the wind got around to the southeast and it began to thicken overhead. At the same time the bites began to diminish, for which I do not think that I was alone in returning heartfelt thanks, as the strain was beginning to tell upon all hands, and Sam had grown so sluggish in his actions as to arouse the sarcasm of Jim, the only one of us who had life enough to talk and fish at the same time.

As the wind freshened, however, the work grew less strenuous, whether because we had hauled up all the fish that were down there, or on account of the easterly wind, I do not know, but suspect the latter. It seems hardly reasonable to suppose that a new-born breeze from any quarter could affect a school of fish living forty fathoms beneath the surface; nevertheless it has been my experience that in our part of the world, at least, as far as hunting and fishing and a good time generally is concerned, nothing good ever yet came out of an east wind. It seems a dispensation provided in the divine order of things to meet the demands of a lot of selfish devotees who get together and pray for rain when I am anxious for fair weather for some sporting event.

In the present case, while it may have been a blessing in disguise, this disguise was so complete that we have never been able to penetrate to the blessing beneath, for it blew the foresail out of us, smashed our dories and, what was worst of all, in the sea which soon arose, our sadly melted ice got adrift and bruised a large proportion of the fish for which we had worked so hard, impairing the market value of many, while some it literally converted into "chum."

We had stopped fishing late in the afternoon, and turned to, to get the fish below. This would have been necessary in any case, as we were working knee deep in fish; a precarious job with the heave coming in from the east as the forerunner of a gale, which, as Neddy predicted, turned out to be one of those that are "born in hell and bred in the Bahamas." Now and again a man in trying to keep his balance would step on a slimy fish, when his feet would shoot from under him and he would go down to land, possibly, on something hard, probably on a rigid dorsal-fin or distended gill which would slash into the flesh and add a new sore spot to his collection. Of these, I had the best assortment.

While some of us were stowing fish, others were double-reefing the foresail, which done, Captain Dave proceeded to pack on superfluous canvas, although he

Saw Fish.

knew that he would probably have to get in again before very long. Truly enough, before morning we were hove to under our double-reefed foresail, which soon left us, however, as it had been weakened in one or two spots, where, when furled, some of the loose bights had caught a spark from the galley stovepipe, the damage from which we had not had time to repair.

The most interesting thing to me about this gale was the spirit in which it was received by Captain Dave. He was a passionate man, with a queer religion of a negative character and acknowledging a Divine supervision which is to be held directly responsible for any calamity that may occur. In the present case, the exquisite satire of the whole performance, which was received by the crew with dogged stoicism, aroused him to a perfect fury. To think that this gale should have been held in check until the time of all times when we were not only least prepared to receive it, but also in a position to have all of our labors count for naught, was a chastisement which he would not meekly and silently endure. Toward morning, to make matters worse, the wind backed around ahead, and in the short sling of the choppy sea Captain Dave could fairly feel the hard-earned dollars slipping through his grasp. He stood by his lashed wheel and, shaking his clenched fist at the flying scud, apostrophized all that lay beyond it in classic terms that caused even the atheistic Neddy to quake in his heelless bedroom slippers.

Rather to the surprise of the rest of us, who were God-fearing men while there was a gale blowing, the weather began to moderate after the damage had been done, and a few days later we slipped over the bar at the mouth of the bay, passing a big square-rigger.

A day or so later, after the fish had been weighed and valued, I scandalized the rest of the complement by declining to receive my share, which was small enough, thanks to the gale. Captain Dave seemed especially disgusted.

"Ye done yer share. What the nation did ye sign on for?" he demanded.

"Just to see how you did it," I answered.

He stared for a moment; then, as the situation began to permeate his gray matter, he broke into forceful profanity, at which I was surprised, for he was a quiet-spoken man except when the wind blew.

"If I'd ha' known that, I never would ha' took ye," says he finally.

"I thought as much, and that's the reason you didn't know," said I; "but if I want to go again you'll take me, won't you now, Captain Dave?"

He answered vigorously in the negative, but just the same I knew that he would.

Making Repairs While at the Dock.

31.
Over the Florida Keys by Rail (1908)

EVERYBODY'S MAGAZINE

FEBRUARY, 1908.

Over the Florida Keys by Rail

By **RALPH D. PAINE**

Author of "The Praying Skipper," "The Greater America," etc.

EDITOR'S NOTE.—Key West, the point of the tail of the American Continent, is attached to the Florida mainland by loose vertebræ called "keys," separated from one another by miles of water. Across these, south from Miami, a railroad is being built. It is the greatest engineering feat of the day. Thirteen miles of the Atlantic, and nineteen more of submerged swamp have already been bridged; and when this veritable railway in the sea is complete, it will mean a forty-eight hour schedule from New York into Havana.

A SPECK of reef set far out in a tropical sea, much nearer to the coast of Cuba than to any port of its own country, Key West has long been the most remote and incongruous city claimed by an American state. In days gone by its spongers, wreckers, and Spanish-speaking cigar-makers no more dreamed of being linked with the mainland by rail than do the people of Honolulu. Until ten years ago their nearest home port was Tampa, 250 miles up the Gulf of Mexico. Then the Flagler railroad, which had been advancing down the strip of wilderness along the Atlantic seaboard, brought Key West within reach of Miami, 157 miles away, by steamers which skirted the far-flung chain of the Florida keys.

This chain of islets swings off from the Everglades of the mainland to stretch down into the Atlantic and the Gulf as far as Key West. Worthless, chaotic fragments of coral reef, limestone, and mangrove swamp, most of them are submerged by high tides and have been aptly called the sweepings

WILSON'S KEY CHANNEL.

The answer lies in Henry M. Flagler's belief that the island of Cuba will some day strike its destined gait of prosperity and growth. For Cuba is the true objective of the railroad to Key West. When the work is finished, huge ferries will carry solid trains to and from Havana; and a through-rail route from New York to Cuba will be completed.

Henry M. Flagler's purpose to stake his fortune on Cuba was the direct result of his visit to the island in company with Sir William Van Horne. Here he learned the scope of the plans for the railroad development of Cuba which seethed in the mind of the great Canadian builder. The man who had constructed more than five thousand miles of wilderness road with 50,000 men in less than five years, who had shoved the Canadian Pacific through to the coast, was sanguine of doing great things in Cuba. Mr. Flagler grasped the fact that his Key West road would be an important transportation link in the far-sighted plans of Sir William Van Horne. He found that the Ann Arbor Railroad was conveying trains of twenty-six freight cars on ferries over one hundred and twelve miles of water on the Great Lakes. It was therefore feasible to carry solid trains between the United States and Cuba. And every inland sugar planter, who had to ship his crop by rail to tide-water before finding steamer transportation, could be offered a competitive rate, for handling and freightage, over the all-rail route via Key West.

A railroad to Key West would serve other purposes as well. As the quickest route for mail and passengers between the United States and the Panama Canal, as a long stride nearer the commerce of South America, as a military and naval base of immense strategic importance for coming generations, a terminus "farthest south" appealed to Mr. Flagler's imagination. Moreover, the idea of a seagoing railroad was, in the last analysis, regardless of the immediate impetus, the logical climax of his prodigal investments along the east coast from Jacksonville to Miami. Here

and débris which the Creator hurled out to sea after He had finished shaping the Florida peninsula. No part of the western frontier or desert is so primitive and unpeopled as was this swarm of seagirt islets until a man with a dream of creative achievement, and millions of money to make it come true, resolved to build a railroad to Key West. It was to be a railroad which, in a distance of 130 miles from mainland to terminus, should bridge no less than thirty miles of open sea, and cross at least thirty miles more of submerged keys and lagoons.

A railroad to be pushed, with stupendous difficulties and at an expense of $15,000,000, through the Atlantic to a remote reef—what is the reason for so monumental an undertaking?

J. R. PARROTT,
In general charge, and director of the entire work.

J. C. MEREDITH,
The construction engineer in charge of the work.

he had already spent $30,000,000 in twenty years extending his chain of magnificent winter resorts farther and farther south and binding them together with his railroad. To make of it a through system he had inevitably to push it on toward the Gulf.

When the Key West extension of his railroad was begun, three years ago, the odds were all against Mr. Flagler's living to see it operated, for he is an old man, seventy-eight years of age. It has been a race against one man's life, and what would ordinarily have required five years to build has been done in three in order that the builder might see his dream come true.

This race against time has been the more dramatic in that the problems were new and of most unusual difficulty. Between some of the keys the tracks must be carried on concrete viaducts so long that from a car window a passenger would be out of sight of land, the horizon closing down to the ocean rim to east and west. The work would have to withstand storms and high seas for mile after mile where there was no barrier to check the assaults of the Atlantic. The construction plant must be put afloat, thousands of men quartered in boats instead of camps, the work inspected in tugs and launches, and a huge fleet maintained for building a railroad. As one engineer summed it up, "It was bound to be a web-footed proposition from start to finish."

Yet, even as the railroad stands today, it is an immense undertaking successfully wrought out and in operation. Within three years this highway of steel has been finished for train service for a distance of 110 miles below Miami, or to within forty-seven miles of Key West. On the remaining stretch eighty per cent. of the construction work has been done. The United States has been given a new railroad terminus far out in the open sea as her southernmost port. From the present terminus at Knight's Key, steamers will run this winter to Havana, 122 miles away, reducing the journey from New York to Cuba to two days—a service as fast as the regular train ferries that will later operate between Key West and Havana, a distance of 90 miles.

LOOKING ACROSS ONE OF THE SOUTHERN KEYS, SHOWING THE STREAK OF RAILROAD GRADING.

The story of this railroad building is quite like a tale from the "Arabian Nights." The viceroy chosen for the work was Joseph R. Parrott, a broad-shouldered, square-jawed man in his forties, who was already carrying enough responsibility to bury several ordinary men. He was a Yale athlete of such ability that he had rowed on five university crews and had been substitute on a sixth. Coming to Florida fresh from the Yale Law School in 1885 to take a berth with the legal department of one of the first railroads in the State, he was induced to join Mr. Flagler's interests twenty years ago. He became the one-man power in direct management of property interests which expanded year by year until they had reached vast proportions. He had to create the East Coast Railroad system, and to equip himself to handle the greatest hotel interests in the world, on top of which tasks he was requested to put a railroad into Key West and was made wholly responsible for the undertaking. Fourteen thousand people have been on his pay-rolls at one time in Florida. And the enterprises controlled by him have involved from thirty to forty millions of capital.

GOING TO SEA BY RAIL—A FOUR-MILE STRETCH OF TRESTLE AND EMBANKMENT.

CARRYING SUPPLIES.

The first plan for extending the railroad south of Miami attempted to find a way across the Everglades to Cape Sable, the southernmost tip of the Florida Peninsula, eighty miles from dry land. Engineering parties spent months at a time in this, the most hostile and inaccessible wilderness left in the United States. They suffered such hardships and torments as have been endured elsewhere only in the heart of Africa. One outfit had to be rescued by a relief expedition and was found on the edge of starvation. The survey was carried through to Cape Sable, the land was found impracticable for railroad building, and the field of action was therefore shifted to the route across the keys. Locating this erratic line was an Alice-in-Wonderland task of itself. The surveying party had to do most of its work afloat, and some of its men were lost among the hundreds of keys for days at a time. They wished to utilize as many of the keys as possible, and finally selected forty-one across which to run the road. There were gaps between them so wide, however, that towers had to be built for sighting the instruments. In other words, these distances which must be bridged were so great that the curvature of the earth hid the rodman on the key from the man with the transit.

The next step was to find the right construction engineer, for upon this official's ability the enterprise must hang in the final issue.

WORKMEN AT LONG KEY VIADUCT RETURNING TO WORK AFTER DINNER.

Down at Tampico, a fragile-looking, sunburned man of middle age was putting three and a half million dollars belonging to the Mexican Government into a pier half a mile long. He was a taciturn, almost diffident person, this quiet little engineer, J. C. Meredith by name. But he knew all about reenforced concrete; he had built bridges all over the face of the map, and his hard-working brother engineers considered him a man of much courage and resourcefulness. After he had finished with his tremendous Tampico pier, he was summoned to confer with the viceroy, J. R. Parrott. The latter expected the engineer to demand a month to look over the ground and another month or so to make up his mind, but to his questions Mr. Meredith replied:

"I'm ready to begin work this afternoon, but I'd like a few days to go home to Kansas City and pack some things and see my family, as I'll have to be on this job for several years."

As soon as the engineer reported for duty, he began to study the surveys of this extraordinary railroad proposition. It had many novel aspects. He had to determine, beyond guesswork, the effects of hurricane winds and tides, to provide the greatest possible wave resistance along every foot of the way, to study and tabulate the data recorded of every West Indian hurricane that has swept the keys since records have been kept, and to lift his work wholly out of the field of experiment. Having satisfied himself that his work would stand the test, he made the plans for his mighty viaducts, and the foremost engineering authorities of this country looked them over and said they were flawless.

Then Mr. Meredith began to build his railroad by the upside-down process of digging more than thirty miles of navigable canals through the Everglades, which barred his progress from the mainland to the keys. These canals were dug by powerful dredges, which were built in holes in the ground. Then water was let in to float them and they began to eat their way toward the sea, throwing up the mud between them to make a railway embankment and leaving two canals in their wake. The grading of the first seventeen miles was accomplished in this fashion. The bed rock was so near the surface that the dredges sometimes stranded and could no longer dig their own way. But presently Engineer Meredith evolved a system of locks by which the stranded dredges were floated over the barriers of rock.

Meanwhile, Mr. Parrott was assembling men and material for the invasion of the keys. At one time he had under charter every available freight steamer flying the American flag on the Atlantic coast, and, still being short of vessels, he had to import cement from Germany to get bottoms to carry it. The crushed rock ordered for the via-

THE LONG KEY VIADUCT, WHICH STRETCHES ACROSS TWO MILES OF OPEN SEA.

THE BEGINNING OF A VIADUCT PIER, SHOWING THE STEEL REENFORCEMENT.

BUILDING THE CONCRETE ARCHES OF THE LONG KEY VIADUCT.

duct construction filled eighty tramp steamers, 200,000 tons of coal freighted another imposing fleet, and the cargoes of steel, lumber, and supplies bannered the sapphire sea with the smoke streamers of deep-laden tramps. Camps and a transportation system had to be arranged to care for 5,000 men far from the mainland, along a hundred-mile fringe of keys with no more than two deep-water harbors in this distance.

Efficient labor was in demand the country over, and good men did not want to fight mosquitoes in the isolation of the Florida keys. Thousands of good-for-nothings, the dregs of sodden and broken humanity, had to be shipped from Northern cities out of sheer necessity. Negro labor could not be obtained in such prosperous times, and the law forbade the importation of blacks from Nassau and Jamaica, or Spaniards from Cuba and their own country. The sources of labor supply depended on for digging the Panama Canal were closed to this American enterprise. Hordes of "hobos," as they were classed, were sent out of the camps as worthless, or because they refused to work at all, scorning even to earn the $12 advanced them for transportation. Although the average number of men employed was about four thousand, the pay-rolls show that 20,000 men were carried to the keys in three years.

In addition to heat and mosquitoes and loneliness, the company's edict against whisky in the camps proved a discouragement to laborers. And the company was able to enforce this mandate because the rum-shops of Key West and Miami could not be reached on foot. To supply the crying demand a fleet of outlaw "booze boats" skulked among the key channels as old-time buccaneers did in these same waters. The engineers waged war against these pirates because they were beyond the law, and the "booze runners" took chances of being peppered with rifle fire or of diving overboard just ahead of a stick of dynamite.

The process of weeding out laborers was costly and disheartening. When the working force had been hammered into something like efficient shape, a hurricane swooped down on the keys in October of 1906 and not only tested to the utmost the work of the engineers, but made havoc in the ranks of the laborers. The construction had been well advanced, however, and embankment, trestle, and viaduct stood the trial without serious damage. The soundness of Mr. Meredith's plans could have had no finer vindication, but the hurricane cost the lives of 130 men, blew the camps to tatters, and swept vessel after vessel of the costly floating equipment out to sea.

Many of the laborers were living in huge barges, or "quarter boats," with two-story superstructures. These craft were towed from key to key as the work advanced. One of them, "Number Four," was torn from its moorings at Long Key before the 145 men aboard could try to get ashore. Shortly before daylight it drove out across the Hawk Channel in a smother of sea and a roaring wind, and was smashed on the back of the Florida Reef. The great barge was pounded to pieces in a twinkling. But there were men in her who showed heroic stuff even in this terrible situation. Bert A. Parlin, one of the resident engineers and the ranking man aboard, might have saved himself, but he went below to try to put heart into his men, and was killed by a flying beam when the superstructure collapsed. The men who had the grit and courage to use their wits crowded out on the balcony to windward to escape this falling wreckage and swore that they would pull through. Those who had the *will* to live were saved under almost incredible circumstances, while the cowards who had crowded into the hold perished to a man.

As the "quarter boat" floundered toward the reef, with the seas breaking clean over her, with death for all on board apparently certain, a barge whirled past her in a fog of spray. Two mechanics, Kelly and Kennedy, stood side by side on the deck of the "quarter boat."

"That barge looks good to me," said Kelly.

"I'll go you," replied Kennedy.

Kelly jumped for the barge as it sped past, and Kennedy was at his heels. A gray sea rose and swallowed them, and their comrades counted them as lost. Almost a week later, the barge was picked up with Kelly and Kennedy aboard, crazed and almost dead for want of food and water. They recovered and returned to the keys. As many as eighty-seven of these "quarter boat" men were picked up out of the sea alive. With remarkable strength and with courage truly indomitable, they had ridden out the hurricane clinging to bits of wreckage, to tables, and to trunks. The Italian steamer Jenny passed them late in the afternoon of the day of the wreck, found forty-four of them, and took them into Key West. Her boats risked the dangerous seas all night long, and it is tragic to record that they heard the voices of others in the darkness, but were unable to locate the calls for help. The British steamer Alton picked up twenty-six more and landed them at Savannah. For days and weeks news of other castaways came from distant ports, Mobile, Galveston, New York, London, Liverpool, and even from Buenos Ayres, whither they had been taken by ships. Without boats or life-preservers, knowing nothing of the sea, undisciplined for such a crisis, these hardy toilers battled for life with a success which makes their story remarkable in the annals of shipwreck.

Of forty-nine men who went out to sea in two house-boats, only one, John Russell, was saved. He floated on a couple of planks for three days, was blinded by salt water, and heard ships pass him in the night before he was seen and picked up and taken into New York.

There was something fine about the finish of one Mullin, left in charge of a cement-mixing plant on board a barge. He was alone when she went out to sea, but there was an electric-light plant on board his craft, and as long as those ashore could see her in the gray dawn, Mullin's lights were blazing like a Coney Island steamboat. He was stoking his boiler and sticking to his job until the moment when the sea swallowed him up. Another lone hero on one of these cement barges found himself blown out into the wild Atlantic. Instead of giving up the game as hopeless, he set to work with his wrench to loosen the bolts which held the cypress box of a water-tank to the deck. Stowing himself in the tank, he stayed there until the barge sank under him; the big box floated off and he drifted in it right side up for several days until he fetched the coast of Nassau.

As swiftly as possible, after the hurricane, the working force was reorganized, and from the clusters of tents and house-boats the working gangs swarmed by night and by day to carry the white trail of the grade southward. Across most of the northern keys they found a bed of coral and limestone; this was blasted and heaped in embankments by hand labor as in ordinary railroad construction. Many of the open-water stretches were crossed by means of ramparts thrown up by suction dredges, which trailed their long lines of pipe across the channels like huge serpents. These crossings were riprapped with rock to buttress them against the wash of the sea. Behind the graders came the track-laying gangs, coupling up one key after another to the mainland, while the camps ahead of them were shifted farther south to invade the islets that swam in wonderful opalescent lagoons. From the top of a derrick frame the finished grade stretched across the green keys like a straight white ribbon.

The line came at length to a bay four miles in width between Lower and Upper Metacumbe Keys. The land is so low that the farther shore almost dipped below the horizon. Across this body of water the railroad pushed its way on trestlework and rock embankment, all of which will be filled in solid before the work is finished. Then the builders brought up at Long Key, where the first great viaduct was constructed.

For two miles across the green sea this structure towers as a wall of masonry carried on noble arches—180 of them, built of concrete reenforced with steel. It has the aspect of a Roman aqueduct built of solid stone, and its colossal strength and dignity of outline are framed in a setting altogether lovely. Seen from the shore of Long Key, its arches march across the water, away, away, until they seem to run sheer into the horizon with nothing to mar their splendid isolation. Save for the low keys at either hand, there is no land in sight anywhere, nothing but ocean shifting from green to blue as it rolls to the Gulf Stream on the one hand, and melts into the western sky on the other. A passenger on a train crossing the Long Key viaduct may be lucky enough to see a school of flying fish skitter past and a porpoise or two hurtling in chase of them. The cost of this one link between the keys was a million and a half dollars for two miles of construction, but unless a ferry is operated so that the traveler may see it from a distance, he will miss any adequate view of this noble and impressive structure.

Only one more stretch of open water comparable with this remains to be bridged. It extends from Knight's Key, the present terminus, to Bahia Honda. Even after seeing the Long Key viaduct, the observer cannot view this great expanse of sea below Knight's Key without a sense of wonder and incredulity at the thought that it is to be bridged. Before him shimmer seven miles of ocean to the farther key, seven miles without a square foot on which a man may walk dry-shod. In fact, Bahia Honda Key is so far distant that it dips below the horizon and is invisible from the water's edge. So far as can be seen, it is a matter of launching a railroad straight at the blank horizon of the Atlantic.

Of this seven miles of sea, three miles will be bridged by two concrete viaducts of equal length, leaving four miles of solid rock embankment to be raised. Omitting this unfinished work, the completed road to Knight's Key has wrought itself over thirteen miles of open water and nineteen miles of submerged swamp in ninety-two miles of track. It is a railroad built of rock and concrete for so much of its length that it is virtually a sea-wall. The Government at Washington became uneasy at the notion of a solid wall stretching from the mainland to Key West, fearing that it might shut off the tidal flow and so disturb the aquatic equilibrium of the Bay of Florida. Thereupon the railroad builders were respectfully informed that they must leave a certain number of bridges by way of openings in their embankments, in order that the immemorial habits of the tide should not be hampered.

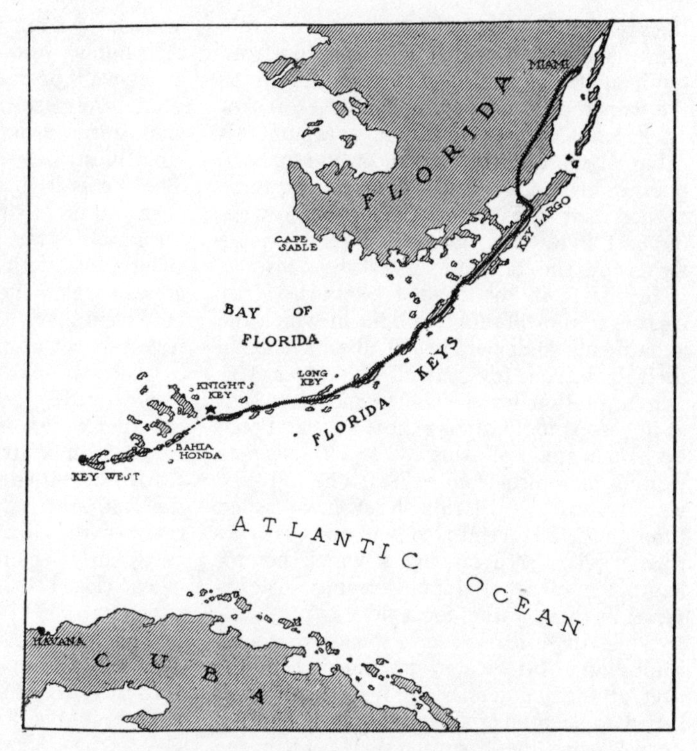

TRAINS NOW RUN TO KNIGHT'S KEY, CONNECTING THERE WITH STEAMERS FOR HAVANA. THE BALANCE OF THE ROAD CAN BE COMPLETED IN ONE YEAR.

While the prevailing shallowness of the water has made it possible to throw up mile after mile of embankment, it has made the problem of transportation immensely difficult. It was found impossible to approach, even in light-draft launches, many of the keys, on which hundreds of men must be camped and fed. A flotilla of stern-wheel steamboats from the Indian River and the Mississippi, reputed to be able to navigate in a heavy dew, was imported to operate on these lagoons, but they ran hard aground miles from the places they sought to reach. "Not quite enough water for swimming and too d—— much for farming," was the way one disgusted skipper voiced his opinion of the Florida keys.

In the forty miles from Bahia Honda south to Key West the island formation differs as radically from the keys to the northward as if they belonged to another geological period. The coral rock disappears and what land there is, is of solid limestone. The keys are so low that many of them are mere swamps densely covered with mangrove. Throwing up embankments across them has been largely a matter of dredging. And for this particular kind of dredging Mr. Meredith designed a new species of amphibious monster. All known methods of railroad building had to be discarded. To feed any of the usual types of dredge with coal and fresh water was impossible because supplies could not be transported over the shoal lagoons and landed within reach. Therefore Mr. Meredith evolved a startling innovation by using a gasoline engine as his dredging power. Six of these gasoline dredges were built on barges. Where there was enough water to float them, they waddled across the key, indefatigably heaping up embankments. When they came to a dry bit of going they were yanked ashore, mounted on wheels, slid on to a steel track, and so progressed as effectively as ever.

As the construction camps floated in among these southern keys, they invaded the haunts of scattered and solitary dwellers in their fastnesses, here a pure-blooded Conch, or native of the keys, whose forefathers had drifted over from the Bahamas, dropping their "h's" en route; there a renegade from some civilization which had cast him out. Or it might be such a picturesque figure as the withered Montenegrin, Nicholas Mackovitch, who has set spring guns around his cabin for some thirty years and who refuses to discuss his past. Such denizens as these sculled their skiffs across the lagoons to wonder at this infernal invasion of their private rights by the railroad grade that rose as if by magic in the flooded swamps. Tiny clearings were brought to light in which the aguardiente smugglers from Cuba have made their rendezvous for generations. Every Cuban revolution for a century past has sent swift vessels to flit among these keys and pick up hidden stores of arms and swarthy leaders waiting to return from exile. The old-time wreckers of the Florida Reef have sailed through these labyrinths to land and to divide their spoil after arranging a wreck beforehand, for many a shipmaster has lost his vessel in these waters for a price.

While these serried keys were dotted with camps and their waters swarmed with the fleet of the builders, Key West itself awakened to such feverish activity as it had not known since the Spanish War. Then the crooked old streets were filled with war correspondents, real and alleged, and with groups of men and officers from the gray cruisers and battle-ships of Sampson's fleet. Now the host that flocked in to arouse the town from its tropical calm was made up of dredging crews and laborers commanded by tanned young engineers. They mobilized their digging machines along the water-front, streaked the island with a railroad grade from end to end, and boosted the prices of real estate by leaps and bounds.

When J. R. Parrott reported to H. M. Flagler that there was no room for deep-water terminals along the harbor front, he was told to go ahead and make enough dry land to serve his purpose. This in itself was a princely undertaking, for it meant filling nearly two hundred acres of salt water, a good-sized town site, with material dredged from the bottom. Suction dredges pushed their tentacles far out to find mud enough to feed their hungry maws, and an army of men built a sea-wall of rock to contain this filling. Already almost a hundred acres have been made terra firma, and the outline map of Key West has been considerably altered. The Federal Government appears to have been afraid that the energy of these railroad makers was likely to play hob with the geography of Florida, for, as the work progressed, again there were signs of uneasiness at Washington. The Navy Department protested that it might some day wish to make a torpedo station of one of the near-by keys, and would need some mud for filling it. At the rate they were working, these railroad dredges would soon scour Key West harbor clean.

Mr. Parrott thereupon agreed to replace all the mud exactly where he had found it, in the event of the Government's needing it. This very courteous offer was accepted, and the incident closed with no mud-slinging by either party.

The tourist journeying south to Knight's Key will find maps and time-tables of little help in getting his bearings. When the road runs through to Key West, however, he will be able to chart his course by the string of lighthouses along the Florida Reef, ten miles out to sea. These spider-legged skeleton towers of steel rise from the open sea, one after the other, visible from the railroad by day, flashing their several beacons by night. Sombrero Reef, Alligator Reef, and American Shoal Lights will serve the traveler in place of mileposts and stations, which is just as it should be on this seagoing railroad. Besides, as he is carried over salt water through long hours of sunshine, with the wind sweeping sweet and cool through the open window, he may watch the stately procession of south-bound ocean steamers which pass close along the Florida Reef in the great tide of traffic to the West Indies, to Central American and South American ports. Nor is it at all fanciful to suppose that if he is wise enough to carry a fishing-line and bait, he may find lively sport from the car platform should the train happen to halt on the Long Key or on the Bahia Honda viaduct.

32.
On No Name Key
(1903)

ON NO-NAME KEY

MAROONED WITH A CREW OF FILIBUSTERS

By RALPH D. PAINE

THE *Three Friends* had been at sea thirteen days in all when, at nightfall, the Sand Key light, off Key West harbor, blinked both a welcome and a warning. The nervous filibuster shied violently and trailed off up the coast with all lights out, and extra watches set for scouting American naval vessels. The cruisers *Raleigh* and *Newark* were looking for filibusters off Key West, and the *Three Friends* had dodged them on her voyage outward bound. At midnight she was feeling her way among a tangle of keys, the lead going, and the captain and mates trying to find a channel by guesswork. When anchor was dropped, there was no land in sight.

Word was passed that No-Name Key lay somewhere off to starboard, but that the vessel could run no nearer than four miles because of shoal water and coral reefs. For the second time the cargo was piled on deck, a back-breaking task, and the forty-odd Cubans and the five Americans of the landing party ordered to tumble the stuff into surf boats. These patriots tugged and strained until daylight, loading the boats. They had started for Cuba two weeks before, had been tossed about without shelter, clutched by sea-sickness almost every day, shot at and chased, had put their necks in imminent peril a dozen times, and they were no nearer the end of the endeavor than when they had slipped out of Fernandina harbor at the outset. And now, in the middle of the night, they were killing themselves breaking out cargo and tugging at oars, to land they knew not where, in what looked like the open sea.

Cases of munitions, hundreds of them, of weapons so packed that every lift was like trying to pull the decks up by the roots, fairly staggered men weakened by exposure and weeks on end of most appalling sea-sickness. The loading of these surf boats was a preliminary to rowing them four miles to the shore of No-Name Key, for the first boat-load found that such an island really lay in the offing. When the boats came within sight of the low line of the key, they stopped abruptly. The water shoaled so gradually that the boats must be unloaded nearly a thousand yards from land, and the packages carried on the backs of the toilers, over ragged reefs that cut, and tripped, and tore through boots and flesh.

Then came the pull of four miles back to the *Three Friends*, and loading again for landing. It was a hard night, and showed impressively how filibustering made for character building. The wind came up with the sun. The surf boats rode high out of water when empty, and were awkward to handle when loaded. The Cuban is an islander, yet he is a sad land-lubber.

The struggles of sundry boat crews after the wind became a reefing breeze were sad and humorous at once. In command of one boat was the former gunner's mate, Mike Walsh. Mike was ablaze with ardor for the life of an amateur pirate until he started for No-Name Key with a boatload of ammunition, and four Cubans as crew. From the stern sheets the gunner's mate swore in amazement, then in anguish, later in alarm. His crew pulled several ways at once when their oars hit the water. The surf boat looked like an epileptic crab. Cubans were on their backs, oars hurtling, feet gesticulating against the sky line.

Tide and wind drove the amazing tangle straight seaward. Mike knocked a Cuban off a seat and took an oar. He pulled as strongly as he swore. His voice filled sea and sky. Yet remorselessly the boat floundered farther away from the shore and from the *Three Friends*. As the distance increased, the clamor of Mike ceased to carry. He and his crew were like some fantastic mechanical toy, in furious action, without any net results. It was expected that revenue cutters and cruisers would swoop in sight at any moment, and Captain O'Brien was bent on getting his cargo ashore. There was no time for a rescue party, and Mike Walsh looked like a sacrifice to the doctrine of the greatest good to the greatest number. Yet his American compatriots in the party had a sublime faith in the ability of Mike to find a way out of any tight corner.

Memories of his previous escapes from more desperate situations were reassuring, then, as I saw Mike vanish seaward, with his Cubans and several thousand rounds of Mauser ammunition for sustenance. From midnight until noon the luckless toilers of the sea, who struggled between ship and shore, were landing the cargo of the *Three Friends*. When they landed they looked back with regret on the wretched days and nights on board the *Three Friends*, for No-Name Key was a strip of sandy reef covered with a dense growth of stunted mangrove bushes, tangled with bits of wreckage where hurricanes had driven the seas clean to the tops of them.

The Place We Called Camp.

When the *Three Friends* vanished in the direction of Key West, the marooned patriots and others began to take account of stock. The Cubans had dropped on the sand whenever they tottered above high-water mark. They were so many dead men with exhaustion, for it had been a terrific twelve hours' toil, coming on the heels of the long voyage. The beach was strewn with cases, many of them in the surf. "Jack" Gorman, the former cavalry bugler, who expected to shoot many Spanish officers with his old Springfield rifle, and who had been conspicuous in the naval surprise of the week before, was the only American comrade-in-arms whom I found in the midst of this sad scene. The resourceful Mike Walsh was careering somewhere beyond the horizon, a raging derelict. There were two more Americans in the party, but they did not count.

"Jack" Gorman and I fell on the beach and slept until nearly sunset, when the limited American colony bestirred itself and began to search for provisions and water. In the litter along the beach, there was found barely enough food and water to last the party three or four days. Gorman and I made shift to fix camp, with rubber blankets for tent roofing, and slung our hammocks. The Cubans were like dead men until into the night. It became evident in our camp that an annual convention of scorpions and tarantulas was in session on No-Name Key. Several times in the night I went sleepily to the beach to see whether the high-water mark had been moved. Studying weather signs soon became a matter for profound consideration.

The morning opened with such animation that it could be truly said to break. The Cuban officers showed symptoms of returning energy. There were sputters of protest and sullen shirking. But the officers felt dry land under them and they became stirred with initiative. Machetes flashed, and the cigar makers from Tampa and Key West got a quick taste of the soldier's life. The mutiny was not fatal, but it went to show that life on No-Name Key was not likely to become monotonous. One meal was enough to indicate that the Cubans would be clamoring for supplies before relief could come. Jack and I buried our few bottles of water in the tent, and hid our cans of beef, beans, and our hardtack in the brush. Scouting parties wandered back from time to time, reporting that there was no fresh water on the key, and the nearest land was a blur on the horizon. This was not so disturbing as the discovery that three of the surf boats had been blown out to sea during the night. Two were left, but they were useless for setting out when heavy weather began to brew, and any attempt to reach other keys was out of the question.

The wind, which veered to the north by noon of this first day, began to increase in a welter of gray and ragged clouds. A yell from the beach drew us from our shelter. A boat was lunging shoreward, a low, inert lump of a craft, wallowing over the climbing seas like a cow over hurdles. A rag of blue fluttered from an oar raised in the bow, and the figure of a solitary occupant seated in the stern gleamed white from the waist up.

"It's nobody but Mike," said Gorman; "but where's his bunch of water-logged patriots? I'll bet a can of beef Mike ate 'em all for breakfast, and topped them off with a Mauser cartridge sandwich."

The surf boat grounded far off shore. Her skipper was seen to flourish an oar in the manner of a harpoon, or as if he were stirring a kettle of soup in the bottom of his craft. Feeble wails arose. "He's wakin' up the crew. He didn't eat 'em after all," commented the appreciative Gorman. "I guess he hove a steamship to, and boarded her single handed for provisions."

The Cubans rose, one by one, and went overboard in close contact with a busy oar handle, followed by a roar from the boat: "Send some o' yer swine out to help me get this stuff out, and report me to the commandante as arrivin' with me cargo in good order."

We stumbled through the surf and fell on the neck of the gunner's mate. His bare chest was burned red, and made a striking background for elaborate devices in tattooing, of which the most conspicuous was the legend, in a wreath, "Home, Sweet Home." Mike threw us off with affectionate protest: "God bless yez, an' I'm glad to reach me happy island, but first let me deliver me cargo, and then I'll tell a few chapters of me log. I've been to the coast uv Africy and back, with a crew that made me weep continuous. An' me only shirt is blown out of the bolt ropes, for I cuddent stop to reef it after I got it set."

Mike carried more ammunition ashore than any three other men, dropped the last case on the beach, reported to the commandante in person, apologized for his delayed arrival, and was made welcome in the American camp, where he ate three meals in one, rerigged the makeshift tent in handy sailor fashion, and insisted on washing the tin plates before he sat himself down to rest.

"I was kind o' circuitous," said Mike, with a grin that was an illumination. "When I went driftin' off like a baby in a bathtub, I addressed me brave but helpless Cubanos until me tongue got stiff, and pulled until me rivets started in siveril places. I saw it was no use, but I told me patriots that if we was goin' to hell in such lubberly fashion, it was me duty to see that they worked their passage all the way; and if you ask 'em, when they come to, I think they'll tell you they did.

"The boat shipped water, and one be one the patriots fell off their perches an' sloshed around in the bilge. They wuz disappointin' shipmates. When day broke, the good ship wuz in the Florida straits, and I begun to worry that I'd fetch the coast of Cuba, and have difficulty in explainin' the presence of me infant filibusterin' expedition, all equipped with arms and rebels, and me the man that passed a few shrapnel into the friendly bosom of the King of Spain. As ye may guess, the wind shifted, and I came drivin' back, and by a mirricle of luck, which has served me in times past, fetched up on this key. It was the smoke of camp-fires that steered me to a landin', and there wuz considerable rowin' done to make it. I don't think me crew will be sittin' up and takin' notice for some time."

Mike Walsh.

The wind increased to a raging "norther" during the night after the return of Mike Walsh, and the party became weather bound. On the third day food and water were almost gone in the Cuban camps, while the three Americans had two days' scant supply.

Men are not altogether lovely when they face a possible struggle for existence in close quarters. We three tent-mates began to hunt the giant crayfish of the Florida coast. Lashing the cleaning-rods of our rifles to the ends of wooden harpoons, we waded through the shallows, and speared our prey, crustaceans that averaged as much as a lobster in weight and size. Boiled in salt water, with green bananas as a side dish, the menu was filling but not various. It was trying to keep the two-hour watches through the night, vigilance that seemed wise, when so many hungry and thirsty men were close at hand. On the fifth day the "norther" weakened, and we began to plan for getting away. Mike and a crew of Cubans were a day and a night in rowing to the nearest key and back. They brought more bananas, and water enough to supply the camps for two days on half allowance. It was decided to attempt to move the expedition to this other key, if possible, but rough weather again made us prisoners for two additional days. Men became peevish, and little mutinies boiled daily, with machete and revolver trimmings. The Cuban surgeon patched the damages, and the officers tried to patch up the differences.

At the end of a week, a schooner hove to off the key, and the boat that came ashore brought food, water, and news that the expedition was to be moved to another key. It was toil to tear the heart out of strong men to move that cargo, and the commandante decided to leave the stuff on No-Name Key, under guard. The party was moved, with the help of the schooner, to an islet almost as desolate. There was fresh water, however, and a change from the diet of crayfish and green bananas.

The perversity of fate ordained that Christmas Day should be passed on No-Name Key. Mike Walsh, with that strain of sentiment which had shown in the incongruous motto tattooed on his chest, hung a tattered sock from a mangrove bush on Christmas eve. He inspected it next morning with an air of cheerful expectancy, then yelled ferociously as he flourished a finger to which was hanging a healthy scorpion. "It's a present to wake a man up," roared Mike, as he hurled it in the camp fire. "You kin laugh, but did you ever see such a fine, big, active scorpion in all yer days? He's the rale Christmas breed. Poor bug, it was crool to toss him in the fire av a Christmas mornin', but he'd a died in turrible agony, annyhow, after bitin' me finger."

When the party had been transferred to Big Pine Key, I thought it best to go to Key West in the sponging schooner employed by the Cubans, and get what information was possible regarding the plans for this lost and castaway expedition.

It was a wearisome wriggle of a sail for a day and a night, beating through innumerable keys, against a strong head wind, to reach Key West in the little schooner.

The brief visit in that town was a succession of violent shocks. Information came faster than it could be handled. The population of Key West is mostly Cuban, and at that time every shred of gossip about the filibustering industry was the leading topic of Key West conversation. I was indeed among friends in the first Cuban café in which I sought for a square meal, a drink and a cigar. The *Tres Amigos* was an open sesame, and money was spurned. In the Cuban club were found the genuine and double-dyed conspirators of the Junta variety. They were uneasy, as usual, and while there was welcome in their reception, there was also something of furtive dread. "You must hide while you are in Key West," they said. "It is not safe. The United States Marshal is looking for you and the others, and two revenue cutters have been sent to find the expedition. The battle of the Rio San Juan was glorious for Cuba Libre; it was the only naval engagement in the history of our struggles for liberty. But it has kicked up a devil of a row. The *Three Friends* came in here for coal. She could not explain herself. There was a hole in her side-works big enough to drive a wagon through, where that magnificent cannon of the splendid Mique Walsh kicked herself backwards, she was so hot against the cursed Spaniards. The American government has the poor, the brave *Tres Amigos* tied up to the dock, with two officers on her night and day. She could not return for you. Food could not be sent to you before because of the devil of a storm that blew so hard for days. We are waiting to hear whether the *Dauntless* or the *Commodore* can escape from Jacksonville to go after you and your devoted comrades on No-Name Key. Maximo Gomez awaits the cargo with impatience, before he storms the very gates of Habana. You must lie low to-day, or you will be arrested for piracy and filibustering at once and together."

Later in the day news came from Jacksonville that the *Dauntless* had put to sea, outwitting the Government officers who were watching her, and taking advantage of her wrecking license to sail without clearance papers. I could not hope to get back to No-Name Key in a schooner before the *Dauntless* should have taken on the expedition and started for the Cuban coast at top speed. Another complication brought additional humiliation. In my luggage on the faraway key, there was a sword, a dazzling, gold-hilted, diamond-studded weapon, which I had been commissioned to carry to General Maximo Gomez. The blade and scabbard of this costly gift were ornamented with such legends as "To the Commander of the Army of Liberation," and "Cuba Libre." It was an emphatically compromising document. For this reason the New York newspaper which had bought this sword at a Cuban fair in Madison Square Garden, at a cost of two thousand dollars, had held it some time before a means of forwarding it to Gomez could be worked out. Jack Gorman had expressed his opinion as follows: "I reckon they waited a long time before they found a dashed enough brand of fool to lug that infernal bric-a-brac around the island of Cuba, with evidence to hang a dozen men sculped all over it."

By a colossal play of good fortune, there came into Key West harbor in the early evening of that eternal day of days the one craft within a thousand miles capable of catching the *Dauntless* at No-Name Key and of keeping the business under cover. The steam yacht *Vamoose* had been chartered by the same newspaper which was responsible for the golden sword and sent south to act as a despatch boat between Key West and Havana, but the weight of the Gulf seas nearly racked and rolled her into wreckage, and the service had to be abandoned.

The swift yacht was placed at my disposal. When the low line of No-Name Key lifted against the morning sky, the sturdy *Dauntless* lay off shore, with a fleet of sloops and small boats streaming between her and the distant beach. The marooned expedition was being transferred with cheering speed, and the sponging crews of the neighboring waters had been called into service under pledges of secrecy. In the early afternoon, cargo and Cubans were once more under hatches and on decks, and amid the cheers of the little fleet of allies the filibuster tore for the dubious track of the transgressor. Captain "Johnny" O'Brien had somehow escaped the fate of the *Three Friends*, and by luck and stratagem had joined the *Dauntless* for the second voyage of the expedition. To those who knew "Johnny" it is superfluous to say that the expedition was landed.

33.
My Winter Game Bag in Florida (1890)

MY WINTER GAME BAG IN FLORIDA.

BY W. E. ANDREWS.

A VISIT to Florida had long been my dearest wish. I had read books without number on that fascinating country, and by the fireside in my far-away home I often dreamed of tropical delights — balmy air, luscious fruits and splendid successes with rod and gun.

We left C—— in a blinding snow storm. In forty-eight hours we found ourselves in another world, as it seemed—green, luxuriant foliage and soft, balmy air took the place of the ice and cold winds.

After a few days' tarry in Jacksonville one of the elegant St. John's River steamers conveyed us to Sanford, every hour bringing forth some new surprise or beautiful bit of scenery to enchant the eye. From Sanford a pleasant carriage ride of seven or eight miles landed us at the fine orange grove owned by Mr. L., whose house was low, with a wide veranda almost entirely around it. A beautiful stretch of water, called Crystal Lake, in which our host informed us lurked many a gamy bass, only waiting to be caught, spread in front of the house.

As we sat on the piazza enjoying our evening smoke and planning for the morrow the moon came up in all her beauty, touching with silvery sparkles the ripples on the quiet lake and lending new glories to the scene. How soft and warm the air felt to our Northern senses, and after the rattle and hurry of travel the absolute quiet seemed a blessed relief.

Our life for the next few weeks was a succession of hunts, varied occasionally with a troll on the lake for bass, and the success that attended on these agreeable pastimes was usually very satisfactory. I particularly remember one of our shooting excursions, not the most successful perhaps, but it is the one most vividly impressed on my memory and will pass as a fair sample of many similar trips. After an early breakfast one bright morning Bernard, Mr. L. and I started for a ten-mile tramp to the "prairie," knowing we were likely to find good snipe shooting there, with perhaps a shot or two at a stray duck. A valuable pointer named Floss went with us. My pet gun was, of course, not forgotten—a double-barreled Parker, 16 gauge, weighing a little over six pounds, but noted for its close, hard shooting qualities and a knack for "getting there" in long shots. My companions carried heavy 12-bore guns, and I did not envy them the extra weight, which in a long day's tramp is quite a serious matter when you are doing the carrying.

Taking an old road but little used, leading through the pine forest, we walked merrily along, drinking in the pure morning air, our guns over our shoulders and Floss obediently trotting along at our heels. After an hour's steady walk we left the road and coming to some scrub palmettos—a likely place for quail—sent

Floss ahead to look the matter up for us, greatly to her satisfaction.

A more beautiful dog I never saw, and it was a pleasure to watch her graceful motions as she quartered the ground to right and left. Suddenly she became motionless, and with eyes that started from her head with excitement, and one foot still in the air, her whole body stiffened until it seemed as if she was carved in marble. We did not stop long to admire her, however, for with guns at full cock we eagerly stepped forward to flush the game she had found; soon it was whirr-whirr-whir-r-r, and a covey of about twenty quail were up and away like a flash of lightning, but the leaden messengers sped quickly after. Three plump birds answered to the call and were gathered in by Floss.

Now the fun began and became very exciting as bird after bird was found and added to our rapidly-growing bag, until a few unaccountable misses on the part of Bernard and myself put a damper on our spirits.

However, when we counted the game and found eleven birds matters commenced to look bright again, and we hurried toward the prairie, resolved, as Bernard said, "to make things hot for each individual snipe in a circuit of five miles."

As we went on, the high rolling ground covered with pine trees was left behind us and gradually gave place to swamps and stagnant pools of water. Here grew the stately palmetto trees, with their beautiful foliage and long slender trunks, giving a more pronounced tropical aspect to the scene, but causing us to look suspiciously around for snakes and other pleasant things peculiar to the greenish water covering our road, a foot or so deep in some places, and through which we were obliged to wade. All nature seemed hushed as our scarcely visible path led us deeper and deeper into the dense mass of luxuriant vegetation covering the swamp we were passing through.

Not a sign of life was visible here, the cheerful note of the meadow lark was no longer to be heard, and only an occasional glimpse of blue sky could be had through the moss and rank growth above our heads. Several times we narrowly missed losing the hardly discernible road, but we persevered and finally reached higher ground. Then the country became more open, the trees fewer, and at last we arrived at our destination—the prairie.

This stretch of open ground hardly deserved the name, not being at all like our Northern idea of a prairie; but the birds we were after were there in plenty, so we heartily echoed Bernard's remark about "what's in a name," and gave ourselves completely up to the sport before us. This particular prairie was nearly a semicircle in shape, fairly level, somewhat wet and muddy land, covered in many places with long, coarse grass not any too green. Behind us and to the right and left this open space was inclosed by a thick growth of palmetto, cypress and other trees, while in front, at a distance of nearly a mile, the St. John's River marked the remaining boundary. This opening was entirely free from trees, except in its very centre, where, clustered closely together on a slight elevation, grew five unusually large palmettos, giving at a distance the effect of a tiny island in a sea of faded green. Scattered here and there could be seen small herds of the lean, gaunt cattle peculiar to Florida, and far away toward the river an occasional flight of ducks darkened the air, causing us to cast longing eyes in that direction.

Agreeing to meet at a certain place on the river's bank for dinner, we each took a different course, but always tending in the same direction.

Carefully examining my gun and finding everything right, I set my face toward the river, expecting every moment to have a snipe rise up from under my very feet, as they sometimes have a trick of doing.

For fully ten minutes I tramped on without a sign of game, and began to think my luck had deserted me, or that I had not yet reached the right ground. As a slight addition to my pleasant feelings I could hear at frequent intervals to my right the boom, boom of my comrades' shots, assuring me that they at least were finding something whereat to shoot.

Things were beginning to look blue for me, when suddenly a well-known "skeep" several yards to my left made every nerve tingle with excitement, and wheeling rapidly I barely caught a glimpse of flying wings before they were hid in the grass again, not over a dozen rods away. "Steady! old boy," I said to myself, and resolving to keep a better lookout next time, slowly and carefully approached the spot I had marked with my eye. With eager, cautious step, bated breath and gun at full cock I crept along until with a whirl and a dart my snipe was a dark, zigzag streak in the air, but only for a second or so, for quickly raising my gun and taking hasty aim, I pulled the trigger, and the dark streak resolved itself into a pair of wings and a ludicrously long bill joined to a plump body that promised many a tender morsel.

With a happy, contented feeling I repressed an inclination to wave my hat and hurrah, and instead I slipped another cartridge in my gun and was then ready to proceed.

The ground I had now reached was just right for snipe, and they were fairly plentiful, but rather inclined to be wild at times; still I had no cause for complaint; my bag was slowly but surely growing, though not quite in the same proportion that my cartridge belt became lighter.

And as the sun marked the hour of noon I kept on toward the river, visions of dinner and other luxuries arising before my eyes at every step. A ten-minutes' walk brought me within a stone's throw of the river, but here my progress seemed stopped by a mass of reeds and water stretching between me and the higher bank beyond.

After vainly looking for some kind of a ford, and seeing no way out of the difficulty but a very wet one, I started to wade across.

Considering all the circumstances, I made splendid time through the muddy water and at length reached dry ground, where I soon had a fire started and proceeded to dry myself, being wet nearly to the waist.

Mr. L. and Bernard had not yet put in an appearance, but it was not long before they reached the unpleasant-looking barrier between us. "Hello, there!" called out Bernard, "where is the ferry?"

Telling them to follow in my footsteps and to look out carefully for certain dangerous holes not down on the chart, after many growls and a prodigious amount of splashing they finally found themselves safely across.

The fire soon dried our wet clothes, and then selecting a shady place we quickly unpacked the necessities of life, with a goodly share of the luxuries as well.

What a glorious dinner we had that day! A hunter's appetite is the best of all seasonings, and with jokes and happy laughter we did full justice to the good things before us, "cleaning the board," according to Bernard; but that idea has since seemed a little far fetched to me, for I am convinced there was not even a shingle to be found within five miles of the spot. Appetites being satisfied pipes were filled and lit, and reclining at our ease close by the river we puffed out clouds of soothing smoke, watching them rise in the warm, quiet air until lost to view among the palmetto leaves above our heads. The events of the morning were duly discussed; every successful shot had to be lived over again, when suddenly Floss set up a loud howl and made a dash for the water, causing us to spring to our feet and grab our guns in a hurry.

Standing on the very edge of the bank, barking with all her might, Floss fairly trembled with excitement, and was with difficulty restrained from jumping into the river. A commotion in the water, not eighteen inches from her nose, partly explained her queer actions; but at first we could not see the true cause of the excitement. Suddenly a reddish brown object appeared among the dark eddies, twisting and coiling in a ludicrous manner, and giving us a partial view of the largest snake we had ever seen. We did not dare risk a shot for fear of hitting Floss, and before she could be dragged a safe distance away the reptile had disappeared.

After waiting a short time for a possible reappearance of our slimy visitor, and firing several useless shots at a sleepy alligator on the opposite bank, we at last concluded to start for home. Keeping together and carefully looking out for chance tempters, we waded back to the prairie. The next half hour added several snipe to our bag, but time would not permit of further indulgence in the fascinating sport, for that day at least, so we reluctantly left the prairie behind us, and finding our road again journeyed back through the swamp lands to the dry ground beyond. Here we left the road, and making a short detour to the right soon reached a pretty little lake nestling among the pine trees and reflecting their stately trunks on its placid bosom. Many of these tiny ponds or "lakes" are scattered all over Florida, and at certain seasons hundreds of plover and an occasional snipe are to be found on the moist ground surrounding the water. Mr. L. and Bernard went one way and I the other, and we made the circuit of the lake.

34.
In a Grove of Oranges (1909)

IN A GROVE OF ORANGES

BY E. P. POWELL

DID you ever find yourself in an orange grove? There is nothing else so fine under the Southern sun; I do not say the sun everywhere, for an apple orchard beats the world for beauty—and a cherry orchard, full of crimson Maydukes and Black Tartarians, is also hard to beat. But under the Southern sky the orange is the best thing the sun and the soil can make, and it is a wonder that grows on the imagination every time you see it. Never ask for an orange, but, just as you would in an apple orchard, name the variety that you prefer, such as Jaffa, or Ruby, or Golden Nugget, or Homosassa. The ground is covered much of the year, just as apples lie in a Northern orchard, and these that have fallen are the richest and the sweetest specimens, if not allowed to lie too long. You may help yourself as freely as you would under my Northern Spy trees and Baldwins. An orange orchard consists of rows of trees reaching about as far as the vision, each tree from twelve to fifteen feet in diameter, and nearly round-headed. The golden globes literally cover the tree, the leaves thrusting themselves out just enough to make the setting perfect. Up and down between the rows are piles of pine logs that look like railroad ties; and in case a frost is threatened these will be kindled to protect the trees.

Early sorts of oranges must be picked in November, and from that time onward the varieties are ripening until April; but there are two or three sorts that will hang on all summer, sweetening every day. The grower, however, expects his shipments to be finished by May first. Oranges and grapefruit, as found in the Northern markets, are almost always plucked before thoroughly sweetened on the trees, and as a consequence Northern buyers rarely find out the delicious flavor of the perfected orange. The grower goes up and down his grove with shears and bag, and cuts enough of the choicest samples to fill his orders for the day. These are carefully poured into boxes in the packing-room, and then placed, one by one, in a sorter, down which the orange rolls until it finds just the slide that fits its size, when it moves to one side and drops into its own box. This sorter grades at least ten different sizes. It is a simple machine, but it works perfectly. The grower who knows his own best interests, never picks up oranges to ship, nor does he allow a single defective fruit to be bought. This leaves a large amount of oranges which can be sold in the town market, or given away. It has little cash value, and yet it consists of the most delicious fruit in the orchard.

An orange grove means simply an orange orchard. The earlier trees found in Florida stood where they came up, making groves, very much as the Iroquois Indians grew their apple trees—building their houses in the middle of the grove. You will still find in Florida some of these old-fashioned orchards, and some of the old-fashioned houses in the heart of the grove. This, of course, prevented that sort of cultivation of which the present orange grower is very fond. He runs his cultivator every few days so as to keep the weeds entirely out of sight, and the whole surface of his orchard is a bed of sand. When he has done picking he spends about one-fourth of his income on commercial fertilizers, which are sowed liberally and then harrowed in. This is a fad, for the old groves in which nothing was done but to dig about the trees and mow down the grasses, bore as fine fruit as ever left the state of Florida. The few old-fashioned groves still standing compete admirably in quantity also as well as quality of fruit with those fussed over and fed to accommodate the manufacturer of high-grade manures. This does not mean that the orange tree does not need food; it means that such food can be provided in the form of natural compost at a rate almost costless.

This beautiful orchard is equally entrancing in blossoming season. Imagine two or three hundred trees, or more, literally one solid mass of crowded orange blossoms; white with a flush of exterior pink, and occasionally red. The volume of fragrance is utterly beyond description by the pen. It rolls, heavy and persuasive, before a dozen playful breezes; for there is almost always a touch of wind from the Gulf or from the ocean playing across the State. A single grove can perfume a square half-mile. You do not go as you do among roses, to smell here and there, for the sweetness comes to you. It offers itself to your senses, and to your judgment. It seems to own and occupy the world, and to have displaced common air. Bees discover it from their homes in the woods, and they come in swarms. Every tree is alive with the honey-gatherers; but they get drunk with the delight, and it is said that they do not make as much honey from orange blossoms as from some of the common weeds. I am not so sure of this; they surely are as happy as even buzzing bees can be. It is a curious sensation that one has, moving through this volume of perfume and listening to the honey-makers. I know of nothing like it in the North, except when the lindens are in blossom; and then you get it, for the bees will work in the lindens all night.

This orange business is the very poetry of both horticulture and commerce. It has a way of fascinating people who are not otherwise excitable. The orange tree is so superbly beautiful, as it stands alone or in the crowd. It is not modest like an apple tree, nor retiring, but its beauty is aggressive and striking. The trees when full of fruit are like piles of gold, and yet you have about them no sensation of Mammon. You clap your hands, and you laugh, and you wander about until you are too weary to go on; and then you sit down on the dry sand or on the log pile. Every day you come back to this feast of color with the same unsatisfied sensation. I am sitting now on my broad veranda, in full sight of a great orange orchard, and it is just at sunset. The sun across the lake is no more golden than the orchard itself. The moon and the evening star are swinging among the pines to the east of the garden, ready to renew the enchantment as soon as the sun has dipped below the horizon. The lake is a vast mirror, and the trees are as perfectly defined in the water as in the air above it. Cows are rambling in the distance along the water's edge, browsing the new grass of January. When will the Northerner learn that the birds are wiser than himself? Here is room for all the frost-bitten farmers, where they may fill their winter months with peace, and also with profit. Those who came here from 1880 to 1890 were merely exploiters, and had no intention of building homes. They proposed to exploit Florida as a place for growing oranges; expecting to get rich quick and then go back to the North to live. They came with money borrowed at twelve to twenty per cent. interest, invested it in pine lands, in which they immediately cleared room for orange groves. These groves grew satisfactorily until 1895. Small crops had been marketed. The trees were loaded with their first full crop; and the outlook was grand indeed. It was already picking time, and some thousands of boxes had already been shipped. Sorrento, my present winter home, could send northward forty thousand boxes during a single winter. Then, just as the harvest was ready, and wealth was full in sight, a blizzard swung around the tip of its wing, and in one night obliterated not only the crop of oranges but froze the trees to the ground.

The shock was more terrible than could have been produced by war or pestilence, for its work was complete. Thousands of settlers had simply nothing left. They had invested every cent of their own, and all they could borrow. They had nothing to show for it but dead trees, and the ground covered with unmarketable oranges. More than one dropped dead in his tracks, as he opened his door in the morning. He had burned his boats behind him, and had neither riches ahead nor could he gain anything by a new venture. The large majority simply fled the State like a flock of sheep—deserting their lands and the cheap houses which they were occupying. There remained a few who were possessed of more or less knowledge of some trade, and could find work in the cities. To this day there are schoolhouses standing in the woods of Florida, where these orange growers sent forty and fifty pupils. The doors swing open to you, the blackboard is on the wall, and the melodeon still stands in the corner; but there is neither a teacher nor a pupil. Those who are now turning toward Florida constitute a very different class of people, and have for their first aim the establishment of homes. They come with sufficient capital to carry them through the making period. Deserted homesteads are taken up, and little villages are strung along the railways. Gardens are made, and culture is divided between a large number of fruits, cereals and vegetables, instead of being entirely concentrated on oranges.

This orange land is right in the heart of Florida. It is totally unlike the border counties, not only in soil but in the character of its vegetation. The land rolls like Michigan, and may be said to be almost hilly; that is, there are very steep places, only they do not climb very high. The strip of land which constitutes the backbone of Florida is about one hundred miles long and about forty miles wide. Every hollow is filled with a lake, and these lakes vary from a few rods to several miles in width. The larger ones are stocked with fine fish; and harmless alligators show themselves occasionally, and have become rather pets and ornaments than otherwise. Nobody fears the ungainly fellow, and he quietly lives on fish and frog, with a possible dinner of duck. Orange groves as they exist to-day are very largely those first planted, and regrafted or budded below the freeze. Such a grove will begin to bear sweet oranges in about three years, and will pay the owner for his work in the course of five or six years. My neighbor Hawkins' grove has been rebudded for over ten years, and from two hundred trees he sold in 1908 twelve hundred dollars' worth of splendid fruit. New groves are desirable, because new sorts of oranges are being created by cross breeding or from seedlings. You may look for many finer sorts in the immediate future, and Florida will very soon cease to send out a single box of oranges of poor or even moderate quality.

Can you make orange growing pay? That of course depends upon the man as well as the grove, but it depends on both. There are apple growers in the North who constantly fail, as there are strawberry growers; and these men will fail in Florida as they do in New York or Massachusetts. The planter must be adaptable to new conditions, for in this sandy soil, and hot climate, he must not expect to do with his trees exactly as he did in the North. More mulching is necessary, and, contrary to the current notion in Florida, less commercial fertilizers should be used. In other words fruit trees must not be whipped up and compelled to do their utmost at a time. The true fruit grower keeps his trees on a steady growth, and asks of them to give him a good average crop. He feeds them with a compost of such material as nature is sure to provide. I am sure that this fertilizer fad will abate. However, the problem is hardly to be answered without considering what else a man can do in Florida. There are some wonderful problems being worked out in this new garden of Eden.

The peaches which we find in our Northern markets are from stock that has been traveling Westward through Asia and Europe for some two thousand years. In some way from Persia it got the name of peach; and these peaches do not fit themselves cheerfully to Florida conditions. A new race has been created by going back to the original Chinese stock, and out of this new race new individual sorts are steadily being originated. Then by the wind and by insects the pollen of the Persian and the Chinese peaches get intermingled, so that in a few years we shall have a race better than both, and suited both to Northern and Southern conditions. The Florida pear has a very similar history and a similar future before it. I have just planted a small orchard of the Magnolia pear, which, with the Kieffer, Le Conte, Smith, and a few more, constitute a new pear race. Meanwhile I am testing with my other citrus fruits, not only new oranges and lemons and grapefruit that have been originated hereabout, but those crosses that are being created by the Agricultural Department at Washington. Something new is cropping out in all these directions every year. Meanwhile Mr. Munson, of Texas, sends me that wonderful new lot of grapes which he has originated from our native stock crossed with foreign. Then we have our figs and quinces and loquats and mulberries, as well as plums and cherries; and there is the apple problem still to solve. Croakers exist everywhere, and there is a cheap race of them in the South. They do not think that anything new can exist under the sun. Unfortunately for their wisdom new things are becoming the order of the day.

So you see that a Northerner may easily combine with orange growing, the growing of many other sorts of fruit, and he has a lot of chances as he has in New York and Ohio. I have a neighbor who has devoted himself to bee-keeping, and does as well here in the winter as he does in Ohio in the summer—that makes a whole year of it. Others find the raising of chickens or turkeys homefully profitable. I cannot see very much difference between the pioneering to the South and that earlier pioneering to the West, only that here the soil is more easily worked, and more attention must be paid to creating humus-compost and mulch. It needs decision of character, trained self reliance, habits of investigation, and it needs also enough capital not to be stranded by the first frost or even freeze. A light frost may be looked for any winter, and a freeze may be looked for about once in ten years.

The pine tree fits to the orange admirably; calm, stately, and commanding, as the orange is homeful and serviceful. Seventy-five great pines, fifty feet to the first limbs, surround my house. In midwinter, when these are in bloom, whole swarms of bees are up there at work, and pine honey is not so bad after all. It has a taste of figs. Twice as many of these old settlers stand at the rear of my garden, running down to the edge of Lake Emerson. To the right of me I have forty acres of pine park, and the lake front is neatly dotted with young pines in groups that look upward aspiringly while they throw their shadows into the mirror-like water of Lake Lucy. Across the lake (about half a mile) the bluffs are crowned superbly with more hundreds and thousands of these health-breathing trees; and when the sun shines through them at night I have a comfortable feeling because they are mine. When the air is quiet below, a murmur and sometimes a roar rolls through the upper limbs of your pines, dropping down occasionally from the upper air to the ground. If you go out among these parks and groves you will find innumerable openings and sometimes half-acres of violets. It is a special charm of these pine woods that the trees rarely stand close as in a Northern deciduous forest, but much as they do in a town park, with plenty of grass and flowers and blueberries. Oaks sometimes get a footing, mostly of the willow-leaved sorts, and occasionally a huge live oak spreads its magnificent limbs, evergreen, and with the densest foliage of any tree I ever beheld.

I wonder always, as I drive through these forests, at the vast display of the beautiful. Who can ever enjoy these wild flowers, reach after reach of them and mile after mile? Is it for the insects alone, and for the birds and the bees that they are painted and perfumed? There is certainly a wonderful reveling here in nature; and I am sorry to say most human beings are unable to understand either the songs in the trees or the flowers on the ground. Yet it is these very things that have made us what we are. They have tuned our ears, quickened our sight, and sent joy into our hearts. They have turned savages into poets. Before the appearance of man on the globe vegetation was flowerless. No apple or orange or oak or maple enlivened the great monotony; not even the grasses that so clothed the fields. No bee made honey, and no flower furnished nectar. At last deciduous trees appeared, broad-leaved forests filled the lower zones; and it was time for man.

I came to Florida wishing to escape the power of Zero. I had foregleams of a log hut, in a pine grove, and simplicity sufficient to satisfy Wagner. I have the simplicity, and have escaped the biting cold. I have spent four winters in Florida, and have never seen a piece of coal, nor a house furnace, and have never longed for such a sight. As a rule the thermometer ranges between sixty and eighty-five at midday, but at night it drops to forty-five or fifty-five, and occasionally, that is three or four times in the winter, it will get down to thirty. The most delightful thing in the world is the big fireplace (I have four of them) and the dashing blaze of pine cones and pine knots. It takes but five minutes to make your bedroom or study delightfully cheerful for a morning bath, or for writing an article to OUTING. But the log house is all a dream; for of all places in the United States Florida is a place for a real house, the heart of a real home—not a costly house, but a retreat. Tourists skirt Florida, buzzing around the coast cities, where the mosquitoes control conditions, and when the conditions are too insistent, they flit for home. They know nothing about the real Florida.

There is always more or less smoke in the atmosphere of Florida after the first of January, for there are fires every day burning over the underbrush and grass within a few miles of you. For a full two months you will see in some direction a broad blaze creeping along the grass, and if the wind blows, sweeping furiously under the pine trees. The trees rarely suffer, unless there is a scar near the ground. Turpentine tappers are on the alert to prevent the flames from spreading among the tapped trees. A precautionary measure is to hoe the grass away from each tree, and before this is done fires are illegal. However, the law is a dead letter and there are fires kindled as early as December. As the sun sets through the smoky atmosphere it becomes a huge globe of crimson, that one may look directly in the face for half an hour. To protect our homes and our orange groves, or gardens and fields that we do not care to have burned, fire lines are necessary, plowed about ten or twelve feet wide. These are a conspicuous feature of the Florida landscape.

Let us be honest, for Florida is not quite Paradise. I think the sour day is less tolerable there than elsewhere. We are not invigorated by the cold, only chilled. The walls of the ordinary Southern house let in mean little drafts that make balloons of the carpets. There is not much comfort in a brisk walk when the thermometer runs between thirty and forty. Many tourists run into spells of nasty coast winds, growl, and hurry back to Boston to get warm. There is, however, very little of this midway weather here in central Florida. We are rather grateful for half a dozen days in the course of the winter that let us down from the elation of sunshine and brightness. Byron asked for one new sensation. Did he ever sit before a big fireplace, blazing with heart pine, a pile of new books at his right hand and a basket of oranges and grape fruit at his left? These are always to be eaten before meals. That is the rule here in Florida, and you may take as many as you choose. There is a fine diversity of method, and while we sit before this blazing fire we shall forget the wind-with-an-edge as we experiment; two or three oranges peeled and sliced; a couple eaten with a spoon; and finally as many more sucked from the blossom end. With oranges, books, and a bright fire, the sense of aloneness is lost, and the out-of-doors is forgotten.

The romance of orange growing I feel myself to the tips of my fingers. I should like to give a life to developing these citrus fruits, but I resolutely turn away, because there are so many more who cannot resist. They will plant orange trees with their last dollar. There is a magic about it, for it turns the roughest sort of folk into poets. It refines, and it quickens imagination. A man must be a clod who can go through my friend Zimmerman's grove and not feel full of worship. Grape fruit, half the size of your head, hanging down in clusters, and the pliant limbs borne down low to the sod; heart-full, arms-full, heads-full; the trees are a solid mass of golden balls—fourteen boxes to a tree; while Zimmerman himself, bent down with age and work, travels down the orchard avenues drinking in the charms of his growing crops, but compelled every fifteen minutes to lie down on the ground and gather a bit of additional strength. Some day some one will pick him up, and he will have gone out of his orchard forever. Everything else in Florida is music. Wild phloxes cover the ground. Mocking birds laugh and whistle in the trees. Red cardinal birds shuttle through the green. The Indians felt all this; they were Seminoles; and not far from here flows the Suwanee River. A little farther are the Kissimmee, the Caloosahatchie and the Withlacoochee, while through the western arm of the State cuts deep the Apalachicola. Almost as soft on the ear are Pensacola and Fernandina and St. Augustine; for the Spaniard caught the spirit of the dream, but the Yankee builds Jacksonvilles and Gainsboros.

35.
A Northern Girl's Huntin' of a 'Gaitah (1900)

A NORTHERN GIRL'S "HUNTIN' OF A 'GAITAH."

BY MARION PRYDE QUAY.

WITHIN the memory of the middle-aged "Crackers,"—as the natives are called—the vast pine-lands of Florida were seamed and threaded with countless trails leading over the grass-grown marshes from one "alligator hole" to another. Now one seldom finds them, and a big alligator is a rare discovery.

This sudden disappearance is owing chiefly to the Seminole Indian. Florida is his "happy hunting ground." Where a white man cannot go, he lives and thrives. He is a nomad, and all through the pine-lands one finds the ashes of his camp-fire, the ridge-pole of his dismantled tent, signs always that the country about has been hunted over, and the "alligator holes" robbed of their booty.

Alligator skins are the Seminole's chief article of barter. They are brought in for miles and traded at the scattered country stores for gaudily colored bandanna handkerchiefs—which are made into a sort of turban—beads, ammunition, knives, etc.; and owing to this near-by depletion the "sob" of the 'gator" grows less in the land.

With the disappearing of the alligator comes an added zest to the hunt. It lends difficulty to the already existing danger and difficulty. Danger and the charm of coming close to Nature, with all her mysteries and moods, are the magnets which for countless ages have drawn men forth from the haunts of men, to slay and spare not.

S— L——, on the Indian River, is a settlement of about a dozen houses. To the right are a few low cottages given over each year to the Northern followers of Izaak Walton, who come South in search of tarpon and winter fishing. In front the wide lovely Indian River stretches away, fringed with palms and weird mangrove trees and pulsing to every heart-beat of the ocean. At the other points of the compass the "Florida Cracker" hath his habitation, and flourisheth like a green bay tree.

It was from one of our house party, Clarence, our guide, fisherman and general factotum, that I learned that here one might go a "huntin' of a 'gaitah" with a reasonable hope of finding one.

One morning I had wandered down to the dock before breakfast and was leaning over the railing, drawing in long breaths of fresh morning air, and viewing the heavens with a would-be fisherman's eye for any sign unfavorable to the plans we had made for the day. Clarence was polishing up the boats and arranging the fishing tackle. The weather was calm and hot and sunshiny, and the river lay so motionless and still that one could hear the faint splash of leaping fish and mark where they had fallen.

"Good morning, Clarence," I called. "A good day for Spanish mackerel; no breeze and no clouds. I think we can count on rare sport out at sea."

Clarence stood still and surveyed the horizon carefully.

"A good day fo' mack'rel, suah, Miss," he said, "and you all suah to get lots of fish; but hit's a bettah day, by *fah*, fo' 'gaitahs."

I examined Clarence carefully for any sign of suppressed amusement—a faintest trace of guile.

"Alligator-hunting, Clarence," I said blandly; "and where would one find them? Here? In the river?"

"*Not yere*, Miss," Clarence laughed amusedly. "Inland huntin' fo' 'gaitahs. Too much salt yere—tho' they do come occasional'. Th'ah some of 'em back in th' country— big uns. You all'd ought to go a huntin' of 'em. I can c'yar yo' wheah yo' suah get a 'gaitah," and Clarence sat down and mused.

He told me stories of 'gators and 'gator hunts, of hair-breadth escapes and odd experiences, until the breakfast bell rang, and I hurried away, filled with a desire to enroll myself in the lists of those valiant hunters who "seek the bubble reputation, even at the alligator's mouth." Reputation there would be, should we be fortunate. I discovered that of twenty men who had gone alligator-hunting from the settlement in the last two years, only two had been successful. My thirst for the fray fired my cousin, V——, to an answering enthusiasm, and she decided to go with me as aid and general voucher for all the tales I *hoped* to tell when we came back. We had several protracted meetings with Clarence in the next few days, and discussed plans and probabilities with a delightful sense of mystery.

There are two ways to hunt alligators. One is to take a small boat and a guide and row up one of the fresh-water streams. Here, lying flat down in the bottom of the boat in the broiling sun, with your rifle cocked and ready for instant action, you calmly allow the mosquitoes to devour you, while you strain your eyes in the blinding light and patiently watch for two little diamond points on the water and may be a tiny rough place—not larger than your hand —for that is what your alligator will look like if you see him. Clarence told me that he went out for four successive days with one man, and each day they lay in the sun for hours at a time and never caught a glimpse of a 'gator. Then the man tired of the sport.

The other and more dangerous way is to drive out to the "alligator holes," where an encounter with a 'gator becomes almost a hand-to-hand fight, as you are on foot and actually in the same water with him. Altogether, at the "holes," one needs a cooler head, and good marksmanship is a necessity. On the latter score, fortunately, I had not much hesitation as I had shot more or less all my life, and knew that I could depend upon the accuracy of my aim.

Inland hunting in the end proved more attractive, and having decided this important question, we arranged with Clarence and with Aiden, his brother— who is a veritable Nimrod—to go with us, provide a conveyance, etc. Then and not until then, we laid our plans before the house party, who amused themselves for the remainder of the evening launching at us dainty shafts of sarcasm and sparkling witticisms, which left us inwardly saddened, but outwardly, most valiant and bold.

The morning of our hunt dawned bright and lovely, and at nine the guides were waiting for us with a two-seated wagon and a "one-time" mustang. They had with them a gun to shoot any moccasin we might encounter, a huge flask of whiskey as an antidote for snake-bites, and two long poles and hooks to land our alligator. We added a kodak, to photograph the spoils, and my rifle and ammunition. I used a Winchester repeating rifle of the '92 model, with 38-calibre, long-distance cartridges.

We drove back into the country for about a mile, over a sandy uninteresting road, which grew suddenly lovely as we reached a small stream, one of the many that drain the swamps. There was a big alligator track along one bank, a long, wet-looking streak through the sand, which Clarence pointed out, and the spirits of hunts-women awoke within us and our hearts beat high! Evidently we were on the trail.

Following the little stream, we drove directly through the pine forest, where the ground was thickly overgrown with palmettos, and came out upon a big, swampy, grassy space, with a circle of willows in the center—our first "alligator hole."

The "alligator holes" are at once curious and lovely. All through the pine-lands there runs a network of marshy ground covered with shallow swamp water and overgrown with tall, willowy, saw-grass. Here and there the waters deepen into little open ponds, and to these the name "alligator hole" is given. The name really refers to the holes the alligators tunnel out in the bottom of the pond, and into which they creep when startled. Here they can lie, safely stowed away, for hours without coming to the surface for air. The ponds are covered with water-lilies and fringed about with willows, which stand out boldly against the wide, flat monotony of the swamps and are very picturesque. Each hole should boast two or three alligators and many tiny ones; and its waters, together with the waters of the swamp around it, are infested with moccasins, only a little less deadly than the Southern rattlesnake.

Clarence and Aiden went to reconnoiter for game. They shot two moccasins not two feet away from us, and we saw some fifteen others, but no alligator; so we stowed the snakes away in the wagon as trophies and set off for another hole. We reached it after an hour's driving, and Clarence went again to look for alligators. He disappeared in the grass, and we could see his head now and again above it. As we reached the hole a flock of blue heron rose from the willows and sailed away, and a white owl cut the air with its lonely cry. We felt how small a part of creation we were in the wilderness, it all looked so wide and lonely, the swamp and all around us pathless forest.

The guide came back in a few moments, all excitement. He had discovered an alligator. He had crept in quite close to the pool without seeing a sign of our quarry, and had just risen to shout to me that there were none to be found, when a huge one, which he had failed to see, and which was sunning itself among the lily pads, jumped out and snapped at him. The boy still looked rather white and shaky. He had thrown himself back on the grass to escape, and the alligator had sunk.

"A fo'teen-foot 'gaitah, *suah*."

I was to come at once.

I came—I jumped out of the wagon into two feet of cold, oozy swamp water, put a dozen cartridges into my rifle and waded off through the swamp, with V—— diligently waving good wishes in the distance.

Clarence kept a close lookout for snakes, and we slipped along as quietly as one can slip through saw-grass, taller than your head, and water which is one moment deep and the next shallow. Finally we reached the hole and I stood and looked at it and felt that cold wave of excitement go over me, which shivers up and down your back and tingles to your very finger-tips. This was alligator-hunting! The black pool of water held all sorts of possibilities for me, and I watched and waited with bated breath.

I waited a long time. I was growing disheartened and weary before I finally saw an alligator; and yet, when he did come, he came so quietly that it was with a little shock of surprise that I looked across the pool and saw him slyly peeping out from beneath a lily leaf. There had been no faintest sound, not the slightest ripple on the water, but there he was. I could just see his eyes, two bright spots, and could imagine his long, dark shape beneath the water. My longing to fire was scarcely controllable and my fingers fairly trembled on the trigger of my rifle; but I was so afraid he might be small and that I might frighten away my big "'gaitah" by the report, if I shot, that I sent the guide around the pool to discover his size. Clarence disappeared, and after what seemed an age of waiting, I saw him creep out on the other side, bend over—then he slipped and fell, and my "'gaitah" quietly sank. I could have wept bitter tears of disappointment. It was the big alligator and it would have been such an easy shot. They tried to bring him up again by imitating the sob of an alligator—"grunting him up," they call it—but in spite of all lures it was an hour before another one appeared. This time I was not too curious as to his size—I fired and he rolled his length over in the water, the inglorious length of three and a half feet!

What a fall was there, my countrymen! He was a "'gaitah," however, and better at least than none, so Clarence hooked him out, and as it was quite late, we waded off to the wagon and V——. That demure maiden, when she saw me, gave way to inexplicable and unrestrained mirth.

"My dear," she said, when she could, "do you mean to tell me you shot that *monster* in *those?*"

"*Those*" were my veil and gloves, and I had—shades of departed hunters forgive!—I had shot my first alligator in my gloves and veil; I was too much excited to notice them.

We drove slowly home after that, fully determined to come again; and over the renewed derision that greeted us upon our arrival I will charitably draw a veil.

That evening I sat on the front steps and plucked the burrs from my hunting skirt. This I did to show to all whom it might concern the supreme indifference with which I received the various wise saws leveled at me by "the party," who also sat on the front steps and were fast making life a burden to me.

Into this scene of agony, there came "Jeems" Ruggles.

"Jeems" Ruggles is our neighboring "Cracker" to the left, and he who knoweth not "Jeems" knoweth not S— L——. This evening he shambled barefooted out of his front gate, with his long, sunburned hair floating back from his brown face, his faded blue shirt widely open at the neck, his trousers short and equally faded, his shoes tied by their strings around his neck.

"Jeems" came along the beach and leaned on our front gate, and I welcomed his advent with joy. Here was relief!

"Good evening, Mr. Ruggles," I said, with a beaming smile.

"Jeems" smiled back as beamingly and swung on the gate.

"By gravvy, Miss Z——," he said, "I year yo' been 'gaitah huntin' this mahnin'!"

I received this remark in stony silence.

"And I year," "Jeems" continued as beamingly, "I year, yo' on'y got a no-'count 'gaitah, and by gravvy, Miss Z——, it's too bad. I jest stopped to tell yo'—yo' bein' dis'pointed 'at way—'at my chillun they got a *pet* 'gaitah down yere in the rivah and they done got him tied to a stake; and, by gravvy! if yo' would like to shoot *him*—he cahn't get away, yo' know, no how, and whenst yo' miss him, yo' can jest fiah away some moah."

I rose and fled, and "the party" laughed loud and long. Mr. Ruggles may have meant well, but after that encounter *nothing* could have kept me from going out for alligators the next day!

We started at the same hour the next morning, and went directly to the farthest pool. When we arrived, Clarence and I crept up, talking in whispers, but there were no fresh trails and no alligators to be seen, except a tiny one, which Aiden caught and shook, head down, until its sobs of grief resounded over the water — all to no avail; and the guides, after examining the "hole," gave up any hope of getting me a quiet shot. The alligator had probably heard us as we crept through the saw-grass; and sunk, frightened, to its tunnel in the pool. The only thing left to do was to try to stir him up with a landing-hook, a dangerous proceeding. A long spiked hook is fastened to a heavy pole, and the entire pool is sounded. When the alligator is struck, he generally comes up with a headlong rush, which creates general havoc.

Clarence cautioned me to be ready to fire at once, as a minute's delay might be fatal, and to be careful in my aim, as I might, in my excitement, shoot him or Aiden. I steadied my nerves for serious work.

One may fire at an alligator half asleep and floating among lily pads, with stoical calm, if one is an experienced hunter; but when you know that the beast, if he comes at all, will come angry, open-mouthed and meaning fight; that he is big; that you are literally in the same water with him, and that water is his element and not yours—the situation yields matter for consideration. Aiden and Clarence prodded and pushed and pushed and prodded with their long spiked poles, but only stirred up lily stems and old logs. Finally, I grew wearied with the long nervous strain of watching, and was just about to call to Clarence to come away, when there was a splash! a yell!—they had struck him, and he came out with his enormous mouth wide open—with a hiss, a jump and a snap, breaking the poles and scattering everything right and left! He looked tremendous! I fired, and he rolled over on the water dead. An eight-and-a-half-foot'gator, and I had shot him.

Oh, the rapture of it all! I laughed and shouted with delight! Then I stood off and surveyed his big bulk with feelings of pride and vain-glory. Clarence's raptures were all for the shot. The bullet had struck the 'gator just between the eyes, and killed him instantly. The skull of an alligator is very thick, and there are just two small spots where one can hit and kill him—one is between the eyes, and the other, a side shot, is just beneath the ear.

The guides dragged the beast out, curled him up in the wagon, and covered him over with willow boughs, as he was a rather gory-looking object. We gave three ringing cheers and fired a salute, and then with infinite glee set off for S— L——. We fired other salutes as we drove in, and hearing them, "the party" gathered in amazement to receive us. Then the neighborhood assembled as the news of our exploit spread, and before them all we stretched out our eight-and-a-half-foot alligator and stood back with negligent ease to receive congratulations.

That evening, after dinner, "Jeems" Ruggles again swung on our front gate and again he beamed.

"Good evenin', Miss Z——. By gravvy, I year yo' cert'ny got a 'gaitah."

I smiled graciously.

"And I jest stopped yere to say 'at I reckon my chillun kin keep thar pet 'gaitah—yo' won't want him *much*."

"I sha'n't want the 'gator, Mr. Ruggles, thank you," I said; "and tell your children for me, that if their live alligator brings them as much pleasure as my dead one has given me, they have a treasure and would better keep him." Then I smiled forgiveness on "the party," and "Jeems" betook himself off.

We started North the next morning, and Clarence surprised and delighted me by appearing with the skin of my alligator, which he had taken off at night that I might have it to take home with me. He brought me, too, the bullet I had used. The entire settlement gathered to see us off, and as we stood at the back of our car waiting for the express to come and carry us away, we felt very much lionized.

Our train came at last. The car was coupled on with a bump, and we waved good-bye to our "Cracker" friends. As we moved, the last words we heard were, from Clarence: "Come down next yeah, Miss Z——, and I'll give yo' a shot at a beah"; from Aiden, "Come down and shoot a wile-cat."

I have my alligator skin tanned as a trophy, I have my memories—a constantly recurring pleasure—and I am going back to add to my experiences a "beah hunt" with Clarence and a shot at a "wile-cat" with Aiden.

I have thoroughly enjoyed my "Cracker" friends. While they are a law unto themselves, this is a quality that develops in the people of any unreclaimed, thinly settled country. It springs up of necessity—in self-defence. I found them always manly, courteous, kind-hearted, and full of resources for the furthering of any pleasure we might plan. They have a rich vein of natural, original humor, and are brave with an unconscious fearlessness most attractive. We felt that we were safe with them always, under any circumstances—even in the midst of the dangers attending the "huntin' of a 'gaitah."

36.
The Haps and Mishaps of a Florida Maroon (1894)

THE HAPS AND MISHAPS OF A FLORIDA MAROON.

BY "LARRY YATT."

URING the palmy days of the buccaneers, when the master found it necessary to restore discipline by punishing one of his cut-throat crew, he used to "maroon" him, that is, set him ashore on some treeless key or coral reef, far out from the mainland. Here the hapless maroon usually anticipated the tardy process of insanity and starvation by drowning himself in the surf. This word "marooning" has been handed down from generation to generation of sallow-faced coast dwellers through the two hundred years that have flown since the last buccaneer of the Spanish main dangled from a man-of-war's yard-arm; until of late some enthusiastic camper-out, with the purpose of making a more poetic name for his favorite pastime, applied it to the life of the midsummer dwellers on the Florida Keys. It was on this subject of marooning that Bob Denison and I were talking, seated in our office overlooking the river front of the busy old town of Savannah, one blazing hot day in September.

"What's the use of pretending to do a day's work while this weather lasts?" said Bob. "Let's find Len Knowles and talk him into a two weeks' maroon at Matanzas inlet."

"Why not Tybee?" I asked.

"For the very good reason that everybody else has gone to Tybee," replied Bob. "Ned Chappel took his wife and babies down there last night, intending to leave them for a month or two. They all came back this morning after spending the night on a billiard-table and taking breakfast off a card-table."

We found Len Knowles over at the Cotton Exchange languidly contemplating, from a back window, a vista of black rice-fields stretching away down-river, until lost in the sweltering mist that made the southern horizon tremulous. He caught eagerly at our joint proposition and was appointed commissary on the spot.

On the following morning we boarded the Florida "Cannonball" Express, which, after eight hours of lively whirling, through fragrant pine forests and whitening cotton fields, set us down, full of dust and enthusiasm, at the gates of the ancient city of San Augustin.

We trudged up a dusty shell road, where the sun beats down in a glare of white heat and into the city, through streets so narrow that belligerent neighbors might whack each other with broomsticks while standing within a yard of their own thresholds, and finally brought up in the office of the "Sea View," where we arranged with our host for a ten-day lease of his new cat-boat the *Eloise*

The natty little craft was soon hauled alongside the hotel landing-stairs, our camp equipage stowed away under the half deck, and when at last the supper gong broke loose on the sea-gallery we had everything in readiness to take advantage of the early morning tide.

The Matanzas River, on the western shore of which San Augustin is located, is simply an arm of the sea, a broad, shallow waterway, with currents that change direction with the ebb and flow of the tide. Its two inlets—San Augustin and Matanzas—are twenty-two miles apart, on the straightest and smoothest stretch of beach on all the eastern shores of the continent. At flood-tide the waters of the Atlantic pour into the inlets, and the two opposing waves rush to meet each other half way. To reach Matanzas inlet by water from San Augustin, you catch the flood-tide at half stage and drop down to the "meeting of the waters" in time to float in on the southern ebb-tide.

After supper we strolled away up the broad sea-wall and finished our cigars on the terra plain of old Fort San Marco, where pretty Minorcan girls, with their dark-browed sweethearts, were tripping to the "trembling string" of a good quadrille band from the artillery garrison. Little did those happy youngsters care that the very stones about were laid in the sweat and blood of hapless ancestors two centuries ago!

Next morning I was awakened by the soft knock and "Daylight, sah!" of the porter, and opened my eyes to find the mosquito-bar rustling in a piping sea-breeze. Fifteen minutes later, as we flew away to meet the sunrise, the only living thing in sight was a sleepy-looking sentinel, pacing up and down in front of the old United States barracks.

As the city sank from view behind the salt-marshes, the wind freshened and hauled round astern. The kettle, under Len's skillful manipulation, sang merrily over the little oil stove, and we had coffee, hot and strong, with chicken sandwiches, while the *Eloise* struck a ten-knot gait, on a three-mile stretch of straight, wide river.

Then there were white sand-dunes close on the port side, and the hoarse roaring of the surf came down on the wind. We felt the little craft heaving under us as the river narrowed and deepened, and passing an old water battery on the starboard side, we glided out into full view of the ocean, with the breakers not three hundred yards away.

We stood close-reefed across the inlet—which is about one mile in width—and came to anchor in the mouth of a deep creek, and camped on the south bank.

We had brought along a nine-by-nine wall tent to sleep in, and a small tent-fly to shelter the cook from sun and rain. These were pitched on the smooth, hard sand, just above high-water mark. Then Bob and I went to look up an old well, marked on a rough chart which I had picked up in San Augustin. After some trouble we found it hidden in the palmetto undergrowth and half full of swamp water. Bob lowered away the bucket and brought up a dead rattlesnake and live mud-turtle. Then I tried my hand at the rope, and landed a lively young water-moccasin. At last we drew a bucketful of the highly-colored fluid, with only tadpoles in it, and returned to camp disgusted. We found Len cleaning the last of a dozen fine mullet, which he had caught with his cast-net. For dinner that day we had fried mullet, roasted sweet potatoes, cold corn dodgers and indigestion.

We had planned to spend the afternoon in surf fishing, but a heavy on-shore wind drove the sea far up the broad beach, and prevented our getting within casting distance of the outer line of breakers. Bob waded far out into the tumbling surf, made an ineffectual attempt to get his line into deep water, and narrowly escaped getting there himself, in the strong undertow.

We had cast off the trammels of fashion, and were unaffectedly happy in our marooning togs of palmetto sombreros, sleeveless balbriggan undershirts and thin jean overalls, rolled up to the knees. We ran races up and down the glistening, sounding shore, and every "splat" of our bare feet on the warm, wet sand was an echo drifting back from the green hills of barefooted boyhood. We slid and rolled down the steep sand dunes and pushed each other into the combing surf, all of which was very undignified, no doubt, in three old fellows, the aggregate of whose years exceeded a century.

On our way into camp Bob unearthed the nest of a loggerhead turtle, out of which he dug a hatful of eggs, and immediately ordered an omelet for supper. So for supper it was turtle egg omelet with hot hominy mush.

Seated around the mush kettle that evening we arranged a seven-day programme of sports of such enchanting promise that even a rough sketch of it sent Bob into a succession of duck fits. There was alligator shooting up the creek and porpoise shooting in the inlet; surf fishing and surf bathing; mullet netting in the lagoons; turtle hunting by moonlight, and turtle egg gathering by daylight. It read like a chapter from "Robinson Crusoe."

The ebb-tide roared itself hoarse, as it ran like a mill-race through the narrow inlet. Far across the salt-marshes the pine forest was aflame with the glory of a Southern sunset. Myriads of screaming sea-gulls darted and circled against the darkening purple of the east. A great flock of pelicans sailed in majestically from the southern swamps and settled down on a neighboring sandbar. The silhouette of palm and pine grew sharp against the west. The shadows deepened in the palmetto jungle, and crept over from the opposite bank. The wind sank to rest with the sun, and a host of brigand mosquitoes swooped down upon the camp, driving us under the mosquito-bar. There we lay awake for hours, listening to the skipping and flopping of the small fry in the shallows.

About midnight a school of disreputable porpoises sailed up the creek to a point opposite the camp, where they proceeded to celebrate. Grunting and snorting like a drove of wild hogs, they bumped into the *Eloise* and churned the water around her into foam. They ran the alligators ashore, picked quarrels with the sharks, and finally got into a free-for-all running fight among themselves, which carried them out into deep water.

I was awakened by the glare of sunlight on the bosom of the sleeping ocean. My companions were snoozing away like healthy infants, so I lowered the tent wall carefully and had just settled myself for another nap when, sweet and clear, a fresh soprano voice fell upon the drowsy stillness, singing that deathless old song of the sea, the "Midshipmite."

"Oh! a long, long pull, and a strong, strong pull;
Cheerily my lads, heave-ho!"

The "lads" were awake in an instant. "Mermaids," said Bob, pulling on his overalls. "Sirens!" cried Len, who had glued his right eye to a little peep-hole in the tent door.

In a desperate struggle for first place at the peep-hole, Bob and I tumbled over our friend, and landed outside in a state of apparel distressingly unconventional. We were just in time to see a white skiff glide into the mouth of the creek, with a pretty young lady in the bow. Her song came to an abrupt end. She gave a pretty little scream. In the stern sheets, a fine-looking old gentleman in white held a large sun-umbrella over a comely old lady in black; while in the rower's seat, two very pretty girls rested smilingly on their oars, as the boat swung around broadside to the shore.

"I trust," said the old gentleman, with a gracious wave of the hand, "that you will pardon this intrusion." Then he explained that they had been camping at Moultrie Creek during the past week, and had just dropped down with the ebb-tide on their way to their last summer's camping-ground, about four miles up the creek. They had hoped to reach their destination in time for a late breakfast, but found the current setting so strongly that they had to land and wait for the tide to turn.

Bob, with a rueful glance at his sunburnt, sprawling feet, advanced to the water's edge and stammered out something about being most happy. As the old gentleman stepped ashore, he introduced himself as Mr. Perkins, of Montgomery, Alabama, and the ladies as his wife and daughters.

The flood-tide rippled around the prow of the *Eloise*, the kettle of dish-water boiled itself dry, and the fire went out while we chatted over our empty coffee-cups.

At last, Mr. Perkins, consulting his watch and a tide-table, announced that the hour for departure had arrived, and arose, extending to us a cordial invitation to visit him in camp and in city.

As the skiff drifted away from the shore a sleek and sleepy-looking young negro thrust his head over the gunwale of a little baggage-punt that the skiff was towing astern, and gazed back wistfully toward a plate full of fried mush, the surface of which the sun had baked to the consistency of a fire-brick.

Bob seized the plate, and dumping its contents into an old newspaper, rolled it up into a ball, and threw it with all his might at the boy. Imagine our feelings, when, instead of hitting its mark, the missile passed high over it and struck Mr. Perkins full in the back of the head, where it burst, knocking off the old gentleman's hat and scattering fried mush in every direction.

The ladies screamed in chorus. As for Mr. Perkins, he simply passed his handkerchief across the back of his head, replaced his hat in the most deliberate manner, and opening the big umbrella, brought it around so as to hide the occupants of the boat from view. We could only stand and gaze helplessly after the receding umbrella. At last Bob found his tongue, and as is usual in such a crisis, succeeded in making himself misunderstood. "Sir!" he cried, in tones which evoked our deepest sympathies, "believe me, I did not mean to hit you!"

Slowly the big umbrella went up, until Mr. Perkins' striking countenance came into view, as he shot an indignant glance backward. "So you were only trying to see how close you could come to me, without hitting me, eh?" said the old gentleman, angrily. "Gentlemen!" he continued, with impressive dignity, and motioning to his daughters to cease rowing, "whenever you shall have framed a suitable apology for this outrage, you will find me not unwilling to take its acceptance under consideration. Again, I wish you good morning."

Then the big umbrella dropped into place, like the falling of the curtain on the last act of a doleful tragedy; the polished oars flashed swiftly in the sunlight, and we soon lost sight of the white skiff in a sharp bend of the creek.

"What are we going to do about it?" I asked, as the boat disappeared.

"Do? Why, we are going to cut across the bend, head them off, and demand an immediate audience!" said Bob.

Hastily drawing on our knee boots, we struck out across country, with Bob in the lead; through swamps where the mud was knee-deep, and water-moccasins not infrequent; through a tangle of live oak and wild grape-vine, where Len got twisted up and hopelessly distanced; bringing up at the river, in a clump of palmetto scrub, just in time to hear a sweet, coaxing voice say: "Now, dear papa, *please* don't scold us for laughing, for we really can't help it."

Then the boat came into view, and we could see Mamma Perkins laughing until the tears ran down her cheeks, and Papa Perkins failing miserably in his efforts to look stern and dignified. Of a sudden the old gentleman leaned back in his seat, and joined so heartily in the laughter of the girls, that the young "coon" in the punt sat up and regarded him apprehensively. "Say, Mars' Perkin!" said the boy, when the old gentleman's risibilities had subsided somewhat, "I spec' dat 'ere passel of frie' mush was tended fo' me all de time, case de strange marse, he look *so* at me, w'en he frowed hit."

"Now or never!" said Bob, as Mr. Perkins went off again at this unexpected sally from the rear. We stepped out on the narrow margin of quicksand, just as the skiff came opposite to us. Bob began at once: "Mr. Perkins," said he "allow me to detain you, while I explain this unfortunate affair."

"Glad to see you, gentlemen—glad to see you, indeed!" said Mr. Perkins, cordially, extending his hand as the boat was laid alongside. "Explanations are quite unnecessary—quite. I see it all plainly, now. It is all right, sirs—all right. Again we will bid you good morning, for the tide slackens. Remember that we shall desire your further acquaintance."

Once more the sun shone and the birds sang for us, as we wended our way back to camp, making the old woods ring with shouts of laughter.

We had arranged to spend the afternoon in surf-fishing; so while Len cooked the dinner, Bob and I netted mullet for bait.

Among all the sports and pastimes of the Florida coast, there are none in my estimation to compare with fishing in the surf. While there is not a positive element of danger in this sport, there is just a spice of it, sufficient always to keep one interested whether the fish bite or not. This feature alone is enough to justify its great popularity.

Passing one end of the line around

my waist, and tying it there, with a loose bow-knot, I coiled the remainder carefully into the left hand and waded out into the surf until arrested by the instinct of self-preservation. Casting the baited hook as far out as possible beyond the line of breakers, and assuring myself of a firm footing, I loosed the line from my waist and took a single turn of it around my right hand.

The surf broke over me in front and the undertow smote me in rear. The crabs nibbled my toes and pinched my heels. The quicksands crawled under my feet, until imagining myself sliding bodily seaward, I gazed involuntarily toward the shore and was much relieved at finding it still there. But how far away it looked across the foam-covered lagoon, above the surface of which the black fins of a pair of ground sharks were plainly visible.

A jerk at the line that took me two steps in quick succession toward deep water, recalled vividly the old tug-of-war game of my school-days. Facing quickly to the rear I brought the line over my left shoulder and struck out for *terra firma*. Casting one swift glance backward I saw just inside the line of breakers a large whitish object leap into the air, flashing in the sunlight like a coat of steel mail and striking the water broadside with a splash which was plainly audible above the roar of the surf.

The water was waist deep in the lagoon, with ugly holes that let me in to the chin. I had hooked a fighter sure enough, for the line never slackened from start to finish. Far out to the right and left it swung, like the play of a mighty pendulum.

I reached the shallows at last, and shortened line, hand over hand, till a bristling back fin showed above the surface. "A long, long pull, and a strong, strong pull," and out of the smother of foam flopped a twenty-pound bass, with the barb of the hook showing through just below the right eye.

After we had landed three fine bass and a drum, a school of wolfish sharks got wind of our bait, and snapped at it till our arms ached, finally getting away with our hooks and all the line that they could reach.

The next day was the Sabbath, and we remained quietly in camp—in anything but a devotional frame of mind, however; for our feet had become so badly swollen and sunburnt that we could scarcely hobble to our meals.

During the next three days we had ample opportunity for testing the old adage about misery loving company, as we lay in the shadow of the palmettoes with our feet encased in poultices composed of hard bread soaked in condensed milk.

On the morning of the fourth day of our confinement to camp we were able to get about in slippers, which Len had improvised from an old Turkish bath-towel. They were nice and easy on the feet, fitted their present proportions fairly well, and left a track in the sand like the winter trail of the *Wendigoos*, of Ojibeway legendary lore.

The day on which we were to begin the return journey was close at hand. Bob, who had engagements which would require his presence in Savannah within three days, advised that we should break camp on the morrow, but was finally persuaded to remain another day, when —it was fondly hoped—we should be able to wear our shoes home. We should have stayed, but after making a careful inventory of subsistence-stores, we had remaining on hand and available for immediate use the following articles: Half-pound can of yeast powder; half pint Bourbon whisky. We went home.

37.
Truck Farming in Florida (1909)

TRUCK FARMING IN FLORIDA

BY E. P. POWELL

YOU do not see all of Florida from the tourist standpoint. These flitters constitute a wonderful tribe, steadily flowing in and out of the State, by three or four main lines of cars, and by three lines of ocean vessels. They begin about the first of December and the hotels are crowded by the middle of that month. Every train unloads a caravan, all furnished with guns, and with fishing tackle, although I have discovered that very few of them know either how to shoot or fish. They are of the Bowser sort largely, and are possessed of very queer notions about having fun. They know little or nothing of the State, even after they have been there for five or six years in succession, and I hear from some of them that they have spent nearer twenty winters in Florida. They go all around the Coast, spending money at the costly resorts, and congratulating themselves as if the joys of this world were measured by the amount of money that goes out of pocket.

Palm Beach is the paradise of this sort of people; it really is a marvel of tropical beauty, and Mr. Flagler is no more celebrated for his railroad activities than for what he has done to turn this place into a Garden of Eden. It is the Mecca of tourists, and no one thinks he has seen Florida till he has spent a few days at Palm Beach. It has the advantage of entire lack of conscience in hotel charges, and has the knack of sifting out the millionaires from common travelers; yet it is a wonderful place that everyone should see. When peripatetics have got through with about three months of winter, and money-spending, along these Coast counties, the mosquitoes set in upon them, and drive them pell-mell out of the State. I find that very few of them ever learn that there is a backbone to Florida, made up of high rolling land, where every hollow is a beautiful lake; a land where the mosquito is sometimes seen but has no control, and where the climate is equable all the year round—that is, the summers are fully as endurable as the winters—I think more so. Nor do these professional tourists know anything about the industries of the State, beyond the fact that oranges grow in Florida, and that grape fruit is served on their hotel menu twice a day. They possibly have acquired some slight knowledge of some of the semi-tropical fruits, like the avocado, and the loquat and the pineapple.

I have told the readers of THE OUTING MAGAZINE about my own winter garden and orange grove, but there remains a phase of agriculture in the State quite as remarkable as anything that can be discovered about the orange orchards; I mean the trucking business. This consists in the growing of early vegetables for the Northern market, and a succession of later vegetables, making three or four crops from a single plat of land. Florida has this unrivaled advantage, that whatever may be undertaken by any other State to the North, even Georgia, we can get our potatoes and vegetables and fruit into Philadelphia, New York, and Boston, or Chicago at least two weeks ahead of any rival. This peninsula, thrust by Nature down into the tropic seas, and watered by showers from both the Atlantic and the Gulf, can defy all the gardens in the world. It has no competition outside its own boundaries, and it is learning co-operation inside its limits. Northerners are finding out this, and are very rapidly taking up hundreds of new acres every year.

The trucking section consists of flat land and rather moist; there are large parts of it that must be drained before they can be put to use. The soil is sandy, but very rich in vegetable matter, much of it almost black. These parts of Florida characterized by the palm, have not been annually burned over, like the pine section, and so have gone on accumulating humus of a very fine quality and a great depth, while the soil below is in need of nothing but heaving up to the sunshine. With proper culture these lands need not be exhausted of fertility in a thousand years. It is a land of small farms, where five acres makes a good-sized homestead, and more likely the owner will be satisfied with what he can get out of one or two acres. Trucking means the intensest culture conceivable. I have heard this black land called Klondike, meaning that it is a mine of wealth. It is a garden in the highest sense of the word.

After you have entered the State and landed at Jacksonville, you can continue your way southward either by any one of three or four lines or cars, or you can take a boat up the St. John's River, which will land you at Sanford or Enterprise, as the end of navigation. It is one of the most thoroughly delightful trips afforded anywhere in the United States. The small steamer winds its way under the sharp eye of a thoroughly trained pilot, following the navigable channel that twists about through a vegetation of the most picturesque and wonderful sort conceivable. Not for two consecutive minutes is the outlook the same. You are in fact simply boating it through tropical forests. The mosses hang down from the trees almost to the smokestack in places, and again the river widens out into a lake, through which you cut your way in the morning sunshine, with ducks in the water and birds overhead, but nowhere a sign that a human being is on the globe apart from the boat. The wilderness is absolute. Then again the channel narrows until you are almost plunging into the wild flowers that literally cover the banks; in fact you are at times among the water hyacinths, that have clogged so many Southern streams with their beauty. Here and there lonesome cabins have been built out on rude piers of logs, and as it is morning you will see the Cracker with his fish pole catching his breakfast out of the river, while his wife kindles a blaze of free driftwood. Neighbors there are none; he looks like a possible Robinson Crusoe. Alligators occasionally lift their noses, and the wealth of wild flowers climbing the trees and tressing the groves together is something marvelous. This trip will be a part of your dream life forever. On and on you go through the laughing lagoons, rarely touching at towns or railroad landings, but occasionally hearing the railroad whistle through some gap in the forest, and once in a while, where the land lies rolling or high, catching a glimpse of orange orchards that indicate a town not far off. For clean, unbroken romance give me a trip up the St. John's.

On the morning of the second day you will reach Sanford, and this is the very heart of the trucking section. You land in a beautiful park, where the palms predominate, but there are orange trees and grape fruit and other semi-tropical fruits growing all about you. The hotel shows that the railroads have gone beyond this point, to exploit the more unique Coast sections, and are carrying the bulk of tourists farther on. The town also bears signs of having been under a deep depression, owing to the orange freeze of 1895. You see, however, some signs of a new impulse. The streets are abundantly supplied with great fountains that throw up waters strong with sulphur. Horses like this water fairly well and many people become fond of it. It is certainly wholesome. There is flatness everywhere. At the depot we see cars laden with lettuce and celery or with cabbage. There is no time when you will not see more or less of this freightage, but the bulk of the shipments are in January and April.

You will be invited to stroll or to ride out into the surrounding country. One mile, two miles, three miles, four miles, and yet you have seen nothing but celery and lettuce, and the negroes and Crackers who are cultivating the fields. As fast as the crop is pulled another is planted. The system of irrigation is simple, for water can be obtained in the form of flowing wells by boring or digging from twelve to twenty feet. The whole country seems to be a floating island. That large sums of money are being made is evident, although one must not believe the advertisements which reach the North. Celery land is not worth thousands of dollars per acre, certainly not as a rule, and no one should invest in this trucking section until he has seen the land and studied the conditions. It is attractive business, mainly because it is quick money. It takes an orange grove ten years to become exceedingly profitable, but a lettuce crop brings in money inside of six months. There are many people who are better adapted to this sort of gardening than to fruit growing, for the problems are less, and less intricate. The insect enemies are fewer, and there remains just this one great danger, a freeze. You may be sure that there will be a touch of frost once or twice every winter, and there is pretty sure to be a bad freeze once in four or five years. Occasionally a whole crop is swept out; thousands of dollars by a single breath of a Northern blizzard. The next day the sun comes out warm and the winds blow in from the ocean, but the mischief is done—lots of work put to naught in a night. The truckers can afford this once in awhile, but not too often. I do not know of any other place either in Florida or elsewhere where gardening literally covers the face of the earth; but here in Sanford the dooryard is a celery bed, and the back yard is another. In one place I found the street side cultivated down to the ditch, but wild phlox Drummond's was smiling up through the paths as a sort of apology for such close domestic economy. It was an admirable way of getting rid of street weeds.

I was invited by a doctor from Pennsylvania, who had gone South for his health, to go out a couple of miles and visit his cucumber houses. I did this the more cheerfully because I wished to know about growing other crops under cover. I had heard a good deal about pineapple culture of this sort, but so far as I had been able to observe, this sort of pineapple growing had been given up through central Florida. I found that my friend had erected very substantial sheds, covering I think something over an acre and a half. Instead of roofs he had arranged rolls of canvas, and a handy mechanical contrivance to unroll these and draw them over the sheds in case of danger. He was planning to grow the new American Wonder Lemon, a remarkable affair that bears lemons weighing from one to two pounds each, on bushy trees of not more than ten feet in height. This lemon was originated in Baltimore a few years ago, and up to the present time is grown mostly in pots in Northern homes. It has not been experimented with much, as yet, as a market fruit. Its quality is superb, and a tree hanging full is a sight to go far to look at. Its very size may, however, debar it from special value in the market. The cucumber sheds were supplied with brick heaters, in which a fire could be quickly started, made of pine knots, and heat generated sufficiently to keep the atmosphere considerably above the freezing point.

Florida is nearly as large as all New England, and of course there is a great diversity of employment. In the northern counties corn, wheat, oats, peaches, pears and apples dominate; in the center we find most of these products growing side by side with oranges, lemons, loquats, sweet potatoes and cassava; and in the southern counties we are among pineapples avocados and other strictly tropical fruits and vegetables. The trucking region is therefore closely associated with orange growing and other citrus products. You cannot drive anywhere about Sanford without coming upon yards that are filled with these golden fruits. Grape fruit hanging six inches in diameter and in huge clusters bends its trees over sometimes to the very soil. Peaches are as common as oranges, and when you get a little nearer the hilly or sloping lands to the west, large peach orchards stand in January and February bursting into bloom. In March you will find a few ripe fruits, but the marketable crop comes not earlier than April and May. The mulberry fills up March, and is the first one of the Southern fruits to ripen. You will find it everywhere; varieties that do not seem to have found any place in our Northern gardens as yet. The fruit is from one to two inches long and three-quarters of an inch in diameter. Nearly every bird in the heavens and every animal on the earth likes the mulberry, and for my part a mulberry pie is the only rival I have ever yet found for a blackberry pie. My whole being turns into a poem when I think of it. You should have just pulp enough not to let the juice run away, and the pie showno sign of stinginess.

This is the way with Florida, that while one industry predominates there is enough else going on to widen out life and make a complete home. With all the rest, of course the St. John's River furnishes a magnificent fishing ground. With the celery and the lettuce are shipped carloads of eggplant and more or less Irish potatoes. One lot on Celery Avenue reports one acre in eggplants, shipping 403 crates, and netting $1.25 per crate; one acre in cauliflower, shipping 300 crates, and netting $1.75 per crate; one acre in cucumbers, shipping 500 crates and netting $1.00 per crate. But, mark you, these three acres were all one acre, and the crops were raised in succession. The owner writes: "I have now a fine crop of corn on the same land." The rule is the same with celery and lettuce, that after shipping three crops, crab grass comes up spontaneously, making splendid autumn fodder, after which the grass is plowed under to add humus to the soil. Another grower reports that he had four acres of celery, from which he shipped 2,000 crates, that netted $1.25 per crate. The same grower had ten acres in tomatoes, from which he shipped 2,000 crates, and netted $1.40 per crate.

From the central counties of the State one may gather reports nearly or quite as attractive, but the products shipped are mainly tomatoes, potatoes, cabbages and melons from the garden, and oranges with grape fruit and peaches from the orchard. The loquat would constitute a splendid article of commerce if it were not too tender for shipment. It is a delicious fruit, ripening all winter; combining the shape of a small pear with the general flavor of a cherry. It is blossoming and ripening during three or four months. The tree is very handsome and the blossoms are highly perfumed. The fruit hangs in large clusters. My impression is that tomato growing and sweet potato growing have by no means reached their maximum, and that the future will develop trucking in this direction enormously. There is a fascination about the growing of celery that leads to an over-stocked market. The prices of one year are not by any means a certain gauge for all years.

Who is doing the work, and is help always obtainable? The negro is a fairly good grade of citizen in every respect. He is not an Anglo-Saxon, and most of the grumbling about him comes from a grade of citizen himself off somewhat from the highest standard. Take the black man as an African, allow somewhat for his instincts, and something more for his superstitions, and you will find him generally industrious, possessed of a little property, and a gentleman. I have not yet met a colored man in Florida who was not courteous. Is it instinct; or is it due to lack of provocation? To me he is a man, and he knows very quickly when he is treated as such. It is a very small sample of humanity that is compelled to prove his superiority to a negro. More than this the black man is a Southern necessity. The South cannot exist without him. The American problem is labor, more help; and this is the same North and South. The negro is needed by the orange grower and by the truck grower, and he is needed also by the migratory farmer who spends only his winters in the South.

The best farmer that I have seen in Florida is a Cracker. With all the peculiarities of his class, he is a careful observer, and quick to apply what lessons he learns. This man runs a milk route, manages several large orange groves, and does a good deal of truck gardening in the bargain. His judgment is inquisitive, but quick and decisive, and his speech is something of the same sort. Roused from their apathy the Crackers make a sort of Southern Yankee. With this exception the most enterprising native that I have discovered is a coal-black African. Caesar is highly respected by all classes, for his forceful and prompt, and every way executive tact. Our lakes constitute sounding boards, and you can hear this fellow half a mile away talking to his mules as he plows, alternately singing a negro melody. Just at this moment I hear him shout, "You old fool mule! Can't you see youse all wrong there? I sure is ashamed of any mule that can't run a straight furrow!" Then another melody rises over the water, followed and interlarded with more objurgations. They tell me that at adolesence this fellow broke out as, and for a year or two remained, all nigger. I think I understand the whites of the South, and am confident that the negro problem is safe in their hands. My plowman is a negro preacher; and his sermons are more nearly up to the times than those preached in the churches for white people, by white ministers. He is a good observer, has keen sympathy with nature, and I should say that for level common sense—a sort of everyday washable religion, Reverend Cole is above the average of white preachers. He does not shout at his horse, for he tells me his religion is practical, a thing for every day life, "Jes to make a man better, Sah! that's all. I reckon nobody knows so very much about another world, Sah! and they might as well not bother themselves too much beyond their knowledge."

Yet the black man has had every conceivable disadvantage. He cannot take advantage of a common church or a common school. There is something in the atmosphere that informs him that he is an inferior. Yet every day I see negroes going by my house, who walk at least two miles with their axes and dinner pails to work, and these fellows are always on time in the morning, nor do they return to their homes before six o'clock at night. They are distinguished for orderly behavior and straightforwardness. That a negro likes steady employment such as is afforded by factories I do not affirm, but he makes a good field hand and a good truck gardener. He is instinctively less fond than the Anglo-Saxon of laying up a large amount of property for the future. Just enough satisfies him, and this he will cheerfully share with his neighbors. One peculiarity is that he will never go to work on the day that he is sent for, but always "tomorrow." The Cracker is a good ways from being the worthless character that he has been represented to be, and the black man is talked about a great deal too much. Let him alone until he can work out some of his instincts, and he will make a fairly good partner in the industries that the South is rapidly developing. The Cracker has bitter prejudices and slouchy ways, but he is capable of progress quite as certainly as the New Englander type. Folk who have been drilled in Massachusetts or New York, or after the Chicago method, must learn that they do not constitute the only type of industry. I have at no time been put out for lack of help in my fields nor do I observe that the truck gardeners lack for laborers.

Around Sanford I noticed that the fields are supplied about equally with blacks and whites as laborers. A good many Germans are found there at work, and they invariably make a good thing of it. An Italian is a novelty, but he is gradually working his way Southward. The speculative interest in Florida has very largely left the orange-growing sections and concentrated about truck growing. Yet for the most part these lands are owned and run by residents. It must, however, be borne in mind that the land is entirely level, and that in wet seasons they are liable to be overflowed —for several days at a time. The climate is not always healthy, and by no means compares with the central part of the State for equability of temperature, while there is no such freedom from insect pests. At the famous resorts the mosquito becomes master of the situation during all the warmer months. It is impossible to remain there after the first of April without protecting your face, and using other precautions not entirely unknown in some sections of the North.

My own partiality for the hilly section is so strong that I would not own a whole county of flat land or Coast land if it were given to me—with the provision that I must occupy it through the whole year. In the center of the State we have no more mosquitoes than we have in central New York, and not so many as in Michigan and Indiana. I quite agree with Mr. Laughlin, of Pittsburg, whose ninety-thousand-dollar establishment is on another of the small lakes not far from my own, that probably the world does not hold a more wholesome section for homes than the lake and hilly region of central Florida. No one need to leave during the hotter months, for at this season there are cool breezes every day from either the Atlantic or the Gulf, and there are daily showers. April is counted the least agreeable of all the months, because the temperature rises a good deal of the time to eighty-five, ninety or even ninety-five, while a shower is a rare thing. We are still eating oranges, however, and we do not find gardening at all oppressive before eleven o'clock in the morning and after three in the afternoon. We soon form the habit of taking long noonings in our hammocks.

I prefer the less speculative and quiet ventures here among the lakes. We can grow all the celery and lettuce that we want for home use, in the bottom lands that border the lakes; and there is considerable shipment of these products. But on the slopes and high lands we grow to better advantage melons and fruit. The demand for these is always good either in Cincinnati or in Jacksonville. A Northern farmer can begin at once with hens, turkeys and ducks, if he likes this sort of employment, and his broilers and eggs will find a good demand in the larger cities. One of my neighbors has been very successful with bees, taking up two thousand pounds in the winter; returning them to his Ohio home where he takes up another two thousand pounds during the summer. This incomparable advantage we have, that we are not only making money, but are establishing homes and securing health. The timber is almost exclusively pine, and you are working all day in or near pine groves. There is no swamp or anything like it, unless it be where a sluggish branch of the Suwanee or Ocala winds its way westward.

However, the migratory farmer is not to be guided by my tastes, nor will his movements be altogether controlled by climatic conditions. In many cases what he wants is money, and this need must control his movements. Trucking is quick work and results are immediate. He can always buy land that is already broken and ready for cropping. Prices will be much higher and profits will accrue in like proportion. In the hilly section good homesteads can be secured for from ten to forty dollars per acre; around Sanford good celery land runs up into the hundreds, and I am told even thousands per acre. In neither case should a Northerner believe the advertiser and make an investment of any size before he has seen the property involved.

38.
Tarpon Fishing, Florida
(1891)

TARPON FISHING, FLORIDA.

BY JOHN MORTIMER MURPHY.

SCALE OF THE SILVER KING.

THE most popular angling in Florida during the winter is capturing the tarpon, or Silver King, with rod and reel. It was deemed impossible to accomplish such a feat a few years ago, but the skill of American salmon fishers has increased so much in recent years that they may now be considered unequaled adepts in the gentle art.

The sport is pursued mainly by Northern gentlemen of wealth and leisure, particularly those who spend part of the summer amid the salmon haunts of Maine and Canada. The favorite winter habitat of this fish in the waters of Florida is the region south of Sarasota Bay, and it is most abundant among the dangerous keys of the Florida reefs, where it can obtain plenty of food. During the spawning season in June and July it travels far to the north in search of favorable nursery grounds, and may then be found along the littoral line of Texas and Louisiana, where it is known as the grandicore. It is now designated by the name of Silver King by the majority of Northern tourists, some poetical sportsman having recently given it that well-deserved appellation to distinguish it from all other members of the family.

The tarpon is one of the most elegantly-formed denizens of the ocean, and certainly among the most brilliant in hue, its scales gleaming like brightly-burnished silver in the sunlight. These average about six inches in circumference on an adult male, and are so clear that I have seen advertisements of hotels stamped on them. They are also used occasionally as visiting cards by lovers of novelty and extensively by those persons who are adepts in the fish-scale work so popular in South Florida and the Bahamas. Few people would think the gigantic tarpon bore any relationship to the pigmy sardine, yet it belongs to the same family, being, in fact, only a colossal herring, and therefore the natural head of the *Clupidæ*. Among its kindred are the shad, alewife, pilchard, menhaden or mossbunker, anchovy and about sixty others, some of which are confined to tropical regions and considered very poisonous. The scientific name of the tarpon is *Megalops thrissoides*. It has only one other representative in its genus; this is a native of the Pacific Ocean and is often called the King Herring, as is also our own fish.

My first introduction to the Silver King was at the extreme south of the peninsula of Florida, where I captured one weighing a little over a hundred pounds with a pair of the graines used by Key West fishermen. We chased it or were pulled about by it for fully an hour before it became exhausted enough to permit us to pull it aboard, and even then it thrashed about so violently that I half expected to see it break through the floor of the boat. I do not know what it would have done had not one of the crew killed it by striking it on the back of the skull with a hatchet. As I gazed upon it I thought it was the handsomest fish I had ever seen, its form indicating strength and speed in about equal proportions, while its dripping scales sparkled in the moonlight.

Although angling for this fish with rod and line is now the "correct thing" among certain sportsmen, yet it cannot, in my opinion, compare with spearing, either in the dexterity required to capture one or in the amusement it affords.

In the former case the angler takes his stand in as light a boat as he can get, and, holding a stout single-jointed rod in his hands, casts in the most favorable spots. Should he hook a tarpon, his line is strong enough to enable the fish to tow the craft about until it yields through exhaustion or breaks away.

It struggles bravely for liberty and makes magnificent bounds into the air to loosen the hook from its jaws, so that it often requires skill and prudence and the patience of a true angler to bring it to gaff. The contest frequently lasts four or five hours, and in some cases the man is compelled to give in before the fish and with every chance of losing it unless he can get an assistant to relieve him.

A couple of anglers had a fight with a

giant off Shark River, not long ago, which lasted five hours, one holding the rod for three hours and the other for the remainder of the time, yet it escaped after all, though not until they tried to haul it into the boat, when they found its weight too great for them in their exhausted condition.

This individual was gravely reported to be twelve feet long and was supposed to be the patriarch of its family.

The only mementos of the fierce struggle which the anglers could show their friends were badly-cut fingers and blistered thumbs, caused by the swift-running line and the hard pressure of the thumbs against the rod.

The tarpon being more lithe and lusty than the salmon can make greater "dead leaps," that is, higher bounds, while apparently at rest. These leaps are so sudden and frequent that the skill of the best anglers is severely taxed to prevent the fish from breaking away, but they cease gradually as its strength begins to wane. Angling of this character would be regarded very laborious exercise by some people, but that only makes it all the more interesting to those who like to conquer with the rod. Tarpon are caught with hand lines also, the bait being usually a part of a mullet or sheepshead, and the hook and line strong enough to hold a porpoise. This style of angling resembles that with rod and reel, but is not so scientific, as it consists chiefly of main strength and stubbornness, with a good deal of vigilance thrown in.

Mr. Hecksher, of New York, is "high rod," so far, in tarpon fishing, having caught the largest specimen yet landed in Florida. Charlotte Harbor is at present the headquarters of those who pay special attention to angling for the Silver King in winter, but a few tourists find their way farther south. The fishing season usually lasts from three to five months, and during that time every man in that section who considers himself a devotee of the rod spends as much of his time on the water as he does on land, for, though the best period in which to angle for tarpon is at half flood, yet it may be captured at any hour in favorable situations. The proprietors of the two leading hotels in Charlotte Harbor report that their guests landed 171 tarpon last winter; of these fifteen were caught with hand lines and the remainder on rods. The largest was 6 feet 1½ inches in length and weighed 116 pounds, and the smallest 5 feet and 64 pounds. Tarpon of same size differ materially in weight. I have known a six footer to turn the scales at 150 pounds, and another of the same length to weigh several pounds less. The most ponderous of the family that I have seen caught north of the Florida Reefs was 6 feet 6 inches long and 4 feet in girth of body; the head had a length of 20 inches and measured 2½ feet around the thickest part. Some seven footers do not attain these all-round dimensions.

The flesh is reddish, with white lines running diagonally through it, if it is cut parallel with the spinal column. Some persons consider it exceedingly palatable, but, for my part, I prefer something more delicate. The crews of the sponging, fishing and coasting vessels plying along the Florida coast dry large quantities of it in the sun, and use it in place of meat to a large extent. It is cut into long strips, and when thoroughly dried bears a close resemblance to the smoked buffalo meat which used to be so common on the Indian hunting grounds a few years ago and was free to every wayfarer who wished to help himself to it. The same generos-

A STARTLING "DEAD LEAP."

ity exists among the sons of Neptune in Florida, nobody need want for food while there is cured tarpon aboard.

Spearing is, in my opinion, far more dangerous and exciting sport than capturing with "still hook" or rod and reel. I distinctly remember how keenly I enjoyed my first attempts at handling the graines, and with what zest I hurled it at the mass of living silver darting through the mirror-like sea beneath me. In this case one man sculled the boat, while I stood in the prow and, with lance uplifted, vigilantly scanned the water until I detected a silvery gleam rushing by, when I cast the missile with my utmost force and hit or missed, according to circumstances. On one occasion the sculler was thrown backward by a fish while he was pulling it aboard and had his ankle so seriously injured that he was compelled to go home. The man who attends to the gaffing must be very careful or the tarpon, on being hauled out of the water, will make such a sudden and powerful leap as to knock him down, and perhaps break his arm or leg, or, it may be, escape. I knew a man who was hit in the breast by one under such circumstances and hurt so badly that he is an invalid to this day, and a neighbor of mine had an arm broken by being hurled suddenly to the bottom of the boat by an unexpected jerk of the tarpon upon the graines line, while he was pulling in the slack.

The fleetness of this fish may be inferred from the fact that one has run out fifty fathoms of line and almost capsized a boat before the sculler, a lusty and experienced sea captain, could turn in pursuit of it. Both harpooner and steersman were pitched to the bottom so violently by this movement that they were stunned, and before they could recover their wits the fish had broken the line and escaped. This giant was supposed to be eleven feet long and to weigh at least 200 pounds. I have heard of one that scaled 180 pounds immediately after being captured, but this fugitive must be considered the giant of its genus — provided the fishermen did not exaggerate.

I could give several examples like these, if necessary, to prove that tarpon fishing with rod or harpoon is no child's play, and that he who would successfully engage in it must be strong, patient and capable of bearing much bodily fatigue. Angling for salmon cannot be compared with it; so I consider that the skillful wielder of the tarpon rod has reached the highest position among the disciples of gentle Izaak.

Those who have never seen a tarpon may get a fair idea of what it looks like by imagining a huge sardine magnificently proportioned and covered with an armor of burnished silver, which reflects every gleam of light and scintillates when fathoms deep in the ocean. Its movements, when alarmed, are so quick that it looks more like a darting streak of sunlight than anything else, especially in shallow water with a darkish bottom, and it is so brave and energetic that it struggles and leaps until completely exhausted. If this noble member of our game fishes deserves the name of Silver King, its most successful captor may be called the king of anglers.

39.
Florida Razorbacks
(1891)

FLORIDA RAZORBACKS.

BY J. M. MURPHY.

SOME portions of South Florida, particularly those regions adjoining the Everglades, are so overrun with wild hogs that even snakes and alligators have sought security in places to which the razorbacks have not yet penetrated.

It would naturally be supposed that the saurians would be only too glad to remain in regions where their prey is so abundant, but the fact is that, however palatable a single hog may be, alligators know they cannot cope with a sounder of frenzied swine with any assurance of success.

It is even dangerous for armed men to pass through the haunts of the hogs, as the brutes seem to be always on guard and to have eyes, ears and nostrils educated to perfection for their purpose.

They are ready to fight with or without provocation, and being stupid, stubborn, daring and malignant, they would rather die in their tracks than yield an inch of ground to a foe.

All wild hogs, especially those of the razorback genus, are so loyal to their kindred that they will die in their defense, and even supply the sick or wounded with food if these cannot forage for themselves.

Cases are known where wild sows brought crippled boars their food, and where boars carefully attended injured sows unable to secure provender.

Being all muscle and activity, and spending the greater part of their lives in foraging for food or fighting their foes, they are as nimble in an assault as so many panthers, and capital strategists, especially in defense. When at bay they form a circle with the most vigorous boars and sows in front and the veteran warriors a little in advance, and await an onslaught with the calmness and rigidity of a Roman phalanx. They look the very image of sourness, bad temper, revenge and hatred as they stand in solid ranks, their little pin-like eyes being apparently immovable, yet carefully watching every motion of the enemy.

They seem more like the rhinoceros in character than any other members of their family, but they have more quickness of apprehension than that ungainly brute and are more prompt in taking advantage of favorable opportunities.

There are two wild species of the *Suidæ* in the United States, one being the peccary of Texas and the other the domestic species, which has relapsed into its primitive state through the inattention of man.

The former, although only a pigmy, has all the daring and stubbornness of its larger congener, and is ready to fight anything from a man to a grizzly bear at a moment's notice.

The razorback is a denizen of the forests and savannas of the lower Southern States, but is most abundant in Louisiana and Florida. It seems to be built specially for unusual activity in a region where food is scarce and enemies numerous, its legs being long, lean and sinewy, its hocks short, its body attenuated to the verge of the ridiculous, its snout prolonged and tapering, its skull low and elongated, its neck scrawny and its back arched in the centre and sloping gradually toward the flanks.

It has a genuine racing look, and its looks do not belie it, for it has greater speed than any ordinary horse.

It is one of the most active foragers in existence, and, as it is omnivorous, seldom lacks for food even in the worst seasons. It preys on birds, rats, mice, hares, and snakes, polecats and young foxes and devours the buds of scrub palmettos, mast of all kind, wild roots, and even pine knots if nothing else is obtainable. No matter how much it eats, however, it can never get fat, its life being too active to permit the accumulation of adipose matter.

These porcine vagrants are the bane of the orange growers in Florida, for no fence is strong enough to keep them out of a grove, and a pack of dogs cannot drive out a small herd—if they once get inside—in twenty-four hours, unless they are helped by a man or several men.

I have had the brutes turn on me while trying to drive them out of the grove and chase me up a tree or else force me to kill them with my rifle. They are not only unmitigated nuisances to fruit growers, but they are the terror of all birds that nest on the ground, as they devour the eggs and young, and even round up an old bird on her nest. It is an old Cracker maxim that wherever hogs are abundant birds and snakes are scarce, and they are the best scavengers in the State, as no offal, no matter how putrid, comes amiss to them.

The wild and half-wild porkers seem to be proof against the poison of even moccasins and rattlesnakes, and they devour the reptiles, head and all, with the greatest impunity.

Wild hogs travel in large sounders while the range is good, but as soon as food gets scarce they break up into small herds and wander over large areas. The greater their numbers the more audacious, pugnacious and sour tempered do they become, and the less their numbers the less their readiness to engage in contests without cause. They are never so few, however, that they are not ready to engage in battle with a dog or a pack of dogs, for they seem to hate these animals with a hatred that can only be satisfied by their annihilation. The moment they see or wind a dog they open on his line, their "music" being a series of fierce grunts and revengeful squeals. On approaching him they charge in a body, and scare the poor wretch so badly that, if he knows their habits, he flees with the terror and speed of a kettle-ornamented cur, and never stops until he is far beyond the reach of their champing, foam-flecked jaws.

They will even attack a man accompanied by a dog, if they overtake him, and rend him to atoms in a few moments, as he has not the ghost of a chance against their numbers, tusks and teeth.

I have known more than one man accompanied by a hound to be sent clambering for dear life up a tree, and a horseman forced to put his steed to its highest speed by these porcine tramps.

When a sounder of swine are preparing for battle they distend their throats, plant their hoofs firmly in the ground, hump up their backs and cause the bristles to become rigid and slightly inclined forward; their eyes gleam with malignant fury, and their muzzles, chests and forelegs are covered with foam churned by their snapping jaws.

The matted covering on their foreheads seems to become denser and sticks out like a protecting shield.

The army forms in columns occasionally, with skirmishers thrown out on each flank, but when placed on the defensive the regular order of battle is a circle, the warriors being tail to tail, thus presenting a formidable and almost impregnable *abatis* of tusks.

When the foe is not deemed very dangerous the formation is very irregular, each hog taking its own position and making a sally whenever it sees a good opportunity for using its weapons. In fighting dogs the boars generally form in open order and rally only when hard pressed or when the assembly is sounded by some combatant in danger of its life. They often charge in a body, and when they grapple with their foe, such, for instance, as a bear, puma or wolf, their screaming is positively terrifying.

Should they prove victorious they devour their enemy promptly; but should they be defeated they rally around their chosen leader and, standing tail to tail, await an assault while getting fresh breath.

When a puma attacks a herd he generally pounces on them from covert; but he is hardly in their midst ere the boars begin ripping him with their ivory scimitars and the shoats and sows to rend him with their fine, short, sharp teeth.

I doubt if there are many old hunters in Florida who would not rather face a pack of wolves or family of pumas than a sounder of razorbacks flushed with a recent victory.

The voice of a wild hog is much deeper, gruffer and more grating than that of its domestic congeners, and the squeals of its young are pitched in a higher key and are far more expressive than those of the barnyard species. An enraged tusker utters a gruff cry, not unlike that of a grizzly bear, but an adult sow grunts in deep, rasping tones.

A series of rapid grunts indicate danger or a challenge to mortal combat; low, infrequent grunts, lazy contentment and a full stomach; high, sharp squeals, either hunger, impatience or punishment from an adversary, and quick, rasping grunts the presence of a foe or some disagreeable object.

They have other cries—such, for instance, as that of endearment by a mother; inquiry, by two meeting after a separation, or the declaration of a good range by the scouts, besides others that have more or less easily understood meanings.

Bears, pumas and wolves are the greatest enemies of wild hogs, and after them alligators and sharks. A saurian will dare almost anything for a meal of fresh pork, but the single grunter takes care to avoid its haunts. A person can readily bring an alligator ashore or within gun range by imitating the squeals or grunts of a pig, and a shoat is probably the most tempting bait that can be employed to lure all species of saurians.

When an alligator captures a hog in water too shallow to drown its prey immediately it turns over and over until it feels the animal give the last gasp, then hastens to its hole to bury its treasure until it becomes putrid enough to be fit for food.

Bears kill hogs by hugging them to death and pumas by jumping on their necks and severing the veins or hewing them with their claws. These animals do not always prove victors, however, for a wild boar has been known to slay bruin by ripping open his abdomen, and another to rout a cougar with the first blow of its tusks.

A boar and a bear have been known to fight for an hour and trample down the grass and bushes on an acre of land and then retreat, being too tired to continue the contest. Both were covered with blood, but the hog was the first to rally. The bear was found dead not far from the battle field the next morning, its sides being ripped open from shoulder to flank and its right leg almost separated from the body. Its antagonist was rather small, which made the victory all the more creditable.

When wolves were plentiful in Florida, about thirty or forty years ago, they captured more hogs than all the other animals combined. Knowing that they were no match for a herd of frenzied hogs, they resorted to stratagems to accomplish their purpose. On meeting a sounder in the woods the wolves would scout around them until they got all the hogs circled in battle array. They would then take positions around the porcine army and, sitting on their haunches, cast hungry looks at the shoats. After gazing at the surging, champing, frenzied but cautious adults in the most apparently indifferent manner for a few minutes one of the wolves, which was known among the settlers as the decoy wolf, would sneak around until he found the weakest spot in the line, or where the shoats were most numerous. Having satisfied himself on this point he would make a feint of charging the young pigs; this would cause all the adult hogs on that side to dash at him. He would allow them to come quite near, then face about suddenly and run for his life, with the hogs close behind him.

The waiting wolves would then rush into the opening made in the ranks, seize some palatable shoats and hasten away with them.

By working this trick repeatedly each wolf could secure a victim, the decoy being generally about the last to secure his prize.

Ferocious animals were so abundant in Florida at one time that the farmers could not raise any stock, it being nothing unusual for them to find all the hogs, sheep and calves in the barnyard destroyed in a night by a bear, puma or pack of wolves. While matters were in this discouraging condition it was accidentally learned that spayed hogs were the most daring fighters in the forest. The farmers promptly availed themselves of this knowledge, and thereafter made these amazons not only the guardians of the sounders but the protectors of every defenseless domestic animal that roamed the forest. They not only held wolves, bears, pumas and alligators at bay, but actually drove them from the vicinity of settlements.

Wild hogs are quite numerous at present along the Fahatchee and Fahnahatchee rivers and other parts of South Florida.

That wolves did not always outwit the hogs is evident from the following story, told by a Western farmer :

"One day, while passin' along the bottoms, I seen such a sight of hogs as I never did see. Thar they stood and squirmed, with their bristles up and steam a risin' out o' their bodies, and their eyes a flashin' and teeth a champin', a mass of bilin' mad hogs a screamin' and a shakin' 'emselves with rage.

"What was a causin' of all this commotion I was not long in seein'. Thar, in the middle of the hogs, was a big oak stump about five feet high, and in the centre of the stump stood a big gray wolf, as gaunt and hungry lookin' a critter as ever I seed.

"He was han'somely treed, and was not in a very pleasin' fix, as he was beginnin' to find out. All about him raged a mass of oneasy hair, fiery eyes, frothin' mouths and gleamin' teeth.

"Poor critter ! Thar he stood ; his tail tucked clost atween his legs and his feet all gathered into the exact centre of the stump, and, Jerusalem ! wasn't he a sick lookin' wolf !

"Right clost about the stump and rairin' up ag'inst it was a crowd of some of the biggest and most onprincipled old sows I ever sot eyes onto. Every half minit one of these big old she fellows would rair up, get her forefeet on top of the stump at one end or tother of the wolf, her jaws comin' together like a flax brake.

"The wolf would turn round to watch that partickerlar sow, when one on tother side of the stump would make a plunge for his tail ; an' so they kep' the poor, cowardly, cornered critter whirlin' round an' round, humpin' up his back, haulin' in his feet and tail, and in every possible way reducin' his general average.

"Almost every instant thar was a charge made on him from some quarter and sometimes from three or four directions at oncet. Jewhittaker ! wasn't it hurryin' times with him then ! When he had a moment to rest and gaze about, all he saw was them two acres of open mouths, restless bristles and fiery eyes. His long red tongue hung out of his open jaws, and as he moved his head from side to side he seemed to have the poorest conceit of his smartness of any wolf I ever seed.

"I determined to try an experiment on that wolf. I raised my gun and fired into the air. At the report the critter forgot himself. He bounded from the stump with the crack of the gun, but he never tetched ground. Half a dozen open mouths reached up for him and there was jest one sharp yell ; then for a rod around was seen flyin' strips of wolf skin, legs and hair ; for half a minit thar was heerd a crunchin' of bones, and then them old sows began a lickin' their chops, rairin' up onto that thar stump and prospectin' about for more wolf.

"'Bout that time I concluded the neighborhood was likely to prove onhealthy, so I got up and peeled it for the nearest clearin's."

40.
An Adventure with a Tarpon (1895)

PAINTED FOR OUTING BY HY. S. WATSON.

"IN A WILD SWIRL OF WATER HE JUMPED CLEAN OVER THE BOAT."

AN ADVENTURE WITH A TARPON.

BY FRED. J. WELLS.

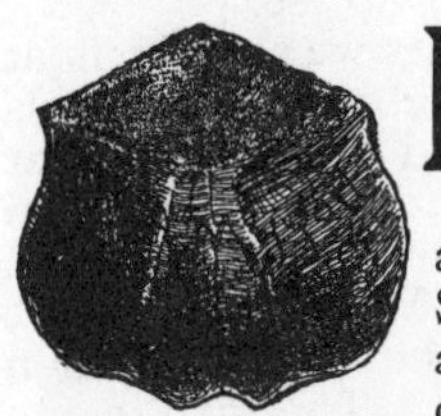

LAST October my friend Beatty came to me, to discuss plans for a fishing trip to the South. As anglers are wont to do, we discussed the advantages and disadvantages of many points, and at last decided in favor of Southern Alabama.

We went to Magnolia Springs on the Fish River. This river, as its name indicates, abounds in fish of various species. It is not very wide, averaging perhaps five hundred yards, but the water is deep and very clear. It flows into Mobile Bay about five miles below the Springs, and large fish, such as tarpon, gar, red-fish, crevalia, shark, etc., ascend the river to feed upon the plentiful smaller fry. We often saw large fish rise to the surface and make a dart through a school of mullets, scattering them in every direction and forcing some to leap several feet into the air. This drama of pursuers and pursued is one of the strange scenes characteristic of Southern waters. The porpoises were also great destroyers. On the mud flats near the mouth of the river, I have seen them rushing through the shallow water with mouths wide open, taking in everything that could not get out of the way.

The river flows through tracts of heavy timber and through broad marshes, its banks bearing live-oak, cypress, and Southern trees embracing more than one hundred varieties. At its mouth it is perhaps two hundred yards wide, with an average depth of from forty to fifty feet. The bottom is composed of fine, hard sand.

We had in our service a colored man, Louis Collins, one of the best guides in the South. He has lived on the banks of Fish River all his life, and is thoroughly acquainted with the habits and peculiarities of the different species of fish. The morning after our arrival we found him waiting for us with his flat-bottomed boat, made especially for fishing. He rowed us to the mouth of the river, and on the way down we trolled with phantom minnows, catching plenty of trout and red-fish, but failing to strike any larger fish. More than once during the day we were electrified by the sight of tarpon, or silver fish as the natives call them, leaping to their full length from the water and falling flat on their sides. The resounding splashes the great fellows made, the gleam of their silvery scales in the sunlight, and the mighty swirl they made as they went under, set our hearts a-thumping, but we were not fortunate enough to have one of them take our hook.

We caught red-fish, one of which weighed full thirty pounds, and made a fight for about forty-five minutes before he could be brought near enough to the boat to be harpooned; several sharks of the smaller species, weighing from twenty to forty pounds, and many smaller fish of different kinds. An exciting feature of this sport is that the tide brings the salt-water fish into the river, so that one seldom knows what kind of a fish he has hooked until it is brought to the surface.

The first fish I caught took the bait and went off with it as if he would never stop. I finally succeeded in turning him, and after about thirty minutes of lively work brought him within view only to find that I had hooked a shark. For several days we fished up and down the river with varied success, seeing many tarpon but not being able to hook one.

One morning we left the Springs about eight o'clock with the intention of spending the day at the mouth of the river. When about half way to the mouth we noticed a swell in the water caused by a large fish swimming slowly up stream near the surface. He was quite a distance away on our left and near the shore, which at that point was marshy and covered with cane brakes and cypress saplings. The guide turned the boat so that it would float in the direction of the fish, and after warning us to keep perfectly still he prepared his harpoon, or gig. The harpoon had a handle about ten feet long and was so arranged that the iron barbed tip would loosen from the handle. A large cord one hundred feet in length was fastened to the harpoon and was wound on a wooden float. After unwinding about twenty-five feet of line and shoving the boat a little more toward shore, the guide stood up ready for action.

The boat was now in such a position that if the fish did not change its course it would pass within a few feet of us. Up to this time the fish had been so deeply submerged that we could not determine his species, but when he was within about six rods of us he came up so near the surface that we could see the narrow elongation of the dorsal fin above the water.

"A silver fish," the guide whispered, and motioned to us not to move. There was a moment of tense excitement as we slowly and silently floated toward our intended victim. Would the fish continue to swim near the surface or would he disappear in the depths? Knowing that the guide was an expert with the harpoon, I felt confident that if we could once get within throwing distance some lively fun would result. Nearer we approached until the fish was nearly opposite and about fifteen feet away, and then suddenly the guide straightened himself up and raising the harpoon above his head, hurled it forward with practiced skill.

For an instant all was still, then the huge fish leaped his full length into the air and we could see that the iron had entered his side just back of the head. He came down with a tremendous splash, turned in a wild swirl of water, rushed head-on like lightning at us and jumped clean over the boat!

I was sitting in the bow and he passed over just in front of me. All that I saw was a silvery something going through the air like a cannon-ball. To say that I dodged would be expressing it mildly. I never came so near falling over backward from a boat, and failed, in my life. As for the guide, who was standing up, he simply dropped.

I had seen fish jump over a boat before, but I never expected to be made a target for a fish weighing over two hundred pounds and I never want to again. As he struck the water he went down out of sight, jerking the line out of the hands of the guide and taking line and float with him. The boat seemed to be going over, but we heard a crash of a broken board and it righted. The line had caught in a crack in the end of one of the short, bottom boards and had split the board about half way and then broken it in two at a large knot. The board being defective was all that saved us from taking a watery bath and in all probability losing the fish, if nothing worse.

After a few moments we saw the float come to the surface about twenty rods away, up the river, and we guessed that the line had unwound of itself. The fish had evidently found the bottom and was moving slowly. We rowed as fast as possible, caught the float, and then made for the shore. The fish came along without struggling very much, although pulling hard. As we neared the shore the guide seized the cord, jumped out into water up to his waist, and made for the bank. He commenced to pull the fish in, and had succeeded in getting about thirty feet of slack line, when the fish turned and went away fast. The guide, seeing he could not hold him, ran and took a half turn around a small cypress sapling about two inches in diameter, but the fish was going so fast and with such force that he bent the tree over, broke the limbs, jerked the line out of the guide's hands, and away he went up stream. The guide got into the boat and we chased the float again. The tarpon jumped out of the water several times, shaking his head as they do when hooked, but the harpoon was in too deep to be loosened. The struggle reminded me more of trying to break a wild mustang than of anything I know of.

We followed the float for fully a quarter of a mile before we overtook it. At last we secured it and rowed again to the shore. The guide jumped out in the marsh and just had time to pass the line around a small tree before the fish started off again. As the guide felt the line straighten out and saw the tree bend over, he noticed a root under which there was room to pass the float and he quickly took a half hitch around it, having just enough slack line to do so. The fish bent the sapling the same as he did the first one and straightened out the line. It was a question whether or not the line, which was a large cord, could stand the pull. All were now on shore and when finally the fish relaxed the strain we kept the line taut and carefully pulled it in. Twice the fish started off, but was quickly turned, it being evident that his strength was fast giving out. We at last hauled him to the bank and found we had a magnificent specimen of the tarpon. The harpoon had gone through the flesh into his vitals, and no doubt that was what sapped his strength, for he died in a very short time.

On measuring him we found he was six feet seven inches in length, with a spread of tail of eighteen inches. The mouth had an expanse of seven inches, and the diameter of the eye was two inches. The narrow extension of the dorsal fin, which we had first seen above the water, was eighteen inches long and about an inch wide. The scales measured as much as four inches in diameter the long way, and twelve inches in circumference. After examining the head and mouth I wondered that tarpon are ever killed with hook and line. The lower jaw is a solid bone, and the flesh, or muscle, is so hard that a hook should be easily shaken loose from it.

We put the fish across the boat near the stern, and pulled back to the Springs, feeling highly elated with our morning's work. The guide told us it was the largest silver fish caught in that section, and I have never heard of a larger one being taken anywhere. The people at Mobile expressed their astonishment at its size, and also at the fact that it was caught so far from the mouth of the river.

We did not have any means of weighing the fish, but it certainly weighed over two hundred pounds. I would have given a great deal for the privilege of taking him North just as he came from the water, but that was impossible. We arranged with a couple of colored men to take off the skin. This we preserved as best we could with arsenic, and succeeded in carrying it home, but as it could not be preserved we had to throw it away, after taking off the scales. The head was mounted, and now adorns the museum in our High School building.